Principles of International Auditing and Assurance

Principles of International Auditing and Assurance

Fifth Edition

Rick Hayes, Philip Wallage and Peter Eimers

Amsterdam University Press

Cover design: Gijs Mathijs Ontwerpers, Amsterdam
Lay-out: Crius Group, Hulshout

ISBN	978 90 4856 415 6
e-ISBN	978 90 4856 416 3
DOI	10.5117/9789048564156
NUR	784

CONTENTS

TOPIC I — THE AUDIT PROFESSION

1 International Auditing Overview 24

2 How the Audit Profession Is Organized 52

TOPIC II — FUNDAMENTAL CONCEPTS

3 Ethics for Professional Accountants 98

4 Exploring the Foundations of Auditing and Assurance 149

TOPIC III — THE AUDIT PROCESS MODEL

5 Client and Engagement Acceptance/Continuance 166

6 Identifying and Assessing Inherent Risk 207

10 Evaluating and Completion 387

11 Reporting 429

LIST OF ILLUSTRATIONS

Since the fourth edition of this book was published in early 2021, a global pandemic disrupted the global economy and altered the way that we work. The pace of technological change and advances in artificial intelligence accelerated with yet to be fully understood long-term impacts. Demands for a broader perspective on company performance have extended beyond pure financial reporting and disclosure, with the advent of the International Sustainability Standards Board (ISSB) under the IFRS Foundation and the passage of the European Union's Corporate Reporting Sustainability Directive (CSRD) as two of the leading examples.

While the pace of change can be disorienting, the value of accounting and auditing remains steadfast. A profession dedicated to the public interest and the highest ethical principles brings clarity and trust to our broader economy. One element that makes accounting and audit nearly unique among the world's professions is its commitment to internationally consistent standards. Over the last two decades, International Financial Reporting Standards (IFRS) have become the norm for financial reporting globally.

The International Standards on Auditing (ISAs) developed by the International Auditing and Assurance Standards Board (IAASB), the body which I chair, serve as the basis for auditing requirements in more than 130 jurisdictions throughout the world. For readers who do not know the IAASB well, the IAASB is an independent standard-setting organization, comprised of globally and professionally diverse professionals committed to the public interest. Our core mission is to enhance confidence in corporate and other external reporting by developing globally accepted auditing and assurance standards.

I am honored to be asked to write a foreword for this edition, joining a tradition started by my predecessors, Bob Roussey, John Kellas, and Arnold Schilder. We are united by a common cause—maintaining a global profession capable of adapting to evolving market developments and addressing the challenging practical and ethical challenges facing auditors and assurance practitioners.

For this reason, I commend Professors Rick Hayes, Philip Wallage, and Peter Eimers for publishing the fifth edition of *Principles of International Auditing and Assurance*. This textbook serves as a benchmark for educators across the globe teaching future professionals how to apply the IAASB's standards and the ethical standards developed by our partner board, the International Ethics Standards Board for Accountants (IESBA).

This publication is both timely and needed for students and educators. The pandemic did not slow the IAASB and the IESBA down, and both boards continue to actively revise existing standards and finalize new standards. This edition enriches the chapters that address risk assessment, which is at the heart of the audit. The authors have taken the opportunity to include deep insights into the concepts embedded in ISA 315, *Identifying and Assessing the Risks of Material Misstatement*. Chapter 6 appropriately focuses on the enhanced risk assessment process, which provides the basis for the identification and assessment of the risks of material misstatement, and the design of further audit procedures. Chapter 7 also provides an in-depth discussion of the auditor's work related to the Entity's System of Internal Control and IT matters.

A second major area of change since the last edition is the IAASB's introduction of a new suite of quality management standards to replace the previous system of quality control. The International Standard on Quality Management (ISQM) 1, ISQM 2, and ISA 220 (Revised) create an integrated package to improve the focus on quality at the firm level, in engagement quality reviews, and at the engagement level, respectively. Importantly, the standards taken together seek to place quality at the heart of audit firm culture and strategy, to create a commitment to continued improvement, and to develop a system for identifying and remediating deficiencies.

In setting our work plan and revising existing standards, the IAASB works closely with regulators, primarily securities regulators and independent audit regulators. Benefiting from this dialogue, we approved a revision to ISA 600, *Special Considerations—Audits of Group Financial Statements (Including the Work of Component Auditors)*. Importantly, the revised ISA 600, covered in Chapter 13, builds off the concepts in ISA 315 and the new quality management standards.

Perhaps the most significant evolution in our work at the IAASB is our dedicated focus on building a specific assurance standard for sustainability reporting. As highlighted above, policymakers, investors, and other stakeholders are calling for reporting from companies and other entities to include sustainability topics. At the same time, there is a recognition that reporting standards alone are insufficient to support the goal of more sustainable and efficient capital allocations. Any trusted corporate reporting system must include external third-party assurance. That is where the IAASB comes into play.

The IAASB has long written standards for assurance of non-financial information. Most notable is International Standard on Assurance Engagements (ISAE) 3000, which can be used for a range of non-financial information, and ISAE 3410, which deals specifically with greenhouse gas statements. Research by the International Federation of Accountants (IFAC) shows that demand for assurance is growing globally, and the IAASB's standards form the basis for the great majority of assurance practices today. In response to calls by policymakers and regulators, in August 2023, the IAASB published the exposure draft – our consultation document – for International Standard on Sustainability Assurance (ISSA) 5000, *General Requirements for Sustainability Assurance Engagements*.

At the time of my writing this foreword, the IAASB is considering its response to the comments received to the proposed ISSA 5000. Our plan is to finalize the standard in the second half of 2024, after the publication of this book. Regardless, readers will be well-prepared for the eventual approval of ISSA 5000 after reading Chapter 15 on Sustainability Assurance Engagements, which provides both the context and a history of the building blocks for the proposed standard. We anticipate that the final approved standard should remain in line with the concepts described in this book.

Observers of standard setting often ask when will standard setters be done with the work. The answer is never. We continue to respond to market events and identified areas for improvement in existing standards. For example, the IAASB is now enhancing existing standards on fraud and going concern. Both standards have been at the heart of perceived audit deficiencies in recent corporate failures. The revisions should further clarify the auditor's role, enhance risk assessment for both topics, and enhance communications directly with management and those charged with governance and externally through the Auditor's Report. We are also considering whether our standards must evolve to account for rapid advances in technology.

One final note is the authors' important and early emphasis on ethics. Ethics is the foundation of quality and trusted audits and assurance. Our partner board, IESBA, continues to improve the *International Code of Ethics for Professional Accountants*, which major accounting firms throughout the world adhere to and national regulators internationally adopt. Because the concepts in the IAASB's and the IESBA's standards are intertwined, the two boards are working more closely together and readers will note increased alignment on concepts that appear in the IESBA Code and our suite of quality management standards and group audits, among others.

I joined the IAASB in July 2019 because I firmly believe in both the relevance and value of audit and assurance. Trust is key to make economies work, and auditors and assurance practitioners at their best are guardians of that trust. Reading and learning from this book, is another step in ensuring that auditors and assurance practitioners continue to contribute to more prosperous and sustainable societies.

Tom Seidenstein
Chair, International Auditing and Assurance Standards Board
March 2024

Welcome to the world of auditors by opening this book!

The audit profession has been relevant to society for several centuries. Living in a complex and dynamic world, there is a growing interest in reliable corporate reporting. Many stakeholders presume that trust is a fundament for doing business. An auditor's work is your window into the heart of an enterprise. Investors, bankers, suppliers, employees, unions, business partners in the value chain, NGOs, governments, and regulators, all make use of the work and reporting by auditors.

Auditing is not like financial or managerial accounting. Accounting is a system where an objective representation of reality is recorded and summarized. Auditing is a set of procedures and techniques by which that representation is 'agreed' to specific criteria. So, accounting endeavors to record economic values, categorize them, and then summarize them in a report. Using a set of proscribed procedures (audit standards), and given specific criteria (financial accounting standards), auditing analyses whether that representation is properly recorded, categorized and reported.

You are studying auditing to further your professional goals, if you are like most people reading this book. In addition to your university or college degree you would like to get a professional credential (such as CPA, CA, RA, CFE, WP, GR, CMA, etc.), or you have heard, correctly, that auditing is a 'high demand' profession. In other words, you would like some practical knowledge which will help you in your career. To fulfil your goals is our wish.

This textbook is written from the view of a professional auditor. Theory and academic concerns are covered. The emphasis is on the professional standards promulgated by the International Auditing and Assurance Standards Board (IAASB) and the practical day-to-day experience of international auditing firms. The authors of both the current and previous editions were all extremely successful professional auditors even before writing this book. The authors are also university professors who have taught hundreds of students from around the world, so this textbook is from the point of view of the international student.

Auditing is not just about accounting issues. Auditors don't just look at (financial and non- financial) information, but also at systems and processes, behavior, and how an enterprise is governed. All sorts of enterprises are audited – profit oriented, not for profit, government, private and public. Auditors may be independent of the enterprise, a valuable internal analyst or working for the government. Audit-trained accountants are also hired to do forensic analysis. Today, as fraudulent schemes become ever larger and more harmful, it is auditors who are an important line of defense. Auditors' detailed analytical skills and professional identity have created jobs in areas as diverse as management, marketing and divorce consulting.

Even before we co-authors began to write the first edition of this book over 30 years ago, we all agreed that our only concern was to produce a high-quality audit text for the international student. This meant that it had to be fully up to date, use outstanding material, have a sound balance of audit theory and real practice, and be based on international auditing and assurance standards. We see the world from a truly global, cross-cultural perspective.

As mentioned in the foreword by Tom Seidenstein, this fifth edition is fully revised and includes the latest developments in the International Standards on Auditing, such as identifying and assessing the risks of material misstatements, the use and impact of technology in the audit, as well as a new chapter on sustainability (ESG) assurance.

The book is engagingly structured around four exciting topics. Topic I dives into the world of the Audit Profession, offering a comprehensive exploration. The second topic enthusiastically delves into Fundamental Concepts, laying a solid foundation. Topic III unfolds the stages of the Audit Process Model, guiding readers through each step with clarity. Finally, Topic IV broadens the horizon with Specific Subjects and Themes, enriching the reader's understanding with diverse insights.

We co-authors have a special place in our hearts for our students. We believe that it is our duty to convey our joy as auditors and audit teachers to you.

ACKNOWLEDGEMENTS

As always, this book was not the work of the co-authors alone, but also of the many professionals who helped us shape our ideas and give depth to the knowledge contained here.

We would like to thank Tom Seidenstein for writing the Foreword. Tom is currently chairman of the IAASB, the global standard setter for 130 countries across the globe that earned respect with various innovations in standard setting reflecting the changing needs in society.

We further would like to thank Jan Thijs Drupsteen for his contributions to chapter 4 about the concepts of auditing and assurance with the drive to tell the story from a helicopter view, Ellen de Koning for her contribution to chapters 6 and 7 with her in-depth knowledge of ISA 315 and reflecting on 'how to tell it our students' and Hans Gortemaker and Wim Bartels reflecting on the new sustainability chapter 15.

This book was created using relevant material from other books. We would like to thank these publishers and professional organizations: American Accounting Association, American Institute of Certified Public Accountants, International Auditing and Assurance Standards Board, International Ethics Standard Board of Accountants, International Federation of Accountants, European Union, US Securities and Exchange Commission, US Public Company Accounting Oversight Board, UK Financial Reporting Council and The Netherlands Royal Institute of Accountants.

Naturally, we could not have undertaken this massive project without the unwavering support of our families, who enabled us to focus on this book through countless co-author video calls and discussions.

Rick Hayes, Philip Wallage, Peter Eimers
Latest updates as per March 2024

THE AUDIT PROFESSION

CHAPTER 1

INTERNATIONAL AUDITING OVERVIEW

1.1 LEARNING OBJECTIVES

After studying this chapter, you should be able to:

1 Understand the basic definition of auditing.
2 Recount requirements relating to an audit of financial statements.
3 Explain the limitations of an audit.
4 Convey the concept of materiality.
5 Relate some of the early history of auditing.
6 Communicate management's influence over financial statements.
7 Convey the theories of the demand for audit services.
8 Describe the four-phase standard audit process model.
9 Discuss some of the audit expectations of society.
10 Be aware of some important developments.

1.2 WHAT IS AN AUDIT?

International auditing education starts with a thorough understanding of what we mean by an audit. There is no definition of an audit, per se, in the International Standards on Auditing. ISA 200, however, describes an audit of financial statements[1], which we will discuss shortly.

A GENERAL DEFINITION OF AUDITING[2]

An audit is a systematic process of objectively obtaining and evaluating evidence regarding assertions about economic actions and events to ascertain the degree of correspondence between these assertions and established criteria and communicating the results to interested users.

Investors and creditors may have different objectives than management of a company (e.g., management prefers higher salaries and benefits (expenses), whereas investors wish higher profits and dividends). Investors and creditors must depend on fair financial statements. To give them confidence in the financial statements, an auditor provides an independent and expert opinion on the fairness of the reports, called an audit opinion.[3]

An audit in accordance with International Standards on Auditing (ISAs) is conducted on the premise that management and those charged with governance have acknowledged certain responsibilities fundamental to the audit's conduct. For instance, the audit of the financial statements does not relieve management or those charged with governance of their responsibilities. Furthermore, the financial statements audited under international standards are the balance sheets, income statements and cash flow statements and the notes thereto.

An audit is an independent, objective and expert examination and evaluation of evidence. Auditors are fair and do not allow prejudice or bias to override their objectivity. They maintain an impartial attitude. As will be discussed in chapter 3, assurance providers such as financial statement auditors must be *independent* and comply with *ethical standards* of principles and rules.

In the audit process, accounting records are analysed using a variety of generally accepted techniques. The audit must be planned and structured in such a way that those carrying out the audit can fully examine and analyse all important evidence. An audit is a systematic process. Its phases are discussed in chapter 4.

To be effective, it is necessary to plan and perform an audit with *professional scepticism*[4] recognizing that circumstances may exist that cause the financial statements to be materially misstated.[5] Professional scepticism is an attitude that includes a questioning mind, being alert to conditions which may indicate possible misstatement due to error or fraud, and a critical assessment of evidence. The auditor shall exercise professional judgement[6] in planning and performing an audit of financial statements. *Professional judgement* is the application of relevant training, knowledge and experience, within the context provided by auditing and accounting standards, in making informed decisions about the courses of action that are appropriate in the circumstances of the audit engagement.

The concept of *materiality*[7] is applied in planning and performing the audit, and in evaluating the effect of misstatements identified on the financial statements. Misstatements, including omissions, are considered material if – individually or aggregated – they could be expected to influence the economic decisions of users taken based on the financial statements. Judgements about materiality are made in the light of surrounding circumstances and are affected by the auditor's perception of needs of users of the financial statements, and by the size or nature of a misstatement, or a combination of both.

The evidence obtained and evaluated concerns assertions about economic actions and events. *Assertions* are representations by management, explicit or otherwise, embodied in the financial statements. One assertion of management about economic actions is that all the assets reported on the balance sheet exist at that date. The assets are real, not fictitious. This is the 'existence' assertion. Furthermore, management asserts that the company owns all these assets. They do not belong to anyone else. This is the 'rights and obligations' assertion. See chapter 8.

The auditor ascertains the degree of correspondence between assertions and established criteria.

In order to design audit procedures to determine whether financial statements are materially misstated due to error or fraud, the auditor considers the risk at two levels. One level of risk is that the overall financial statements may be misstated. The second risk is misstatement in relation to classes of transactions (asset, revenue, etc.), account balances and disclosures. See chapters 7, 8 and 9.

The *risk of material misstatements* at the overall financial statement level often relates to the entity's control environment[8] (although these risks may also relate to other factors, such as declining economic conditions). This overall risk may be especially relevant to the auditor's consideration of fraud (see chapter 12). The auditor must obtain *sufficient appropriate audit evidence*[9] to draw conclusions on which to base the auditor's opinion. To this end the auditor will take the following steps:

- ▶ studying and evaluating accounting systems and internal controls on which she[10] wishes to rely and testing those internal controls to determine the nature, extent and timing of other auditing procedures (further discussed in chapter 7); and
- ▶ carrying out such other tests, inquiries and other verification procedures of accounting transactions and account balances, as she considers appropriate in the particular circumstances (chapter 8).

In communicating the results to intended users the auditor must state that in her opinion the financial statements 'give a true and fair view' or 'present fairly, in all material respects' the financial position of the company. The communication of such a written auditor's opinion in the United States is called an attestation report. In an international context the audit report is an example of an 'assurance' report.

The form of opinion expressed by the auditor will depend upon the applicable financial reporting framework and any applicable law or regulation (chapter 11). The auditor may also have certain other communication and reporting responsibilities to users, management, those charged with governance, or parties outside the entity.

LIMITATIONS OF AN AUDIT

There are certain inherent limitations in an audit that affect the auditor's ability to detect material misstatements. These limitations result from such factors as the use of testing (sampling risk), and the inherent limitations of any accounting and internal control system. For example, in some cases, management can override internal controls designed to prevent and detect fraud. Also, auditors rely on third-party information but are not experts in determining the authenticity of documents. Furthermore, most audit evidence is persuasive rather than conclusive and is the work performed by an auditor to form an opinion permeated by judgement. Judgement is required to determine the nature and extent of audit evidence and the drawing of conclusions based on the audit evidence gathered. Finally, auditors are required to assess whether an entity can continue as a going concern for the foreseeable future. However, predicting the future financial performance and viability of an organization involves uncertainties, and auditors may not always identify issues that could threaten the entity's ability to continue operating Because of these factors and the fact that people make mistakes, an audit is no guarantee that the financial statements are free of material misstatements.

HISTORY

▶ **AUDITING THROUGH HISTORY**

Auditing predates the Christian era. Anthropologists have found records of auditing activity dating back to early Mesopotamian times (around 3000 BC). There was also auditing activity in ancient China, Greece and Rome. The Latin meaning of the word 'auditor' was a 'hearer or listener' because in Rome auditors heard taxpayers, such as farmers, give their public statements regarding the results of their business and the tax duty due.

SCRIBES OF ANCIENT TIMES

Auditors[11] existed in ancient China and Egypt. They were supervisors of the accounts of the Chinese Emperor and the Egyptian Pharaoh. The government accounting system of the Zhao (1046–221 BC) dynasty in China included an elaborate budgetary process and audits of all government departments. From the dawn of the dynastic era in Egypt (3000 BC) the scribes (accountants) were among the most esteemed in society and the scribal occupation was one of the most prestigious occupations.

Egyptian Pharaohs were very severe with their auditors. Each royal storehouse used two auditors. One counted the goods when they came in the door and the second counted the goods after they were stored. The supervisor looked at both accounts. If there was a difference, the auditors were both killed.

Bookkeeping as a support mechanism for the determination of profit or wealth, or as a decision support system for achieving profit maximization, was basically unknown in ancient cultures like the Mesopotamian, Egyptian, Greek or Roman. Auditing in English-speaking countries dates to AD 1130. Then, although they had highly developed economic systems, registration of economic facts or events was limited to the recording of single transactions whose sole purpose was to support the short-term memory of the trading partner.

Rational maximization of wealth or profit did not fit into the systems of these cultures. Wealth was not a function of keen entrepreneurship or of smart cost-benefit trade-offs. It was merely a reward for one's loyalty to the government or for living in accordance with religious and moral principles and rules.

MIDDLE AGES

During the Middle Ages, auditing practices were informal and often performed by church and state officials. The focus was on verifying compliance with laws and regulations. As trade and commerce expanded, the need for more systematic auditing processes increased.

In medieval Europe, guilds began conducting internal audits to ensure members adhered to established rules and regulations. This practice helped maintain quality standards in various trades.

The attitude of profit maximization developed at the end of the Middle Ages, with the emergence of large merchant houses in Italy. Trading was no longer the domain of the individual commercial traveller; it was now coordinated centrally at the luxurious desks of the large merchant houses in Venice, Florence or Pisa. As a result, communication became vital.

Not unexpectedly, therefore, the system of double-entry bookkeeping was first described in Italy, used by a Genoa commune in 1340 AD. The first book on double entry accounting was Luca Pacioli's *Summa de Arithmetica* dated 20 November 1494.

INDUSTRIAL REVOLUTION

The Industrial Revolution in the 18th and 19th centuries led to the emergence of joint-stock companies. With an increasing number of shareholders and complex business structures, the demand for external audits grew to ensure the accuracy of financial reporting.

MODERN CORPORATION

The practice of modern auditing dates back to the beginning of the modern corporation at the dawn of the Industrial Revolution. In 1853, the Society of Accountants was founded in Edinburgh. Several other institutes emerged in Great Britain, merging in 1880 into the Institute of Chartered Accountants in England and Wales. This nationwide institute was a predecessor to institutes that emerged all over the Western world at the end of the nineteenth century, for example, in the USA[12] (in 1886) or in the Netherlands (in 1895).

Further developments of the separation between provision of capital and management and in the complexity of companies, along with the occurrence of several fraud cases and financial scandals (e.g. City of Glasgow Bank, 1883; Afrikaansche Handelsvereeniging, 1879),[13] have led to a steady growth of the audit profession and regulation. The British Companies Acts (1845–62) were models for US auditing. The first US authoritative auditing pronouncement was issued in 1917.

ECONOMIC CONDITIONS FOR AUDIT REPORTS

At the same time, companies across the world experienced growth in technology, improvement in communications and transportation, and the exploitation of expanding worldwide markets. As a result, the demands of owner-managed enterprises for capital rapidly exceeded the combined resources of the owners' savings and the wealth-creating potential of the enterprises themselves. It became necessary for industry to tap into the savings of the community as a whole. The result has been the growth of sophisticated securities markets and credit-granting institutions serving the financial needs of large national, and increasingly international, corporations.

The flow of investor funds to the corporations and the whole process of allocation of financial resources through the financial markets have become dependent to a very large extent on financial reports made by company management. One of the most important characteristics of these corporations is the fact that their ownership is almost totally separated from their management. Management has control over the resources including the accounting systems. They are not only responsible for the financial reports to investors, but they also have the authority to determine the way in which the information is presented.

1.4 THEORY

▶ THEORIES ON THE DEMAND OF AUDIT SERVICES[14]

The demand for audit services may be explained by several different theories. Some theories like the Agency Theory have been well researched and reported on. Other theories based on public perceptions such as the Policeman Theory, the Lending Credibility Theory and the Legal Liability Theory serve more as a point of reference than as a researched construct.

THE POLICEMAN THEORY

Is an auditor responsible for discovering fraud, like a policeman? Think of this idea as the Policeman Theory. Up until the 1940s it was widely held that an auditor's job was to focus on arithmetical accuracy and on prevention and detection of fraud. However, from the 1940s until the turn of the 21st century there was a shift of auditing to mean verification of truth and fairness of the financial statements. Financial statement frauds such as those at Société Générale, Satyam, Ahold, Enron, etc. have resulted in careful reconsideration of this theory. There is an ongoing public debate on the auditor's responsibility for detection and disclosure of fraud and non-compliance with laws and regulation, returning us to the basic public perceptions on which this theory derives.

THE LENDING CREDIBILITY THEORY

Another public perception is that the primary function of auditing is the addition of credibility to the financial statements. We may think of this as the Lending Credibility Theory. Audited financial statements are used by management to enhance the stakeholders' faith in management's stewardship. If stakeholders such as stockholders, government, or creditors have to make their judgements based on the information they receive, they must have faith that this is a fair representation of the economic value and performances of the organization. In audit research terms, an audit reduces the 'information asymmetry' (the fact that management knows more than the stakeholders). Investors and creditors use audited financial statements as a signal that the information disclosed is credible and trustworthy (also referred to as 'signalling theory' or 'information economics theory'). This enhances the value of financial information in decision-making processes.

LEGAL LIABILITY THEORY

Auditors are subject to legal liability if they fail to detect material misstatements in financial statements. This theory suggests that the fear of legal consequences motivates auditors to exercise due professional care and scepticism in their work. Regulatory requirements, such as those outlined in the U.S. Sarbanes-Oxley Act, impose obligations on companies to undergo external audits, contributing to the demand for audit services. Because accountants must insure themselves properly against claims, this theory is also called the 'deep pocket theory of liability'.

29

AGENCY THEORY

In the agency theory, originally proposed by Watts and Zimmerman,[15] a reputable auditor – an auditor who is perceived to meet expectations – is appointed not only in the interest of third parties, but also in the interest of management. A company is viewed as the result of more or less formal 'contracts', in which several groups make some kind of contribution to the company, given a certain 'price'. Company management tries to get these contributions under optimum conditions for management: low interest rates from bankers, high share prices for stockholders, and low wages for employees.

In these relationships, management is seen as the 'agent', trying to obtain contributions from 'principals' such as bankers, stockholders and employees. Costs of an agency relationship are monitoring costs (the cost of monitoring the agents), bonding costs (the costs, incurred by an agent, of 'insuring' that agents will not take adverse actions against the principals), and residual loss (effective loss that results despite the bonding and monitoring costs incurred).

Agency Theory also includes consideration of 'moral hazard'. A moral hazard occurs when entering into a contract with another company or an agent being deliberately skewed or altered in order to attempt to make a profit.

A clear example of a moral hazard occurs in the case of a salesperson who is compensated at an hourly rate with no commission. The salesperson in this situation may be inclined to put less effort into his performance, as the rate of pay doesn't change regardless of how hard he works. Typically, this sort of situation can be avoided by an (independent) audit or altering the pay structure to include both an hourly salary and commission to serve as a performance incentive.

INFORMATION ASYMMETRY

Several types of complexities arise in these agent-principal relationships, such as information asymmetry. The agent (management) has a considerable advantage over the principals regarding information about the company. Hidden action[16] (or *moral hazard*) refers to a situation where one party in a transaction takes actions that are not observable or verifiable by the other party. For example, in an employment contract, an employee may engage in behaviours or activities that the employer cannot easily monitor, such as exerting less effort or taking risks that may not be apparent. Hidden information (or *adverse selection*) occurs when one party possesses private information that is not known to the other party during a transaction. In the context of insurance, a policyholder may have information about their health status that the insurance company is not aware of. This hidden information can lead to adverse selection, as the insurance company may not accurately assess the risk associated with insuring that individual. In summary, hidden action relates to unobservable actions taken by one party after an agreement is in place, while hidden information involves one party having private information before entering into a transaction, which may impact the outcome and decisions made by the other party. Both concepts are part of the broader study of information asymmetry in economics.

In order for the principals (who buy shares in the company, loan the company money, or work for them) to have faith in the information given by management, it must be reliable. This means there is an incentive for both managers and outside investors to engage independent experts ('monitoring' in agency theory terms).

The contribution of an audit to shareholders is basically determined by the probability that the auditor will detect errors in the financial statements (or other irregularities, such as fraud or illegal acts) and the auditor's willingness to report these errors (e.g., by qualifying the auditor's report), even against the wish of the auditee (auditor independence). Costs as a result of reputation damage have been demonstrated in several empirical studies, which showed that audit firms, having suffered a public rebuke, were confronted with a decline in their market share.

The auditors are very important to the directors of these corporations. As Sir Adrian Cadbury commented[17]:

The external auditors are not part of the company team, but the chairmen (members of a corporate board of directors) have a direct interest in assuring themselves of the effectiveness of the audit approach within their companies. No chairman appreciates surprises, least of all in financial matters. The relationship between auditors and managers should be one where the auditors work with the appropriate people in the company but do so on a strictly objective and professional basis, never losing sight of the fact that they are there on the shareholders' behalf. Chairmen need auditors who will stand up to management when necessary and who will unhesitatingly raise any doubts about the people or procedures with the audit committee. Weak auditors expose chairmen to hazards.

1.5 AUDITING PROCESS AND PRACTICE

▶ THE OBJECTIVE ON AN AUDIT

In conducting an audit of financial statements, the overall objectives of the auditor are:
- ▶ To obtain reasonable assurance about whether the financial statements as a whole are free from material misstatement, whether due to fraud or error, thereby enabling the auditor to express an opinion on whether the financial statements are prepared, in all material respects, in accordance with an applicable financial reporting framework; and
- ▶ To report on the financial statements, and communicate as required by the ISAs, in accordance with the auditor's findings.

In all cases when reasonable assurance cannot be obtained and a qualified (financial statements materially misstated) opinion in the auditor's report is insufficient in the circumstances for purposes of reporting to the intended users of the financial statements, the ISAs require that the auditor disclaim an opinion or withdraw (or resign) from the engagement, if withdrawal is possible under applicable law or regulation.

In the international environment today, the professional auditor audits financial statements, internal control, compliance with policies, compliance with laws and regulations, and codes of best practice. However, no matter what subject matter the audit is designed to evaluate, the audit process is a well-defined methodology to help the auditor accumulate sufficient competent evidence.

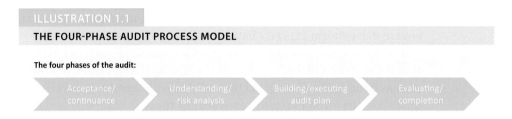

ILLUSTRATION 1.1

THE FOUR-PHASE AUDIT PROCESS MODEL

The four phases of the audit:

Acceptance/continuance → Understanding/risk analysis → Building/executing audit plan → Evaluating/completion

EMPIRICAL SCIENTIFIC CYCLE AND THE AUDIT

The audit process may be compared to the empirical scientific cycle.[18] The empirical scientific cycle is a systematic process of experimenting that starts with a research question, then a plan for an empirical test of the question is made, the test is done, feedback is analysed, and the scientist makes a judgement. The scientist's opinion is that the experimental hypothesis is false or not false, or perhaps that the test is inconclusive.

Although the numerous judgements made during a financial audit (about audit approach, sampling, audit risk, etc.) make it more of an art than a science, the audit process follows a systematic process. The audit process begins with a client's request for an audit of financial statements, which is followed by a plan of the audit and tests of evidence, culminating in a judgement or opinion. The auditor's judgement is whether the financial statements are as to their fairness, unmodified (unqualified)[19], qualified[20], adverse[21] or disclaimed[22].

A scientist poses a question – this is similar to the client asking an auditor to audit a set of financial statements. A plan is drawn up for the experiment (an audit plan). The scientist tests his theory and evaluates the evidence, and an auditor tests the assertions made in the financial statements. The scientist writes up a report on the experiment and an auditor writes a report on the representational quality of the financial statements based on the underlying accounting evidence.

Assessing risk is the core of the audit. The rest of the audit is designed to provide a response to these identified risks. In this book, we will provide a 'business risk' orientated approach. Business risks result from significant conditions, events, circumstances, actions, or inactions that could adversely affect a company's ability to execute its strategies. For example, risks may include changes in customer demand, government regulations, etc. Most business risks will eventually have financial consequences and, therefore, an effect on the financial statements. As such, the auditors are required to discuss business risks as part of the planning process.

▶ STANDARD AUDIT PROCESS MODEL IN FOUR PHASES

In this book a four-phase standard audit process model is used based on the scientific empirical cycle. The phases of the audit are:

1 Acceptance and continuance of audit client and engagement.
2 Planning through understanding and risk analysis.
3 Building and executing the audit plan.
4 Evaluating evidence and completion.

Illustration 1.1 shows the four-phase audit process model and its major sub-components.

▶ PHASE I: CLIENT AND ENGAGEMENT ACCEPTANCE AND CONTINUANCE

An audit firm carries out audits for both existing clients and new clients. For existing clients, there is in general not much activity involved in accepting the client for another year's audit. The audit firm is familiar with the company and has a great deal of information for making an acceptable decision. However, if the auditor's business risk is unacceptably high (for example, client is a fraudster or acts illegally), the auditor reconsiders continuation of the agreement. Audit firms have strict procedures for reconsidering high-risk engagements.

When prospective clients approach the audit firm with a request to bid on their financial audits, audit firms must investigate the business background, financial statements, and industry of the client. The firm must also convince the client to accept them. The process of client acceptance involves evaluation of the client's background, selecting personnel for the audit, and evaluating the need and requirements for using the work of other professionals. (The client acceptance phase of the auditing methodology is discussed in detail in chapter 5, 'Client and Engagement Acceptance / Continuance'.)

▶ PHASE II: PLANNING THROUGH UNDERSTANDING AND RISK ANALYSIS

The auditor must plan her work to enable her to conduct an effective audit in an efficient and timely manner. Plans should be based on knowledge of the client's business.

Plans are developed after assessing risk of financial material misstatement by obtaining a basic understanding of the business background, control environment, and control activities (procedures)[23] and the client's accounting system, which might include performing analytical procedures[24]. The second part of the planning process is to determine the riskiness of the engagement and set materiality levels.

Finally, the auditor prepares an audit plan[25] which outlines the nature, timing and extent of audit procedures required to gather evidence that responds to the identified risks.

As will be explained in chapters 6 and 7, ISA 315 sets out the risk assessment procedures that form the foundation for an audit of financial statements. ISA 315 offers detailed guidance for auditors to perform consistent and effective identification of the risks of material misstatement.

One of the most widely accepted concepts on auditing is the importance of the client's internal control system[26] to reliable financial information. If the client has adequate internal controls for proving reliable data and safeguarding assets and records, the amount of audit evidence required, and planned for, is significantly less than where internal controls are inadequate. Therefore, assessing the design and operating effectiveness of internal controls is a very important part of the planning process.

An entity's internal control structure includes five basic categories of policies and procedures. Management designs and implements this to provide reasonable assurance that its control objectives will be met. These components of internal control are[27]:

1　the control environment
2　risk assessment
3　control procedures
4　information system
5　monitoring

Planning concepts are discussed in chapter 6, 'Identifying and Assessing Inherent Risk', and chapter 7, 'Identifying and Assessing Control Risk'.

▶ PHASE III: BUILDING AND EXECUTING THE AUDIT PLAN

The audit should be performed, and the report prepared with due professional care by persons who have adequate training, experience and competence in auditing. The auditor should also be independent of the audit and keep the results of the audit confidential, as required by international ethics. 'Due professional care' means that the auditor is a professional responsible for fulfilling her duties diligently and carefully. Due care includes the completeness of the working papers, the sufficiency of the audit evidence and the appropriateness of the audit report.

The testing and evidence-gathering phase of the audit requires first planning the audit procedures. Then testing is done of any controls that the auditor expects to rely upon. Once the controls are tested, the auditor must decide on additional, substantive, tests. Prior to this, understanding of controls is needed to determine what kind of tests (the nature), when they should be done (timing), and what the number (extent) of the tests should be.

GATHERING EVIDENCE

The auditor should obtain sufficient appropriate audit evidence through the performance of control and substantive procedures[28] to enable her to draw reasonable conclusions on which to base her audit opinion. Tests of controls[29] are audit procedures designed to evaluate the operating effectiveness of controls in preventing, or detecting and correcting, material misstatements at the assertion level; substantive procedures are designed to obtain evidence as to the completeness, accuracy, and validity of the data produced by the accounting system. A substantive procedure is an audit procedure designed to detect material misstatements at the assertion level. Substantive procedures comprise: (1) Tests of details (of classes of transactions, account balances, and disclosures) and (2) Substantive analytical procedures.

There are three types of tests: details of transactions, account balances, and analytical review. (Audit evidence is discussed in chapter 8 and chapter 9.)

▶ PHASE IV: EVALUATING EVIDENCE AND REPORTING FINDINGS

After the fieldwork is almost complete, a series of procedures are generally carried out to 'complete the audit'. The intent of these procedures is to review the audit work, get certain assurances from the client, uncover any potential problems, check compliance with regulations, and check the consistency of the material that is to be presented to the users of financial statements. We will discuss this further in chapter 10.

The auditor must perform final audit procedures before the audit report can be written. The auditor must:
- ▶ obtain legal letters,
- ▶ identify subsequent events,
- ▶ carry out an overall review,
- ▶ review all material that goes into the annual report, report to the board of directors
- ▶ obtain a written representation from management (management representations letter)[30],
- ▶ carry out wrap up procedures.

The auditor should review and assess the conclusions drawn from audit evidence on which she will base her opinion on the financial information. We discuss this in chapters 10 and 11. This review and assessment involves forming an overall conclusion as to whether:

- ▶ the financial information has been prepared using acceptable accounting policies, consistently applied;
- ▶ the financial information complies with relevant regulations and statutory requirements;
- ▶ the view presented by the financial information as a whole is consistent with the auditor's knowledge of the business of the entity; and
- ▶ there is adequate disclosure of all material matters relevant to the proper presentation of the financial information.

THE AUDIT OPINION

The audit report should contain a clear written expression of opinion on the financial information. An unmodified (unqualified) opinion indicates the auditor's satisfaction in all material respects with the matters. When a qualified opinion, adverse opinion or disclaimer of opinion is given, the audit report should state the reasons in a clear and informative manner.

Completing the audit is discussed in chapter 10. Audit reports are discussed in detail in chapter 11.

1.6   DUTIES, EXPECTATIONS AND DEVELOPMENTS

The development of the auditor's duties, linked to changes in the audit market, is since the origin of the profession an object of public debate, often referred to as the audit expectation gap debate. The *expectations-performance gap* is defined as the gap between society's expectations of auditors and auditors perceived performance, comprising 'reasonableness' and 'performance' components. This gap results from the fact that users of audit services have expectations regarding the duties of auditors that exceed the current practice in the profession.

A good deal of research has been done on the audit expectation-performance gap by Brenda Porter and others (illustration 1.2)[31]. Early empirical research was conducted by Porter to investigate the audit expectation-performance gap. The study highlighted the duties which constitute the reasonableness[32], deficient standards and deficient performance components of the gap. The research provided insights into the structure, composition and extent of the audit expectation-performance gap and suggested a rational, comprehensive approach towards narrowing the gap.

The users of audit services can broadly be classified as intended users[33] (shareholders, bankers, creditors, employees, customers, and other groups) and 'auditees' (management, the board of directors). Each group has its own set of expectations for an auditor's duties. To be trustworthy to the intended users it is required that the auditor to be independent of the auditee, who is accountable through the annual report to be audited but also pays the bill.[34] The resulting requirements for the auditor's integrity are discussed in chapter 3.

Expectation gap studies demonstrate that public expectations are high. Basically, it seems that a large part of the financial community (users of audit services) expects for

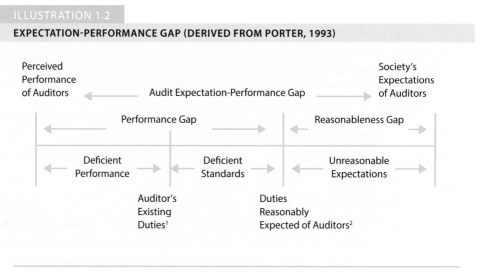

ILLUSTRATION 1.2

EXPECTATION-PERFORMANCE GAP (DERIVED FROM PORTER, 1993)

[1] Duties defined by the law and professional promulgations
[2] Duties which are cost-beneficial for auditors to perform

example that financial statements with an unmodified (unqualified) audit opinion are completely free from error and fraud.

Public expectations include questions such as:

▶ Is the company a going concern?
▶ What is the risk that an 'unfortunate mistake' brings this company to its knees?
▶ Are there adequate controls?
▶ Is the entity free of fraud?
▶ What effect do the company's products and by-products have on the environment?

Current developments in each of these 'duties' will be described in the remainder of this chapter.

REPORTING ON THE COMPANY'S ABILITY TO CONTINUE AS A GOING CONCERN

Perhaps the most disturbing events for the public's trust in the audit profession are cases where an unmodified (unqualified) audit report has been issued shortly before a company's bankruptcy.

Under ISA 570[35] and most national regulations, auditors need to determine whether the audited entity is able to continue as a going concern. Although warning the financial statement users of any threatening financial distress is appropriate, the disclosure of a possible future bankruptcy – especially when the future course of events is hard to predict – may prove to be a self-fulfilling prophecy which deprives management of its means to save the company. We refer to chapters 10 and 11 for further discussion.

REPORTING ON EFFECTIVENESS OF INTERNAL CONTROL

The issue of testing and reporting on the quality of a company's internal control system has been recognized as one of the focal issues in auditing. There has been much discussion in Europe, Canada and the USA about reporting on the effectiveness and functioning of internal controls[36]. Support for reporting lies in the belief that users of financial information have a legitimate interest in the condition of the controls over the accounting system and management's response to the suggestions of the auditors for correction of weaknesses. Those who argue against reporting on controls say that such reporting increases the cost of audits, increases auditor (and director) liability and is not relevant information.

The United States Sarbanes–Oxley Act of 2002 requires that company officers certify that internal controls are effective and requires that an independent auditor verify management's analysis[37]. Section 404 of the Act requires each annual report of a company to contain an 'internal control report' which should:

1 state the responsibility of management for establishing and maintaining an adequate internal control structure and procedures for financial reporting;
2 contain an assessment, as of the end of the fiscal year, of the effectiveness of the internal control system and procedures for financial reporting;
3 contain an 'attestation' to management's assessment by the company's independent, outside auditors; and
4 contain an attestation by an independent auditor to any difference between management's required assertions and the audit evidence on internal controls.

US Public Company Accounting Oversight Board (PCAOB) has promulgated Audit Standard 2201 An Audit of Internal Control Over Financial Reporting That Is Integrated with An Audit of Financial Statements'[38] that addresses internal control audits. Such an assurance engagement is further discussed in section 14.5.

The UK Corporate Governance Code 2018 required boards to monitor a company's risk management and internal control framework and carry out annual reviews of its effectiveness. The 2024 Code includes more prescriptive requirements as to how boards should report on this review. In the annual report, boards need to include[39]:

▶ disclosure on how the board has monitored and reviewed the effectiveness of the framework
▶ a declaration as to the effectiveness of the material controls as at the balance sheet date, and
▶ a description of any material controls which have not operated effectively as at the balance sheet date, any remedial action taken (or proposed) to improve them and any action taken to address previously reported issues.

The Code expressly refers to reporting controls, together with financial, operation and compliance controls, when detailing the material controls to be covered by the board's monitoring and review.

BARINGS BANK EXAMPLE

Barings Bank is an example of a company whose breakdown in internal controls, specifically segregation of duties, led to the ultimate destruction of the company.[40] In 1995 Nicholas Leeson, manager of the Singapore Branch of Barings, not only made investments in the Nikkei exchange index derivatives, but also was able to authorize and account for his investment (account settling). This ultimately led to the multi-billion-dollar collapse of Barings and a jail sentence for Leeson.

For developing and evaluating the effectiveness of internal controls there has been a landmark study published by the Committee of Sponsoring Organizations of the Treadway Commission (COSO Report)[41]. This report envisaged (see illustration 1.3):

▶ harmonizing the definitions regarding internal control and its components;

▶ helping management in assessing the quality of internal control;

▶ creating internal control benchmarks, enabling management to compare the internal control in their own company to the state-of-the-art; and

▶ creating a basis for the external reporting on the adequacy of the internal controls.

Although all of these objectives might have an influence on the audit service, the latter subject is particularly relevant, because it might lead to certification by the auditor of management's assertions regarding the quality of a company's internal control system but also regarding the risk of a material misstatement in (non[42]) financial reporting due to fraud or error. (The COSO report is discussed in more detail in chapter 7.)

ILLUSTRATION 1.3

THE COSO REPORT OBJECTIVES

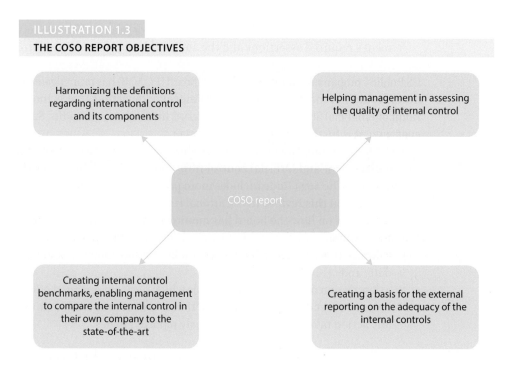

Harmonizing the definitions regarding international control and its components

Helping management in assessing the quality of internal control

COSO report

Creating internal control benchmarks, enabling management to compare the internal control in their own company to the state-of-the-art

Creating a basis for the external reporting on the adequacy of the internal controls

▶ REPORTING ON THE OCCURRENCE OF FRAUD

The audit expectation gap is frequently associated with the fraud issue. Both governments and the financial community expect the auditor to find existing fraud cases and report them. The fact that this part of the expectation gap has attracted so much attention is partly attributable to the evolution of auditing. As stated in our brief description of the history of auditing, the detection of fraud has been one of the profession's cornerstones. (See chapter 12, 'Fraud and Other Considerations of Law and Regulation in an Audit'.)

FAMOUS FRAUDS

One of the largest non-financial statement frauds of all time was the Ponzi scheme of Bernard Madoff, who ran a $60 billion fraudulent hedge fund.[43] Major companies that issued fraudulent financial statements in the early twenty-first century included: US companies Enron, WorldCom, Xerox, Tyco, Health South, Bristol Myers and NextCard; European firms Ahold, Parmalat and Comroad; Japanese bank Resona; and Australian insurance company HIH. More recent examples are Satyam, FTX, Steinhoff, Wirecard, Theranos, Patisserie Valerie, Luckin Coffee and Adani Group[44]. Some of these cases are discussed in 'Concept and a Company' cases throughout this book.

The current position of the audit profession as to fraud is described in International Standards on Auditing (ISA) 240[45]. According to ISA 240, the primary responsibility for the prevention and detection of fraud and error rests with both those charged with the governance and the management of an entity. Fraud may involve sophisticated and carefully organized schemes designed to conceal it, such as forgery, deliberate failure to record transactions, or intentional misrepresentations being made to the auditor. The auditor is responsible for obtaining reasonable assurance that the financial statements are free from material statements, whether caused by fraud or error.

OCCURRENCE OF ILLEGAL ACTS

Closely related to the subject of fraud is the auditor's reaction to the occurrence of illegal acts in a company. Both ISA 250[46] and most national regulators state that the auditor's responsibility in this area is restricted to designing and executing the audit in such a way that there is a reasonable expectation of detecting material illegal acts like bribery and corruption which have a direct impact on the form and content of the financial statements. In reporting illegal acts, national regulators require the auditor to assess the potential impact on the financial statements and determine the consequences of the uncertainty or error in the financial statements for the opinion.

The professional regulations in some countries require the auditor to inform members of the audit committee or board of directors. Informing third parties is allowed in certain circumstances. (See chapter 12, 'Fraud and Other Considerations of Law and Regulation in An Audit'.) ISA 240 and ISA 250 address what should be reported in auditor communication of illegal acts. Most expectation gap studies reveal that respondents expect the auditor to detect and report illegal acts that have a significant impact on the financial statements.

▶ SUSTAINABILITY REPORTING

The importance of the company as a potential generator of wealth is understood, but awareness of the impact that a company's activities have on society and the environment is becoming more and more prevalent. This has led to the expectation by investors that more information than just financial statements should be provided about a company.

As a consequence, the landscape of sustainability reporting and assurance has witnessed significant developments, reflecting a broader shift towards corporate responsibility and accountability. Organizations increasingly adopt the Global Reporting Initiative (GRI) standards for comprehensive disclosure of economic, environmental, and social impacts. Integrated Reporting (IR) is gaining traction, combining financial and non-financial information to provide a holistic perspective on performance.

The Task Force on Climate-related Financial Disclosures (TCFD) recommendations has prompted companies to disclose climate-related risks and opportunities in financial reporting. Aligning with the United Nations' Sustainable Development Goals (SDGs) has become a common practice, showcasing commitment to global sustainability objectives.

Technology plays a crucial role, with reporting platforms and data analytics facilitating efficient and transparent sustainability reporting. Stakeholder engagement is emphasized, recognizing the importance of involving diverse stakeholders to capture concerns and expectations.

Supply chain transparency is increasingly integrated into sustainability reporting, necessitating disclosure of responsible sourcing, fair labour practices, and environmental considerations throughout the supply chain.

Emerging reporting frameworks, such as the European Sustainability Reporting Standards (ESRS) and standards issued by the International Sustainability Standards Board (ISSB) and Sustainability Accounting Standards Board (SASB), address industry-specific disclosure of financially material sustainability information.

In summary, the evolution of sustainability reporting and assurance reflects a dynamic and multifaceted landscape, with organizations embracing transparency, stakeholder engagement, and innovative frameworks to communicate their commitment to sustainable business practices.

As will be discussed in chapter 15, assurance services are on the rise, with independent third-party verification enhancing the credibility of sustainability reports. Regulatory changes in various jurisdictions are compelling companies to disclose environmental and social impacts, reinforcing the integration of sustainability into core business operations and have this information verified.

▶ EXAMPLES OF LANDMARK LEGISLATION THAT INFLUENCED THE INTERNATIONAL AUDIT MARKET

The international audit market has been shaped by landmark studies and legislation that have played a crucial role in establishing standards and regulations. The following are some examples that will be explored in greater detail throughout this book.

Sarbanes-Oxley Act (SOX) – 2002 (United States)
▶ One of the most significant pieces of legislation in the accounting and auditing industry.
▶ Enacted in response to corporate accounting scandals, such as Enron and WorldCom.
▶ Enhanced corporate governance and financial disclosures, impacting audit committees, auditor independence, and internal controls.

EU Audit Reform – 2014 (European Union)
▶ The reform aimed to enhance the quality and transparency of audits.
▶ Introduced mandatory audit firm rotation and restrictions on non-audit services to improve auditor independence.
▶ Encouraged competition in the audit market by limiting the market share of audit firms.

IFRS Adoption – Early 2000s (International)
▶ The widespread adoption of International Financial Reporting Standards (IFRS) has profoundly impacted global financial reporting and auditing.

▷ Promotes consistency and comparability in financial statements across countries, affecting how audits are conducted and reported.

Public Company Accounting Oversight Board (PCAOB) – 2002 (United States)
▷ Created by the Sarbanes-Oxley Act, the PCAOB oversees the audits of public companies to protect investors.
▷ Sets auditing and professional practice standards for registered public accounting firms.

International Standards on Auditing (ISA)
▷ Developed by the International Auditing and Assurance Standards Board (IAASB) under the International Federation of Accountants (IFAC).
▷ Provides a set of international standards that guide auditors in conducting audits and issuing audit reports.

These examples illustrate how legislative actions and standards-setting bodies have shaped the international audit market by addressing issues of transparency, accountability, independence, and quality in financial reporting and auditing practices.

1.7 FUTURE OF AUDITING

In the future, as is the case today, a comprehensive report on a company's activities, financial statements, notes and auditors' reports will be required. In addition to these, however, there will also be a director's report on corporate governance (including effectiveness of internal control systems, going concern, and fraud), and sustainability reports. These reports will not only be retrospective, but more prospective information will be disclosed.

As a result, auditing spreads to audit of non-financial, textual and electronic data such as emails, phone messages, social media, human resources, intellectual capital, brand valuation and management, and other intangibles.

With the explosion in the use of information technology the auditor needs sufficient expertise, coupled with the knowledge of her client's affairs, to enable her to obtain and interpret all the evidence needed to provide reasonable assurance that the financial statements are fairly presented.

The impact of Artificial Intelligence (AI) on financial statement auditors is transformative, introducing efficiencies, improving accuracy, and influencing the overall audit process. Some aspects of how AI is affecting auditors in the context of financial statement auditing are the automation of routine tasks, data analytics and pattern recognition, enhanced risk assessment, and fraud detection. AI tools are increasingly being used for fraud detection. Machine learning algorithms can identify unusual patterns and anomalies in financial transactions, aiding auditors in detecting potential fraud or irregularities that might be challenging to uncover through traditional methods. But of course, fraudsters will also use the latest (AI) technologies as is illustrated in 'Concept and a Company 1.1'.

The new auditing environment will demand new skills of auditors if they are to be reporters and assessors of governance and measurements. They must have a questioning mind and be able to analyse and critically assess evidence.

Professor J.P. Percy outlined a challenging perspective on the auditor's future[47]. He predicted that auditors would account for information not only in financial but also non-financial terms. The public desire will be for external and internal assessors on the board of directors. External assessors will appraise the integrity of information and business conduct, and internal assessors will appraise the efficiency and effectiveness of systems and their adequacy. Independent directors or assessors working on behalf of the shareholders within the board will ensure proper governance is being observed. (See chapter 14 for further discussion of assurance services.)

CONCEPT AND A COMPANY 1.1

FINANCE WORKER PAYS OUT $25 MILLION AFTER VIDEO CALL WITH DEEPFAKE 'CHIEF FINANCIAL OFFICER BY HEATHER CHEN AND KATHLEEN MAGRAMO, CNN, SUN FEBRUARY 4, 2024

Concept	Authorities are increasingly concerned at the damaging potential posed by artificial intelligence technology.
Story	A finance worker at a multinational firm was tricked into paying out $25 million to fraudsters using deepfake technology to pose as the company's chief financial officer in a video conference call, according to Hong Kong police.

The elaborate scam saw the worker duped into attending a video call with what he thought were several other members of staff, but all of whom were in fact deepfake recreations, Hong Kong police said at a briefing.

"(In the) multi-person video conference, it turns out that everyone [he saw] was fake," senior superintendent Baron Chan Shun-ching told the city's public broadcaster RTHK.

Chan said the worker had grown suspicious after he received a message that was purportedly from the company's UK-based chief financial officer. Initially, the worker suspected it was a phishing email, as it talked of the need for a secret transaction to be carried out.

However, the worker put aside his early doubts after the video call because other people in attendance had looked and sounded just like colleagues he recognized, Chan said.

Believing everyone else on the call was real, the worker agreed to remit a total of $200 million Hong Kong dollars – about $25.6 million, the police officer added.

The case is one of several recent episodes in which fraudsters are believed to have used deepfake technology to modify publicly available video and other footage to cheat people out of money.

At the press briefing, Hong Kong police said they had made six arrests in connection with such scams.

Chan said that eight stolen Hong Kong identity cards – all of which had been reported as lost by their owners – were used to make 90 loan applications and 54 bank account registrations between July and September last year.

On at least 20 occasions, AI deepfakes had been used to trick facial recognition programs by imitating the people pictured on the identity cards, according to police.

The scam involving the fake CFO was only discovered when the employee later checked with the corporation's head office.

Hong Kong police did not reveal the name or details of the company or the worker.

Authorities across the world are growing increasingly concerned at the sophistication of deepfake technology and the nefarious uses it can be put to.

Discussion Questions	▶ What measures can organizations implement to enhance their employees' awareness of emerging technological threats like deepfake technology? Provide specific examples and recommendations to mitigate the risk of falling victim to such scams.
	▶ Consider both technological and procedural safeguards that auditors can recommend to ensure the integrity of financial transactions and protect against deepfake-related fraud. How can auditors work collaboratively with IT and cybersecurity teams to strengthen controls in the face of evolving technological threats?
References	https://edition.cnn.com/2024/02/04/asia/deepfake-cfo-scam-hong-kong-intl-hnk/index.html
	Adoption of artificial intelligence in auditing: An exploratory study, Ravi Seethamraju and Angela Hecimovic, Australian Journal of Management, July 2022, Volume 48, Issue 4, https://doi.org/10.1177/03128962221108440
	Artificial intelligence and auditing in small- and medium-sized firms: Expectations and applications Pall Rikhardsson, Kristinn R. Thórisson, Gudmundur Bergthorsson, Catherine Batt, AI Magazine, August 2022, https://doi.org/10.1002/aaai.12066

1.8 SUMMARY

A general definition of auditing is 'An audit is a systematic process of objectively obtaining and evaluating evidence regarding assertions about economic actions and events to ascertain the degree of correspondence between these assertions and established criteria and communicating the results to interested users.'

An audit is an independent, objective and expert examination and evaluation of evidence. Auditors are fair and do not allow prejudice or bias to override their objectivity. They maintain an impartial attitude. To be effective, the auditor plans and performs an audit with professional scepticism recognizing that circumstances may exist that cause the financial statements to be materially misstated. Professional judgement is the application of relevant training, knowledge and experience, within the context provided by auditing and accounting standards, in making informed decisions about the courses of action that are appropriate to the audit engagement.

The concept of materiality is applied by the auditor in planning and performing the audit, and in evaluating the effect of identified misstatements on the financial statements. Misstatements, including omissions, are considered to be material if, individually or in the aggregate, they could reasonably be expected to influence the economic decisions of users based on the financial statements.

Auditing predates the Christian era. Anthropologists have found records of auditing activity dating back to early Mesopotamian times (around 3000 BC). There was also auditing activity in ancient China, Greece and Rome. The Latin meaning of the word 'auditor' was a 'hearer or listener' because in Rome auditors heard taxpayers, such as farmers, give their public statements regarding the results of their business and the tax duty due. Auditors existed in ancient China and Egypt. They were supervisors of the accounts of the Chinese Emperor and the Egyptian Pharaoh. The government accounting system of the Zhao (1046–221 BC) dynasty in China included an elaborate budgetary process and audits of all government departments. From the dawn of the dynastic era in Egypt (3000 BC) the scribes (accountants) were among the most esteemed in society and the scribal occupation was one of the most prestigious occupations.

The attitude of profit maximization emerged at the end of the Middle Ages, with the emergence of large merchant houses in Italy. A system of double entry bookkeeping was first described in Italy, used by a Genoa commune in 1340 AD. The first book on double entry accounting was Luca Pacioli's *Summa de Arithmetica* dated 20 November 1494.

The practice of modern auditing dates back to the beginning of the modern corporation at the dawn of the Industrial Revolution. In 1853, the Society of Accountants was founded in Edinburgh. Several other institutes emerged in Great Britain, merging in 1880 into the Institute of Chartered Accountants in England and Wales.

Today the flow of investor funds to the corporations and the whole process of allocation of financial resources through the securities markets have become dependent to a very large extent on financial reports made by company management. One of the most important characteristics of these corporations is the fact that their ownership is almost totally separated from their management. Management has control over the accounting systems. They are not only responsible for the financial reports to investors, but they also have the authority to determine the way in which the information is presented.

The demand for audit services may be explained by several different theories. Agency Theory has been well researched and reported on. Other theories based on public perceptions such as the Policeman Theory, the Lending Credibility Theory and the Legal Liability Theory serve more as a point of reference than as a researched construct.

In the agency theory, originally proposed by Watts and Zimmerman, a reputable auditor – an auditor who is perceived to meet expectations – is appointed not only in the interest of third parties, but also in the interest of management. A company is viewed as the result of more or less formal 'contracts', in which several groups make some kind of contribution to the company, given a certain 'price'. Company management tries to get these contributions under optimum conditions for management: low interest rates from bankers, high share prices for stockholders, and low wages for employees. Agency Theory also includes consideration of 'moral hazard'. A moral hazard occurs when entering into contract with another company or an agent being deliberately skewed or altered in order to attempt to make a profit.

In conducting an audit of financial statements, the overall objectives of the auditor are: (a) To obtain reasonable assurance about whether the financial statements as a whole are free from material misstatement, whether due to fraud or error, thereby enabling the auditor to express an opinion on whether the financial statements are prepared, in all material respects, in accordance with an applicable financial reporting framework; and (b) To report on the financial statements, and communicate as required by the ISAs, in accordance with the auditor 's findings.

In this book a four-phase standard audit process model is used based on the scientific empirical cycle. The phases are: 1 client acceptance and audit engagement (pre-planning); 2 assess the risk of material misstatement (planning basis for an audit approach); 3 respond to identified risks (tests for evidence) and 4 evaluate evidence and report findings.

The users of audit services can broadly be classified as auditees (management, the board of directors) and third parties (shareholders, bankers, creditors, employees, customers, and other groups). Each of these groups has its own set of expectations with regard to an auditor's duties. Expectations were found with regard to the following duties of auditors in giving an opinion on the: (a) fairness of financial statements; (b) company's ability to continue as a going concern; (c) company's internal control system; (d) occurrence of fraud; and (e) occurrence of illegal acts.

Partly as a response to some of the expectation gap issues, there have been two landmark studies (the COSO Report and the Cadbury Report which led to the Combined Code and the Turnbull Report) and most recently responses have been legislated into the US accounting profession by the Sarbanes–Oxley Act of 2002.

The impact that a company's activities have on society and the environment has led to the expectation by investors that more information than just financial statements should be provided about a company. The landscape of sustainability reporting and assurance has witnessed significant developments, reflecting a broader shift towards corporate responsibility and accountability reporting by audit firms. Standards for sustainability have been contributed by several organizations including Task Force on Climate-related Financial Disclosures (TCFD), United Nations' Sustainable Development Goals (SDG), European Sustainability Reporting Standards (ESRS), International Sustainability Standards Board (ISSB), and Sustainability Accounting Standards Board (SASB).

In the future there will be a director's report on corporate governance (including effectiveness of internal control systems, going concern, and fraud), and sustainability reports in addition to the currently required annual report, financial statements, notes and auditors' reports. These reports will not only be retrospective, but more prospective information will be disclosed.

1.9 QUESTIONS, EXERCISES AND CASES

QUESTIONS

1.2 What Is an Audit?
1-1 Based on the ISAs, what are the general principles governing an audit of financial statements? Discuss materiality and professional scepticism.

1-2 What is meant by 'economic actions and events' and why are they relevant in the context of auditing?

1-3 What are the limitations of an audit? Why must these limitations be considered?

1.3 History
1-4 Why have fraud scandals contributed to the development of the audit profession?

1-5 Why do you think owner-managed companies decide to have their financial statements audited by an auditor?

1.4 Theory
1-6 Agency Theory. Identify principals and agents in the cases mentioned below. Describe the contributions and 'prices' associated with these relationships, identify potential risks for the principal and give suggestions for limiting these risks:

    A.   The Pasadena Bank lends money to the Alhambra Construction Company.

    B.   Employee Mario Auditorio considers leaving his current job and starting a new career with Instituto Milanese.

C.   Manager Yu-Chang receives an annual bonus, based on last year's profit of company Shang-Zu.

D.   Supplier 'Vite et Juste' delivers goods to company 'Merci'. Payment is due 60 days after the date of the invoice.

1-7   Explain the difference between moral hazard and adverse selection in a financial reporting setting. How can the financial statement auditor help to reduce these forms of information asymmetry?

1.5 Auditing Process

1-8   What is meant by the 'empirical scientific cycle' and how does this link to the audit process?

1-9   Audit Process Model. What are the four Phases of an Audit? Discuss each. Determine which is the most important of the four and explain why.

1-10 What are the components of internal controls?

1.6 Duties, Expectations and Developments

1-11 What are the duties and tasks of a (financial statement) auditor?

1-12 What are reasons auditors do not (always) meet expectations and what can be the consequences for the audit profession?

1.7 Future of Auditing

1-13 In what way can AI tools help an auditor in their audits?

PROBLEMS AND EXERCISES

1.2 What Is an Audit?

1-14 Based on the ISAs what are the general principles governing an audit of financial statements? Discuss materiality and professional scepticism.

1-15 The evidence in an audit concerns assertions about economic actions and events. Discuss management assertions.

1-16 Why do you think an auditor wishes to rely on internal controls?

1.3 History

1-17 In this chapter, the history of auditing has been briefly described from an international perspective. Identify the major differences with the developments specific for your country and try to explain these based on differences in the economic system or development.

1-18 Why does it follow that the emergence of joint stock companies during the Industrial Revolution would lead to more business focus on audits and a founding of public audit firms?

1.4 Theory

1-19 Legal Liability Theory. Explain how the Legal Liability Theory shapes audits acceptance of the following auditees?

A.   A business in a high-risk industry.

B.   A Netherlands non-profit NGO whose director is a convicted criminal.

C.   A NGO headquartered in Zaire whose director is a convicted criminal.

QUESTIONS, EXERCISES AND CASES

1.5 Auditing Process

1-20 Objectives of an Audit. Tracy Keulen, the sole owner of a small bakery, has been told that the business should have financial statements reported on by an independent Registerac-countant (RA). Keulen, having some bookkeeping experience, has personally prepared the company's financial statements and does not understand why such statements should be examined by an RA. Keulen discussed the matter with Petra Dassen, an RA, and asked Dassen to explain why an audit is considered important.

Required:

A.   Describe the objectives of the independent audit.

B.   Identify five ways in which an independent audit may be beneficial to Keulen.

1-21 Why should an audit opinion be in writing? As each auditee differs, do you expect auditors' opinions to differ as well[48]? Explain.

1-22 Audit Process Model. Based on the standard Audit Process Model, trace the procedures an auditor would use to audit a retail clothing business (continuing client) from the initial client contact to the audit opinion.

1.6 Duties, Expectations and Developments

1-23 Opinion on the Occurrence of Illegal Acts. Ostling, Auktoriserad Revisor, accepted an engagement to audit the financial statements of Sandnes Company of Göteborg, Sweden. Ostling's discussions with Sandnes's new management and the predecessor auditor indicated the possibility that Sandnes's financial statements may be misstated due to the possible occurrence of errors, irregularities and illegal acts.

Required:

A.   Identify and describe Ostling's responsibilities to detect Sandnes's errors and ir-regularities. Do not identify specific audit procedures.

B.   Identify and describe Ostling's responsibilities to report Sandnes's errors and irregularities.

C.   Describe Ostling's responsibilities to detect Sandnes's material illegal acts. Do not identify specific audit procedures.

1-24 Give an example of the performance gap and of the reasonableness gap as sketched in illustration 1.2.

1.7 Future of Auditing

1-25 Do you think auditors will become 'policeman/ woman' in the near future? Motivate.

1-26 Explain what is meant by sustainability assurance.

CASES

1-27 International Standards on Auditing (ISA). International Standards on Auditing (ISA). Download the latest version of Handbook of International Quality Control, Auditing Review, Other Assurance, And Related Services Pronouncements from the IAASB website https://www.iaasb.org/standards-pronouncements. Pick one ISA and discuss how that standard would influence the work of an auditor.

1-28 Qualifications of Auditors. Look for the text of the EC Eighth Company Law Directive which is about the qualifications and work of auditors.

Required:

Based on the Eighth Directive, answer the following questions.

A.   How many years of work experience must an auditor have before he can receive an auditing credential?

B.   How many years of education must an auditor have before certification?

1-29 Generative AI can be a threat and an opportunity for financial statement audits. Explain.

1-30 What role does explainability and interpretability of AI algorithms play in the context of financial statements audits, and how can auditors ensure transparency and trustworthiness in their assessments when utilizing advanced AI technologies in the audit process?

1.10   NOTES

1.   International Auditing and Assurance Standards Board (IAASB), 2023, International Standard on Auditing 200 (ISA 200) 'Overall Objectives of the Independent Auditor and the Conduct of an Audit in Accordance with International Standards on Auditing', paragraphs 1–9. International Federation of Accountants, New York, *Handbook of International Quality Management, Auditing Review, Other Assurance, and Related Services Pronouncements*, 2022 ed, Volume I, International Federation of Accountants, New York.

2.   American Accounting Association, 1973, *A Statement of Basic Auditing Concepts*, Studies in Accounting Research (6), American Accounting Association, Sarasota, Florida, p. 2.

3.   As will be explained in chapters 14 and 15, auditors can also examine non-financial information, such as effectiveness of internal controls or compliance with company policies or environmental regulations.

4.   Professional scepticism – an attitude that includes a questioning mind, being alert to conditions which may indicate possible misstatement due to error or fraud, and a critical assessment of evidence (discussed in more detail in chapter 4).

5.   Material misstatement – a significant mistake in financial information which would arise from errors and fraud if it could influence the economic decisions of users taken on the basis of the financial statements.

6.   Professional judgement – the application of relevant training, knowledge and experience, within the context provided by auditing, accounting and ethical standards, in making informed decisions about the courses of action that are appropriate in the circumstances of the audit engagement. (Discussed in more detail in chapter 4.)

7.   Materiality – information is material if its omission or misstatement could influence the economic decisions of users taken on the basis of the financial statements. Materiality depends on the size of the item or error judged in the particular circumstances of its omission or misstatement. Thus, materiality provides a threshold or cut-off point rather than being a primary qualitative characteristic, which information must have if it is to be useful. (We discuss materiality in greater depth in chapter 5.)

8.   Control environment – includes the governance and management functions and the attitudes, awareness and actions of those charged with governance and management concerning the entity's internal control and its importance in the entity. The control environment is a component of internal control.

9.   Sufficient appropriate audit evidence – *sufficiency* is the measure of the quantity (amount) of audit evidence. *Appropriateness* is the measure of the quality of audit evidence and its relevance to a particular assertion and its reliability. (We will discuss evidence at some length in chapters 8 and 9.)

10. Throughout this book, as a matter of convenience, we will use the terms 'she' and 'her' and 'hers' which will be meant to indicate all genders: she, he, him, her, his, hers, and any persons whatsoever.

11. The term 'auditore' is an Italian word that translates to 'auditor' in English. The word is derived from the Latin term 'auditor,' which means a listener or a hearer.

12. In the latter half of the 19th century, the US railway was built from east to west, requiring financial support from the UK. Investors supplied the necessary capital for the railway's construction and dispatched their accountants to oversee the project (Wallage, P, Methodology and Degree of Structure: A Dissertation on the Audit Process (University of Amsterdam, 1991).

13. The Afrikaansche Handelsvereeniging was a company controlled by a very reputable citizen of Rotterdam, the Netherlands. He managed to conceal important losses of his company to bankers, creditors and stockholders by providing false balance sheets.

14. See chapter 2 for the supply side of the audit market.

15. See Watts, R.L. and Zimmerman, J.L., 1978, 'Towards a Positive Theory of the Determination of Accounting Standards', *The Accounting Review*, January, pp. 112–134; and Watts, R.L. and Zimmerman, J.L., 1979, 'The Demand for and Supply of Accounting Theories: The Market for Excuses', *The Accounting Review*, April, pp. 273–305.

16. K.J. Arrow. 'The Economics of Agency.' Stanford University IMSSS Technical Report No. 451, October 1984.

17. Cadbury, Adrian, 1995, *The Company Chairman*, 2nd ed, Prentice Hall, Hemel Hempstead, England, p. 116.

18. Wallage, Philip, 1993, 'Internationalizing Audit: A Study of Audit Approaches in the Netherlands', *European Accounting Review*, 1993, No. 3, pp. 555–578.

19. Unmodified (unqualified opinion) – an audit opinion expressed when the auditor concludes that the financial statements give a true and fair view (or are presented fairly, in all material respects) in accordance with the identified financial reporting framework.

20. Qualified opinion – a qualified opinion is expressed when the auditor concludes that an unqualified opinion cannot be expressed but that the effect of any disagreement with management, or limitation on scope, is not so material and pervasive as to require an adverse opinion or a disclaimer of opinion.

21. Adverse opinion – an adverse opinion is expressed when the possible effect of a misstatement is material and pervasive.

22. Disclaimer of opinion – a disclaimer of opinion is expressed when the possible effect of a limitation on scope is so material and pervasive that the auditor has not been able to obtain sufficient appropriate audit evidence and accordingly is unable to express an opinion on the financial statements.

23. Control activities – those policies and procedures that help ensure that management directives are carried out. Control activities are a component of internal control.

24. Analytical procedures – evaluations of financial information through analysis of plausible relationships among both financial and non-financial data. Analytical procedures also encompass such investigation as is necessary of identified fluctuations or relationships that are inconsistent with other relevant information or that differ from expected values by a significant amount.

25. Audit plan – a work plan that reflects the design and performance of all audit procedures, consisting of a detailed approach for the nature, timing and extent of audit procedures to be performed (including the performance of risk assessment procedures) and the rationale for their selection. The audit plan begins by planning risk assessment procedures and

once performed, it is updated and changed to reflect the further audit procedures needed to respond to the results of the risk assessments. Also called audit program.

26. Internal control structure – the set of policies and procedures designed to provide management with reasonable assurance that the goals and objectives it believes are important will be met.

27. Committee of Sponsoring Organizations of the Treadway Commission (COSO), 1992, Chapter 1 'Definition' *Internal Control Integrated Framework – Framework*, American Institute of Certified Public Accountants, Jersey City, New Jersey, 1992.

28. Substantive procedure – an audit procedure designed to detect material misstatements at the assertion level. Substantive procedures comprise: (a) Tests of details (of classes of transactions, account balances, and disclosures); and (b) Substantive analytical procedures.

29. Tests of controls – an audit procedure designed to evaluate the operating effectiveness of controls in preventing, or detecting and correcting, material misstatements at the assertion level.

30. Written representation – a written statement by management provided to the auditor to confirm certain matters or to support other audit evidence. Written representations in this context do not include financial statements, the assertions therein, or supporting books and records.

31. Porter, Brenda, 'An Empirical Study of the Audit Expectation-Performance Gap', *Accounting and Business Research*, Volume 24, 1993 – Issue 93 and others: Richard T. Fisher and Samuel T. Naylor (2016), 'Corporate reporting on the Internet and the expectations gap: new face of an old problem', *Accounting and Business Research* 46:2, pp. 196–220. / Klaus Ruhnke, Martin Schmidt (2014), 'The audit expectation gap: existence, causes, and the impact of changes', *Accounting and Business Research* 44:5, pp. 572–601 / Ivo Blij IV, Harold Hassink, Gerard Mertens, Reiner Quick (1998), 'Disciplinary practices and auditors in Europe: a comparison between Germany and the Netherlands', *European Accounting Review* 3, pp. 467–491.

32. The inherent limitations of the audit of the financial statements (see section 1.2) are not always entirely accepted and/or understood by all groups of users.

33. In terms of agency theory' Principals' but sometimes also referred to as stakeholders or society-at-large.

34. People often refer to the saying in this context 'He who pays the piper calls the tune.' Meaning that the person who provides the money for something decides what will be done or has a right to decide what will be done.

35. International Auditing and Assurance Standards Board (IAASB), 2023, International Standard on Auditing (ISA 570) 'Going Concern', *Handbook of International Quality Management, Auditing, Review, Other Assurance, and Related Services Pronouncements*, 2022 edn, Volume I, International Federation of Accountants, New York.

36. On 22 January 2024, the Financial Reporting Council (FRC) published a revised UK Corporate Governance Code (2024 Code). The 2024 Code includes a limited number of targeted changes, with the primary revision being the new requirement for boards to make an annual declaration as to the effectiveness of their internal controls (Provision 29). This change is representative of the increasing importance of non-financial disclosures. In The Netherlands proposed additions to the Corporate Governance Code include:
    · a statement about the level of certainty the internal controls provide on the effective management of operational and compliance risks.
    · a statement that the internal controls provide limited assurance that the (CSRD) sustainability reporting does not contain material inaccuracies.

- an explanation of how the assessment of the effectiveness of the internal controls with regard to operational, compliance and reporting risks has taken place. https://www.debrauw.com/articles/proposal-to-include-risk-management-statement-vor-in-dutch-corporate-governance-code-published

37. Congress of the United States, 2002, Sarbanes–Oxley Act of 2002, s 404 'Management Assessment of Internal Controls', Washington DC.

38. PCAOB, 2007, Audit Standard No. 5, (currently Audit Standard 2201) 'An Audit of Internal Control Over Financial Reporting That Is Integrated with An Audit of Financial Statements', Public Company Accounting Oversight Board.

39. https://www.frc.org.uk/library/standards-codes-policy/corporate-governance/uk-corporate-governance-code/

40. A movie was made in 1999 about this event called *Rogue Trader* (Warner Brothers).

41. Committee of Sponsoring Organizations of the Treadway Commission (COSO), 1992, *Internal Control – Integrated Framework,* American Institute of Certified Public Accountants.

42. In 2023 COSO issued supplemental guidance for organizations to achieve effective internal control over sustainability reporting (ICSR), using the globally recognized COSO Internal Control-Integrated Framework (ICIF). See chapter 15.

43. US Securities and Exchange Commission Office of Investigations, 2009, 'Investigation of Failure of the SEC to Uncover Bernard Madoff's Ponzi Scheme', Report No. OIG–509, April 31, 2009, Washington DC.

44. https://en.wikipedia.org/wiki/Accounting_scandals

45. International Auditing and Assurance Standards Board (IAASB), 2023, International Standard on Auditing 240 (ISA 240) 'The Auditor's Responsibilities Relating to Fraud in an Audit of Financial Statements', *Handbook of International Quality Management, Auditing Review, Other Assurance, and Related Services Pronouncements*, 2022 edn, Volume I, International Federation of Accountants, New York.

46. International Auditing and Assurance Standards Board (IAASB), 2023, International Standard on Auditing 250 (ISA 250) 'Consideration of Laws and Regulations in an Audit of Financial Statements', *Handbook of International Quality Management, Auditing Review, Other Assurance, and Related Services Pronouncements*, 2022 edn, Volume I, International Federation of Accountants, New York.

47. J.P. Percy, Auditing and Corporate Governance – A Look Forward into the 21st Century, International Journal of Auditing 1(1), 3–12 (1997).

48. The fact that every situation is different is referred to as 'contextual variability' or 'situational specificity.' Also indicated by contingency theory, a behavioural theory that claims there is no one best way to organize a corporation, to lead a company, or to make decisions. Instead, the optimal course of action is contingent upon the internal and external situation.

CHAPTER 2

HOW THE AUDIT PROFESSION IS ORGANIZED

2.1 LEARNING OBJECTIVES

After studying this chapter, you should be able to:

1   Differentiate the different types of audits.
2   Distinguish between the types of auditors and their training, licensing and authority.
3   Understand drivers for audit regulation.
4   Understand characteristics of audit firms.
5   Identify organizations that affect international accounting and auditing.
6   Name the standards set by International Auditing and Assurance Standards Board (IAASB).
7   Give an overview of the International Standards on Auditing (ISA).
8   Understand the basic definition of auditing in an international context.
9   Comprehend auditor liability.
10 Understand disciplinary actions for accountants and firms.
11 Understand the system of audit firm oversight.
12 Discuss the requirements of International Standards on Quality Management (ISQM).

2.2 INTRODUCTION

In this chapter we will discuss how the audit profession is organized, what types of auditors there are and what types of audit they perform. We will sketch standards and auditing standard setters but also several mechanisms that drive and control audit quality.

2.3 TYPES OF AUDITORS

There are two basic types of auditors: independent external auditors and internal auditors. Governmental auditors take both the functions of internal and external auditor having the government as 'auditee'. The independent auditor and her qualifications will be discussed in the next section.

WORLDCOM INTERNAL AUDITOR DISCOVERS MISSTATEMENTS

Concept	The work of internal auditors in the review of financial statements.
Story	To illustrate the importance of internal auditors to companies we can look at what happened at WorldCom (now merged with Verizon Business, a US telecommunications company). It was the $9 billion fraud that was perpetrated at WorldCom, at the time the Number 2 long-distance telephone carrier in the USA, that formed the motivation to pass the first US accounting law since 1934. At the time the fraud was disclosed, US President George W. Bush said, 'I'm deeply concerned … There is a need for renewed corporate responsibility in America' (Wolffe 2002). One month later Bush signed the Sarbanes–Oxley Act.

The fraud that created, at that time, the largest bankruptcy in US history and resulted in the payment of the largest fine ever imposed up until that time by the Securities and Exchange Commission ($500 million (Larson and Michaels 2003)) involved transferring on the corporate books some $9 billion of telephone line leases and other expenses to 'capital investments', an asset. This allowed the expenses to be spread over 40 years. The accounting effect was to increase four crucial financial numbers: operating profit, cash flow from operations, total assets and retained earnings. This, in turn, increased WorldCom's share price and made those who exercised low-cost stock options rich. Chief Executive Officer (CEO) Bernard Ebbers made $35 million in June 1999, Chief Financial Officer Scott D. Sullivan made $18 million in August 2000, and chairman of the audit committee, Max Bobbitt, made $1.8 million in 1999 (Romeo and Norris 2002).

Cynthia Cooper, vice president for internal auditing, was the one who discovered the fraud at WorldCom and reported it to the board of directors. She may be the only internal auditor in history to be named *Time* magazine's person of the year (2002).

The story begins when a worried executive in the wireless division told Cooper in March 2002 that corporate accounting had taken $400 million out of his reserve account and used it to boost WorldCom's income. Cooper went to Arthur Andersen, the CPA firm. They told her it was not a problem. When she didn't relent, CFO Sullivan told Cooper that everything was fine and she should back off. Cooper, concerned that her job might be in jeopardy, cleaned out personal items from her office. Cooper told *Time* magazine, 'when someone is hostile, my instinct is to find out why' (Ripley, 2002).

As the weeks went on, Cooper directed her team members to widen their net. Having watched the Enron implosion and Andersen's role in it, she was worried they could not necessarily rely on the accounting firm's audits. So they decided to do part of Andersen's job over again. She and her team began working late into the night, keeping their project secret. And they had no allies. At one point, one of Cooper's employees bought a CD burner and started copying data, concerned that the information might be destroyed before they could finish.

In late May, Cooper and her group discovered a gaping hole in the books. In public reports the company had categorized billions of dollars as capital expenditures in 2001, meaning the costs could be stretched out over a number of years into the future. But in fact the expenditures were for regular fees WorldCom paid to local telephone companies to complete calls and therefore were not capital outlays but operating costs, which should be expensed in full each year. The trick allowed WorldCom to turn a $662 million loss into a $2.4 billion profit in 2001.

On 11 June, CFO Sullivan called Cooper and gave her ten minutes to come to his office and describe what her team was up to. She did, and Sullivan asked her to delay the audit. She told him that would not happen. The next day, Cooper told the head of the audit committee of the board of directors about her findings. On 25 June, after firing Sullivan, the board revealed the fraud to the public.

Nowadays, the SEC has its own Office of the Whistle-blower, which was formed as a part of the Dodd–Frank Act (2010). See http://www.sec.gov/whistleblower for more information.

Discussion Questions	▶ What advantages does an internal auditor have over an external auditor in discovering fraud? ▶ And what disadvantages?

References	Larsen, Peter and Adrian Michaels, 2003, 'MCI Fined $500m Over Fraud Charges', *Financial Times*, p. 1, 20 May. Ripley, Amanda, 2002, 'The Night Detective', *Time*, Vol. No. 160, 27, p. 58, 30 December. Romeo, Simon and Floyd Norris, 2002, 'New Bookkeeping Problems Disclosed by WorldCom', *New York Times*, pp. A1–C8, 2 July. Spiegel, Peter, 2003, 'WorldCom Finance Chief "Tried to Delay Inquiry"', *Financial Times*, p. 1, 9 July. Wolffe, Richard, 2002, 'Bush Condemns New Scandal as Outrageous', *Financial Times*, p. 1, 27 June.

▶ INTERNAL AUDITORS

Many large companies and organizations maintain an internal auditing staff. Internal auditors are employed by individual companies to investigate and appraise the effectiveness of company operations for management. Much of their attention is often given to the appraisal of internal controls. A large part of the internal auditor's work consists of operational audits (reviews of operations). In addition, they may conduct compliance audits (reviews of compliance with policies and regulations). In many countries internal auditors are heavily involved in financial audits. If the internal auditor performs financial audits the external auditor should review their work.

The internal audit function ordinarily reports directly to management. According to good corporate governance, the chief internal auditor can also directly report to the board of directors and more specifically to the audit committee. An internal auditor must be independent of the department heads and other executives whose work she reviews. Internal auditors, however, can never be independent in the same sense as the independent auditors because they are employees of the company they are examining.

Internal auditors have two primary effects on a financial statement audit:

1   Their existence and work may affect the nature, timing, and extent of audit procedures by the external auditor.
2   External auditors may use internal auditors to provide direct assistance in performing the audit. If this is the case the external auditor must assess internal auditor competence (education, experience, professional certification, etc.) and objectivity (organizational status within the company). However, such use can be prohibited by law or regulations, but ISA 610 provides a robust framework to ensure that direct assistance is obtained only in appropriate circumstances, that the external auditor considers the relevant limitations and safeguards, and that the auditor's responsibilities are clearly set out.

▶ **THE INDEPENDENT EXTERNAL AUDITOR: TRAINING, LICENSING AND AUTHORITY**

Independent auditors have primary responsibility to the performance of the audit function on published financial statements of publicly traded companies and non-public companies. Some countries have several classes of auditors who have different functions.

Independent auditors are typically certified either by a professional organization or a government agency.

The authority for auditors to carry out the attest function (certifying the financial statements) comes from national commercial or company law in most countries, but in some cases (e.g., the USA and Canada) the individual provinces or states exercise considerable control over who the auditor is and how she becomes qualified. All Certified Public Accountants (CPA) in the USA are licensed by the individual states. Most countries have strong professional accountant organizations which may also influence who becomes an auditor.

Certified designations for auditors in different countries are listed in illustration 2.1.

ILLUSTRATION 2.1

AUDITOR CERTIFICATION DESIGNATIONS AROUND THE WORLD

Certified Public Accountants (CPA)	Australia, Belize, El Salvador, Guatemala, Hong Kong, Israel, Japan, Kenya (CPA (K)), Korea, Malaysia, Malawi, Myanmar, Philippines, Singapore, Taiwan, Western Samoa and the USA.
Chartered Accountants (CA)	Australia (ACA), Bahamas, Bermuda, Botswana, Canada, Cayman Islands, Channel Islands, Cyprus, Fiji, Guyana, Hungary, India, Jamaica, Nigeria, Trinidad, New Zealand, Papua New Guinea, Saudi Arabia, South Africa (CA-SA), Swaziland (CA (SD)), United Arab Emirates, the UK and Zimbabwe.
Contador Publico (CP)	Argentina, Brazil (Contador), Chile, Columbia (CP Titulado), Costa Rica (CP Autorizado -CPA), Dominican Republic (CPA), Ecuador (CPA), Mexico, Panama (CPA) and Peru.
Expert Comptable	France (or Commissaire aux comptes), Luxembourg and Senegal.
Auditors	Bahrain, Czech Republic, Qatar and Solomon Islands.
Other titles	Register accountants (RA) and Accountants Administratie-Consulenten (AA) in the Netherlands and Netherlands Antilles; Wirtschaftsprufer in Austria and Germany; Statautoriseret Revisor in Denmark and Norway; Dottore Commercialista in Italy; Revisor Official de Contas (ROC) in Portugal; Auktoriserad Revisor (AR) in Sweden; Wirtschaftsprufer and Expert Comptable in Switzerland; Reviseur d'Entreprises in Belgium; KHT or CGR in Finland; Soma Orkoton Logiston (SOL) in Greece; Licenciado en Contaduria Publico in Venezuela; Akuntan Publik in Indonesia; Loggilturendurskodandi in Iceland; Licensed Accountant (LA) in Iraq; Technician Superior in Lebanon; and Sworn Financial Advisor (SFA) in Turkey.

▶ **LICENSING REQUIREMENTS**

The auditor is someone who is trained in an academic program and who meets certain licensing requirements. Countries may have requirements for minimum age, citizenship, university degree and completion of a qualifying examination. The Eighth European Union (EU) Directive[1] has a minimum experience requirement (internship) of three years, whereas the USA only requires one or two years.

It is common for people in the USA and Canada to become professional accountants in their early twenties, but in Germany and Japan many people do not attain their credentials until their mid-thirties. The EU Eighth Company Law Directive sets minimum qualifications for statutory auditors. This directive specifies that an individual must attain at least entrance-level qualifications at university level, engage in a program of theoretical instruction, receive at least three years' practical training and pass an examination of professional competence. Similar requirements exist in China although candidates must demonstrate proficiency in the required languages, particularly Mandarin, as much of the accounting documentation and communication may be in Chinese.

Furthermore, the Eighth Directive puts an obligation on Member States to ensure that statutory audits are carried out with professional integrity and that there are appropriate safeguards in national law to protect the independence of auditors.

2.4 TYPES OF AUDITS

Audits are typically classified into three types: audits of financial statements, operational audits and compliance audits.

▶ AUDITS OF FINANCIAL STATEMENTS

A Financial statement audits involve analyzing, testing fand reporting on inancial statement records. The criteria for financial statement audits may be, for example, International Financial Reporting Standards (IFRS), United States generally accepted accounting principles (US GAAP), national company laws as in Northern Europe, or the tax code in South America. This book primarily discusses audits of financial statements.

In addition to the audit of financial statements, audits of non-financial information are increasingly taking place, especially audits of sustainability information (see chapter 15).

▶ OPERATIONAL AUDITS

An operational audit is a study of a specific unit of an organization for the purpose of measuring its performance. Audit of the inventory from the initial order to shipping out the door with a goal of one-day shipping is an operational audit. So is an audit of production methods used in a manufacturing process. Operational audits review all or part of the organization's operating procedures to evaluate effectiveness and efficiency of the operation. Effectiveness is a measure of whether an organization achieves its goals and objectives. Efficiency shows how well an organization uses its resources to achieve its goals. Operational reviews may not be limited to accounting. They may include the evaluation of organizational structure, marketing, production methods, computer operations or whatever area the organization feels needs evaluation. Recommendations are normally made to management for improving operations.

▶ **COMPLIANCE AUDITS**

A compliance audit may not necessarily be related to accounting. It is a review of an organization's procedures to determine whether the organization is following specific procedures, i.e., rules or regulations set out by some higher authority (e.g., tax codes, corporate governance codes, employee safety, or environmental regulations). The performance of a compliance audit is dependent upon the existence of verifiable data and recognized criteria or standards. Results of compliance audits are generally reported to management within the organizational unit being audited.

Government auditors are usually associated with compliance audits – for example, the tax authority, the government internal auditing arm, or audit of a bank by banking regulators. An example of a compliance audit is an audit of a bank to determine if they comply with capital reserve requirements. Another example would be an audit of taxpayers to see if they comply with national tax law such as the audit of an income tax return by an auditor of the government tax agency such as the Internal Revenue Service (IRS) in the USA.

Compliance audits are quite common in not-for-profit organizations funded at least in part by government. Many government entities and non-profit organizations that receive financial assistance from the federal government must arrange for compliance audits. Such audits are designed to determine whether the financial assistance is spent in accordance with applicable laws and regulations.

Illustration 2.2 summarizes the three types of audits. Each of these types of audits has a specialist auditor, namely the independent auditor (including the government auditor), and internal auditor. The independent auditor is mainly concerned with financial statement audits, the internal auditor concentrates on operational audits, and the governmental auditor is most likely to determine compliance. However, given information technology developments, the different processes are becoming more and more integrated, and as a consequence the split between these categories may become theoretical.

ILLUSTRATION 2.2

TYPES OF AUDIT

Audits of financial statements	Operational audits	Compliance audits
Examine financial statements, determine if they give a true and fair view or fairly present the financial position, results and cash flows.	A study of a specific unit of an organisation for the purpose of measuring its performance.	A review of an organisation's procedures and financial records performed to determine whether the organisation is following specific procedures, rules or regulations set out by some higher authority.

2.5   AUDIT FIRMS

In the previous chapter we have extensively discussed the demand side of the audit market. But what about the supply side? How is it structured? Usually, audit firms are classified into two distinct categories:

- ▶ the Big Four firms; and
- ▶ the Non-Big Four firms.

▶ THE BIG FOUR FIRMS

The four largest accountancy firms in the world (known as 'the Big Four') influence international auditing because of their day-to-day operations in many countries and their membership in most of the world's professional accounting organizations. All of these firms have revenues of billions of dollars. The Big Four are: Deloitte, EY, KPMG, and PricewaterhouseCoopers.

These firms resulted partially from several major mergers in the late 1980s. These audit firms have a global network of affiliated firms. Actually, there were the Big Five firms after a series of mergers, including Arthur Andersen. However, because of the Enron accounting scandal, the market lost its confidence in Arthur Andersen and this firm had to forfeit its business in 2002 after almost 90 years of having been a highly respected firm (see Concept and a company 2.7). This case study demonstrates how crucial it is for auditors to fully respond to the inspired confidence of their stakeholders[2]. (We discuss these ethics issues in chapter 3.)

Although most of these firms are still structured as national limited liability partnerships with national instead of international profit sharing, these national member firms participate in an international head office, in which global technologies, procedures, and directives are developed. In addition to sharing the methodology, the networks are also used for the coordination of international audit engagements. The group auditor of a worldwide operating company uses the services of auditors of the member firms in the countries where the client has subsidiaries. As a result of the developments in communications technology, the effectiveness of these networks and the efficiency of the coordination of international engagements have increased significantly.

For the Big Four firms, audit and accounting services represent approximately half of the firms' total fee income.

▶ THE NON – BIG FOUR FIRMS

Non-Big Four firms can hardly be treated as a homogeneous group. At one extreme there are a very large number of small local firms, with only a handful of professionals. At the other extreme there are a small number of *second-tier* firms, which also have an international network, although not quite as extensive as the Big Four network. In between, there are a large number of medium-sized national or regional audit firms with several offices. The second-tier firms include BDO International, RSM International, Grant Thornton, Crowe Global and Baker Tilly International. To give you an idea of size: Grant Thornton International is the seventh largest accounting network in the world by combined fee income[3]. Member firms within the global organization operate in over 130 countries employing over 56,000 personnel for combined global revenue of US$5.72 billion (Grant Thornton corporate website https://www.grantthornton.com/).

THE BASIC THEORY

Concept	**Auditor's search for materiality.**
Story	There was once a group of very famous accountants and auditors who joined together as a mutual study group. They determined that they could find the basic truths of auditing. They read all manner of philosophical, scientific and religious works and discussed those theories amongst themselves. They felt that knowledge of the pure truths of auditing would form a basis for discovering the core truths of business and, indeed, life itself.

They studied the great works of accounting for many years, but felt that they were getting nowhere. Finally, they decided to take leave of their day jobs and search the world to find the answer. They sought the advice of great teachers all over the world. They would ask each great teacher to recommend one who was even wiser. Thus, they collected these recommendations until their search pointed to one man – a teacher of teachers.

The group journeyed to an isolated area in the great desert wastes of Africa. There they met the great man and, paying their respects, they told him of their heart-felt desire and long suffering to find the pure truths of auditing. He said, 'I cannot give you the answers. These you must find yourself.' He instructed them to collect the entire world's accounting knowledge, encompassing everything from the Sarbanes–Oxley Act 2002 back to cuneiform tablets of 3400 BCE. Then they were to condense all that knowledge to ten volumes.

The group went away and gathered and summarized knowledge for all the ages. After years of work, they again sat at the feet of the teacher of teachers and presented their ten volumes. The sage picked up the volumes and thumbed through them. He handed the volumes back to the group and then said, 'Go and make this into one volume.'

After years of toil, the group, whose membership was now thinning appreciably, returned with their one volume of the world's audit truths. The teacher of teachers said, 'Make this into one sentence.'

Taking on this almost impossible task, the remaining members of the group locked themselves into a cave and ate nothing but soup made of nettles to sustain them until they came up with the one true answer. When they returned to the guru with this sentence, he smiled and said to them, 'You got it.' This was the sentence:

'There is no such thing as a free lunch.'

Discussion Questions	▶ Why can we expect that a fraud that works now may not work in the future?
	▶ Why can a company not continue to grow indefinitely at 15 per cent per year?
	▶ Why can a management that make up fictitious sales not profit in the long run?
	▶ Why does every form of earnings manipulation have its cost?
	▶ Based on this one sentence, how would you justify the existence of ethics?
References	The great audit works.

▶ ORGANIZATION OF THE AUDIT

In the earliest days of multinational accountancy firms, the organizational form of audit firms was a partnership or professional corporation. Today legal forms vary around the world between countries as well as between firms. Limited liability forms of organization, such as Limited Liability Partnership (LLP), have come into widespread use to limit liability of individual accountants, to enlarge confidence of clients and society and to improve regulatory compliance.

PROFESSIONAL STAFF

The partners hire professional staff to assist them in their work. The organizational hierarchy in a typical international auditing firm (shown in illustration 2.3) includes partners, managers, supervisors, seniors or in-charge auditors, and staff accountants. A new employee usually starts as a staff accountant and spends several years at each classification before eventually achieving partner status. A new employee must acquire accounting knowledge as they learn (see Concept and a Company 2.2).

In the remainder of this section the allocation of personnel to an audit is discussed. However, it must be remembered that human resource models will vary between auditing firms. The following describes the common threads of work.

ILLUSTRATION 2.3

BIG FOUR ORGANIZATIONAL PYRAMID

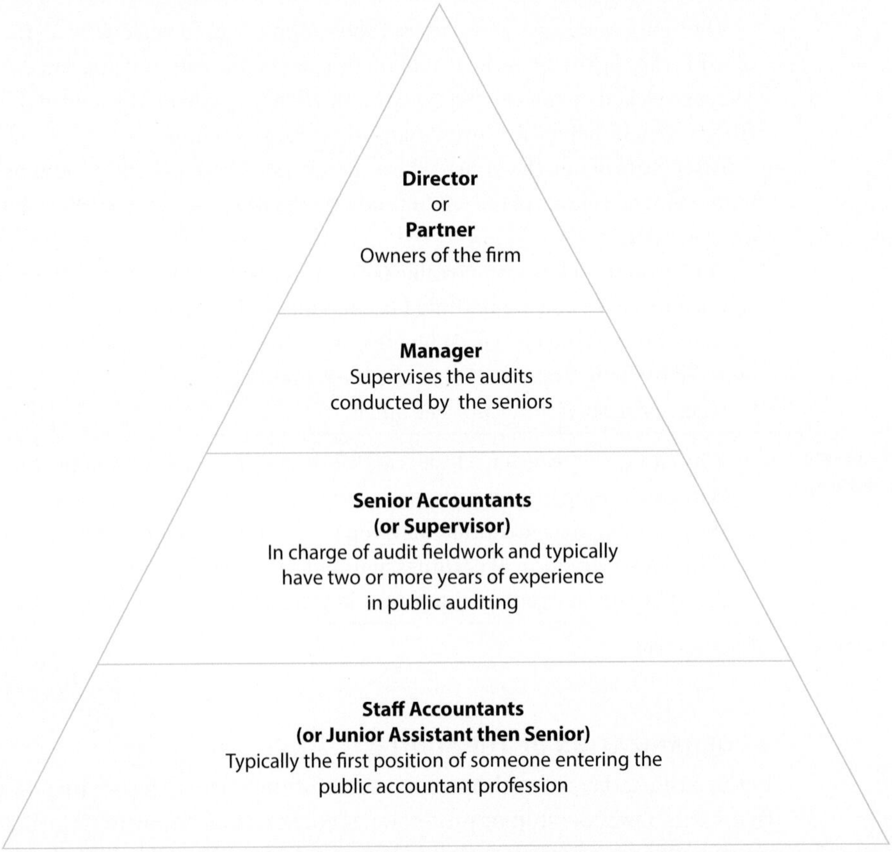

Director
or
Partner
Owners of the firm

Manager
Supervises the audits
conducted by the seniors

**Senior Accountants
(or Supervisor)**
In charge of audit fieldwork and typically
have two or more years of experience
in public auditing

**Staff Accountants
(or Junior Assistant then Senior)**
Typically the first position of someone entering the
public accountant profession

STAFF ACCOUNTANTS

The first position when someone enters the public accounting profession is that of staff accountant (also called assistant or junior accountant). The staff accountant often performs the more detailed routine audit tasks.

SENIOR ACCOUNTANTS (OR SUPERVISOR)

The senior ('in-charge') auditor or 'supervisor' oversees audit fieldwork and typically has two or more years' experience in public auditing. The senior takes a major part in planning the audit and is primarily responsible for conducting the audit engagement at the client's place of business. Planning and supervision of more complex audits may involve the partner or director in planning and the manager in supervising the engagement.

The senior supervises the work of the audit staff, reviews working papers and time budgets, and assists in drafting the audit report. The senior maintains a continuous record of staff hours in each phase of the audit examination and maintains professional standards of fieldwork. This work is subject to review and approval by the manager and partner.

MANAGERS

The manager supervises the audits conducted by the seniors. The manager helps the seniors plan their audit programs, reviews working papers periodically, and provides other guidance. The manager is responsible for determining the audit procedures applicable to specific audits and for maintaining uniform standards of fieldwork. Often managers have the responsibility of compiling and delivering the firm's billings to the audit client. The manager, who typically has at least five years' experience, needs a broad and current knowledge of tax laws, accounting standards and government regulations. A manager is likely to specialize in accounting requirements of a specific industry. Most firms also include so-called senior managers who are typically senior-level professionals who play a crucial role in managing and overseeing audit engagements. The role of a senior manager in an audit team involves a combination of technical, managerial, and client-facing responsibilities.

PARTNERS/DIRECTORS

Partners are the owners of the auditing firm. The change in legal structure means that in some countries those formerly known as partners are directors. They are heavily involved in the planning of the audit, evaluation of the results and determination of the audit opinion. The degree to which they are involved in the audit will vary between firms and assignments because firms must ensure that partners allocate their time in an appropriate way. Partners will delegate as much of the work as possible to experienced managers and seniors. Moreover, the larger the accountancy firm the more variation there is likely to be in practice depending on the nature of the engagement.

Other partner or director duties include maintaining contacts with clients, resolving controversies that may arise, and attendance at the client's stockholders' meetings to answer any questions regarding the financial statements or the auditor's report. They may also recruit new staff members, review audit working papers, supervise staff and sign the audit reports, depending on the complexity of the engagements. Partners may specialize in a particular area such as tax laws or a specific industry. The partner is the person who must make the final decisions involving complex judgements.

Many audit firms include equity partners who share in ownership and in profits and losses and salary partners who receive a fixed salary without direct ownership. The decision between the two is influenced by factors like financial capacity, career goals, and the firm's structure. Both contribute to the firm's success, and individuals may transition from salary to equity partnership based on performance.

CONCEPT AND A COMPANY 2.3

HISTORY OF DELOITTE

Concept	**Founding fathers and international mergers of Big Four audit firms.**
Story	In 1990 Deloitte Touche Tohmatsu was created following a number of earlier mergers. In 2003 the names of Touche and Tohmatsu were dropped, leaving Deloitte as the firm's full name. Deloitte was established by three founders: William Welch Deloitte, George Touche and Admiral Nobuzo Tohmatsu.
	In 1845, at the age of 25, W.W. Deloitte opened his own office opposite the Bankruptcy Court in Basinghall Street, London. At that time three Companies Acts created joint-stock companies, laying the foundation for modern company structures. Deloitte made his name with the industry of the day – the railways – and in 1849 the Great Western Railway appointed Deloitte the first independent auditor in that industry. He discovered frauds on the Great North Railway, invented a system for railway accounts that protected investors from mismanagement of funds, and was to become the grand old man of the profession. As president of the newly created Institute of Chartered Accountants, Deloitte found a site for its headquarters in 1888. In 1893 he opened offices in the USA.
	Financial disasters in the new and booming investment trust business in England gave George Touche his business opportunity. His reputation for flair, integrity, and expertise brought him a huge amount of work setting these trusts on the straight and narrow. A similar flair for saving doomed businesses from disaster and restructuring them led to the formation of George A. Touche & Co. in 1899. In 1900, along with John Niven, the son of his original Edinburgh accounting mentor, Touche set up the firm of Touche, Niven & Co. in New York. Offices spread across the USA and Canada and were soon attracting clients like R.H. Macy, a large US nationwide department store. In the UK, General Electric Company was an important client and still is. Meanwhile Touche himself took his reputation for probity and ran for public election in England and became MP for North Islington, England, in 1910, and was knighted in 1917. He died in 1935.
	After Tohmatsu qualified as a certified public accountant at the age of 57 in 1952, he became a partner in a foreign-affiliated accounting firm and a director of a private corporation. In 1967, he became president of the Japanese Institute of Certified Public Accountants. In the 1960s, the Japanese government wanted to see national audit corporations established, and Tohmatsu asked Iwao Tomita, a former student and a graduate of the Wharton School in Chicago, to respond to that challenge. In May of 1968, Tohmatsu & Co. (formerly Tohmatsu Awoki & Co.) was incorporated.
Discussion Question	▶ What events and circumstances contributed to the growth and international scope of Deloitte's operations?
References	http://www.Deloitte.com.

CONCEPT AND A COMPANY 2.4

A HISTORY OF EY

Concept	**Founding fathers and international mergers of Big Four audit firms.**
Story	The founders of Ernst & Young (EY) were Arthur Young, who had an interest in investments and banking which led to the foundation in 1906 of Arthur Young & Co. in Chicago, USA, and A.C. Ernst, who was a bookkeeper while still in high school, joined his brother and started Ernst & Ernst in 1903.

Ernst pioneered the idea that accounting information could be used to make business decisions – the forerunner of management consulting. He also was the first to advertise professional services. Young was profoundly interested in the development of young professionals. In the 1920s he originated a staff school; in the 1930s, his firm was the first to recruit from university campuses.

Both firms were quick to enter the global marketplace. As early as 1924, they allied with prominent British firms – Young with Broads Paterson & Co. and Ernst with Whinney Smith & Whinney. In 1979, Ernst's original agreement led to the formation of Ernst & Whinney. These alliances were the first of many for both firms throughout the world – and they are the roots of the global firm today.

Young and Ernst, never having met, both died in 1948 within only a few days of each other. In 1989, the firms they started combined to create Ernst & Young (later shortened to EY). |
| **Discussion Questions** | ▸ What is the impact today of Ernst's innovation of advertising professional services?
▸ What do you think Young's staff school taught to professional accountants in 1920?
▸ What do you think Ernst & Young teach today in their staff school? |
| **References** | www.ey.com. |

CONCEPT AND A COMPANY 2.5	
HISTORY OF KPMG	
Concept	Founding fathers and international mergers of Big Four audit firms.
Story	KPMG was formed in 1987 with the merger of Peat Marwick International (PMI) and Klynveld Main Goerdeler (KMG) and their individual member firms. Spanning three centuries, the organization's history can be traced through the names of its principal founding members – whose initials form the name 'KPMG.' K stands for Klynveld. Piet Klijnveld founded the accounting firm Klynveld Kraayenhof & Co. in Amsterdam in 1917. P is for Peat. William Barclay Peat founded the accounting firm William Barclay Peat & Co. in London in 1870. M stands for Marwick. James Marwick founded the accounting firm Marwick, Mitchell & Co. with Roger Mitchell in New York City in 1897. G is for Goerdeler. Dr Reinhardt Goerdeler was for many years chairman of Deutsche Treuhand-Gesellschaft and later chairman of KPMG. He is credited with laying much of the groundwork for the Klynveld Main Goerdeler (KMG) merger. In 1911, William Barclay Peat & Co. and Marwick Mitchell & Co. joined forces to form what would later be known as Peat Marwick International (PMI), a worldwide network of accounting and consulting firms. William Barclay Peat & Co. was founded in 1870 in London; Marwick Mitchell & Co. was founded in 1897 in New York City. Klynveld Kraayenhof & Co. was founded in Amsterdam in 1917. In 1979, Klynveld Kraayenhof & Co. joined forces with Deutsche Treuhand-Gesellschaft and the international professional services firm McLintock Main Lafrentz & Co. to form Klynveld Main Goerdeler (KMG). Goerdeler was Dr Reinhard Goerdeler, the chairman of Deutsche Treuhand-Gesellschaft. In 1987, PMI and KMG and their member firms joined forces. Today, all member firms throughout the world carry the KPMG name exclusively or include it in their national firm names.
Discussion Question	▶ What types of problem could result from combining four firms from different nations with different cultures into a working environment?
References	http://www.KPMG.nl.

HISTORY OF PRICEWATERHOUSECOOPERS

Concept	**Founding fathers and international mergers of Big Four audit firms.**
Story	A merger in 1998 of Coopers & Lybrand and Price Waterhouse created PricewaterhouseCoopers. These two firms have historical roots going back some 150 years.
	PricewaterhouseCoopers employs about 125,000 people in more than 142 countries throughout the world.
	In 1849, Samuel Lowell Price started an accounting business in London. In 1865, William H. Holyland and Edwin Waterhouse joined him in partnership, and by 1874 the company name changes to Price, Waterhouse & Co. (or PW for short). In 1873, the firm conducted their first US project. The growing US practice lead to the establishment of permanent PW presence in the Western hemisphere, which began with the opening of the office in New York City in 1890. By the turn of the century, it had a register of clients that covered a wide range of industrial and commercial fields in most sections of the USA. Branch offices began to open throughout the USA and then in other parts of the world. In 1982 Price Waterhouse World Firm was formed.
	In 1854, William Cooper established his own practice in London, which seven years later became Cooper Brothers. The firm's history in the USA began in 1898, when Robert H. Montgomery, William M. Lybrand, Adam A. Ross Jr, and his brother T. Edward Ross formed Lybrand Ross Brothers and Montgomery in Philadelphia. During the early twentieth century their offices spread around the country and then in Europe.
	From 1953, the firm experienced a major transformation from a medium-size company, focused on auditing and primarily national in scope, into a multinational player with a growing mix of consulting services. The boldest step was a 1957 merger between Cooper Brothers & Co. (UK), McDonald, Currie and Co. (Canada), and Lybrand, Ross Bros, & Montgomery (US), forming Coopers & Lybrand, which had 79 offices in 19 countries. In 1990, Coopers & Lybrand merged with Deloitte Haskins & Sells in a number of countries around the world. Finally, in 1998 Price Waterhouse and Coopers & Lybrand merged worldwide to become PricewaterhouseCoopers, and the trading name of the firm was shortened to PwC in 2010.
Discussion Question	▶ Why did the Western hemisphere operations of Price and Coopers grow rapidly in the twentieth century?
References	http://www.columbia.edu/cu/libraries/indiv/rare/guides/PWC/main.http://www.pwcglobal.com.

2.6 STANDARD SETTING

▶ INTERNATIONAL FINANCIAL REPORTING STANDARDS (IFRS)

Financial accounting standards are unique and separate from audit standards. By its nature, auditing requires that the real-world evidence of financial transactions be compared to financial standards. The standards to which an international auditor compares financial statements are generally standards in the reporting country (e.g. Financial Accounting Standards (FAS) in the USA, or national standards in European Union (EU) Member States which are based on EU Directives). In the future, companies and auditors in many additional countries will use International Financial Reporting Standards (IFRS) which are set by the International Accounting Standards Board (IASB).

Standards issued by the IASB are called International Financial Reporting Standards (IFRS). For the great majority of the world IFRS are required for domestic public companies. For even more of the world's countries IFRS are required or permitted for public listings of foreign companies[4].

Although all the European Union Directives influence international accounting, the Eighth Company Law Directive is especially applicable to auditing. The Eighth Directive sets the minimum requirements for accounting training and experience for the community.

▶ INTERNATIONAL AUDITING STANDARDS

As international financial reporting standards acquired more authority, logic dictated a set of international auditing standards collateral to them. Auditing standards were very important for multinational corporations that wanted consistent auditing throughout the world.

With a set of international standards adopted for the world, international investors can be more confident in financial statements prepared in another country. The non-domestic auditor's opinion will lend as much credibility as a domestic auditor's opinion.

IAASB AUDITING, ASSURANCE, QUALITY MANAGEMENT, AND RELATED SERVICES STANDARDS

The International Auditing and Assurance Standards Board (IAASB) is an independent standards board supported by the International Federation of Accountants (IFAC). Their objective is to improve the degree of uniformity of auditing practices and related services throughout the world by issuing pronouncements on a variety of audit and attest functions.

The IAASB consists of a full-time chairman and volunteer members from around the world. The board is balanced between practitioners in public practice with significant experience in the field of auditing and other assurance services and individuals who are not in public practice; in addition, at least three members are nominated by the public. See illustration 2.4 'IAASB at a glance' below[5]:

IAASB AT A GLANCE

IAASB AT A GLANCE

18 IAASB Members
3 IAASB Observers
17 Technical Advisors

10 IAASB Meetings
(9 virtual and 1 hybrid)

12 Technical Staff
and Consultants

12 Task Forces and
Working Groups

3 IAASB CAG Meetings

27 CAG Member Organizations

1 IAASB-NSS Meeting

3 IAASB CAG Observers

123 Task Force / Working
Group Meetings

17 IAASB-NSS Members

5 IAASB Liaison
Representatives

IAASB

Members are appointed by the IFAC Board based on recommendations from the IFAC Nominating Committee and are approved by the Public Interest Oversight Board (PIOB). In addition, there are a small number of observer members who have speaking rights at IAASB meetings but no voting rights. The IAASB is supported by technical staff with a wide range of standard-setting experience. IAASB members are required to sign an annual statement declaring they will act in the public interest and with integrity in discharging their roles within IFAC, while nominating organizations of members of the IAASB are asked to sign independence declarations. IAASB issues several sets of standards to be applied to international auditing and assurance services. IAASB Standards contain basic principles and essential procedures together with related guidance in the form of explanatory and other material. See illustration 2.5:

▷ *International Standards on Quality Management* (ISQMs) as the standards to be applied for all services falling under the standards of the IAASB.

▷ *International Standards on Auditing* (ISAs) as the standards to be applied by auditors in reporting on historical financial information.

▷ *International Standards on Assurance Engagements* (ISAEs) as the quality control standards to be applied by practitioners in assurance engagements dealing with information other than historical financial information.

▷ *International Standards on Sustainability Assurance* (ISSA) as the quality control standards to be applied by practitioners dealing with sustainability information (see chapter 15).

▷ *International Standards on Related Services* (ISRSs) as the standards to be applied to related services; and

▷ *International Standards on Review Engagements* (ISREs) as the standards to be applied to the review of historical financial information.

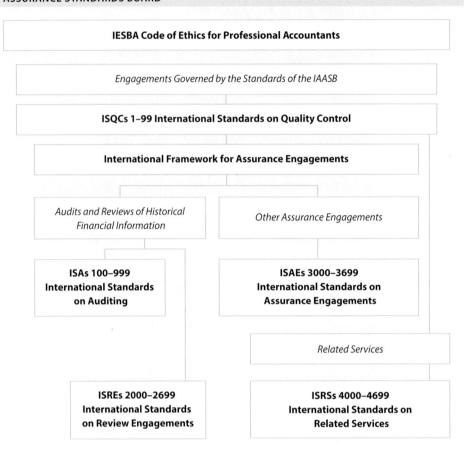

ILLUSTRATION 2.5[6]

STRUCTURE OF PRONOUNCEMENTS ISSUED BY THE INTERNATIONAL AUDITING AND ASSURANCE STANDARDS BOARD

IESBA Code of Ethics for Professional Accountants

Engagements Governed by the Standards of the IAASB

ISQCs 1–99 International Standards on Quality Control

International Framework for Assurance Engagements

Audits and Reviews of Historical Financial Information

Other Assurance Engagements

ISAs 100–999 International Standards on Auditing

ISAEs 3000–3699 International Standards on Assurance Engagements

Related Services

ISREs 2000–2699 International Standards on Review Engagements

ISRSs 4000–4699 International Standards on Related Services

▶ INTERNATIONAL STANDARDS ON AUDITING (ISA)

The International Auditing and Assurance Standards Board (IAASB) seeks worldwide recognition for the International Standards on Auditing (ISAs), though they're not meant to supplant local laws. By December 2021, over 135 countries had adopted ISAs[7]. This book uses ISAs as foundational standards, as they're seen as the premier global auditing norms. ISAs serve to harmonize auditing practices globally, ensuring consistency. The practice and theory of international auditing includes, in addition to knowledge of ISAs, consideration of quality control standards, allocating materiality, performing the audit, coordinating international reports and personnel, etc.

A listing of the International Standards on Auditing is given in illustration 2.6.

ILLUSTRATION 2.6

LIST OF 2022 INTERNATIONAL STANDARDS ON AUDITING

INTERNATIONAL STANDARDS ON QUALITY Management (ISQMs)

ISQM 1   I Quality Management for Firms That Perform Audits or Reviews of Financial Statements, or Other Assurance or Related Services Engagements

ISQM 2   Engagement Quality Reviews

AUDITS OF HISTORICAL FINANCIAL INFORMATION

200–299   General Principles and Responsibilities

ISA 200   Overall objectives of the Independent Auditor and the conduct of an Audit in Accordance with International standards on Auditing

ISA 210   Agreeing the Terms of Audit Engagements

ISA 220   (Revised) Quality Control for an Audit of Financial statements

ISA 230   Audit Documentation

ISA 240   The Auditor's Responsibilities Relating to Fraud in an Audit of Financial Statements

ISA 250   (Revised) Consideration of Laws and Regulations in an Audit of Financial Statements

ISA 260   (Revised) Communication with Those Charged with Governance

ISA 265   Communicating Deficiencies in Internal Control to Those Charged with Governance and Management

300–499   Risk Assessment and Response to Assessed Risks

ISA 300   Planning an Audit of Financial Statements

ISA 315   Identifying and Assessing the Risks of Material Misstatement

ISA 320   Materiality in Planning and Performing an Audit

ISA 330   The Auditor's Responses to Assessed Risks

ISA 402   Audit Considerations Relating to an Entity using a Service Organization

ISA 450   Evaluation of Misstatements Identified during the Audit

500–599   Audit Evidence

ISA 500   Audit Evidence

ISA 501   Audit Evidence – Specific Considerations for Selected Items

ISA 505   External Confirmations

ISA 510   Initial Audit engagements – Opening Balances

ISA 520   Analytical Procedures

ISA 530   Audit Sampling

ISA 540   (Revised) Auditing Accounting Estimates and Related Disclosures

ISA 550	Related Parties
ISA 560	Subsequent Events
ISA 570	(Revised) Going Concern
ISA 580	Written Representations
600–699	**Using the Work of Others**
ISA 600	Special Considerations – Audits of Group Financial Statements (Including the Work of Component Auditors)
ISA 610	Using the Work of Internal Auditors
ISA 620	Using the Work of an Auditor's Expert
700–799	**Audit Conclusions and Reporting**
ISA 700	(Revised) Forming an Opinion and Reporting on Financial Statements
ISA 701	Communicating Key Audit Matters in the Independent Auditor's Report
ISA 705	(Revised) Modifications to the Opinion in the Independent Auditor's Report
ISA 706	(Revised) Emphasis of Matter Paragraphs and Other Matter Paragraphs in the Independent Auditor's Report
ISA 710	Comparative Information – Corresponding Figures and Comparative Financial statements
ISA 720	(Revised) The Auditor's Responsibilities relating to other Information\
800–899	**Specialized Areas**
ISA 800	(Revised) Special Considerations – Audits of Financial statements Prepared in Accordance with special Purpose Frameworks
ISA 805	(Revised) Special Considerations – Audits of Single Financial statements and Specific Elements, Accounts or Items of a Financial statement
ISA 810	(Revised) Engagements to Report on Summary Financial Statements

2.7 AUDIT REGULATION

▶ **INTERNATIONAL PERSPECTIVE**

In the previous section, the supply side of the audit market has been described. In most countries, the demand has long been on a voluntary basis, i.e., it was left to the companies to decide whether they had their financial statements audited or not. As for the supply side, the provision of audit services has been left open to the free market in some countries, without any official legal requirements for auditors. Although regulation and legislation differ, both the demand and the supply of audit services are currently regulated to some degree in most countries. Accounting and finance research suggests that national legal environments are among the key determinants of financial market development, corporate ownership structures, corporate policies, and the properties of accounting information around the world.[8]

In most countries, audits are legally required for some types of companies. For example, in the USA listed entities and the European Union, large, and medium-sized companies, are required by law to provide audited financial statements. The European Union audit rules apply to all companies within the individual Member States that are required to be audited. The requirements may vary from state to state. The major bourses (including NYSE, NASDAQ, London Stock Exchange, Euronext Stock Exchange, Shanghai Stock Exchange (SSE), Tokyo NIKKEI, National Stock Exchange of India (NSE) and Frankfurt (DAX) have listing rules that require all listed companies to have their annual report (including financial statements) audited.

The supply of audit services is currently also regulated in most countries. In the European Union, *statutory audits*, i.e., audits required by law, can only be performed by auditors who have met specific technical requirements with regard to education and experience. Laws in other countries require audits of companies issuing public equity or debt, companies receiving government money, and companies in certain industries (like banking and utilities).

► US SARBANES-OXLEY ACT

The accounting scandals begun by the Enron collapse and extending to such giant companies as WorldCom, Xerox and Tyco, caused a backlash in the USA, resulting in legislation being signed into law by the US President in July 2002. The Sarbanes-Oxley Act is the first accounting law passed by the US since the Securities and Exchange Act of 1934.

The Act had new requirements for audit firms and audit committees. Auditors must report to the audit committee, not management. The lead audit partner and audit review partner must be rotated every five years. A second partner must review and approve audit reports. It is a felony with penalties of up to ten years in jail to wilfully fail to maintain 'all audit or review work papers' for at least five years. Destruction of documents carries penalties of up to 20 years in jail. The Act lists eight types of services that are 'unlawful' if provided to a publicly held company by its auditor: book-keeping, information systems design and implementation, appraisals or valuation services, actuarial services, internal audits, management and human resources services, broker/dealer and investment banking, and legal or expert services related to audit service.

As mentioned in chapter 1, The Public Company Accounting Oversight Board (PCAOB), created by the Act, oversees and investigates the audits and auditors of public companies, and sanctions both firms and individuals for violations of laws, regulations and rules. The Board may also determine by regulation other services it wishes to prohibit. Non-audit services not banned by the Act must be pre-approved by the audit committee. Management must assess and make representations about the effectiveness of the internal control structure and their auditor will be required to attest to the assessment and describe the tests used.

► EUROPEAN UNION REGULATION

The statutory audit of financial statements in the European Union (EU) is governed by the EU Audit Regulation (Regulation (EU) No 537/2014)[9] and the EU Audit Directive (Directive 2014/56/EU)[10]. These regulations set out the framework for the statutory audit of annual and consolidated financial statements of companies in the EU.

Key points related to statutory financial statements audits in the EU include:

▶ Mandatory Audit Requirement: The regulations require certain companies to undergo a statutory audit of their financial statements. This includes public-interest entities (PIEs) such as listed companies, credit institutions, and insurance undertakings.

▶ Independence and Rotation: The regulations emphasize the independence of auditors and include provisions on mandatory audit firm rotation to ensure objectivity and prevent conflicts of interest.

▶ Audit Quality and Professional Scepticism: Auditors are required to adhere to high-quality auditing standards and exercise professional scepticism during the audit process. This is to enhance the reliability and credibility of financial statements.

▶ Audit Report and Transparency: Auditors are required to issue an audit report expressing their opinion on the financial statements. The audit report provides transparency to stakeholders about the fairness and accuracy of the financial information.

▶ Supervision by National Competent Authorities: National competent authorities in each EU member state oversee the implementation of the regulations and supervise audit firms to ensure compliance.

2.8 LEGAL LIABILITY

There are many stakeholders who rely on audited financial statements: the client (with which there is a privity relationship), and third parties such as actual and potential stockholders, vendors, bankers and other creditors, employees, customers, and the government (like the tax authorities). Legal liability of the auditor to each stakeholder varies from country to country, district to district. This liability can generally be classified as based on one or more of the following: common law, civil liability under statutory law, criminal liability under statutory law, and liability as members of professional accounting organizations.

▶ LIABILITY UNDER COMMON LAW

Liability for auditors under common law generally falls in two categories: liabilities to clients and third-party liability.

LIABILITY TO CLIENTS

A typical civil lawsuit filed by a client involves a claim that the auditor did not discover financial statement fraud or employee fraud (defalcation) because the auditors showed *negligence*[11] in the conduct of an audit. The legal action can be for *breach of contract*[12] or, more likely, a *tort*[13] action for negligence. Tort actions are the most common, for generally they generate larger monetary judgements than breach of contract.

LIABILITIES TO THIRD PARTIES

Third parties include all stakeholders in an audit other than the audit client. An audit firm may be liable to third parties such as banks that have incurred a loss due to reliance on misleading financial statements.

ULTRAMARES

The most famous US audit case in third party liabilities happened with the 1931 *Ultramares-Touche* case (*Ultramares Corporation* v *Touche et al.*).[14] In this case, the court held that although the accountants were negligent in not finding that a material amount of accounts receivable had been falsified when careful investigation would have shown the amount to be fraudulent, they were not liable to a third party bank because the bank creditors were not a primary beneficiary, or known party, of whom the auditor was informed before conducting the audit. This precedent is called the Ultramares doctrine, that ordinary negligence (the failure to use reasonable care) is not sufficient for a liability to a third party because of lack of *privity of contract*[15] between the third party and the auditor.

CAPARO

The 1990 *Caparo* case (*Caparo Industries, PLC* v *Dickman and Others*)[16] is a leading English tort law case on the test for a duty of care of an auditor. Prior to the decision, if a statement (like an audit opinion) was made negligently, then the person making the statement was liable for any resulting loss. The question in Caparo had to do with the scope of the assumption of responsibility, and what the limits of liability ought to be.

The UK House of Lords, following the Court of Appeal, set out a 'threefold test'. In order for an obligation (duty of care)[17] to arise in negligence: (1) harm must be reasonably foreseeable because of the defendant's conduct; (2) the parties must be in a relationship of proximity; and (3) it must be fair, just and reasonable to impose liability. In the case of annual financial statements, this purpose was to give the shareholders the information necessary to enable them to question the past management of the company, to exercise their voting rights and to influence future policy and management.

GERMAN LIABILITY

In Germany, auditors have an unlimited liability to the client if there is an intentional violation of duties, but the liability is capped by law at €1,000,000 to €4,000,000, depending on circumstances, for negligent violation of duties. Liability to third parties as described by the Tort Law (§ 823–826 BGB) is restricted to certain prerequisites such as intent and violation of morality. There is also liability to third parties under Contract Law, which has less restrictive prerequisites than Tort Law.

As a reaction to the spectacular collapse of Wirecard, a then listed financial service provider, in June 2020, an Act on Strengthening the Financial Market Integrity (Finanzmarktintegritätsstärkungsgesetz – FISG) establishes new requirements for the corporate governance and the audit of listed companies as well as other public-interest entities. One aspect being the increase of the liability caps for auditors (16 million Euro for listed companies) and tightened criminal liability.

▷ CIVIL LIABILITY UNDER STATUTORY LAW

Statutory civil liabilities are liabilities under laws that require a *preponderance of evidence* to convict resulting in a civil penalty such as a fine or suspension of license to operate. Preponderance of evidence means that the proposition is more likely to be true than not true. In other words, the standard is satisfied if there is a greater than fifty percent chance that the proposition is true. Most countries have laws that affect the civil liabilities of auditors. Securities laws, for example, may impose strict standards on professional accountants. In the USA, the Securities Act of 1933 not only created the Securities and Exchange Commission (SEC), it established the first US statutory civil recovery rules for third parties against auditors. Original purchasers of securities of a firm newly registered to make a public offering have recourse against the auditor for up to the original purchase price if the financial statements are false or misleading.

Anyone who purchased securities described in the SEC registration statement (S1) may sue the auditor for material misrepresentations or omissions in financial statements published in the S1. The auditor has the burden of demonstrating that reasonable investigation was conducted or that the loss of the purchaser of securities (plaintiff) was caused by factors other than the misleading financial statements. If the auditor cannot prove this, the plaintiff wins the case.

The United States Sarbanes-Oxley Act of 2002 also prescribes civil penalties for Chief Financial Officers (CFOs) and Chief Executive Officers (CEOs). If there is a material restatement of a company's reported financial results due to the material noncompliance of the company, as a result of misconduct, the CEO and CFO must reimburse the company for any bonus or incentive, or equity-based compensation received within the 12 months following the filing with the financial statements subsequently required to be restated.[18]

Financial statements filed with the SEC by any public company must be certified by CEOs and CFOs. If all financials do not fairly present the true condition of the company, CEOs and CFOs may receive fines up to $1 million or up to $5 million for fraud.[19]

▶ CRIMINAL LIABILITY UNDER STATUTORY L AW

Statutory criminal law generally requires evidence *beyond a reasonable doubt* to convict resulting in loss of freedom, imprisonment and fines. Proof beyond a reasonable doubt is met if there is no plausible reason to believe otherwise. If there is a real doubt, based upon reason and common sense after careful and impartial consideration of all the evidence, or lack of evidence, in a case, then the level of proof has not been met. A professional auditor may be held criminally liable under the laws of a country or district that make it a criminal offence to defraud another person through knowingly being involved with false financial statements.

US SECURITIES AND EXCHANGE ACT OF 1934 AND SARBANES-OXLEY ACT OF 2002

The Securities and Exchange Act of 1934 in the USA requires every company with securities traded on national and over-the-counter exchanges to submit audited financial statements annually (SEC form 10-K) as well as other reports for quarterly financials (10-Q), unusual events (8-K) and other events. The Act also sets out (Rule 10b-5) criminal liability conditions if the auditor employs any device, scheme or artifice to defraud or make any untrue statement of a material fact or omits to state a material fact, i.e., the auditor intentionally or recklessly misrepresents information for third party use. The SEC also has authority to sanction or suspend an auditor from doing audits for SEC-registered companies.[20]

Several court cases have been subjected to an application of the Act's criminal liability section. In *United States* v *Natelli* (1975) two auditors were convicted of criminal liability for certifying financial statements of National Student Marketing Corporation that contained inadequate disclosures pertaining to accounts receivable. In *United States* v

Weiner (1975) three auditors were convicted of securities fraud in connection with their audit of Equity Funding Corporation of America. The fraud the company perpetrated was so massive and the audit work so sub-standard that the court concluded that the auditors must have been aware of the fraud. Management revealed to the audit partner that the prior years' financials were misstated, and the partner agreed to say nothing in *ESM Government Securities* v *Alexander Grant & Co.* (1986). The partner was convicted of criminal charges for his role in sustaining the fraud and was sentenced to a 12-year prison term.

The Sarbanes-Oxley Act of 2002 attaches criminal penalties to CEOs, CFOs and auditors. To knowingly destroy, create, manipulate documents and/or impede or obstruct federal investigations is considered a felony, and violators will be subject to fines or up to 20 years' imprisonment, or both.[21] All audit reports or related workpapers must be kept by the auditor for 7 years. Failure to do this may result in 10 years' imprisonment. CFOs and CEOs who falsely certify financial statements or internal controls are subject to 10 years' imprisonment. Wilful false certification may result in a maximum of 20 years' imprisonment.[22]

CONCEPT AND A COMPANY 2.7

ARTHUR ANDERSEN AND OBSTRUCTION OF JUSTICE

Concept	Auditor statutory legal liability – illegal acts.

Story	Arthur Andersen, LLP, one of the former Big Five audit firms with 2,311 public company clients and 28,000 US employees, was found guilty of 'obstruction of justice'. The obstruction of justice statute, 18 USC s 1512(b), makes it a crime for anyone to 'corruptly persuade' 'another person' to destroy documents 'with intent to impair' the use of the documents 'in an official proceeding'. The US District Court for the Southern District of Texas sentenced Andersen to pay a $500,000 fine and serve five years of probation (WSJ, 2002).

The charge resulted from Andersen's destruction of thousands of documents and email messages relating to work performed for Enron. The court found that Andersen illegally destroyed the documents with the intent of thwarting an investigation by the US Securities and Exchange Commission. On 15 June 2002, the tenth day of deliberations, the jury met for only 30 minutes, and then delivered its fatal verdict. This was the first time a major accounting firm had ever been convicted of a criminal charge (Manor, 2002).

Andersen contended that the document destruction was done in the standard course of business and was not illegal. The prosecution introduced evidence that Andersen billed Enron about $720,000 for consultation services relating to 'SEC Inquiry' at the same time the firm was destroying documents relating to the Enron audit. The Department of Justice said that the Andersen billing records presented strong evidence that the firm knew about the SEC investigation at the same time they were shredding documents that might have been subpoenaed in that investigation. This establishes that many people at Andersen who were involved in the document destruction had direct, personal knowledge of the investigation (Fowler, 2002).

The document destruction was precipitated by a memo from Nancy Temple in Andersen's legal department which stated that, under the Andersen document retention policy, superseded drafts of memos should be discarded. David Duncan, the Andersen lead audit partner on the Enron account, ordered employees to adhere to the firm's guidelines on 'document retention' and destroy irrelevant documents. In the trial, prosecution produced a binder of handwritten notes from Temple, taken from numerous conference calls with Andersen executives, to show that the attorney realized that the SEC would probably open an investigation into Enron (Beltran *et al.*, 2002).

Andersen appealed the judgment on several grounds. Andersen complained that the judge allowed the government to tell jurors about SEC actions against Andersen for faulty audits of Waste Management and Sunbeam, thereby prejudicing the jury. They also said that the judge gave improper instructions to the jury. The jury gave a message to the judge asking for guidance on making their decision. The question they asked was: 'If each of us believes that one Andersen agent acted knowingly and with a corrupt intent, is it for all of us to believe it was the same agent? Can one believe it was agent A, another believe it was agent B, and another believe it agent C?' (*Houston Chronicle*, 2003).

Over strenuous objections from the prosecution, Judge Harmon returned a message to the jury, telling them they could find Andersen guilty of obstructing justice even if they could not agree on which employee committed the crime (McNulty, 2002).

However, in May 2005 the Supreme Court reversed the previous conviction of Andersen. This was a symbolic victory for Andersen, as by then the firm was already nearly out of business due to the previous conviction. In a statement, Andersen said they were 'very pleased with the Supreme Court's decision, which acknowledges the fundamental injustice that has been done to Arthur Andersen and its former personnel and retirees.' As an audit firm, Andersen was not back in business as its reputation as an independent, high-quality auditor was pretty much gone.

Discussion Questions	▶ Should the whole audit firm be charged with an offence by a few of its auditors? ▶ In what ways can auditor working papers (correspondence, plans and audit notes) be beneficial to an investigation of company fraudulent practices?

References	Beltran, L., J. Rogers and P. Viles, 2002, 'U.S. Closes in Andersen Trial,' *CNNMoney*, 5 June. Fowler, Tom, 2002, 'Soul Searching Led to Plea, Duncan Says,' *Houston Chronicle*, 16 May. Manor, R., 2002, 'Andersen Finally Admits Demise,' *Chicago Tribune*, 17 June. McNulty, S., 2002, 'Andersen Guilty in Enron Obstruction Case,' *Financial Times*, 16 June. WSJ, 2002, 'Andersen Sentenced To 5 Years' Probation,' *Wall Street Journal*, 17 October.

To hold the auditor legally liable successfully in a civil suit, the following conditions must be met:

▶ An audit failure/neglect must be proven (*negligence* issue). A verdict by the disciplinary court is often the basis for meeting this condition.
▶ The auditor should owe a duty of care to the plaintiff (*due professional care* issue).
▶ The plaintiff must prove a causal relationship between his losses and the alleged audit failure (*causation* issue).
▶ The plaintiff must quantify his losses (*quantum* issue).

TRAFIGURA AND THE ILLEGAL DUMPING OF TOXIC WASTE

Concept	Auditor's responsibilities regarding laws and regulation – illegal acts.
Story	TrafiguraBeheer BV is a Dutch multinational commodity trading company founded in 1993 and trading in base metals and energy, including oil.

On 2 July 2006, the *Probo Koala*, a ship leased by the company, entered a port in Amsterdam to unload several hundred tonnes of toxic waste. Amsterdam Port Services BV, the company that had been contracted to take the waste, raised their price to process the waste twenty-fold soon after determining the waste was more toxic than previously understood. So, after baulking at a competitor's 1000 euro per cubic metre disposal charge near Amsterdam, Trafigura decided to have the ship take back the waste and have it processed en route to different offloading sites, which all refused it until Abidjan, Côte d'Ivoire, one of Africa's largest seaports. According to Trafigura the waste was then handed over to a local newly formed dumping company, Compagnie Tommy, which illegally dumped the waste instead of processing it. Many people there became sick due to exposure to the waste, and investigations were begun to determine whether it was intentionally dumped by Trafigura. Trafigura stated in a press statement that their tests showed the waste not to be as toxic as had been claimed, and that they were unsure why so many people had become ill from exposure to it. The *New York Times* reported on 3 October 2006 that the dumping of the waste by Compagnie Tommy was indeed illegal.

On 13 February 2007, to release its jailed executives in response to the deaths of ten people and the various illnesses of over 100,000 people attributed to the waste, Trafigura paid €152 million to Côte d'Ivoire in compensation. The payment also exonerated Trafigura from further legal proceedings in Côte d'Ivoire.

On 16 November 2012 Trafigura and the Dutch authorities agreed to a settlement. The settlement obliges Trafigura to pay the existing €1 million fine and in addition the company must also pay Dutch authorities a further €300,000 in compensation – the money it saved by dumping the toxic waste in Abidjan rather than having it properly disposed of in the Netherlands. The Dutch also agreed to stop the personal court case against Trafigura's chairman, Claude Dauphin, in exchange for a €67,000 fine.

Discussion Questions	▶ Do you think the auditor of TrafiguraBeheer BV should have discovered the illegal activities of TrafiguraBeheer BV, given the attention in the international press during 2006 and early 2007?
	▶ Do you think the financial statements of TrafiguraBeheer BV for the year ending 31 December 2006 are materially incorrect, if the contingent liability of €152 million is not included in these financial statements?
References	http://en.wikipedia.org/wiki/Trafigura.

▶ SUGGESTED SOLUTIONS TO AUDITOR LIABILITY

In the last two decades, several auditor litigation cases have resulted in multi-million dollar claims to be paid by auditors. For example, some Big Four audit firms made settlements with the US government for more than US $500 million, because of audit failures regarding several US hedge funds and financial institutions. The requirement for audit firms to carry insurance against litigation varies significantly depending on the jurisdiction. However, it's important to note that mandatory insurance requirements for audit firms may not specifically target litigation, but rather liability insurance to cover potential damages arising from professional errors or negligence. Insurance against litigation is now common for audit firms (and in some countries like the Netherlands[23], mandatory). Even though the premium rates for these insurance policies have risen dramatically over the last decade, these policies only cover damage to a certain amount. Claims paid above this 'cap' are not covered and have to be paid by the audit firm itself.

It is widely acknowledged that the financial risks resulting from litigation for audit firms and partners might be a threat to the viability of the audit profession. Former European Union Internal Market and Services Commissioner Charlie McCreevy has said:

We have concluded that unlimited liability combined with insufficient insurance cover is no longer tenable. It is a potentially huge problem for our capital markets and for auditors working on an international scale. The current conditions are not only preventing the entry of new players in the international audit market but are also threatening existing firms. In a context of high concentration and limited choice of audit firms, this situation could lead to damaging consequences for European capital markets[24].

To reduce these risks several measures are considered:

▶ A limit or *cap* on claims (a maximum settlement amount) is known in advance and limits settlements. Liability is now capped in Austria, Belgium, Germany, Greece and Slovenia.

▶ In some countries, a system of *proportionate liability* is under study. In such a system, an audit firm is not liable for the entire loss incurred by plaintiffs (as is the case under *joint and several liability*), but only to the extent to which the loss is attributable to the auditor. The US has a system of proportionate liability, but only under the federal acts.

▶ Exclude certain activities with a higher risk profile from the auditors' liability. A mechanism to achieve this outcome would be to introduce so-called safe harbour provisions by legislation.

▶ In order to protect the personal wealth of audit partners, some audit firms are structured as a limited liability partnership (e.g., in the UK).

2.9 DISCIPLINARY ACTION

Nearly all national audit professions have some sort of disciplinary court. In most countries, anyone can lodge a complaint against an auditor, regardless of one's involvement with the auditor. The disciplinary court typically consists of representatives of the audit and legal professions, and sometimes representatives of the public. Having heard the arguments of the plaintiffs and the defendant, the court makes its judgment and determines the sanction – if any – against the auditor.

In some countries, the trials of these disciplinary courts are public. In most countries, the verdicts are made public, if the verdict is either a suspension or a lifetime ban. Appeal against the verdict of the disciplinary court is usually possible.

Disciplinary action ordinarily arises from such issues as: failure to observe the required standard of professional care, skills or competence; non-compliance with rules of ethics; and discreditable or dishonourable conduct. Sanctions commonly imposed by disciplinary bodies include reprimand, fine, payment of costs, withdrawal of practising rights, suspension, and expulsion from membership. Other sanctions can include a warning, the refund of the fee charged to the client, additional education, and the work to be completed by another member at the disciplined member's expense. The effectiveness of enforcing ethical standards varies from country to country.

In the USA expulsion from a state society or the American Institute of Certified Public Accountants (AICPA) does not mean that the expelled member cannot practise public accounting because only the state boards of public accountancy have the authority to revoke a license. As illustrated in the case of Arthur Andersen,[25] if a company is convicted of a felony, the US Security and Exchange Commission (SEC) prohibits them from auditing publicly traded companies. In other countries, such as Japan, France and Germany, government often takes a formal role in the enforcement of the standards.

ILLUSTRATION 2.7

EXAMPLES OF VIOLATIONS OF INDEPENDENCE (DERIVED FROM SEC PRESS RELEASES)

According to the SEC's order, RSM US repeatedly represented that it was 'independent' in audit reports issued on the clients' financial statements, which were included or incorporated by reference in public filings with the commission or provided to investors. Instead, the SEC found that RSM US or its associated entities, including other member firms of the RSM International network, provided non-audit services to, and had an employment relationship with, affiliates of RSM US audit clients, which violated the sec's auditor independence rules. The prohibited non-audit services included corporate secretarial services, payment facilitation, payroll outsourcing, loaned staff, financial information system design or implementation, bookkeeping, internal audit outsourcing, and investment adviser services. The prohibited employment relationship concerned a partner at an RSM member firm in Australia serving on a voluntary basis as a non-discretionary member of the board of an affiliate of an RSM US issuer audit client. RSM US agreed to pay a $950,000 penalty and be censured.
Source: SEC charges RSM US LLP with violating Auditor Independence rules. For Immediate release, 2019-161, https://www.sec.gov/news/press-release/2019-161

The SEC's order finds that PwC violated the SEC's auditor independence rules by performing prohibited non-audit services during an audit engagement, including exercising decision-making authority in the design and implementation of software relating to an audit client's financial reporting, and engaging in management functions. In connection with performing non-audit services for 15 sec-registered audit clients. The order states that PwC violated Public Company Accounting Oversight Board (PCAOB) rule 3525, which requires an auditor to describe in writing to the audit committee the scope of work, discuss with the audit committee the potential effects of the work on independence, and document the substance of the independence discussion. According to the order, PwC's actions deprived numerous issuers' audit committees of information necessary to assess PwC's independence. PwC agreed to pay disgorgement of $3,830,213, plus prejudgment interest of $613,842 and a civil money penalty of $3.5 million, and to be censured.
Source: sec charges PwC LLP with violating Auditor Independence rules and engaging in Improper Professional conduct, https://www.sec.gov/news/press-release/2019-184.

Disciplinary actions by professional accounting associations differ around the world. As an example, the following are disciplinary actions that may be taken by the American Institute of Certified Public Accountants (AICPA). Membership in the AICPA is suspended or terminated automatically without a hearing if a member is (1) convicted of a crime punishable by imprisonment for more than one year; (2) wilfully fails to file an income tax return that he or she is required to file; (3) files a false or fraudulent income tax return on the member's or a client's behalf; or (4) wilfully aids in the preparation and presentation of a false and fraudulent income tax return for a client.[26] AICPA bylaw Section 760R[27] requires publication of a disciplinary action taken against a member of the AICPA. This public notice gives the member's name, city and state of residence, the type of sanction, and a short statement of the reasons for the action.

In the **UK**, disciplinary law for accountants is governed primarily by regulatory bodies such as the Financial Reporting Council (FRC) and professional accountancy organizations like the Institute of Chartered Accountants in England and Wales (ICAEW) and others. Any of these bodies are themselves subject to oversight by the independent Financial Reporting Council (FRC), which is responsible for, amongst other things, considering cases that raise public interest considerations.

In **Germany**, the disciplinary law for accountants and auditors is primarily regulated by the Wirtschaftsprüferordnung (Public Accountants Act) and the Berufsordnung der Wirtschaftsprüfer (Professional Code of Conduct for Public Accountants), which are overseen by the Wirtschaftsprüferkammer (Chamber of Public Accountants). Additionally, there are different levels of disciplinary bodies within the profession, such as the Professional Courts for Public Accountants, which handle more severe disciplinary cases.

In **Japan**, the disciplinary law and regulations for accountants are overseen by several organizations, with the primary body being the Certified Public Accountants and Auditing Oversight Board (CPAAOB).

In **Italy**, the disciplinary law and regulations for accountants, including Certified Public Accountants (Commercialisti) and Statutory Auditors (Revisori Contabili), are overseen by various regulatory and professional bodies. Some aspects of disciplinary procedures may vary at the regional or local level due to the presence of regional chambers of accountants (Consigli Regionali dei Dottori Commercialisti e degli Esperti Contabili).

The disciplinary procedures for accountants in **the Netherlands** are governed by both the AFM (firms) and the Accountantskamer (individuals), which is a special chamber of the Dutch court system responsible for handling disciplinary cases related to accountants and auditors.

2.10 AUDIT FIRM OVERSIGHT

Because of the public need for high audit quality. there are many accounting oversight boards (government or professional committees) to review the work of auditors and take an active part in setting and enforcing standards. Similar boards are in Australia (Financial Reporting Council), the Netherlands Authority for the Financial Markets (AFM), France Autorité des marchés financiers (AMF) and the USA (the Public Company Accounting Oversight Board). These boards are mentioned in illustration 2.8[28].

ILLUSTRATION 2.8

SPECIFIC COUNTRY OVERSIGHT BOARDS

In **Australia**, the Corporate Law Economic Reform Program Act 1999 established the **Financial Reporting Council (FRC)** which is responsible for overseeing the effectiveness of the financial reporting framework in Australia. Its key functions include the oversight of the accounting and auditing standards setting processes for the public and private sectors, providing strategic advice in relation to the quality of audits conducted by Australian auditors, and advising the Minister on these and related matters to the extent that they affect the financial reporting framework in Australia. The FRC monitors the development of international accounting and auditing standards, works to further the development of a single set of accounting and auditing standards for world-wide use and promotes the adoption of these standards. http://www.frc.gov.au/

Netherlands Authority for the Financial Markets (AFM) has been responsible for supervising the operation of the financial markets since 1 March 2002. This means that AFM supervises the conduct of the entire financial market sector: savings, investment, insurance and loans. AFM is the successor of the STE (Securities Board of the Netherlands/Stichting Toezicht Effectenverkeer), which supervised all of the participants in the securities trade. AFM is responsible for supervision of financial institutions and financial markets. https://www.afm.nl/en

In **France** the **Autorité des marchés financiers (AMF)** monitors the information disclosed by listed corporates, paying particular attention to quality and transparency. It investigates special topics on an ongoing basis such as enhancing the competitiveness of the Paris financial center, replacing the traditional French concept of public issuance of securities (*appel public à l'épargne*) with the European notion of 'public offer', and the security and attractiveness of markets for small and mid-sized companies. https://www.amf-france.org/en_US/

In the **United States of America,** the **Public Company Accounting Oversight Board** (PCAOB) was created by the Sarbanes–Oxley Act of 2002. The PCAOB is empowered to regularly inspect registered accounting firms' operations and will investigate potential violations of securities laws, standards, consistency and conduct. Accounting firms headquartered outside the USA that 'prepare and furnish' an audit report involving US firms registered with the SEC are subject to the authority of the PCAOB. The PCAOB is very influential as all corporations, no matter in what country they are headquartered, are subject to PCAOB audit standards if that company is traded on a US exchange (such as New York Stock Exchange, NASDAC, etc.). https://pcaobus.org/

The oversight of auditors by regulators involves monitoring and evaluating the activities of audit firms to ensure compliance with professional standards, legal requirements, and ethical norms. Regulators typically conduct inspections, investigations, and reviews of audit engagements to assess the quality of audits and safeguard the interests of investors and the public. Findings from these oversight activities can reveal areas of improvement, compliance issues, or potential risks in the audit process.

Regulators publish their findings and reports based on inspections and audit quality reviews. Audit firms are often required to address identified deficiencies and implement remedial actions. This could involve improving internal controls, enhancing training programs, or making changes to audit methodologies[29]. Regulators may have enforcement powers to impose sanctions, fines, or other disciplinary measures if audit firms fail to address identified issues or if there are serious violations of auditing standards.

The International Forum of Independent Audit Regulators (IFIAR), whose membership includes the audit regulators from 55 jurisdictions representing Africa, North America, South America, Asia, Oceania, and Europe, was established on 15 September 2006. Its mission is to serve the public interest and enhance investor protection by improving audit quality globally. To this end IFIAR develops strategic and operational plans, along with thought leadership papers on key audit quality oversight matters and annually publishes global inspection findings. its 2022 report IFIAR encourages audit firms to continue implementing quality management activities to:

> ▶ Identify areas for improvement to the systems of quality control that support their audit practices.
> ▶ Perform root cause analysis and implement responsive actions.
> ▶ Monitor the impact of such actions; and
> ▶ Leverage the results to adjust or refine their improvement strategies.[30]

2.11 AUDIT FIRM'S QUALITY MANAGEMENT SYSTEM

▶ QUALITY MANAGEMENT (ISQM 1, ISQM 2, AND ISA 220)

Quality control is a very important consideration for auditors. International Standard on Quality Management 1 (ISQM 1) and ISQM 2[31] apply to all firms of professional accountants in respect to audits and reviews, other assurance, and related services engagements. ISQM 1 gives the requirements designed to enable the accounting firm to meet the objective of quality control. In addition, it contains related guidance in the form of application and other explanatory material. ISQM 2 deals with the appointment and eligibility of the engagement quality reviewer, and the performance and documentation and performance of the engagement quality review. ISA 220 sets out the engagement partner's responsibilities with respect to ethical requirements. These include remaining alert for evidence of non-compliance with ethical requirements of the members of the engagement team determining appropriate action if there is non-compliance.

A major objective of the audit firm is to establish and maintain a system of quality control to provide it with reasonable assurance that the accounting firm and its personnel comply with professional standards, legal and regulatory requirements, and that reports issued are appropriate in the circumstances. The audit firm must establish and communicate to their personnel a system of quality control that includes policies and procedures that address each of the following elements:

> ▶ Leadership responsibilities for quality within the firm.
> ▶ Relevant ethical requirements.
> ▶ Acceptance and continuance of client relationships and specific engagements.
> ▶ Human resources.
> ▶ Engagement performance.
> ▶ Monitoring.

▶ INTERNATIONAL STANDARD ON QUALITY MANAGEMENT 1 (ISQM 1)

International Standards on Quality Management (ISQMs) are to be applied for all services falling under the IAASB's Engagement Standards.

Under ISQM 1, firms are required to design a system of quality management to manage the quality of engagements performed by the firm.[32] ISQM 1 applies to all firms that perform audits or reviews of financial statements, or other assurance or related services engagements.[33] ISQM 1 applies to managing quality for those engagements.

Under ISQM 1, a system of quality management addresses the following eight components:[34]

1 The firm's risk assessment process[35];
2 Governance and leadership;
3 Relevant ethical requirements;
4 Acceptance and continuance of client relationships and specific engagements;
5 Engagement performance;
6 Resources;
7 Information and communication; and
8 The monitoring and remediation process.

The risk-based assessment is carried out through:

▶ Establishing quality objectives. The accounting firm is required to establish the quality objectives specified by ISQM1 and ISQM2.
▶ Identifying and assessing risks to the achievement of the quality objectives (called 'quality risks'). The firm is required to identify and assess quality risks to provide a basis for the responses.[36]

To promote good governance, this ISQM requires that, at least annually, the individual(s) assigned ultimate responsibility and accountability for the system of quality management, evaluates the system and concludes that the objectives of the system are being achieved.[37] Ultimate responsibility and accountability for the system of quality management to the firm's chief executive officer or the firm's managing partner or the firm's managing board of partners. Operational responsibility for specific aspects of the system of quality management, including compliance with independence requirements[38]; and the monitoring and remediation process[39] must be assigned to a firm employee.

The audit firm shall include the following responses to quality management: establish policies or procedures for identifying and addressing threats to compliance with ethical requirements; and reporting of any breaches of ethical requirements.[40] The firm should obtain, at least annually, a documented confirmation of compliance with independence requirements from all personnel required to be independent. A process for complaint resolution should be established.[41] Policies or procedures should be set that address circumstances when the firm becomes aware of information after accepting a client relationship that would have caused it to decline the client relationship had that information been known before that acceptance. Also policies must address when the firm is obligated by law or regulation to accept a client relationship or specific engagement.[42]

► INTERNATIONAL STANDARD ON QUALITY MANAGEMENT 2 (ISQM 2)

ISQM 2 deals with the appointment and eligibility of the engagement quality reviewer, and the performance and documentation and performance of the engagement quality review.[43] This ISQM applies to all engagements for which an engagement quality review is required to be performed in accordance with ISQM 1. An engagement quality review is an objective evaluation of the significant judgments made by the engagement team and the conclusions reached. An engagement quality review performed in accordance with this ISQM 2 is a specified response that is designed and implemented by the firm in accordance with ISQM 1.[44]

The engagement quality reviewer is a partner, other individual in the firm, or an external individual, appointed by the firm to perform the engagement quality review. The engagement quality reviewer and individuals who assist the engagement quality reviewer must not be members of the engagement team.[45] The engagement quality reviewer must have appropriate authority to perform the engagement quality review[46] and comply with relevant ethical requirements and with provisions of law and regulation relevant to their eligibility.[47] Before the engagement partner can assume the role of engagement quality reviewer firm policies should specify a cooling-off period of at least two years.

To ensure completeness of reporting, the engagement partner is precluded from dating the engagement report until notification has been received from the engagement quality reviewer that the engagement quality review is complete.

The engagement quality reviewer should examine selected engagement documentation relating to the significant judgments made by the engagement team. Based on that documentation they should evaluate:

- ► The basis for making those significant judgments, including the exercise of professional scepticism by the engagement team;
- ► Whether the engagement documentation supports the conclusions reached;
- ► Whether the conclusions reached are appropriate.
- ► For audits of financial statements, that ethical requirements relating to independence have been fulfilled and the basis for determining significant judgments made and conclusions reached are appropriate in the circumstances of the engagement.

In the process of their evaluation, the engagement quality reviewer should review:

- ► For audits of financial statements, the financial statements and the auditor's report.
- ► For review engagements, the financial statements or financial information and the engagement report.
- ► For other assurance and related services engagements, the engagement report, and when applicable, the subject matter information.

► INTERNATIONAL STANDARD ON AUDITING 220 (ISA 220)

ISA 220 (Revised)[48] sets out the engagement partner's responsibilities with respect to relevant ethical requirements, including those related to independence.[49] In accordance with ISA 200[50] the engagement team is required to plan and perform an audit with professional scepticism and to exercise professional judgment. Professional judgment is exercised in making informed decisions about the courses of action that are appropriate to manage and achieve quality given the nature and circumstances of the audit engagement.

Professional scepticism supports the quality of judgments made by the engagement team. Under ISA 220 the engagement partner takes overall responsibility for managing and achieving quality on the audit engagement, including taking responsibility for creating an environment for the engagement that emphasizes the firm's culture and expected behaviour of engagement team members.

2.12 AUDIT SERVICES: AN EXAMPLE

Isle & Oblivion (I&O) is a fairly large regional audit firm. They like to offer clients a bundle of audit and advisory services such as income tax preparation, financial consulting, mergers and acquisitions, computer accounting systems set up and maintenance, internal audit and, of course the bread-and-butter financial audit services. In illustration 2.9 we sketch services that are offered by a US Big Four firm. Most of these services, except tax preparation and limited advisory services, they cannot offer to their audit clients because it may create self-interest, self-review, advocacy, or even intimidation threats. (See chapter 3, Ethics for Professional Accountants, for more detail.)

ILLUSTRATION 2.9

CAPABILITIES OF A US BIG FOUR AUDIT FIRM (2023)[51]

Assurance
Financial statement audit, Digital Assurance and Transparency, SOC reporting services

Board and Governance Issues
Audit committee, Board performance and practices, ESG oversight, Shareholder insights, Strategy

Sustainability consulting and climate transition
Climate risk modelling, Decarbonization and net zero, ESG deals and reporting, Sustainability assurance, Sustainable Value Governance, ESG tax, technology and digital

Tax Services
Global Structuring, International Tax Reporting, Legal Business Solutions, Mergers and acquisitions Tax, Tax Accounting Services, Reporting and Strategy, Tax Compliance
Tax Transfer pricing
Wealth Management Tax Services

Consulting
Alliances and ecosystems
Cloud and digital
Cloud strategy
Analytics Insights
Cybersecurity, Privacy and Forensics

Strategy, Risk and Compliance

Investigations and Forensics and Financial Crime and Compliance

Info Governance and Privacy

Deals and Acquisitions and Divestitures

Capital markets

Turnaround and restructuring

Application Security and Controls Monitoring

Controls Testing and Monitoring

Cyber

Legal

Procurement

Risk and regulatory

Financial services and health industries risk and regulatory

Enterprise risk, controls and tech solutions

Enterprise Strategy and Value

Customer and Operations Transformation

Operations Transformation

Financial Services Transformation

Health, Finance, Workforce Transformation

We will not discuss all the different services that I&O as an accountancy firm offers. Here we concentrate on two basic types of auditors: independent external auditors and internal auditors. Governmental auditors take both the functions of internal and external auditor with governmental bodies as 'client' like departments, parliaments, counties, municipalities, etc.

As we will give more coverage to the external audit of I&O throughout this book, we will only give a brief example of internal audits here. Some of I&Os clients have an Internal Auditing Function (IAF). These internal auditors are employed by the client to investigate and appraise the effectiveness of operations and internal controls to help management decision making as well as performing special investigations at the request of the board. Ordinarily internal auditors are full-time employees of a client company.

One of I&O's clients with an internal audit function is Heiligenstadt, a cultural consulting service located in Vienna, Austria. Head of the IAF is Fleur Hague, WP (Wirtschafstprüfer). Her team consists of two managers (WPs), one IT auditor, one environmental auditor and 5 staff and junior auditors who follow extensive training and have at least a bachelor's university degree. The Board of Heiligenstadt ordered Fleur Hague and her team recently to review and analyse their computerized data collection operations to determine profitability, strengths and weaknesses of each service Heiligenstadt offers.

The internal audit team starts preparing an audit plan that will be discussed with the board. One of the audit procedures is interviewing the management and getting their key objectives and a history of the construction and use of the database to be examined. Fleur prepares a rough draft audit plan emphasizing examination of the most and least profitable of Heiligenstadt's services and a random sample of their 'standard competitive services'. After the audit following the audit plan, the internal audit team prepares a report to management and Fleur presents it to the Board of Directors. According to good corporate governance, it is the Audit Committee that appoints and evaluates the chief IAF. There is also a direct communication line with the Audit Committee.

2.13   SUMMARY

There are two basic types of auditors: independent external auditors and internal auditors. Governmental auditors take both the functions of internal and external auditor having the government as 'auditee'.

Internal auditors are employed by individual companies to investigate and appraise the effectiveness of company operations for management. Much of their attention is often given to the appraisal of internal controls. A large part of the internal auditor's work consists of operational audits (reviews of operations). In addition, they may conduct compliance audits (reviews of compliance with policies and regulations)

Independent auditors have primary responsibility to the performance of the audit function on published financial statements of publicly traded companies and non-public companies. External and internal auditors are typically certified or licensed either by a professional organization or a government agency.

Audits are typically classified into three types: audits of financial statements, operational audits and compliance audits. An operational audit is a study of a specific unit of an organization for the purpose of measuring its performance. A compliance audit may not necessarily be related to accounting. It is a review of an organization's procedures to determine whether the organization is following specific procedures, i.e., rules or regulations set out by some higher authority (i.e., tax codes, corporate governance codes, employee safety, or environmental regulations).

Audit firms are often classified into two distinct categories: the Big Four firms and the Non-Big Four firms. The Big Four are Deloitte, Ernst & Young (EY), KPMG, and PricewaterhouseCoopers (PwC), the four largest accountancy firms in the world with billions of dollars in revenues. Although most of these firms are still structured as national limited liability partnerships with national instead of international profit sharing, these national member firms participate in an international head office, in which global technologies, procedures, and directives are developed.

Non-Big Four includes audit firms of all sizes and is not a homogeneous group. At one extreme there are a very large number of small local firms, with only a handful of professionals. At the other extreme there are a small number of second-tier firms, which also have an international network, although not quite as extensive as the Big Four network.

The organizational hierarchy in a typical international auditing firm (Big Four and second-tier firms) includes partners (or directors), managers, supervisors, seniors or in-charge auditors, and staff accountants. A new employee usually starts as a staff accountant and spends several years at each classification before eventually achieving partner status.

Financial accounting standards are unique and separate from audit standards. By its nature, auditing requires that the real-world evidence of financial transactions be compared to financial standards. The standards to which an international auditor compares financial statements are generally standards in the reporting country (e.g., Financial Accounting Standards (FAS) in the USA, or national standards in European Union (EU) Member States which are based on EU Directives). Countries may use International Financial Reporting Standards (IFRS), formerly called International Accounting Standards (IAS), which are set by the International Accounting Standards Board (IASB).

The International Auditing and Assurance Standards Board (IAASB) is an independent standards board which issues several sets of standards to be applied to international auditing and assurance services. IAASB issues:

- ▶ International Standards on Auditing (ISAs) as the standards to be applied by auditors in reporting on historical financial information;
- ▶ International Standards on Assurance Engagements (ISAEs) as the quality control standards to be applied by practitioners in assurance engagements dealing with information other than historical financial information;
- ▶ International Standards on Quality Management (ISQMs) as the standards to be applied for all services falling under the standards of the IAASB;
- ▶ International Standards on Related Services (ISRSs) as the standards to be applied on related services; and
- ▶ International Standards on Review Engagements (ISREs) as the standards to be applied to the review of historical financial information.

Although regulation and legislation differ, both the demand and the supply of audit services are currently regulated to some degree in most countries. Recent accounting and finance research suggests that national legal environments are among the key determinants of financial market development, corporate ownership structures, corporate policies, and the properties of accounting information around the world.

The supply of audit services is regulated in most countries. In the European Union, statutory audits, i.e., audits required by law, can only be performed by auditors who have met specific technical requirements with regard to education and experience under the Eighth Council Directive and Directive 2006/43. The United States changed the demand and supply for audit services by enacting the Sarbanes-Oxley Act.

Legal liability of the auditor to each stakeholder varies from country to country, district to district. This liability can generally be classified as based on one or more of the following: common law, civil liability under statutory law, criminal liability under statutory law, and liability as members of professional accounting organizations.

Liability for auditors under common law includes liabilities to clients and third-party liability. Statutory civil liabilities are liabilities under laws that require a preponderance of evidence to convict resulting in a civil penalty such as a fine or suspension of license to operate. A professional auditor may be held criminally liable under the laws of a country or district that make it a criminal offence to defraud another person through knowingly being involved with false financial statements. Statutory criminal law requires evidence beyond a reasonable doubt to convict resulting in loss of freedom, imprisonment and fines.

Nearly all national audit professions have some sort of disciplinary court. In most countries, anyone can lodge a complaint against an auditor, regardless of one's involvement with the auditor. If a conviction results, the defendant may be sanctioned with a fine, reprimand, suspension of license or ban from profession.

The Securities and Exchange Act of 1934 in the USA requires every company with securities traded on national and over-the-counter exchanges to submit audited financial statements annually (SEC form 10-K) as well as other reports for quarterly financials (10-Q), unusual events (8-K) and other events. The U.S. Sarbanes-Oxley Act of 2002 attaches criminal penalties to CEOs, CFOs and auditors. To knowingly destroy, create, manipulate documents and/or impede or obstruct federal investigations is considered a felony, and violators will be subject to fines or up to 20 years' imprisonment, or both. All audit reports or related workpapers must be kept by the auditor.

To hold the auditor legally liable successfully in a civil suit, the following conditions have to be met:

▶ An audit failure/neglect must be proven (*negligence* issue). A verdict by the disciplinary court is often the basis for meeting this condition.
▶ The auditor should owe a duty of care to the plaintiff (*due professional care* issue).
▶ The plaintiff must prove a causal relationship between his losses and the alleged audit failure (*causation* issue).
▶ The plaintiff must quantify his losses (*quantum* issue).

The global oversight organization is the International Forum of Independent Audit Regulators (IFIAR). Similar boards are in Australia (Financial Reporting Council), the Netherlands Authority for the Financial Markets (AFM), France Autorité des marchés financiers (AMF) and the USA (the Public Company Accounting Oversight Board).

Quality management is a very important consideration for auditors. International Standard on Quality Management 1 (ISQM 1) and ISQM 2 apply to all firms of professional accountants in respect to audits and reviews, other assurance, and related services engagements. ISQM 1 gives the requirements designed to enable the accounting firm to meet the objective of quality control. In addition, it contains related guidance in the form of application and other explanatory material. ISQM 2 deals with the appointment and eligibility of the engagement quality reviewer, and the performance and documentation and performance of the engagement quality review. ISA 220 sets out the engagement partner's responsibilities with respect to ethical requirements. These include remaining alert for evidence of non-compliance with ethical requirements of the members of the engagement team determining appropriate action if there is non-compliance.

A major objective of the audit firm is to establish and maintain a system of quality control to provide it with reasonable assurance that the accounting firm and its personnel comply with professional standards, legal and regulatory requirements, and that reports issued are appropriate in the circumstances. The audit firm must establish and communicate to their personnel a system of quality control that includes policies and procedures that address leadership, ethical requirements, acceptance and continuance of client, human resources, engagement performance and monitoring.

2.14   QUESTIONS, EXERCISES AND CASES

2.3   Types of Auditors

2-1   What are differences between an accountant and an auditor?

2.4   Types of Audits

2-2   How many types of audits are there? Name each and briefly define them.

2-3   What are the differences and similarities in audits of financial statements, compliance audits and operational audits?

2.5   Audit Firms

2-4   What are the names of the Big Four firms?

2-5   What is meant by second-tier firms?

2-6   List the four basic positions within the organizational structure of an audit firm and describe the duties of each position.

2-7   Give a brief history of each of the Big Four firms.

2.6   Standard Setting

2-8   How do International Financial reporting standards (IFRS) differ from International Standards on Auditing (ISA)?

2-9   Why is the adoption of International Auditing standards important for developing nations?

2.7   Audit Regulation

2-10   Describe the major US and European regulations discussed in this section.

2.8   Auditor's Legal Liability

2-11   What are four major sources of auditors' legal liability? Briefly discuss them.

2-12   What measures are possibilities to reduce auditors' unlimited legal liability?

2.9   Disciplinary Action

2-13   Can IESBA discipline an accountant for violation of the Code of Ethics? What sanctions are commonly imposed by disciplinary bodies?

2-14   What are the disciplinary sanctions employed by the American Institute of Certified Public Accountants (AICPA)?

2.10   Audit Firm Oversight

2-15   Give the names of four national accounting oversight boards (government or professional committees) to review the work of auditors and take an active part in setting and enforcing standards.

2-16   Describe the activities of the International Forum of Independent Audit regulators (IFIAR).

2.11   Audit Firms' Quality Management system

2-17   Explain the difference between the three standards that deal with quality management.

2-18 What areas must policies and procedures on quality management address?

2-19 Discuss quality management policies for engagement performance.

2.3 Types of Auditors

2-20 Independent External Auditors. Give reasons why the following organizations should have annual audits by an independent external auditor:

a.   The US Federal Reserve Board

b.   A retail company traded on the London stock exchange

c.   Walt Disney Company

d.   Amnesty International

e.   A small grocery store in Ponta Grossa, Brazil

f.   A local Baptist church in Lubbock, Texas, USA.

2.4 Types of Audits

2-21 Operational Audits. List four examples of specific operational audits that could be conducted by an internal audit in a manufacturing company. Describe how you would conduct each.

2-22 Auditing Tasks. Each of the following represents tasks that auditors frequently perform:

1   Compilation of quarterly financial statements for a small business that does not have any accounting personnel capable of preparing financial statements.

2   Review of tax return of corporate president to determine whether she has included all taxable income.

3   Review of the activities of the receiving department of a large manufacturing company, with special attention to the efficiency of the materials inspection.

4   Evaluation of a company's computer system to determine whether the computer is being used effectively.

5   Examination on a surprise basis of Topanga Bank. with emphasis placed on verification of cash and loans receivable and observation of the California banking code.

6   Examination of vacation records to determine whether employees followed company policy of two weeks' paid vacation annually.

7   Audit of a small college to determine that the college had followed requirements of a bond indenture agreement.

8   Examination of financial statements for use by stockholders when there is an internal audit staff.

9   Audit of a German government agency to determine if the agency has followed policies of the German government.

10   Audit of annual financial statements to be filed with the US Securities and Exchange Commission (SEC).

11   Examination of a French government grants to a private company to determine whether it would have been feasible to accomplish the same objective at less cost elsewhere.

12   Audit of a statement of cash receipts and disbursements to be used by a creditor.

Required:

For each of the above, identify the most likely type of auditor (independent, government or internal) and the most likely type of audit (financial, compliance or operational).

2-23 Internal and External Audits. Khaled Al-Zubari, an executive recruiter, is a member of the Board of Directors of Mantilla Corporation. At a recent board meeting, called to discuss the financial plan for 20x4, Mr Al-Zubari discovered two planned expenditures for auditing. In the controller's department budget he found an internal audit activity, and in the treasurer's budget he found an estimate for the 20x4 annual audit by the company's external auditing firm. Mr Al-Zubari could not understand the need for two different expenditures for auditing. Since the fee for the annual external audit was less than the cost of the internal audit activity, he proposed eliminating the internal audit function.

Required:

A. Explain to Mr Al-Zubari the different purposes served by the two audit activities.

B. What benefits does the audit firm conducting an audit of financial statements derive from the existence of an internal audit function?

2.5 Audit Firms

2-24 How do the markets for the Big Four differ from second-tier firms? Describe a typical audit client for each group including average revenue, global nature, number of employees, government regulation and governance mechanism.

2-25 Auditor Responsibility. Four friends who are auditing students have a discussion. Jon says that the primary responsibility for the adequacy of disclosure in the financial statements and footnotes rests with the auditor in charge of the audit fieldwork. Mailing says that the partner in charge of the engagement has the primary responsibility. Abdul says the staff person who drafts the statements and footnotes has the primary responsibility. Yolanda contends that it is the client's (auditee's) responsibility.

Required: Which student is correct and why?

2.6 Standard Setting

2-26 International Auditing Standards. The London, Tokyo and New York stock exchanges, among others, require an annual audit of the financial statements of companies whose securities are listed on it. What are the possible reasons for this?

2-27 Describe the International Federation of Accountants (IFAC). Discuss the function of the groups within IFAC.

2.7 Audit Regulation

2-28 Comment on the following statements:

A. In most countries audits are legally required for every type of company.

B. The PCAOB sanctions firms, but not individuals, for violations of laws, regulations, and rules.

C. The European Eighth Directive's objective is to register all auditors and audit firms and make such information accessible to the public.

D. Three areas of audit regulation that are essential are (1) the independence of the profession; (2) opening up the audit market, and (3) creating a more integrated European market and stepping up its supervision.

E. Auditing is a profession and regulation of professionals should be principles based instead of rules based.

F. National regulation is conflicting with the existence of a global profession.

G. There is no reason to have national regulations in addition to international regulations for auditors.

2.8 Legal Liability

2-29 Legal Liability to Third Parties. Suppose you are a judge in the following civil case. Plaintiff Sue Banco, a banker, accuses auditor Big Zero of having performed a negligent audit in the financial statements of Trouble Company. Five months after the financial statements (with an unqualified opinion) were published, Trouble Company filed for bankruptcy, leaving the bank with unrecovered loans amounting to $ 20 million.

Required:

Describe the relevant issues to be addressed in this case.

2.9 Disciplinary Action

2-30 AICPA Actions Membership in the AICPA is suspended or terminated automatically without a hearing if a member is (1) convicted of a crime punishable by imprisonment for more than one year; (2) wilfully fails to file an income tax return that he or she is required to file; (3) files a false or fraudulent income tax return on the member's or a client's behalf; or (4) wilfully aids in the preparation and presentation of a false and fraudulent income tax return for a client.

Required:

Consulting the AICPA website, give an example of each of the above four disciplinary actions taken in the last two years.

2.10 Audit Firm Oversight

2-31 Comment on the following statements

A. The core principles of IFAR are comprehensive.

B. The FRC has broad oversight for setting accounting standards in the public and private sectors.

C. Oversight bodies of auditor's should be chaired by auditors.

D. Audit firm oversight increases a culture of fear, which makes it difficult for auditors to learn from mistakes.

2.11 Audit Firm's Quality Control System

2-32 Quality Review. Charalambos Viachoutsicos is assigned the responsibility of setting up a quality review program at his St Petersburg, Russian Federation, audit firm, Levenchuk.

Required:

A. What should the verification procedures include? Who should perform the procedures?

B. What type of documentation is required?

C. What should be covered in the report on the quality review program?

D. What organizational authority is required for the personnel who carry out the quality audit?

E. What qualifications should the personnel have?

CASE

2-33 Legal Responsibilities of Auditors. Pick five countries. Assume that you are the head of an international commission to determine legal responsibilities of accountants in various countries. use your university library and the Internet to research accounting in these five countries.

Required:

A. List the country, concept of independence and functions generally not allowed.

B. List the ethical standards, enforcement, legal liabilities and responsibility for the detection of fraud.

C. Using the library, LexisNexis, or Internet find one recent legal case in each country that impacts auditor independence or resulted from fraud. summarize each case.

D. Write a brief comparing the recent legal case and auditor ethical standards in each country.

2.15 NOTES

1. Council of European Communities, Eighth Council Directive of 10 April 1994, Article 24, *Official Journal of the European Communities*, No. L 126, 1994.
2. Gaining trust takes time, but losing it can happen quickly.
3. Smith, Philip, 'Top 20 International Networks 2018'. www.accountancyage.com. *Accountancy Age*. Retrieved 2019-02-18.
4. The Chinese Accounting Standards (CAS) are since 2006 largely replaced by the International Financial Reporting Standards (IFRS), to bring China more in line with the rest of the world.
5. https://www.iaasb.org/about-iaasb
6. Derived from IAASB, adapted by the authors incorporating (ED) ISSA 5000 and visualizing services not governed by the standards of IAASB. Sources: Handbook of International Quality Management, Auditing, Review, Other Assurance and Related Services Pronouncements 2022 Edition Volume I, International Federation of Accountants (IFAC). New York., volume I, page 5 combined with volume III, page 57.
7. https://www.ifac.org/who-we-are/membership#:~:text=IFAC%20membership%20comprises%20over%20180,most%20important%20stakeholders%20and%20constituent
8. See Ball, R., Kothari, S. and Robin, A. (2000), 'The Effect of International Institutional Factors on Properties of Accounting Earnings', *Journal of Accounting and Economics*, 29 (February), pp. 1–52; and Shleifer, A. and Vishny, R. (1997), 'A Survey of Corporate Governance', *Journal of Finance*, 52 (July), pp. 737–783.
9. https://eur-lex.europa.eu/legal-content/EN/TXT/PDF/?uri=CELEX:32014R0537#:~:text=This%20Regulation%20lays%20down%20requirements,independence%20and%20the%20avoidance%20of
10. https://eur-lex.europa.eu/legal-content/EN/TXT/PDF/?uri=CELEX:32014L0056
11. Negligence (ordinary negligence) is the failure to use reasonable care. The doing of something which a reasonably prudent person would not do, or the failure to do something which a reasonably prudent person would do under like circumstances (the 'Lectric Law Library, Lectlaw.com).
12. Breach of contract means failing to perform any term of a contract, written or oral, without a legitimate legal excuse. This may include not completing a job, not paying in full or on

time, failure to deliver all the goods, substituting inferior or significantly different goods, not providing a bond when required, being late without excuse, or any act which shows the party will not complete the work ('anticipatory breach'). Breach of contract is one of the most common causes of lawsuits for damages and/or court-ordered 'specific performance' of the contract (http://legal-dictionary.thefreedictionary.com).

13. Tort is French for wrong, a civil wrong, or wrongful act, whether intentional or accidental, from which injury occurs to another. Torts include all negligence cases as well as intentional wrongs which result in harm. Therefore, tort law is one of the major areas of law (along with contract, real property and criminal law), and results in more civil litigation than any other category. Some intentional torts may also be crimes, such as assault, battery, wrongful death, fraud, conversion (a euphemism for theft) and trespass on property, and form the basis for a lawsuit for damages by the injured party. Defamation, including intentionally telling harmful untruths about another, either by print or broadcast (libel) or orally (slander), is a tort and used to be a crime as well (http://legal-dictionary.thefreedictionary.com).

14. 255 NY 170, 174 NE 441 (1931); See also Knapp, Michael C. (2010), Contemporary Auditing: Real Issues and Cases, 8th Ed.

15. Privity of contract is the relation which subsists between two contracting parties.

16. Caparo Industries PLC v Dickman and Others, 1990, 1 All ER 568. See Cooper, B.J. and Barkoczy, M.L. (1994), 'Third Party Liability: The Auditor's Lament', Managerial Auditing Journal, Bradford, Vol. 9. Is. 5. p. 31.

17. In tort law, a duty of care is a legal obligation imposed on an individual requiring that they adhere to a standard of reasonable care while performing any acts that could foreseeably harm others. It is the first element that must be established to proceed with an action in negligence. The claimant must be able to show a duty of care imposed by law which the defendant has breached. In turn, breaching a duty may subject an individual to liability.

18. Congress of the United States, 2002, Sarbanes-Oxley Act of 2002 (SoX), s 304, 'Forfeiture of certain bonuses and profits', Washington DC.

19. Ibid. SoX, 906, paragraph 1350, 'Failure of corporate officers to certify financial reports.

20. Rule 3(e) of the SEC's Rules of Practice states: 'The commission can deny, temporarily or permanently, the privilege of appearing or practicing before it in any way to any person who is found by the commission ... (1) not to possess the requisite qualifications to represent others, or (2) to be lacking in character of integrity or to have engaged in unethical or improper professional conduct.'

21. Ibid, SoX, s 801, paragraph 1520, 'Destruction of corporate audit records'.

22. Ibid, SoX, s 906, paragraph 1350, 'Failure of corporate officers to certify financial reports'.

23. Verordening Accountantsorganisaties (VAO) Article 12, outlines the mandatory insurance requirements for accounting firms and their employees regarding professional liability. The insurance must meet certain criteria, including solvency standards, coverage amounts based on turnover, deductible limits, coverage of all firm activities, and inclusion of legal defence costs. The accounting firm must ensure coverage for at least two years for run-off and run-on risks. Additionally, the insurance should cover liability for all individuals involved in the firm's activities. The firm is responsible for assessing any need to exceed the minimum requirements outlined in the article.

24. European Union, press release 'Auditing: Commission issues Recommendation on limiting audit firms' liability (see MEMO/08/366)', 6 June 2008, Brussels.

25. Arthur Andersen was one of the largest auditing firms in the world (one of the Big Five) when they were convicted by the U.S. Department of Justice of obstruction of justice (a felony) when in 2001, the Houston, Texas branch office shredded documents relating to their audit client, Enron.

26. Code of Professional Conduct. 2013. BL Section 730. American Institute of Certified Public Accountants, Inc. New York, NY 10036-8775.

27. Code of Professional Conduct. 2013. BL Section 760R. American Institute of Certified Public Accountants, Inc. New York, NY 10036-8775.

28. Information in this illustration was combined from the separate websites of the specific accounting oversight boards mentioned. Their websites are given in the illustration text.

29. International Auditing and Assurance Standards Board (IAASB), 2023.
    ▷ International Standards on Quality Management 1 (ISQM 1). Quality Management for Firms that Perform Audits or Reviews of Financial Statements, or Other Assurance or Related Services Engagements.
    ▷ International Auditing and Assurance Standards Board (IAASB). 2023. International Standards on Quality Management 2 (ISQM 2). 'Engagement Quality Reviews'.
    Handbook of International Quality Management, Auditing, Review, Other Assurance and Related Services Pronouncements 2022 Edition Volume I, International Federation of Accountants (IFAC). New York.

30. https://www.ifiar.org/activities/annual-inspection-findings-survey/

31. Ibid. ISQM 1 and ISQM 2.

32. Ibid. ISQM 1 para. 7.

33. Ibid. ISQM 1 para. 5.

34. Ibid. ISQM 1 para. 6.

35. Auditor's business risks 'result from significant conditions, events, circumstances or actions that could adversely affect the auditor's ability to achieve her objectives and execute its strategies, or through the setting of inappropriate objectives and strategies'. Put more simply, anything that pushes a business away from its core objectives and in the direction of failure can be called a business risk. There are several ways of subdividing business risk. Sometimes risks are classified between operating risks, financial risks, and compliance risks.

36. Ibid. ISQM 1 para. 8.

37. Ibid. ISQM 1 para. 20.

38. Ibid. ISQM 1 para. 29, A65.

39. Ibid. ISQM 1, para. 35.

40. Ibid. ISQM 1 para. 30.

41. Ibid. ISQM 1 para. 34.

42. Ibid. ISQM 1 para. 34.

43. Ibid. ISQM 2 para. 1.

44. Ibid. ISQM 2 para. 1.

45. Ibid. ISQM 2 para. 9.

46. Ibid. ISQM 2 para. 17.

47. Ibid. ISQM 2 para. 18.

48. International Auditing and Assurance Standards Board. 2023. International Standard on Auditing 220 (Revised) 'Quality Management for an Audit of Financial Statements', Handbook of International Quality Management, Auditing, Review, Other Assurance and Related Services Pronouncements 2022 Edition Volume I, International Federation of Accountants (IFAC). New York.

49. Ibid. ISA 220 (Revised), paragraph 16.

50. ISA 200, Overall Objectives of the Independent Auditor and the Conduct of an Audit in Accordance with International Standards on Auditing, 2023, paragraphs 15–16, Handbook of International Quality Management, Auditing, Review, Other Assurance and Related Services Pronouncements 2022 Edition Volume I.

51. https://www.pwc.com/us/en/services.html

TOPIC II

FUNDAMENTAL CONCEPTS

CHAPTER 3

ETHICS FOR PROFESSIONAL ACCOUNTANTS

3.1 LEARNING OBJECTIVES

After studying this chapter, you should be able to:

1. Explain the three general subject areas of ethics.
2. Understand normative theories about ethics.
3. Explain what ethics means to an accountant in public practice.
4. State the purpose for a professional code of ethics.
5. Explain purpose and content of the IESBA Code of ethics for Professional Accountants.
6. Identify and discuss the fundamental principles of ethics as described by the IESBA Code of ethics.
7. Discuss what threats to the fundamental principles are.
8. Define safeguards and give some examples.
9. Explain the concept of independence and identify the principles-based approach for resolving appearing issues.
10. Describe non-audit services prohibited by the Code of ethics.
11. Discuss the responsibilities of an accountant in public practice in dealing with ethical conflicts that apply to his clients and colleagues.
12. State the topics of guidance that are particularly relevant to professional accountants in business.
13. Summarize the possible disciplinary actions for violation of ethics codes.

3.2 WHAT ARE ETHICS?

Morality is what people believe to be right and good, while ethos/ethics involves systematizing, defending, and recommending concepts of right and wrong behavior. Ethics is a discipline dealing with values relating to human conduct, with respect to the rightness and wrongness of certain actions and to the goodness and badness of the motives and ends of such actions. Ethics apply when an individual has to make a decision from various alternatives regarding moral principles. All individuals and societies possess a sense of ethics in that they have some sort of agreement as to what right and wrong are, although this can be influenced by cultural differences. Ethical questions you can think of are: 'Do I always have to keep my promise?' and 'Do I need to put my own interest aside in favour of others?' Illustration 3.1 incorporates the characteristics most people associate with ethical behavior.[1] Ethical behavior is necessary for society to function in an orderly manner. The need for ethics in society is sufficiently important that many commonly held ethical values are incorporated into laws. The law is an expression of ethical beliefs of society, but law and ethics are not the same thing. The law cannot codify all ethical requirements. Therefore, an action might be unethical, yet not necessarily illegal. For example, it might be unethical to lie to your family, but it is not necessarily illegal.

Similarly, just because an act is illegal does not necessarily mean it is immoral. By establishing a code of ethics, a profession assumes self-discipline beyond the requirements of the law.

In the following section, we will explore various ethical theories in depth, highlighting their significant relevance to auditors. They serve society's interests, and it's essential they conduct themselves with integrity amid various ethical challenges encountered in their day-to-day practice. Understanding ethical theories equips them with the necessary tools to navigate and resolve these dilemmas effectively. This knowledge not only aids in making informed decisions but also upholds the trust and credibility essential in their role.

In other words, understanding ethical theories is invaluable for resolving ethical dilemmas. This knowledge equips individuals with the insights needed to navigate complex moral challenges effectively. Knowledge of theories can be helpful in ethical dilemmas!

ILLUSTRATION 3.1

CHARACTERISTICS OF ETHICAL BEHAVIOR

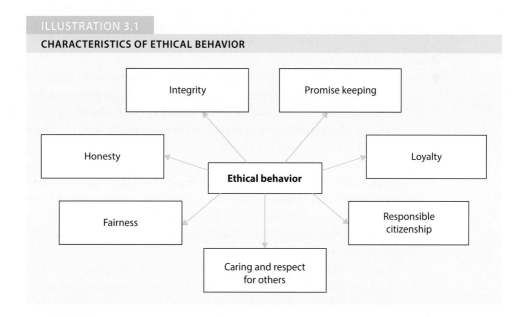

▶ THEORIES OF ETHICS

Philosophers today usually divide ethical theories into three general subject areas: metaethics, normative ethics, and applied ethics.

Metaethics investigates where our ethical principles come from, and what they mean. Are they merely social inventions? Do they involve more than expressions of our individual emotions? Metaethical answers to these questions focus on the issues of universal truths, the will of God, the role of reason in ethical judgements, and the meaning of ethical terms themselves.

Normative ethics takes on a more practical task, which is to arrive at moral standards that regulate right and wrong conduct. This may involve articulating the good habits that we should acquire, the duties that we should follow, or the consequences of our behaviour on others. Moral theories serve two main purposes in the study of ethics:

▶ They provide reasons or justifications for our own actions and decisions.
▶ We can rely on them to evaluate the actions and decisions of others.

Finally, applied ethics involves examining specific controversial issues, such as abortion, infanticide, animal rights, environmental concerns, homosexuality, capital punishment, or nuclear war.

By using the conceptual tools of metaethics and normative ethics, discussions in applied ethics try to resolve these controversial issues. The lines of distinction between metaethics, normative ethics, and applied ethics are often blurry. For example, the issue of abortion is an applied ethical topic since it involves a specific type of controversial behaviour. But it also depends on more general normative principles, such as the right of self-rule and the right to life, which are litmus tests for determining the morality of that procedure. The issue also rests on metaethical issues such as, 'where do rights come from?' and 'what kinds of beings have rights?'[2]

Normative ethics involves arriving at moral standards that regulate right and wrong conduct. In a sense, it is a search for an ideal litmus test of proper behaviour.

Important normative theories are:

▶ *Virtue Ethics* tells us what kind of person one ought to be, rather than what they do. The focus is on the character (goodness) of the person. Less emphasis on learning rules but developing good habits of character (moral education since virtuous character traits are developed in one's youth and regulate our emotions). According to Aristotle the character of people can be formed through upbringing and education and by setting good examples. To this end, developing good qualities is necessary. Both intellectual and character traits (acting according to good intentions and motives). These are called virtues and as explained by Aristotle they can be found in the Golden Mean. In this traditional virtue ethics this is the balance of extremes of virtues and vices, a balance between excess and deficiency (see illustration 3.2).
▶ *Teleological ethics* employs certain standards (purpose or end) against which consequences of an action are judged. Actions are not right or wrong in themselves. In other words, there is no need to consider the motives or intentions for which people do what they do. For example, an act of lying is not intrinsically wrong; it is wrong only if it leads to bad consequences. This kind of Utilitarian-type theories hold that the end consists in an experience or feeling produced by the action (19th-century English philosophers like Jeremy Bentham and John

ILLUSTRATION 3.2

TRADITIONAL VIRTUE ETHICS

Aristotle's Concept of the Golden Mean

Deficiency (–)	BALANCE	Excess (+)
cowardice	COURAGE	rashness
stinginess/miserliness	GENEROSITY	extravagance
sloth	AMBITION	greed
humility	MODESTY	pride
secrecy	HONESTY	loquacity
moroseness	GOOD HUMOR	absurdity
quarrelsomeness	FRIENDSHIP	flatteryinsensibility
self-indulgence	TEMPERANCE	irritability
apathy	COMPOSURE	impulsiveness
indecisiveness	SELF-CONTROL	

Stuart Mill), with its formula the 'greatest happiness [pleasure] of the greatest number.'

▶ *Deontological ethics* holds that we should act in ways circumscribed by moral rules irrespective of consequences and was proposed by Immanuel Kant[4]. Is the philosophical practice of defining and adhering to an absolute set of standards by which ethical behaviour can be measured. It defines universal duties that serve as moral guides to decision making. The act of carrying out that duty is more important than the consequences of the act. Considers that some acts are right or wrong independent of their consequences. Looks to one's obligation to determine what is ethical and answers the question: What should I do and why should I do it? Deontology demands that we do what is intrinsically right and refrain from doing what is intrinsically wrong. The Golden Rule is a classic example of a normative principle and establishes a single principle against which we judge all actions: We should do to others what we would want others to do to us, and therefore it would be wrong for me to lie to, harass, victimise, assault or kill others. Other normative theories focus on a set of foundational principles, or a set of good character traits.[5] See illustration 3.3 for the contrast with the teleological view.

ILLUSTRATION 3.3

DEONTOLOGICAL VERSUS TELEOLOGICAL ETHICS[6]

Deontological	**Teleological**
Ruled-based view of ethics was first proposed by Immanuel Kant which therefore commonly known as **Kantian ethics**.	**Consequence-based view** of ethics was introduced by Jeremy Bentham and developed by John Stuart Mill which is also known as **utilitarianism**.
Goodness or badness is determined by the **action**.	Goodness or badness is determined by the results or **outcomes**.
The only behavior that can be considered ethical is the one that has **good will** behind it.	Can justify the behavior as ethical if it produces **greatest good for the greatest number**.

▶ **ETHICS IN THE ACCOUNTANCY PROFESSION**

The attitude and behaviour of professional accountants in providing auditing and assurance services[7] have an impact on the economic well-being of their community and country.

Professional accountants can remain in this advantageous position only by continuing to provide the public with these unique services at a level that demonstrates that the public confidence is well founded.

The distinguishing mark of the profession is acceptance of its responsibility to the public. Therefore, the standards of the accountancy profession are heavily determined by the public interest. One could say in accountancy 'the public and the auditees are our clients, and our main product is credibility'.

It is in this context that the International Ethics Standards Board of Accountants (IESBA) Code of Ethics for Professional Accountants[8] states that it is an auditor's responsibility to act in the public interest – it is a distinguishing 'moral guide' of the accountancy profession. The professional auditors' responsibility (and virtue) is not to satisfy only their client or employer, but to consider the public interest.

To achieve these objectives, the Code of Ethics covers several fundamental principles for the behavior of professional accountants and for those who are undertaking reporting assignments, which is discussed in the balance of this chapter. Of course, quality of performance and appropriate behavior are primarily driving intrinsic motivation of professionals like accountants but are also guarded by external oversight and legal (disciplinary) convictions in case of non-compliance.

3.3 THE INTERNATIONAL CODE OF ETHICS FOR PROFESSIONAL ACCOUNTANTS

The ethical standards are set out by International Ethics Standards Board of Accountants (IESBA) after research and appropriate consultation with exposure drafts. The guidance is incorporated into *the Handbook of the Code of Ethics for Professional Accountants* (the Code). The Code is intended to serve as a model on which to base national ethical guidance[9]. It sets standards of conduct for professional accountants and states the fundamental principles that should be observed by professional accountants in order to achieve common objectives.

The IESBA Code of Ethics is divided into four parts (illustration 3.4):
  ▶ Part 1 establishes the fundamental principles of professional ethics for professional accountants and provides a conceptual framework that is applied to:
    ▶ identify threats to compliance with the fundamental principles;
    ▶ evaluate the significance of the threats identified; and
    ▶ employ safeguards, when necessary, to eliminate the threats or reduce them to an acceptable level.
  ▶ Parts 2, 3 and 4 describe how the conceptual framework applies in certain situations. They provide examples of safeguards that may be appropriate to address threats to compliance with the fundamental principles. They also describe situations where safeguards are not available to address the threats.
  ▶ Part 2 applies to professional accountants in business. Professional accountants in public practice may also find part 2 relevant to their particular circumstances.

▶ Part 3 and 4 apply to professional accountants in public practice. Part 3 addresses applying the general principles in public practice. Part 4A is about independence for audit and review engagements. Part 4B is about independence for assurance engagements other than audit and review engagements. The process of establishing ethical principles is complicated. In France and Japan, the ethical code is a matter of law. In the USA, Singapore, Mexico and the UK, the standards are developed and regulated by professional bodies. The IESBA *Handbook of the Code of Ethics for Professional Accountants* offers fundamental principles that are of a general nature which may be threatened and safeguards that may be applied.

ILLUSTRATION 3.4

OVERVIEW OF THE IESBA CODE OF ETHICS

OVERVIEW OF THE CODE

PART 1
COMPLYING WITH THE CODE, FUNDAMENTAL PRINCIPLES AND CONCEPTUAL FRAMEWORK
(ALL PROFESSIONAL ACCOUNTANTS - SECTIONS 100 TO 199)

PART 2	PART 3
PROFESSIONAL ACCOUNTANTS IN BUSINESS (SECTIONS 200 TO 299) (PART 2 IS ALSO APPLICABLE TO INDIVIDUAL PROFESSIONAL ACCOUNTANTS IN PUBLIC PRACTICE WHEN PERFORMING PROFESSIONAL ACTIVITIES PURSUANT TO THEIR RELATIONSHIP WITH THE FIRM)	**PROFESSIONAL ACCOUNTANTS IN PUBLIC PRACTICE** (SECTIONS 300 TO 399)

INTERNATIONAL INDEPENDENCE STANDARDS (PARTS 4A AND 4B)
PART 4A – **INDEPENDENCE FOR AUDIT AND REVIEW ENGAGEMENTS** (SECTIONS 400 TO 899)
PART 4B – **INDEPENDENCE FOR ASSURANCE ENGAGEMENTS OTHER THAN AUDIT AND REVIEW ENGAGEMENTS** (SECTIONS 900 TO 999)

GLOSSARY
(ALL PROFESSIONAL ACCOUNTANTS)

▶ **CONCEPTUAL FRAMEWORK APPROACH**

Rather than a list of rules that must be obeyed to be an ethical accountant, the so-called 'rule based' approach which holds sway in many countries, the IESBA has chosen to use a 'conceptual framework' approach. The objective of the conceptual framework is to:

▶ Identify threats to compliance with the fundamental principles;
▶ Evaluate the threats identified; and
▶ Address the threats by eliminating or reducing them to an acceptable level.

A conceptual framework requires a professional accountant to identify, evaluate and address threats to compliance with the fundamental principles, rather than merely comply with a set of specific rules which may be arbitrary.

When a professional accountant identifies threats to compliance with the fundamental principles and determines that they are at an unacceptable level, she shall determine whether appropriate safeguards are available and can be applied to eliminate the threats or reduce them to an acceptable level.[10] Identifying a threat may depend on the auditor's perspective but the auditor should always consider the situation conservatively. If you put a safeguard in place that you believe will reduce the impact of a threat on a fundamental principle to an acceptable level, then the fundamental principle is not impaired. If the accountant believes that a threat impairs the fundamental principle, then you should consider that the only safeguard is to end the activity.

There are five fundamental principles of ethics applicable to *all* professional accountants, as they are stated in part 1 of the Code. They are:

- ► Integrity – to be straightforward and honest in all professional and business relationships.
- ► Objectivity –not to compromise professional or business judgments because of bias, conflict of interest or undue influence of others.
- ► Professional Competence and Due Care – to:
    (i) Attain and maintain professional knowledge and skill at the level required to ensure that a client or employing organization receives competent professional service, based on current technical and professional standards and relevant legislation; and
    (ii) Act diligently and in accordance with applicable technical and professional standards.
- ► Confidentiality – to respect the confidentiality of information acquired as a result of professional and business relationships.
- ► Professional Behavior – to comply with relevant laws and regulations and avoid any conduct that the professional accountant knows or should know might discredit the profession.

The professional accountant shall apply the conceptual framework to identify, evaluate and address threats to compliance with the fundamental principles as set out in part 1 of the Code. Additional requirements and application material that are relevant to the application of the conceptual framework are set out in parts 2–4 of the Code.

3.4 PART 1 – COMPLYING WITH THE CODE, FUNDAMENTAL PRINCIPLES AND CONCEPTUAL FRAMEWORK

The IESBA Code of Ethics offers further discussion on these five fundamental principles. Each concept is the topic of sections (111–115) in the Code.

► INTEGRITY (SEC. 111)

The principle of integrity imposes an obligation on all professional accountants to be straightforward and honest in all professional and business relationships. Integrity also implies fair dealing and truthfulness and having the strength of character to act appropriately, even when facing pressure of when doing so may create adverse personal or organizational consequences.

A professional accountant must avoid reports and other information if she believes that the material contained is false or misleading, it includes information that was not verified, or leaves out information that makes the report misleading.

▶ OBJECTIVITY (SEC. 112)

The principle of objectivity imposes an obligation on all professional accountants not to compromise their professional or business judgement because of bias, conflict of interest or the undue influence of others. A professional accountant may be exposed to situations that may impair her objectivity. She should not perform a professional service if a circumstance or relationship biases or unduly influences the accountant's professional judgement.

But how does the auditor know if she is biased? A wealth of evidence suggests that judgements are often clouded by a number of cognitive and motivational biases. Individuals consistently rate themselves above average across a variety of domains, take credit for their successes but explain away their failures, assume they are more likely than their peers to experience the good things in life and avoid the bad, and tend to detect more support for their favoured beliefs than is objectively warranted.[11] Although the Code of Ethics does not address these (unconscious) biases explicitly, auditors can be influenced by financial incentives, e.g. if possible gains of wealth, prospects of a better income, as well as personal relationships with client's management, may bias an auditor's judgements. Religious and cultural biases may also affect an auditor's work. Psychologists at Harvard, the University of Virginia and the University of Washington created 'Project Implicit' to develop Hidden Bias Tests – to measure unconscious bias primarily of this sort.[12]

▶ PROFESSIONAL COMPETENCE AND DUE CARE (SEC. 113)

The principle of professional competence and due care requires that the professional accountant maintains her professional skill and knowledge to that of a competent professional. This means that professional accountants understand and implement technical and professional standards when doing their work.

Professional competence can be divided into separate phases: (a) Attainment of professional competence; and (b) Maintenance of professional competence. Professional competence requires a high standard of general education followed by specific education, training, examination in relevant subjects, and work experience. The maintenance of professional competence requires a continuing awareness and an understanding of relevant technical, professional and business developments through continuing professional education. Diligence is the responsibility to act in accordance with the requirements of an assignment, carefully, thoroughly and on a timely basis. Where appropriate, the professional accountant should inform clients and users about inherent limitations in the services or activities.

▶ CONFIDENTIALITY (SEC. 114)

Professional accountants have an obligation to respect confidentiality of information about a client's (or employer's) affairs acquired in the course of professional services. The principle of confidentiality requires that professional accountants refrain from disclosing, without the permission of the client or employer or legal requirement, confidential information gathered while performing their duties. Furthermore, professional accountants should not use this confidential information to their own personal advantage.

Professional accountants should respect the confidentiality of information acquired during the course of performing professional services, including in a social environment. The auditor should be alert to the risk of inadvertent disclosure, particularly to a close business associate or a close or immediate family member. The responsibility to keep the information confidential continues even after the accountant–client (or accountant–employer) relationship ends. Professional accountants must also ensure that staff and outside advisers under their control understand and comply with the principle of confidentiality.

PERMITTED DISCLOSURE OF CONFIDENTIAL INFORMATION

Confidential information may be disclosed when disclosure is authorized by the client, required by law, or where there is a professional duty or right to disclose (such as in a peer review quality control program)[13]. When disclosure is authorized by the employer or client, professional accountants should consider the interests of all the parties, including third parties, that might be affected.

EXAMPLES OF DISCLOSURE

One example of when disclosure of client information is required by law is when the professional accountant produces documents or provides evidence in legal proceedings. Another example is disclosure of infringements of law to appropriate public authorities. In the USA, accountants in public practice may be required to disclose evidence in court and in the Netherlands and UK auditors may be required to report fraud to governmental authorities.

There is also a professional duty to disclose information, when not prohibited by law, in the following circumstances:

- ▶ In response to an inquiry from regulatory bodies.
- ▶ To participate in a quality control review of a peer auditing firm or professional body.
- ▶ In compliance with technical and professional standards, encompassing ethical requirements.
- ▶ Confidentiality of information is part of statute or common law and therefore requirements of confidentiality will depend on the law of the home country of each accountant.

▶ PROFESSIONAL BEHAVIOR (SEC. 115)

The principle of professional behavior means compliance with relevant laws and regulations and avoidance of any action that may discredit the accounting or auditing profession. Acts that discredit the profession are those that a reasonable and well informed third party upon consideration of the facts and circumstances at the time, would conclude that the act adversely affects the reputation of the profession.

For example, in marketing and promoting themselves and their work, professionals should be honest and truthful and not:

- ▶ make exaggerated claims for the services they are able to offer, the qualifications they possess, or experience they have gained; or
- ▶ make disparaging references or unsubstantiated comparisons to the work of others.

▶ **CONCEPTUAL FRAMEWORK (SEC 120.5)**

Applying the IESBA Code of Ethics conceptual framework the professional accountant shall:

- ▶ Have an inquiring mind
- ▶ Exercise professional judgment; and
- ▶ Use the reasonable and informed third party test[14]

▶ **IDENTIFYING THREATS (SEC 120.6)**

Compliance with the fundamental principles may potentially be threatened by a broad range of circumstances and relationships. The nature and significance of the threats may differ depending on whether the audit client is a public interest entity an assurance client that is not an audit client, or a non-assurance client. The conceptual framework of the IESBA Code of Ethics discusses ways to identify threats to fundamental principles, determine the significance of those threats, and, if they are significant, identify and apply safeguards to reduce or eliminate the threats.

Threats fall into one or more of the following categories:

- ▶ self-interest
- ▶ self-review
- ▶ advocacy
- ▶ familiarity
- ▶ intimidation

SELF-INTEREST THREAT

A 'self-interest threat' occurs when an auditor could benefit from a financial interest in, or other self-interest conflict with, an assurance client. Examples of circumstances that create self-interest threats for a professional accountant in public practice include:

- ▶ A member of the assurance team having a direct financial interest in the assurance client.
- ▶ A firm having undue dependence on total fees from a client.
- ▶ A member of the assurance team having a significant close business relationship with an assurance client.
- ▶ A firm being concerned about the possibility of losing a significant client.
- ▶ A member of the audit team entering into employment negotiations with the audit client.
- ▶ A firm entering into a contingent fee arrangement relating to an assurance engagement.
- ▶ A professional accountant discovering a significant error when evaluating the results of a previous professional service performed by a member of the professional accountant's firm.

SELF-REVIEW THREAT

A 'self-review threat' occurs when (1) results of a previous engagement need to be re-evaluated in reaching conclusions on the present assurance engagement or (2) when a member of the assurance team previously was an employee of the client (especially a director or officer) in a position to exert significant influence over the subject matter[15] of the assurance engagement. Examples of circumstances that create self-review threats for a professional accountant in public practice include:

- A firm issuing an assurance report on the effectiveness of the operation of financial systems after designing or implementing the systems.
- A firm having prepared the original data used to generate records that are the subject matter of the assurance engagement.
- A member of the assurance team being, or having recently been, a director or officer of the client.
- A member of the assurance team being, or having recently been, employed by the client in a position to exert significant influence over the subject matter of the engagement.
- The firm performing a service for an assurance client that directly affects the subject matter information of the assurance engagement.

ADVOCACY THREAT

An 'advocacy threat' occurs when a member of the assurance team promotes, or seems to promote, an assurance client's position or opinion. That is, the auditor subordinates her judgement to that of the client. Examples of circumstances that may create this threat include:

- Selling, underwriting or otherwise promoting financial securities or shares of an assurance client.
- Acting as the client's advocate in a legal proceeding.

FAMILIARITY THREAT

A 'familiarity threat' occurs when an auditor becomes too sympathetic to the client's interests because she has a close relationship with an assurance client, its directors, officers or employees. Examples of circumstances that may create this threat include:

- A member of the engagement team having an immediate family member or close family member who is a director or officer of the assurance client.
- A member of the engagement team having a close family member who is an employee of the assurance client and in a position to significantly influence the subject matter of the assurance engagement.
- A director or officer of the client or an employee in a position to exert significant influence over the subject matter of the engagement having recently served as the engagement partner.
- A professional accountant accepting gifts or preferential treatment from a client, unless the value is trivial or inconsequential.
- Senior personnel having a long association with the assurance client.

In some countries, 'immediate family member' may mean the engagement member's spouse and dependent. In other countries immediate family member may be the engagement member's child, or her spouse, her parent or grandparent, parent-in-law, brother, sister, or brother-in-law or sister-in-law of the client. For example, a CPA firm that prepares a tax return for a client who is an immediate family member, for example, a spouse or a sister, and gives a tax deduction in which adequate evidence for the deduction is not provided, could be in violation of independency law.

INTIMIDATION THREAT

An 'intimidation threat' occurs when a member of the assurance team may be deterred from acting objectively and exercising professional scepticism by threats, actual or perceived, from the directors, officers or employees of an assurance client. Examples of circumstances that create intimidation threats for a professional accountant in public practice include:

> A firm being threatened with dismissal from a client engagement.
> An audit client indicating that it will not award a planned non-assurance contract to the firm if the firm continues to disagree with the client's accounting treatment for a particular transaction.
> A firm being threatened with litigation by the client.
> A firm being pressured to reduce inappropriately the extent of work performed in order to reduce fees.
> A professional accountant feeling pressured to agree with the judgement of a client employee because the employee has more expertise on the matter in question.
> A professional accountant being informed by a partner of the firm that a planned promotion will not occur unless the accountant agrees with an audit client's inappropriate accounting treatment.

> ### ADDRESSING THREATS/SAFEGUARDS (SEC. 120.10)

If the professional accountant determines that the identified threats to compliance with the fundamental principles are not at an acceptable level, the accountant shall address the threats by eliminating them or reducing them to an acceptable level. The accountant must do so by:

> Eliminating the circumstances, including interests or relationships, that are creating the threats;
> Applying safeguards, where available and capable of being applied, to reduce the threats to an acceptable level; or
> Declining or ending the specific professional activity.

When threats are identified, other than those that are clearly insignificant, appropriate safeguards should be identified and applied to eliminate the threats or reduce them to an acceptable level. If elimination or reduction is not possible the auditor should decline or terminate the engagement. When deciding what safeguards should be applied one must consider what would be unacceptable to an informed third-party having knowledge of all relevant information.

Safeguards fall into two broad categories:
1 safeguards created by the profession, legislation or regulation; and
2 safeguards in the work environment.

SAFEGUARDS CREATED BY THE PROFESSION, LEGISLATION OR REGULATION: EXAMPLES

Safeguards created by the profession, legislation or regulation may include educational, training and experience requirements to become a certified member of the profession; continuing education requirements; professional accounting, auditing and ethics standards and monitoring and disciplinary processes; peer review of quality control; and professional rules or legislation governing the independence requirements of the firm.

SAFEGUARDS WITHIN THE WORK ENVIRONMENT: EXAMPLES

In the work environment, the relevant safeguards will vary depending on the circumstances. Work environment safeguards comprise firm-wide safeguards (corporate culture) and engagement-specific safeguards. Examples of firm-wide safeguards in the work environment include:[16]

▶ Leadership of the firm that promotes compliance with the fundamental principles and establishes the expectation that assurance team members will act in the public interest.

▶ Policies or procedures for establishing and monitoring compliance with the fundamental principles by all personnel.

▶ Compensation, performance appraisal and disciplinary policies and procedures that promote compliance with the fundamental principles.

▶ Management of the reliance on revenue received from a single client.

▶ The engagement partner having authority within the firm for decisions concerning compliance with the fundamental principles, including decisions about accepting or providing services to a client.

▶ Educational, training and experience requirements.

▶ Processes to facilitate and address internal and external concerns or complaints.

Safeguards within the firm's own systems and procedures may also include engagement-specific safeguards such as:

▶ Using an additional professional accountant not on the assurance team to review the work done.

▶ Consulting an outside third party (e.g. a committee of independent directors or a professional regulatory body).

▶ Rotation of senior assurance team personnel.

▶ Communicating to the audit committee the nature of services provided and fees charged.

▶ Involving another audit firm to perform or re-perform part of the assurance engagement.

To mitigate the effect of bias these safeguards could be employed:

▶ Seeking advice from experts to obtain additional input.

▶ Consulting with others to ensure appropriate challenge as part of the evaluation process.

▶ Receiving training related to the identification of bias as part of professional development.

Depending on the nature of the engagement, the engagement team may be able to rely on safeguards that the client has implemented. However, it is not possible to rely solely on such safeguards to reduce threats. The audit client (auditee) may be biased or restrictive in what safeguards they implement, or the safeguards may not be followed in the ordinary course of events. Illustration 3.5 gives an overview of principles, threats and safeguards in the Code of Ethics.

ILLUSTRATION 3.5

OVERVIEW OF PRINCIPLES, THREATS AND SAFEGUARDS IN THE CODE OF ETHICS

Principles	Threats	Safeguards
▸ Integrity ▸ Objectivity ▸ Professional Competence and Due Care ▸ Confidentiality ▸ Professional Behavior	▸ self-interest ▸ self-review ▸ advocacy ▸ familiarity ▸ intimidation	1) Eliminating the circumstances, including interests or relationships, that are creating the threats; 2) Applying safeguards, where available and capable of being applied, to reduce the threats to an acceptable level; or 3) Declining or ending the specific professional activity.

3.5 PART 2 – PROFESSIONAL ACCOUNTANTS IN BUSINESS

Part 2 of the IESBA Code of Ethics describes how the conceptual framework contained in Part 1 applies in certain situations to professional accountants in business. Part 2 also addresses circumstances in which compliance with the fundamental principles may be compromised under the topics of potential conflicts, preparation and reporting information, acting with sufficient expertise, financial interests, and inducements. Part 2 does not contain discussion of independence. This is because accountants in business do not provide assurance in any form and do not play a role in society at large. Also, because accountants in business are employees it is difficult to require independence from the organization that is the source of their income. See illustration 3.6 for a summary of topics in Part 2.

ILLUSTRATION 3.6

PART 2: PROFESSIONAL ACCOUNTANTS IN BUSINESS

CONTENTS

200 Applying the Conceptual Framework – Professional Accountants in Business

210 Conflicts of Interest

220 Preparation and Presentation of Information

230 Acting with Sufficient Expertise

240 Financial Interests, Compensation and Incentives Linked to Financial Reporting and Decision Making

250 Inducements, Including Gifts and Hospitality

260 Responding to Non-compliance with Laws and Regulations

270 Pressure to Breach the Fundamental Principles

A professional accountant in business may be a salaried employee, a partner, director, an owner manager, a volunteer or another working for one or more employing organization. Professional accountants in business may be responsible for the preparation and reporting of financial and other information or for providing effective financial management and competent advice on a variety of business-related matters. The accountant has a responsibility to further the legitimate aims of the accountant's employing organization. A professional accountant in business is expected to encourage an ethics-based culture in an employing organization that emphasizes the importance that senior management places on ethical behaviour. A professional accountant in business shall not knowingly engage in any business, occupation, or activity that impairs or might impair integrity, objectivity or the good reputation of the profession and as a result would be incompatible with the fundamental principles[17].

As we discussed in the Part 1 section of this chapter, compliance with the fundamental principles may potentially be threatened by a broad range of circumstances and relationships[18]. Threats fall into one or more of the following categories: self-interest, self-review, advocacy, familiarity and intimidation.

Self-interest threats are perhaps the most frequent for a professional accountant in business:

- ▶ Holding a financial interest in or receiving a loan or guarantee from the employing organization.
- ▶ Participating in incentive compensation arrangements offered by the employing organization.
- ▶ Having access to corporate assets for personal use.
- ▶ Being offered a gift or special treatment from a supplier of the employing organization.

Some examples of circumstances leading to self-review and advocacy threats for a professional accountant in business can be mentioned. Determining the appropriate accounting treatment for a business combination after performing the feasibility study that supported the acquisition decision creates a self-review threat. Any false or misleading statements made when furthering the goals and objectives of their employing organizations creates an advocacy threat.

Examples of circumstances that may create familiarity threats for professional accountants in business include:

- ▶ Being responsible for the financial reporting of the employing organization when an immediate or close family member employed by the organization makes decisions that affect the financial reporting of the organization.
- ▶ Having a long association with individuals influencing business decisions.

Examples of circumstances that may create intimidation threats for a professional accountant in business include:

- ▶ A professional accountant or immediate or close family member facing the threat of dismissal or replacement over a disagreement about:
  - ▶ The application of an accounting principle.
  - ▶ The way in which financial information is to be reported.
- ▶ An individual attempting to influence the decision-making process of the professional accountant, for example with regard to the awarding of contracts or the application of an accounting principle.

As previously discussed in the Part 1 section of this chapter, safeguards that may eliminate or reduce threats to an acceptable level fall into two categories: (1) safeguards created by the profession, legislation or regulation; and (2) safeguards in the work environment. Safeguards in the work environment for the professional accountant include:[19]

- Leadership that stresses the importance of ethical behaviour and the expectation that employees will act in an ethical manner.
- Policies and procedures to empower and encourage employees to communicate ethics issues that concern them to senior levels of management without fear of retribution.
- Policies and procedures to implement and monitor the quality of employee performance.
- Systems of corporate oversight or other oversight structures and strong internal controls.
- Recruitment procedures emphasizing the importance of employing high calibre competent personnel.
- Timely communication of policies and procedures, including any changes to them, to all employees, and appropriate training and education on such policies and procedures.
- Ethics and code of conduct policies.

To ensure effective communication, when a professional accountant interacts with specific management or Those Charged With Governance (TCWG) members, they should be certain that such communication adequately informs all individuals in a governance position with whom the accountant would typically engage.

In those situations where all available safeguards have been exhausted and it is not possible to reduce the threat to an acceptable level, a professional accountant in business may conclude that it is appropriate to resign from the employing organization.

3.6 PART 3 – PROFESSIONAL ACCOUNTANTS IN PUBLIC PRACTICE

Whereas the ethics guidance discussed above (Part 1 of the Code) is applicable to all professional accountants, Part 3 of the IESBA Code of Ethics is only applicable to accountants in public practice. Part 3 describes how the conceptual framework contained in Part 1 applies in certain situations to professional accountants in public practice. A professional accountant in public practice is a professional accountant, irrespective whether they provide assurance services or not (for example, audit, tax or consulting) in a firm that provides professional services. This term is also used to refer to a firm of professional accountants in public practice.

Ethical guidance for accountants in public practice is offered in the areas of professional appointment, conflicts of interest, second opinions, fees and other remuneration, marketing professional services, gifts and hospitality, custody of client assets, objectivity, and independence.

▶ CONFLICTS OF INTEREST (SEC. 310)

An accountant in public practice must develop procedures to identify circumstances that would lead to a conflict of interest and apply safeguards when necessary to eliminate the threats. For example, a threat to objectivity may be created when a professional accountant in public practice competes directly with a client or has a joint venture or similar arrangement with a major competitor of a client. If a conflict of interest may exist, application of one of the following safeguards is appropriate:

- ▶ notifying the client of the audit firm's activities that may represent a conflict of interest; or
- ▶ notifying all known relevant parties that the professional accountant in public practice is acting for two or more parties in respect of a matter where their respective interests are in conflict and obtaining their consent to so act; or
- ▶ notifying the client that the professional accountant in public practice does not act exclusively for any one client in the provision of proposed services (for example, in a particular market sector or with respect to a specific service).

CONCEPT AND A COMPANY 3.1

ACCOUNTANT FALSIFIES ACCOUNTS FOR BOSSES AT WORLDCOM

Concept	**Ethics and the employed accountant – caving into pressure from your bosses.**
Story	On 10 October 2002 the US attorney's office announced that Betty Vinson, former Director of Management Reporting at WorldCom, had pleaded guilty to two criminal counts of conspiracy and securities fraud, charges that carry a maximum sentence of 15 years in prison. One year later, 10 October 2003, she was charged with breaking Oklahoma securities laws by entering false information on company documents – a charge that potentially carries a ten-year prison sentence (English, 2003).

Over the course of six quarters Vinson made illegal entries to bolster WorldCom's profits at the request of her superiors. Each time she worried. Each time she hoped it was the last time. At the end of 18 months she had helped falsify at least $3.7 billion in profits (Lacter, 2003).

In 1996, Ms Vinson got a job in the international accounting division at WorldCom making $50,000 a year (equivalent to $100,000 today). Ms Vinson developed a reputation for being hardworking and diligent. Within two years Ms Vinson was promoted to be a senior manager in WorldCom's corporate accounting division where she helped compile quarterly results and analysed the company's operating expenses and loss reserves. Ten employees reported to her (Pulliam, 2003).

Work began to change in mid-2000. WorldCom had a looming problem: its huge line costs – fees paid to lease portions of other companies' telephone networks – were rising as a percentage of the company's revenue. Chief Executive Bernard Ebers and Chief Financial Officer Scott Sullivan informed Wall Street in July that the company's results for the second half of the year would fall below expectations.

A scramble ensued to try to reduce expenses on the company's financial statements enough to meet Wall Street's expectations for the quarter. But the accounting department was able to scrape together only $50 million, far from the hundreds of millions it would take to hit the company's profit target. In October, her boss told Vinson to dip into a reserve account set aside to cover line costs and other items for WorldCom's telecommunications unit and use $828 million to reduce expenses, thereby increasing profits (Pulliam, 2003).

Ms Vinson was shocked by her bosses' proposal and the huge sum involved. She worried that the adjustment wasn't proper. She agreed to go along. But afterwards Ms Vinson suffered pangs of guilt. On 26 October, the same day the company publicly reported its third-quarter results, she told her colleagues who were also involved that she was planning to resign. A few suggested that they, too, would quit.

CFO Sullivan heard of the mutiny in accounting and called Vinson and other employees into his office. He explained that he was trying to fix the company's financial problems. Think of it as an aircraft carrier, he said; we have planes in the air. Let's get the planes landed. Once they are landed, if you still want to leave, then leave. But not while the planes are in the air. Mr Sullivan assured them that nothing they had done was illegal and that he would assume all responsibility. He noted that the accounting switch wouldn't be repeated (Pulliam, 2003).

That night, she told her husband about the meeting and her worries over the accounting. Mr Vinson urged her to quit. But in the end, she decided not to quit. She was the family's chief support, earning more than her husband. She, her husband and daughter depended on her health insurance. She was anxious about entering the job market as a middle-aged worker.

By the end of the first quarter of 2001, it was clear Ms Vinson could find no large pools of reserves to transfer to solve the profit shortfall. Sullivan suggested that rather than count line costs as part of operating expenses in the quarterly report, they would shift $771 million in line costs to capital-expenditure accounts which would result in decreased expenses and increased assets and retained earnings. Accounting rules make it clear that line costs are to be counted as operating leases, not capital assets.

Ms Vinson felt trapped. That night she reviewed her options with her husband and decided to put together a resumé and begin looking for a job. Nevertheless, she made the entries transferring the $771 million, backdating the entries to February by changing the dates in the computer for the quarter. She faced the same dilemma in the second, third and fourth quarters of 2001. Each subsequent quarter she made more fraudulent entries (Pulliam, 2003).

Ms Vinson began waking up in the middle of the night, unable to go back to sleep because of her anxiety. Her family and friends began to notice she was losing weight and her face took on a slightly gaunt look. At work she withdrew from co-workers, afraid she might let something slip. In early 2002, she received a promotion, from senior manager to director, along with a raise that brought her annual salary to about $80,000 (equivalent to $160.000 today) (Pulliam, 2003).

In March 2002 the SEC made requests for information from WorldCom and Cynthia Cooper, head of internal auditing (see Chapter 1), started asking questions. Ms Vinson and two other professional accountants hired an attorney and told their story to federal officials from the FBI, SEC and US attorney, hoping to get immunity from prosecution for their testimony.

On 1 August 2002, Ms Vinson received a call from her attorney telling her that the prosecutors in New York would probably indict her. In the end, they viewed the information Ms Vinson had supplied at the meeting with federal officials as more of a confession than a tip-off to wrongdoing. Within hours, WorldCom fired her because of the expected indictment. The only thing she was allowed to take with her was a plant from her desk (Pulliam, 2003).

Two of her colleagues pleaded guilty to securities fraud. Unable to afford the legal bill that would result from a lengthy trial, Betty Vinson decided to negotiate a guilty plea as well.

Discussion Questions

▶ Was Betty Vinson justified in her actions because they were at the request of her superiors? Why?

▶ If you were in Ms Vinson's situation, what would you have done?

References English, S., 2003, 'City – WorldCom Boss on Fraud Charges', *The Daily Telegraph*, 4 September.

Lacter, M., 2003, 'Looking the Other Way (Comment) (Editorial)', *Los Angeles Business Journal*, 30 June.

Pulliam, S., 2003, 'Over the Line: A Staffer Ordered To Commit Fraud Baulked, Then Caved – Pushed by WorldCom Bosses, Accountant Betty Vinson Helped Cook the Books – A Confession at the Marriott', *The Wall Street Journal*, 23 June, p. 1.

The professional accountant must also determine whether to apply one or more of the following additional safeguards:

▶ The use of separate engagement teams.

▶ Procedures to prevent access to information (for example, strict physical separation of such teams, confidential and secure data filing).

▶ The use of confidentiality agreements signed by employees and partner of the firm.

▶ Regular review of the application of safeguards by a senior individual not involved with relevant client engagements.

When there is a conflict-of-interest threat to the fundamental ethics principles that cannot be reduced to an acceptable level by employing safeguards, the auditor should not accept the engagement or, if already engaged, resign from the assurance engagement.

▶ PROFESSIONAL APPOINTMENTS (SEC. 320)

Before auditors in public practice take on a new client relationship, they should decide whether acceptance of the client would create any threats to compliance with the fundamental principles of ethics.

The fundamental principle of professional competence and due care imposes an obligation on a professional accountant in public practice to provide only those services that they are competent to perform. Competence is important in engagement acceptance and the acceptance of the client themselves. Before accepting a specific client engagement, the auditor must determine whether acceptance would create any threats to compliance with the fundamental principles. A self-interest threat to professional competence and due care is created if the engagement team does not possess, or cannot acquire, the competencies necessary to properly carry out the engagement. When evaluating whether to accept the client, the auditor should consider that potential threats to integrity or professional behavior may be created from questionable issues associated with that client (its owners, management or activities), client involvement in illegal activities (such as money laundering), or questionable financial reporting practices.

Basic safeguards against client acceptance and engagement acceptance threats include obtaining knowledge of the client and its governance and business activities or ensuring the client's commitment to improve corporate governance practices or internal controls. Examples of such safeguards include the following (some safeguards are also discussed in ISA 220.9 and 11 on quality control)[20]:

CONCEPT AND A COMPANY 3.2

LINCOLN SAVINGS & LOAN – EMPLOYMENT OF A FORMER AUDITOR

Concept	Independence in Fact and Appearance.
Story	Upon completion of the 1987 Arthur Young (later Ernst & Young, EY) audit of Lincoln Savings & Loan Association (Lincoln) which resulted in an unqualified opinion, the engagement audit partner, Jack Atchison, resigned from Arthur Young and was hired by Lincoln's parent American Continental Corporation (ACC) for approximately $930,000 annual salary. His prior annual earnings as a partner at Arthur Young were approximately $225,000 (Knapp, 2001).

Charles Keating Jr syphoned money out of Lincoln Savings and Loan for his own benefit from the day he acquired Lincoln in 1984 until the Federal Home Loan Bank Board (FHLBB) seized control on 14 April 1989. At the time of the seizure nearly two-thirds of Lincoln's asset portfolio was invested in high-risk land ventures and Keating had used fraudulent accounting methods to create net income. In the end, Lincoln's demise involved investors' losses of $200 million and its closure cost US taxpayers $3.4 billion in guaranteed deposit insurance and legal costs, making it the most costly savings and loan failure in US history. For their part in the Lincoln failure, Ernst & Young paid the California State Board of Accountancy (the state agency which registers California CPAs) $1.5 million in 1991 to settle negligence complaints and in 1992 paid the US Government $400 million to settle four lawsuits (Knapp, 2001).

In the court case *of Lincoln S&L* v *Wall*, it was suggested that Atchison might have known about the financial statement problems during his audit of Lincoln. ACC was in dire need of obtaining $10 million because of an agreement with the Bank Board to infuse an additional $10 million into Lincoln. Thus, Lincoln was actually the source of its own $10 million cash infusion. Ernst & Young LLC learnt of these facts from Jack Atchison after Atchison had become a top official at Lincoln (USDC – DC, 1990).

At the time Atchison made his move, the practice of 'changing sides' was not against the AICPA's ethics standards; however, the Securities and Exchange Commission (SEC) stated that Atchison's move should certainly be examined by the accounting profession's standard setting authorities as to the impact such a practice has on an accountant's independence. Furthermore, they stated that it would seem that a 'cooling-off period' of one to two years would not be unreasonable before the client can employ a senior official on an audit (SEC, 1990).

Ultimately, the Sarbanes-Oxley Act of 2002 required a cooling-off period of one year after a company's last audit before clients can hire as an officer any member of the audit team.

Discussion Questions	▶ What impact does employment of former independent auditors by an audit client have on that auditor's independence during the audit?
	▶ Were Atchison's actions ethical?

References	Knapp, M., 2001, 'Lincoln Savings and Loan Association', *Contemporary Auditing Real Issues & Cases*, South Western College Publishing, Cincinnati, Ohio, pp. 57–70.
	SEC, 1990, Final rule release 33-7919, *Final Rule: Revision of the Commission's Auditor Independence Requirements*, Securities and Exchange Commission, February 5.
	USDC – DC, 1990, *Lincoln Savings & Loan Association* v *Wall*, 'Consolidated Civil Action Nos. 89-1318, 89-1323', 743 F. Supp. 901; 1990 US Dist. LEXIS 11178, United States District Court for the District of Columbia, 22 August 1990; Decided, 22 August 1990, Filed.

▷ Acquiring an appropriate understanding of the nature of the client's business, the complexity of its operations, the specific requirements of the engagement and the purpose, nature and scope of the work to be performed.

▷ Acquiring knowledge of relevant industries, subject matters and relevant regulatory or reporting requirements.

▷ Assigning sufficient staff with the necessary competencies.

▷ Using experts where necessary. (When an auditor in public practice intends to rely on the advice or work of an expert, she should consider the expert's reputation, expertise, availability of resources and compliance with applicable ethical standards.) See ISA 620.10[21].

▷ Accepting specific engagements only when they can be performed competently.

REPLACING AN EXISTING AUDITOR

An auditor who is asked to replace another auditor, or who is considering a new engagement for a company currently audited by another auditor, must consider whether there are any reasons, professional or otherwise, for not accepting the engagement. There may be a threat to professional competence and due care if an auditor accepts the engagement before knowing all the pertinent facts. Determining possible reasons for not accepting a new client may require direct communication with the existing auditor to establish the facts and circumstances regarding the proposed change in auditors.

Safeguards to deal with a threat to due professional care include:

▷ When requested by a prospective client to submit a proposal to perform the audit, stating in the tender that, before accepting the engagement, contact with the existing auditor[22] will be made.

▷ Asking the existing auditor to provide known information on any facts or circumstances that, in the existing accountant's opinion, the proposed auditor needs to be aware of before deciding whether to accept the engagement; or obtaining necessary information from other sources.

▷ A professional accountant in public practice will generally need to obtain the client's permission, preferably in writing, to initiate discussion with an existing accountant. The existing accountant should provide information to the proposed auditor honestly and unambiguously. If the proposed accountant for whatever reason is unable to communicate with the existing accountant, the proposed accountant should take reasonable steps to obtain information such as through inquiries of third parties or background investigations of senior management or those charged with governance of the client.

▷ ### SECOND OPINIONS (SEC. 321)

Sometimes a professional accountant in public practice is asked to provide a second opinion on the application of accounting, auditing, reporting or other standards or principles to specific circumstances on behalf of a company that is not an existing client.

This may create threats to compliance with the fundamental principles. For example, there may be a threat to professional competence and due care in circumstances where the second opinion is not based on the same set of facts that were made available to the existing accountant or is based on inadequate evidence. When asked to provide such an opinion, the auditor should consider any threats that may arise and apply safeguards. Examples of possible safeguards include seeking client permission to contact the existing accountant, describing the limitations surrounding any opinion in communications with the client, and providing the existing accountant with a copy of the opinion.

▶ OBJECTIVITY OF AN ENGAGEMENT QUALITY REVIEWER AND OTHER APPROPRIATE REVIEWERS (SEC. 325)

Appointing an engagement quality reviewer who is involved in the work being reviewed or has close relationships with those responsible for performing that work might create threats to compliance with the principle of objectivity. An example of an action that might be a safeguard to address a self-review threat is implementing a period of sufficient duration (a cooling-off period) before the individual who was on the engagement is appointed as an engagement quality reviewer.

▶ FEES AND OTHER TYPES OF REMUNERATION (SEC. 330)

When negotiating to provide services to an assurance client, a professional accountant in public practice may quote whatever fee is deemed appropriate. The fact that one professional accountant in public practice may quote a fee lower than another accountant is not in itself unethical. Nevertheless, there may be threats to compliance with the fundamental principles arising from the level of fees quoted. For example, a self-interest threat to professional competence and due care is created if the fee quoted is so low that it may be difficult to perform the engagement in accordance with applicable technical and professional standards for that price. Examples of safeguards against possible threats would include making the client aware of the terms of the engagement and the basis of the fees. Contingent fees are widely used for certain types of non-assurance engagements. However, they may create threats to compliance with the fundamental principles in certain circumstances. They may create a self-interest threat to objectivity. The existence and significance of such threats will depend on a number of factors including nature of the engagement, fee range, and the basis for determining the fee.[23]

Accepting a referral fee or commission relating to a client creates a self-interest threat to objectivity and professional competence and due care. For example, safeguards must be set up for a fee received for referring a continuing client to another accountant or other expert or receiving a commission from a third party (for example, a software vendor) in connection with the sale of goods or services to a client. Similarly, safeguards must be made for payments by a professional accountant in public practice such as a referral fee to obtain a client.

Examples of safeguards for receiving and paying fees include disclosing to the client any arrangements either to pay a referral fee to another professional accountant for the work referred or to receive a referral fee for referring the client to another. Another safeguard would be to obtain advance agreement from the client for commission arrangements.

A professional accountant in public practice may purchase all or part of another accounting firm on the basis that payments will be made to individuals formerly owning the firm or to their heirs or estates. Such payments are not regarded as commissions or referral.

▶ INDUCEMENTS INCLUDING GIFTS AND HOSPITALITY (SEC. 340)

An offer of gifts and hospitality from a client to a professional accountant in public practice, or an immediate or close family member, may create threats to compliance with the fundamental principles. For example, a self-interest or familiarity threat to objectivity may be created if a gift from a client is accepted; an intimidation threat to objectivity may result from the possibility of such offers being made public. However, if a reasonable and informed third party, weighing all the specific facts and circumstances would consider specific gifts or hospitality trivial and inconsequential, the offers would be considered part of the normal course of business which was not intended to influence the auditor's decision making.

An inducement can take many different forms, for example:
- ▶ Gifts.
- ▶ Hospitality.
- ▶ Entertainment.
- ▶ Political or charitable donations.
- ▶ Appeals to friendship and loyalty.
- ▶ Employment or other commercial opportunities.
- ▶ Preferential treatment, rights or privileges.

▶ CUSTODY OF CLIENT ASSETS (SEC. 350)

Unless permitted to do so by law, the professional accountant in public practice should not have custody of client money or assets. If asset custody is permitted by law, the accountant should comply with legal duties required by regulation. The holding of client assets creates threats to compliance with the fundamental principles; for example, there is a self-interest threat to professional behavior and may be a self-interest threat to objectivity arising from holding client assets. An accountant entrusted with money (or other assets) belonging to others must:
- ▶ Keep other's assets separately from personal or accounting firm assets.
- ▶ Use such assets only for the purpose for which they are intended.
- ▶ At all times be ready to account for those assets and any income, dividends or gains generated to any persons entitled to such accounting.
- ▶ Comply with all relevant laws and regulations relevant to the holding of and accounting for such assets.
- ▶ Make appropriate inquiries about the source of such assets and consider legal and regulatory obligations.

▶ RESPONDING TO NON-COMPLIANCE WITH LAWS AND REGULATIONS (SEC. 360)

The backbone of the accountancy profession is its responsibility to act in the public interest. A professional accountant might encounter non-compliance or suspected non-compliance in the course of providing a professional service to a client. Examples of relevant laws and regulations include those that deal with:
- ▶ Fraud, corruption and bribery.
- ▶ Money laundering, terrorist financing and proceeds of crime.
- ▶ Securities markets and trading.
- ▶ Banking and other financial products and services.

- Data protection.
- Tax and pension liabilities and payments.
- Environmental protection.
- Public health and safety.

Non-compliance might result in fines, litigation or other consequences for the client, potentially materially affecting its financial statements. Importantly, such non-compliance might have wider public interest implications in terms of potentially substantial harm to investors, creditors, employees or the general public. According to the IESBA Code of Ethics Sec 360 (5A3) an act that causes substantial harm is one that results in serious adverse consequences to any of these parties in financial or non-financial terms. Examples include the perpetration of a fraud resulting in significant financial losses to investors, and breaches of environmental laws and regulations endangering the health or safety of employees or the public.

When encountering such non-compliance or suspected non-compliance, the accountant shall obtain an understanding of those legal or regulatory provisions and comply with them, including (IESBA Code of Ethics Sec 360.6):

- Any requirement to report the matter to an appropriate authority; and
- Any prohibition on alerting the client. A prohibition on alerting the client might arise, for example, pursuant to anti-money laundering legislation.

Non-compliance with law and regulations related to corruption and money laundering is also discussed in section 12.11.

3.7 PART 4 – INDEPENDENCE STANDARDS

▶ INDEPENDENCE IN A GLOBAL CONTEXT

The independence of the auditor from the firm that she is auditing is one of the basic requirements to keep public confidence in the reliability of the audit report. Independence adds credibility to the audit report on which investors, creditors, employees, government and other stakeholders depend to make decisions about a company. The benefits of safeguarding an auditor's independence extend so far as to the overall efficiency of the capital markets.

Across the world, national rules on auditors' independence differ in several respects such as: the scope of persons to whom independence rules should apply; the kind of financial, business or other relationships that an auditor may have with an audit client; the type of non-audit services that can and cannot be provided to an audit client; and the safeguards which should be used. The European Commission has issued independence standards to be applied throughout the European Union (EU). The USA enacted the Sarbanes-Oxley Act of 2002, which describes independence requirements of US auditors.

The European Commission Council Directive 2006/43/EC[24] gives discretionary power to Member States to determine the conditions of independence for a statutory auditor. Article 22 requires that Member States shall ensure that when carrying out a statutory audit[25], the statutory auditor and/or the audit firm is independent of the audited entity and

ILLUSTRATION 3.7

INDEPENDENCE IN THE SARBANES–OXLEY ACT OF 2002

TITLE II – AUDITOR INDEPENDENCE

Sec. 201. Services outside the scope of practice of auditors.

Sec. 202. Pre-approval requirements.

Sec. 203. Audit partner rotation.

Sec. 204. Auditor reports to audit committees.

Sec. 205. Conforming amendments.

Sec. 206. Conflicts of interest.

Sec. 207. Study of mandatory rotation of registered public accounting firms.

Sec. 208. Commission authority.

Sec. 209. Considerations by appropriate State regulatory authorities.

Prohibited non-audit service contemporaneously with the audit include:

(1) bookkeeping or other services related to the accounting records or financial statements of the audit client;

(2) financial information systems design and implementation;

(3) appraisal or valuation services, fairness opinions, or contribution-in-kind reports;

(4) actuarial services;

(5) internal audit outsourcing services;

(6) management functions or human resources;

(7) broker or dealer, investment adviser, or investment banking services;

(8) legal services and expert services unrelated to the audit; and

(9) any other service that the Board determines, by regulation, is impermissible.

is not involved in the decision-taking of the audited entity.[26] The following independence measures apply to all statutory auditors and audit firms, regardless of whether the audited entity is a public-interest entity or not:

▶ Introducing stronger requirements on independence, notably by improving the organizational requirements of statutory auditors and audit firms.

▶ In addition, the following stricter requirements apply to the statutory audit of Public Interest Entities (PIEs).

▶ Introducing mandatory tender for statutory auditors and audit firms every 10 years.

▶ Establishing a list of non-audit services that cannot be provided by the statutory auditor or audit firm to the audited entity.

▶ Imposing limitations on the fees charged for non-audit services.

Accounting firms that audit US publicly traded companies must adhere to the regulations of the Sarbanes-Oxley Act,[27] Title II, *Auditor Independence*, as interpreted by the Public Company Accounting Oversight Board (PCAOB).[28] the Independence sections and the prohibited services are listed in illustration 3.7. According to PCAOB AS 1005, to be independent, the auditor must be intellectually honest. To be recognized as independent, he must be free from any obligation to, or interest in, the client, its management, or its owners. Independent auditors should not only be independent in fact; they should avoid situations that may lead outsiders to doubt their independence. See illustration 3.7 for independence topics in the Sarbanes-Oxley Act.

Under PCAOB rules all non-audit services to clients, which are not specifically prohibited, must be pre-approved by the Audit Committee and disclosed to the shareholders. Audit partners must be rotated every five years. Clients (auditees) cannot hire as an officer any member of the independent auditors' team within one year after their last audit. The US profession has established, through the AICPA's Code of Professional Conduct, precepts to guard against the presumption of loss of independence. 'Presumption' is stressed because the possession of intrinsic independence is a matter of personal quality rather than of rules that formulate certain objective tests. Insofar as these precepts have been incorporated in the profession's code, they have the force of professional law for the independent auditor. Determination of independence of auditors who audit non-publicly traded firms is left up to the regulatory authorities of the 50 states of the USA.

As sketched in illustration 3.8 below, independence rules and standards for financial auditors in China are primarily governed by the China Securities Regulatory Commission (CSRC) and the Ministry of Finance (MOF).

In Russia they are primarily overseen and regulated by several key entities such as the Ministry of Finance, the Federal Financial Monitoring Service (Rosfinmonitoring), Russian Audit Chamber[29] and so-called Self-Regulatory Organizations (SROs).

ILLUSTRATION 3.8

ETHICAL RULES AND OVERSIGHT IN RUSSIA AND CHINA

Russia

Ethical Guidelines: Auditors are expected to follow a strict code of ethics that emphasizes integrity, objectivity, and professional behaviour.

Independence from Clients: Auditors should maintain complete independence from the organizations they are auditing. They must avoid any financial or personal relationships that could compromise their objectivity.

Prohibition of Certain Services: Auditors are restricted from providing certain non-audit services to their audit clients to prevent conflicts of interest.

Rotation of Auditors: In certain cases, there may be mandatory rotation requirements to ensure that audit firms do not become too closely aligned with their clients.

Audit Committee Oversight: Publicly traded companies are often required to have an independent audit committee overseeing the auditor's work to enhance accountability.

Regulatory Oversight: Auditors in Russia are subject to regulatory oversight by organizations like the Federal Financial Monitoring Service (Rosfinmonitoring) and the Ministry of Finance.

China

Prohibition of Conflicts of Interest: Auditors are required to avoid any financial or personal interests that could compromise their objectivity and independence. They should not hold any financial stake in the companies they audit.

Rotation of Auditors: To prevent long-term relationships that might compromise independence, there are requirements for the rotation of audit firms at regular intervals.

Code of Ethics: Auditors are expected to adhere to a strict code of ethics that promotes integrity, objectivity, confidentiality, and professional behaviour.

Client Restrictions: There are rules about auditors not providing certain non-audit services to their audit clients, to prevent potential conflicts of interest.

Independence Checks: Audit firms are required to perform independence checks to ensure that there are no compromising relationships or interests that could affect their ability to provide an unbiased opinion.

Disclosure of Fees: Audit firms must disclose the fees they receive for audit and non-audit services for transparency.

Regulatory Oversight: Regulatory bodies in China closely monitor compliance with independence rules and take necessary actions in case of violations.

▶ PART 4A – INDEPENDENCE STANDARDS FOR AUDIT OR REVIEW ENGAGEMENTS

The IESBA Code of Ethics for Professional Accountants, addresses the independence requirements for audit engagements and review engagements in Part 4A (see illustration 3.9 for contents). Independence requirements for assurance engagements that are not audit or review engagements are addressed in Part 4B of the Code. The Code discusses independence in assurance services in terms of a principles-based, conceptual approach that takes into account threats to independence, accepted safeguards and the public interest.

CONCEPTS-BASED APPROACH

IFAC strongly believes that a high-quality principles-based approach to independence will best serve the public interest by eliciting thoughtful auditor assessment of the particular circumstances of each engagement.[30] However, the Code gives related guidance and explanatory material as well.

Professional accountants in public practice must not only maintain an independent attitude in fulfilling their responsibilities, but the users of financial statements must also have confidence in that independence.

The conceptual framework involves two views of independence to which the auditor must comply: (1) independence of mind and (2) independence in appearance. Independence of mind (historically referred to as independence in fact) is a state of mind that allows one to draw conclusions that are unaffected by influences that compromise professional judgment. Independence in mind allows the professional accountant to act with integrity, objectivity, and professional scepticism. Independence in appearance involves avoidance of significant circumstances in which a reasonable and informed third party, considering all the facts and circumstances, might conclude that the professional accountant's integrity, objectivity or professional scepticism has been compromised.

The Ethics Code discusses independence in assurance services in terms of a principles-based approach that takes into account threats to independence, accepted safeguards and the public interest. The Section states principles that members of assurance teams should use to identify threats to independence (self-interest, self-review, advocacy, familiarity and intimidation threats), evaluate the significance of those threats, and, if the threats are other than clearly insignificant, identify and apply safeguards created by the profession, legislation or regulation, safeguards within the assurance client, and safeguards within the firm's own systems and procedures to eliminate the threats or reduce them to an acceptable level.

A professional accountant shall use professional judgement in applying this conceptual framework to:
- identify threats to independence;
- evaluate the significance of the threats identified; and
- apply safeguards, when necessary, to eliminate the threats or reduce them to an acceptable level.

Independence for audit and review services and possible threats and safeguards are given in detail in Part 4A, the largest section of the Code. See illustration 3.9. Review and

---

ILLUSTRATION 3.9

PART 4A INDEPENDENCE – AUDIT AND REVIEW ENGAGEMENTS

Paragraph

400 Applying the Conceptual Framework to Independence for Audit and Review Engagements

410 Fees

411 Compensation and Evaluation Policies

420 Gifts and Hospitality

430 Actual or Threatened Litigation

510 Financial Interests

511 Loans and Guarantees

520 Business Relationships

521 Family and Personal Relationships

522 Recent Service with an Audit Client

523 Serving as a Director or Officer of an Audit Client

524 Employment With an Audit Client

525 Temporary Personnel Assignments

540 Long Association of Personnel (Including Partner Rotation) with an Audit Client

600 Provision of Non-Assurance Services to an Audit Client

601 Accounting and Bookkeeping Services

602 Administrative Services

603 Valuation Services

604 Tax Services

605 Internal Audit Services

606 Information Technology Systems Services

607 Litigation Support Services

608 Legal Services

609 Recruiting Services

610 Corporate Finance Services

800 Reports on Special Purpose Financial Statements that Include a Restriction on Use and Distribution (Audit and Review Engagements)

---

audit independence is discussed on the topics of conceptual framework, network firms, public interest entities, documentation, engagement period, financial interests, loans and guarantees, business relationships, family and personal relationships, employment with an audit client, temporary staff assignments, recent service with an audit client, serving as director or officer of an audit client, long association of senior personnel with audit clients, and other topics not covered in this chapter, including mergers and acquisitions and related entities. The sub-section on non-assurance services discusses safeguards and threats of non-assurance services to the audit client including the following topics: management responsibilities, preparing accounting records and financial statements, taxation services, internal audit services, IT systems services, litigation support services, legal services, recruiting services, and valuation and corporate finance services. The independence section ends with a discussion of general topics including fees, compensation and evaluation policies, gifts and hospitality, actual or threatened litigation, and restricted reports (not discussed in this chapter).

The Code emphasizes that during audit engagements it is in the public interest and required that members of audit teams must be independent of audit clients.

The audit firm assigns operational responsibility for compliance with independence requirements to an individual(s) in accordance with International Standard on Quality Management (ISQM 1). Under ISQM 1, relevant ethical requirements are those related to the firm, its personnel and, when applicable, others subject to the independence requirements to which the firm and the firm's engagements are subject. In addition, the individual professional accountant remains responsible for compliance with any provisions that apply to that accountant's activities, interests or relationships. If a firm is a network firm,[31] the firm must be independent of the audit clients of the other firms within the network. The independence requirements that apply to a network firm apply to any entity, such as a consulting practice or professional law practice, which meets the definition of a network firm irrespective of whether the entity itself meets the definition of a firm.

ISA 600 requires the group engagement partner to take responsibility for confirming whether the component auditors understand and will comply with the relevant ethical requirements, including those related to independence, that apply to the group audit (see chapter 13).

▶ APPLICATION OF THE CONCEPTUAL FRAMEWORK APPROACH TO INDEPENDENCE FOR AUDIT AND REVIEW ENGAGEMENTS (SEC. 400)

A firm or network firm must refrain from taking on management responsibilities for an audit client. When engaging in professional activities for an audit client, it is crucial for the firm to ensure that the client's management is exclusively responsible for making appropriate judgments and decisions. It's important to note that for a listed entity serving as an audit client, this encompasses all associated entities. In the case of other entities, the term 'audit client' in this context includes related entities over which the client has direct or indirect control.

DOCUMENTATION OF INDEPENDENCE

The auditor has to document conclusions regarding compliance with independence requirements as well as the discussions that support these conclusions. The documentation requirements are made explicit in the various sections of part 4 of the Code. Conceptually:

- ▶ when safeguards are required, the auditor shall document the nature of the threat and the safeguards in place or applied that reduce the threat to an acceptable level; and
- ▶ when a threat required significant analysis to determine whether safeguards were necessary and the conclusion was that they were not because the threat was already at an acceptable level, the professional accountant must document the nature of the threat and the rationale for the conclusion.

▶ ENGAGEMENT PERIOD (400.30)

Independence from the audit client is required both during the engagement period and the period covered by the financial statements.[32] The engagement period starts when the audit team begins to perform audit services. The engagement period ends when the audit report is issued. When the engagement is of a recurring nature, it ends at the later of the notification by either party that the professional relationship has terminated or the issuance of the final audit report. During or after the period covered by the financial statements the audit firm must consider threats to independence created by financial or business relationships with the audit client or previous services provided to the audit client. Auditors should consider threats if a non-assurance service that would not be permitted during the period of the audit engagement was provided to the audit client before the audit. Safeguards include:

▶ excluding personnel who provided the non-assurance service as members of the audit team;

▶ having a professional accountant review the audit and non-assurance work as appropriate; or

▶ engaging another audit firm to evaluate the results of the non-assurance service or having another firm re-perform the non-assurance service to the extent necessary to enable it to take responsibility for the service.

In the remainder of this section we will only briefly discuss paragraphs 420-430, 510-520 and 600-610 of Part A of the Code of Ethics (illustration 3.9) and focus on relevant threats and safeguards.

▶ FEES (SEC. 410)

Professional fees should be a fair reflection of the value of the professional service performed for the client, taking into account the skills and knowledge required, the level of training and experience of the persons performing the services, the time necessary for the services and the degree of responsibility that performing those services entails. The IESBA Code of Ethics discusses threats to independence in pricing auditing services in terms of size, whether fees are overdue and contingent fees.

When the total audit fees for a specific client represent a large proportion of the firm's total fees, the dependence on that client and concern about losing the client create a self-interest or intimidation threat. These threats are also created when the fees generated from one audit client represent a large proportion of the revenue from an individual partner's clients or a large proportion of the revenue of an individual office of the audit firm. Safeguards must be applied to eliminate the threat or reduce it to an acceptable level. Examples of such safeguards include reducing the dependency on the client; internal or external quality control reviews; or consulting a third party to review key audit judgements.

The Code of Ethics refers to a specific situation of a client's fees as a proportion of total fees. If an audit client is a public interest entity and, for two consecutive years, the total fees from the client represent more than 15 per cent of the total fees received by the audit firm, the firm must disclose that fact to the audit client and discuss which safeguards it will apply.

The Code warns that a self-interest threat may be created if fees due from an assurance client for professional services remain unpaid for a long time, especially if a significant part is not paid before the issue of next year's assurance report. The firm should also consider whether the overdue fees might be regarded as being equivalent to a loan to the client and whether, because of the significance of the overdue fees, it is appropriate for the firm to be reappointed.

Contingent fees are fees (except those established by courts) calculated on a predetermined basis relating to the outcome of a transaction or the result of the services performed by the firm. A contingent fee charged directly or indirectly by an audit firm for an audit or non-assurance engagement creates a self-interest threat that is so significant that no safeguards could reduce the threat to an acceptable level. Some non-assurance engagements may be acceptable under certain safeguards.[33]

Fees are distinct from reimbursement of expenses. Out-of-pocket expenses, in particular travelling expenses, attributable directly to the professional services performed for a particular client would normally be charged in addition to the professional fees.

▶ COMPENSATION AND EVALUATION POLICIES (SEC. 411)

A self-interest threat is created when a member of the audit team or a key audit partner is evaluated on or compensated for selling non-assurance services to that audit client. The significance of the threat must be evaluated and, if the threat is not at an acceptable level, the firm shall either revise the compensation plan or evaluation process for that individual or apply safeguards to eliminate the threat or reduce it to an acceptable level. Examples of such safeguards include removing such members from the audit team or having a professional accountant review the work of the audit team member.

CONCEPT AND A COMPANY 3.3	
INDEPENDENCE OF THE EXTERNAL AUDITOR – RENTOKIL AND KPMG UK	
Concept	Auditor independence – auditors should be aware of significant threats to independence that may arise and the appropriate safeguards to apply in an attempt to eliminate those threats.
Story	On 31 July 2009 KPMG UK raised the eyebrows of competitors in the UK and elsewhere in the world with their agreement with Rentokil Initial. Rentokil hired KPMG as their new external auditor, replacing PwC. However, KPMG also replaced Deloitte, who handled much of the internal audit, along with Rentokil's own internal audit team. Other audit firms questioned whether the combination of offering external and internal audit services could be provided by the same firm, without the creation of conflicting interests and threatening independence.
	'The arrangement is controversial, since the Enron and WorldCom accounting scandals have resulted in new rules largely designed to split external and internal audit roles to avoid auditors becoming too tied to their clients', the *Financial Times* wrote.
	Oliver Tant, head of audit for KPMG UK, argued the arrangement was ethically sound. According to Tant, 'the internal audit work does not replace, conflict with, or undermine the independence of the external audit – it simply extends our understanding of the business and its controls and hence the breadth and depth of insight we can offer'. Tant said the arrangement did not merge internal and external audit functions.

In the US under SOX legislation, external auditors are not allowed to combine internal audit services and external audit services to the same client.

This combo deal was favorable for Rentokil, as the new deal saved about £1 million per year in total (internal and external) audit fees.

Discussion Questions	▶ To what extent would providing both internal and external audit services to an audit client be considered a threat to independence? ▶ What safeguards could KPMG have put in place to compensate for this threat?
References	http://www.ft.com/cms/s/0/ae47504a-7fc4-11de-85dc-00144feabdc0.html#axzz2Ms9NDegv. http://www.accountancyage.com/aa/news/1749104/kpmg-audit-head-defends-controversial-rentokil-role.

▶ GIFTS AND HOSPITALITY (SEC. 420)

Accepting gifts or hospitality from an audit client may create self-interest and familiarity threats. If a firm or a member of the audit team accepts gifts or hospitality, unless the value is trivial and inconsequential, the threats created would be so significant that no safeguards could reduce the threats to an acceptable level.

▶ ACTUAL OR THREATENED LITIGATION (SEC. 430)

When litigation takes place, or appears likely, between the audit firm or a member of the audit team and the audit client, self-interest and intimidation threats are created. The relationship between client management and the members of the audit team must be characterised by complete candour and full disclosure regarding all aspects of a client's business operations. When the firm and the client's management are placed in adversarial positions by actual or threatened litigation, affecting management's willingness to make complete disclosures, self-interest and intimidation threats are created. The significance of the threats shall be evaluated, and safeguards applied when necessary to eliminate the threats or reduce them to an acceptable level. Examples of such safeguards include removing the individual involved in litigation from the audit or having a professional review the work performed. If such safeguards do not reduce the threats to an acceptable level, the only appropriate action is to withdraw from, or decline, the audit engagement.

▶ FINANCIAL INTERESTS (SEC. 510)

The self-interest threat created when an auditor, her firm, or a member of her immediate family has direct or material indirect financial interest in an audit client is such that no safeguards could reduce it to an acceptable level. None of the following shall have a direct financial interest or a material indirect financial interest in the client: a member of the audit team; a member of that individual's immediate family; or the firm. If other partners and managerial employees who provide non-audit services to the audit client, or their immediate family members, hold a direct financial interest or a material indirect financial interest in the audit client, the self-interest threat created would be so significant that no safeguards could reduce the threat to an acceptable level.

A loan, or a guarantee of a loan, to a member of the audit team, or a member of that individual's immediate family, or the firm from an audit client that is a bank, a similar institution, or non-bank entity (except if the non-bank loan is immaterial) may create a threat to independence. The loan or guarantee must not be made except under normal lending procedures, terms and conditions, otherwise a self-interest threat would be created that would be so significant that no safeguards could be sufficient. If the loan or guarantee is made under normal lending procedures, terms and conditions safeguards must be applied such as having the work reviewed by a professional accountant from a network firm that is neither involved with the audit nor received the loan.

▶ BUSINESS, FAMILY AND PERSONAL RELATIONSHIPS (SEC. 520-521)

A close business relationship between a firm, or a member of the audit team, or a member of that individual's immediate family, and the audit client or its management, arises from a commercial relationship or common financial interest and may create self-interest or intimidation threats. Unless the financial interest is immaterial and the business relationship is insignificant, the business relationship must not be entered into because *no* safeguards would be sufficient and the individual with the relationship must be removed from the audit team. Examples of close business relationships include:

- ▷ Having a financial interest in a joint venture with either the client or a controlling owner, director, officer or other individual who performs senior managerial activities for that client.
- ▷ Arrangements to combine one or more services or products of the firm with one or more services or products of the client and to market the package with reference to both parties.
- ▷ Distribution or marketing arrangements under which the firm distributes or markets the client's products or services, or the client distributes or markets the firm's products or services.

Family and personal relationships between a member of the audit team and a director or officer or certain employees (depending on their role) of the audit client may create self-interest, familiarity or intimidation threats. If an immediate family member of a member of the audit team is a director or officer of the audit client, or an employee in a position to exert significant influence over the preparation of the client's accounting records or the financial statements or was in such a position during any period covered by the engagement, the threats can only be reduced to an acceptable level by removing that individual from the audit team.

If a director or officer of the audit client, or a significant employee, has been a member of the audit team or partner of the firm, familiarity or intimidation threats may be created. The threat would be so significant that no safeguards could reduce the threat to an acceptable level unless: the individual is not entitled to any benefits or payments from the audit firm and any amount owed to the individual is not material to the firm; and that individual does not continue to participate in the audit firm's business activities. Furthermore, a self-interest threat is created when a member of the audit team participates in the audit engagement while knowing that the member of the audit team will, or may, join the client at some time in the future.

The lending of staff by a firm to an audit client may create a self-review threat. Such assistance may be given, but only for a short period of time, and the firm's personnel shall not be involved in providing non-assurance services not permitted under Section B of the IESBA Code of Ethics or assuming management responsibilities.

Familiarity and self-interest threats are created by using the same senior personnel on an audit engagement over a long period of time. Examples of such safeguards include:

▶ rotating the senior personnel of the audit team;

▶ having a professional accountant who was not a member of the audit team review the work of the senior personnel; or

▶ regular independent internal or external quality reviews of the engagement.

In respect to an audit of a public interest entity, an individual shall not be a key audit partner for more than seven years. After such time, the individual shall not be a member of the engagement team or be a key audit partner for the client for two years.

▶ PROVISION OF NON-ASSURANCE SERVICES TO AUDIT CLIENTS (SEC. 600-610)

Firms have traditionally provided to their audit clients a range of non-assurance services that are consistent with their skills and expertise. Providing non-assurance services may, however, create threats to the independence of the firm or members of the audit team. The threats created are most often self-review, self-interest and advocacy threats. Providing certain non-assurance services to an audit client may create a threat to independence so significant that no safeguards could reduce the threat to an acceptable level.

PUBLIC INTEREST ENTITIES (PIES)

For public interest entities, there are often stricter regulations and guidelines in place to limit the provision of these services by their external auditors. This is to safeguard the independence and objectivity of the auditor when performing their primary assurance role. Regulatory bodies and accounting standards-setters typically establish rules and requirements to manage and disclose non-assurance services for PIEs effectively. EU regulation explicitly list certain services that external auditors are prohibited from providing to PIEs. These prohibited services include, for example, bookkeeping, financial information systems design, and certain legal services.[34]

The Sarbanes-Oxley Act of 2002 Section 201 also prohibits bookkeeping, financial information systems design and implementation as well as valuation services, actuarial services, internal audit outsourcing services and certain other services to be provided to public companies.

NON-PUBLIC INTEREST ENTITIES

If a firm were to assume a management responsibility[35] for an audit client, the threats created would be so significant that no safeguards could reduce the threats to an acceptable level. For example, deciding which recommendations of the firm to implement will create self-review and self-interest threats. Further, assuming a management responsibility creates a familiarity threat because the firm becomes too closely aligned with the views and interests of management. Therefore, the firm shall not assume a management responsibility for an audit client.

Providing an audit client with accounting and bookkeeping services, such as preparing accounting records or financial statements, creates a self-review threat when the audit firm subsequently audits the financial statements. An audit firm shall not provide to an audit client that is a public interest entity accounting and bookkeeping services, including payroll services, or prepare financial statements or financial information which forms the basis of the financial statements. However, the firm may provide some services related to the preparation of accounting records and financial statements to an audit client that is not a public interest entity. Examples of such services include:

- ▶ Providing payroll services based on client-originated data.
- ▶ Recording transactions for which the client has determined or approved the appropriate account classification.
- ▶ Posting transactions coded by the client to the general ledger.
- ▶ Posting client-approved entries to the trial balance.
- ▶ Preparing financial statements based on information in the trial balance.

Tax return preparation services involve assisting clients with their tax reporting obligations by drafting and completing information, including the amount of tax due (usually on standardised forms) required to be submitted to the applicable tax authorities. The tax returns are subject to whatever review or approval process the tax authority deems appropriate. Accordingly, providing such service does not generally create a threat to independence if management takes responsibility for the returns including any significant judgments made.

Tax planning or other tax advisory services such as advising the client how to structure its affairs in a tax efficient manner or advising on the application of a new tax law or regulation may create a self-review threat where the advice will affect matters to be reflected in the financial statements. For example, where the effectiveness of the tax advice depends on a particular accounting treatment or presentation in the financial statements and the audit team has reasonable doubt as to the appropriateness of the related accounting treatment and the outcome or consequences of the tax advice will have a material effect on the financial statements, the self-review threat would be so significant that no safeguards could reduce the threat to an acceptable level.

The existence and significance of any threat will depend on a number of factors. For example, providing tax advisory services where the advice is clearly supported by tax authority or other precedent does not generally create a threat to independence. If safeguards are required, they may include:

- ▶ using professionals who are not members of the audit team to perform the service;
- ▶ having a tax professional, who was not involved in providing the tax service, advise the audit team on the service and review the financial statement treatment;
- ▶ obtaining advice on the service from an external tax professional; or
- ▶ obtaining pre-clearance or advice from the tax authorities.

An advocacy or self-review threat may be created when the firm represents an audit client in the resolution of a tax dispute. Where the taxation services involve acting as an advocate for an audit client before a public tribunal or court in the resolution of a tax matter and the amounts involved are material to the financial statements the advocacy threat created would be so significant that no safeguards could eliminate or reduce the threat to an acceptable level. Therefore, the firm shall not perform this type of service for an audit client.

The provision of internal audit services to an audit client creates a self-review threat to independence if the firm uses the internal audit work in the course of a subsequent external audit. Performing a significant part of the client's internal audit activities increases the possibility that firm personnel providing internal audit services will assume a management responsibility. Assuming management responsibility when providing internal audit services to an audit client creates a threat that would be so significant that no safeguards could reduce the threat to an acceptable level.

To avoid assuming a management responsibility, the firm shall only provide internal audit services to an audit client if it is satisfied that:

▶ Client senior management always takes responsibility for internal audit activities and acknowledges responsibility for designing, implementing and maintaining internal control.

▶ Client management reviews, assesses and approves the scope, risk and frequency of the internal audit services.

▶ The client's management evaluates and determines which recommendations resulting from internal audit services to implement and manages the implementation process.

▶ The client's management reports to those charged with governance the significant findings and recommendations resulting from the internal audit services.

In the case of an audit client that is a public interest entity, a firm shall not provide internal audit services that relate to:

▶ a significant part of the internal controls over financial reporting;

▶ financial accounting systems that generate information that is significant to the client's accounting records or financial statements; or

▶ amounts or disclosures that are material to the financial statements on which the audit firm will express an opinion.

Providing IT systems services may create a self-review threat depending on the nature of the services and the IT systems. Providing services to an audit client involving the design or implementation of IT systems that form a significant part of the internal control over financial reporting or generate accounting records or financial statements creates a self-review threat. For a non-public interest entity, other IT systems services may not create a threat to independence if the audit firm's personnel do not assume management responsibility, but safeguards must be put in place.

Performing valuation services or litigation support services for an audit client may create a self-review threat. The existence and significance of any threat will depend on several factors such as whether the services will have a material effect on the financial statements, the active participation of the client's in determining and approving the methodology and other significant matters of judgement, the degree of subjectivity inherent in the service, and the extent and clarity of the disclosures in the financial statements.

Legal services that support an audit client in executing a transaction (for example, contract support, legal advice, legal due diligence and restructuring) may create self-review threats. Acting in an advocacy role for an audit client in resolving a dispute or litigation when the amounts involved are material to the financial statements on which the firm will express an opinion would create advocacy and self-review threats so significant that no safeguards could reduce the threat to an acceptable level. Therefore, the firm shall not perform this type of service for an audit client. However, when the amounts involved are not material to the financial statements, the audit firm may provide the service if safeguards are in place.

Providing recruiting services to an audit client may create self-interest, familiarity or intimidation threats. The audit firm may generally provide such services as reviewing the professional qualifications of a number of applicants and providing advice on their suitability for the post. In addition, the firm may interview candidates and advice on a candidate's competence for financial accounting, administrative or control positions. The audit firm cannot provide search services or reference checks for a director, officer or senior management who has influence over the accounting records or financial statements.

Advocacy and self-review threats may be created if the auditor provides the audit client corporate finance services such as assisting in developing corporate strategies, identifying possible targets for the audit client to acquire, advising on disposal transactions, assisting finance raising transactions, or providing structuring advice. If the effectiveness of corporate finance advice depends on a particular accounting treatment or presentation in the financial statements and the audit team has reasonable doubt as to the appropriateness and the consequences of the corporate finance advice, and the treatment will have a material effect on the financial statements, the self-review threat would be so significant that no safeguards could reduce the threat to an acceptable level.

Providing corporate finance services involving promoting, dealing in, or underwriting an audit client's shares would create an advocacy or self-review threat that no safeguards could reduce to an acceptable level.

ILLUSTRATION 3.10

PART 4B: INDEPENDENCE – OTHER ASSURANCE ENGAGEMENTS

CONTENTS

▶ **PART 4B – INDEPENDENCE REQUIREMENTS FOR ASSURANCE ENGAGEMENTS OTHER THAN AUDIT OR REVIEW ENGAGEMENTS**

Part 4B of the IESBA Code of Ethics (see illustration 3.10 for contents) addresses independence requirements for assurance engagements that are not audit or review engagements. If the assurance client is also an audit or review client, the requirements in the prior section of this chapter (including part 4A of the Code of Ethics) also apply to the firm, network firms and members of the audit or review team. Although part 4B is described separately from part 4A, the concepts of independence are the same. We will not explore the non-financial statement audit or review assurance ethics in this book.

3.8 ENFORCEMENT OF ETHICAL REQUIREMENTS

Disciplinary action ordinarily arises from such issues as: failure to observe the required standard of professional care, skills or competence; non-compliance with rules of ethics; and discreditable or dishonourable conduct. Sanctions commonly imposed by disciplinary bodies include: reprimand, fine, payment of costs, withdrawal of practising rights, suspension, and expulsion from membership. Other sanctions can include a warning, the refund of the fee charged to the client, additional education, and the work to be completed by another member at the disciplined member's expense. The effectiveness of enforcing ethical standards varies from country to country.

In many countries an auditor who violates the ethical standard may be disciplined by law (a special disciplinary court) or by the professional organization. The penalties range from a reprimand to expulsion or fine. In the USA expulsion from a state society or the American Institute of Certified Public Accountants (AICPA) does not mean that the expelled member cannot practise public accounting because only the state boards of public accountancy have the authority to revoke a license. As illustrated in the case of Arthur Andersen,[36] if a company is convicted of a felony, the US Security and Exchange Commission (SEC) prohibits them from auditing publicly traded companies. See illustrations 3.11 and 3.12.

ILLUSTRATION 3.11

EXAMPLES OF VIOLATIONS OF INDEPENDENCE (DERIVED FROM SEC PRESS RELEASES)

According to the SEC's order, RSM US repeatedly represented that it was 'independent' in audit reports issued on the clients' financial statements, which were included or incorporated by reference in public filings with the Commission or provided to investors. Instead, the SEC found that RSM US or its associated entities, including other member firms of the RSM International network, provided non-audit services to, and had an employment relationship with, affiliates of RSM US audit clients, which violated the SEC's auditor independence rules. The prohibited non-audit services included corporate secretarial services, payment facilitation, payroll outsourcing, loaned staff, financial information system design or implementation, bookkeeping, internal audit outsourcing, and investment adviser services. The prohibited employment relationship concerned a partner at an RSMI member firm in Australia serving on a voluntary basis as a non-discretionary member of the board of an affiliate of an RSM US issuer audit client. RSM US agreed to pay a $950,000 penalty and be censured.

Source: SEC Charges RSM US LLP With Violating Auditor Independence Rules. For Immediate Release, 2019-161, https://www.sec.gov/news/press-release/2019-161

The SEC's order finds that PwC violated the SEC's auditor independence rules by performing prohibited non-audit services during an audit engagement, including exercising decision-making authority in the design and implementation of software relating to an audit client's financial reporting, and engaging in management functions. In connection with performing non-audit services for 15 SEC-registered audit clients, the order states that PwC violated Public Company Accounting Oversight Board (PCAOB) Rule 3525, which requires an auditor to describe in writing to the audit committee the scope of work, discuss with the audit committee the potential effects of the work on independence, and document the substance of the independence discussion. According to the order, PwC's actions deprived numerous issuers' audit committees of information necessary to assess PwC's independence. PwC agreed to pay disgorgement of $3,830,213, plus prejudgment interest of $613,842 and a civil money penalty of $3.5 million, and to be censured.

Source: SEC Charges PwC LLP With Violating Auditor Independence Rules and Engaging in Improper Professional Conduct. SEC For Immediate Release 2019-184, https://www.sec.gov/news/press-release/2019-184.

ILLUSTRATION 3.12

EXAMPLE OF VIOLATION OF INTEGRITY

Ernst & Young (EY), agreed to pay a $100 million fine after U.S. securities regulators found that hundreds of its auditors had cheated on various ethics exams they were required to obtain or maintain professional licenses — and that the firm did not do enough to stop the practice. The penalty is the largest ever imposed by the Securities and Exchange Commission against a firm in the auditing business, which occupies a unique ethical perch in the financial world. These firms are in charge of verifying the accuracy of companies' financial statements and issuing warnings to investors if they identify dubious accounting practices. Regulators said EY had misled investigators, withheld evidence and violated public accounting rules designed to maintain the integrity of the profession.

Source: Matthew Goldstein, 28 June 2022, *New York Times*

3.9   SUMMARY

The attitude and behavior of professional accountants in providing auditing and assurance services have an impact on the economic well-being of their community and country. Professional accountants can remain in this advantageous position only by continuing to provide the public with these unique services at a level that demonstrates that the public confidence is well-founded. The standards of the accountancy profession are heavily determined by the public interest. Therefore, a professional accountant's responsibility is not exclusively to satisfy the needs of an individual client or employer.

The International Ethics Standards Board of Accountants (IESBA) Code of Ethics is divided into four parts:

Part 1 establishes the fundamental principles of professional ethics for all professional accountants and provides a conceptual framework that is applied to: identify threats to compliance with the fundamental principles; evaluate the significance of the threats identified; and apply safeguards, when necessary, to eliminate the threats or reduce them to an acceptable level.

Parts 2,3 and 4 describe how the conceptual framework applies in certain situations. They provide examples of safeguards that may be appropriate to address threats to compliance with the fundamental principles. They also describe situations where safeguards are not available to address the threats. Part 2 applies to employed professional accountants. Part 3 applies only to those professional accountants in public practice. Part 4 describes independence matters.

Rather than a list of rules that must be obeyed to be an ethical accountant, the so called 'rule-based' approach which holds sway in many countries, the IESBA has chosen to use a 'conceptual framework' approach. A conceptual framework requires a professional accountant to identify, evaluate and address threats to compliance with the fundamental principles, rather than merely comply with a set of specific rules which may be arbitrary. The fundamental principles of ethics are described in Part 1 of the Code and are applicable to all professional accountants. They are: integrity, objectivity, professional competence and due care, confidentiality, and professional behaviour. Part 1 of the Code offers further discussion on these principles. Each concept is the topic of subsequent Sections (111–115) in the Code.

Compliance with the fundamental principles may potentially be threatened by a broad range of circumstances and relationships. The nature and significance of the threats may differ depending on whether the audit client is a public interest entity, to an assurance client that is not an audit client, or to a non-assurance client. The conceptual framework of the IESBA Code of Ethics discusses ways to identify threats to fundamental principles, determine the significance of those threats, and, if they are significant, identify and apply safeguards to reduce or eliminate the threats.

Threats fall into one or more of the following categories: self-interest; self-review; advocacy; familiarity; and intimidation. When threats are identified, other than those that are clearly insignificant, appropriate safeguards should be identified and applied to eliminate the threats or reduce them to an acceptable level. If elimination or reduction is not possible the auditor should decline or terminate the engagement.

When deciding what safeguards should be applied one must consider what would be unacceptable to an informed third-party having knowledge of all relevant information. Safeguards fall into two broad categories: (1) safeguards created by the profession, legislation or regulation; and (2) safeguards in the work environment.

Part 2 of the IESBA Code of Ethics describes how the conceptual framework contained in Part 1 applies in certain situations to professional accountants in business. A professional accountant in business may be a salaried employee, a partner, director, an owner manager, a volunteer or another working for one or more employing organizations.

Professional accountants in business may be responsible for the preparation and reporting of financial and other information or for providing effective financial management and competent advice on a variety of business-related matters. The accountant has a responsibility to further the legitimate aims of the accountant's employing organization. A professional accountant in business is expected to encourage an ethics-based culture in an employing organization that emphasizes the importance that senior management places on ethical behaviour.

Part 3 of the IESB Code of Ethics is only applicable to accountants in public practice. A professional accountant in public practice is a professional accountant, irrespective of functional classification (for example, audit, tax or consulting) in a firm that provides professional services. Part 3 describes how the conceptual framework (Part 1) applies to professional accountants in public practice. Ethical guidance is offered in the areas of professional appointment, conflicts of interest, second opinions, fees and other remuneration, marketing professional services, gifts and hospitality, custody of client assets, objectivity, and independence for both audit and review engagements and other assurance engagements.

An auditor who is asked to replace another auditor, or who is considering a new engagement for a company currently audited by another auditor, must consider whether there are any reasons, professional or otherwise, for not accepting the engagement. Evaluating reasons for not accepting a new client may require direct communication with the existing auditor to establish the facts and circumstances regarding the proposed change in auditors.

Across the world, national rules on auditors' independence differ in several respects such as: the scope of persons to whom independence rules should apply; the kind of financial, business or other relationships that an auditor may have with an audit client; the type of non-audit services that can and cannot be provided to an audit client; and the safeguards which should be used. The European Commission has issued independence standards to be applied throughout the EU. The USA enacted the Sarbanes-Oxley Act of 2002 that describes independence requirements of US auditors.

The IESBA Code of Ethics for Professional Accountants, Part 4A, addresses the independence requirements for audit and review engagements. Independence requirements for assurance engagements that are not audit or review engagements are addressed in Part 4B. The Code discusses independence in assurance services in terms of a principles-based, conceptual approach that takes into account threats to independence, accepted safeguards and the public interest.

Accountants in public practice must not only maintain an independent attitude in fulfilling their responsibilities, but the users of financial statements must have confidence in that independence. These two objectives are frequently identified as 'independence of mind' and 'independence in appearance.' Independence of mind (historically referred to as independence in fact) exists when the accountant is able to maintain an unbiased attitude throughout the audit, so being objective and impartial, whereas independence in appearance is the result of others' interpretations of this independence.

The Ethics Code defines the two views. Independence of mind is the state of mind that permits the expression of a conclusion without being affected by influences that compromise professional judgement, thereby allowing an individual to act with integrity and exercise objectivity and professional scepticism. Independence in appearance is the avoidance of facts and circumstances that are so significant that a reasonable and informed third party would be likely to conclude, weighing all the specific facts and circumstances, that a firm's, or a member of the audit team's, integrity, objectivity or professional scepticism has been compromised.

The Ethics Code discusses independence in assurance services in terms of a principles-based approach that considers threats to independence, accepted safeguards and the public interest. The section states principles that members of assurance teams should use to identify threats to independence (self-interest, self-review, advocacy, familiarity and intimidation threats), evaluate the significance of those threats, and, if the threats are other than clearly insignificant, identify and apply safeguards created by the profession, legislation or regulation, safeguards within the assurance client, and safeguards within the firm's own systems and procedures to eliminate the threats or reduce them to an acceptable level.

Independence for audit and review services and possible threats and safeguards are sketched in Part 4A, the largest section of the Code. Independence is discussed with regards to network firms, public interest entities, documentation, engagement period, financial interests, loans and guarantees, business relationships, family and personal relationships, employment with an audit client, temporary staff assignments, recent service with an audit client, serving as director or officer of an audit client, long association of senior personnel with audit clients, and other topics not covered in this chapter, including mergers and acquisitions and related entities. Safeguards and threats of non-assurance services are discussed regarding the following topics: management responsibilities, preparing accounting records and financial statements, taxation services, internal audit services, IT systems services, valuation and litigation support services, legal services, recruiting services, and corporate finance services. Finally, some general independence issues like fees, compensation and evaluation policies, gifts and hospitality, actual or threatened litigation are discussed.

The effectiveness of enforcing ethical standards varies from country to country. In many countries an auditor who violates the ethical standard may be disciplined by law or by the professional organization. The penalties range from a reprimand to expulsion or fine.

3.10 ETHICS: AN EXAMPLE

The attitude and behavior of professional accountants in providing auditing and assurance. Ethics is one of the crucial considerations of Isle & Oblivion Accountants (I&O) because their reputation, and therefore the future of their firm, depends on it. The ethical standards followed by I&O and other auditors and accountants is given in the International Ethics Standards Board of Accountants (IESBA) Code of Ethics for Professional Accountants (the Code). The IESBA Code states that it is an auditor's responsibility to act in the public interest – it is a distinguishing mark of the accountancy profession. The professional auditors' responsibility is not to satisfy only their client or employer but putting the public interests first.

The Code sets standards of conduct for professional accountants and states the fundamental principles that should be observed by professional accountants in order to achieve common objectives. Independence is required for all assurance services and is closely linked to the principles of integrity and objectivity and is an important element of serving the public interest. Part 1 of the Code establishes the fundamental principles of professional ethics for professional accountants and provides a conceptual framework that is applied to:

- ▶ identify threats to compliance with the fundamental principles as spelled out in the Code;

> ▶ evaluate the significance of the threats identified; and
> ▶ employ safeguards, when necessary, to eliminate the threats or reduce them to an acceptable level.

Fleur Ltd., a client of I&O, is a virtual reality company that sells software and hardware that immerse the product user in an artificial world that they experience as reality. Dalia Desdemona, CA is an audit partner new to I&O whose first engagement is a financial audit of Fleur. The prior engagement partner had taken a job at another audit firm. If there is a change in engagement partner or certain auditors I&O's audit plan requires that the current engagement partner (Dalia Desdemona, in this case) discuss any Fleur issues with the prior partner during the first meeting. During the discussion with CEO Jeff Scribble, Dalia learns that the previous engagement partner had so much good to say about Fleur that his nephew Dario, on hearing the good comments, purchased several OTC shares in Fleur. The CEO Jeff said he was sorry to see that the prior partner was not handling his company because Jeff had known him for twenty years since they both graduated from London Business School. As a matter of fact, the prior partner had done Jeff a favour by appearing before the Council committee to get Fleur building permits for their factory. Jeff said that a local TV station had been after him to do an interview and he felt he should mention the great help that I&O and the prior engagement partner had given them.

One day Jeff Scribble, the founder and CEO, tells Dalia Desdemona that the prior engagement partner used to offer his luxury stadium seat to see the local football team and asks Dalia if she can offer him the same thing. Jeff tells Dalia that he has a ski chalet in the closest mountain resort and he is offering whenever she needs a vacation. When the two are discussing the bookkeeping system, Dalia casually says that her husband is a bookkeeper and he uses a similar system. Jeff says that they are looking for an accounting manager and maybe her husband should apply. Fleur's IT Supervisor said he had known the previous partner for five years since the time that the partner entered the set up for the present accounting system.

There are several threats to I&O's compliance with the fundamental principles based on the description above: Self-interest threats, self-review threats, advocacy threats, familiarity threats, and intimidation threats. The procedure to minimize or eliminate these threats involves identifying the threats, evaluating the threats, addressing the threats with safeguards, and then communicating with those charged with governance like management and the board of directors.

The prior engagement partner used to offer his luxury stadium seat for football matches. Any audit employee should not accept staying free at CEO Jeff's ski chalet. Both offers are in violation of the integrity ethics standard. As the Standard says: 'A breach of the fundamental principle of integrity arises when a professional accountant offers or accepts, or encourages others to offer or accept, an inducement where the intent is to improperly influence the behaviour of the recipient or of another individual.' The integrity threat resulting from offers of valuable gifts and hospitality can only be mediated by refusing the offers.

One ethical threat of self-interest might be that the prior engagement partner's nephew purchased several OTC shares in Fleur. The auditor and her immediate family should not have a direct financial interest in the client. In some countries, such as the US, a nephew is not considered immediate family.

The CEO and the prior engagement partner had known each other for twenty years since they both graduated from London Business School which could be considered a familiarity threat because of their long personal association.

An advocacy threat arose when the prior partner appeared before the Council committee to get Fleur building permits for their factory. The Fleur CEO Jeff may suggest that he could mention the advocacy that I&O showed Fleur to a local TV station. Jeff might feel that he is doing I&O a favour, but he is threatening them. The permits that he helped secure might be considered an intimidation threat.

Fleur's IT Supervisor said he had known the previous partner for five years since the time that the partner entered the year end journal entries into the accounting system. Basing your audit on data you have created in the accounting system is a self-review threat.

The following are safeguards that might be initiated by I&O to moderate or reduce the threat. As Fleur is not a publicly traded company which is prohibited from offering this service to such an audit client, any threat can be resolved by having an appropriate reviewer who was not a member of the team review the work performed or advise as necessary. I&O disclosed in the notes to the financial statement that they had helped with building permits to minimize the impact of an advocacy action. I&O could have declined to audit Fleur if the ethics breach had been more severe (for instance acting as a witness for the defence in a bankruptcy or divorce case). Disclosure of the long friendship between the prior auditor and Fleur CEO might manage the familiarity threat, but this is quite an unresolved issue.

What can the auditor do if it is concluded that independence is breached in prior audits? The PCAOB has in the past, in some circumstances, required a re-audit. What do you think?

3.11 QUESTIONS, EXERCISES AND CASES

QUESTIONS

3.2 What are ethics?

3-1 What are ethics?

3-2 What ethical principles incorporate characteristics used by society as good moral behavior?

3-3 Why are normative theories about ethics 'relevant' for auditors?

3-4 According to the IESBA Code of ethics, what is the ethics objective of the accountancy profession?

3.3 The International Code of Ethics for Professional Accountants

3-5 Describe each of the four parts of the IESBA Code of ethics.

3-6 Name and define the five fundamental principles of ethics applicable to all professional accountants.

3.4 Part 1 – Complying with the Code, Fundamental Principles and Conceptual Framework

3-7 Conduct that might discredit the profession includes conduct that a reasonable and informed third party would be likely to conclude adversely affects the good reputation of the profession. Does 'conduct' also include behavior in the private sphere? Motivate.

3-8 Confidential client information may generally be disclosed only with the permission of the client. What are the exceptions to this rule?

3-9 Can a professional accountant claim that the returns he prepares are always acceptable to the taxing authorities? Why?

3-10 Name and define the basic categories of threats.

3-11 Safeguards fall into two broad categories. What are the categories? Give examples of each.

3.5 Part 2 – Professional Accountants in Business

3-12 What self-interest threats do you think are the most frequent for a professional accountant in business?

3-13 What should an employed accountant do if they feel they are being asked to do something that is contradictory to accounting standards?

3.6 Part 3 – Ethics Applicable to Professional Accountants in Public Practice

3-14 Give an example of a threat and corresponding safeguard for each of the following activities of a professional accountant in public practice.
- A. Professional appointment
- B. Conflicts of interest
- C. Second opinions
- D. Fees and other types of remuneration
- E. Marketing professional services
- F. Gifts and hospitality
- G. Custody of client assets
- H. Objectivity – all services

3-15 What are contingent fees? Give two examples and explain why accountants in public practice should or should not take them.

3-16 An auditor who is asked to replace another auditor, or who is considering a new engagement for a company currently audited by another auditor must consider what safeguards are appropriate. discuss which safeguards would apply to such circumstances.

3.7 Part 4 Independence Standards

3-17 Discuss the differences between the European Commission Council directive on independence and the Sarbanes-Oxley Act's view of auditor independence.

3-18 What is the difference between 'independence in mind' and 'independence in appearance'? State two activities that may not affect independence in fact but are likely to affect independence in appearance.

3-19 Describe two threats and related safeguards associated with each of the following independence activities (Code section):
- A. Engagement Period (400.30)
- B. Fees (410)
- C. Compensation and evaluation policies (411)
- D. Gifts and hospitality (420)

E.   Actual or threatened litigation (430)

F.   Financial interests (510)

G.   Business, family and personal relationships (520-521)

H.   Provision of non-assurance services to audit clients (600)

3-20 Name some forms of financial involvement with a client that may affect independence.

3.8   Enforcement of Ethical Requirements

3-21 Can IESBA discipline an accountant for violation of the Code of ethics? What sanctions are commonly imposed by disciplinary bodies (see section 2.9)?

PROBLEMS AND EXERCISES

3.2   What Are Ethics?

3-22 Ethics Code. Why is there a need for an ethics code for professional accountants? Explain. In what ways should the ethics code for professional accountants be different from that of other groups such as physicians or attorneys? Should the Ethics Code apply to all sustainability assurance practitioners regardless of their professional backgrounds, as well as professional accountants involved in sustainability reporting as well as in sustainability assurance? Motivate.

3-23 Can auditors always be independent and objective (see endnote 11)? Answering this question you could also read the paper 'Why Good Accountants Do Bad Audits' by Max H. Bazerman, George Loewenstein and Don A. Moore, *Harvard Business Review* (November 2002)[37].

3.3   The International Code of Ethics for Professional Accountants

3-24 Discuss the differences between a conceptual framework and a rules-based approach to ethics.

3.4   Part 1 – General Application of the IESBA Code of Ethics for Professional Accountants

3-25 Violations of Code of Ethics. For each of the following situations involving relations between auditors and the companies they audit indicate whether it violates the IESBA Code of ethics for Professional Accountants and the rationale for the applicable guideline.

A.   Yaping Lei, CPA, discloses confidential information in a peer review of the firm's quality control procedures.

B.   Frank Smith, CPA, prepares and submits a tax return to the Internal Revenue Service which he believes omits income his client receives from trading goods on eBay.com.

C.   El-Hussein El-Masery, CA, is auditing a company in Nigeria that has offered to send him and his wife on a holiday in Hawaii for two weeks.

D.   Tabula Gonzales, CP, says in an interview in the local paper that Emilio Rios, CP, misleads his clients about the quality of his audit work.

3.5   Part 2 – Professional Accountants in Business

3-26 Jemmy Le, CPA, worked for Barrelon corporation, a manufacturer of wine and beverage oak barrels. He has been a good employee, so when he got married the CEO of Barrelon loaned him the down payment for a house. Instead of a bonus last year, the company gave Mr Le a compensation arrangement that is based on the profits of the company. The company also gave Mr Le a Lexus RX350 for business use which makes a good ride when he goes skiing on vacation. Part of the reason for Mr Le's success is the influence of his stepbrother who is on the board of directors.

Required:

Describe any threats that Mr Le's working relationship may have and what safeguards may be put in place to compensate.

3.6 Part 3 – Ethics Applicable to Professional Accountants in Public Practice

3-27 Professional Accountants in Public Practice. Galati and Brambila formed a corporation called Financial Fitness Systems, each woman taking 50 per cent of the authorised common stock. Galati is a Dottore Commercialista (Consob), a public accountant, and Brambila is an insurance underwriter. The corporation provides auditing and tax services under Galati's direction and insurance services under Branbila's direction. The opening of the corporation's office was announced by a 15 cm, 2-column announcement in the local newspaper.

One of the corporation's first audit clients was the Galore Company. Galore had total assets of €923,820,000 and total liabilities of €415,719,000. In the course of her examination, Galati found that Galore's building with a book value of €369,528,000 was pledged as security for a ten-year term note in the amount of €307,940,000. Galore's statements did not mention that the building was pledged as security for the ten-year term note. However, as the failure to disclose the lien did not affect either the value of the assets or the amount of the liabilities and her examination was satisfactory in all other respects, Galati rendered an unqualified opinion on Galore's financial statements. About two months after the date of her opinion, Galati learned that an insurance company was planning to loan Galore €230,955,000 in the form of a first mortgage note on the building. Galati had Brambila notify the insurance company of the fact that Galore's building was pledged as security for the term note.

Shortly after the events described above, Galati was charged with a violation of professional ethics.

Required:

Identify and discuss the ethical implications of those acts by Galati that were threats according to the IESBA Code of ethics for Professional Accountants.

3.7 Part 4 – Independence Requirements

3-28 Independence in Fact and Appearance. Auditors must not only appear to be independent; they must also be independent in fact.

Required:

A. Explain the concept of auditor's independence as it applies to third-party reliance upon financial statements.
    - ▶ What determines whether or not an auditor is independent in fact?
    - ▶ What determines whether or not an auditor appears to be independent?
B. Explain how an auditor may be independent in fact but not appear to be independent.
C. Would an accountant in public practice be considered independent for a review of the financial statement of (1) A church in which the accountant is serving as treasurer without compensation? (2) A club for which the accountant's spouse is serving as a treasurer-bookkeeper if the accountant is not to receive a fee for the review.

3-29 Independence and Gifts. Samantha Seekineau, Soma Orkoton Logiston (SOL), is in charge of the audit of Olympic Fashions. Five young assistant auditors are working with Seekineau on the engagement, and several are avid windsurfers. Olympic Fashions owns two villas on Mikonos, which it uses to entertain clients. The comptroller of Olympic Fashions has told Seekineau that she and her audit staff are welcome to use the villas at no charge any time they are not already in use. How should Seekineau respond to this offer? Explain.

CASES

3-30 Ethical Issues. The following situation involves Kevin Smith, staff accountant with the local CPA firm of Hobb, Mary, and Khang (HM&K). the bookkeeper of Mirage Manufacturing Company resigned three months ago and has not yet been replaced. As a result, Mirage's transactions have not been recorded and the books are not up to date. Mirage must prepare interim financial statements to comply with terms of a loan agreement but cannot do so until the books are posted. To help them with this matter, mirage turns to HM&K, their independent auditors. Mirage wants Kevin Smith to update their books because Kevin had audited them last year.
Required:
A. Identify the ethical issues that are involved.
B. Discuss whether there has or has not been any violation of ethical conduct.

3-31 Ethical Issues. You are the lead auditor working for a reputable midsized audit firm. One of your firm's longstanding clients is DELTA, a large manufacturing company that has been experiencing financial difficulties. The company's management has been under pressure to show improved financial performance to shareholders and potential investors. During the audit process, you uncover evidence of financial irregularities that suggest the company may be manipulating its financial statements to present a more favourable picture of its financial health. However, the management insists that the discrepancies are merely accounting errors and urges you to overlook them to avoid negative repercussions for the company. Upon further investigation, you realize that if you report the irregularities accurately, it could damage DELTA's reputation, potentially leading to loss of investor confidence, plummeting stock prices, and even bankruptcy. On the other hand, turning a blind eye to these discrepancies would compromise your professional integrity and ethical obligations as an auditor. As the deadline for submitting the audit report approaches, you find yourself torn between your duty to your client and its employees and your responsibility to uphold the principles of integrity and transparency in auditing.
Questions for consideration:
▶   What ethical principles are at stake in this situation?
▶   How might your decision impact various stakeholders, including shareholders, employees, creditors, and the general public?
▶   What actions could you take to navigate this ethical dilemma while preserving your professional integrity?
▶   What are the potential consequences of each course of action, both for you personally and for your firm?
▶   How might relevant professional standards and regulatory requirements influence your decision-making process?

3.12 NOTES

1. Developed by the Josephson Institute for the Advancement of Ethics, a US not-for-profit foundation to encourage ethical conduct of professionals in the fields of government, law, medicine, business, accounting and journalism.

2. Internet Encyclopedia of Philosophy: http://www.iep.utm.edu/ethics

3. https://philosophyfinds.wordpress.com/2017/06/24/traditional-virtue-ethics/

4. Groundwork of the Metaphysics of Morals (1785; German: Grundlegung zur Metaphysik der Sitten; also known as the Foundations of the Metaphysics of Morals, Grounding of the Metaphysics of Morals, and the Grounding for the Metaphysics of Morals) is the first of Immanuel Kant's mature works on moral philosophy and remains one of the most influential in the field.

5. For further information about ethical theories we refer to Michael Sandel, Justice, What's the right thing to do? New York: Farrar, Straus and Giroux, 2010.

6. Source Google Image as well as https://culcnambotak.wordpress.com/2017/07/27/deontology-vs-teleontology/

7. An assurance service or assurance engagement is an engagement in which a practitioner expresses a conclusion designed to enhance the degree of confidence of the intended users other than the responsible party about the outcome of the evaluation or measurement of a subject matter against criteria.

8. International Ethics Standards Board of Accountants (IESBA), Introduction – Objectives, para. 100.1, Handbook of the International Code of Ethics for Professional Accountants 2021 Edition, International Federation of Accountants, New York.

9. IESBA issued an Exposure Draft (2024) regarding International Ethics Standards for Sustainability Assurance (IESSA) and other revisions to the code relating to sustainability assurance and reporting. The proposed standard aims to establish clear ethical frameworks for sustainability assurance practitioners and professional accountants involved. https://www.ethicsboard.org/publications/proposed-international-ethics-standards-sustainability-assurance-including-international?utm_source=Main+List+New&utm_campaign=28a2abd83f-EMAIL_CAMPAIGN_2024_02_06_08_37&utm_medium=email&utm_term=0_-28a2abd83f-%5BLIST_EMAIL_ID%5D

10. International Ethics Standards Board of Accountants (IESBA), Handbook of the International Code of Ethics for Professional Accountants 2023 Edition, para. 100.4, International Federation of Accountants, New York.

11. One can challenge whether 'being objective' (unbiased) is possible. See for example Ehrliner, J., Gilovich, T. and Ross, L., (2005), 'Peering into the Bias Blind Spot: People's Assessments of Bias in Themselves and Others', p. 2, Personality and Social Psychology Bulletin, 31, pp. 1–13 as well as The Impossibility of Auditor Independence, Bazerman, M.H., Morgen, K.P., Lowenstein, G.F., Sloan Management Review, Summer 1997.

12. Project Implicit website: https://implicit.harvard.edu/implicit/

13. From the Code Ethics (ICAEW): A professional accountant should respect the confidentiality of information acquired as a result of professional and business relationships and should not disclose any such information to third parties without proper and specific authority unless there is a legal or professional right or duty to disclose. Confidential information acquired as a result of professional and business relationships should not be used for the personal advantage of the professional accountant or third parties. https://www.icaew.com/for-current-aca-students/applying-for-membership/code-of-ethics.

14. The reasonable and informed third party test is a consideration by the professional accountant about whether the same conclusions would likely be reached by another party.

Such consideration is made from the perspective of a reasonable and informed third party, who weighs all the relevant facts and circumstances that the accountant knows, or could reasonably be expected to know, at the time the conclusions are made. (120.5A.6)

15. A subject matter of an assurance is the topic about which the assurance is conducted.

16. International Ethics Standards Board of Accountants (IESBA), Handbook of the International Code of Ethics for Professional Accountants 2021 Edition, paragraph 300.7A5, International Federation of Accountants (IFAC), New York.

17. Ibid. IESBA 2023, para. R115.1.

18. Ibid. IESBA 2023, para. 200.6A1.

19. Ibid. IESBA 2023, para. 200.7A3.

20. International Auditing and Assurance Standards Board (IAASB), 2023, International Standard on Auditing 220 (ISA 220) 'Quality Control For An Audit Of Financial Statements', Handbook of International Quality Management, Auditing, Review, Other Assurance, and Related Services Pronouncements, 2022 edn., Volume I, International Federation of Accountants, New York.

21. International Auditing and Assurance Standards Board (IAASB), 2023, International Standard on Auditing 620 (ISA 620) 'Using the Work of an Auditor's Expert', Handbook of International Quality Control, Auditing, Review, Other Assurance, and Related Services Pronouncements, 2022 edn, Volume I, International Federation of Accountants, New York.

22. Existing auditor is the auditor who is currently holding an audit or assurance services appointment with the prospective client.

23. International Ethics Standards Board of Accountants (IESBA), Handbook of the International Code of Ethics for Professional Accountants 2023 Edition, paragraph 330.4A2, International Federation of Accountants (IFAC), New York.

24. Directive 2006/43/EC of the European Parliament and of the Council of 17 May 2006 on statutory audits of annual accounts and consolidated accounts, Article 22, https://eur-lex.europa.eu/legal-content/EN/TXT/?uri=CELEX%3A32006L0043&qid=1717544315104

25. Statutory audits are audits of financial statements required by law.

26. Regulation (EU) No 537/2014 of the European Parliament and of the Council of 16 April 2014 on specific requirements regarding statutory audit of public-interest entities and repealing Commission. Directive 2014/56/Eu of the European Parliament and of the Council of 16 April 2014. https://eur-lex.europa.eu/legal-content/EN/TXT/?uri=CELEX%3A32014R0537&qid=1717544630311

27. The Senate and House of Representatives of the United States of America, Sarbanes–Oxley Act of 2002, Public Law, 107–204, 30 July 2002.

28. US Securities and Exchange Commission (SEC), 2003, Final Rule: Strengthening the Commission's Requirements Regarding Auditor Independence; Rel. Nos. 33-8183, 34-47265; 35-27642; IC-25915; IA-2103; File No. S7-49-02, Securities and Exchange Commission, January 28.

29. The Russian Audit Chamber is a government agency that supervises the audit industry in Russia. It sets professional standards for auditors and conducts quality control reviews of audit firms.

30. Pendergast, Marilyn A., 'Strengthening the Commission's Requirements Regarding Auditor Independence: file s7-49-02', International Federation of Accountants, New York, 10 January 2003.

31. A network firm is a firm or entity that belongs to a network. A network is a larger structure that is aimed at cooperation and is clearly aimed at profit or cost-sharing or shares common ownership, control or management, common quality control policies and procedures, common business strategy, the use of a common brand name, or a significant part of professional resources.

32. International Ethics Standards Board of Accountants (IESBA), 2021 Handbook of the International Code of Ethics for Professional Accountants 2021 Edition, paragraph 400.30, International Federation of Accountants (IFAC), New York.

33. International Ethics Standards Board of Accountants (IESBA), Handbook of the International Code of Ethics for Professional Accountants 2021 Edition, paragraph 600.7A2 and 8, International Federation of Accountants (IFAC), New York.

34. Regulation (EU) No 537/2014 on specific requirements regarding statutory audit of public-interest entities. https://eur-lex.europa.eu/legal-content/NL/ALL/?uri=celex%3A32014R0537.

35. International Ethics Standards Board of Accountants (IESBA), Handbook of the International Code of Ethics for Professional Accountants 2021 Edition, paragraph R600.7A1, International Federation of Accountants (IFAC), New York.

36. Arthur Andersen was one of the largest auditing firms in the world (one of the Big Five) when they were convicted by the US Department of Justice of obstruction of justice (a felony) when in 2001, the Houston, Texas, branch shredded documents relating to their audit client, Enron Corporation.

37. https://hbr.org/2002/11/why-good-accountants-do-bad-audits

CHAPTER 4

EXPLORING THE FOUNDATIONS OF AUDITING AND ASSURANCE

4.1 LEARNING OBJECTIVES

After studying this chapter, you should be able to:

1. Describe the objectives of an audit.
2. Explain the concepts of reasonable and limited assurance.
3. Understand the concept of sufficient appropriate evidence.
4. Explain how materiality is set and affects the scope of audit work.
5. Describe the importance of the internal control environment.
6. Explain the importance of understanding the business and risk assessment.
7. Explain why ethical behaviour is key for the auditor.
8. Recognize the importance of professional judgement and professional scepticism.
9. Describe the two levels of quality control.
10. Understand the need for documentation.
11. Discuss the similarities and differences between audit engagements and assurance engagements.

An audit is an assurance engagement in the public interest. If successful it provides reasonable assurance to the public that the financial statements are free of material misstatement due to fraud or error. Important concepts in an audit are materiality, professional scepticism and professional judgement. The auditor needs to behave ethically and needs to be independent of the auditee. The audit process is about understanding the risks, understanding how they are managed by the auditee, and performing tests of controls and substantive procedures to gather sufficient appropriate audit evidence. Documentation should tell the story of the audit.

4.2 THE OBJECTIVES OF AUDITING IN AN ELEVATOR PITCH

When an auditor issues an auditor's report on financial statements, she declares with reasonable assurance that the financial statements give a true and fair view[1] of the financial statements as a whole in accordance with the applicable financial reporting framework. True – implicating that what is in the financial statements is correct, considering a certain threshold. Fair – implicating that all required/relevant information is included, and an overall balanced view is presented. A true and fair view incurs that the financial statements are free from material misstatements due to error (unintentional mistakes) or fraud (intentional mistakes).

THE OBJECTIVE OF AN AUDIT OF THE FINANCIAL STATEMENTS IS, ACCORDING TO ISA 200:[2]

1 to obtain reasonable assurance about whether the financial statements as a whole are free from material misstatement, whether due to fraud or error, thereby enabling the auditor to express an opinion on whether the financial statements have been prepared, in all material respects, in accordance with an applicable financial reporting framework; and

2 to report on the financial statements and to communicate as required by the ISAs in accordance with the auditor's findings.

Issuing the auditor's report is the final step in an extensive due process. Broadly speaking the financial statements audit consists of the following phases:

Phase 1: Client/engagement acceptance/continuance (*chapter 5*)
  ▶ Deciding to accept or continue with the client.
  ▶ Deciding to accept and continue the engagement.

Phase 2: Planning through understanding and risk analysis (*chapters 6 and 7*)
  ▶ Understanding the organization whose financial statements are audited and, on that basis determine the risks of material misstatement in the financial statements.
  ▶ Identifying which internal control measures the organization has taken to manage these risks.

Phase 3: Building and executing the audit plan (*chapter 8 and 9*)
  ▶ Testing the effectiveness of these identified internal control measures insofar as you intend to rely on them.
  ▶ Performing substantive audit procedures that are still required to obtain the required reasonable level of assurance.

Phase 4: Evaluating and reporting (*chapters 10 and 11*)
  ▶ Evaluating and communicating the findings, including misstatements found, and articulating the opinion in the form of an auditor's report.

THE FOUR PHASES OF THE AUDIT

The four phases of the audit:

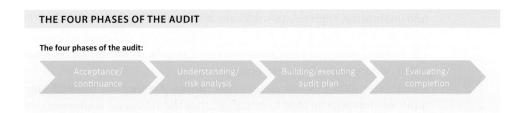

These main concepts will be addressed in the sections below.

4.3 REASONABLE ASSURANCE

The auditor's objective is to provide reasonable assurance that the financial statements are free of material misstatement. ISA 200 defines 'reasonable assurance' as 'a high level of assurance but not absolute'[3]. The difference between a high level of assurance and absolute assurance results from the inherent limitations to the work of an auditor:

▶ From an economic perspective it is not justifiable to test every item or transaction flow completely. Also, given the relevance of the financial statements, it is sometimes impossible to await the availability of more audit evidence. Concluding a financial statement audit after two years has limited relevance for users.

▶ Financial statements consist of many judgmental items. Consider, for example, the valuation of trade receivables. An auditor can evaluate whether the management's estimate seems plausible based on experiences with previous estimates made by management and market conditions. But the chance that the estimate is 100% accurate is unlikely.

▶ The majority of the audit evidence on which the auditor bases her opinion is persuasive rather than conclusive[4].

Although an auditor might have gathered sufficient appropriate audit evidence to issue an unqualified (unmodified) opinion, the financial statements might be materially misstated as a result of fraud or errors. This is possible since the auditor bases her opinion on reasonable, not absolute, assurance. However, these inherent limitations do not justify an auditor being satisfied with less than persuasive audit evidence. In other words, reasonable assurance is the ultimate an auditor can do, notwithstanding circumstances for which she cannot be held responsible. On the other hand, the financial statements may be correct, although the audit has not been carried out in accordance with the ISAs.

4.4 SUFFICIENT APPROPRIATE AUDIT EVIDENCE

The auditor must obtain sufficient appropriate audit evidence to keep the risk of an undetected material misstatement in the financial statements to an acceptable level, in isolation or in combination with other statements. Audit evidence is all the information that the auditor uses to base her opinion upon. Audit evidence has quantitative ('sufficient') and qualitative (appropriate – relevant and reliable) aspects. The auditor can obtain this evidence when accepting a client and an engagement, while collecting knowledge about the audited entity, when performing risk analysis, while testing internal controls and when performing substantive procedures.

It is important that the auditor determines whether she has sufficient appropriate audit evidence to be able to conclude that the financial statements give a true and fair view. In making this determination the auditor includes the effect individually and collectively that uncorrected misstatements might have on her conclusion that the financial statements are not materially misstated and thus that she has sufficient appropriate audit evidence.

See chapter 8 for details.

4.5 MATERIALITY

A material misstatement is a deviation that makes it likely that the judgment of a reasonable person, who relies on the information, will be influenced or affected by misrepresentation or omission. For example, financial statements may impact the judgment of investors as to whether they should continue to invest in a company. But also impacted may be the judgement of a potential client who wants to have a house built by a contractor when she evaluates the financial statements of a construction company. Not all misstatements have relevance to all users.

There is no magic formula for determining which misstatement is material to which users, and which is not. The auditor must determine this amount based on her professional judgment. She will choose an amount that takes into account the interests of a larger group of users and not of one specific user. She often uses benchmarks (for example, a percentage of equity, profit before tax or a percentage of turnover). The materiality calculated this way is called quantitative materiality.

Materiality might not be the same for all account balances and classes of transactions. For example, decision making by users may be more affected by a misstatement in management fees than by a misstatement in inventory. The auditor then might decide to test management fees with a lower materiality. This is called qualitative materiality. Materiality is not an auditing concept by nature. It reflects the materiality concept in reporting frameworks, such as IFRS.

Setting materiality in the planning stage determines whether there are volumes of transactions to which the auditor pays no (or little) attention in his audit. Specifically, when scoping the transaction streams, the substantive analytics threshold and the samples size. Materiality has no effect on effectiveness testing of controls, nevertheless the effectiveness of controls limits the risk of material misstatement and influences the level of substantive procedures needed to assess that with reasonable assurance no material misstatement exists.

See chapter 6 for more details.

4.6 THE IMPORTANCE OF INTERNAL CONTROL MEASURES

Doing business involves risk taking. Some risks can be managed, others not. For example, you can put valuable goods in a safe so that the risk of these goods being stolen is managed. Nevertheless, it is almost impossible to manage the risk that potatoes will rot due to excessive rainfall, and as a result cannot be harvested. You may irrigate the land, but that does not exclude this risk in full.

Companies will consciously or unconsciously try to manage (most) risks that business objectives will not be met. Some measures are more effective than others. A warehouse employee who signs a shipping document for goods receipt without understanding what she is doing may not check if all pallets are present. Nevertheless, she probably has received certain goods. This control activity is more effective when the warehouse employee counts the pallets and simultaneously checks whether they are in good condition.

Often it is a combination of mitigating factors that manage risks. The risk of a cashier making a mistake or committing a fraud is, for example, limited when goods are being scanned. It is then more difficult for this employee to adjust prices manually. Counting the cash register at the end of each day makes it harder to steal money. And eye surveillance (even if this is only done by customers) means that the risk that articles are not being scanned decreases. Some measures have a direct effect (for instance counting the contents of a cash register to determine whether there is a cash deficit), some have an indirect effect, (for example monitoring by management).

All these procedures can be classified as internal controls on which the auditor can rely in the context of his audit. She will have to determine how much audit evidence she can derive from an internal control, assuming it operates as expected. It is important to remember that it is often not black or white. There are often many shades of grey regarding effectiveness.

See chapter 7 for more details.

4.7 THE AUDITOR BEHAVES ETHICALLY

An important precondition for adding value and carrying out an audit according to the ISAs is that the auditor complies with the Code of Ethics, issued by the International Ethics Standards Board for Accountants (IESBA). As the auditor needs to be trustworthy, her behaviour should reflect that trust. Parts 1 and 3 of the Code of Ethics are applicable to accountants in public practice. Part 1 and 2 applies to accountants in business. Part 2 is in certain situations also applicable to accountants in public practice. The independence section is only applicable for professional accountants providing audit and assurance services.

Refer to chapter 3 for more background on ethics. A professional accountant, and thus an auditor, must adhere to 5 fundamental principles according to the Code of Ethics:

Fundamental Principles	
Integrity	The integrity ensures that the professional accountant acts honestly and that she is not allowed to attach her name to misleading information.
Objectivity	Objectivity essentially means that the professional accountant does not perform a service if she is unable to do so objectively.
Professional competence and due care	Professional accountants in public practice must execute their engagement professionally and carefully.
Confidentiality	The professional accountant receives a lot of information that is sensitive to the company or the engagement. The professional accountant treats this information confidentially and in principle keeps it secret. In principle, because sometimes based on legislation or regulations the company and the professional accountant have to disclose information and therefore the professional accountant has to comply, sometimes even if the organization does not.
Professional behaviour	Behaviour also means that the professional accountant acts professionally and does not discredit the accounting profession.

When performing audit and assurance engagements, the auditor needs to be independent, which is a path to objectivity.

4.8 THE AUDITOR EXERCISES PROFESSIONAL SCEPTICISM

An auditor is critical of the audit evidence obtained. For example, if a client claims that no write-off of outdated inventory[5] is required, the auditor will ask critical questions about this and search for corroborative or contradictory information. This is referred to as professional scepticism. This does not mean that the auditor assumes that all information obtained is incorrect, but she must be objective and professionally sceptical. In that context, it was stated earlier that much audit evidence is persuasive rather than conclusive.

4.9 THE AUDITOR EXERCISES PROFESSIONAL JUDGEMENT

Not everything is black and white in an audit. An auditor will therefore regularly make judgements during the audit. Her professional judgement is relevant, for example, if an auditor estimates the likelihood and impact of a misstatement in the valuation of a financial derivative. The consideration of whether management's assessment is acceptable, but also the consideration of whether there is sufficient appropriate audit evidence requires professional judgment. Such decisions require the auditor's expertise and experience.

4.10 QUALITY MANAGEMENT

▶ **ENGAGEMENT LEVEL**

Probably the most important aspect of quality management at the engagement level is that a partner actively takes responsibility for the engagement. She must verify that relevant ethical and independence requirements are being complied with, that the client and the engagement have been correctly accepted and that there have been no indications later on that question the acceptance, that the team has the necessary knowledge and experience. She must ensure that the team is properly managed, that team members are assessed in accordance with the firm policies, where necessary she involves specialists/experts in accordance with the firm's policies, a quality control reviewer has been appointed where required and that the engagement quality control review is carried out in accordance with the standards. Finally, she must evaluate whether the findings from the firm's monitoring system are relevant to her audit and, where necessary, followed up and whether reasonable assurance is obtained.

▶ **AUDIT FIRM LEVEL**

Auditors perform their work within audit firms. These firms set up a quality management system that facilitates their auditors in conducting a high-quality audit. Further, the firm might provide an audit methodology and supportive tools like an electronic file. The firm also provides training and education for staff. In most cases the auditor leverages the firm's quality management system and is dependent on it.

4.11 THE AUDITOR IS ACCOUNTABLE WITH ROBUST DOCUMENTATION

The purpose of documentation is twofold. On the one hand, the documentation must support the substantiation of the auditor's report, On the other hand, the documentation must confirm that the audit has been planned and conducted in accordance with laws and regulations.

Based on the audit file, an experienced auditor (with knowledge of the industry) must be able to understand audit procedures that have been carried out, what audit information was obtained, findings including significant matters addressed during the audit and the discussions and rationale of the conclusions.

It is neither necessary nor practical to document everything. For example, it is not necessary to document that certain matters have been done if this is apparent from the file itself. Further, the audit file does not have to explain why something is not a risk if that is evident to an experienced auditor.

4.12 AUDIT VERSUS ASSURANCE

An audit engagement is an example of an assurance engagement. Assurance engagements differentiate by subject matter, level of assurance, whether they are historical or future-based and whether they are assertion-based. Subject matters can be financial and non-financial. Assurance engagements on historical financial information aimed to obtain a reasonable level of assurance are labelled as 'audit'. In all these situations it is important that the auditor or practitioner collects sufficient appropriate evidence to substantiate here conclusion, applies materiality, behaves ethically, can apply professional judgement and professional scepticism, has established quality control, and documents properly in order to be accountable after the audit. A prerequisite for all assurance engagements is the availability of suitable criteria or benchmarks used to evaluate the subject matter.

4.13 LIMITED VERSUS REASONABLE ASSURANCE

Where a financial audit is aimed at reaching a reasonable level of assurance (high level but not absolute – see section 4.3), assurance engagements can be aimed at reaching either a reasonable or a limited level of assurance. ISAE 3000 defines a limited assurance engagement as 'an assurance engagement in which the practitioner reduces engagement risk to a level that is acceptable in the circumstances of the engagement but where that risk is greater than for a reasonable assurance engagement (...)[6]. In other words: the auditor's efforts are less at a limited assurance engagement (we define this as 'plausible evidence') as compared to a reasonable assurance engagement (we define this as 'convincing evidence'). Auditors use negative wording when expressing limited assurance: 'nothing has come to our attention that X is not ok'.

Limited versus reasonable assurance

Assume someone claims: 'there are currently 5 blue cars driving on the highway from A to B'.

Variant 1 (reasonable assurance)
In order to assess that is correct, the auditor flies in a helicopter 300 meters above the highway. The auditor counts and makes pictures. Physical counting becomes straightforward due to the distinct colours of the cars, which can be easily distinguished and later verified through high-density overall pictures. When done, the auditor can conclude 'I am convinced that there are 5 blue cars on the highway'.

Variant 2 (limited assurance):
The auditor flies at 750 meters (about 2460.63 ft) above the highway. The auditor counts and makes pictures. Counting physically is less clear as the different colours of the cars cannot easily be distinguished. The pictures afterwards facilitate, but the pictures are less granular. When done, the auditor cannot conclude more than 'It's plausible that there are 5 dark blue cars on the highway'.

See chapter 14 on assurance engagements and chapter 15 specifically on sustainability assurance engagements.

SUMMARY

An audit is an assurance engagement in the public interest. If successful it provides reasonable assurance to the public that the financial statements are free of material misstatement due to fraud or error. Important concepts in an audit are materiality, professional scepticism and professional judgement. The auditor needs to behave ethically and needs to be independent of the auditee. The audit process is about understanding the risks, understanding how they are managed by the auditee, and performing tests of controls and substantive procedures to gather sufficient appropriate audit evidence. Documentation should tell the story of the audit.

The objective of an audit is to obtain reasonable assurance about whether the financial statements as a whole are free from material misstatement, thereby enabling the auditor to express an opinion on whether the financial statements have been prepared in all material respects in accordance with the applicable financial reporting framework (ISA, GAAS, etc.). The auditor must also report on the financial statements and communicate her findings as required by the audit standards.

Broadly speaking, the financial statements audit consists of the following phases:

▶ Phase 1 – Client/engagement acceptance/continuance;
▶ Phase 2 – Planning through understanding and risk analysis;
▶ Phase 3 – Building and execution of the audit plan; and
▶ Phase 4 – Reporting.

An auditor seeks reasonable assurance as the basis for the financial statements. ISA 200 defines 'reasonable assurance' as 'a high level of assurance but not absolute'. The difference between a high level of assurance and absolute assurance results from the inherent limitations to the work of an auditor. These limitations are: Because of economic costs it is not justifiable to test every item or transaction flow completely. Financial statements consist of many judgmental items. Most of the audit evidence is persuasive rather than conclusive. The financial statements might be materially misstated as a result of fraud or errors.

The auditor must obtain sufficient appropriate audit evidence to keep the risk of an undetected material misstatement in the financial statements to an acceptable level. Audit evidence has quantitative ('sufficient') and qualitative (appropriate – relevant and reliable) aspects.

A material misstatement is a deviation that makes it likely that the judgment of a reasonable person, who relies on the information, will be influenced or affected by misrepresentation or omission. The auditor must determine this amount based on her professional judgment.

An important precondition for adding value and carrying out an audit is that the auditor complies with the Code of Ethics, issued by the International Ethics Standards Board for Accountants (IESBA). As the auditor needs to be trustworthy, her behaviour should reflect that trust. Parts 1 and 3 of the Code of Ethics are applicable to accountants in public practice. Part 1 and 2 applies to accountants in business.

An auditor is critical of the audit evidence obtained. The auditor will ask critical questions about evidence and search for corroborative or contradictory information. This is referred to as professional scepticism.

Probably the most important aspect of quality management at the engagement level is that an audit partner actively takes responsibility for the engagement. She must verify that relevant ethical and independence requirements are being complied with and that the team has the necessary knowledge and experience. She must ensure that the team is properly managed, a quality control reviewer has been appointed where required and that the engagement quality control review is carried out in accordance with the standards.

The purpose of documentation is twofold. On the one hand, the documentation must support the substantiation of the auditor's report. On the other hand, the documentation must confirm that the audit has been planned and conducted in accordance with laws and regulations.

An audit engagement is an example of an assurance engagement. Assurance engagements differentiate by subject matter, level of assurance, whether they are historical or future-based and whether they are assertion-based. Subject matters can be financial and non-financial. Assurance engagements on historical financial information aimed to obtain a reasonable level of assurance are labelled as 'audit'.

Assurance engagements can be aimed at reaching a reasonable or a limited level of assurance. A limited assurance engagement is 'an assurance engagement in which the practitioner reduces engagement risk to a level that is acceptable in the circumstances of the engagement but where that risk is greater than for a reasonable assurance engagement. That is, the auditor's efforts are less at a limited assurance engagement as compared to a reasonable assurance engagement.

4.15   QUESTIONS, EXERCISES AND CASES

QUESTIONS

4.2   The Objectives of Auditing in an Elevator Pitch

4-1   Assume you have just one minute, how would you describe the key objectives of an audit?

4.3   Reasonable Assurance

4-2   What is the definition of reasonable assurance?

4-3   Why is it not possible to obtain an absolute level of assurance?

4.4   Sufficient Appropriate Audit Evidence

4-4   What is the difference between sufficient and appropriate in the context of audit evidence? Give an example of each.

4.5   Materiality

4-5   Explain the concept of materiality in the context of a financial statements audit.

4.6   The Importance of Internal Control Measures

4-6   Why are internal control measures important for a company? Why is it also relevant for the auditor?

4.7   **The Auditor Behaves Ethically**

4-7   Why are the auditor's ethics important in the context of a professional service?

4.8   **The Auditor Exercises Professional Scepticism**

4-8   Why is exercising professional scepticism important for the auditor? Give an example how to apply.

4.9   **The Auditor Exercises Professional Judgement**

4-9   What is your view on the following statement: *'Professional judgement is key for a high-quality audit'*?

4.10   **Quality Management**

4-10   On which two levels should Quality Control be effective? Give an example of each.

4.11   **The Auditor is Accountable with Robust Documentation**

4-11   What is your view of the following statement: *'Robust documentation is a means for the auditor to take the credit for the comprehensive work done in the audit.'*

4.12   **Audit Versus Assurance**

4-12   What are the similarities and differences between Audit and Assurance?

4.13   **Limited Versus Reasonable Assurance**

4-13   Can you express the difference between Limited Assurance and Reasonable Assurance?

PROBLEMS AND EXERCISES

4.2   **The Objectives of Auditing in an Elevator Pitch**

4-14   The audit process is an iterative process. What does that mean? Illustrate the iterative nature with an example.

4.3   **Reasonable Assurance**

4-15   Why does the auditor's report not provide more than reasonable assurance? If you had to quantify reasonable assurance, is it 50%, 70% or 90%? Why not 100%?

4.4   **Sufficient Appropriate Audit Evidence**

4-16   You are conducting an audit of XYZ Company, a manufacturing firm. The management claims that the inventory valuation is accurate and reflects the current market value of their goods. As an auditor, you need to gather evidence to verify the accuracy of this claim. Questions:

a.   Propose specific audit procedures you would employ to gather the necessary evidence.

b.   How would you ensure that the evidence collected is appropriate for this audit objective?

c.   Discuss any potential limitations or challenges you might encounter in obtaining sufficient and appropriate audit evidence in this scenario.

4.5 Materiality

4-17 Scenario: You are assigned as the auditor for ABC Corporation, a mid-sized retail company. Your task is to conduct a financial statement audit for the fiscal year ending December 31st. ABC Corporation operates in a competitive market and has shareholders and creditors with varying interests in the company's financial performance.

Questions:

a. Define materiality in the context of financial statement audits.

b. Explain why materiality is important in the audit process.

c. Discuss how the determination of materiality influences audit planning decisions, such as the nature, timing, and extent of audit procedures.

d. Evaluate the potential impact of misstatements below the materiality threshold on the audit opinion.

Note: Engage in discussions with your peers or instructor to compare different approaches to determining materiality and its implications in the audit process.

4.6 The Importance of Internal Control Measures

4-18 Do you think gathering sufficient and appropriate evidence:

a. Can be gathered without an understanding of design of Internal Control Measures

b. Can be gathered by understanding of design of Internal Control Measures only (without any other audit procedure). Motivate!

4.7 The Auditor Behaves Ethically

4-19 Check (on internet) what is meant by 'Underreporting of Time' and 'Premature signing off' as examples of 'dysfunctional behaviour'. Do you think both are also 'unethical'? Motivate. What can be the effect on appropriateness and sufficiency of gathered audit evidence?

4.8 The Auditor Exercises Professional Scepticism

4-20 Michael, a financial auditor, is reviewing the financial statements of Bike AG, a software development company. Bike AG has recently launched a new product and reported a significant increase in revenue. Michael notices that the revenue from the new product seems unusually high compared to previous years. Additionally, there's a lack of detailed information provided by management regarding the product's sales and customer base. Management is very busy and doesn't have time to provide detailed information.

Give an example of a professionally critical attitude on the part of Michael.

4.9 The Auditor Exercises Professional Judgement

4-21 Eva completed her economics studies with honours and subsequently obtained her accounting degree with high marks. Her colleagues praise her for her knowledge and expertise. She has 3 years of practical experience in the retail industry. She has now been asked to become an audit manager for a client in the banking sector. When asked by the engagement partner whether she can apply professional judgment in the audit process, she answers with a resounding yes.

Do you agree? Motivate.

4.10 **Quality Management**

4-22 What do you think is more important: Quality management at the engagement level or firm level? Motivate.

4.11 **The Auditor is Accountable with Robust Documentation**

4-23 Why do you think auditing standards require auditors to document all activities of the audit process in detail in their audit files?

4.12 **Audit Versus Assurance**

4-24 Mention some assurance services that are not audit services and explain why they are no audit service. Can you give an example of an audit service that is no attestation service?

4.13 **Limited Versus Reasonable Assurance**

4-25 In the realm of financial reporting and auditing, assurance services play a pivotal role in instilling confidence in the accuracy and reliability of financial information. However, within the spectrum of assurance, there exists a crucial distinction between two fundamental levels: limited assurance and reasonable assurance. This case aims to elucidate the disparities between these two levels of assurance through a hypothetical scenario involving a small business seeking financial assurance services.

Tech4all Corporation, a burgeoning startup in the technology sector, is preparing to launch its initial public offering (IPO) to attract investors and fuel its expansion plans. As part of its IPO readiness strategy, Tech4all Corporation engages you (as partner of a big 4 audit firm) services to conduct an assurance engagement on its interim financial statements. The board of Tech4all asks you to prepare a quote for both limited and reasonable assurance and explain the differences in degree of assurance, work to be carried out and fee.

a. Sketch the main differences between the two offers.

b. Suppose you are in the middle of carrying out the reasonable assurance assignment and due to unexpected signals of fraud you want to carry out more work, which of course entails more costs. The board therefore asks you to change the assignment to a limited level of assurance assignment. How are you going to respond to that? Motivate.

CASE

Champions NV[7]

Champions NV is a national soccer club playing in the top division of the territory soccer league. Its shares are listed on the Amsterdam Stock Exchange. The company has a fiscal year ending 30 June each year and the company is required to publish interim summarized financial statements each quarter. The company is preparing its financial statements in accordance with IFRS as adopted in the EU.

Your audit firm has been the auditor of Champions for six years. You are in the role of senior staff in the audit team preparing some work on behalf of the engagement manager and engagement partner. Assume on each question that you aim to convince the manager and partner based on your comprehensive and to-the-point analysis.

Governance is as follows:
- ▶ An independent supervisory board including an audit committee and a remuneration committee.
- ▶ Board of directors comprising a CEO and a CFO and CTM (chief soccer matters)

The company has the following departments:
- ▶ Technical (15 persons)– headed by CTM
- ▶ Commercial (10 persons) – headed by CEO
- ▶ Finance (5 persons) – headed by CFO
- ▶ Operations (25 persons) – headed by CFO

Champions uses two separate applications for the financial administration (off the shelf product- no source code available at Champions) versus the operations (tailor-made by an external software supplier). These systems are linked via an interface. During this fiscal year, the Champions had issues with the operations system, resulting in a one-week-offline period.

The stadium is owned by an international brewery. The rental fee is a fixed amount per year. The contract will terminate on 30 June 20X9; during 20X8/20X9 the new contract will be negotiated.

The summarized financial statements of last fiscal year are as follows:

PROFIT & LOSS ACCOUNT (amounts x € 1.000)		
	20X7/20X8	20X6/20X7
Revenues	**91.949**	**118.223**
Purchases	7.452	6.994
Wages & Salaries	52.836	55.096
Depreciation fixed assets	3.175	3.180
Other expenses	41.691	44.581
Total expenses	**105.154**	**109.851**
Operating result before transfer fees	**(13.205)**	**8.372**
Amortization transfer fees	(24.979)	(18.082)
Result from player transfers	39.361	78.616
Other	584	310
Result before tax	**1.761**	**67.016**
Corporate tax	(328)	(17.277)
Net result after tax	**1.186**	**49.461**

BALANCE SHEET (amounts x € 1.000)					
	30/6/X8	30/6/X7		30/6/X8	30/6/X7
Capitalized transfer fees	89.050	55.761	Equity	158.937	158.873
Tangible fixed assets	20.311	14.390	Long term liabilities	20.323	15.052
Financial fixed assets	46.070	14.390	Short term liabilities	93.064	72.155
Inventory	4.590	2.519			
Receivables	76.172	58.107			
Investment portfolio	23.941	23.326			
Cash & banks	12.190	64.499			
	272.324	**246.080**		**272.324**	**246.080**

Transfer fees

When contracting new players, in a number of cases transfer fees have to be paid to the soccer club the player has been playing with before joining Champions. Transfer fees are capitalized at the start and amortized over the remaining contracting period on a straight-line basis. When leaving Champions before the end of the contract, a transfer fee received is considered as realized in the profit & loss account under 'result from player transfers'. Any remaining capitalized transfer fee for this player is then deducted from this result.

Revenues

Champions has 5 regular revenue categories (with percentage of total revenues):
a. Broadcasting/television rights (25%)
b. Shirt sponsoring (10%)
c. Fan shop sales (30%)
d. Entrance fees (30%)
e. Drinks during the games (5%)

Note a) **Broadcasting/television rights**: Champions receives revenues from television rights on a yearly basis based on a contract the soccer league has with the broadcasting company. This revenue per soccer club depends on the ranking in the competition each season. On a monthly basis, Champions receives an advance payment amounting to 1/12th based on the revenue on the actual ranking last season. Each year in July after the season, the final revenue is calculated and settled for the amount not yet paid in advance.

Note c) **The fan shop sales** comprise the sale of mainly shirts, shorts etc. in the fan shop, on the website and to a wholesaler for further distribution to individual sport stores in Netherlands and abroad. All articles are entered in the tailor-made operations software as mentioned above.

Once a year in spring, Champions purchases in bulk the articles from one Chinese supplier. All articles are tagged with a bar code. Sales prices in the fan store and on the website are offered based on a pricing list authorized by the CFO. No discounts are given until the end of the playing season (in May).

▷ A contract is signed with a wholesaler, who is the reseller of the goods to individual sport stores. The contract comprises the agreed price per article, the minimum number per category of articles to be purchased by the wholesaler and a bonus incentive correlated with the number of articles sold.

▷ On a monthly basis, an integral inventory count is organized by scanning all articles individually. Any stock count differences are booked in the P&L account as 'inventory difference' under 'Purchases'.

Question A

You are in the process of planning your audit 20X8/20X9 and considering an appropriate level of materiality based on the historical figures above. Assume the budget 20X8/20X9 (finalized in May 20X8) includes a budgeted revenue of 100 million euro, total expenses of 110 million euro and net effect from transfers (realized transfer fees minus amortization) of 15 million euro, resulting in profit before tax of 5 million euro.

▶ *Consider the (overall) materiality level(s) including the rationale for the benchmark and the nominal amount.*

Question B

During a team meeting prior to your final audit, you understand that additional revenue is expected from UEFA revenues amounting to 100 million euro (budget: only 10 million euro on a yearly basis).

▶ *Reconsider your materiality level(s) as mentioned under question 1a. Which considerations do you have to reassess the materiality level set and which consequences for the audit procedures?*

4.16 NOTES

1. When the reporting framework is a compliance framework, the auditor concludes that the financial statements present fairly, in all material aspects.
2. International Audit and Assurance Standards Board 2023,International Standard on Auditing 200 (ISA 200) 'Overall Objectives of the Independent Auditor and the Conduct of an Audit in Accordance with International Standards on Auditing', para. 11 in: International Auditing and Assurance Standards Board (IAASB), 2023, *Handbook of International Quality Management, Auditing, Review, Other Assurance, and Related Services Pronouncements*, 2022 edn, Volume I, International Federation of Accountants, New York.
3. Ibid. ISA 200, para. 13(m).
4. Ibid. ISA 200, para. 5.
5. International Standard on Auditing 501 (ISA 501) 'Audit Evidence–Specific Considerations for Selected Items', para. 4–8, *Handbook of International Quality Management, Auditing Review, Other Assurance, and Related Services Pronouncements*, 2022 edn, Volume I, International. Federation of Accountants, New York.
6. International Auditing and Assurance Standards Board (IAASB), 2023, *Handbook of International Quality Management, Auditing, Review, Other Assurance, and Related Services Pronouncements*, 2022 edn, Volume II, International Federation of Accountants, New York.
7. The case Champions NV is derived from the May 25, 2019 Audit & Assurance exam of the International Executive Master of Auditing, hosted by Maastricht University/Vrije Universiteit Amsterdam, www.iema-edu.org.

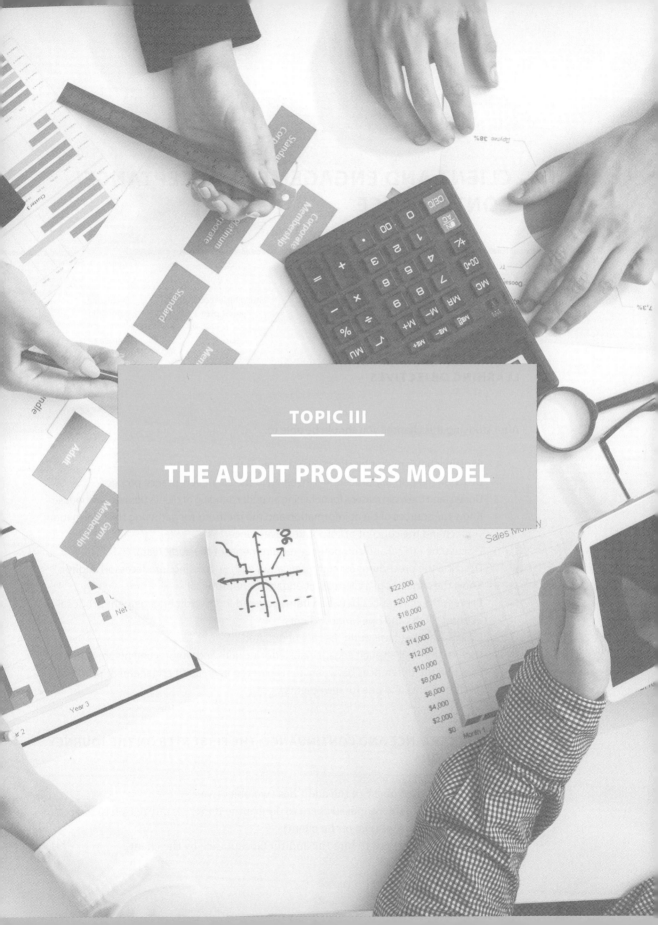

TOPIC III

THE AUDIT PROCESS MODEL

CHAPTER 5

CLIENT AND ENGAGEMENT ACCEPTANCE/ CONTINUANCE

The four phases of the audit:

Acceptance/ continuance	Understanding/ risk analysis	Building/executing audit plan	Evaluating/ completion
Phase 1	Phase 2	Phase 3	Phase 4

5.1 LEARNING OBJECTIVES

After studying this chapter, you should be able to:

1   Explain what is meant by client acceptance.
2   Describe the primary procedures involved in the client acceptance process.
3   Understand the main reasons for obtaining an understanding of client's business and industry.
4   Know the sources of client information and the methods for gathering the information.
5   Understand the concept of corporate governance.
6   Discuss the ethical and competency requirements of the audit team.
7   Describe the procedures for communicating with an existing (predecessor) auditor.
8   Know the contents of a client audit engagement proposal.
9   Express the differences between items covered in an audit engagement proposal to existing clients and one for new clients.
10 Explain on what basis audit fees are negotiated.
11 Understand what an audit engagement letter includes and why its contents are important.
12 Describe the differences between items covered in an audit engagement proposal to existing clients and one for new clients.

5.2 CLIENT ACCEPTANCE AND CONTINUANCE: THE FIRST STEP ON THE JOURNEY TO AN OPINION

The client acceptance phase of the audit has two objectives:
1   Examination of the proposed client to determine if there is any reason to reject the engagement (acceptance of the client).
2   Convincing the client to hire the auditor (acceptance by the client).

▶ GENERAL CLIENT ACCEPTANCE PROCEDURES

In general terms, the procedures towards acceptance of the client are: acquiring knowledge of the client's business; examining the audit firm's ethical requirements and technical competence; determining possible use of other professionals (including outside specialist) in the audit; communication with the predecessor auditor; preparation of client proposal; assignment of staff and the submission of the terms of the engagement in the form of an audit engagement letter. See illustration 5.1.

ILLUSTRATION 5.1	
STANDARD AUDIT PROCESS MODEL – PHASE I CLIENT ACCEPTANCE	
Objective	Determine both acceptance of a client and acceptance by a client. Decide on acquiring a new client or continuation of relationship with an existing one and the type and number of staff required.
Procedures	1　Evaluate the client's background and reasons for the audit [chapter 5.3]. 2　Determine whether the auditor is able to meet the ethical requirements regarding the client [chapter 5.5]. 3　Determine need for other professionals [chapter 5.5]. 4　Communicate with predecessor auditor [chapter 5.6]. 5　Prepare client proposal [chapter 5.7]. 6　Select staff to perform the audit. 7　Obtain an engagement letter [chapter 5.8].

An auditor must exercise care in deciding which clients are acceptable. An audit firm's legal and professional responsibilities are such that clients who lack integrity can cause serious and expensive problems. In the 1990s, auditing firms in the USA and Northern Europe became cautious about auditing financial institutions due to legal issues from audits of Lincoln Savings, Standard Chartered Bank, and BCCI. By the early 2000s, various sectors faced significant challenges: energy (Enron, Dynergy, Pacific Gas and Electric, State of California), telecommunications (WorldCom, Global Crossing, Qwest), healthcare (HealthSouth, ImClone), investment banks, hedge funds (Bear Sterns, Lehman Brothers, MF Global), retailing (K-mart, Ahold), and food products (Parmalat).

To control auditors' business risks, auditing firms sometimes refuse to accept clients in certain high-risk industries. Other reasons are the continuous pressure to enhance audit quality by standard setters, regulators and oversight bodies, forcing the increasingly risk-averse auditors away from certain clients. Lack of resources can also be a legitimate reason not to accept new clients or to discontinue audit engagements[1].

▶ AUDIT CLIENTS

The client-audit firm relationship is *not* a one-way street where the audit firm evaluates the client and then, judging the client 'acceptable', sends out an engagement letter closing the deal. The audit services market is competitive, and, as with any business, there are highly sought-after clients that every audit firm aspires to establish an auditing relationship with. Although not always the case, audit firms prepare and submit engagement proposals to many of their (potential) clients, especially the large ones.

▸ STEPS IN THE CLIENT ACCEPTANCE PROCESS

The next section in this chapter discusses the importance of obtaining a preliminary understanding of the client, to evaluate the client's background and the risks associated with accepting the engagement. There must also be an understanding of the auditors' relationship to the client to enable the auditor to consider if the ethical and professional requirements (independence, competence, etc.) typical to the specific engagement can be met. That is the second step in the client acceptance process.

The balance of the chapter concerns acceptance by the client (called 'responsible party' in assurance services terms). The audit firm must write and present to the client an engagement proposal (some auditors consider this a beauty contest). The chapter also discusses the components of a client engagement proposal for existing and new clients; and briefly discusses the International Organization for Standardization (ISO) quality control standard 9000 and how that applies to an auditing firm and its engagement services.

As discussed in section 2.11, The International Standards on Audit Firm Quality Management (ISQM 1 & 2) outline requirements for audit firms to maintain quality in their operations. ISQM 1 emphasizes the need for a quality management system covering risk assessment, client and engagement acceptance, and engagement performance. It mandates the establishment of quality objectives related to client relationships and engagements, ensuring consideration of factors like engagement nature, client integrity, firm's capability, and financial priorities.

5.3 EVALUATE THE CLIENT'S BACKGROUND

The auditor should obtain knowledge of the client's business that is sufficient to enable her to identify and understand the events, transactions, and practices that may have a significant effect on the financial statements or on the audit report. More specifically, the ISAs[2] put client acceptance in terms of identifying risk threats that may emerge in taking on clients and suggest that safeguards be put in place. The main reasons for obtaining this understanding, from the auditor's view, are (1) to evaluate the engagement risks associated with accepting the specific engagement and (2) to help the auditor in determining whether all professional and ethical requirements (including independence, competence, etc.) regarding this client can be met.

Auditors do not just obtain knowledge of the client preliminary to the engagement, during the client acceptance phase. Once the engagement has been accepted, auditors will do a more extensive search for knowledge of the client, its business and industry in the planning phase (Phase II of the audit model – see chapters 6 and 7 (ISA 300, 315, 320)).

The information obtained about the nature and circumstances of the engagement may include:[3]

 ▸ The industry of the entity for which the engagement is being undertaken and relevant regulatory factors.
 ▸ The nature of the entity, for example, its operations, organizational structure, ownership and corporate governance, its business model and how it is financed; and

▶ The nature of the underlying subject matter and the applicable criteria. For example, the underlying subject matter may include social, environmental or health and safety information; and the applicable criteria may be performance measures.

'Corporate governance' is about what the board of a company does and how it sets the values of the company, and it is to be distinguished from the day-to-day operational management of the company by full-time executives[4]. Understanding the auditee's corporate governance is key for assessing the risk of material misstatements (see chapter 6) and for effective communication with those charged with governance (see chapter 11). An engagement to provide assurance on internal control statements respectively on non-financial information, will be discussed in the text (see chapter 14 and 15). The concept of corporate governance is discussed in appendix 5.1.

Auditors may do a preliminary examination of both new and existing clients by visiting their premises, reviewing annual reports, having discussions with client's management and staff, and accessing public news and public information databases, usually via the Internet. If the client is an existing one, prior years' working papers should be reviewed. If the client is new, the auditor should consult prior auditors and increase the preliminary information search. (See illustration 5.2.)

ILLUSTRATION 5.2

PRELIMINARY INFORMATION SEARCH

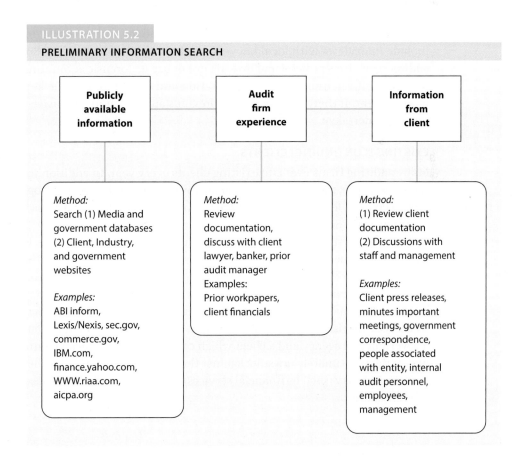

Publicly available information	Audit firm experience	Information from client
Method: Search (1) Media and government databases (2) Client, Industry, and government websites	*Method:* Review documentation, discuss with client lawyer, banker, prior audit manager	*Method:* (1) Review client documentation (2) Discussions with staff and management
Examples: ABI inform, Lexis/Nexis, sec.gov, commerce.gov, IBM.com, finance.yahoo.com, WWW.riaa.com, aicpa.org	*Examples:* Prior workpapers, client financials	*Examples:* Client press releases, minutes important meetings, government correspondence, people associated with entity, internal audit personnel, employees, management

▶ **SUBJECTS FOR DISCUSSION**

Discussions with client's management and staff are important to evaluate governance, internal controls and possible risks. These discussions might include such subjects as:

- ▶ changes in management, organizational structure, and activities of the client;
- ▶ current government regulations;
- ▶ current business developments affecting the client such as social, technical and economic factors;
- ▶ current or impending financial difficulties or accounting problems;
- ▶ susceptibility of the entity's financial statements to material misstatement due to error or fraud;
- ▶ existence of related parties;
- ▶ new or closed premises and plant facilities;
- ▶ recent or impending changes in technology, types of products or services and production or distribution methods;
- ▶ changes in the accounting system and the system of internal control.

NEW CLIENT INVESTIGATION

Before accepting a new client, an audit firm will do a thorough investigation to determine if the client is acceptable and if the auditor can meet the ethical requirements of independence, specific competence, etc.

Sources of information outside those mentioned for both new and existing clients include interviews with local lawyers, banks and other businesses. Sometimes the auditor may hire a professional investigator or use its forensic accounting department to obtain information about the reputation and background of the key members of management. If there has not been a previous auditor, more extensive investigation may be undertaken.

EXISTING (CONTINUING) CLIENTS

Many auditing firms evaluate existing clients every year. In addition to the research discussed above, the auditor will consider any previous conflicts over scope of the audit, type of opinion, fees, pending litigation between the audit firm and client, and management integrity. (See illustration 5.3.)

These factors strongly influence whether the relationship will continue. For continuing engagements, the auditor would update and re-evaluate information gathered from the prior years' working papers. The auditor should also perform procedures designed to identify significant changes that have taken place since the last audit.

The auditor may also choose not to continue conducting audits for a client because she feels excessive risk is involved. For example, there may be regulatory conflict between a governmental agency and a client which could result in financial failure of the client and perhaps ultimately lawsuits against the auditor. It may be that the auditor feels that the industry (such as financial services) offers more risk than is acceptable to the specific auditor.

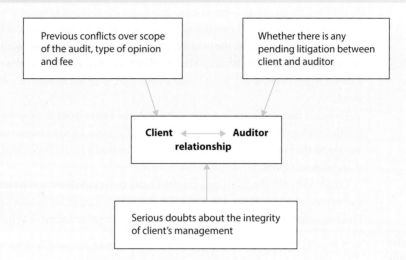

ILLUSTRATION 5.3

INFLUENCES ON THE CLIENT-AUTOR RELATIONSHIP

Previous conflicts over scope of the audit, type of opinion and fee

Whether there is any pending litigation between client and auditor

Client ←→ Auditor relationship

Serious doubts about the integrity of client's management

CONCEPT AND A COMPANY 5.1

RESONA, THE AUDITOR AND JAPAN'S BANKING INDUSTRY

Concept	An auditor must consider company and industry background before accepting an audit client.
Story	'Auditors shouldn't be allowed to act like God,' said Hideyuki Aizawa, a senior member of Japan's major political party, the LDP. 'Resona should be the first and last time this happens.' Mr Aizawa's comments came in reaction to the government's decision to inject ¥2,000 billion ($17 billion, £10.4 billion) into Resona after auditors found that Japan's fifth largest bank was badly undercapitalized (Pilling, 2003).

The Resona filing was the first-ever test of emergency assistance under the Deposit Insurance Law. Resona had already received around ¥1,000 billion ($8.5 billion) from the government in two previous rounds of fund injections (Nikkei Weekly, 2003).

Auditor Says No

Shin Nihon, one of Japan's Big Four accounting firms, in effect forced Resona to seek government help by refusing to accept the bank's estimate of how much deferred tax assets it should be allowed to include as capital. This was after co-auditor Asahi & Co refused to sign off on the bank's accounts. Shin Nihon's move stunned the Japanese business community, which had been accustomed to more lenient treatment from auditors.

Troubles at Resona

Resona Bank was created after the integration of Daiwa Bank and Asahi Bank, and began operating 3 March 2003. Neither bank wanted to merge, but both were forced to do so by the combined efforts of the Ministry of Finance and the Financial Services Agency, which were overseeing the consolidation of Japan's banking industry from 13 large lenders to five mega-lenders (Ibison, 2003).

Resona admitted that its capital-adequacy ratio (i.e. its capital divided by its assets, weighted by risk) had fallen to around 2 per cent, half the required minimum for domestic banks that do not have international operations.

Resona's Tier 1 capital comprised of 70 per cent deferred tax assets (DTAs) according to Moody's Investors Service, the credit rating company. This compares with about 40 per cent at Japan's four other largest banks – Mizuho, SMFG, MTFG and UFJ – and is enormous compared with US regulations, which limit banks to using DTAs of just 10 per cent of their capital (Ibison, 2003).

Deferred tax assets are generated through the losses from taxable bad-loan write-offs by entities such as banks. The losses can be set off against future taxable income. Since the tax burden on the bank is effectively reduced, the deferred amount is counted towards the entity's shareholders' equity.

Combined with the dual pressures of a more strict calculation of its non-performing loans and exposure to a declining stock market, the circumstances for Resona's bailout were created. Their solvency was also affected by participation in government development schemes.

Discussion Questions	▷ Assuming that another bank was in similar circumstances to Resona, what concerns would a replacement auditor have? ▷ What kind of industry risks would have been encountered by audit firms wishing to audit a Japanese bank in 2004?
References	*The Accountant*, 2003, 'Japan's Top Seven Banks Slash Deferred Tax Assets by 18 per cent', 31 December. Ibison, D., 2003, 'Unholy Japanese Alliance Ends in Tears', *Financial Times*, 19 May, p. 23. *Nikkei Weekly*, 2003, 'Resona Accepts 2 Trillion Yen Bailout', Nihon Keizai Shimbun, 19 May. Pilling, D., 2003, 'Japanese Bailout Prompts Political Backlash', *Financial Times*, 22 May.

5.4   ABILITY TO MEET ETHICAL AND SPECIFIC COMPETENCE REQUIREMENTS

Based on the evaluation obtained regarding the background of the client, the auditor should determine whether all ethical requirements [as discussed in chapter 3 'Ethics for Professional Accountants'] can be met with regard to the specific engagement. Probably the most important procedure in this step of the engagement acceptance process is verification of the auditor's independence. Given the facts and circumstances, a determination is made whether the auditor and the audit team possess the specific competence required to deal with the issues that the auditor is likely to encounter in the audit.

This audit team evaluation is also important for Step 6 in the client acceptance process – selecting staff to perform the audit.

NEW CLIENT ACCEPTANCE – PENN SQUARE BANK

Concept	Evaluation of a client and the audit firm for client acceptance.
Story	In late November 1981, without prior warning, B.P 'Beep' Jennings, CEO of Penn Square Bank, notified Harold Russell, managing partner of audit firm Arthur Young Oklahoma City, that they were no longer the auditors for Penn Square Bank. He said Peat Marwick (predecessor of KPMG) would be the new auditor for the bank's 1981 financial statements. For the years ending 31 December 1976, through 31 December 1979, Penn received unqualified (clean) opinions from Arthur Young (predecessor of Ernst & Young). In 1980, Arthur Young issued a qualified opinion on Penn Square's financial statements stating that the auditors were unable to satisfy themselves 'as to the adequacy of the reserve for possible loan losses.

Penn Square Bank – Loans to Wildcatters

Penn Square Bank, in Oklahoma City, USA, was named after a shopping mall and served small business and residents of the surrounding community until 1974 when the bank was acquired by Jennings. From that date onward, the bank expanded its deposit base by offering interest rate premiums on 'jumbo' bank certificates of deposit that carried interest rates 25 to 150 basis points above prevailing market rates.

The money deposited was loaned to the highest risk oil and gas speculators ('wildcatters'). Because of the rapid growth in their loan portfolio that doubled the bank's assets every two years from 1976 to 1982, they joint-ventured the loans with major metropolitan banks around the country. Penn Square performed all necessary administrative functions for these loans, including obtaining appraisals and engineering estimates of oil reserves.

Oil and gas prices worldwide plummeted in 1980. Many of the Penn Square-backed exploration ventures were aimed at recovering oil and gas from the deepest reservoirs. However, due to large exploration costs these were not economically feasible when the price of crude oil dropped.

Also in 1980, the bank's large profits and rapidly increasing high-risk loan volume caused an investigation by the US Office of the Comptroller of the Currency (OCC), federal bank examiners. The investigation uncovered numerous violations of banking laws by Penn Square, including insufficient liquidity, inadequate capital and poor loan documentation. In late 1980, the OCC forced the bank's directors to sign an 'administrative agreement' that required them to take remedial measures to correct these problems (Knapp, 2001).

Qualified Opinion – Management Not Pleased

Russell reported (US Congress, 1982) that there were loan considerations that led to the qualification of the 1980 audit opinion. The bank's loan documentation practices had deteriorated between 1979 and 1980. Many loans did not have current engineering reports documenting oil reserves. Other loans had engineering reports that did not include an opinion of the engineer or did not list the assumptions used in estimating the reserves. When Russell discussed these problems with client management they were 'not pleased'.

Peat Marwick Steps In

Peat Marwick officials testified (US Congress, 1982) that their firm made the standard inquiries required of predecessor auditor Arthur Young. Arthur Young responded to these inquiries by stating that its relationship with Penn Square Bank had been 'free of significant problems'. However, Arthur Young did bring to Peat Marwick's attention the qualified opinion that it had issued on Penn Square's 1980 financial statements.

Jim Blanton, the managing partner of Peat Marwick's Oklahoma City office, told the US Congress committee (US Congress, 1982) that several members of his firm were well-acquainted with Penn Square's top executives. Peat Marwick disclosed that several Oklahoma City audit firm partners had previously obtained more than $2 million in loans and a $1 million line of credit from Penn Square. To resolve a possible independence problem an agreement reached between the two parties required Penn Square to 'fully participate out' (sell) the loans and the line of credit to other banks.

The results of the Peat Marwick 1981 Penn Square audit were an unqualified (clean) opinion. On 5 July 1982, bank examiners from the Federal Deposit Insurance Corporation (FDIC) locked the doors of the Penn Square Bank. The more than $2 billion in losses suffered by Penn Square, its affiliated banks, uninsured depositors, and the FDIC insurance fund made this bank failure the most costly in US history at that time.

Discussion Questions	▶ When Penn Square Bank replaced Arthur Young in late 1980, what concerns should have been apparent to any proposed new auditor?
	▶ What independence issues were at stake for the new auditor Peat Marwick?

References	Knapp, M., 2001, 'Penn State Bank', Contemporary Auditing Real Issues & Cases, South Western College Publishing, Cincinnati, Ohio.
	US Congress, 1982, House Committee on Banking, Finance and Urban Affairs, Penn Square Bank Failure, Part 1, US Government Printing Office, Washington, DC.

▶ ETHICAL REQUIREMENTS

The members of the auditor team as well as the entire audit firm must meet the relevant ethics requirements (see chapter 3, 'Ethics for Professional Accountants'). This will require procedures to check the personal financial investments of partners and employees and the business relationships with the potential audit client. The auditor should review the non-audit services her audit firm is providing or has recently been providing to this potential client.

The firm's ability to perform the engagement in accordance with professional standards and applicable legal and regulatory requirements may be affected by:[5]

▶ The availability of appropriate resources to perform the engagement.

▶ Having access to information to perform the engagement, or to the persons who provide such information; and

▶ Whether the firm and the engagement team can fulfil their duties in relation to the relevant ethical requirements.

Audit firms may focus on the profitability of the firm from the engagement, and fees obtained for the performance of engagements have an effect on the firm's financial resources. There may be circumstances when the firm is satisfied with the fee quoted for an engagement, but it is not appropriate for the firm to accept or continue the engagement or client relationship (e.g., when the client lacks integrity and ethical values)[6]. There may be other circumstances when the fee quoted for an engagement is not sufficient given the nature and circumstances of the engagement, and it may diminish the firm's ability to perform the engagement in accordance with professional standards and applicable legal and regulatory requirements.

IESBA's Handbook of the International Code of Ethics for Professional Accountants addresses fees and other types of remuneration, including circumstances that may create a threat to compliance with the fundamental principle of professional competence and due care if the fee quoted for an engagement is too low[7]. IESBA's commentary on fees[8] suggests a self-interest threat to independence may be created if a significant part of fees is not paid before the audit report for the following year. Generally, the audit firm is expected to require payment of these fees before the audit report is issued. If fees remain unpaid after the report has been issued, safeguards need to be applied. For instance, a possible safeguard is having an additional professional accountant who does not take part in the audit engagement, provide advice, or review the work performed.

▶ LITIGATION AND INDEPENDENCE

Another influence on the continuance of the relationship is whether there is any pending litigation between client and auditor. If the client is involved in litigation with the auditor, to continue to audit the client could jeopardize independence.[9] The commencement by a client or other third party of proceedings against the auditor would compromise independence. The commencement of litigation by the auditor alleging, for example, fraud or deceit by the officers of a company, or substandard performance of the client's audit by the accountant, would also impair independence. On the other side of the legal fence, acting as an advocate on behalf of an assurance client in litigation or in resolving disputes with third parties is an 'advocacy threat' to independence.[10]

▶ SPECIFIC COMPETENCIES

The issue of specific competence needs consideration in the light of client evaluation in the previous step of the engagement process. Based on the specific circumstances of the client and its industry, the auditor should determine if the necessary expertise regarding the industry, specific GAAP issues, or certain non-audit skills are available to the audit team.

Audit team members must have a degree of technical training and proficiency required in the circumstances. When determining that the engagement has appropriate competence and capabilities, the engagement partner may take into consideration the audit team's[11].

- ▶ Understanding of, and practical experience with, audit engagements of similar nature and complexity through appropriate training and participation.
- ▶ Understanding of professional standards and applicable legal and regulatory requirements.
- ▶ Expertise in specialized areas of accounting or auditing.
- ▶ Expertise in IT used by the entity or automated tools or techniques that are to be used by the engagement team in planning and performing the audit engagement.
- ▶ Knowledge of the relevant industries in which the entity being audited operates.
- ▶ Ability to exercise professional scepticism and professional judgment.
- ▶ Understanding of the forms policies or procedures.

5.5 USE OF OTHER PROFESSIONALS IN THE AUDIT

International Standard on Auditing 600 (ISA 600) 'Special Considerations – Audits of Group Financial Statements (Including the Work of Component Auditors)' provides practical assistance to auditors in the audit of group financial statements[12]. For more information see section 13.3.

Judgments by the audit firm about whether to accept or continue a client relationship or specific engagement are appropriate are based on the firm's ability to perform the engagement in accordance with professional standards and applicable legal and regulatory requirements.[13] If the audit firm does not have the requisite competencies or would have difficulties personally examining the client (because of, for instance, an important client division located in another country) the audit firm may need the services of another audit firm or expert. The audit firm may require an outside specialist such as IT, environmental or tax specialists to do a proper audit. To promote reasonable assurance, international standards dictate certain procedures required to investigate the background of these other professionals. We discuss use of other professionals in further detail in section 13.4.

CONCEPT AND A COMPANY 5.3

SUREBEAM NOT SURE OF ITS AUDITOR

Concept	Client acceptance.

Story	SureBeam Corporation, before going out of business in 2004, made systems that irradiate food to remove harmful bacteria. Using SureBeam's system, a food company could scan a food product and break down the DNA chains of bacteria that can cause illnesses such as E. coli, Listeria Monocytogenes, Salmonella and Campylobacter (PR Newswire, 2003).

In 2003, Big Four firm Deloitte & Touche was dismissed from its role as auditor for SureBeam Corporation after expressing concern over SureBeam's compliance with generally accepted accounting principles. Before they hired Deloitte, the company discharged Andersen and KPMG in the span of less than a year. As they were publicly traded, SureBeam needed audited financial statements (Wallmeyer, 2003).

After Andersen was prohibited from auditing listed firms in 2002, SureBeam hired KPMG to carry on its audit work, but in June 2003 KPMG was fired for charging too much for the audit work. Deloitte was hired to replace KPMG (Freeman, 2004).

After a preliminary examination of SureBeam's accounting records, Deloitte questioned SureBeam's accounting treatment of the sale of equipment to an international company in 2000. Millions of dollars of revenue were recognized on the sale, but the money was ultimately not recovered. According to SureBeam's chief executive officer, John C. Arme, Deloitte 'said they could not come to a conclusion as to whether accounting for that contract was proper.' Deloitte also questioned the accounting treatment of a barter transaction whereby SureBeam recognised revenue from the exchange of equipment for services with Texas A&M University (AcccountingWeb.com, 2003).

Some of SureBeam's accounting practices have been questioned by the Securities and Exchange Commission, but no request for a change in the company's accounting methods occurred right up until they went bankrupt in 2004 (Freeman, 2004; Norris, 2003).

Discussion Question	▶ SureBeam has approached your audit firm to do their current audit. What client acceptance procedures should be carried out? What risks are involved in taking on this client?
References	AccountingWeb.com, 2003, 'Deloitte Relieved of Duties After Questioning Accounting Methods', AccountingWeb.com, 4 September. Freeman, M., 2004, 'Accounting Dispute Led to Demise of SureBeam', *San Diego Union-Tribune*, 14 January. Norris, F. 2003, 'Don't Like the Audit? Then Fire the Auditor; SureBeam Searches for Accountant No. 4', *International Herald Tribune*, 23 August, p.13. PR Newswire, 2003, 'SureBeam Corporation Appoints Peterson & Co., LLP as Independent Auditor', PR Newswire Association LLC, 3 December. Wallmeyer, A., 2003, 'SureBeam Says It Won't Meet Targets for Revenue and Profit', Wall Street Journal (Eastern edition), New York, NY, 17 September, p. A.22.

5.6 COMMUNICATING WITH THE PREDECESSOR (EXISTING) AUDITOR

If there is an existing auditor, the International Ethics Standard Board for Accountants (IESBA) Handbook of the International Code of Ethics for Professional Accountants (discussed in chapter 3) suggests that, depending on the circumstance, the new auditor communicate directly with the predecessor auditor.[14] In cases when a new auditor will replace an existing auditor, the code of ethics advises that the new, proposed auditor communicate with the existing accountant (auditor).[15] The extent to which an existing accountant can discuss the affairs of the client with the proposed accountant will depend on receipt of the client's permission and the legal or ethical requirements relating to this disclosure. The purpose of this communication is to reduce or eliminate threats by getting information on any facts or circumstances that the proposed accountant needs to be aware of before deciding whether to accept the engagement. This requirement is an important measure to prevent 'opinion shopping', or to notify the new auditor of the circumstances under which the predecessor auditor has ended the relationship with the client.

▶ REQUEST PERMISSION OF CLIENT

As stated in the Code of Ethics for Professional Accountants (the Code), a professional accountant in public practice will generally need to obtain the client's permission, preferably in writing, to initiate discussion with an existing accountant (auditor). Once the permission of the client is obtained, the existing accountant shall comply with the request. Where the existing accountant (auditor) provides information, the auditor must provide it honestly and unambiguously. If the client denies the existing auditor permission to discuss its affairs with the proposed successor auditor or limits what the existing auditor may say that fact should be disclosed to the proposed successor auditor.

When the predecessor (existing) auditor receives the communication of the newly proposed auditor, professional courtesy dictates that the existing auditor should reply, preferably in writing, advising of any professional reasons why the proposed accountant should not accept the appointment. If the proposed accountant is unable to communicate with the existing accountant, the proposed accountant shall take reasonable steps to obtain information about any possible threats by other means, such as through inquiries of third parties or background investigations of senior management or those charged with governance of the client.

▷ FIRST TIME ENGAGEMENTS

For first-time engagements, ISA 510 indicates:

> The auditor shall obtain sufficient appropriate audit evidence about whether the opening balances contain misstatements that materially affect the current period's financial statements[16].

Of course, one of the best ways to be assured that the opening balances and accounting policies are correct when the prior period financial statements were audited by another auditor, is to review the predecessor auditor's working papers. This should allow the new auditor to obtain sufficient appropriate evidence. The new auditor should also consider the professional competence and independence of the predecessor auditor. If the prior period's auditor's report was not the standard unqualified opinion, the new auditor should pay particular attention in the current period to the matter which resulted in the modification.

5.7 ACCEPTANCE BY THE CLIENT – THE ENGAGEMENT PROPOSAL

The auditor has determined that the client is acceptable from a risk and ethics perspective and has concluded that the ethical requirements regarding the specific client engagement can be met. Then, typically, significant effort will be devoted to gaining the auditee as a client, given the competitive pressure that exists in the current audit environment (see chapter 1, 'International Accounting Overview'). This requires a carefully prepared engagement proposal.

Aspects of the procedures for the engagement proposal may be found in ISA 210 'Agreeing the Terms of Audit Engagements'.[17] The auditor and the client should have a mutual understanding of the nature of the audit services to be performed, the timing of those services, the expected fees, audit team, audit approach, audit quality, use of client's internal auditors, and the transition needs.

References to the quality aspects of the client proposal may be found in ISO 9001,[18] which suggests that the auditing firm should define and document its policy and objectives for, and commitment to, quality. The auditor should ensure that this policy is understood, implemented, and maintained at all levels in the organisation.

There are two basic types of audit engagement proposals: those to continuing clients and those for new clients.

▷ CONTINUING CLIENT AUDIT PROPOSAL

The continuing client proposal will differ between firms, but generally it discusses the following:

- ▷ a review of how the auditing firm can add value, both to the company in general and to those directly responsible for the engagement of the auditor, for example the Audit Committee;
- ▷ plans for further improvement in value added including discussion of present regulatory trends, audit scope, and any recent changes in the company that may affect the audit;

- a description of the audit team and any changes in the audit team from the previous year;
- a detailed fee proposal.

► A REVIEW OF HOW THE AUDITING FIRM CAN ADD VALUE

The introductory part of the client proposal is a discussion of how the proposing firm can benefit (add value to) the client firm. There is a discussion of the focus of the firm, its management philosophy, and quality control policies. The relationship with the client's internal audit department and accounting department may be discussed.

This section on plans for further improvement in value added might identify the client's requirements and discuss how the audit firm meets these requirements. The audit scope and materiality limits may also be discussed. Reliance on audit regulatory requirements – local, national and international – should be discussed. The extent of reliance on the client's internal audit staff should be spelt out. Finally, it is important to review any changes in client company management, new projects undertaken, and the general regulatory environment. Especially important are those changes that affect the audit.

► AUDIT TEAM

An important part of the proposal is a description of members of the audit team and summary of their work experience. Special emphasis may be placed on the members of the team returning from previous engagements. Selecting the audit team is Step 6 in the client acceptance process (see illustration 5.1).

► FEE PROPOSAL

The detailed description of the proposed fee is traditionally a separate part of the proposal, presented as a separate document. The fee proposal may involve several levels of detail or a few depending on type. The core audit requires the most time and detail. It will show costs for operation audits including, perhaps, audits of subsidiaries and quarterly audits. Less level of detail would be required for statutory audits and potential future developments.

► NEW CLIENT AUDIT PROPOSAL

A proposal to audit a new client is very important to audit firms because new clients are the primary growth engine for firms. Obtaining more prestigious clients is the desire of most firms. A proposal to a large, solid client may be very complex, requiring many hours of staff time to prepare, especially if it is a competitive situation. A sample table of contents for a new client proposal is shown in illustration 5.4.

The executive summary gives a brief summary of the proposal with special emphasis on client expectation, audit approach, firm selling points and coordination of the audit with staff internal auditors.

The general proposal may begin with a description of client business sectors, technology, financial strengths and divisions. The client's objectives as the basis of the audit strategy[19] could be outlined. It may point out audit requirements relating to securities exchange, environmental, governmental and other regulations, including items in the company's policies that go beyond existing statutory requirements.

ILLUSTRATION 5.4

SAMPLE TABLE OF CONTENTS OF NEW CLIENT PROPOSAL

ABC Company Engagement Proposal

▶ Executive summary
▶ ABC Company business and audit expectations
▶ Strengths of Big One, LLP
▶ The audit team
▶ The audit approach
▶ ABC Company internal auditors
▶ ABC Company transition needs and management
▶ After service monitoring
▶ Fee details
▶ Appendix

Big One, LLP CPAs

Strengths of the audit firm may explore client service attitudes, technical competency, experience, desire to exceed expectations, and advice and assistance. This section might also emphasise report quality, continuity of audit teams, worldwide service, cost effectiveness of audits, and audit firm's quality standards.

The audit team section includes a description of members of the team and a summary of their work experience. This section might also detail how the team will communicate with management, the role of the team and supervisors, and team meetings and communications. Choosing the audit team is generally done well ahead of writing the client proposal.

The audit approach is an important section because it allows a discussion of how the audit is tailored to this one, specific client. The section could explain audit emphasis or concentration on specific audit risks, the use of information technology on the audit, the involvement of other auditors or experts, and the number of locations or components reviewed. The section could address terms of the engagement, any statutory responsibilities, and internal control and client systems. The nature and timing of reports or other communications (e.g., audit opinion, review, special procedures, governmental reporting, oral and written reports to the audit committee) expected under the engagement is also important.

The client's internal auditors' work[20] must be relied upon to a certain extent in all audits. However, the external auditor has sole responsibility for the audit opinion expressed, and that responsibility is not reduced by the external auditor's use of the work of the internal auditors. This section may include reference to the internal auditors' work and production, supplier selection, and supplier failure. Other issues explored may include safeguarding of assets, internal controls, management information systems, systems security, adherence to corporate policy, due diligence reviews, and opportunities for improvement.

A discussion of the transition needs of the company in terms of accommodating the new auditor may be very important in convincing a new client to switch auditors. This section of the proposal might include a transition schedule detailing meetings with management and former auditors. Other areas addressed might include permanent file documentation, understanding of internal control, and benefits of the change.

After the audit is complete there are still opportunities for the auditor to offer service to the client. These after-service monitoring activities may include monitoring the audit performance, audit firm self-evaluation (usually at closing meetings), questionnaires for management to evaluate the audit performance, and written summaries of what was done in the audit (i.e. audit and satisfaction survey) can be given to the client.

An appendix might include further information about the audit team, an outline of the audit plan and a list of representative publications. The outline of the audit plan usually shows the degree of audit time required for fieldwork, confirmation of controls, and validation of both balances and transactions. In particular, the outline of the audit plan will provide an overview of the audit risks, and the auditor's suggested response to those risks, in the form of detailed audit procedures.

▷ ESTABLISHING AND NEGOTIATING AUDIT FEES

According to the IESBA International Code of Ethics,[21] when entering into negotiations regarding professional services, a professional accountant in public practice may quote whatever fee is deemed appropriate. Professional fees should be a fair reflection of the value of the professional services performed for the client, taking into account: the skill and knowledge required, the level of training and experience of the persons engaged in performing the professional services, the time required, and the degree of responsibility that performing those services entails. These factors can be influenced by the legal, social and economic conditions of each country.

Sometimes an auditing firm charges a lower fee when a client is first signed up. This is called 'low balling'. The fact that one professional accountant in public practice may quote a fee lower than another is not in itself unethical. Nevertheless, there may be threats to compliance with the fundamental principles arising from the level of fees quoted. For example, a self-interest threat to professional competence and due care is created if the fee quoted is so low that it may be difficult to perform the engagement in accordance with applicable technical and professional standards for that price.[22]

▷ CONTINGENT FEES[23]

A contingent (or contingency) fee is an arrangement whereby no fee will be charged unless a specified finding or result is obtained, or when the fee is otherwise contingent on the findings or results of these services. Fees charged on a percentage or similar basis are regarded as a contingent fee. Contingent fees are widely used for certain types of non-assurance engagements. They may, however, create threats to compliance with the fundamental principles in certain circumstances. They may create a self-interest threat to objectivity. The existence and significance of such threats will depend on factors including: the nature of the engagement, range of possible fee amounts, the basis for determining the fee, and whether the outcome will be reviewed by an independent third party. If the threats are significant, safeguards are applied such as: an advance written agreement with the client as to the basis of remuneration. Some countries do not allow auditors to charge contingent fees. (They are prohibited by the US Securities and Exchange Commission, for example).

▶ **COMMISSIONS AND REFERRAL FEES**

In certain circumstances, an auditor in public practice may receive a referral fee or commission relating to a client. For example, when the auditor does not provide the specific service required, a fee may be received for referring a continuing client to another professional accountant in public practice or other expert. An auditor in public practice may receive a commission from a third party (for example, a software vendor) in connection with the sale of goods or services to a client. However, accepting such a referral fee or commission creates a self-interest threat to objectivity and professional competence and due care. If the threat is significant, safeguards should be applied to eliminate the threat or reduce it to an acceptable level. Examples of safeguards include: disclosing to the client any arrangements to pay or receive referral fees or obtaining advance agreement from the client for commission arrangements.

A professional accountant in public practice may also pay a referral fee to obtain a client, for example where the client continues as a client of another professional accountant in public practice but requires specialist services not offered by the existing accountant. The payment of such a referral fee also creates a self-interest threat to objectivity and professional competence and due care.

5.8 **THE AUDIT ENGAGEMENT LETTER**

It is in the interests of both client and auditor that the auditor sends an engagement letter.[24] Preferably, before the commencement of the engagement, to help in avoiding misunderstandings. An engagement letter is an agreement between the accounting firm and the client for the conduct of the audit and related services. An auditor's engagement letter documents and confirms her acceptance of the appointment, the objective and scope of the audit, the extent of auditor responsibilities to the client, and the form of any reports.

The engagement letter may affect legal responsibilities to the client. In litigation, the auditor may use an engagement letter as a contract stating its scope, responsibilities, and limitations. The letter describes the auditor's purpose, that the audit entails study of internal control, the time schedule of the engagement, and fees.

▶ **CONTENTS OF THE ENGAGEMENT LETTER**

The form and content of the audit engagement letter may vary for each client, but they should be recorded in an audit engagement letter or other suitable form of written agreement and should include:[25]

- ▶ The objective of the audit of financial information.
- ▶ The responsibilities of the auditor.
- ▶ Management's responsibility.
- ▶ The applicable financial reporting framework.
- ▶ Reference to the expected form and content of any reports issued by the auditor and a statement that a report may differ from its expected form and content.

The auditor may also wish to include in the letter:[26]

▶ Elaboration of the scope of the audit, including reference to applicable legislation, regulations, ISAs, and ethical and other pronouncements of professional bodies to which the auditor adheres.[27]

▶ The form of any other communication of results of the audit engagement.

▶ The fact that because of the test nature and other inherent limitations of an audit, together with the inherent limitations of any system of internal control, there is an unavoidable risk that even some material misstatement may remain undiscovered.

▶ Arrangements regarding the planning and performance of the audit, including the composition of the audit team.

▶ The expectation that management will provide written representations.[28] (See ISA 580 'Written Representations'.)

▶ The agreement of management to make available to the auditor draft financial statements and any accompanying other information in time to allow the auditor to complete the audit in accordance with the proposed timetable.

▶ The agreement of management to inform the auditor of facts that may affect the financial statements, of which management may become aware during the period from the date of the auditor's report to the date the financial statements are issued.

▶ A request for the client to confirm the terms of the engagement by acknowledging receipt of the engagement letter.

▶ The basis on which fees are computed and any billing arrangements.

When relevant, the following points could also be made:

▶ Arrangements concerning the involvement of other auditors and experts in some aspects of the audit.

▶ Arrangements concerning the involvement of internal auditors and other client staff.

▶ Arrangements to be made with the predecessor auditor, if any, in the case of an initial audit.

▶ Any restriction of the auditor's liability.

▶ A reference to any further agreements between the auditor and the client.

▶ Any obligations to provide audit working papers to other parties.

On recurring audits, the auditor may decide not to send a new engagement letter each year. However, she should consider sending a letter in any of the following circumstances:

▶ where there is an indication that the client misunderstands the objective and scope of the audit;

▶ where the terms of the engagement are revised;

▶ where there has been a recent change in management;

▶ where the size or nature of the business has changed; and

▶ where there are legal requirements that an engagement letter be written.

If the auditor reviews both the parent and a subsidiary, branch or division of the company, she may consider sending a separate engagement letter to that component business. The auditor should consider who appoints the auditor of the component, legal requirements, degree of parent ownership and the extent of any work performed by the auditors.

Illustration 5.5 shows a sample engagement letter[29].

▶ **FINANCIAL REPORTING FRAMEWORK**

The form of opinion expressed by the auditor will depend upon the applicable financial reporting framework[30] and any applicable law or regulation. The auditor may also have certain other communication and reporting responsibilities to users, management, those charged with governance, or parties outside the entity based on the audit. These may be established by the ISAs or by applicable law or regulation[31]. ISA 200 describes how the financial reporting frameworks are acceptable for general purpose financial statements[32].

5.9 CLIENT ACCEPTANCE AN EXAMPLE

For examples of how the client acceptance process works we introduce the audit firm Isle & Oblivion, CAs. (I&O). I&O have a new client, Titan Tec, Inc. Isle & Oblivion, CAs, are approached by Titan Tec, Inc., to bid on undertaking an audit. They wish to change from their current auditor, Starkweather and Gendu, CPAs.

Titan Tec is a data service firm that collects social media and internet data internationally and sells it to corporate customers. They have been in operation since May 2010 and have a profitable business. They offer data to several international companies including General Motor's subsidiary GMC Middle East and Unilever Dove division. Ownership is privately held with shares controlled by several private equity and sovereign wealth funds. Titan Tec has hired professional, experienced management from the beginning. Their headquarters is in Silverstrand, California. They have a subsidiary in Edinburgh, U.K. Titan Tec have had the same auditors, Starkweather and Gendu, who do quarterly and annual financial statement audits, for the last five years.

EVALUATE THE NEW CLIENT'S BACKGROUND AND REASONS FOR THE AUDIT

Suggested procedures for evaluating prospective clients include (1) obtaining financial statements, (2) performing third-party inquiries, (3) communicating with predecessor auditors, (4) evaluating independence issues, and (5) reviewing pertinent regulatory rules.

Isle & Oblivion obtain Titan Tec financial statements, board of director minutes, tax returns and government filings. An examination indicates financial statements and accounting appear conservative and follows US GAAP. The company has just this year become profitable as they have attracted more customers because their data analysis has become more accepted. Their present auditor will not bid on the contract and suggested the need for a new auditor with both USA and UK experience.

The engagement Partner of I&O contacts the prior auditor, Starkweather and Gendu, Titan Tec's service providers, attorneys, and representatives of one private equity firm and one sovereign fund. The response is positive and reinforces what the Engagement Partner had already discovered – Titan Tec is well funded, management is competent, and their data gathering techniques are efficient and proprietary. The company is well respected in the industry. Communications with the prior auditor reaffirm that the present auditor is not bidding for the audit. The prior auditor had a good relationship with Titan Tec.

I&O employees have no financial interests in Titan Tec nor are there issues with related parties between I&O and Titan Tec. They are independent of their client. I&O auditors are familiar with US laws for data analysis firms and I&O has an attorney on staff who has worked with several US data analysis firms.

On the negative side, data acquisition and resale are subject to a great deal of risk because technology is changing rapidly, laws in UK and USA are very different as regards the industry, and because of privacy issues, Titan Tec may face litigation obstacles. The audit will be costly because first client audits require a good deal of transition issues including learning the accounting system, controls and personnel which is not the custom to charge for. Also, financial reporting is complicated by the necessity of reporting to each of private equity and sovereign wealth funds.

Despite the low expectations for profit from this audit, the engagement partner believes that this is a good company to work for and will eventually be very profitable. The company can afford the audit services and will add status to I&O's audit portfolio. After consulting with the senior partners, the engagement partner produces a client proposal to perform the audit.

NEW CLIENT PROPOSAL

ISA 210 'Agreeing the Terms of Audit Engagements' suggests the auditor and the client should have a mutual understanding of the nature of the audit services to be performed, the timing of those services, the expected fees, audit team, audit approach, audit quality, use of client's internal auditors, and the transition needs.

I&O uses the following 'new client proposal' format.

Executive Summary: The New Client Proposal begins with a summary of the proposal. It starts with a description of the online data analysis industry. It next describes Titan Tec's financial strengths such as its strong equity position and the UK and USA divisions. The Titan Tec's objectives of providing current audited financials to their equity supplier is the basis of the I&O audit. Audit requirements are providing a financial basis for state and federal income tax, preparing special reports to equity firms, all required reports that go beyond existing statutory requirements. Titan Tec reports to all their private equity and sovereign wealth funds – some are special reports for that fund only – in addition to government agencies. The Executive Summary highlights that I&O is an excellent choice for auditor due to I&O's strengths, staff expertise, global experience, and deep knowledge of Titan Tec's sector.

Strengths of the audit firm may explore I&O's competency, experience in the data industry, projecting a desire to exceed expectations. The proposal lists some impactful advice and assistance they have provided other companies. This section also emphasizes report quality, the low turnover and depth of knowledge held by their audit teams, their worldwide service experience and the audit firm's adherence to quality management standards.

The audit team section includes a description of members of the team and a summary of their work experience. This section details that the engagement partner will be the main contact for management. The audit team will be responsible for specified sections of the audit plan and supervisors will coordinate. The team will meet at least once weekly, and any issues will be communicated to management.

The audit approach explains audit emphasis will be on assets and equity accounts in view of the equity funds support. I&O have propriety software specifically for the data collection industry, which it will use. Other auditors or experts may be called as required, but it is expected that I&O has the expertise in house. I&O will review both company locations. The terms of the engagement are expected in field time of one month plus audit completion procedures lasting three weeks. The audit opinion should be issued in 2 ½ months in writing to the audit committee and special reporting should add another two weeks.

The internal auditors' work at Titan Tec must be relied upon even though I&O has sole responsibility for the audit opinion. This section states that the internal auditors' work will be reviewed, especially regarding production, supplier selection, and supplier failure. As the internal audit department pays attention to safeguarding of assets, internal controls, management information systems, systems security, adherence to corporate policy, due diligence reviews, I&O will also review these activities and offer opportunities for improvement.

The transition needs of Titan Tec are to explain accounting systems and personnel to the new auditor, I&O. This can be expensive if all the hours expended by I&O to bring them up to date are charged. I&O will outline a transition schedule detailing meetings with management and former auditors.

After-service monitoring: I&O will monitor the audit performance and meet at audit closing for an audit firm self-evaluation. I&O provides questionnaires for management to evaluate the audit performance, and written summaries of what was done in the audit will be given to the Titan Tec.

An *appendix* might include detailed resumes of the audit team, an outline of the audit plan and a list of representative publications. The outline of the audit plan shows the degree of audit time required for fieldwork, confirmation of controls, and validation of both balances and transactions. The outline of the audit plan will provide an overview of the audit risks, and the I&O's suggested response to those risks in the form of detailed audit procedures.

Professional fees should be a fair reflection of the value of the professional services performed for the client, taking into account: the skill and knowledge required, the level of training and experience of the persons engaged in performing the professional services, the time required, and the degree of responsibility that performing those services entails. The engagement partner has estimated the time and personnel required to do the audit. The partner gives the rate per person depending on position (staff are less than senior staff who are billed at less than supervisors, etc.). After adding it all up, the partner reduces the amount by a discount on the cost of ordinary transition tasks like familiarizing the new auditor with Titan Tec personnel and accounting systems.

ENGAGEMENT LETTER

Titan Tec accepts Isle & Oblivion's offer and decides to retain them. The engagement partner immediately puts together an engagement letter. An engagement letter is the agreement between the accounting firm and client for the audit and related services. Isle & Oblivion's engagement letter documents and confirms I&O's acceptance of the appointment, the objective and scope of the audit, the extent of auditor responsibilities to Titian Tech, and the form of any reports. See illustration 5.5.

ILLUSTRATION 5.5

ISLE & OBLIVION AUDIT ENGAGEMENT LETTER

Audit Committee of Board of Directors Titian Tec, Inc.:

You have requested that we audit the financial statements of Titan Tec, which comprise the balance sheet as at 31 December 20X1, and the income statement, statement of changes in equity and cash flow statement for the year then ended, and a summary of significant accounting policies and other explanatory information. We are pleased to confirm our acceptance and our understanding of this audit engagement by means of this letter. Our audit will be conducted with the objective of our expressing an opinion on the financial statements.

We will conduct our audit in accordance with International Standards on Auditing (ISAs) and International Standards on Quality Management (ISQM). Those standards require that we comply with ethical requirements and plan and perform the audit to obtain reasonable assurance about whether the financial statements are free from material misstatement. An audit involves performing procedures to obtain audit evidence about the amounts and disclosures in the financial statements. The procedures selected depend on the auditor's judgement, including the assessment of the risks of material misstatement of the financial statements, whether due to fraud or error. An audit also includes evaluating the appropriateness of accounting policies used and the reasonableness of accounting estimates made by management, as well as evaluating the overall presentation of the financial statements.

Because of the inherent limitations of an audit, together with the inherent limitations of internal control, there is an unavoidable risk that some material misstatements may not be detected, even though the audit is properly planned and performed in accordance with ISAs.

In making our risk assessments, we consider internal control relevant to the entity's preparation of the financial statements in order to design audit procedures that are appropriate in the circumstances, but not for the purpose of expressing an opinion on the effectiveness of the entity's internal control. However, we will communicate to you in writing concerning any significant deficiencies in internal control relevant to the audit of the financial statements that we have identified during the audit.

Our audit will be conducted on the basis that the audit committee and Board of Directors acknowledge and understand that they have responsibility:

A. For the preparation and fair presentation of the financial statements in accordance with International Financial Reporting Standards;

B. For such internal control as management determines is necessary to enable the preparation of financial statements that are free from material misstatement, whether due to fraud or error; and

C. To provide us with:

(i) Access to all information of which [management] is aware that is relevant to the preparation of the financial statements such as records, documentation and other matters;

(ii) Additional information that we may request from [management] for the purpose of the audit; and

(iii Unrestricted access to persons within the entity from whom we determine it necessary to obtain audit evidence.

As part of our audit process, we will request from management written confirmation concerning representations made to us in connection with the audit.

We look forward to full cooperation from your staff during our audit.

We understand that reports of our findings require special formats for equity investors.

The form and content of our report may need to be amended in the light of our audit findings.

Please sign and return the attached copy of this letter to indicate your acknowledgement of, and agreement with, the arrangements for our audit of the financial statements including our respective responsibilities.

Isle & Oblivion
(Signed by partner)

Acknowledged and agreed on behalf of Titan Tec by
(Signed)

5.10 SUMMARY

The Client Acceptance phase of the audit has two objectives: 1. Examination of the proposed client to determine if there is any reason to reject the engagement (acceptance of the client) and 2. Convincing the client to hire the auditor (acceptance by the client).

Components of acceptance of the client are: acquiring knowledge of the client's business; examination of the audit firm's ethical requirements and technical competence; possible use of other professionals (including outside specialists) in the audit; communication with the predecessor auditor; preparation of client proposal; assignment of staff; and the submission of the terms of the engagement in the form of an audit engagement letter.

The auditor should obtain knowledge of the client's business that is sufficient to enable her to identify and understand the events, transactions and practices that may have a significant effect on the financial statements or on the audit report. More specifically, the ISAs put client acceptance in terms of identifying threats that may emerge in taking on clients and suggest that safeguards be put in place. There must also be an understanding of the auditors' relationship to the client to enable the auditor to evaluate risks and consider if the ethical and professional requirements (independence, competence, etc.) typical to that specific engagement can be met.

The information obtained about the nature and circumstances of the engagement may include: the industry of the entity including relevant regulatory factors; the nature of the entity, for example, its operations and corporate governance, how it is financed; and the nature of the underlying subject matter and the applicable criteria. For example, the underlying subject matter may include social, environmental or health and safety information; and the applicable criteria may be performance measures.

'Corporate governance' is about what the board of a company does and how it sets the values of the company, and it is to be distinguished from the day-to-day operational management of the company by full-time executives. Discussions with client's management and staff are important to evaluate governance, internal controls and possible risks. These discussions might include such subjects as: changes in management, organizational structure, government regulations, financial difficulties, accounting problems, etc.

Based on the evaluation obtained regarding the client's background, the auditor should determine if all ethical requirements can be met regarding the specific engagement. Probably the most important procedure in this step of the engagement acceptance process is verification of the auditor's independence.

IESBA's Handbook of the International Code of Ethics for Professional Accountants addresses fees and other types of remuneration, including circumstances that may create a threat to compliance with the fundamental principle of professional competence and due care if the fee quoted for an engagement is too low. IESBA's commentary on fees suggests a self-interest threat to independence may be created if a significant part of fees is not paid before the audit report for the following year.

Another influence on the continuance of the relationship is whether there is any pending litigation between client and auditor. If the client is involved in litigation with the auditor, to continue to audit the client could jeopardize independence. The commencement by a client or other third party of proceedings against the auditor would compromise independence. On the other side of the legal fence, acting as an advocate on behalf of an assurance client in litigation or in resolving disputes with third parties is an 'advocacy threat' to independence.

Judgments by the audit firm about whether to accept or continue a client relationship or specific engagement are based on the firm's ability to perform the engagement. If the audit firm does not have the required competencies, the audit firm may need the services of another audit firm ('a component auditor') or expert. The audit firm may require an outside specialist such as IT, environmental or tax specialists to do a proper audit. If the auditor uses a component auditor, she becomes the 'group auditor'. The group auditor is responsible for expressing an audit opinion on whether the group financial statements give a true and fair view (or are presented fairly, in all material respects) in accordance with the applicable financial reporting framework.

If there is an existing auditor, the IESBA Code of Ethics for Professional Accountants suggests that, depending on the circumstance, the new auditor communicate directly with the predecessor auditor. The extent to which an existing accountant can discuss the affairs of the client with the proposed accountant will depend on receipt of the client's permission and the legal or ethical requirements relating to this disclosure.

The auditor has determined that the client is acceptable from a risk and ethics perspective and has concluded that the ethical requirements regarding the specific client engagement can be met. Then, typically, significant effort will be devoted to gaining the auditee as a client, given the competitive pressure that exists in the current audit environment. This requires a carefully prepared engagement proposal. The auditor and the client should have a mutual understanding of the nature of the audit services to be performed, the timing of those services, the expected fees, audit team, audit approach, audit quality, use of client's internal auditors, and the transition needs.

The continuing client proposal will differ between firms, but generally it discusses the following:

▶ a review of how the auditing firm can add value, both to the company in general and to those directly responsible for the engagement of the auditor, for example the Audit Committee;

▶ plans for further improvement in value added including discussion of present regulatory trends, audit scope, and any recent changes in the company that may affect the audit;

▶ a description of the audit team and any changes in the audit team from the previous year;

▶ a detailed fee proposal.

According to the IESBA International Code of Ethics, when entering into negotiations regarding professional services, a professional accountant in public practice may quote whatever fee is deemed appropriate. Professional fees should be a fair reflection of the value of the professional services performed for the client, taking into account: the skill and knowledge required, the level of training and experience of the persons engaged in performing the professional services, the time required, and the degree of responsibility that performing those services entails. These factors can be influenced by the legal, social and economic conditions of each country.

It is in the interests of both client and auditor that the auditor sends an engagement letter preferably, before the commencement of the engagement, to help in avoiding misunderstandings. An engagement letter is an agreement between the accounting firm and the client for the conduct of the audit and related services. An auditor's engagement letter documents and confirms her acceptance of the appointment, the objective and scope of the audit, the extent of auditor responsibilities to the client, and the form of any reports.

APPENDIX 5.1   THE CONCEPT OF CORPORATE GOVERNANCE

Corporate governance has been defined in many different ways by many different authors in many different countries. All aspects of corporate governance are subject to discussion in many parts of society, in both the private and the public sector. An audit firm system of quality management must also address governance and leadership[33].

We can liken 'governance' to a game of darts[34]. The board of directors sets the mission, vision, objectives and strategy of the entity. (These are like the target in the game of darts.) Governance deals with managing as a key responsibility of the board. (Managing includes coordination and skill required to hit the bull's eye of the target.) It is also the board's responsibility to design and monitor controls that reasonably assure that objectives are met (the darts player should ensure a good night's rest, make sure that all windows are closed and that the audience is quiet). The third element of governance is supervision. Independent supervision of management performance and remuneration is especially crucial (the umpire should supervise the darts game as crossing the line with your foot is not permitted).

We all know that conflicts of interest between management and stakeholders do exist on a day-to-day basis and can result in bankruptcies or major frauds. These potential conflicts of interests are one of the major reasons of incorporating monitoring by non-executive board members as well as introducing external (stock exchange or banking) oversight and external auditors as important gatekeepers. Governance also includes transparency[35] to all stakeholders that can be recognised (principles and rules of the darts match should be disclosed).

According to the UK Institute of Chartered Accountants (ICAEW), corporate governance is the system by which companies are directed and controlled. Boards of directors are responsible for the governance of their companies. The shareholders' role in governance is to appoint the directors and the auditors and to satisfy themselves that an appropriate governance structure is in place.

The responsibilities of the board include setting the company's strategic aims, providing the leadership to put them into effect, supervising the management of the business and reporting to shareholders on their stewardship.

Corporate governance is therefore about what the board of a company does and how it sets the values of the company, and it is to be distinguished from the day-to-day operational management of the company by full-time executives[36].

CONCEPT AND A COMPANY 5.4	
LI & FUNG THIRD GENERATION CORPORATE GOVERNANCE	
Concept	**'The techniques are modern, but the culture is still Confucian,' Victor Fung, Chairman (*Economist*, 2000).**
Story	A 2001 study of 495 companies by CLSA Emerging Markets found a strong link between good corporate governance, earnings and stock values. According to the study, the correlation between good corporate governance and share performance for the largest companies is 'a near perfect fit'. In that study, Li & Fung were rated as one of the top companies (Day, 2001). A corporate governance poll conducted by *Euromoney* magazine rated Li & Fung fourth highest globally in corporate governance and second highest in Asia (*Euromoney*, 2003).

Li & Fung, a family-owned company founded in 1906 during the Ching Dynasty, acted as a trader – basically a broker, charging a fee to put buyers and sellers together. As of 2016, apparel makes up around two-thirds of the business, with furniture and home furnishings, beauty and personal care products, fashion accessories and general merchandising, such as seasonal gifts, constituting the rest. ('At a glance – Li & Fung Limited' 2017.)

When they decided to make a public stock offering on the Hong Kong Stock Exchange in 1973, they had already begun changing their governance. William Fung, managing director of the company put it this way, 'We typify the transition from a first-generation entrepreneurial firm to a company that is being made more professional to compete with Japan and the multinationals' (Kraar, 1994).

In 1989, to pay relatives who wanted to cash out, William Fung and his elder brother Victor, who is chairman of both the family company and Prudential Asia, arranged a leveraged buy-out (LBO) with bank financing. After cleaning up the privatized company and selling off fringe businesses like chartered boats, the brothers took it public again in 1992 (Kraar, 1994).

At Li & Fung, the Harvard-trained management has replaced family members in the company with professional managers, imported performance-related pay and instituted an open, western-style management regime. It accepts the need for stakeholding and transparent governance (Caulkin, 1996). Victor Fung explains, 'You can run a large empire with very few people making few decisions. Now you need a large number of small decisions' (*Economist*, 2000).

Li & Fung represent good corporate governance in several ways: leadership in outsourcing to customize customer products, leadership in employee management and fiscal controls, and encouraging best practices among its suppliers.

Distributed Manufacturing around the Customer's Needs

Li & Fung performs the high-value-added tasks such as design and quality control in Hong Kong, and outsources the lower-value-added tasks to the best possible locations around the world. For example, to produce a garment the company might buy yarn from Korea, have it woven and dyed in Taiwan, then shipped to Thailand for final assembly, using zippers from Japan. For every order, the goal is to customize the product to meet the customer's specific needs. They call this supply chain outsourcing 'distributed manufacturing' (Magretta, 1998).

Li & Fung is uniquely organized around the customer. They are divided into divisions and each division is structured around an individual customer or a group of customers with similar needs. Consider, for example, the Gymboree division where everyone is focused solely on meeting Gymboree's needs. On every desk is a computer with direct software links to Gymboree. The staff is organized into specialized teams in such areas as technical support, merchandising, raw material purchasing, quality assurance and shipping (Magretta, 1998).

People Management and Fiscal Controls

For the creative parts of the business, Li & Fung gives people considerable operating freedom. Substantial financial incentives tied directly to the unit's bottom line motivate the division leaders. There's no cap on bonuses. On the other hand, when it comes to financial controls and operating procedures, Li & Fung does not want creativity or entrepreneurial behavior. In these areas, Li & Fung centralizes and manages tightly. They have a fully computerized operating system for executing and tracking orders, and everyone in the company uses the system (Magretta, 1998).

Since 1993, Li & Fung have changed from a Hong Kong-based Chinese company that was 99.5 per cent Chinese into a truly regional multinational with a workforce from at least 30 countries. Victor Fung says, 'We are proud of our cultural heritage. But we don't want it to be an impediment to growth, and we want to make people comfortable that culturally we have a very open architecture' (Magretta, 1998).

Best Practices at Suppliers

Wherever Li & Fung operates, it follows local rules and best practices. It makes sure its suppliers are doing the right thing when it comes to issues such as child labor, environmental protection and country-of-origin regulations. If it finds factories that don't comply, it will not work with them. This generally does not happen because of the company's long relationship with the suppliers (Magretta, 1998).

Li & Fung, in the course of monitoring its supplier network, constantly compares the performance of hundreds of different companies. It then shares the information with all of them, giving them a detailed understanding of their performance gaps, ideas for addressing them, and strong incentives for taking action. Benchmarking, rather than being an occasional event, is an intrinsic part of process management (Hagel, 2002).

Discussion Questions	▶ How might Li & Fung's reputation for good corporate governance impact its on-going business?
	▶ As Li & Fung's auditor, which areas of the business would require the greatest test of controls?
	▶ Which are the most significant substantive tests?

References	'At a glance – Li & Fung Limited'. 2017. *Li & Fung Limited*. Retrieved 13 February 2017.
	Caulkin, S., 1996, 'Chinese walls', *Management Today*, London, September, p. 62.
	Day, P., 2001, 'Corporate Governance Can Be Strong Indicator of Stock Performance within Emerging Markets', *Wall Street Journal*, New York, 1 May, p. C14.
	Economist, 2000, 'The End of Tycoons', 29 April, Vol. 355, Issue 8168, p. 67.
	Euromoney, 2003, 'Good Practice Boosts Performance', September, Vol. 34, Issue 412, p. 222.
	Hagel III, J., 2002, 'Leveraged Growth: Expanding Sales without Sacrificing Profits', *Harvard Business Review*, October, Vol. 80, Issue 10, p. 68.
	Kraar, L., 1994, 'The Overseas Chinese', *Fortune*, New York, 31 October, Vol. 130, Issue 9, p. 91.
	Magretta, J., 1998, 'Fast, Global, and Entrepreneurial: Supply Chain Management, Hong Kong Style. An interview with Victor Fung', *Harvard Business Review*, September/October, Vol. 76, Issue 5, p.102.

Good corporate governance helps to build an environment of trust, transparency and accountability necessary for fostering long-term investment, financial stability and business integrity, thereby supporting stronger growth and more inclusive societies[37].

▶ STAKEHOLDERS

As is widely recognized, directors of the business should also consider the impact of their decisions on other stakeholders.

Usually, a list of stakeholders would also include the community, the general public, consumer groups, etc. However, these groups have no legal rights and no legal power to enforce any contract. The stakeholder relationships include a relationship between the community and the firm, between governments and firms, and between community and governments. Through this legal network, members of the community can influence the firm and express their opinion.

By some opinions, members of the community are not direct stakeholders of the firm but mediated stakeholders through the government. However, in some cases, members of community may believe that the legal network does not provide them with adequate or sufficiently efficient means to be heard. They choose to bypass the legal system with legitimate actions like consumer boycotts or even illegitimate and illegal actions.

Summarising, corporate governance essentially focuses on the dilemmas that result from the separation of ownership and control, and addresses, in particular, the principal–agent relationship between shareholders and directors on the one hand and the relationship between company agents and stakeholders on the other hand. Other parties are: lenders to the corporation, its trading partners (workers, customers and suppliers) as well as competitors and the general public. All of these parties have an interest in the success of the corporation. All except competitors (and possibly the general public and analysts) stand to lose financially as a result of corporate failure.

▸ GOVERNANCE BOARDS

Another difference between the market-oriented and the network-oriented corporate governance structures is the two-tier separation between the board of management and the supervisory board in the network structure. In the market-oriented, one-tier system, the complete board (that is, both executive and non-executive directors) is formally responsible for day-to-day operating activities. However, this responsibility is delegated to the executive members, while the non-executive board members have a supervisory role. This means that non-executives supervise and, at the same time, are jointly responsible for day-to-day operations. In the two-tier system, supervising and management are formally separated: the monitoring of executive board members is exclusively the responsibility of the supervisory board. Therefore, supervisory board members seem to be more independent than their non-executive counterparts. Despite these differences in structure, role and tasks of boards are generally accepted and characterised by differentiating decision management and decision control[38].

Given these worldwide developments, in many countries special corporate governance committees have been installed to prepare principles and best practices for 'good' corporate governance[39]. The interesting conclusion that can be derived from the different reports is the ongoing convergence of corporate governance structures. In other words, globalising financial and investment markets seeks the best of both worlds in corporate practices and policies, and hence 'best practice behaviour'.

▸ LAWS AND REGULATIONS

As already mentioned in section 2.7 in response to corporate scandals, the Sarbanes-Oxley Act of 2002 (SOX) established new standards for corporate governance, accounting, and financial disclosure. It emphasizes the role of audit committees and enhances the independence of boards and auditors[40].

SOX consists of 11 'Sections':

1　Public Company Accounting Oversight Board
2　Auditor Independence

3 Corporate Responsibility
4 Enhanced Financial Disclosures
5 Analyst Conflicts of Interest
6 Commission Resources and Authority
7 Studies and Reports
8 Corporate and Criminal Fraud Accountability Act of 2002
9 White-Collar Crime Penalty Enhancements
10 Corporate Tax Returns
11 Corporate Fraud and Accountability.

A main characteristic is its legal force. Deviation from law leads to clear punishments. Company executives who fraudulently report financial statements are subject to criminal penalties if they 'knowingly' violate the law ($1 million or ten years' imprisonment) or if they are 'wilful and knowing' in their violation ($5 million or 20 years' imprisonment).

Another characteristic of the law is its scope. All US-listed companies (domestic and foreign registrants and auditors) must comply with the Sarbanes–Oxley Act, despite the differences in culture and laws of foreign companies.

Specific laws and regulations related to corporate governance may vary by jurisdiction. Here are references to some important and widely recognized regulations that have a global impact:

- The UK Corporate Governance Code sets out principles of good governance for listed companies in the UK. It covers various aspects, including board composition, leadership, accountability, and remuneration.
- While primarily focused on data protection and privacy, EU General Data Protection Regulation (GDPR) has implications for corporate governance, particularly in terms of how organizations handle and protect sensitive information.
- The King IV Report on Corporate Governance provides guidelines on corporate governance for South African companies. It emphasizes the integrated nature of governance, considering economic, social, and environmental factors.
- Introduced in 2015 and revised in subsequent years, the Japanese Corporate Governance Code aims to enhance the governance practices of Japanese companies, with a focus on transparency, accountability, and shareholder engagement.
- Chinese Corporate Governance Code (China) sets out guidelines for governance practices in Chinese companies. It emphasizes the role of the board, transparency, and protection of shareholder rights.
- Securities and Exchange Board of India (SEBI) Listing Obligations and Disclosure Requirements (LODR) Regulations (India) outline governance and disclosure norms for listed entities in India, covering aspects such as board composition, audit committees, and related-party transactions.

▶ TRANSPARENCY AND INTEGRITY

Transparency forms the backbone of good corporate governance. Transparency within governance is like a 'lubricant' for an engine. Transparency includes concepts like openness, reporting and disclosure. Integrity is also one of the fundamental principles of good corporate governance. This means that the leaders and the management should commit to the company's core values and mission instead of their own personal interests. Integrity is the consistency and transparency of each leader's deeds and actions. Leaders should act their words. It also means taking appropriate action and accountability to do what is right for the company's reputation, needs, and interests.

In a business environment, transparency requires a sophisticated system of accounting. Such an accounting system should:

- ▶ allow investors to assess the magnitude and timing of future cash flows to be generated by a business;
- ▶ encourage efficient operations and maximisation of results;
- ▶ provide an early warning of problems in meeting objectives of the firm; and
- ▶ lead to quick corrective action whenever things go bad.

▶ CORPORATE GOVERNANCE STRUCTURES

To understand current developments, one should understand differences in national corporate governance structures as well. These differences are caused by factors such as culture, history, legal systems, and so on. In other words, corporate behaviour is influenced by the history and culture of the country. Geert Hofstede, a social economist, characterised the Anglo-Saxon culture as masculine and European continental culture as feminine[41].

Market and network corporate governance structures exhibit notable distinctions (see illustration 5.6). Market-oriented countries like the USA and Commonwealth nations favour aggressive, confrontational approaches, while network-oriented countries such as those in Continental Europe and parts of Asia prioritize consensus over conflict. Market-oriented nations typically operate under common law, while network-oriented countries adhere to civil law principles. Cultural factors heavily influence these differences.

For instance, in Germany and Japan, there's a tradition of long-term shareholder support, influenced by banks that serve as both equity providers and lenders. France and Italy, on the other hand, have a tradition of family-oriented businesses, often with founding families as major shareholders represented on the board. This familial involvement leads

---

ILLUSTRATION 5.6

CORPORATE GOVERNANCE STRUCTURES

Market-oriented (Anglo-Saxon)	Network-oriented (Continental)
• Confrontation • Shareholders: 　– greater spread, 　　individual private investors • Shareholder relations • One-tier boards	• Consensus • Shareholders: 　– banks 　– individual investors • Stakeholder approach • One-tier boards

to a focus beyond shareholder interests, with profits often reinvested into the company. Moreover, the absence of an aggressive takeover culture fosters a more stable, long-term business environment, shielding against the fear of hostile takeovers and displacement.

▶ CORPORATE GOVERNANCE AND THE ROLE OF THE AUDITOR

The external auditor plays a central role in good corporate governance. Despite the fact that auditors are indirect stakeholders, their core role is to provide assurance regarding:

- ▶ financial and non-financial information;
- ▶ internal control statements; and
- ▶ corporate governance statements.

CONCEPT AND A COMPANY 5.5

HIH INSURANCE BOARD FAILURE TO 'SEE, REMEDY AND REPORT THE OBVIOUS'

Concept	Corporate culture, poor corporate governance model, the role of the auditor.
Story	HIH was one of Australia's biggest home-building market insurers selling home warranty insurance and builders' warranty insurance. Raymond Williams and Michael Payne established the business in 1968.

Despite Australian regulation designed to detect solvency problems at an early stage, 'the corporate officers, auditors and regulators of HIH failed to see, remedy or report what should have been obvious.' Poor leadership, inept management and indifference to company problems marked the last years of HIH. Those involved in HIH management ignored or concealed the true state of the company's steadily deteriorating financial position, which led by 2001 to the largest corporate failure in Australian history at that time (HIH Royal Commission, 2003).The problematic aspects of the corporate culture of HIH were caused by a number of factors. One was blind faith in a leadership that was ill-equipped for the task. Risks were not properly identified and managed. Unpleasant information was hidden, filtered or sanitized. Finally, there was no skeptical questioning and analysis.

Underwriting Losses

The main reason for HIH's financial decline was several billion dollars in underwriting losses based on claims arising from insured events in previous years. Past claims on policies that had not been properly priced had to be met out of present income, i.e. a deficiency resulted from 'under-reserving' or 'under-provisioning'. The reserves were based on reports of independent actuaries and the assessment of those reports by the auditors. Actuaries were never called in before the board of directors to describe the report.

From as far back as 1997 their underwriting losses increased dramatically. In the year ending 31 December 1997 HIH made an underwriting loss of $33.8 million on net premium earned of $1,233.5 million. The comparative figures for the year ending 30 June 2000 are $103.5 million and $1,995.4 million respectively. Between 1997 and 1999 the underwriting loss was up 206 per cent while the net earned premium rose by only 25 per cent. The reported underwriting losses were high, but without several one-off entries they would have been much worse. On 12 September 2000 Andersen, HIH's auditor, made a presentation to the HIH audit committee. They said that in the 12 months to December 1999, one-off adjustments reduced the underwriting loss by $157 million; and at 30 June 2000 they reduced the loss by $360 million.

Reliance on intangibles

Another feature of the financial trend was the increasing reliance on intangible assets to support shareholders' equity. In addition to goodwill and management rights, HIH had on its balance sheet future income tax benefits, deferred information technology costs, and deferred acquisition costs. Goodwill alone represented 50 per cent of HIH's shareholders funds. By way of comparison, QBE and NRMA (two comparable Australian insurance companies) had a ratio of goodwill to shareholders funds of 4.9 per cent and 0.4 per cent respectively.

Acquisitions

At board level, there was little, if any, analysis of the future strategy of the company. Indeed, the company's strategy was not documented. As one director conceded, if he had been asked to commit to writing what the long-term strategy was, he would have had difficulty doing so. Examples of this lack of strategy were the acquisition of a UK branch (where losses amounted to $1.7 billion), reacquisition of US operations (causing losses of $620 million), and a joint venture with Alliance Australia Limited.

The most disastrous business transaction involved joint venture arrangements agreed between HIH and Allianz which ultimately caused HIH to experience an insurmountable cash flow crisis in early 2001 and largely dictated the timing of HIH's collapse. In addition to the transfer of HIH's most profitable retail lines to the joint venture, HIH was required to contribute $200 million received for the retail lines plus an additional $300 million in cash and assets to a trust to cover claims. All premium income (about $1 billion) was paid into the trust, and HIH was not allowed access to the funds until an actuarial assessment, about five months after the transfer.

The agreement to proceed with the Allianz proposal took a mere 75 minutes of the board of directors' meeting. The trust provisions and their potential adverse effect on cash flow were either completely overlooked or not properly appreciated.

Corporate Governance Model

The corporate governance model at HIH was deficient in a number of ways. There was a dearth of clearly defined and recorded policies or guidelines. There were no clearly defined limits on the authority of the chief executive in areas such as investments, corporate donations, gifts and staff emoluments. The board did not have a well-understood policy on matters that would be reserved to itself, but depended on the chief executive. In addition, it was heavily dependent on the advice of senior management. There were very few occasions when the board either rejected or materially changed a proposal put forward by management. The board was reluctant to disclose related-party transactions. The Chairman of the board gave board agendas to the CEO, but not to the board members, for comments.

Discussion Questions	▷ What were the warning signs of financial decline that the auditors should have addressed in their procedures?
	▷ Describe why assessment of the corporate governance model is important to the audit.
	▷ What types of strategy and action could the board of directors initiate which could have changed the outcome?

References	HIH Royal Commission, Justice Owen, R., 2003, *The Failure of HIH Insurance*, Commonwealth of Australia.

The auditor's role of auditing financial statements, including the identification and communication of deficiencies in internal control to those in charge of governance, is discussed throughout this book. Understanding the business, and its environment is key for assessing the risk of material misstatements (see chapter 6), while an engagement to provide assurance on non-financial information and an audit of internal control statements have been elaborated on later in the text (see chapter 14 and 15).

That leaves the third important governance role – the audit or review of corporate governance statements. Stock Exchange Listing Rules typically do not mandate auditors to specifically review a Corporate Governance Statement. However, auditors are often required to assess the directors' statement regarding compliance with corporate governance principles and practices as part of their broader audit responsibilities.

See illustration 5.7 which gives requirements for the auditor's review of the management's statement regarding compliance with the code of best practice[42].

If, in the opinion of the auditors, the listed company has not complied with any of the requirements set out in the code, the listed company must ensure that the auditor's report includes, to the extent possible, a statement giving details of the non-compliance.

ILLUSTRATION 5.7

REVIEW OF CORPORATE GOVERNANCE STATEMENT (UK)

The Listing Rules require us to review the directors' statement in relation to going concern, longer-term viability and that part of the Corporate Governance Statement relating to the [entity]'s compliance with the provisions of the UK Corporate Governance Statement specified for our review.

Based on the work undertaken as part of our audit, we have concluded that each of the following elements of the Corporate Governance Statement is materially consistent with the financial statements or our knowledge obtained during the audit:

▶ Directors' statement with regards the appropriateness of adopting the going concern basis of accounting and any material uncertainties identified [set out on page …];

▶ Directors' explanation as to its assessment of the entity's prospects, the period this assessment covers and why they period is appropriate [set out on page …].

▶ Directors' statement on fair, balanced and understandable [set out on page …];

▶ Board's confirmation that it has carried out a robust assessment of the e-merging and principal risks [set out on page …];

▶ The section of the annual report that describes the review of effectiveness of risk management and internal control systems [set out on page …]; and;

▶ The section describing the work of the audit committee [set out on page …]

5.11 QUESTIONS, EXERCISES AND CASES

5.2 Client Acceptance: The First Step on the Journey to an Opinion

5-1 What is the difference between acceptance of the client and acceptance by the client?

5.3 Evaluate the Client's Background

5-2 What are the major sources of client information auditors have available? Which source would prove the best for new businesses? Why?

5.4 Ability to Meet Ethical and Specific Competence Requirements

5-3 Consideration of whether the firm has the competencies and resources to undertake a new engagement includes reviewing existing partner and staff competencies. What competencies are these?

5.5 Use of Other Professionals in the Audit

5-4 What is a group auditor? What must she consider when the work of another auditor is used?

5-5 How is an 'expert' defined? When should an auditor bring in an expert?

5.6 Communicating With the Predecessor (Existing) Auditor

5-6 To what extent can an existing auditor discuss the affairs of their client with a new auditor?

5.7 Acceptance by the Client – The Engagement Proposal

5-7 List four things an auditor must consider when establishing professional fees. What is meant by 'low balling'?

5-8 Define a contingency fee. Why should a contingency fee not be used? What are the two exceptions for using contingency fees?

5-9 Briefly list the four items found in a continuing client audit proposal. List and define the items that may be found in an audit proposal for a new client.

5.8 The Audit Engagement Letter

5-10 What should be included in an engagement letter? What are some reasons a client might change the terms of the engagement?

5-11 Under what circumstances will an auditor send a new engagement letter each year to a continuing client?

5-12 List the ISAs used in this chapter and briefly define them.

Appendix 5.1 Corporate Governance

5-13 Explain the concept of Corporate Governance.

5-14 Describe the difference between shareholders and stakeholders and discuss why differences play a central role in the corporate governance discussion.

5-15 Describe the positive and negative effects the corporate governance components 'Transparency' and 'Internal Control' could have in meeting the company objectives.

5-16 Describe the differences between a market-oriented and a network-oriented corporate governance structure.

5-17 What are advantages and disadvantages of a one-tier board structure?

5-18 Should a corporate governance code be developed by governmental bodies and enforced by law or should a code be developed by private institutions such as companies, shareholder representatives, lawyers and accountants and compliance be left to self-regulation? Describe the motivation for your answer.

5-19 List major differences between the internal and external audit.

5-20 What is meant by the statement 'Corporate governance is not an end in itself'?

5-21 Why is corporate governance relevant for planning the financial statements audit?

5-22 Describe the role of the external auditor in corporate governance.

PROBLEMS AND EXERCISES

5.2 **Client and Engagement Acceptance**

5-23 In the context of International Standards on Auditing (ISAs), the term 'client' is commonly used to refer to the entity that commissions an audit of the financial statements. However, this entity is often also the auditee. With an emphasis on maintaining auditor independence, suggest a rationale for referring to the entity as 'auditee' instead of 'client'. Discuss the potential benefits of this terminology change in the audit process.

5.3 **Evaluate the Client's Background**

5-24 The audit firm of F.A. Bloch and Co. has been approached by the following companies who wish to retain Bloch for audit work:

1   Interlewd, an internet company, whose website features explicit images of male nudes and which operates male strip clubs on the west coast of Australia.

2   Dreamtime, a company that operates gambling casino boats offshore and video game machines in major Australian cities.

3   Bernadette, an entertainment company, whose chief executive officer has been investigated by the Italian government for taking bribes, violating public securities laws, conspiring to commit bodily harm and issuing bad checks. The CEO has not been convicted of any of these charges. The board of directors claims that this happened many years ago, and since then the CEO has run several companies successfully.

Required:

A.   What procedures should F.A. Bloch and Co. use to investigate these potential clients?

B.   What would F.A. Bloch and Co. consider in determining whether to accept these clients?

5.4 **Ability to Meet Ethical and Specific Competence Requirements**

5-25 The audit firm of Giuseppe Mulciber, Dottore Commercialista, has been asked to bid on an annual audit of the financial statements of Mammon, a publicly traded gold jewellery manufacturer. The Mulciber firm has been performing assurance services for Mammon over the past three years. Almost everyone on the audit team has investments in stocks and mutual funds. Mammon and Mulciber had disputes in the past about the extent of assurance services provided. One of the members of the proposed audit staff was an employee of Mammon until 14 months ago. Only one person on the proposed audit team had audited a jewellery manufacturer.

Required:

A.   What procedures would Mulciber conduct to determine independence of the firm and audit team?

B.   Does the Mulciber audit team have the proper competencies? Explain.

C.   What circumstances might disqualify Mulciber from serving as an auditor for Mammon?

5.5   Use of Other Professionals in the Audit

5-26 Use of Other Auditor. Rene Lodeve, Reviseur d'Entreprises, has been hired by BelleRei, N.V., a Liege, Belgium, company. Lodeve will audit all accounts except those of a subsidiary in Spain, which represents 15 per cent of the total sales of BelleRei, which is audited by an 'other accountant', Jeme Indigena.

Required:

A.   What procedures would Lodeve perform to determine whether Indigena has sufficient professional competence to perform the work?

B.   If Lodeve concludes that he cannot depend on the work of Indigena, and he cannot perform additional procedures, what sort of audit opinion should Lodeve give?

5.6   Communicating With the Predecessor (Existing) Auditor

5-27 Preparation and Planning. Roger Buckland was recently appointed auditor of Waterfield, Ltd, a public company. He had communicated with the company's previous auditor before accepting the audit. Buckland attended the company's shareholders meeting at which he was appointed but he has not yet visited the company's offices.

Required:

List the matters that Buckland should attend to between the time of his appointment and the commencement of his audit work in order to effectively plan the audit.

5.7   Acceptance by the Client – The Engagement Proposal

5-28 Audit Proposals. Juao Castelo, Revisor Oficial de Contas (ROC), is required to write a client audit proposal for two clients, one continuing (Jinne) and one new (Autodafe).

Required:

A.   Based on the proposal for a continuing client and a new client discussed in this chapter, list the contents of the proposal to Jinne and Autodafe.

B.   What do the two proposals have in common? What is different?

C.   Describe what is discussed in each section of the proposal to Autodafe.

5-29 Audit Fees. Ursula Chona, Contador Publico (CP Titulado), an auditor from Medellin, Columbia, was referred a client by a local attorney and she has agreed to accept the client for a financial statements audit. She must now determine what fee she will charge.

Required:

A.   According to international ethics, the fee should be a fair reflection of effort, taking what conditions into account?

B.   On what basis should the fee be calculated? Should out-of-pocket expenses be included or listed separately?

C. What are the circumstances under which Chona can ask for a contingency fee?

D. Can Chona pay a 'finder's fee' to the attorney who referred the client to her?

5.8 The Audit Engagement Letter

5-30 Engagement Letter. Stephen Hu, CPA, from Taipei, Taiwan, has just accepted a new client, Kiwan Xou. The company will be audited under the ISA and IAS standards. The client will be given an audit opinion and a management letter. The fees are based on hourly fees, will take 125 hours, and will involve one senior (TD 3,500 per hour), two staff auditors (TD 2,800 per hour), and a partner (TD 5,000 per hour). Out-of-pocket expense is estimated at TD 65,000. The payments will be 33 per cent at the beginning of the audit with the balance at the end of the audit.

Required:

Based on the above information, write an engagement letter to Kiwan Xou from Stephen Hu.

Appendix 5.1 Corporate Governance

5-31 Bakka Bee is a Canadian construction firm, of which 30 per cent of the shares are listed at the Toronto Stock Exchange and 70 per cent are held by management. They are a firm with 200 employees in five countries. One of their divisions – in Peru – has encountered difficulties linked to the statutory accounts and might be involved in violating human rights. Because of recent discussions about the company in the national parliament, it may have to be liquidated.

Required:

Discuss Bakka Bee in terms of three of the four causes of the current corporate governance discussion: (1) bankruptcies, fraud and mismanagement; (2) the influence of public, customers and media; (3) globalisation of capital markets.

5-32 Pick one listed US-based company and one listed continental European company and compare and contrast their board of directors and other supervisory boards.

5-33 According to the US Sarbanes-Oxley Act, auditors should audit the internal controls of financial reporting (SOX 404). However, from prior research it can be concluded that users of the auditor's opinion on financial statements assume an unqualified opinion implicates internal controls being adequately designed and operating. Explain why this expectation cannot be met by an audit of financial statements. Describe major differences in evaluating internal controls over financial reporting in a financial statements audit and auditing internal controls over financial reporting as a separate engagement.

5-34 Why is self-regulation by the audit profession in the US no longer in place? Find some arguments 'pro and con' self-regulation.

CASES

5-35 Description of the business: Compu Group Corporation designs, develops, manufactures and markets a wide range of personal computing products, including desktop personal computers, portable computers, network servers and peripheral products that store and manage data in network environments. The company markets its products primarily to business, home, government and education customers. The company operates in one principal industry segment across geographically diverse markets.

The company is subject to legal proceedings and claims which arise in the ordinary course of its business. Management does not believe that the outcome of any of those matters will have a material adverse effect on the company's consolidated financial position or operating results.

Required:

A.   Based on the information presented, evaluate the company for acceptance. List criteria that must be reviewed in order to determine acceptability.

B.   Make a checklist for areas covered.

C.   Outline your audit approach.

5.12   NOTES

1.   https://www.accountingweb.co.uk/business/financial-reporting/audit-risks-trickle-down-to-smaller-firms

2.   See IESBA, 2021, paragraph Part 3 Section 320, Handbook of the International Code of Ethics for Professional Accountants. And International Auditing and Assurance Standards Board (IAASB), 2023, International Standard on Auditing 315 (ISA 315) 'Identifying and Assessing the Risks of Material Misstatement through Understanding the Entity and Its Environment', paragraphs 5-10, Handbook of International Quality Management, Auditing, Review, Other Assurance and Related Services Pronouncements, 2022 edn, Volume I. Both International Federation of Accountants, New York.

3.   International Auditing and Assurance Standards Board. 2023. International Standard on Quality Management 1 (ISQM 1). 'Quality Management for Firms that Perform Audits or Reviews of Financial Statements, or Other Assurance or Related Services Engagements', Paragraph A67, Handbook of International Quality Management, Auditing, Review, Other Assurance and Related Services Pronouncements, 2022 edn, Volume I. International Federation of Accountants, New York.

4.   https://www.icaew.com/technical/corporate-governance/principles/principles-articles/does-corporate-governance-matter

5.   Ibid. ISQM 1 para. A72.

6.   Ibid. ISQM 1 para. A73.

7.   Ibid. ISQM 1 para. A74.

8.   International Ethics Standards Board of Accountants (IESBA), 2021, Section 410 'Fees', para. 410.7A1, Handbook of the International Code of Ethics for Professional Accountants, 2021 edn, International Federation of Accountants, New York.

9.   See, for example, American Institute of Certified Public Accountants (AICPA), 2013, Code of Professional Conduct, .08 101-6 'The Effect of Actual or Threatened Litigation on Independence (Revised)', para. 05, American Institute of Certified Public Accountants, New York, states: 'Independence may be impaired whenever the covered member and the covered member's client company or its management are in threatened or actual positions of material adverse interest by reason of threatened or actual litigation.'

10. International Ethics Standards Board of Accountants (IESBA), 2021, Handbook of the International Code of Ethics for Professional Accountants, Part 4A, Independence for Audit and Review Engagements, Section 607, para. 607.1, International Federation of Accountants, New York.

11. Ibid. ISQM 1, para. A71.

12. International Auditing and Assurance Standards Board (IAASB), 2023, International Standard on Auditing 600 (ISA 600) 'Special Considerations – Audits of Group Financial Statements (Including the Work of Component Auditors)', Handbook of International Quality Management, Auditing, Review, Other Assurance and Related Services Pronouncements, 2022 edn, Volume I, International Federation of Accountants, New York.

13. Ibid. ISQM 1 Para. 30, A72.

14. International Ethics Standard Board for Accountants (IESBA), 2021, Handbook of the International Code of Ethics for Professional Accountants, para. 320.4 A3 –A4 and paragraphs 320.5 A1 and R320.6, International Federation of Accountants, New York.

15. Existing accountant (or auditor) is a professional accountant in public practice currently holding an audit appointment or carrying out accounting, taxation, consulting or similar professional services for a client.

16. International Auditing and Assurance Standards Board (IAASB), 2023, International Standards on Auditing 510 (ISA 510) 'Initial Audit Engagements – Opening Balances', para. 6, Handbook of International Quality Management, Auditing, Review, Other Assurance and Related Services Pronouncements, 2022 edn, Volume I, International Federation of Accountants, New York.

17. International Auditing and Assurance Standards Board (IAASB), 2023, International Standards on Auditing 210 (ISA 210) 'Agreeing the Terms Audit Engagements'. Handbook of International Quality Management, Auditing, Review, Other Assurance and Related Services Pronouncements, 2022 edn, Volume I, International Federation of Accountants, New York.

18. International Standards Organization (ISO), 2000, ISO 9001:2000(E) 'Quality Management Systems – Requirements', ISO copyright office, Geneva.

19. Audit strategy is the design of an optimized audit approach that seeks to achieve the necessary audit assurance at the lowest cost within the constraints of the information available.

20. International Auditing and Assurance Standards Board (IAASB), 2023, International Standards on Auditing 610 (ISA 610) 'Using the Work of Internal Auditors', para. 1-5, Handbook of International Quality Management, Auditing, Review, Other Assurance and Related Services Pronouncements, 2022 edn, Volume I, International Federation of Accountants, New York.

21. International Ethics Standards Board of Accountants (IESBA), 2021, Handbook of the International Code of Ethics for Professional Accountants, Section 240, International Federation of Accountants, New York.

22. Ibid. IESBA Section 240.

23. Ibid. IESBA Section 330.4 A1 to 330.4 A4 'Fees and Other Types of Remuneration' and Section 905.5 A1 to 905.7 A3 'Independence for Assurance Engagements Other than Audit and Review Engagements' discuss fees including contingent fees and referral fees.

24. In the USA and other national contexts, an engagement letter is not required, although it is usually recommended.

25. Ibid. International Standards on Auditing 210 (ISA 210) 'Agreeing the Terms of Audit Engagements', para. 10.

26. Ibid. ISA 210, paras A24–A24.

27. In some jurisdictions (such as the USA), the auditor may have responsibilities to report separately on the entity's internal control. In such circumstances, the auditor reports on that responsibility as required in that jurisdiction. The reference in the auditor's report on the financial statements to the fact that the auditor's consideration of internal control is not for the purpose of expressing an opinion on the effectiveness of the entity's internal control may not be appropriate in such circumstances. See section 14.5.

28. Written representation – A written statement by management provided to the auditor to confirm certain matters or to support other audit evidence. Written representations in this context do not include financial statements, the assertions therein, or supporting books and records.

29. Ibid. ISA 210. Appendix 1 'Example of an Audit Engagement Letter'.

30. Applicable financial reporting framework is the financial reporting framework adopted by management and, where appropriate, those charged with governance in the preparation of the financial statements that is acceptable in view of the nature of the entity and the objective of the financial statements, or that is required by law or regulation.

31. See, for example, ISA 260 'Communication with Those Charged with Governance' para. A33 and ISA 240, 'The Auditor's Responsibilities Relating to Fraud in an Audit of Financial Statements', para. 43. 2023, Handbook of International Quality Management, Auditing, Review, Other Assurance and Related Services Pronouncements, 2022 edn, Volume I, International Federation of Accountants, New York.

32. International Auditing and Assurance Standards Board (IAASB), 2023, International Standards on Auditing 200 (ISA 200) 'Overall Objectives of the Independent Auditor and the Conduct of an Audit in Accordance With International Standards On Auditing', paras A2–A10.

33. Ibid. ISQM 1, para. 6.

34. Darts is a game in which darts (slender, pointed missiles with tail fins) are thrown by hand at a target of concentric circles.

35. Transparency – for corporations, practices that make rules, regulations and accounting methods open and accessible to the public. Transparency includes concepts like openness, reporting and disclosure.

36. https://www.icaew.com/technical/corporate-governance/principles/principles-articles/does-corporate-governance-matter

37. https://www.oecd.org/corporate/

38. Business Sector Advisory Group on Corporate Governance, 1998, Corporate Governance, Improving Competitiveness and Access to Capital in Global Markets, A Report to the OECD by the Business Sector Advisory Group on Corporate Governance, Ira M. Millstein (Chairman) et al., OECD. Also see OECD, 2004, OECD Principles of Corporate Governance, Organisation for Economic Cooperation and Development, Paris. http://www.oecd.org/

39. https://www.ecgi.global/content/codes

40. US Congress, 2002, Sarbanes-Oxley Act of 2002, Public Law 107–204, Senate and House of Representatives of the United States of America in Congress assembled, Washington, DC, 30 July.

41. Hofstede, Geert, 1980, 'International Differences in Work-Related Values', Culture's Consequences, Sage Publications, California.

42. Financial Reporting Council, 2020, Illustrative Auditor's Reports on United Kingdom Private Sector Financial Statements, https://media.frc.org.uk/documents/Illustrative_Auditors_Reports_Bulletin_March_2020.pdf

CHAPTER 6

IDENTIFYING AND ASSESSING INHERENT RISK

The four phases of the audit:

Acceptance/ continuance	Understanding/ risk analysis	Building/executing audit plan	Evaluating/ completion
Phase 1	Phase 2	Phase 3	Phase 4

6.1 LEARNING OBJECTIVES

After studying this chapter, you should be able to:

1 State what the general objective is of planning an audit.
2 Discuss the relevant aspects of understanding the entity and its environment.
3 Describe what is done during initial interviews, discussions and site visits with the auditee.
4 Give examples of a management objective, the related strategy and the resulting business risk.
5 Explain the structure of the audit process model.
6 Understand the audit risk model.
7 Sketch the risk assessment process.
8 Be able to determine materiality.
9 Describe audit procedures to understand entity and its environment.
10 Discuss other planning activities.

6.2 PLANNING OBJECTIVE AND PROCEDURES

International Standards on Auditing 300 (ISA 300) 'Planning an Audit of Financial Statements' states:[1] 'the objective of the auditor is to plan the audit so that it will be performed in an effective manner', and 'The auditor shall establish an overall audit strategy that sets the scope, timing and direction of the audit, and that guides the development of the audit plan'.

▶ PLANNING OBJECTIVE AND PROCEDURES

In planning an audit, the auditor must determine timing and scope of the audit and the amount and type of evidence required to assure the auditor that there is no material misstatement of the financial statements due to fraud or error. This is phase II in the Audit Process Model transitioning into Phase III when preparing the detailed audit plan containing the auditor's response to the identified risks (see illustration 6.1).

The planning procedures are:

1   Perform audit procedures to understand the entity and its environment, including the entity's internal control.
2   Assess the risks of material misstatements of the financial statements.
3   Determine materiality.

This chapter discusses the planning process through understanding and risk analysis aimed to assess the inherent risks. We start conceptually with the audit risk model (section 6.3) followed by the risk assessment process following ISA 315 (section 6.4) and determining materiality (section 6.5). Additional considerations are included in the remaining sections. Chapter 7 is focused on a specific part of this process – the auditor's assessment of internal control and control risk, including IT. Chapter 8 describes building and execution of the audit plan, following the risk assessment process described in this chapter and chapter 7.

ILLUSTRATION 6.1

AUDIT PROCESS MODEL

Phase I: Client & engagement acceptance/continuance

Objective	Determine both acceptance of a client and acceptance by a client. Decide on acquiring a new client or continuation of relationship with an existing one and the type and number of staff required.
Procedures	1 Evaluate the client's background and reasons for the audit.
	2 Determine whether the auditor is able to meet the ethical requirements regarding the client.
	3 Determine need for other professionals.
	4 Communicate with predecessor auditor.
	5 Prepare client proposal.
	6 Select staff to perform the audit.
	7 Obtain an engagement letter.

Phase II: Planning through understanding, risk analysis, design & implementation of controls

Objectives	1 Plan the audit so that it will be performed in an effective manner.
	2 Establish an overall audit strategy that sets the scope, timing and direction of the audit, and that guides the development of the audit plan.
	3 Identify and asses the risks of material misstatement, whether due to fraud or error, at the financial statement levels thereby providing a basis for designing and implementing responses to the assessed risks of material misstatement.
Procedures	1 Perform audit procedures to understand the entity and its environment, including the entity's internal control.
	2 Assess the risks of material misstatements of the financial statements.
	3 Determine materiality.

Phase III: Building & executing of the audit plan

Objective   Obtain sufficient appropriate audit evidence regarding the assessed risks of material misstatement, through designing and implementing appropriate responses to those risks.

Procedures   1 Prepare the planning memorandum and audit plan containing the auditor's response to the identified risks.
2 Tests of controls.
3 Substantive tests:
   – Analytical procedures
   – Tests of details including sampling

Phase IV: Evaluating and Completion

Objective   Complete the audit procedures and issue an auditor's report.

Procedures   1 Evaluate governance matters.
2 Perform procedures to identify subsequent events.
3 Review financial statements and other report material.
4 Perform wrap-up procedures.
5 Report to the board of directors.
6 Prepare auditor's report.

6.3   THE AUDIT RISK MODEL

As introduced in chapter 4, when issuing the auditor's report, the auditor opines with reasonable assurance whether the financial statements as a whole are free from material misstatement due to fraud or error. There is a risk that the auditor retrospectively issued the incorrect opinion. That's called 'audit risk'.

▶ **AUDIT RISK**

Audit risk[2] is the risk that the auditor gives an inappropriate audit opinion when the financial statements are materially misstated. The higher the audit risk, the more evidence must be gathered in order to obtain sufficient appropriate assurance as a basis for expressing an opinion on the financial statements.

Audit risk has three components[3]: inherent risk, control risk[4] and detection risk. These components are traditionally defined as follows:

1 Inherent risk is the susceptibility to misstatement of an assertion about a class of transaction, account balance or disclosure to a misstatement that could be material, either individually or when aggregated with other misstatements before consideration of any related controls. Inherent risk is higher for some assertions and related classes of transactions, account balances, and disclosures than for others. For example, it may be higher for complex calculations or for accounts consisting of amounts derived from accounting estimates that are subject to significant estimation uncertainty.

2 Control risk is the risk that a misstatement that could occur in an account balance or class of transactions and that could be material – individually or when aggregated

with misstatements in other balances or classes – will not be prevented or detected and corrected on a timely basis by accounting and internal control systems. To be able to assess control risk, the auditor must perform procedures to obtain an understanding of accounting and internal control systems. Procedures to obtain an understanding (risk assessment procedures) may be used to support the assessments of the risks of material misstatement of the financial statements.

3 Detection risk is the risk that auditor's procedures will not detect a misstatement that exists in an account balance or class of transactions that could be material, individually or when aggregated with misstatements in other balances, or classes of transactions, or disclosures.

ISA 315 separates the assessment of inherent risk and control risk. The entity's system of internal control may lead to control deficiencies that need to be considered when identifying the risks of material misstatements. The combination of inherent and control risk is called the risk of a material misstatement (RMM).

When inherent and control risks are high – and therefore result in high RMM – acceptable detection risk needs to be low to reduce audit risk to an acceptably low level. For example, if the internal control structure prevents and or detects errors (i.e. control risk is low), the auditor can perform less effective substantive tests (detection risk is high). Alternatively, if the account balance is more susceptible to misstatement (inherent risk is higher), the auditor must apply more effective substantive testing procedures (to lower detection risk). In short, the higher the assessment of inherent and control risk, the more audit evidence the auditor should obtain from the performance of substantive procedures.

Illustration 6.2[5] shows how a symbolic graphic may be used to illustrate how audit risk works. The potential pool of material errors is represented by the tap[6] at the top of the illustration. The sieves[7] represent how the client and the auditor attempt to remove material errors from the financial statements. In illustration 6.2, the first sieve represents the internal control system. The client may install a system of internal accounting control to detect material errors and correct them. Ideally, the control system should detect any material errors before they enter the financial statements. However, there is some risk that errors will either pass undetected through the control system (perhaps because of a breakdown or weakness) or will bypass the control system altogether (e.g. where there are no controls in place such as an unusual exchange of non-monetary assets). The liquid falling through the sieve represents the errors not detected and the spill over represents those errors that bypass the control system. If the internal control system does not detect and correct the errors, they will be included in the financial statements. The auditor must design audit procedures that will provide reasonable assurance that material errors will be detected and removed from the financial statements. In illustration 6.2, the second sieve represents the auditor's procedures. Despite internal controls and auditors' procedures to detect misstatement, there will always be the possibility that some misstatements will be undetected. This is audit risk.

Illustrations 6.3 and 6.4 show the relationship between inherent, control and detection risks.

HOW AUDIT RISK WORKS

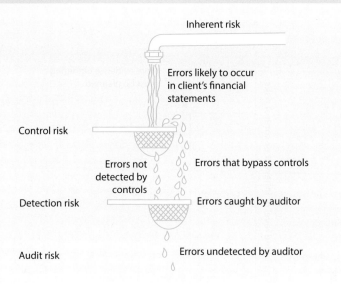

INTERRELATIONSHIP OF THE COMPONENTS OF AUDIT RISK

The following table shows how the acceptable level of detection risk may vary based on assessments of inherent and control risks.

		Auditor's assessment of control risk		
		High	Medium	Low
Auditor's assessment of inherent risk	High	Lowest	Lower	Medium
	Medium	Lower	Medium	Higher
	Low	Medium	Higher	Highest

The darker shaded areas in this table relate to detection risk.

There is an inverse relationship between detection risk and the combined level of inherent and control risks. For example, when inherent and control risks are high, acceptable levels of detection risk need to be low to reduce audit risk to an acceptably low level. On the other hand, when inherent and control risks are low, an auditor can accept a higher detection risk and still reduce audit risk to an acceptably low level.

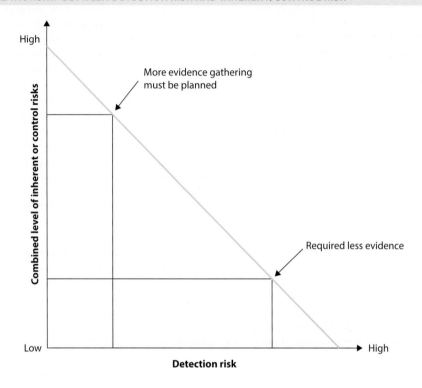

ILLUSTRATION 6.4

RELATIONSHIP BETWEEN DETECTION RISK AND INHERENT/CONTROL RISK

6.4 THE RISK ASSESSMENT PROCESS

ISA 315 requires the auditor to design and perform risk assessment procedures to obtain audit evidence that provides an appropriate basis for the identification and assessment of risks of material misstatement, whether due to fraud or error, at the financial statement and assertion; and for the design of further audit procedures in accordance with ISA 330. ISA 315 has a structured approach for identifying and assessing the risks of material misstatement. This storyline shown in an 8-step approach in illustration 6.5.

Understanding the entity's system of internal controls including IT (steps 6-8 in illustration 6.5) is an integral part of risk assessment. Given the complexity and extent of this topic, it will be dealt with separately in chapter 7, 'Identifying and Assessing Control Risk'.

ILLUSTRATION 6.5

HOW TO IDENTIFY RISKS OF MATERIAL MISSTATEMENT (RMM)

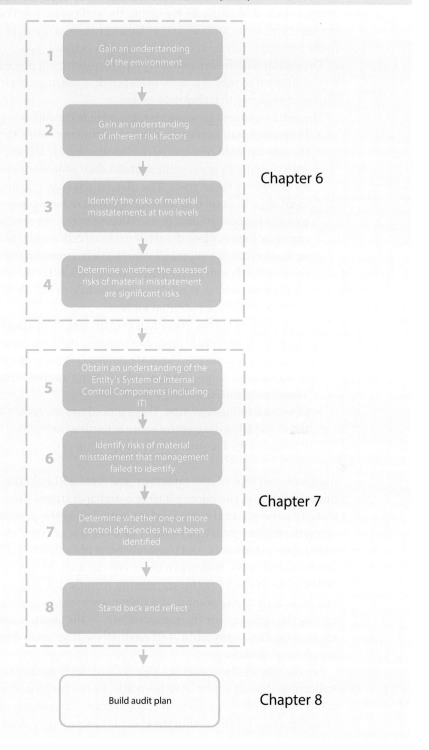

1. Gain an understanding of the environment

2. Gain an understanding of inherent risk factors

3. Identify the risks of material misstatements at two levels

4. Determine whether the assessed risks of material misstatement are significant risks

Chapter 6

5. Obtain an understanding of the Entity's System of Internal Control Components (including IT)

6. Identify risks of material misstatement that management failed to identify

7. Determine whether one or more control deficiencies have been identified

8. Stand back and reflect

Chapter 7

Build audit plan

Chapter 8

▶ RISK ASSESSMENT PROCEDURES AND RELATED ACTIVITIES

ISA 315 outlines the steps an auditor should take to gain sufficient understanding to assess risks and incorporate them into the audit plan. It sets a foundation for planning the audit and using professional judgment to assess the risks of material misstatement in the financial statements and how to address those risks.

The auditor must design and carry out risk assessment procedures impartially, avoiding any inclination to seek out audit evidence that confirms their initial assumptions or to disregard evidence that contradicts them.

The risk assessment procedures must include the following[8]:

- *Inquiries* of management and others within the entity, including individuals within the internal audit function (if the function exists). It is important to have discussions with the client's management about their objectives and expectations and plans for achieving these goals. The discussions may encompass short-term management objectives such as increasing profit, reducing investment in working capital, introducing new product lines, reducing taxes, or reducing selling and distribution expenses. Expectations should be explored concerning the company's external agents such as customers, suppliers, shareholders, financial institutions, government, etc. However, although management will typically be the most effective and efficient information source, it might be worthwhile to obtain information from others, in order to reduce the potential for bias.
- *Analytical procedures.* These may help the auditor in identifying unusual transactions or positions. Analytical procedures usually involve a comparison of company results to that of the industry. There are publications of major industry ratios and trends that might be helpful to the auditor doing analytical procedures (see chapter 7 'Identifying and Assessing Control Risk').
- *Observation and inspection.* These procedures may cover a broad area, ranging from the observation of an entity's core activities, the reading of management reports or internal control manuals to the inspection of documents.

A visit to, and tour of, the company premises will help the auditor develop a better understanding of the client's business and operations. Viewing the facilities helps to identify some internal control safeguards. Seeing the production process will help in assessing the inventory movement and the use of fixed assets. Observations of the orderliness, cleanliness, and physical layout of facilities and of the employees' routine functions and work habits can often tell the auditor more about the client than can be learnt from studying the accounting records. Knowledge of the physical facilities and plant layout may point to the right questions to ask during the planning phase or getting the right answers to questions later in the audit. Knowing the layout will assist in planning how many audit staff members will be needed to participate in observing the physical inventory.

On the site visit one may see signs of potential problems. Rust on equipment may indicate that plant assets have been idle. Excessive dust on raw materials or finished goods may indicate a problem of obsolescence. The auditors can see the physical extent of segregation of duties within the client organisation by observing the number of office employees.

OTHER INFORMATION SOURCES

▷ In addition, the auditor must consider other information gathered during the acceptance or continuance process and – when applicable – information gathered during prior client engagements. She shall evaluate whether such information remains relevant and reliable as audit evidence for the current audit.

▷ The auditor might consider obtaining information from other sources, for example, the entity's external legal counsel, or externally available data sources, including analysts' reports, industry journals, government statistics, surveys, texts, financial newspapers, etc. Professional institutes distribute industry audit guides, and most industries have trade magazines and books describing their business. Most large audit firms also have industry groups following the developments in those industries and creating newsletters on industry-specific items.

▷ If the engagement is a continuing one, prior year's working papers are reviewed, and reliance can be placed on the observations from prior periods. Based on a roll forward, the prior year's audit file frequently contains information on company history and records of most important accounting policies in previous years. Under certain circumstances, the auditor may use the outcomes of controls testing in the current audit file. However, before relying on existing working papers, the auditor needs to make sure that there have been no significant changes in the relevant aspects of the client's entity or environment and – of course – must remain professionally sceptical.

▷ If the client/engagement is new, the auditor needs to perform additional procedures with respect to opening balances. Inquiries at the predecessor auditor's and reviewing her working papers are common practice as the objective of ISA 510[9] is to obtain sufficient appropriate audit evidence about whether:

  ▷ Opening balances contain misstatements that materially affect the current period's financial statements; and

  ▷ Appropriate accounting policies reflected in the opening balances have been consistently applied in the current period's financial statements, or changes thereto are appropriately accounted for and adequately presented and disclosed in accordance with the applicable financial reporting framework.

AUDIT TEAM DISCUSSION

ISA 315 requires a team-wide discussion of the susceptibility of the financial statements to material misstatement[10]. An important reason for this requirement is the consideration that the team members collectively have a broader access to people within the organisation and their insights. As they say, the most interesting information may typically be obtained in elevators and on the car park, and, again, there might be a better balance in the team's insights if the perspectives on the entity are not just confined to those conveyed by top management.

6.4.1 **GAIN AN UNDERSTANDING OF THE ENVIRONMENT**

(Step 1, illustration 6.5)

ISA 315 distinguishes the following relevant aspects in the understanding of the entity and its environment[11]:

1 the entity's organizational structure, ownership and governance and its business model, including the extent to which the business model integrates the use of IT;

2 industry, regulatory and other external factors;

3 the measures used, internally and externally, to assess the entity's financial performance;

4 the applicable financial reporting framework, and the entity's accounting policies and the reasons for any changes thereto. The auditor evaluates whether the entity's accounting policies are appropriate and consistent with the applicable financial reporting framework.

Some of the typical considerations of the auditor developing an understanding of an entity are as follows:

▷ The entity's *organizational structure, ownership* and *governance*, and its business model (including the extent to which the business model integrates the use of IT). This aspect of the understanding phase deals with the entity's core operations, types of investments, its financing/ownership, and how management applies and discloses accounting policies.

▷ Information acquired about *business operations* may include nature of revenue sources (retailer, manufacturer, and professional services); products and services (e.g. pricing policies, locations and quantities of inventory, profit margins, warranties, order book); market (exports, contracts, terms of payment, market share, franchises,

ILLUSTRATION 6.6

CONSIDERATIONS WHEN OBTAINING AN UNDERSTANDING OF THE NATURE OF THE ENTITY

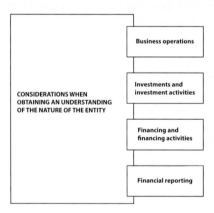

Business operations (derived from the Business Model) such as	Investments and investment activities such as	Financing and financing activities such as	Financial reporting such as
– Products, services and markets, resources, value drivers – Conduct of operations like production, sales, transport – Joint ventures, alliances – Governance structure, market position, locations – Key customers, suppliers, employee arrangements	– Mergers and acquisitions – Investments and divestments in capital, loans, securities and assets – Investments in non consolidated entities – Market conditions and opportunities	– Debt structure, solvency and liquidity policies – Debt arrangements and convenants – Ownership structure – Use of derivatives – Subsidiaries and contingent obligations	– Accounting principles – Industry and company specific standards and rules – (Inter) national accounting standards, law, rules, guidance – Revenue recognition practice – Accounting for fair values, unusual or complex transactions

licences, patents, composition of customer group), and location of company facilities (warehouses, offices); employment (wage levels, supply, union contracts, pensions), key suppliers, and customers.

▶ *Investments that have reduced in value.* Recent examples have been the crypto currency debacle of FTX[12] and the Theranos investment scandal[13]. Important transactions for which information could be gathered include: acquisitions, mergers and disposals of business divisions; use of derivative financial instruments; type of major investments by the company; capital investment activities (in plant and equipment, technology, etc.) and investment in non-consolidated entities such as joint ventures, special purpose entities[14] and partnerships.

▶ *The entity's choice and application of financial reporting policies* is one of the core considerations of the auditor, because these are the criteria on which the financial statements have been prepared and the auditor gives her assurance. The auditor must review company accounting policies including revenue recognition, inventories, research and development, important expense categories, judgmental accounting valuations, and financial statement presentation and disclosure. Foreign currency assets, liabilities, and transactions require special attention.

THE ENTITY'S OBJECTIVES, STRATEGIES AND RELATED BUSINESS RISKS

Client's 'business risk' refers to the potential for conditions or events that could impact the client's ability to achieve its objectives and execute its strategies. This includes risks that could affect the financial reports' reliability but goes beyond just financial risks. It encompasses a wide range of factors such as changes in the industry, new competitors, regulatory changes, technological advancements, and operational challenges. Auditors assess these risks to plan their audit, focusing on areas where the risk of material misstatement is higher due to these business risks. Understanding the client's business risk helps auditors make informed decisions about the nature, timing, and extent of audit procedures to apply.

The auditor will consider the entity's objectives and strategies, and the related business risks that may affect the financial statements. The entity's objectives are the overall plans for the company as determined by those charged with governance[15] and management.

One could compare a business entity to a living system. The communications network (formal and informal) is like a central nervous system where important direction is given from the brain to the body to perform work. In an organisation, management or those responsible for governance (e.g. the board of directors) formulate a strategy which, in turn, influences how employees perform work. Any living organism has a symbiotic relationship with the environment. Events such as severe weather may engender survival risks for an entity. Searching for food in the environment modifies the work an organism does and shapes its survival strategy. Similarly, in business organisations there exists a symbiotic alliance between the business processes of the organisation and external economic agents. Customers, suppliers, shareholders and the general public are external economic agents who impact on a company's profitability and ultimate survival. Financial statements are the communications that describe, on a monetary level, the company's dynamic interrelationship with external agents.

Understanding the entity and its environment, is a critical step in the risk assessment process[16]. Illustration 6.7 gives a global systems perspective of client's risks[17].

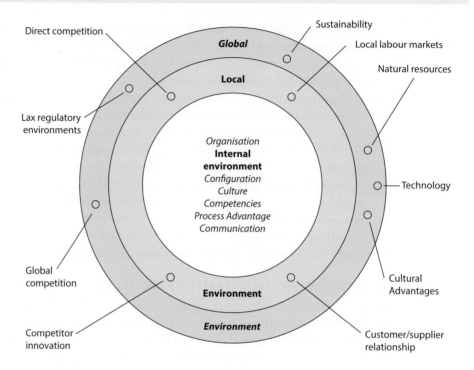

ILLUSTRATION 6.7

GLOBAL PERSPECTIVE OF CLIENT RISK

An interesting interpretation of this part of the 'understanding and risk assessment' phase is taken in a strategy-orientated framework[18] which involves the following steps:

1 Understand the client's strategic advantage. What are the entity's plans? What market niches do they control?

2 Understand the risks that threaten the client's business objectives. What forces are challenging the entity's competitive advantages?

3 Understand the key processes and related competencies to realise strategic advantage. What advantages and competencies are needed to increase market share in their business area? What are the risks and safeguards?

4 Measure and benchmark process performance. What is the evidence that the expected value is being created by the strategy?

5 Document the understanding of the client's ability to create value and generate future cash flows using a client business model, process analysis, key performance indicators, and a business risk profile.

6 Use the comprehensive business knowledge decision frame to develop expectations about key assertions embodied in the overall financial statements.

7 Compare reported financial results to expectations and design additional audit test work to address any gaps between expectations.

Illustration 6.8 shows what an auditor might consider in determining objectives, strategies and risks of the firm.

CONSIDERATIONS CONCERNING ENTITY OBJECTIVES, STRATEGIES AND RELATED BUSINESS RISKS

Existence of objectives (i.e. how the entity addresses industry, regulatory and other external factors) relating to, for example, the following:

- ▶ Industry developments (potential related business risk – entity does not have the personnel or expertise to deal with the changes in the industry)
- ▶ New products and services (potential related business risk – increased product liability)
- ▶ Expansion of the business (potential related business risk – demand has not been accurately estimated)
- ▶ New accounting requirements (potential related business risk – incomplete or improper implementation, increased costs)
- ▶ Regulatory requirements (potential related business risk – increased legal exposure)
- ▶ Current and prospective financing requirements (potential related business risk – loss of financing due to inability to meet requirements)
- ▶ Use of IT (potential related business risk – systems and processes not compatible)
- ▶ Effects of implementing a strategy, particularly any effects that will lead to new accounting requirements (potential related business risk – incomplete or improper implementation)

In the following sections, we discuss elements that are part of understanding the client and risk assessment procedures.

INDUSTRY, REGULATORY AND OTHER EXTERNAL FACTORS

It is important to understand the client's industry because their industry has specific risks created by the nature of the business, accounting conventions, and industry regulation. Understanding inherent risks common to all companies in a certain industry helps the auditor identify the inherent risks of the individual company. For example, the telecommunications industry has certain risks because it is globally competitive, technological changes may render certain assets obsolete at a quicker pace than anticipated, and telecommunication laws control a client's base and service fees. In other words, the industry gives rise to risks that may result in material misstatement of the financial statements of an individual company.

One of the relevant factors in this regard is the financial reporting framework (e.g. International Financial Reporting Standards (IFRS), Egyptian Accounting Standards (EAS), Brazil Accounting Norms, Russian Accounting Principles. etc.) that is applicable to the jurisdiction in which the company operates. Other factors relevant to the industry understanding could be the competition, supplier and customer relationships, technological developments and energy costs. The regulatory environment issues relevant to understanding the industry are accounting principles (and their industry specific application), taxation, environmental requirements, and the laws and government policies affecting the industry. Industries are also affected by external factors such as general economic conditions, interest rates, and availability of capital and debt. A list of matters that an auditor might consider when obtaining an understanding of the industry, regulatory and other external factors affecting an entity is given in illustration 6.9.

ILLUSTRATION 6.9

INDUSTRY, REGULATORY AND OTHER EXTERNAL FACTORS, INCLUDING THE APPLICABLE FINANCIAL REPORTING FRAMEWORK AUDITORS MIGHT CONSIDER

Industry conditions

▶ The market and competition, including demand, capacity and price competition

▶ Cyclical or seasonal activity

▶ Product technology relating to the entity's products

▶ Energy supply and cost

Regulatory environment

▶ Accounting principles and industry specific practices

▶ Regulatory framework for a regulated industry

▶ Legislation and regulation that significantly affect the entity's operations

　▶ Regulatory requirements

　▶ Direct supervisory activities

▶ Taxation (corporate and other)

▶ Government policies currently affecting the conduct of the entity's business

　▶ Monetary, including foreign exchange controls

　▶ Financial incentives (e.g. government aid programs)

　▶ Tariffs, trade restrictions

▶ Environmental requirements affecting the industry and the entity's business

Other external factors currently affecting the entity's business

▶ General level of economic activity (e.g. recession, growth)

▶ Interest rates and availability of financing

▶ Inflation, currency revaluation

▶ Technology (influence social media, cloud, cyber, AI)

LEGAL DOCUMENTS AS PART OF UNDERSTANDING THE CLIENT AND ITS ENVIRONMENT

Many of these aspects of the nature of the entity can be affected by legal considerations. Therefore, it is important, at an early stage, to consider specific legal documents, including corporate charter and bylaws, minutes of the board of directors and stockholders' meetings, and contracts. Local standards may require disclosure of contracts in the financial statements. Examples are listed in illustration 6.10.

Auditors are interested in all contracts in relation to the assessment of inherent risk. Contracts that are of particular interest to auditors are long-term notes and bonds payable, stock options, pension plans, contracts with vendors for future delivery of supplies, government contracts for completion and delivery of manufactured products, royalty agreements, union contracts, and leases.

ILLUSTRATION 6.10

EXAMPLES OF LEGAL DOCUMENTS AND RECORDS TO CONSIDER IN THE CONTEXT OF UNDERSTANDING THE ENTITY'S NATURE

Corporate charter – generally gives the name of the corporation, the date of incorporation, the kinds and amounts of capital stock the corporation is authorised to issue, and the types of business activities the corporation is authorised to conduct.

Bylaws – includes rules and procedures of the corporation including fiscal year, frequency of stockholder meetings, method of voting for board of directors, and the duties and powers of the corporate officer.

Corporate minutes – official record of the meetings of the board of directors and stockholders. Include authorisation of compensation of officers, new contracts, acquisition of fixed assets, loans and dividends payments.

Contracts – include long-term notes and payables, stock options, pension plans, contracts with vendors, government contracts, royalty agreements, union contracts, and leases.

MEASUREMENT AND REVIEW OF THE ENTITY'S FINANCIAL PERFORMANCE WHEN PERFORMING ANALYTICAL PROCEDURES

In order to assess the risk of material misstatements in the financial statements, an auditor should examine internally generated information used by management and external (third party) evaluations of the company. Internal measures provide management with information about progress towards meeting the entity's objectives. Internal information may include key performance indicators, budgets, variance analysis, segment information, and divisional, departmental or other level performance reports, and comparisons of an entity's performance with that of competitors. External information, such as analysts' reports and credit rating agency reports, may be useful to the auditor. Internal or external performance measures may create pressures on management to misstate the financial statements. A deviation in the performance measures may indicate a risk of misstatement of related financial statement information[19]. See illustration 6.11.

ILLUSTRATION 6.11

MEASUREMENT AND REVIEW OF THE ENTITY'S FINANCIAL PERFORMANCE

The following are internally generated information used by management for analysing financial performance that an auditor might consider before performing analytical procedures during the planning phase:
  ▶ Key performance indicators (financial and non-financial) and key ratios, trends and operating statistics
  ▶ Employee performance measures and incentive compensation policies
  ▶ Use of forecasts, budgets variance analysis, segment information and divisional, departmental or other level performance reports
  ▶ Comparisons of an entity's performance with that of competitors
  ▶ Period-on-period financial performance (revenue growth, profitability, leverage)

Analytical procedures are so important to the audit, and so universally employed, that a separate chapter is needed to describe them (chapter 9, 'Analytical Review', Phase 3). Analytical procedures[20] are performed at least twice in an audit – in the planning phase and near the end of the audit. During the gathering evidence phase the auditor may also use analytical procedures.

In this phase of understanding the client and its environment, analytical procedures focus on potential red flags when confronted with the latest (unaudited) figures rather than collecting persuasive audit evidence. So, the auditor applies analytical procedures at the planning stage to assist in understanding the business and in identifying areas of potential risk. Application of analytical procedures may indicate aspects of the business of which the auditor was unaware. Analytical procedures in planning the audit use information that is both financial and non-financial (e.g. the relationship between sales and square footage of selling space or volume of goods sold).

In order to better understand the client's business and industry, the auditor will calculate typical ratios and compare the company ratios to those of the industry. If the auditor is concerned about possible misstatements the ratios can be compared to prior years and looked at for fluctuations. To learn about liquidity or going concern, one may compare the current or quick ratio to previous years and to the industry.

When analytical procedures identify significant fluctuations or relationships that are inconsistent with other relevant information or that deviate from predicted amounts, the auditor should increase procedures to obtain adequate explanations and appropriate corroborative evidence.

6.4.2   GAIN AN UNDERSTANDING OF INHERENT RISK FACTORS

(Step 2, illustration 6.5)

Doing business involves risk taking. External circumstances giving rise to business risks may also influence inherent risk, but not every business risk will translate directly in a risk of a material misstatement in the financial statements. For example, the fact that an engineering company has difficulty finding sufficient engineers is clearly a business risk, without there being an obvious direct link to audit risk.

For example, technological developments might make a particular product obsolete, thereby causing inventory to be more susceptible to overstatement. Factors in the entity and its environment that impact several or all the classes of transactions, account balances, or disclosures may also influence the inherent risk. Such factors may include, for example, a lack of sufficient working capital to continue operations or a declining industry characterized by many business failures. Although the concept of business risks is broader than the concept of risks of material misstatements in the financial statements, most business risks will typically have a financial consequence, and hence will find their way into the financial statements.

Therefore, the auditor needs to gain an understanding how so-called *inherent risk factors*[21] affect the susceptibility of assertions to misstatement and the degree to which they do so. Inherent risk factors are defined as:

▷ Characteristics of events or conditions that affect susceptibility to misstatement, whether due to fraud or error, of an assertion about a class of transactions, account balance or disclosure, before consideration of controls.

▷ Taking into account qualitative or quantitative factors including complexity, subjectivity, change, uncertainty or susceptibility to misstatement due to management bias or other fraud risk factors.

The process how to assess these risk assessments, is visualized in illustration 6.12. It shows the comprehensiveness of the range to look at: it starts with a broad range of events and conditions, followed by peeling using the specific characteristics or conditions. The final step is to consider the likelihood and magnitude of misstatements. ISA 315 uses the concept of 'spectrum of inherent risk' to assist the auditor making a judgement, based on the likelihood and magnitude of a possible misstatement, on a range from higher to lower[22].

The illustration ends with the inner circle of inherent risks. Note that risks of material misstatements (RMM) are the same as inherent risks (IR), unless the auditor assesses control risks (CR) and is planning to test the operating effectiveness of controls[23].

Assessment of CR and its implications for the further audit plan are discussed in chapters 7 (Identifying and Assessing Control Risk) and 8 (Building and Execution of the Test Plan).

ILLUSTRATION 6.12

THE FRAMEWORK FOR THE IDENTIFICATION AND ASSESSMENT OF RISKS OF MATERIAL MISSTATEMENTS

Events and conditions identified when performing risk assessment procedures

Inherent risk factors (characteristics of events or conditions):
- Complexity
- Subjectivity
- Change
- Uncertainty
- Susceptibility to misstatement due to management bias or other fraud risk factors

Events and conditions that affect the susceptibility of (an) assertion(s) to misstatements

Inherent risks

Consideration of likelihood of occurrence and magnitude of misstatement

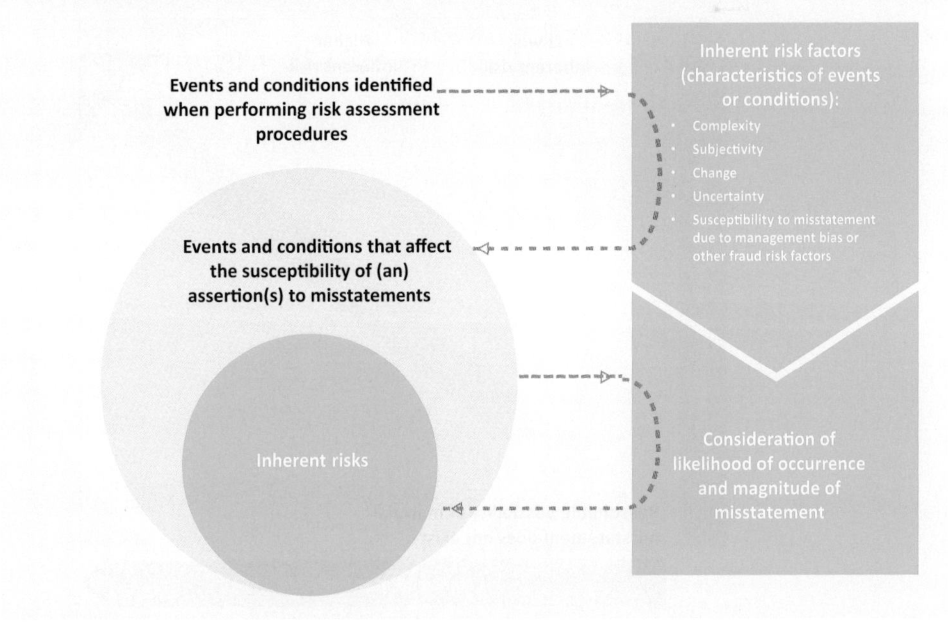

6.4.3 IDENTIFY THE RISKS OF MATERIAL MISSTATEMENTS AT TWO LEVELS

(Step 3, illustration 6.5)

The auditor needs to identify RMMs at two levels[24]:
- ▶ At financial statement level taking into account the effect on assertion level and potential pervasiveness on the financial statements.
- ▶ At assertion level based on the assessment of likelihood and magnitude of misstatement taking into account how and to the degree which:
  1 Inherent risk factors affect the susceptibility of relevant assertions to misstatement; and
  2 The risks of material misstatement at the financial statement level affect the assessment of inherent risk for risks of material misstatement at the assertion level.

A relevant assertion is defined[25] as: 'assertion about a class of transactions, account balance or disclosure is relevant when it has an identified risk of material misstatement'. The determination of whether an assertion is a relevant assertion is made before consideration of any related controls.

The audit evidence obtained might also apply to classes of transactions, account balances and disclosures at financial statement level as well as at the assertion level. Risks that exist at the financial statement level are pervasive, i.e. they have a potential impact on many items in the financial statements. An example is the risk that a company is unable

ILLUSTRATION 6.13

THE RISK SPECTRUM

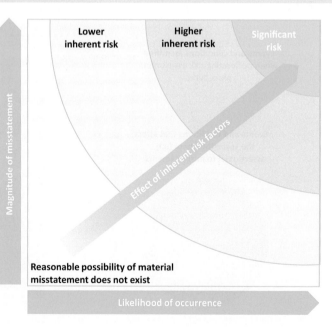

to continue as a going concern. This risk would not just have an impact on one item of the financial statements but would be of importance on the recognition and valuation of many items. Other risks are confined to one or only a few assertions in the financial statements, e.g. the risk of theft from a specific warehouse A could have an impact on the existence of the items recorded on account balance 'Inventory warehouse A'. 'Inventory' is the financial statement account balance, and the related class of transaction would be 'Goods in' or 'Goods out'.

For all RMMs, proper audit procedures must be designed and executed to mitigate those risks to an acceptable level. Depending on the likelihood and magnitude of the potential misstatements there is a *spectrum* of lower to higher inherent risks. Significant risks are at the upper end of this spectrum (as described in the next paragraph).

Building on the above, several events or conditions do not require follow-up during the audit because they do not present a risk of a material misstatements. This risk spectrum is visualized in illustration 6.13. Significant risks – which are part of inherent risk – are the upper end of the spectrum.

6.4.4 **DETERMINE WHETHER THE ASSESSED INHERENT RISKS ARE SIGNIFICANT RISKS**
(Step 4, illustration 6.5)

ISA 315 defines a significant risk as an identified RMM where 'the inherent risk is close to the upper end of the spectrum of inherent risk due to the degree to which inherent risk factors affect the combination of the likelihood of a misstatement occurring and the magnitude of the potential misstatement should that misstatement occur'[26]. An identified RMM is also to be treated as a significant risk in accordance with the requirements of other ISAs[27]. The latter is applicable for RMMs related to fraud (chapter 12) and related parties (section 10.7).

Significant risks are risks that require special audit consideration. Significant risks generally relate to judgmental matters and significant non-routine transactions. Judgement is used, for example, in the development of significant accounting or fair value estimates. Such non-routine transactions may arise from management intervention in specifying the accounting treatment for a transaction, manual intervention for data collection and processing, complex calculations or accounting principles, transactions for which there is difficulty in implementing effective controls, and significant related party transactions. Inherent risks may be greater for significant judgmental matters requiring accounting estimates or revenue recognition and for assumptions about the effects of future events (e.g. fair value) than for ordinary transactions.

SPECIAL AUDIT CONSIDERATIONS FOR SIGNIFICANT RISKS
As part of risk assessment, the auditor may determine some of the risks identified are significant risks that require special audit consideration. Classification of a risk as requiring special consideration is important in the context of the auditor's response to the risk (see chapter 7, 'Identifying and Assessing Control Risk'). In particular, it is even more important for significant than for non-significant risks that the auditor evaluates the design of the entity's controls, including relevant control procedures, and obtains contemporaneous evidence as to whether or not they have been implemented. Further, it is required that the auditor performs substantive procedures that are specifically responsive to the risks.

CONCEPT AND A COMPANY 6.1

BUSINESS RISK AND SIGNIFICANT RISK – LEHMAN BROTHERS AND ERNST & YOUNG

Concept	What is business risk? What is significant risk? When does a business turn out to become an audit risk?
Story	The financial market turmoil in 2007 and 2008 has led to the most severe financial crisis since the Great Depression and also had large repercussions on the real economy. The bursting of the US housing bubble forced banks to write down several hundred billion dollars in bad loans caused by mortgage delinquencies. At the same time, the stock market capitalization of the major banks declined by more than twice as much.
	Lehman Brothers Holdings Inc. was a global financial services firm. It was the fourth-largest investment bank in the US (behind Goldman Sachs, Morgan Stanley, and Merrill Lynch), doing business in investment banking, equity and fixed-income sales and trading (especially US Treasury securities), research, investment management, private equity and private banking, until it filed for bankruptcy on 15 September 2008.
	Lehman borrowed significant amounts to fund its investing in the years leading to its bankruptcy in 2008, a process known as leveraging or gearing. A significant portion of this investing was in housing-related assets, making it vulnerable to a downturn in that market.
	In March 2008, Lehman Brothers had survived the fallout (in which competitor Bear Stearns went bankrupt), but only narrowly. It subsequently made heavy use of the Fed's new Primary Dealer Credit Facility and had to issue new equity to strengthen its balance sheet. The inability to do so was a significant business risk for Lehman, resulting from the failure to mitigate other business risks.
	In order to avoid this business failure, Lehman Brothers used an accounting procedure termed 'repo 105' to temporarily exchange $50 billion of assets into cash just before publishing its financial statements. This conclusion was drawn by Anton R. Valukas, a court-appointed examiner, in a report in which he published the results of a year-long investigation into the finances of Lehman Brothers.
	Repo 105 is an accounting manoeuvre where a short-term loan is classified as a sale.
	In December 2010, New York's attorney general, Cuomo, filed a lawsuit in the New York Supreme Court claiming that Ernst & Young (E&Y), a Big Four firm, helped hide Lehman's 'fraudulent financial reporting'. As the auditor of Lehman Brothers, Ernst & Young approved the use of repo 105 transactions and approved the financial statements of Lehman Brothers.
	In a press release, Ernst & Young stated: 'Lehman's bankruptcy occurred in the midst of a global financial crisis triggered by dramatic increases in mortgage defaults, associated losses in mortgage and real estate portfolios, and a severe tightening of liquidity. Lehman's bankruptcy was preceded and followed by other bankruptcies, distressed mergers, restructurings, and government bailouts of all of the other major investment banks, as well as other major financial institutions. In short, Lehman's bankruptcy was not caused by any accounting issues.'
Discussion Questions	▶ Do you believe it is possible that Lehman Brothers was able to borrow more money thanks to the use of repo 105 transactions?
	▶ Did Ernst & Young put too much emphasis on the form of repo 105 transactions and neglected the substance of repo 105 transactions?
	▶ Do you blame Lehman Brothers for trying almost anything to avoid bankruptcy?

References   Brunnermeier, M.K. (2008), 'Deciphering the Liquidity and Credit Crunch 2007–08', NBER Working Paper No. 14612, National Bureau of Economic Research, Cambridge, MA.

http://en.wikipedia.org/wiki/Lehman_Brothers.

http://www.accountingweb.com/topic/accounting-auditing/did-ernst-young-really-assist-financial-fraud.

As addressed before, understanding the entity's system of internal controls is an integral part of risk assessment. Given the complexity and extent of this topic, it will be dealt with in chapter 7, 'Identifying and Assessing Control Risk'.

6.5   MATERIALITY

The auditor's responsibility is to express an opinion on whether the financial statements are prepared, in all material respects, in accordance with financial accounting standards. Materiality is the degree of inaccuracy or imprecision that is still considered acceptable given the purpose of the financial statements[28].

Although financial reporting frameworks may discuss materiality in different terms, in the context of an audit, they generally explain that:

1   Misstatements, including omissions, are material if they, individually or in the aggregate, could reasonably be expected to influence the economic decisions of users taken based on the financial statements.

2   Judgements about materiality are made in light of surrounding circumstances and are affected by the size or nature of a misstatement, or a combination of both.

3   Judgements about matters that are material to users of the financial statements are based on a consideration of the common financial information needs of users as a group. The possible effect of misstatements on specific individual users, whose needs may vary widely, is not considered[29].

▶ PLANNING MATERIALITY

Planning materiality is a concept that is used to design the audit such that the auditor can obtain reasonable assurance that any error of a relevant (material) size or nature will be identified. There are additional costs for an auditor to audit with a lower materiality. The lower the materiality, the more costly is the audit. If any error of whatever small size needs to be found in the audit, the auditor would spend significantly more time than when a certain level of imprecision (higher materiality level) is considered acceptable.

What is material is often difficult to determine in practice. However, four factors are generally considered: size of item; nature of item; the circumstances; and the cost and benefit of auditing the item.

SIZE OF THE ITEM

The most common application of materiality concerns the size of the item considered. A large dollar amount item omitted from the financial statements is generally material. Size must be considered in relative terms, for example as a percentage of the relevant base (net income, total assets, sales, etc.) rather than an absolute amount. The view that size is an essential determinant of materiality means that, for financial reporting purposes, materiality can only be judged in relation to items or errors which are quantifiable in monetary terms.

NATURE OF THE ITEM

The nature of an item is a qualitative characteristic. An auditor cannot quantify the materiality decision in all cases; certain items may have significance even though the dollar amount may not be quite as large as the auditor would typically consider material. For example, a political bribe by an auditee, even though immaterial in size, may nevertheless be of such a sensitive nature and have such an effect on the company financial statement that users would need to be told. It has been suggested[30] that in making judgements about materiality, the following aspects of the nature of a misstatement should be considered:

▶ the events or transactions giving rise to the misstatement;
▶ the legality, sensitivity, normality and potential circumstances of the event or transaction;
▶ the identity of any other parties involved; and
▶ the accounts and disclosure notes affected.

CIRCUMSTANCES OF OCCURRENCE

The materiality of an error depends upon the circumstances of its occurrence. There are two types of relevant circumstances:

1 the users of the accounting information's economic decision-making process;
2 the context of the accounting information in which an item or error occurs.

Since materiality means the impact on the decisions of the user, the auditor must have knowledge of the likely users of the financial statements and those users' decisions process. If a company is being audited prior to listing on a national stock exchange or a large loan or merger, the users will be of one type. If statements of a closely held partnership are being audited, users will be of a different type.

For example, if the primary users of the financial statements are creditors, the auditor may assign a low materiality threshold to those items on financial statements that affect liquidity[31] such as current assets and current liabilities. On the other hand, if the primary users are investors or potential investors, the auditor may assign a low materiality threshold to income.

RELIABILITY, PRECISION AND AMOUNT OF EVIDENCE

The auditor should consider materiality and its relationship with audit risk when conducting an audit, according to ISA 320[32]. What does this mean? In statistical sampling, there is a fixed relationship between:

▶ the reliability of an assertion based on the sampling (in auditing this is determined by audit risk);
▶ the precision of this statement (in auditing it is determined by materiality); and
▶ the amount of evidence that should be gathered in order to make this assertion.

Changes in one of these three items have implications for (one of) the other two.

▷ **PERFORMANCE MATERIALITY**

Performance materiality is the amount or amounts set by the auditor at less than materiality for the financial statements as a whole. This reduces to an appropriately low level the probability that the total of uncorrected and undetected misstatements exceeds materiality for the financial statements as a whole. If applicable, performance materiality also refers to the amounts set by the auditor at less than the materiality levels for particular classes of transactions, account balances or disclosures[33].

Examples of considerations for determining performance materiality are outcome of risk assessments, complexity and volatility, financial health and stability, audit procedures and evidence. In practice, performance materiality is in general between 50 (higher risks) and 80 (lower risks) percent of planning materiality.

EXAMPLE: THREE ASSUMPTIONS IN THE SAME CIRCUMSTANCE

A real-life example might illustrate this relationship between reliability, precision and amount of evidence. Suppose you are asked to make an assertion about the average taxable income of randomly selected people, shopping at the Champs Elysees in Paris. Also suppose that gathering information regarding the taxable income of these people is costly. Consider the following three situations:

1 You are asked to make, with a high degree of reliability (you were asked to bet quite some money on the correctness of your assertion), the assertion that the average annual taxable income of ten people will be between minus and plus €30,000,000. Even though a high degree of reliability is requested (i.e. a lot is at stake for you), you will probably do little or no investigative work because you were allowed to make a very imprecise statement (i.e. a very high level of tolerance is allowed).

2 You are asked to make, with a low degree of reliability (you were asked to bet only a symbolic €1 on the correctness of your assertion), the assertion that the average annual taxable income of these random ten people will be between €0 and €70,000. Even though this time a high degree of precision is requested, you will probably only do little or no (costly) investigative work, since you were only asked to make your assertion with a low degree of reliability (not a lot at stake for you).

3 You are asked to make, with a high degree of reliability (again, you were asked to bet quite some money on the correctness of your assertion), the assertion that the average annual taxable income of these ten people will be between €0 and €70,000. Because of the high degree of reliability and precision requested (i.e. a lot is at stake for you and only a relatively low degree of tolerance is accepted in your statement), you will probably do extensive investigative work.

These examples might clarify how there is an inverse relationship between audit risk (as a measure of reliability) and materiality (as a measure of precision). (See also illustration 6.14.)

What degree of imprecision or materiality is acceptable in auditing financial statements? To decide this, the imprecision tolerated should be related to the size of the audited company's business and its profitability. Try to determine how much error or misstatement auditors would be willing to tolerate and still render an opinion that the financial statements were not materially misleading in Case One and Case Two, following.

ILLUSTRATION 6.14

RELATIONSHIP BETWEEN AUDIT RISK AND MATERIALITY

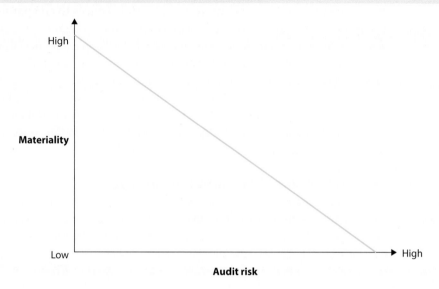

MATERIALLY MISSTATED OR NOT?

CASE ONE

A few days before the end of 20X1, $1,000 expenditure for the repair of equipment was incorrectly charged to the equipment account in the balance sheet rather than to operating expenses in the income statement. As a result (ignoring depreciation), total assets should be stated at $1,589,000 instead of $1,590,000 and income before taxes should be stated at $107,000 instead of $108,000. Are the financial statements still fairly presented and not materially misleading?

CASE TWO

A few days before the end of 20X1, $50,000 expenditure for the repair of equipment was incorrectly charged to the equipment account rather than to operating expenses. As a result (ignoring depreciation), total assets should be stated at $1,490,000 rather than $1,540,000 and income before taxes should be stated at $58,000 rather than $108,000? Are the financial statements fairly presented and not materially misleading?

ANALYSIS

In Case One the financial statements are fairly presented and not materially misstated because the $1,000 difference in assets and net income will not make a difference to the financial statement user, i.e. it is not material. Case Two is different. The financial statements are materially misstated, primarily because net income, an important basis of materiality, is overstated by 86 per cent. This overstatement of net income is something that could definitely change the decisions of a financial statement user, i.e. it is material.

▶ **WHERE TO SET MATERIALITY?**

Considering all these materiality factors, then, at what amount should materiality be set? In practice, every accounting firm has its own set of guidelines, or 'rules of thumb' related to a financial statement base such as net income, total revenues, etc. Rules of thumb commonly used in practice include:

- ▶ 5 to 10 per cent of net income before taxes.
- ▶ 5 to 10 per cent of current assets.
- ▶ 5 to 10 per cent of current liabilities.
- ▶ 0.5 to 2 per cent of total assets.
- ▶ 0.5 to 2 per cent of total revenues.
- ▶ 1 to 5 per cent of total equity.

The appropriate financial statement base for computing materiality will vary based on the nature of the client's business. For example, if a company is near break-even, net income for the year will be much too small to use as the financial statement base. In that case the auditors will often choose another financial statement base or use an average of net income over a number of prior years.

CONCEPT AND A COMPANY 6.2

ARTHUR ANDERSEN, WASTE MANAGEMENT AND MATERIALITY

Concept	What is material and how is materiality determined?

Story	In 1993 and early 1994, Arthur Andersen audited Waste Management's 1993 financial statements. By 1 February 1994, the engagement team quantified current and prior period misstatements totaling $128 million, which, if recorded, would have reduced net income before special items by 12 per cent.

The engagement team prepared Proposed Adjusting Journal Entries (PAJEs) in that amount for Waste Management to record in 1993. A PAJE is an adjustment proposed by the auditor to the company during the audit that, if accepted by the company, would correct a misstatement in the books.

The engagement team also identified 'accounting practices that gave rise to other known and likely misstatements' involving understatements of operating expenses for which no PAJEs were prepared. These misstatements included, among other things:

1 amounts for deferred costs of impaired projects that should have been written off;
2 land carrying values in excess of net realizable value;
3 improper purchase acquisition accruals in connection with the establishment of environmental remediation reserves (liabilities);
4 reversals of the environmental remediation reserves (liabilities) to income; and
5 unsupported changes to the salvage values of waste vehicles and containers.

The engagement team also knew of the company's capitalized interest methodology, which Andersen knew did not conform to GAAP but which it had determined was 'not materially inaccurate'.

Waste Management refused to record the PAJEs or to correct the accounting practices giving rise to the PAJEs and other misstatements and likely misstatements.

The engagement team informed Andersen's risk management partner of the PAJEs and questionable accounting practices. Andersen's Audit Objectives and Procedures Manual required that risk management partners consult with senior partners when cumulative PAJEs exceeded 8 per cent of net income from continuing operations. These partners reviewed and discussed the unrecorded PAJEs as well as 'continuing audit issues'. They determined that Andersen would nonetheless issue an unqualified audit report on Waste Management's 1993 financial statements.

Applying an analytical procedure for evaluating the materiality of audit findings referred to as the 'roll-forward' method, these partners determined that, because the majority of PAJEs concerned prior period misstatements, the impact of the PAJEs relating to current period misstatements on Waste Management's 1993 income statement was not material. They would issue an unqualified audit report. But they also warned Waste Management that Andersen expected the company to change its accounting practices and to reduce the cumulative amount of the PAJEs in the future.

Waste Management later paid US$457 million to settle a shareholder class-action suit. The SEC fined Waste Management's independent auditor, Arthur Andersen, US$7 million for its role.

Discussion Questions	▶ What analysis do you think the engagement team did to determine the amount of the PAJEs?
	▶ By what reasoning did the audit team determine the accounting practices that gave rise to other known and likely misstatements mentioned that did not need adjustment?
	▶ What items do you think the senior partners discussed when determining that Andersen would issue an unqualified opinion?
	▶ ISA 450 did not exist when this case occurred. If it had existed, did Arthur Andersen meet all requirements of ISA 450?

| **References** | SEC, 2001, Release No. 44444, Accounting And Auditing Enforcement Release No. 1405, 'In the Matter of Arthur Andersen LLP Respondent', Securities and Exchange Commission, 19 June. |
| | http://en.wikipedia.org/wiki/Waste_Management,_Inc#Accounting_improprieties. |

US SEC RESPONSE TO WORLDCOM ILLEGAL ACTS

Concept	Liability under statutory law – involving auditors in the disciplinary process.
Story	WorldCom's illegal activities, which included providing falsified financial information to the public, led to the company's downfall in 2002.

WorldCom misled investors from at least as early as 1999 through the first quarter of 2002, and during that period, as a result of undisclosed and improper accounting, WorldCom materially overstated the income it reported on its financial statements by approximately $9 billion (SEC, *Litigation Release*, 2002).

WorldCom was ordered to hire a qualified consultant, acceptable to the SEC, to review the effectiveness of its material internal accounting control structure and policies, including those related to line costs, reserves and capital expenditures, as well as the effectiveness and propriety of WorldCom's processes, practices and policies to ensure that the company's financial data was accurately reported in its public financial statements. The company hired KPMG to launch a comprehensive audit of its financial statements for 2001 and 2002 (Ulick, 2002).

WorldCom was also ordered to provide reasonable training and education to certain officers and employees to minimize the possibility of future violations of federal securities laws.

The SEC proposed a settlement in its civil action against WorldCom Inc. in a federal district court. The proposed settlement was for WorldCom to pay a civil penalty of $1.5 billion. As a result of the company's pending bankruptcy case, the proposed settlement provides for satisfaction of the Commission's judgment by WorldCom's payment, after review and approval of the terms of the settlement by the bankruptcy court, of $500 million (SEC, *Litigation Release*, 2003).

Discussion Questions	▷ What security procedures should WorldCom have taken overall in order to prevent these illegal acts from happening?
	▷ What steps should innocent middle management have taken in order to stop or prevent top executives who performed the illegal acts?
	▷ Should they have reported to officials at the first sign of improper accounting? Or should they have just quit the company immediately?
References	SEC, 2002, Litigation Release 17866, 'In *SEC* v *WorldCom*, Court Imposes Full Injunctive Relief, Orders Extensive Reviews of Corporate Governance Systems and Internal Accounting Controls', US Securities and Exchange Commission, November 2002.
	SEC, 2003, Litigation Release 18147, 'In WorldCom Case, SEC Files Proposed Settlement of Claim for Civil Penalty', US Securities and Exchange Commission, May 2003.
	Ulick, Jake, 2002, 'WorldCom's Financial Bomb', *CNN/Money*, 26 June.

6.6 FRAUD AND IRREGULARITIES

When performing audit procedures according to ISA 315, the auditor includes the considerations on the risks of material misstatements due to fraud. ISA 240 'The Auditor's Responsibilities Relating to Fraud in an Audit of Financial Statements', deals with the auditor's responsibilities relating to fraud. Specifically, it expands on how risk assessment and response are to be applied in relation to risks of material misstatement due to fraud.

The thought process from inherent risk factors to inherent risks is mirrored with the journey from fraud risk factors to fraud risks. We refer to chapter 12 (Fraud and Other Considerations of Law and Regulation in An Audit).

6.7 USING THE WORK OF OTHERS AND CONSIDERING AUDITEE USE OF SERVICE ORGANISATIONS

In the course of an audit engagement an auditor may rely on the work of the company's internal auditors, and in some cases, they may hire an expert external to their firm to provide expertise necessary for the audit but not available at the audit firm. The auditor may also find it necessary to review the work of any outsourced services which may impact the financial statement. As part of the auditor's risk assessment phase, the auditor assesses whether the entity has an internal auditor, uses a management expert or uses a service organization for outsourced services.

As these topics are relevant to multiple stages of the audit, we have grouped those in chapter 13.3.

6.8 OTHER PLANNING ACTIVITIES

Other planning activities include planning discussions with those charged with governance (like the board of directors) and preparing the audit planning memorandum.

▶ DISCUSSIONS WITH THOSE CHARGED WITH GOVERNANCE

As part of the planning process, it may be appropriate to have discussions with those charged with governance. The auditor should understand where the entity has an internal audit function, the extent to which the auditor will use the work of internal audit, and how the external and internal auditors can best work together in a constructive and complementary manner. Further, the auditor may seek the views of those charged with governance about the appropriate person(s) in the entity's governance structure with whom to communicate, the allocation of responsibilities between those charged with governance and management, the entity's objectives and strategies, and the related business risks that may result in material misstatements. Also see section 5.3.

Discussion with those charged with governance will be helpful in planning audit procedures. The attitudes, awareness, and actions of those charged with governance concerning the entity's internal control and its importance in the entity, including how they oversee the effectiveness of internal control, and the detection or possibility of fraud will shape the assessment of control risk and planned procedures for fraud detection. The actions of those charged with governance in response to developments in accounting standards, corporate governance practices, exchange listing rules and related matters will determine how much accounting practices should be considered. Their responses to previous communications with the auditor will say a lot about whether prior year problems have been resolved.

▷ **AUDIT PLAN**

According to ISA 300[34] 'Planning an audit involves establishing the overall audit strategy for the engagement and developing an audit plan.'

The audit plan sets out the nature, timing and extent of planned audit procedures required by ISA 315 and ISA 330[35] to implement the overall audit strategy into a comprehensive description of the work to be performed. It serves as a set of instructions to staff involved in the audit and as a means to control and record the proper execution of the work. The auditor should document the overall audit strategy and the audit plan, including reasons for significant changes made during the audit engagement.

ISA 300 does not prescribe the format of the audit plan. The format used may be dependent on the electronic documenting system of the audit firm, which may prefer whether a memorandum, a documentation per specific topic, or a combination of both.

Chapter 7 describes Control Risk and IT. Chapter 8 explores building the audit (test) plan, based on the elements of understanding and risk analysis as described in chapters 6 and 7.

▷ **DOCUMENTATION**

The auditor's documentation of reasons for significant changes to the overall audit strategy and audit plan includes the auditor's response to the events, conditions or results of audit procedures that resulted in such changes. The manner in which these matters are documented is for the auditor to determine based on professional judgement. Nevertheless, ISA 315[36] requires documenting at least:

▷ The discussion among the engagement team and the significant decisions reached.
▷ Key elements of the auditor's understanding, the sources of information from which the auditor's understanding was obtained and the risk assessment procedures performed.
▷ The evaluation of the design of identified controls, and determination whether such controls have been implemented; and
▷ The identified and assessed risks of material misstatement at the financial statement level and at the assertion level, including significant risks and risks for which substantive procedures alone cannot provide sufficient appropriate audit evidence, and the rationale for the significant judgments made.

ISA 320[37] about materiality requires the auditor to document at least the amounts and factors considered in their determination:

▷ Materiality for the financial statements as a whole.
▷ If applicable, the materiality level or levels for particular classes of transactions, account balances and disclosures.
▷ Performance materiality.
▷ Any revisions of the above as the audit progressed.

EXAMPLE ILLUSTRATING AUDIT PLANNING

Binheim GmbH is a designer clothing company which designs, manufactures and distributes internationally several apparel brand names including Pinakothek and Natur. Binheim is privately held by the von Ansbach family. The family sold 10 percent of its shares during the audit year to a new division of Adidas AG, a multi-billion-euro international company. Binheim has awarded a bid to perform the audit to Isar & Ludwig, Wirtschaftsprüfers. The management of Binheim told the partner that they want an audit because of the new equity position and the demands by Adidas that the company must be audited.

As Binheim is a new client of Isar & Ludwig (I&L) and I&L does not have an established understanding of Binheim and the von Ansbach family, inherent risk is higher than normal.

During the client acceptance phase, the audit partner looked at documents and interviewed professionals who served the firm to get a feeling for the background of Binheim. The partner reviewed a report prepared by the team on Binheim's internal controls. The management was generally considered to be ethical and the internal controls were strong.

The audit team also examined the entity's organizational structure, ownership and governance and its business model, including the extent to which the business model integrates the use of IT.

Also reviewed was current information on the industry, regulatory and other external factors, including the applicable financial reporting framework. They considered the measures used, internally and externally, to assess the entity's financial performance. These factors could represent some inherent risk. To get this data, the audit team discussed with the management their objectives and expectations and plans for achieving these goals. Expectations were also explored with a sample of the company's external agents such as customers, suppliers, shareholders, financial institutions, government.

The accounting system and premises were reviewed for any unusual transactions. Binheim GmbH's key ratios were compared to those of the industry. The audit team read management reports and internal control manuals. The audit team visited and toured the company premises. Inventory seemed well organized.

The fact that the von Ansbach family approached Adidas and sold them on the idea that they were a good investment increased the risk of the company overstating revenue, assets or profit and understating liabilities and expenses. I&L would likely consider the possibility of a related party issue because the von Ansbach family approached Adidas with the joint venture idea and Adidas owns 10% of the venture.

There might also be differences between computerized systems between the two companies. All these increase the risk of material misstatement. Materiality is set at 1% of revenue, as that could be a crucial account. These factors may contribute to control risk.

The team held a team-wide discussion on the susceptibility of the financial statements to material misstatement.

All the collected data and the audit team discussion should provide a basis for drawing up the audit plan. The plan should establish tests to reduce the risk of material misstatement to a reasonable level.

6.9 SUMMARY

The objective of the auditor is to plan the audit so that it will be performed in an effective manner. The auditor shall establish an overall audit strategy that sets the scope, timing and direction of the audit, and that guides the development of the audit plan. The objective of planning is to determine the amount and type of evidence and review required to give the auditor assurance that there is no material misstatement of the financial statements.

The planning procedures are:

1 Perform audit procedures to understand the entity and its environment, including the entity's internal control.
2 Assess the risks of material misstatements of the financial statements.
3 Determine materiality.

This chapter discusses the planning process through understanding and risk analysis aimed to assess the inherent risks. It starts conceptually with the audit risk model (section 6.3) followed by the risk assessment process following ISA 315 (section 6.4) and determining materiality (section 6.5). Additional considerations are included in the remaining sections.

Audit risk is the risk that the auditor gives an inappropriate audit opinion when the financial statements are materially misstated. The higher the audit risk, the more evidence must be gathered in order to obtain sufficient appropriate assurance that serves as a basis for expressing an opinion on the financial statements. Audit risk has three components: inherent risk, control risk and detection risk. They are defined:

▷ Inherent risk is the susceptibility of an account balance or class of transactions to misstatements that could be material, assuming that there were no related internal controls.

▷ Control risk is the risk that a misstatement that could occur in an account balance or class of transactions and that could be material will not be prevented or detected and corrected on a timely basis by accounting and internal control systems.

▷ Detection risk is the risk that auditor's procedures will not detect a misstatement that exists in an account balance or class of transactions that could be material, individually or when aggregated with misstatements in other balances, or classes of transactions, or disclosures.

In the ISAs, the combination of inherent and control risk is called the risk of a material misstatement (RMM). When inherent and control risks are high – and therefore result in high RMM – acceptable detection risk needs to be low to reduce audit risk to an acceptably low level. For example, if control risk is low, the auditor can perform less effective substantive tests (detection risk is high). Alternatively, if inherent risk is higher, the auditor must apply more effective substantive testing procedures to lower detection risk. In short, the higher the assessment of inherent and control risk, the more audit evidence the auditor should obtain from the performance of substantive procedures.

ISA 315 provides an overview of the procedures that the auditor should follow in order to obtain an understanding sufficient to assess the risks and consider these risks in designing the audit plans. The risk assessment procedures shall include the following: inquiries of management, analytical procedures, and observation and inspection. Further, a visit to, and tour of, the company premises will help the auditor develop a better understanding of the client's business and operations. Viewing the facilities helps to identify some internal control safeguards. Seeing the production process will help in assessing the inventory movement and the use of fixed assets.

ISA 315 also requires an audit team-wide discussion of the susceptibility of the financial statements to material misstatement. The most interesting information may typically be obtained in elevators and on the car park, and, again, there might be a better balance in the team's insights if the perspectives on the entity are not just confined to those conveyed by top management.

ISA 315 distinguishes the following relevant aspects in the understanding of the entity and its environment:

▶ the entity's organizational structure, ownership and governance and its business model, including the extent to which the business model integrates the use of IT;

▶ industry, regulatory and other external factors, including the applicable financial reporting framework;

▶ the measures used, internally and externally, to assess the entity's financial performance;

▶ the applicable financial reporting framework, and the entity's accounting policies and the reasons for any changes thereto. The auditor evaluates whether the entity's accounting policies are appropriate and consistent with the applicable financial reporting framework.

The auditor applies analytical procedures at the planning stage to assist in understanding the business and in identifying areas of potential risk. Application of analytical procedures may indicate aspects of the business of which the auditor was unaware. Analytical procedures in planning the audit use information that is both financial and non-financial (e.g. the relationship between sales and square footage of selling space or volume of goods sold). In order to better understand the client's business and industry, the auditor will calculate typical ratios and compare the company ratios to those of the industry. If the auditor is concerned about possible misstatements the ratios can be compared to prior years and looked at for fluctuations. To learn about liquidity or going concern, one may compare the current or quick ratio to previous years and to the industry.

Based on gaining an understanding of the environment, the auditor needs to gain an understanding how *inherent risk factors* affect the susceptibility of assertions to misstatement and the degree to which they do so. Inherent risk factors are defined as a characteristic of events or conditions that affect susceptibility to misstatement of an assertion about a class of transactions, account balance or disclosure, before consideration of controls.

Significant risks are audit risks that require special audit consideration. ISA 315 defines a significant risk as an identified risk of material misstatement where 'the inherent risk is close to the upper end of the spectrum of inherent risk' Significant risks generally relate to judgmental matters and significant non-routine transactions. Judgement is used, for example, in the development of significant accounting or fair value estimates. Non-routine transactions are transactions that are unusual, either due to size or nature, and that therefore occur infrequently. Risks of material misstatement may be greater for significant judgmental matters requiring accounting estimates or revenue recognition and for assumptions about the effects of future events (e.g. fair value) than for ordinary transactions.

The auditor's responsibility is to express an opinion on whether the financial statements are prepared, in all material respects, in accordance with financial accounting standards. Materiality is the degree of inaccuracy or imprecision that is still considered acceptable given the purpose of the financial statements. What is material is often difficult to determine in practice. However, four factors are generally considered: size of item; nature of item; the circumstances; and the cost and benefit of auditing the item. For example, the nature of an item might be important -a political bribe by an auditee, even though immaterial in size, may nevertheless be of such a sensitive nature and have such an effect on the company financial statement that users would need to be told.

At what amount should materiality be set? In practice, every accounting firm has its own set of guidelines, or 'rules of thumb' related to a financial statement base such as net income, total revenues, etc. In the course of an audit engagement an auditor may rely on the work of the company's internal auditors, and in some cases, they may hire an expert external to their firm to provide expertise necessary for the audit but not available at the audit firm. The auditor may also find it necessary to review the work of any outsourced services which may impact the financial statement.

As part of the planning process, it may be appropriate to have discussions with those charged with governance. The auditor should understand where the entity has an internal audit function, the extent to which the auditor will use the work of internal audit, and how the external and internal auditors can best work together in a constructive and complementary manner. Further, the auditor may seek the views of those charged with governance as to the appropriate person(s) in the entity's governance structure with whom to communicate, the allocation of responsibilities between those charged with governance and management, the entity's objectives and strategies, and the related business risks that may result in material misstatements.

Planning an audit involves establishing the overall audit strategy for the engagement and developing an audit plan. The audit plan sets out the nature, timing and extent of planned audit procedures required to implement the overall audit strategy into a comprehensive description of the work to be performed. It serves as a set of instructions to staff involved in the audit and as a means to control and record the proper execution of the work.

The auditor should document the overall audit strategy and the audit plan, including reasons for significant changes made during the audit engagement. The auditor's documentation should include at least the significant discussion among the engagement team; key elements of the auditor's understanding and the sources of that understanding; the risk assessment procedures performed; the evaluation of the design of identified controls; the assessed risks of material misstatement at the financial statement level including significant risks and risks for which substantive procedures alone cannot provide sufficient appropriate audit evidence; and the rationale for the significant judgments made.

6.10 QUESTIONS, EXERCISES AND CASES

6.2 Planning Objective and Procedures

6-1 What is the objective of audit planning?

6-2 List the planning procedures.

6.3 Audit Risk Model

6-3 What are the definitions of the three audit risk components?

6-4 What components of the audit risk exist independently of the audit? What does an auditor do in this situation?

6-5 Distinguish between business risk and significant risk.

6.4 The Risk Assessment Process

6-6 ISA 315 provides an overview of the procedures that the auditor should follow in order to obtain an understanding sufficient to assess the risks and consider these risks in designing the audit plans. Describe the procedures.

6-7 How can understanding of a certain industry help an auditor?

6-8 What is a business risk that is no inherent risk?

6-9 What are inherent risk factors?

6-10 When is RMM = IR?

6.5 Materiality

6-11 How is materiality defined in the ISAs (specifically ISA 320)?

6-12 What four factors are generally considered in determining materiality? Briefly discuss them.

6-13 What guidelines or 'rules of thumb' related to a financial statement base such as net income, total revenues, etc. are commonly used in practice?

6.6 Fraud and Irregularities

6-14 Describe why fraud matters are an integral part of understanding the entity and its environment.

6.7 Using the Work of Others and Considering Auditee Use of Service Organisations

6-15 What is the relevance of taking into account the internal audit function during the risk assessment phase?

6-16 How does the auditee use of service organisations have an effect on the auditor's risk assessment?

6.2 Planning Objective and Procedures

6-17 Planning Procedures. Constantijn & Nianias, Soma Orkaton Logistons (SOLs), have been hired to audit Eidola Company, a biochemical company listed on the Athens Stock Exchange. Constantijn & Nianias is auditing the client for the first time in the current year as a result of a dispute between Eidola and the previous auditor over the proper booking of sales and accounts receivable for sales of inventory that has not been delivered but has for practical purposes been completed and sold.

Eidola has been grown from a small start-up to a highly successful company in the industry in the past seven years, primarily as a result of many successful mergers negotiated by Lev Panis, the president and chairman of the board. Although other biotech firms have had difficulty in recent years, Eidola continues to prosper, as shown by its constantly increasing earnings and growth. Bayer, the large German chemical company, has a special discount contract with them and represents 15 per cent of their sales. In the last year, however, the company's profits turned downward.

His board of directors that include many of his old university classmates generally supports Lev. The board, which meets twice annually, recently issued a policy on corporate ethics conduct. Lev says he owes much of his success to the hiring of aggressive young executives paid relatively low salaries combined with an unusually generous profit-sharing plan. The corporate structure is very informal, as Lev does not believe than any employee should have a title or a specific job description as it 'gives people airs'. Lev's only corporate objective is 'to make large profits so our stock price will increase and our shareholders will be happy'. The management information system at Eidola is very limited and they lack sophisticated accounting records for a company that size. The information system will be updated this year. The personnel in the accounting department are competent but somewhat overworked and underpaid relative to the other employees, and therefore turnover is high. The most comprehensive records are for production and marketing because Lev Panis believes these areas are more essential to operations than accounting. There are only four internal auditors and they spend the majority of their time taking inventories, which is time consuming because inventories are located at 11 facilities in four countries.

The financial statements for the current year include a profit 20 per cent less than the last year, but the auditors feel it should be a larger decrease because of the reduced volume and the disposal of a segment of the business, Kata-Karpos. The disposal of this segment was considered necessary because it had become increasingly unprofitable over the past three years. When it was acquired from Christopher Panis, Lev Panis's brother, it was considered profitable even though its largest customer was Kata-Klino, also owned by Christopher Panis.

Eidola is considered under-financed by market analysts. There is excessive current debt and management is reluctant to sell equity on the capital markets because increasing the number of shares will decrease share price. Lev Panis is now talking to several large companies in hopes of a merger.

Required:

A.   Briefly discuss which matters Constantijn & Nianias, SOLs, should consider for each of the first three planning procedures.

B.   What techniques should the auditors use to gather the needed information?

6.3   **The Audit Risk Model**

6-18 Explain why, given a specific Audit Risk (AR) and a high Risk of Material Misstatement (RMM), extensive audit procedures must then be carried out.

6-19 Risk Analysis. Four tasks are required to assess the risk of misstatement. They are (1) identify risk by developing an understanding of the entity and its environment, (2) relate the risk to what could go wrong in management's assertion, (3) determine whether risks could result in material misstatement of the financial statements, and (4) consider that risks will result in material misstatement.

Required:

Using these tasks, analyse the following risks:

A.   Cash receipts from sales in an office supply store are not recorded.

B.   Investment in securities by the treasury department of a small manufacturing firm result in large losses.

C.   Financial statement disclosures do not comply with IASs.

D.   Pollution equipment in a large international steel refinery does not comply with local pollution control laws.

E.   Bank statements do not correlate with cash receipts and disbursements.

6.4 The Risk Assessment Process

6-20 Nature of the Entity. To get information about the core processes of the entity an auditor examines its business operations, investments, capital structure and financing activities, and financial reporting policies. Why are these business operations considered 'core processes'?

6-21 Client Facilities Tour. When an auditor has accepted an engagement from a new client who is a manufacturer, it is customary for the auditor to tour the client's plant facilities. Discuss the ways in which the auditor's observations made during the course of the plant tour would be of help in planning and conducting the audit.

6.5 Materiality

6-22 Materiality and Risk. Dag Nilsson, Auktoriserad Revisor (AR), considers the audit risk at the financial statement level in the planning of the audit the financial statements of Lycksele Lappmark Bank (LLB) in Storuman, Sweden, for the year ended 31 December 20X5. Audit risk at the financial statement level is influenced by the risk of material misstatements, which may be indicated by a combination of factors related to management, the industry, and the entity. In assessing such factors, Nilsson has gathered the following information concerning LLB's environment.

LLB is a nationally insured bank and has been consistently more profitable than the industry average by making mortgages on properties in a prosperous rural area, which has experienced considerable growth in recent years. LLB packages its mortgages and sells them to large mortgage investment trusts. Despite recent volatility of interest rates, LLB has been able to continue selling its mortgages as a source of new lendable funds.

LLB's board of directors is controlled by Kjell Stensaker, the majority stockholder, who is also the chief executive officer (CEO). Management at the bank's branch offices has authority for directing and controlling LLB's operations and is compensated based on branch profitability. The internal auditor reports directly to Hakon Helvik, a minority stockholder, who is chairman of the board's audit committee.

The accounting department has experienced little turnover in personnel during the five years Nilsson has audited LLB. LLB's formula consistently underestimates the allowance for loan losses, but its controller has always been receptive to Nilsson's suggestions to increase the allowance during each engagement.

During 20X5, LLB opened a branch office in Ostersund, 300 km from its principal place of business. Although this branch is not yet profitable due to competition from several well-established regional banks, management believes that the branch will be profitable by 20X7.

Also during 20X5 LLB increased the efficiency of its accounting operations by installing a new computer system.

Required:

Based only on the information above, describe the factors that most likely would have an effect on the risk of material misstatement. Indicate whether each factor increases or decreases the risk. Use the format illustrated below:

Environmental factor	Effect on risk of material misstatements
Branch management has authority for directing and controlling operations	Increase

CASES

6-23 **Materiality.** Via Internet get the latest balance sheet and income statement of Nokia, an international manufacturer of portable telephones headquartered in Finland. At the www. Nokia.com website click investors, click reports, click financial reports, finally click annual information or use the site search box using the terms Nokia's financial statements.

Required:

A. Use professional judgement in deciding on the initial judgement about materiality for the basis of net income, current assets, current liabilities and total assets. State materiality in both percentages of the basis and monetary amounts.

B. Assume materiality for this audit is 7 per cent of earnings from operations before income taxes. Furthermore, assume that every account in the financial statements may be misstated by 7 per cent and each misstatement is likely to result in an overstatement of earnings. Allocate materiality to these financial statements.

C. Now, assume that you have decided to allocate 80 per cent of your preliminary judgement (on the basis of earnings from operations before taxes) to accounts receivable, inventories and accounts payable. Other accounts on the balance sheet are low in inherent and control risk. How does this allocation of materiality impact evidence gathering?

D. After completing the audit, you determine that your initial judgement about materiality for current assets, current liabilities and total assets has been met. The actual estimate of misstatements in earnings exceeds your preliminary judgement. What should you do?

NOTES

1. International Auditing and Assurance Standards Board (IAASB), 2023, International Standard on Auditing 300 (ISA 300) 'Planning an Audit of Financial Statements', para. 4 and 6, *Handbook of International Quality Control, Auditing, Review, Other Assurance, and Related Services Pronouncements*, 2022 edn, Volume I, International Federation of Accountants, New York.

2. International Auditing and Assurance Standards Board (IAASB), 2023, International Standard on Auditing 000 (ISA 200) 'Overall Objectives Of The Independent Auditor And The Conduct Of An Audit In Accordance With International Standards On Auditing', par 35 and 36, *Handbook of International Quality Control, Auditing, Review, Other Assurance, and Related Services Pronouncements*, 2022 edn, Volume I, International Federation of Accountants, New York.

3. International Auditing and Assurance Standards Board (IAASB), 2023, Glossary of Terms, Handbook of International Quality Control, Auditing, Review, Other Assurance, and Related Services Pronouncements, 2022 edn, Volume I, International Federation of Accountants, New York.

4. Inherent risk and control risk are the entity's risks which exist independently of the audit of the financial statements.

5. AICPA, 1985, Auditing Procedures Study *Audits of Small Business*, AICPA, New York, p. 44, reproduced in: Dan M. Guy, C. Wayne Alderman and Alan J. Winters, Harcourt Brace Janovich, San Diego, California, 1996, p.131.

6. Tap – an apparatus used for controlling the flow of liquid or gas from a pipe: *Oxford Student's Dictionary*, 2003.

7. Sieve – utensil with wire network, used for separate small and large lumps, etc.: *Oxford Student's Dictionary*, 2003.

8. International Auditing and Assurance Standards Board (IAASB), 2023, International Standard on Auditing 315 (ISA 315) 'Identifying and Assessing the Risks of Material Misstatement', *Handbook of International Quality Control, Auditing, Review, Other Assurance, and Related Services Pronouncements*, 2022 edn, Volume I, International Federation of Accountants, New York., para. 14.

9. International Auditing and Assurance Standards Board (IAASB), 2023, International Standard on Auditing 510 (ISA 510) 'Initial Audit Engagements—Opening Balances', *Handbook of International Quality Control, Auditing, Review, Other Assurance, and Related Services Pronouncements*, 2022 edn, Volume I, International Federation of Accountants, New York.

10. Ibid. ISA 315, para. 17.

11. Ibid. ISA 315 para. 19-20.

12. Cryptocurrency scandals dominated the financial headlines for much of 2023, culminating with the conviction in early November of Sam Bankman-Fried, the once-lauded founder of FTX. FTX rates among the greatest financial frauds of all time. Currently, around US$30 billion to US$35 billion worth of crypto is locked up in cryptocurrency bankruptcies, with around 15 million people affected. Some US$16 billion was entrusted to FTX when it collapsed. Source: website Transparantly.AI, February 28, 2024.

13. The Theranos investment scandal was a major case of corporate fraud involving the health technology company Theranos, which was founded in 2003 by Elizabeth Holmes. The company claimed to have developed a groundbreaking blood testing technology that could conduct a wide range of tests using only a few drops of blood from a fingerstick, as opposed to traditional methods that require larger blood samples drawn from veins. This

technology was touted as a faster, cheaper, and less invasive alternative to conventional blood tests.

14. Special Purpose Entity (SPE) is defined as an entity (e.g. corporation, partnership, trust, joint venture) created for a specific purpose or activity. SPEs may be used to transfer assets and liabilities from an entity – accounted for as a gain for that entity. Between 1993 and 2001, Enron created over 3,000 SPEs.

15. Governance – the term 'governance' describes the role of persons entrusted with the supervision, control and direction of an entity. Those charged with governance ordinarily are accountable for ensuring that the entity achieves its objectives, financial reporting, and reporting to interested parties. Those charged with governance include management only when it performs such functions.

16. Ibid. ISA 315, para. 21-26.

17. Derived from: Bell, T., et al., 1997, *Auditing Organizations Through a Strategic-Systems Lens: The KPMG Business Measurement Process*, KPMG, p. 27 and enriched with the terms sustainability and technology.

18. Ibid. Bell (1997), p. 31.

19. Ibid. ISA 315 (revised 2019), para. A76-A77.

20. For the purposes of the ISAs, the term 'analytical procedures' means evaluations of financial information through analysis of plausible relationships among both financial and non-financial data. Analytical procedures also encompass such investigation as is necessary of identified fluctuations or relationships that are inconsistent with other relevant information or that differ from expected values by a significant amount. See International Auditing and Assurance Standards Board (IAASB), 2023, International Standard on Auditing 520 (ISA 520) 'Analytical Procedures', para. 4, *Handbook of International Quality Control, Auditing, Review, Other Assurance, and Related Services Pronouncements*, 2022 edn, Volume I, International Federation of Accountants, New York.

21. Ibid. ISA 315 para.19.c.

22. International Auditing and Assurance Standards Board (IAASB), 2019, Factsheet: Introduction to ISA 315 (Revised 2019) 'Identifying and Assessing the Risks of Material Misstatement', International Federation of Accountants, New York.

23. Ibid. ISA 315 para. 34.

24. Ibid. ISA 315 para. 30-31.

25. Ibid. ISA 315 para. 12h.

26. Ibid. ISA 315, para. 12l.

27. International Auditing and Assurance Standards Board (IAASB), 2023, International Standard on Auditing 240 (ISA 240) 'The Auditor's Responsibilities Relating to Fraud in an Audit of Financial Statements', para. 27 and and International Standard on Auditing (ISA 550) 'Related Parties', para. 18, *Handbook of International Quality Control, Auditing, Review, Other Assurance, and Related Services Pronouncements*, 2022 edn, Volume I, International Federation of Accountants, New York.

28. Public Company Accounting Oversight Board (PCAOB) Audit Standard number 11, 2010, para. 2, gives yet another definition of materiality: in interpreting the federal securities laws, the Supreme Court of the United States has held that a fact is material if there is 'a substantial likelihood that the … fact would have been viewed by the reasonable investor as having significantly altered the 'total mix' of information made available.' As the Supreme Court has noted, determinations of materiality require delicate assessments of the inferences a 'reasonable shareholder' would draw from a given set of facts and the significance of those inferences to him.

29. International Auditing and Assurance Standards Board (IAASB), 2023, International Standard on Auditing 320 (ISA 320) 'Materiality in Planning and Performing an Audit', para, 2. *Handbook of International Quality Control, Auditing, Review, Other Assurance, and Related Services Pronouncements*, 2022 edn, Volume I, International Federation of Accountants, New York.

30. Financial Reporting and Auditing Group, *Of International Auditing, Assurance and Ethics Release FRAG 1/9, Materiality in Financial Reporting – A Discussion Paper*, para. 27, the Institute of Chartered Accountants in England and Wales, January 1995.

31. A liquid company has less risk of being able to meet debt than an illiquid one. Also, a liquid business generally has more financial flexibility to take on new investment opportunities.

32. Ibid. ISA 320, para. A1.

33. Ibid. ISA 320, para. 9.

34. Ibid. ISA 300, para 7-9.

35. Ibid. ISA 330, para 9.

36. Ibid. ISA 315, para. 38.

37. Ibid. ISA 320, para. 14.

IDENTIFYING AND ASSESSING CONTROL RISK

The four phases of the audit:

Acceptance/ continuance	Understanding/ risk analysis	Building/executing audit plan	Evaluating/ completion
Phase 1	Phase 2	Phase 3	Phase 4

7.1 LEARNING OBJECTIVES

After studying this chapter, you should be able to:

1   Understand the basic definition of internal control.
2   Discuss why internal controls are important to the auditor.
3   Distinguish between the different components of internal control.
4   Characterize the differences between general and application IT controls.
5   Describe the elements of the control environment.
6   Evaluate how management's objectives are related to risk assessment.
7   Explain the effects of information and communication on the internal control system.
8   Distinguish between the major types of control activities.
9   Give examples of major types of control activities (procedures).
10 Identify monitoring controls.
11 Distinguish between hard and soft controls.
12 Know what is meant by design of controls.
13 Sketch what an auditor does in preliminary planning assessments of internal control risk.

7.2 INTRODUCTION

This chapter delves into the crucial aspect of 'identifying and assessing control risk,' constituting the second phase of the audit process. It builds upon chapter 6, which centred on identifying and assessing inherent risk. ISA 315 defines the risk of material misstatement (RMM) as inherent risk, unless the auditor intends to evaluate the effectiveness of internal controls[1]. In this chapter we focus on the importance of the auditor's understanding of these controls. As information technology (IT) has a central place in systems of Internal Control, design and implementation of IT controls and processes are embedded in the next sections.

Internal Control is not only essential to maintaining the accounting and financial records of an organisation, but also to manage the entity. All stakeholders have an interest in internal controls. In many parts of the world regulators emphasize the importance of internal control by requiring management to make annual public statements about the effectiveness of internal controls[2].

Reinforcing internal controls is generally seen as one of the most important steps in avoiding negative surprises. Even a company that is considered 'in control' will face risks. Effective internal controls ensure that likelihood and impact of risks are identified at an early stage. Company risk management procedures will identify ways to deal with these risks, to the extent possible.

As we discussed earlier in chapter 6, the consideration of internal control is an important part of Phase II (Planning through understanding, risk analysis, design & implementation of controls) of the Audit Process Model. It was also noted that the first two steps in the planning procedures are:

▶ Perform audit procedures to understand the entity and its environment, including the entity's internal control.
▶ Assess the risks of material misstatements of the financial statements.

We continue with our 'How to identify risks of material misstatement RMM' 8-step approach with the steps 5-8 in this chapter. See illustration 7.1. This chapter will concentrate on the importance of internal control, on general concepts in internal control, and on its components (the control environment, risk assessment, control activities, information and communication, and monitoring). As technology is in the middle of the entity's operations, IT considerations are an integral part of this chapter.

ISA 315[3] requires the auditor to obtain an understanding of the components of the entity's system of internal control relevant to the preparation of the financial statements. Based on this understanding, the auditor identifies[4] risks of material misstatement that management failed to identify:

▶ Determine whether any such risks are of a kind you would have identified by the entity's risk assessment process and, if so, obtain an understanding of why the entity's risk assessment process failed to identify such risks of material misstatement; and
▶ Consider the implications for your evaluation of the entity's risk assessment process.

Based on this evaluation of each of the components of the entity's system of internal control, the auditor determines[5] whether one or more control deficiencies have been identified.

As highlighted in chapter 6, the assessment of RMM is the same as the assessment of inherent risks, unless the auditor plans to test the operating effectiveness of controls[6]: she then has to assess initial control risk. So: Controls are *not* part of the assessment of inherent risks but can only decrease the risk of material misstatement *after* testing the operating effectiveness of the controls.

ILLUSTRATION 7.1

HOW TO IDENTIFY RISKS OF MATERIAL MISSTATEMENT (RMM)

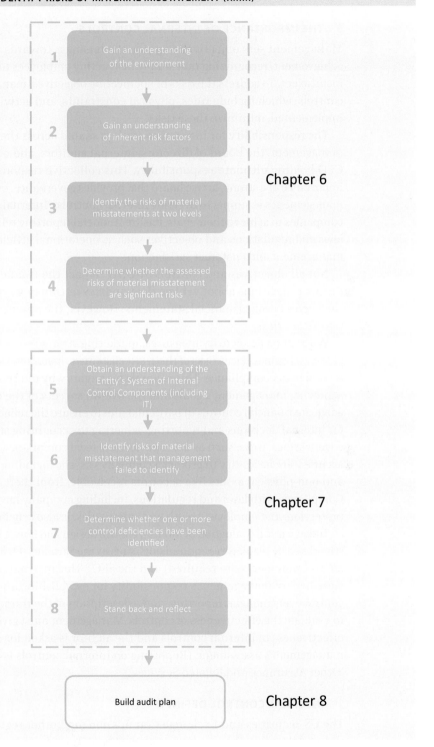

INTERNAL CONTROL DEFINED

▶ **THE IMPORTANCE OF INTERNAL CONTROLS**

Management sets objectives to guide the business towards profitability or mission achievement, recognizing that simply instructing employees to meet these objectives is insufficient. To address the risks of not meeting objectives, management designs internal controls, which include rules, physical constraints, and activities that, when properly implemented, minimize these risks.

The responsibility for internal controls is shared across the organization, including management, the board of directors, internal auditors, and other personnel, with the CEO holding ultimate responsibility. This collective responsibility underscores the importance of a strong, active board that provides governance, oversight, and can address management's attempts to override internal controls[7]. Internal controls are essential for companies to achieve their goals, ensure financial reporting reliability, and comply with laws and regulations and objectives such as operational efficiency, effective employee management and customer satisfaction.

Not all objectives and controls directly impact the financial statement audit. For instance, decisions about vehicle fleet updates or transport efficiency may not affect the current year's financial statements. However, the absence of controls can lead to significant risks.

Without basic security measures, marketing strategies, or an adequate accounting system, a business faces risks of theft, lost customers, inventory issues, and legal challenges related to tax compliance. This example highlights why internal controls are integral to achieving management's goals and the overall success of the organization. Therefore, adequate financial controls in particular aim to ensure the reliability of information used for internal decisions and reporting, adhering to accounting standards. These controls cover various areas, such as asset protection, legal compliance, and financial reporting accuracy are necessary to protect a company's assets, including physical assets like cash and non-physical assets like accounts receivable, from theft, misuse, or destruction. Compliance with laws and regulations, including company law, tax law, environmental protection, and employee health and safety rules, is also crucial.

Today, careful evaluation of internal control design and how it is operating in practice, is stimulated by regulatory requirements, such as the Sarbanes-Oxley Act[8] (in which internal control statements are required) and the SEC.[9] This internal control report contains a statement of management's responsibility for establishing and maintaining adequate control over financial reporting, and a description of the framework management uses to evaluate the effectiveness of controls. Management must give their assessment of the effectiveness of internal controls and the auditor is asked for an attestation report on management's assessment. (Reporting on internal controls is discussed in chapter 14, 'Other Assurance and Related Services'.)

▶ **INTERNAL CONTROL DEFINED**

The US Securities and Exchange Commission (and other regulatory agencies around the world) require that management must base its evaluation of the effectiveness of the company's internal control over financial reporting on a suitable, recognized control framework established by a body or group that followed due-process procedures, including the broad distribution of the framework for public comment.[10] For example, the COSO (Committee of Sponsoring Organizations of the Treadway Commission) framework provides a comprehensive structure for internal control practices within organizations. It was developed to address the need for a standardized approach to internal control, particularly in response to financial reporting scandals and regulatory requirements[11] as does the report published by the Financial Reporting Council, 'Internal Control Revised Guidance for Directors on the Combined Code', October 2005 (known as the Turnbull Report)[12].

To be effective and efficient, to evaluate the design and operating effectiveness of internal controls in a financial statements audit or when performing an audit of internal control over financial reporting, the auditor uses the same suitable, recognized control framework as management[13.]

According to COSO internal control is:

> 'a process, effected by an entity's board of directors, management and other personnel, designed to provide reasonable assurance regarding the achievement of objectives in the following categories: effectiveness and efficiency of operations, reliability of financial reporting, compliance with applicable laws and regulations, and safeguarding of assets against unauthorized acquisition, use or disposition'[14]

This definition reflects certain fundamental concepts:
  ▷ Internal control is a 'process'. Internal control is not one event or circumstance, but a series of actions that permeate an entity's activities. These actions are pervasive and are inherent in the way management runs the business.
  ▷ Internal control is affected by people. A board of directors, management, and other personnel in an entity affect internal control. The people of an organization accomplish it, by what they say and do. People establish the entity's objectives and put control mechanisms in place.
  ▷ ISA 315[15] makes clear that internal control, no matter how effective, can only provide an entity with reasonable assurance about achieving the entity's objectives. The likelihood of achievement is affected by limitations inherent in all internal control systems. These limitations include the realities that human judgement can be faulty, breakdowns may occur because of human failures such as simple error, and controls may be circumvented by collusion of two or more people. Finally, management has the ability to override the internal control system. For example, management may enter into side agreements[16] with customers that alter the terms and conditions of the entity's standard sales contract in ways that would preclude revenue recognition.
  ▷ Internal control is geared to the achievement of objectives in one or more separate but related categories:
    1 *operations* – relating to effective and efficient use of the entity's resources;
    2 *financial reporting* – relating to preparation of reliable published financial statements;

3 *compliance* – relating to the entity's compliance with applicable laws and regulations;

4 *safeguarding of assets.*

ISA 315 describes the system of internal control in a way that closely aligns with the COSO definition:

> The system designed, implemented and maintained by those charged with governance, management and other personnel to provide reasonable assurance about the achievement of an entity's objectives with regard to reliability of financial reporting, effectiveness and efficiency of operations, and compliance with applicable laws and regulations.

Standard 315 requires that the auditor obtains an understanding of internal control relevant to the audit[18] and[19] distinguishes the following components of internal control:

▸ the control environment;
▸ the entity's risk assessment process;
▸ control activities;
▸ the information system and communication;
▸ the entity's process to monitor the system of internal control.

ILLUSTRATION 7.2

THE COSO FRAMEWORK

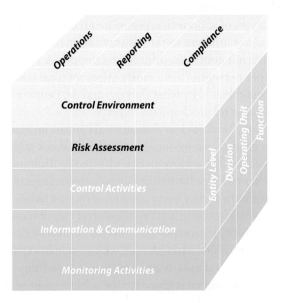

Illustration 7.2 shows internal control components from the COSO report[20].

Illustration 7.3 gives more detail on each component including a description. IAASB considers these components as the Entity's system of internal controls[21]. In other words: these components need to be considered comprehensively and form the backbone of this chapter (see section 7.4).

ILLUSTRATION 7.3

COMPONENTS OF INTERNAL CONTROL FRAMEWORK

Components	Description of component	Component elements
Control environment	Actions, policies and procedures that reflect the overall attitude of top management, directors and owners of an entity about controls and its importance	▸ Management's philosophy and operating style, integrity and ethical values ▸ Participation of those charged with governance (board of directors or audit committee) ▸ Assignment of authority and responsibility ▸ Attract, develop and maintain competent individuals ▸ Accountability for internal control responsibilities
Management's risk assessment	Management's identification and analysis of risks relevant to the preparation of financial statements in accordance with IFRS	Management's assertions: existence, completeness, valuation, presentation and disclosure, measurement, occurrence
Monitoring	Management's ongoing and periodic assessment of the effectiveness of the design and operation of an internal control structure to determine if it is operating as intended and modified when needed	Not applicable
Information system and communication	Methods used to identify, assemble, classify, record and report an entity's transactions and to maintain accountability for related assets	Transaction-related audit objectives: existence, completeness, accuracy, classification, timing, posting and summarization
Control activities (control procedures)	Policies and procedures that management established to meet its objectives for financial reporting	▸ Adequate segregation of duties ▸ Proper authorization of transactions and activities (specific computer controls) ▸ Adequate documents and records (general computer controls) ▸ Physical control over assets and records ▸ Independent checks on performance

INTERNAL CONTROLS OVER FINANCIAL REPORTING

Internal controls that are important for the auditor are those that ensure the financial statements reflect the true economic condition of the entity. These include controls to ensure the accuracy of input data, access controls to restrict access to authorized personnel only, and segregation of duties controls to prevent fraud.

If the auditor can assess the quality of accounting and internal control systems and verify their proper operation throughout the audit year, the risk of material misstatement due to fraud or error (RMM) may be reduced.

The rationale for relying on a company's accounting and internal control systems is twofold. First, reliance on these activities enhances the efficiency of the external audit. Effective internal controls can mitigate inherent risks, leading to lower control risk and reducing the need for substantive testing to gather audit evidence. Additionally, by testing the operational effectiveness of these activities, the auditor can identify control deficiencies and provide recommendations for improvement, thus adding value to the client. In some countries, a third rationale for relying on controls is the requirement for management, the external auditor, or both, to report on internal controls over financial reporting (ICFR), as outlined in section 14.5.

The auditor's primary consideration is whether and how a specific control prevents, detects, or corrects material misstatements in classes of transactions, account balances, or disclosures.

Auditors emphasize understanding controls over classes of transactions rather than account balances or disclosures. The rationale behind this prioritization is that the accuracy of the accounting system's output (account balances) hinges on the accuracy of inputs and processing (transactions). For instance, if controls effectively ensure the accuracy of billings, cash receipts, charge-offs, returns, and allowances, then the ending balance in accounts receivable is likely to be correct. Additionally, disclosures typically depend on the accuracy of account balances.

INTERNAL CONTROLS OVER OPERATIONS AND COMPLIANCE

Auditors primarily rely on financial controls, but controls relating to the effectiveness of operations, and controls for compliance objectives may also be relevant to an audit. Auditors have responsibility for the discovery of management and employee fraud and certain types of illegal acts, even though management has the primary responsibility regarding fraud and illegal acts. Controls over non-financial data that the auditor uses in analytical procedures or controls over compliance with income tax laws may be relevant to an audit. The extensive use of general information system controls like restricted access (i.e. password controls) that limit access to the data are also relevant. Conversely, controls to prevent the excessive use of materials in production generally are not relevant to a financial statement audit, as the auditor provides a judgement on the true and fair view of the financial statements and not a judgement on the effectiveness or efficiency of operations.

Auditors primarily rely on financial controls, but controls related to the effectiveness of operations and compliance objectives may also be relevant to an audit. Auditors bear responsibility for detecting management and employee fraud, as well as certain types of illegal acts, notwithstanding that management holds primary responsibility for fraud and illegal acts. Controls over non-financial data used by auditors in analytical procedures or controls ensuring compliance with income tax laws may also be relevant to an audit of financial statements. Also of significant importance are general IT controls, such as restricted access (e.g., password controls) limiting data access.

Conversely, controls aimed at preventing the excessive use of materials in production are generally not relevant to a financial statement audit. This is because the auditor's assessment focuses on determining the true and fair view of the financial statements, rather than evaluating the effectiveness or efficiency of operations.

▶ **DESIGN AND IMPLEMENTATION OF INTERNAL CONTROLS**

To understand the entity's system of internal control the auditor will evaluate its effectiveness of the design of controls and whether they have been implemented. She determines whether the control, individually or in combination with other controls, is capable of effectively preventing, or detecting and correcting, material misstatements due to error or fraud[22]. Implementation of a control means that the control exists, and that the entity is using it. There is little point in assessing the implementation of a control that is not effective, and so the design of a control is considered first. An improperly designed control may represent a significant deficiency in the system of internal control. Further, if more controls are capable of effectively preventing, or detecting and correcting the same material misstatements, the auditor will test only the controls that are most efficient to test.

Given the assessment of inherent risk (initial assessment of RMM), the auditor has to determine whether any such risks will be prevented or detected by the entity's risk assessment process and obtain an understanding of why the entity's risk assessment process fail to identify such risks of material misstatement) and consider the implications for her evaluation of the entity's risk assessment process (initial assessment of control risk).

In the upcoming section, we'll delve into comprehending the components of internal control. This understanding serves as the foundation for assessing RMM and determining control deficiencies.

7.4 OBTAIN AN UNDERSTANDING OF INTERNAL CONTROL COMPONENTS (INCLUDING IT)

(Step 5, illustration 7.1)

7.4.1 CONTROL ENVIRONMENT

The control environment includes the governance and management functions and the attitudes, awareness and actions of those charged with governance and management concerning the entity's internal control and its importance in the entity. The control environment has a pervasive influence on the way business activities are structured, the way objectives are established, and the way risks are assessed. The control environment is influenced by the entity's history and culture. Culture plays a crucial role in shaping the control environment by influencing the integrity, ethical values, and competence of the entity's people. It affects the processes by which strategies and objectives are established, and the structure in which business and control activities are conducted.

Cultural elements, such as shared values, beliefs, and behaviours, determine how employees perceive the importance of controls within the organization. A strong ethical culture, endorsed and practiced by management, reinforces the importance of controls, compliance, and ethical behaviour throughout the organization. This includes how authority and responsibility are defined and respected, the attention and direction provided by the board of directors, and the commitment to competence.

A positive control environment, influenced by a supportive culture, encourages employees to report deviations, fosters open communication, and promotes a proactive approach to assessing and managing risks. Conversely, a weak or negative culture can undermine the control environment, leading to disregard for internal controls, increased risk of fraud, and non-compliance with policies and procedures.

CUMULATIVE EFFECT OF CONTROLS

When analysing the control environment, the auditor must think about the collective effect of various control environment elements. Strengths in one of the elements might mitigate weaknesses in another element. For example, an active and independent board of directors may influence the philosophy and operating style of senior management. Alternatively, human resource policies directed towards hiring competent accounting personnel might not mitigate a strong bias by top-management to overstate earnings.

ELEMENTS OF THE CONTROL ENVIRONMENT

There are a number of specific elements that may be relevant when obtaining an understanding of the control environment and which may be used as indicators of the quality of the control environment of a particular organization. These elements include[23]:

- ▶ How management's responsibilities are carried out, such as creating and maintaining the entity's culture and demonstrating management's commitment to integrity and ethical values.
- ▶ When those charged with governance are separate from management, how those charged with governance demonstrate independence from management and exercise oversight of the entity's system of internal control.
- ▶ How the entity assigns authority and responsibility in pursuit of its objectives.
- ▶ How the entity attracts, develops, and retains competent individuals in alignment with its objectives.
- ▶ How the entity holds individuals accountable for their responsibilities in pursuit of the objectives of the entity's system of internal control.

MANAGEMENT PHILOSOPHY, INTEGRITY, AND ETHICAL VALUES

As mentioned above, the attitude of an organization's management (tone-at-the-top), its management style, corporate culture, and values are the essence of an efficient control. If management believes control is important, others in the company will observe the control policies and procedures. If employees in the organization feel control is not important to management, it will not be important to them. The control environment consists of the actions, policies and procedures that reflect the overall attitudes of top management, directors and owners.

Management's philosophy and operating style is their attitude about, and approach to, financial reporting, accounting issues, and to taking and managing business risk. A personal example set by top-management and the board provides a clear signal to employees about the company's culture and the importance of control. In particular, the chief executive plays a key role in determining whether subordinates decide to obey, bend or ignore company rules, and the kinds of business risks accepted.

Management philosophy may create significant risk. A key element of risk is dominance of management by a few individuals. Dick Fuld, the CEO of Lehman Brothers when it declared bankruptcy in 2008 leading to the worse financial crisis in the United States since the Great Depression, was so domineering that against the advice of Lehman executives he turned down two offers to save the company (one from billionaire Warren Buffett). Auditors may consider key questions, such as: Does management take significant risk or are they risk adverse? What is management's attitude towards monitoring of business risk?

The integrity and ethical values of the people who create, administer, and monitor controls determines their effectiveness. The communication of company integrity and ethical values to employees and reinforcement in practice affects the way in which employees view their work. Setting a good example is not enough. Top-management should verbally communicate the entity's values and behavioural standards to employees.

CONCEPT AND A COMPANY 7.1

WEAKNESSES IN THE CONTROL ENVIRONMENT – THE CASE OF XEROX (1997–2000)

Concept   A control environment in which there is motivation to misstate financial statements may lead to problems.

Story   Xerox is a US copy machine manufacturing company that saw its market share eroded in the USA in the 1990s because of foreign competition. The management, in order to cash in on a compensation scheme that would net them $35 million if Xerox's stock price rose to more than $60 per share, developed a scheme to artificially increase revenue.

To settle charges that included fraud, the Securities and Exchange Commission (SEC) required that Xerox pay a $10 million civil penalty – at that time, the largest ever by a company for financial-reporting violations. The SEC also required that Xerox restate its financial statements for the years 1997 to 2000 (SEC, *Litigation release*, 2002).

Most of the improper accounting – involving $2.8 billion in equipment revenue and $660 million in pre-tax earnings – resulted from improper accounting for revenue. On some sales, service revenue was immediately recognized, in violation of GAAP. The revenue associated with the servicing component of multi-year lease contracts was recognized during the first year, instead of recognized over the life of the lease. To increase revenue, Xerox increasingly booked more revenue associated with the equipment.

Xerox also increased earnings by nearly $500 million by improperly setting aside various reserves, then gradually adding them back as gains to make up for profit shortfalls. In one instance Xerox changed its vacation policy by limiting the amount of time off employees could carry over from one period to the next, saving $120 million. But instead of taking the gain immediately as required by US GAAP, Xerox systematically and improperly released the money at a rate of $30 million per year (Bandler and Hechinger, 2002).

Discussion Questions   ▶ What impact does this weakness in the control environment have on Xerox, its auditors, its management and its shareholders?
▶ What audit procedures in this case should the auditor perform to reduce the risk of misstatement?

References   Bandler, J. and Hechinger, J., 2001, 'Fired Executive Questioned Xerox's Accounting Practices', *The Wall Street Journal*, 6 February.
SEC, 2002, Litigation Release 17465, 'Xerox Settles SEC Enforcement Action Charging Company with Fraud', US Securities and Exchange Commission, 11 April.

Management can act to maximize control integrity and reduce misstatement. Management might remove incentives and temptations that prompt personnel to engage in fraudulent or unethical behaviour. Incentives for unethical behaviour include pressure to meet unrealistic performance targets, high performance-dependent rewards, and upper and lower cut-offs on bonus plans. Temptations for employees to engage in improper acts include: non-existent or ineffective controls; top-management who are unaware of actions taken at lower organizational levels; ineffective board of directors; and insignificant penalties for improper behaviour.

Communication and enforcement of integrity and ethical values are essential elements which influence the effectiveness of the design, administration, and monitoring of internal controls. The auditor uses information gathered by performing risk assessment procedures to obtain an understanding of the design of controls as audit evidence to support the risk assessment. The effectiveness of controls cannot rise above the integrity and ethical values of the people who create, administer and monitor them. Integrity and ethical values are essential elements of the control environment that influence the design of other components.

PARTICIPATION OF THOSE CHARGED WITH GOVERNANCE

The participation of those charged with governance, especially the entity's board of directors and audit committee, significantly influences the control environment and 'tone at the top'. The guidance and oversight responsibilities of an active and involved board of directors who possess an appropriate degree of management, technical and other expertise are critical to effective internal control.

Because the board must be prepared to question and scrutinize management's activities, present alternative views and have the courage to act in the face of obvious wrongdoing, it is necessary that the board contain at least a critical mass of independent (non-executive) directors.[24] For instance, the Sarbanes-Oxley Act requires that members of the audit committee be independent. In order to be considered to be independent, a member of an audit committee may not accept any consulting, advisory or other compensatory fee from the company they govern or be affiliated with any company subsidiary[25].

The responsibilities of those charged with governance are of considerable importance for publicly traded companies. This is recognized in codes of practice such as the London Stock Exchange Combined Code and other regulations such as the Sarbanes-Oxley Act. The board of directors usually has a compensation committee charged with executive and management compensation. If the compensation is performance-related the board must counterbalance the pressures for management to manipulate financial reporting.

Important factors to consider in evaluating a board of directors, board of trustees, or comparable body is experience and stature of its members, extent of its involvement, scrutiny of activities and the appropriateness of its action. Another factor is the degree to which difficult questions are raised and pursued with management regarding plans or performance. Interaction of the audit committee with internal and external auditors, existence of a written audit committee charter and regularity of meetings are other factors affecting the control environment.

ASSIGNMENT OF AUTHORITY AND RESPONSIBILITY

A company's control environment will be more effective if its culture is one in which quality and competence are openly valued. Competence is the knowledge and skills necessary to accomplish tasks that define the individual's job. Management needs to specify the competence levels for particular jobs and make sure those possessing the necessary training, experience, and intelligence perform the job.

The entity's organizational structure provides the framework within which business activities are planned, executed, controlled and monitored. Important considerations are clarity of lines of authority and responsibility; the level at which policies and procedures are established; adherence to these policies and procedures; adequacy of supervision and monitoring of decentralized operations; and appropriateness of organizational structure for size and complexity of the entity. By understanding the entity's organizational structure, the auditor can discover the management and functional elements of the business and how control policies are carried out.

How authority and responsibility are assigned throughout the organization and the associated lines of reporting has an impact on controls. For example, a bank may require that two officers sign all cheques written for more than a certain amount. Computer users are only allowed to access certain parts of the accounting system. Responsibility and delegation of authority should be clearly assigned. How responsibility is distributed is usually spelt out in formal company policy manuals.

These manuals describe policies such as business practice, employee job responsibilities, duties and constraints (including written job descriptions). The auditor should consider whether management may have established a formal code of conduct but nevertheless acts in a manner that condones violations of that code or authorizes exceptions to it.

ATTRACT, DEVELOP AND MAINTAIN COMPETENT INDIVIDUALS

A very important element of the control environment is personnel, which is why human resource policies and practices are essential. With trustworthy and competent employees, weaknesses in other controls can be compensated and reliable financial statements might still result. Honest, efficient people are able to perform at a high level even when there are few other controls to support them.

A company should take care in hiring, orientation, training, evaluation, counselling, promoting, compensating, and remedial actions. Recruiting practices that include formal, in-depth employment interviews and evidence of integrity and ethical behaviour result in hiring high-quality employees. Training improves employee technical skills and communicates their prospective roles in the enterprise. Rotation of personnel and promotions driven by periodic performance appraisals demonstrate the entity's commitment to its people. Competitive compensation programs that include bonus incentives serve to motivate and reinforce outstanding performance. Disciplinary actions send a message that violations of expected behaviour will not be tolerated.

'CHAINSAW AL', SUNBEAM AND CONTROL ENVIRONMENT

Concept	'Tone at the top' sets the control environment. Big egos and greed can destroy a company.

Story   The SEC filed a civil injunctive action charging five former officers of Sunbeam Corporation, including CEO 'Chainsaw Al' Dunlap, and the former engagement partner of Arthur Andersen LLP with fraud, resulting in billions of dollars of investor losses. The complaint alleged that management of Sunbeam, a US manufacturer of small appliances, security devices and camping gear, engaged in a fraudulent scheme to create the illusion of a successful restructuring of Sunbeam and thus facilitate a sale of the company at an inflated price (SEC, 2001).

Sunbeam management employed a laundry list of fraudulent techniques, including creating 'cookie jar' revenues, recording revenue on contingent sales, accelerating sales from later periods into the present quarter, and using improper bill and hold transactions. For fiscal 1997, at least $60 million of Sunbeam's record setting $189 million earnings came from accounting fraud (SEC, 2001).

The biggest problem was Sunbeam's practice of overstating sales by recognizing revenue in improper periods, including its 'bill and hold' practice of billing customers for products, but holding the goods for later delivery. One famous example was Sunbeam sales of $58 million worth of barbecue grills at cut-rate prices in December (giving stores until June to pay for them). Barbecue grills are ordinarily sold in summer.

When he became CEO of Sunbeam, a faltering manufacturer in an overcrowded business with low profit margins, Albert (Chainsaw Al) Dunlap had just orchestrated a successful turn-around of Scott Paper and had a reputation for ruthless cost cutting (hence the name 'chainsaw'). He was also a tireless self-promoter. When the Sunbeam board awarded him a three-year, $70 million contract, he boasted, 'You can't overpay a great executive. Don't you think I'm a bargain?' (Harrop, 1998).

At his first press conference Dunlap announced that he had already begun firing executives (Schifrin, 1996). Three months later, Dunlap said he would fire half of Sunbeam's 12,000 employees, sell or consolidate 39 of the company's 53 facilities, divest the company of several business lines, eliminate six regional headquarters in favor of a single office in Florida, and scrap 87 per cent of Sunbeam's products. In July 1996 when Dunlap became CEO, Sunbeam had already been through a bankruptcy and years of cost cutting. In October 1997, Dunlap hired Morgan Stanley to find potential suitors or takeover targets (*Weekly Corporate Growth Report*, 1998).

Dunlap believed in carrots and sticks. Dunlap preached sales at any cost and in any way. He gave people great incentives to perform and fired them when they did not. The need to overpower was also present in the executive suite. In fact, as a biographer puts it, 'working with Al Dunlap was a lot like going to war ... The pressure was brutal, the hours exhausting, and the casualties high ... At Sunbeam, Dunlap created a culture of misery, an environment of moral ambiguity, indifferent to everything except the stock price. He would throw papers or furniture, bang his hands on his desk, knock glasses of water off a table, and shout so ferociously that a manager's hair could lift from his head by the stream of air that rushed from Dunlap's screaming mouth' (Byrne, 1999).

The bullying and outrageous sales targets left Sunbeam with no idea of what its real inventory was. Divisional managers would report sales that met the targets, whether they had been effected or not. By early 1998, routine operational functions within the company were breaking down. Assembly lines were not working at peak efficiency. Supplies were not arriving on time. Maintenance was not being performed when it was needed. So goods were not getting shipped to the shops (Uren, 1998).

Discussion Questions	▶ When Dunlap became CEO of Sunbeam in 1996, the share price shot up from $12.12 to $18.58 in a day. What aspect of Dunlap's management style could have caused this?
	▶ If you were auditing Sunbeam in 1996, what financial statement accounts do you believe would be susceptible to misstatement?
References	Byrne, J.A., 1999, *Chainsaw: The Notorious Career of Al Dunlap in the Era of Profit-at-Any-Price*, HarperCollins Publishing Inc., New York.
	Harrop, F., 1998, 'Dunlap Backers Had it Coming', *Rocky Mountain News*, 22 June, p. 35A.
	Schifrin, M., 1996, 'Chain Saw Al to the Rescue? (Corporate turn-around expert Albert Dunlap hired to help Sunbeam Corp.)', *Forbes*, Vol. 158, No. 5, 26 August, p. 42.
	SEC, 2001, Litigation News Release 2001–49, 'SEC Sues Former CEO, CFO, Other Top Former Officers of Sunbeam Corporation in Massive Financial Fraud', Securities and Exchange Commission, 15 May.
	Uren, D., 1998, 'Dunlap Style No Match for Tough Times', *The Australian*, 20 June, p. 57.
	'Sunbeam to Acquire Coleman Co. for 1.3 Times Revenue', *Weekly Corporate Growth Report*, 9 March 1998.

Performance is measured and incentives help to drive accountability for the achievement of internal control objectives. Management and the board of directors must evaluate and adjust pressures associated with the achievement of objectives as they assign responsibilities, develop performance measures, and evaluate performance. Performance evaluation of internal control responsibilities should include adherence to standards of conduct and expected levels of competence and provide rewards or exercise disciplinary action as appropriate.

▶ HARD AND SOFT CONTROLS

To minimize risks, management establishes a framework of rules, physical constraints and activities. Due to the explicit, formal and tangible character of these controls, they are generally referred to as *hard controls*. However, the dynamic environment with its rapidly changing technology, increasing regulatory requirements and globalization requires more than rigorous adherence to policy, procedures and protocols, which may be referred to as *soft controls*[26].

SOCIAL-PSYCHOLOGICAL FACTORS

The 2008 financial and economic crisis exposed the more human factor, the so-called soft controls, in the inner workings of organizations as never before. Soft controls are the intangible factors in an organization that influence the behaviour of managers and employees. Whereas soft controls are founded in the culture or climate of an organization, the hard controls are more explicit, formal and visible. The control environment includes soft controls like tone-at-the-top, risk-awareness, openness to raise issues and discuss ideas, trust and loyalty, stakeholder focus, and enforcement.

Based on scientific research, Muel Kaptein[27] distinguishes seven social-psychological factors which influence people's behaviour within organizations. These factors highly influence the effectiveness of internal control measures and procedures. The factors are as follows:

1   *Clarity* for directors, managers and employees as to what constitutes desirable and undesirable behaviour: the clearer the expectations, the better people know what they must do, how to perform the control and the more likely they are to act on it.

2   *Role-modelling* among administrators, management or immediate supervisors: the better the examples given in an organization, the better people behave, while the worse the example, the worse the behaviour.

3   *Achievability* of goals, tasks and responsibilities set: the better equipped people in an organization are, the better they are able to execute the control activities that are expected from them.

4   *Commitment* on the part of directors, managers and employees in the organization: the more the organization treats its people with respect and involves them in the organization, the more these people will try to serve the interests of the organization and reach the internal control objectives.

5   *Transparency of behaviour*: the better people observe their own and others' behaviour, and its effects, the more they take this into account and the better they are able to control and adjust their behaviour to the expectations of others.

6   *Openness to discussion* of viewpoints, emotions, dilemmas and transgressions: the lower the bar for people within the organization to talk about moral or ethical issues regarding internal control, the more they will be likely to do this, and the more they will learn from one another.

7   *Enforcement* of behaviour, such as appreciation or even reward for desirable behaviour, sanctioning of undesirable behaviour and the extent to which people learn from mistakes, near misses, incidents, and accidents: the better the enforcement, the more people tend towards what will be rewarded and avoid what will be punished.

TESTING SOFT CONTROLS

While it's a crucial step outlined in 'Building an Audit Plan' (chapter 8), acquiring adequate evidence of the operating effectiveness of soft controls may prove challenging with traditional testing methods and tools.

Instead, the auditor will need to think 'outside-the-box' to gather sufficient, competent evidential matter in such audits. Observations, self-assessments, surveys, workshops, or similar techniques may be better suited than traditional methods. Specifically[28]:

▶ Employee surveys are frequently used in evaluating the success of management's efforts in establishing an effective control environment. These surveys provide useful measurements of the effectiveness of one or more control environment elements. Annual employee ethics compliance forms are another example.

▶ The Chief Audit Executive should use her network within the organization. The network is critical in discerning whether communication, tone at the top, management walking the talk, and effective supervision are present on a day-to-day basis.

▶ Audit team discussion with the secretaries of executives can be a useful source of information about behaviour in the organization.

▶ The internal auditor's knowledge of the organization's inner working is useful to further corroborate the effectiveness of soft controls.

▶ The value of 'auditing by walking around' cannot be overstated. By being present, visible and observant across the organization, auditors can identify those intangible clues that may lead to deeper assessments. Associates who trust they can provide concerns to auditors with an appropriate degree of anonymity are also valuable.

▶ Past audit results over control activities and the reaction and remediation from management are also good indicators.

▶ Internal auditors' participation in committees, taskforces, workgroups, and involvement in ethics and compliance program implementation and assessments provide valuable insights over extended periods of time.

FACTORS ON WHICH TO ASSESS INTERNAL CONTROL ENVIRONMENT

Illustration 7.4 lists issues that might be focused on to assess the internal control environment, based on the COSO report[29]. These elements are cited as factors to consider when doing a control environment assessment to determine whether a positive control environment exists, but the absence or opposite of these factors indicate negative control environment. Elements of a negative control environment such as unethical management, management with low integrity, incompetent management, or governance promoting a 'cowboy culture' in the company increase the risk of financial misstatement. If the boards of directors seldom meet or are lax in their oversight responsibility, risk increases. Poor training, retention or morale of employees increases the risk that controls will not be implemented.

ILLUSTRATION 7.4

FACTORS ON WHICH TO ASSESS INTERNAL CONTROL ENVIRONMENT

How management's responsibilities are carried out, such as creating and maintaining the entity's culture and demonstrating management's commitment to integrity and ethical values
(Management philosophy and style, integrity and ethical values)

▶ Nature of business risks accepted, for example, whether management often enters into particularly high-risk ventures, or is extremely conservative in accepting risks.

▶ Frequency of interaction between senior management and operating management, particularly when operating from geographically removed locations.

▶ Attitudes and actions towards financial reporting, including disputes over application of accounting treatments (e.g. selection of conservative versus liberal accounting policies, whether accounting principles have been misapplied, important financial information not disclosed, or records manipulated or falsified).

▶ Existence and implementation of codes of conduct and other policies regarding acceptable business practice, conflicts of interest, or expected standards of ethical and moral behavior.

▶ Dealings with employees, suppliers, customers, investors, creditors, insurers, competitors and auditors, etc. (e.g. whether management conducts business on a high ethical plane, and insists that others do so, or pays little attention to ethical issues).

▶ Pressure to meet unrealistic performance targets – particularly for short-term results – and extent to which compensation is based on achieving those performance targets.

How those charged with governance demonstrate independence from management and exercise oversight of the entity's system of internal control

▶ An entity's control consciousness is influenced significantly by those charged with governance. Independence from management.

▶ Frequency and timeliness with which meetings are held with chief financial and/or accounting officers, internal auditors and external auditors.

▶ Sufficiency and timeliness with which information is provided to board or committee members, to allow monitoring of management's objectives and strategies, the entity's financial position and operating results, and terms of significant agreements.

▶ Sufficiency and timeliness with which the board or audit committee is apprised of sensitive information, investigation and improper acts (e.g. travel expenses of senior officers, significant litigation, investigations of regulatory agencies, defalcations, embezzlement or misuse of corporate assets, violations of insider trading rules, political payments, illegal payments).

▶ Oversight of the design and effective operation of whistle blower procedures and the process for reviewing the effectiveness of the entity's internal control.

How the entity assigns authority and responsibility in pursuit of its objectives

▶ Appropriateness of the entity's organizational structure and its ability to provide the necessary information flow to manage its activities.

▶ Adequacy of definition of key managers' responsibilities and their understanding of these responsibilities.

▶ Formal or informal job descriptions or other means of defining tasks that comprise particular jobs.

▶ Analysis of the knowledge and skills needed to perform jobs adequately.

How the entity attracts, develops, and retains competent individuals in alignment with its objectives

▶ Extent to which policies and procedures for hiring, training, promoting, and compensating employees are in place.

▶ Appropriateness of remedial action taken in response to departures from approved policies and procedures.

▶ Adequacy of employee candidate background checks, particularly with regard to prior actions and activities considered to be unacceptable by the entity.

▶ Adequacy of employee retention and promotion criteria and information-gathering techniques (e.g. performance evaluations) and relation to the code of conduct or other behavioral guidelines.

How the entity holds individuals accountable for their responsibilities in pursuit of the objectives of the entity's system of internal control (Accountability for internal control responsibilities)

▶ Mechanisms to communicate and hold individuals accountable for performance of controls responsibilities and implement corrective actions as necessary;

▶ Establishing performance measures, incentives and rewards for those responsible for the entity's system of internal control, including how the measures are evaluated and maintain their relevance;

▶ How pressures associated with the achievement of control objectives impact the individual's responsibilities and performance measures; and

▶ How the individuals are disciplined as necessary.

7.4.2 RISK ASSESSMENT

All components of internal control, from control environment to monitoring, should be assessed for risk. Management's risk assessment differs from, but is closely related to, the auditor's risk assessment discussed in chapter 6. Management assesses risks as part of designing and implementing the internal control system to minimize errors and irregularities. Auditors assess risks to decide the evidence needed in the audit. The two risk assessment approaches are related in that if management effectively assesses and responds to risks, the auditor will typically need to accumulate less audit evidence than when management fails to, because RMM is lower.

INTERNAL AND EXTERNAL BUSINESS RISK

Risks to the organization may arise from external or internal factors. Externally, technological developments can affect the nature or timing of research and development or lead to changes in procurement. Changing customer needs affect product development, pricing, warranties and service. New legislation and regulation can force changes in operating policies and strategies. Economic changes have an impact on decisions relating to financing, capital expenditures and expansion. Risks arising from internal factors might include a disruption of information systems processing; the quality of personnel and training; changes in management responsibilities; misappropriation opportunities because of the nature of the entity's activities or employee accessibility to assets; and an ineffective audit committee.

Many techniques have been developed to identify general risks to a business. The majority involve identifying and prioritizing high-risk activities. One method[30] follows this procedure:

1 identify the essential resources of the business and determine which are most at risk;
2 identify possible liabilities that may arise;
3 review the risks that have arisen in the past;
4 consider any additional risks imposed by new objectives or new external factors;
5 seek to anticipate change by considering problems and opportunities on a continuing basis.

To illustrate, let us take as an example. Feats, an importer of apparel and footwear, established an objective of becoming an industry leader in high-quality fashion merchandise. Entity-wide risks are: supply sources (including quality, stability and number of foreign suppliers); currency rate fluctuations; timeliness of receiving shipments (including customs delays); availability, reliability and costs of shipping; and likelihood of trade embargoes caused by political instability. Other more generic business risks such as economic conditions, market acceptance, competitors and changes in regulations also have to be considered.

CONDITIONS THAT MAY INCREASE RISK

Certain conditions may increase risk and, therefore, deserve special consideration. These conditions are: changed operating environment; new personnel; new or revamped information systems; rapid growth; new technology; new lines, products and activities; corporate restructuring; and foreign operations.

A sample blank risk assessment internal control questionnaire is shown in illustration 7.5.[31]

ILLUSTRATION 7.5

RISK ASSESSMENT BLANK EVALUATION TOOL

Considerations	Comments Yes/No
Entity-Wide Objectives and Strategies	
1 Management has established entity-wide objectives.	1
2 Information on the entity-wide objectives is disseminated to employees and the board of directors.	2
3 Management obtains feedback from key managers, other employees, and the board signifying that communication to employees is effective.	3
Strategies	
4 Are strategies related to and consistent with entity-wide objectives?	4
5 The strategic plan supports the entity-wide objectives.	5
6 The strategic plan addresses high-level resource allocations and priorities.	6
Plans and Budgets	
7 Are business plans and budgets consistent with entity-wide objectives, strategic plans and current conditions?	7
8 Assumptions inherent in the plans and budgets reflect the entity's historical experience and current conditions.	8
9 Plans and budgets are at an appropriate level of detail for each management level.	9
Activity-Level Objectives	
Are objectives established for each of the following activities?	
10 Operations	10
11 Marketing and Sales	11
12 Service	12
13 Process Accounts Receivable	13
14 Procurement	14
15 Process Accounts Payable	15
16 Process Funds	16
17 Fixed Assets	17
18 Benefits and Retiree Information	18
19 Payroll	19
20 Product Costs	20
21 Tax Compliance	21
22 Financial and Management Reporting	22
23 Human Resources and Administrative Services	23
24 External Relations	24
25 Information Technology	25
26 Technology Development	26
27 Legal Affairs	27
28 Are those activity-level objectives consistent with each other?	28
29 Are activity-level objectives linked with entity-wide objectives and strategic plans?	29
30 Activity-level objectives are reviewed from time to time for continued relevance.	30
31 Are activity-level objectives complementary and reinforcing within activities?	31

7.4.3 CONTROL ACTIVITIES

Control activities (sometimes called 'control procedures')[32] are policies and procedures that help ensure management directives are carried out. They help ensure that necessary actions are taken to address risks to the achievement of the entity's objectives for operations, financial reporting, or compliance. Generally, control activities fall into five broad categories: authorization, performance reviews, information processing, physical controls and segregation of duties[33].

▶ POLICIES AND PROCEDURES

Each control activity may be divided into two elements: a policy establishing what should be done and procedures to effectuate that policy. A policy, for example, might be that a securities dealer retail branch manager must monitor (conduct performance reviews of) customer trades. The control activity to effectuate that policy is a review of a report of trade activities by the customer, performed in a timely manner and with attention given to the nature and volume of securities traded. Control activity implements the control policies by specific routine tasks, performed at particular times by designated people, held accountable by adequate supervision and evidence of performance.

The categories of control activities noted in ISA 315[34] are:

- ▶ authorization and approvals;
- ▶ reconciliations;
- ▶ verifications (such as edit and validation check or automated calculations);
- ▶ segregation of duties;
- ▶ physical and logical controls including those addressing safeguarding of assets;
- ▶ management controls on disclosures.

We have highlighted two categories below.

PHYSICAL CONTROLS

Physical controls are procedures to ensure the physical security of assets. Assets and records that are not adequately protected can be stolen, damaged, or lost. In highly computerized companies damaged data files could be costly or even impossible to replace. For these reasons, only individuals who are properly authorized should be allowed access to the company's assets. Direct physical access to assets may be controlled through physical precautions, for example: storerooms guard inventory against pilferage; locks, fences and guards protect other assets such as equipment; and fireproof safes and safety deposit vaults protect assets such as currency and securities.

SEGREGATION OF DUTIES

Segregation of duties seeks to prevent persons with access to readily realizable assets from being able to adjust the records that record and thereby control those assets. Duties are divided, or segregated, among different people to reduce the risks of error or inappropriate actions. For instance, responsibilities for authorizing transactions, for recording them, and for handling the related assets (called custody of assets) are separated.

Segregation of duties entails three fundamental functions (acronym ARC) that must be separated and adequately supervised:

1 *Authorization* is the delegation of initiation of transactions and obligations on the company's behalf.
2 *Recording* is the creation of documentary evidence of a transaction and its entry into the accounting records.
3 *Custody* is physical control over assets or records.

A separation of these three functions is an essential element of control. Let us use the example of wages. Authorization is required for hiring of staff and is a function of the personnel department. The accounting department handles the recording of the time records and the payroll in the payroll journals. The receipt of pay cheques and issuance of them to the employees is handled by work supervisors.

Illustration 7.6 shows an overview of segregation of duties.

ILLUSTRATION 7.6

OVERVIEW OF SEGREGATION OF DUTIES

Transaction type	Controls
Authorization	Controls that ensure that only necessary transactions based on the entity's objectives are undertaken. They prevent unnecessary and fraudulent transactions. Examples: organizational chart, accounting procedures manual, chart of accounts, conflict of interest policy, signatures on cheques limited to that of president, etc.
Recording	Controls which ensure that all authorized transactions are allowed in the accounting records, they are properly entered, and are not deleted or amended without proper authorization. Examples: entries in journals then ledgers, posting reference in journals, rotation of accounting personnel, listing of mail receipts, cash register tapes, reconciliation of bank statements, etc.
Custody	Controls that ensure that assets cannot be misused. Examples: pre-numbered forms, access to records (computer or manual) limited to authorized personnel, individuals handling cash do not keep the accounting records of cash, bonding of employees, locked storage, people responsible for assets should not be authorized to sell them, daily deposits of cash, etc.

People who authorize transactions should not have control over the related asset. Jérôme Kerviel, a derivative trader, brought one of the world's largest banks, Société Générale, to its knees with fraud worth €4.9 billion in early 2008. 'Le rogue trader' made €50 billion of unauthorized trades and futures positions – more than SocGen's own stock market value. Kerviel tried to conceal the activity by creating losing trades intentionally so as to offset his early gains[35]. In 1995 another investment bank, Barings, a British bank founded in 1762 and the investment bank that financed the 'Louisiana Purchase' from Napoleon by US President Thomas Jefferson's administration, was forced into insolvency by losses. Nicholas Leeson, the head derivatives trader of the Singapore branch, lost £827 million in speculative trading, mainly on the futures markets. He not only made investments in Nikkei exchange indexed derivatives, but also was able to authorize his own investments[36]. The authorization of a transaction and the handling of the related asset by the same person increases the possibility of *defalcation* within the organization.

Another example of when duties were not separated with a disastrous result was the bond trading loss in the New York Office of Daiwa Bank in 1995. Over 11 years, 30,000 unauthorized trades were made resulting in a $1.1 billion loss (an average of $400,000 in losses for every trading day). Daiwa allowed Toshihide Iguchi, a bond trader, to authorize sales, have custody of the bond assets and record these transactions[37]. Daiwa Bank paid fines of $340 million, and closed its American operations, after being sued by US authorities. Mr Iguchi was convicted and jailed for four years and required to pay $2.5 million in fines in 1996[38]. Four years later, in 2000, a court in Osaka, Japan ordered 11 senior executives at the bank to repay a total of $775 million in damages to their own bank.

If an individual has custody of assets and also accounts for them, there is a high risk of that person disposing of the asset for personal gain and adjusting the records to cover the theft. The basic control imposed by double-entry bookkeeping means that in order to conceal the theft or fraudulent use of an asset, the perpetrator must be able to prevent the asset being recorded in the first place or to write it off. If the theft cannot be permanently written off, it may still be temporarily concealed by being carried forward in preparing inventory sheets, in performing the bank reconciliation, or in reconciling the debtor or creditor control accounts.

IT SEGREGATION OF DUTIES

Operations responsibility and record keeping, and the information technology (IT) duties should be separate. Information systems are crucially important to control, so it is suggested that those duties be segregated for programmer, computer operator, librarian and data reviewer. A programmer wrote (or configured) the software. Giving the programmer access to input data creates temptation. The computer operator (who inputs the accounting data) should not be allowed to modify the program. A librarian maintains and is custodian of the records and files that should only be released to authorized personnel. The person who tests the efficiency of all aspects of the system should be independent of the other computer jobs.

CONCEPT AND A COMPANY 7.3	
WEAKNESSES IN THE CONTROL ENVIRONMENT – THE CASE OF SOCIÉTÉ GÉNÉRALE	
Concept	A control environment in which the motivation to misstate financial statements may lead to problems.
Story	In 2000, Jérôme Kerviel graduated from University Lumière Lyon with a Master of Finance specializing in organization and control of financial markets. Subsequently, he found employment with the bank Société Générale in the summer of 2000. He started out in the compliance department.
	In 2005 he was promoted to the bank's Delta One products team in Paris where he was a junior trader. Société Générale's Delta One business includes program trading, exchange-traded funds, swaps, index futures and quantitative trading. Kerviel was assigned to arbitrage discrepancies between equity derivatives and cash equity prices.
	In January 2008, Société Générale announced they had lost approximately €4.9 billion closing out positions over three days of trading beginning 21 January 2008, a period in which the market was experiencing a large drop in equity indices. Bank officials also claim that throughout 2007, Kerviel had been trading profitably in anticipation of falling market prices; however, they have accused him of exceeding his authority to engage in unauthorized trades totaling as much as €49.9 billion, a figure far higher than the bank's total market capitalization. Bank officials claim that Kerviel tried to conceal the activity by creating losing trades intentionally so as to offset his early gains. So, Société Générale concluded these positions were fraudulent transactions created by Jérôme Kerviel.

On 24 January 2008, Société Générale filed a lawsuit against Kerviel. On 5 October 2010, he was found guilty and sentenced to at least three years' imprisonment and was ordered to pay back the damages Société Générale suffered (€4.9 billion). Kerviel appealed, claiming his supervisors knew what he was doing. However, on 24 October 2012, a Paris appeals court upheld the October 2010 sentence.

In an interview with German newspaper *Der Spiegel*, Kerviel said: 'In the process, I didn't make a penny, I didn't enrich myself personally and I didn't commit any fraud. I only wanted to be a good employee who generated as much profit as possible for his employer. I was merely a small cog in the machine – and now I'm suddenly supposedly the main person responsible for the financial crisis.' Also, he pointed out that 'having more controls and regulations goes against efforts to pursue consistently higher profits at a time when all banks want to maximize their return on equity.' In the same interview, Kerviel explained how it was possible for him to make trades of this size, since the maximum official risk exposure for that trader in Jérôme's department was €125 million. Kerviel stated: 'My supervisors had deactivated the system of alerts. If I had wanted to, I could have even invested €100 billion in a single day. My bosses removed all the safeguards off my computer.'

Earlier on 21 February 2008, the London *Sunday Times* reported that according to an independent report Société Générale had missed 75 warning signs on the activities of rogue trader Jérôme Kerviel. Risk control activities were followed correctly, the report said, but compliance officers rarely went beyond routine checks and did not inform managers of anomalies, even when large sums were concerned. Nor were follow-up checks made on cancelled or modified transactions.

Discussion Questions	▷ What controls were in place, but not operating? ▷ If Jérôme Kerviel had managed to deactivate the system of alerts by himself, given his previous experience at the compliance department of the bank, do you believe he was the only person responsible for the loss?

References	Seib C., 2008, 'Société Générale Missed 75 Warnings on Trader Kerviel', *Sunday Times*, 21 February. http://en.wikipedia.org/wiki/J%C3%A9r%C3%B4me_Kerviel. http://en.wikipedia.org/wiki/2008_Soci%C3%A9t%C3%A9_G%C3%A9n%C3%A9rale_trading_loss. http://richardbrenneman.wordpress.com/2010÷11/19/jerome-kerviel-rogue-trader-or-the-perfect-patsy/. http://www.spiegel.de/international/business/rogue-trader-jerome-kerviel-i-was-merely-a-small-cog-in-the-machine-a-729155.html.

7.4.4 INFORMATION AND COMMUNICATION (INCLUDING IT)

Every enterprise must capture pertinent information related to both internal and external events and activities in both financial and non-financial forms. The information must be identified by management as relevant and then communicated to people who need it in a form and time frame that allows them to do their jobs.

The information relevant to financial reporting is recorded in the accounting information system and is subjected to procedures that initiate, record, process and report entity transactions. The quality of information generated by the system affects management's ability to make appropriate decisions in controlling the entity's activities and preparing reliable financial reports.

Not just a matter of reporting, communication occurs in a broader sense, flowing down, across and up the organization. All personnel must receive a clear message from top-management that control responsibilities must be taken seriously. Employees must understand their own role in the internal control system, as well as how individual activities relate to the work of others, and how to report significant information to senior management. There also needs to be effective communication with external parties such as customers, suppliers and regulators.

As the computer is in the middle of almost any entity nowadays, understanding the importance of it and IT related risks and control are key in the context of the financial statement audit.

Illustration 7.7 shows how IT related procedures are embedded into the audit approach.

ILLUSTRATION 7.7

UNDERSTANDING AND RESPONDING TO IT IS AN INTEGRAL PART OF UNDERSTANDING AND RISK ANALYSIS

Audit Phase	IT related procedures
Understand the entity and its environment, including the entity's internal control	▶ Understand the role of IT within the entity
	▶ Understand the IT landscape and organization
	▶ Identify the relevant IT (dependent) controls
	▶ Relate the controls to applications/systems
	▶ Identify the relevant IT General Controls
	▶ Assess design and implementation of the relevant IT General Controls
Assess the risks of material misstatements	▶ Identify and assess the risks related to IT
Respond to the risk of material misstatements	▶ Determine if and how the IT (dependent) controls will be tested (also depending on reliance on IT General Controls)
	▶ Test operating effectiveness of relevant IT General Controls
	▶ Test effectiveness IT (dependent) controls
Evaluate findings and follow up	▶ Evaluate the nature and impact of IT (dependent) controls deficiencies
	▶ Re-assess the audit plan responding to the identified risks and deficiencies

WHAT IS INCLUDED IN INFORMATION SYSTEMS?

An organization uses an array of information. The information systems used by companies include the accounting system; production system; budget information; personnel system; systems software; applications software for word-processing, calculating, presentations, communications and databases; and all the records and files generated by this software such as customer and vendor records. The information system also includes information about external events, activities, and conditions necessary to make informed business decisions and comply with external reporting.

Illustration 7.8 shows the typical input, subsystems and output of an information system.

TYPICAL INPUT, SUBSYSTEMS AND OUTPUT OF AN INFORMATION SYSTEM

Input
- ▶ accounting transactions
- ▶ correspondence
- ▶ personnel information
- ▶ customer and vendor information
- ▶ entity objectives and standards
- ▶ procedure manuals
- ▶ information about external events, activities and conditions

Subsystems
- ▶ accounting system
- ▶ customer and vendor records
- ▶ production system
- ▶ budget system
- ▶ personnel system
- ▶ computer systems software
- ▶ computer applications software (word processing, spreadsheet, presentation, communication, computer languages and database)

Output
- ▶ accounting reports
- ▶ budget reports
- ▶ production reports
- ▶ operating reports
- ▶ correspondence
- ▶ all the records and files generated by applications software

For an audit, the auditor should obtain an understanding of the information systems and the related business processes relevant to financial reporting in the following areas[39]:
- ▶ the classes of transactions in the entity's operations that are significant to the financial statements;
- ▶ the procedures, within both IT and manual systems, by which those transactions are initiated, recorded, processed and reported from their occurrence to their inclusion in the financial statements; this includes the correction of incorrect information and how information is transferred to the general ledger;
- ▶ the related accounting records, supporting information, and specific accounts in the financial statements and how they initiate, record, process and report transactions;
- ▶ how the information system captures events and conditions, other than transactions, that are significant to the financial statements;

▶ controls surrounding journal entries, including non-standard journal entries used to record non-recurring, unusual transactions or adjustments;

▶ the financial reporting process used to prepare the entity's financial statements, including significant accounting estimates and disclosures.

For internal control and documentation purposes the auditor may view an accounting system as a series of steps by which economic events are captured by the enterprise, recorded and assembled in a normal ledger and ultimately reflected in the financial statements. Controls are needed to ensure that all the relevant economic events are captured by the accounting system, and that processes that modify and summarize financial information do not introduce errors.

To understand the accounting system sufficiently, the auditor should identify major classes of transactions in the client's operations and understand the accounting and financial reporting process thoroughly – from how the transactions are initiated to their inclusion in the financial statements. The auditor should identify significant accounting records, supporting documents and accounts in the financial statements. The critical points of interest for an auditor are where financial information *changes* along the path of recording and assembling a ledger.

FINANCIAL REPORTING PROCESS (COMMUNICATION)

The auditor should know how the company communicates significant matters relating to financial reporting. Open communication channels help ensure that exceptions are reported and acted on. When evaluating the communication system, the auditor will consider:

▶ Effectiveness with which employees' duties and control responsibilities are communicated.

▶ Existence of channels of communication for people to report suspected improprieties.

▶ Receptivity of management to employee suggestions of ways to enhance productivity, quality or other similar improvements.

▶ Adequacy of communication across the organization (e.g. between procurement and production activities), and the completeness and timeliness of information and its sufficiency to enable people to discharge their responsibilities effectively.

▶ Openness and effectiveness of channels with customers, suppliers, and other external parties for communicating information on changing customer needs.

▶ Timely and appropriate follow-up action by management resulting from communications received from customers, vendors, regulators or other external parties.

▶ IT RISK AND CONTROLS

The procedures by which transactions are initiated, recorded, processed and reported from their occurrence to their inclusion in the financial statements include entries of transaction totals into the general ledger (or equivalent records) and an understanding of recurring and infrequent or unusual adjustments to the financial statements.

IT may be used to transfer information automatically from transaction processing systems to general ledger to financial reporting. The automated processes and controls in such systems may reduce the risk of inadvertent errors but create new risk. When IT is used to transfer information automatically, there may be little or no visible evidence of unauthorized intervention in the information systems if it occurs.

The auditor should also understand how the incorrect processing of transactions is resolved. For example, is there an automated suspense file and, if so, how are suspense items cleared out on a timely basis? How are system overrides or bypasses to controls accounted for?

As IT poses specific risks to an entity's internal control the auditor should be aware of the following:

- ▶ Reliance on systems or programs that are inaccurately processing data, processing inaccurate data, or both. For instance, individuals may inappropriately override such automated processes, by changing the amounts being automatically passed to the general ledger or to the financial reporting system. Furthermore, where IT is used to transfer information automatically, there may be little or no visible evidence of such intervention in the information systems.
- ▶ Unauthorized access to data that may result in destruction of data or improper changes to data, including the recording of unauthorized or non-existent transactions or inaccurate recording of transactions. Particular risks may arise where multiple users access a common database.
- ▶ The possibility of IT personnel gaining access privileges beyond those necessary to perform their assigned duties thereby breaking down segregation of duties. A frequent problem in audits of small to medium-sized businesses is that there is only one IT employee and she has unlimited access to all computer systems hardware and software, all security systems and all back-ups. A response to this risk is to have someone periodically review the security and access logs to monitor the IT employee's activity.
- ▶ Unauthorized changes to data in master files.
- ▶ Unauthorized changes to systems or programs.
- ▶ Failure to make necessary changes to systems or programs.
- ▶ Inappropriate manual intervention.
- ▶ Potential loss of data or inability to access data as required.
- ▶ Management's failure to commit sufficient resources to address IT security risks may adversely affect internal control by allowing improper changes to be made to computer programs or to data, or unauthorized transactions to be processed.
- ▶ Inconsistencies between the entity's IT strategy and its business strategies.
- ▶ Changes in the IT environment.

INPUT RISKS

Risk exists at all levels of the information system, but especially related to input. Input should be only by those people and systems with authorized access. Data entry should be secure from unauthorized access. Input should be accurate (correct data is entered correctly), valid (transaction is approved or authorized), and complete (all valid transactions should be entered and captured by the system). Subsystems should process transactions completely (all data that should be transacted into the general ledger is there) and accurately (data that is entered is reflected in the general ledger). Lack of controls or insufficient controls on authorization, data input and processing by subsystems increases risk.

The heart of any internal control system is the information technology (IT) upon which so much of the business processes rely. ISA 315 defines General IT controls[40] as: 'controls over the entity's IT processes that support the continued proper operation of the IT environment, including the continued effective functioning of information processing controls and the integrity of information (i.e., the completeness, accuracy and validity of information) in the entity's information system.'

General IT controls commonly include controls over datacenter and network operations; system software acquisition, change and maintenance; access security; back-up and recovery; and application system acquisition, development, and maintenance. A good example of a general control in accounting software is an error message if there is a problem in using the operating system. The IT environment is the policies and procedures that the entity implements and the IT infrastructure (hardware, operating systems, etc.) and application software that it uses to support business operations and achieve business strategies.

Controls in IT systems consist of a combination of automated or application controls (for example, controls embedded in computer programs) and manual controls. In manual systems, general controls are controls over proper authorization of transactions and activities. Further, manual controls may be independent of IT, may use information produced by IT, or may be limited to monitoring the effective functioning of IT and of automated controls, and to handling exceptions. An entity's mix of manual and automated elements in internal control varies with the nature and complexity of the entity's use of IT.

Generally, IT benefits an entity's internal controls by enabling them to consistently apply predefined business rules and perform complex calculations in processing large volumes of transactions or data; enhance the timeliness, availability, and accuracy of information; and facilitate the additional analysis of information. IT systems enhance the ability to monitor the performance of the entity's activities and its policies and procedures; reduce the risk that controls will be circumvented; and enhance the ability to achieve effective segregation of duties by implementing security controls in applications, databases, and operating systems.

Information processing control activities are primarily of two types: application controls and general controls. Application controls are controls that apply to applications that initiate, record, process and report transactions (such as MS Office, SAP, QuickBooks), rather than the computer system in general. Examples of application controls are edit checks of input data, numerical sequence checks, and manual follow-up of exception reports. In manual systems, applications controls may be referred to as adequate document and record controls.

There is a multitude of risks associated with IT, so auditors must expend a good deal of effort analysing these systems for issues that may affect the financial statements and the auditor's opinion.

GENERAL IT CONTROLS

General IT controls assure that access to the computer system is limited to people who have a right to the information. Appropriate delegation of authority sets limits on what levels of risk are acceptable and these limits determine the discretion of the employees delegated to authorize the main types of business transactions. Authorization may be general or specific. An example of general limits set by policy is product price lists, inventory reorder points and customer credit limits. Specific authorization may be made on a case-by-case basis such as authorization of reduction in the price of a dress with buttons missing in a retail-clothing store.

APPLICATION CONTROLS

There are several standard application controls. The chart of accounts is an important application control because it provides the framework for determining the information presented on to financial statements. An example of such an applicable control device is the use of serial numbers on documents and input transactions. Serial numbering provides control over the number of documents issued. Cheques, tickets, sales invoices, purchase orders, stock certificates, and many other business papers use this control. Documents should be recorded immediately because long periods between transaction and recording increase the chance of misstatement. Systems manuals for computer accounting software should provide sufficient information to make the accounting functions clear.

COMPUTER FACILITY CONTROLS

Computer facilities may have several types of controls. General controls such as access controls or application controls such as passwords allow only authorized people admittance to the computer software. A very important general control is back-up and recovery procedures, as anyone who has had a system go down without current records being adequately backed up will tell you. Physical controls such as locks on the doors to the computer room and locked cabinets for software and back-up tapes protect the tangible components of a computer system.

7.4.5 MONITORING

Internal control systems need to be monitored. Monitoring is a process that deals with ongoing assessment of the quality of internal control performance. The process involves assessing the design of controls and their operation on a timely basis and taking necessary corrective actions. By monitoring, management can determine that internal controls are operating as intended and that they are modified as appropriate for changes in conditions.

Ongoing monitoring information comes from several sources: exception reporting on control activities, reports by government regulators, feedback from employees, complaints from customers, and most importantly from internal auditor reports. For large companies, an internal audit department is essential to effective monitoring[41].

The internal audit department plays a crucial role in an organization's governance structure as a part of the 'Three Lines of Defence' model. This model is designed to ensure effective risk management and control by clearly defining responsibilities across three lines of defence (illustration 7.9):

> ▶ First Line of Defence: Operational management, which is directly responsible for maintaining internal controls and managing risks within their specific operations. This includes implementing and maintaining proper procedures, controls, and measures to mitigate risks in daily activities.
> ▶ Second Line of Defence: Various risk management and compliance functions established by the organization to help build and support the internal controls

implemented by the first line. This includes risk management, compliance, quality assurance, and other oversight functions that monitor and facilitate the implementation of effective risk management practices by operational management.

▶ Third Line of Defence: The Internal Audit Department, which provides an independent and objective assurance and consulting service. As the third line, internal audit evaluates and improves the effectiveness of governance, risk management, and control processes. This role encompasses assessing the adequacy and effectiveness of the first and second lines of defence in managing risks to the organization. Monitoring internal controls by the internal auditors may also help to assess control risk by external auditors and reduce evidence requirements.

ILLUSTRATION 7.9

THREE LINES OF DEFENCE MODEL (INSTITUTE OF INTERNAL AUDITORS)[42]

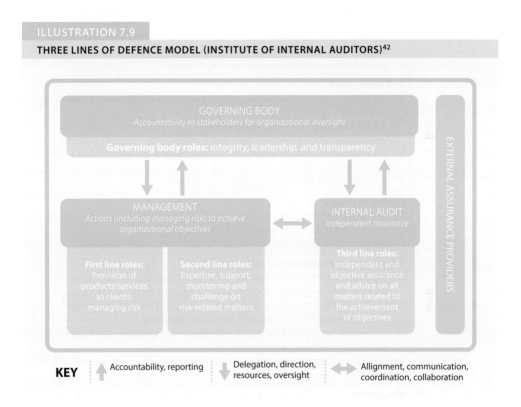

Management's monitoring activities may include using information from communications from external parties such as customer complaints and regulator comments that may indicate problems or highlight areas in need of improvement. Two more examples of monitoring activities are management's review of *bank reconciliations*, and an internal auditors' evaluation of sales personnel's compliance with the company's human resource policies.

INTERNAL CONTROLS OVER TIME

Internal control systems change over time. The way controls are applied may evolve. Some procedures can become less effective or perhaps are no longer performed. This can be due to the arrival of new personnel, the varying effectiveness of training and supervision,

ILLUSTRATION 7.10

OVERALL INTERNAL CONTROL EVALUATION TOOL

THIS EXHIBIT IS A BLANK TOOL (WORK PAPER) FOR THE EVALUATION OF AN ENTITY'S CONTROL ENVIRONMENT. THIS FORM IS TO BE FILLED IN AFTER THE DETAILED FORMS SUCH AS THAT SHOWN IN ILLUSTRATION 7.4 ARE COMPLETE.

Internal control components	*Comments* *Yes/No*
Control Environment	
1 Does management adequately convey the message that integrity cannot be compromised?	1
2 Does a positive control environment exist, whereby there is an attitude of control consciousness throughout the organization and a positive 'tone at the top'?	2
3 Is the competence of the entity's people commensurate with their responsibilities?	3
4 Is management's operating style, the way it assigns authority and responsibility, and organizes and develops its people appropriate?	4
5 Does the board provide the right level of attention?	5
Risk Assessment	
6 Are entity-wide objectives and supporting activity-level objectives established and linked?	6
7 Are the internal and external risks that influence the success or failure of the achievement of the objectives identified and assessed?	7
8 Are mechanisms in place to identify changes affecting the entity's ability to achieve its objectives?	8
9 Are policies and procedures modified as needed?	9
Control Activities	
10 Are control activities in place to ensure adherence to established policy and the carrying out of actions to address the related risks?	10
11 Are there appropriate control activities for each of the entity's activities?	11
Information and Communication	
12 Are information systems in place to identify and capture pertinent information – financial and non-financial, relating to external and internal events – and bring it to personnel in a form that enables them to carry out their responsibilities?	12
13 Does communication of relevant information take place?	13
14 Is information communicated clear with respect to expectations and responsibilities of individuals and groups, and reporting of results?	14
15 And does communication occur down, across and upwards in the entity, as well as between the entity and other parties?	15
Monitoring	
16 Are appropriate procedures in place to monitor on an ongoing basis, or to periodically evaluate the functioning of the other components of internal control?	16
17 Are deficiencies reported to the right people?	17
18 Are policies and procedures modified as needed?	18
Overall Conclusion	

time and resource constraints, or additional pressures. Furthermore, circumstances for which the internal control system originally was designed may also change. Accordingly, management needs to determine whether the internal control system continues to be relevant and able to address new risks. This is the monitoring function.

EVALUATION OF MONITORING ACTIVITIES

When evaluating the ongoing monitoring the following issues might be considered[43]:

▶ periodic comparisons of amounts recorded with the accounting system with physical assets;

▶ responsiveness to internal and external auditor recommendations on means to strengthen internal controls;

▶ extent to which training seminars, planning sessions, and other meetings provide management with information on the effective operation of controls;

▶ whether personnel are asked periodically to state whether they understand and comply with the entity's code of conduct and regularly perform critical control activities;

▶ effectiveness of internal audit activities;

▶ extent to which personnel, in carrying out their regular activities, obtain evidence as to whether the system of internal control continues to function.

Evaluations of all the components are taken together for an overall evaluation and a sample blank evaluation form is shown in illustration 7.10.[44]

7.5 IDENTIFY RMM AND DETERMINE CONTROL DEFICIENCIES

(Steps 6 and 7, illustration 7.1)

To gain an understanding of the entity's internal control and assess initial control risk (CR), the auditor is required to evaluate the design of controls and determine whether they have been implemented. Evaluating the design of a control involves considering whether the control is capable of effectively preventing, or detecting and correcting, material misstatements.

Errors in design occur when crucial internal control activities are designed by individuals with limited knowledge of accounting. For instance, if an entity's IT personnel do not completely understand how an order entry system processes sales transactions, they may erroneously design changes to the system. On the other hand, good designs may be poorly implemented. An IT controls change may be correctly designed but misunderstood by individuals who translate the design into program code. IT controls may be designed to report transactions over a predetermined dollar amount to management, but individuals responsible for conducting the review may not understand the purpose of such reports and, accordingly, may fail to review them or investigate unusual items. For example, there may be an error in the design of a control. Equally, the operation of a control may not be effective, such as where information produced for the purposes of internal control is not effectively used because the individual responsible for reviewing the information does not understand its purpose or fails to take appropriate action.

Limitations inherent to internal control include the faultiness of human judgement in decision-making and simple human failures such as errors or mistakes.

There are no standard procedures for assessing the design of internal controls, but all controls are created to assure that an objective be met. When assessing control design, the auditor will start with the objective. Then she will ask herself what controls should and could be in place to assure that this objective is met and in what way these controls may be implemented. This is the design of the control.

In other words, based on her understanding of the design and the deficiencies and weaknesses identified therein, the auditor assesses the risk of material errors not being prevented or detected internally in the financial statements.

As sketched in chapter 6, the risk of a material misstatement (RMM) is equal to inherent risk (IR) unless that risk is mitigated by adequately designed internal controls. In that case, the initial CR (Control Risk) is relatively low, and it may be decided to test the operational effectiveness of these controls to assess final CR (see chapter 8).

CONTROLS ADDRESSING SIGNIFICANT RISK

It is especially important to evaluate the design of controls that address significant risks and controls for which substantive procedures alone are not sufficient. For significant risks, the auditor should evaluate the design of the entity's controls, including relevant control activities. Implementation of a control means that the control exists, and that the entity is using it. We will discuss tests of controls' operating effectiveness in chapter 8.

FINANCIAL STATEMENT ASSERTIONS AND CONTROLS

There are standard financial statement objectives, or *assertions*, that are assumed to be in place for a financial statement that fairly represents the underlying financial condition of the entity. For example, the assertion existence may be applied to sales, i.e. 'revenue exists'. The objective is that all sales that sum to the revenue account balance actually exist – each sales transaction composing the revenue meets the definition of 'revenue' and actually occurred (sales were not fictitious). Controls such as cash registers, restricted access for recording sales in the general ledger, and control activities such as segregation of duties and monitoring of unusual transactions should be designed and implemented to assure that the revenue account balance is correct. Inputting revenue transactions through the cash register is a design to assure revenue exists. In addition to using a cash register, an additional part of the design of the control is that all employees are trained to use the cash register. We refer to chapter 8 for a further discussion on assertions.

METHODS FOR OBTAINING CONTROLS AUDIT EVIDENCE

Obtaining audit evidence about the design and implementation of relevant controls may involve[45]:

> ▶ *Inquiring of entity personnel.* Inquiries directed towards internal audit personnel may relate to their activities concerning the design and effectiveness of the entity's internal control. Ordinarily, only inquiring of entity personnel will not be sufficient to evaluate the design of a control or to determine whether a control has been implemented.
> ▶ *Observing the application of specific controls.* The auditors may observe the application of the control or re-perform the application themselves.

- *Inspecting documents and reports.*
- *Selecting transactions and tracing them* through the application process of the information system relevant to financial reporting (i.e. walkthrough).

▶ THE USE OF TECHNOLOGY IN RISK ASSESSMENT PROCEDURES

As auditors increasingly utilize technology in conducting risk assessment procedures, ISA 315 explicitly notes the use of automated tools & techniques. Illustration 7.11 provides the references to the sections in ISA 315 and how to apply.

Some risk assessment procedures may already provide audit evidence and, consequently, serve as tests of controls of design. For instance, in obtaining an understanding of the control environment, the auditor may make inquiries about management's use of budgets, observe management's comparison of monthly budgeted and actual expenses, and inspect reports pertaining to the investigation of variances between budgeted and actual amounts. These procedures provide knowledge about the design of the entity's budgeting policies and may also provide audit evidence about the effectiveness of the operation of budgeting policies in preventing or detecting material misstatements.

▶ IDENTIFY CONTROL DEFICIENCIES

When evaluating each of the components of the entity's system of internal control, the auditor may find that some of the entity's policies in a component are not appropriate to the nature and circumstances of the entity. Identifying such mismatches can signal potential control deficiency, as per ISA 315, which then requires auditors to respond accordingly[47]. If the auditor has identified one or more control deficiencies, the auditor may consider the effect of those control deficiencies on the design of further audit procedures in accordance with ISA 330.

Deficiencies internal control must be reported to management and those charged with governance in accordance with ISA 265. Deficiency in internal control exists when: (a) a control is designed, implemented or operated in such a way that it is *unable to prevent, or detect and correct, misstatements* in the financial statements on a timely basis; or (b) a control necessary to prevent, or detect and correct, misstatements in the financial statements on a timely basis is *missing*. The auditor must communicate in writing significant deficiencies in internal control identified during the audit to those charged with governance on a timely basis. The auditor must also communicate in writing to management on a timely basis significant deficiencies in internal control that the auditor will communicate to those charged with governance, unless circumstances make it inappropriate. The auditor is responsible for considering what the timing of the reporting on internal control deficiencies should be. It is possible the timely basis for reporting internal control deficiencies is before the year-end audit.

ILLUSTRATION 7.11

EXPLICIT USE OF AUTOMATED TOOLS & TECHNIQUES IN ISA 315

Where	How	Ref
Risk assessment procedures (315.14)	On large volumes of data (from the general ledger, sub-ledgers or other operational data) including for analysis, recalculations, reperformance or reconciliations.	315.A21
	Performing analytical procedures with data analytics.	315.A31
	To observe or inspect, in particular assets, for example through the use of remote observation tools (e.g., a drone).	315.A35
Understanding the entity and its environment (315.19)	To understand flows of transactions and processing as part of the auditor's procedures to understand the information system. An outcome of these procedures may be that the auditor obtains information about the entity's organizational structure or those with whom the entity conducts business (e.g., vendors, customers, related parties).	315.A57
Obtaining an understanding of the information system (315.25)	To obtain direct access to, or a digital download from, the databases in the entity's information system that store accounting records of transactions. Confirm the understanding obtained about how transactions flow through the information system by tracing journal entries, or other digital records related to a particular transaction, or an entire population of transactions, from initiation in the accounting records through to recording in the general ledger. Analysis of complete or large sets of transactions may also result in the identification of variations from the normal, or expected, processing procedures for these transactions, which may result in the identification of risks of material misstatement.	315.A137
Journal entry testing (315.26aii)	In manual general ledger systems, non-standard journal entries may be identified through inspection of ledgers, journals, and supporting documentation. When automated procedures are used to maintain the general ledger and prepare financial statements, such entries may exist only in electronic form and may therefore be more easily identified through the use of automated techniques.	315.A161
Identification of significant classes of transactions, account balances and disclosures. (315.29)	An entire population of transactions may be analyzed using automated tools and techniques to understand their nature, source, size and volume. By analyzing the flows of an entire population of revenue transactions, the auditor may more easily identify a significant class of transactions that had not previously been identified.	315.A203
Understanding the Entity's Use of Information Technology in the Components of the Entity's System of Internal Control (315 appendix 5)	Use of validation software tools, which systematically check formulas or macros, such as spreadsheet integrity tools.	315 appendix 5, para 14

7.6 STAND BACK AND REFLECT

(Step 8, illustration 7.1)

After understanding and assessing control risks, it's time to evaluate the risk assessment process (step 8 in illustration 7.1).

▶ CLASSES OF TRANSACTIONS, ACCOUNT BALANCES AND DISCLOSURE THAT ARE NOT SIGNIFICANT BUT WHICH ARE MATERIAL

ISA 315[48] mandates auditors to reassess whether their initial evaluation of material classes of transactions, account balances, or disclosures, previously not considered significant, still holds. This 'stand back' procedure is logical, as auditors might encounter new or differing information during the audit that substantially deviates from the initial risk assessment basis. ISA 315 mentions the example 'that the entity's risk assessment may be based on an expectation that certain controls are operating effectively. In performing tests of those controls, the auditor may obtain audit evidence that they were not operating effectively at relevant times during the audit. Similarly, in performing substantive procedures the auditor may detect misstatements in amounts or frequency greater than is consistent with the auditor's risk assessments. In such circumstances, the risk assessment may not appropriately reflect the true circumstances of the entity and the further planned audit procedures may not be effective in detecting material misstatements.[49]

7.7 FINAL REFLECTIONS ON THE PRELIMINARY ASSESSMENT OF CONTROL RISK

It is difficult for an auditor to prepare an audit plan if she does not get a preliminary idea of the risks that internal controls may not be operating. One needs to have a certain faith that the data in the accounts and transactions was initiated and processed accurately. It is the controls that give an auditor some assurance that the data is accurate. For example, the auditor has to have assurance that people who input the data were authorized to do so, did not have segregation of duties conflicts and were supervised or reviewed by another party.

In order to assess control risk, the auditor undertakes a number of tasks when planning an audit. First, she considers the results of previous audits that involved evaluating the operating effectiveness of internal control, including the nature of identified deficiencies and action taken to address them. She will also discuss the possibility of audit risk with audit firm personnel responsible for performing other services to the entity. She will interview entity personnel to find evidence of management's commitment to the design, implementation and maintenance of sound internal control and the importance attached to internal control throughout the entity. She may also try to get a good idea of the volume of transactions, which may determine whether it is more efficient for the auditor to rely on internal controls.

Knowledge of the industry and the environment might also help in determining control risk. There are obvious questions. For instance, what is the impact on controls of significant business developments affecting the entity, including changes in information technology and business processes, changes in key management, and acquisitions, mergers and divestments? Have controls adapted to significant industry developments such as changes in industry regulations and new reporting requirements? Were there changes in the financial reporting framework, such as changes in accounting standards? Are there other relevant developments, such as changes in the legal environment affecting the entity?

If the entity uses service organizations[50] the auditor may want to discover the control risks at the service organization. She can get either a Type 1 or Type 2 report[51] which may assist the auditor in obtaining a preliminary understanding of the controls implemented at the service organization[52]. (See chapter 13 for further details.) If there is no report available or the report is too old, the auditor may perform procedures to update the information, such as discussing the changes at the service organization with auditee personnel who would be in a position to know of such changes, reviewing current documentation and correspondence issued by the service organization, or discussing the changes with service organization personnel.

7.8   STARTING POINT FOR PREPARING AUDIT PLAN

Once finalized the risk assessment procedures, the auditor finalised an extensive exercise identifying a comprehensive list of all RMMs. IAASB summarized this journey as shown in illustration 7.12.

Next step is that the auditor prepares the audit plan responding to the RMMs in accordance with ISA 330. This will be addressed in chapter 8. Tests of the operating effectiveness of controls may be performed on controls that the auditor has determined are suitably designed to prevent, or detect and correct, a material misstatement.

7.9   SUMMARY

Internal control is not only essential to maintaining the accounting and financial records of an organization, but it is also essential to managing the entity. For that reason, everyone from the external auditors to management to the board of directors to the stockholders of large public companies to government has an interest in internal controls. In many parts of the world, regulators have emphasized the importance of internal control by requiring management to make annual public statements about the effectiveness of internal controls.

Internal control, according to the Committee of Sponsoring Organizations of the Treadway Commission (COSO), is a process, effected by an entity's board of directors, management and other personnel, designed to provide reasonable assurance regarding the achievement of objectives in the following categories: effectiveness and efficiency of operations, reliability of financial reporting, compliance with applicable laws and regulations, and safeguarding of assets against unauthorized acquisition, use or disposition.

The reason a company establishes a system of control is to help achieve its performance and profitability goals and prevent loss of resources by fraud and other means. Internal control can also help to ensure reliable financial reporting and compliance with laws and

ILLUSTRATION 7.12

OVERVIEW OF ISA 315[53]

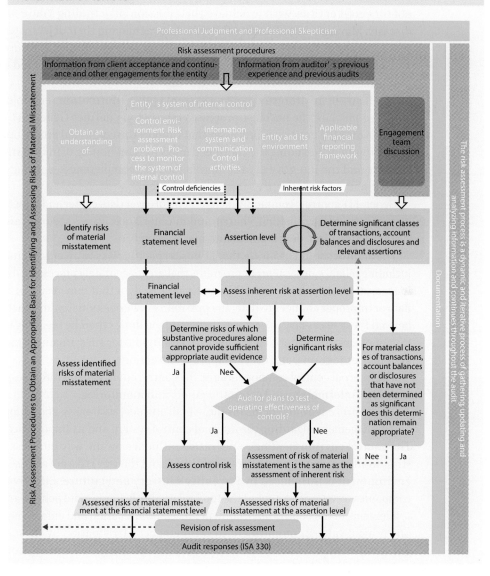

regulations. The entity's internal control system consists of many specific policies and procedures designed to provide management with reasonable assurance that the goals and objectives it believes important to the company will be met. Controls are especially important in preventing fraud, supporting management objectives, ensuring accuracy of transactions, and supporting assessment of the financial statements.

To understand the entity's internal controls the auditor will evaluate the design of a control and judge whether it has been implemented. She determines whether the control, individually or in combination with other controls, is capable of effectively preventing, or detecting and correcting, material misstatements.

Whether formally or informally, management sets objectives that they expect their business to achieve. For example, profit-making organizations have profit as a goal and not-for-profit entities wish to achieve their mission (like finding a cure for Alzheimer's disease). Management identifies the risk of not achieving their objectives. To minimize these risks, management designs and puts in place a set of rules, physical constraints and activities called 'internal controls' which, if they are implemented properly, will minimize the risks of not meeting objectives.

The heart of any internal control system is the information technology (IT) upon which so much of the business processes rely. ISA 315 defines General IT controls[54] as: 'controls over the entity's IT processes that support the continued proper operation of the IT environment, including the continued effective functioning of information processing controls and the integrity of information (i.e., the completeness, accuracy and validity of information) in the entity's information system.'

General IT controls commonly include controls over data center and network operations; system software acquisition, change and maintenance; access security; and application system acquisition, development and maintenance.

The auditor should be aware that IT poses specific risks to an entity's internal control including reliance on systems or programs that are inaccurately processing data, processing inaccurate data, or both, unauthorized access to data that may result in destruction of data or improper changes to data; the possibility of IT personnel gaining access privileges beyond those necessary to perform their assigned duties thereby breaking down segregation of duties; unauthorized changes to data in master files; unauthorized changes to systems or programs, and other inappropriate actions.

The internal control components are: the control environment, risk assessment, control activities, information and communication, and monitoring.

The control environment means the overall attitude, awareness, and actions of directors and management regarding the internal control system and its importance in the entity. The control environment has a pervasive influence on the way business activities are structured, the way objectives are established, and the way risks are assessed. The control environment is influenced by the entity's history and culture. Effectively controlled companies set a positive 'tone at the top' and establish appropriate policies and procedures.

Elements of the control environment are: communication and enforcement of integrity and ethical values; commitment to competence; participation by those charged with governance; management's philosophy and operating style; organizational structure; assignment of authority and responsibility; and human resource policies and practices.

All components of internal control, from control environment to monitoring, should be assessed for risk. Certain conditions may increase risk and, therefore, deserve special consideration. These conditions are: changed operating environment; new personnel; new or revamped information systems; rapid growth; new technology; new lines, products and activities; corporate restructuring; and foreign operations.

Management's risk assessment differs from, but is closely related to, the auditor's risk assessment. Management assesses risks as part of designing and operating the internal control system to minimize errors and irregularities. Auditors assess risks to decide the evidence needed in the audit. The two risk assessment approaches are related in that if management effectively assesses and responds to risks, the auditor will typically need to accumulate less audit evidence than when management fails to, because control risk is lower.

Information is needed at all levels of the organization: financial information; operating information; compliance information; and information about external events, activities, and conditions. This information must be identified, captured, and communicated in a form and time frame that enables people to carry out their responsibilities. The information system controls should be tested because there are general IT and input risks that the accounting system does not produce sufficient audit evidence.

Control activities (sometimes called 'control procedures') are policies and procedures that help ensure management directives are carried out. They help ensure that necessary actions are taken to address risks to the achievement of the entity's objectives for operations, financial reporting or compliance. Generally, control activities fall into five broad categories: authorization, performance reviews, information processing, physical controls and segregation of duties.

Internal control systems need to be monitored. Monitoring is a process that deals with ongoing assessment of the quality of internal control performance over time. The process involves assessing the design of controls and their operation on a timely basis and taking necessary corrective actions. By monitoring, management can determine that internal controls are operating as intended and that they are modified as appropriate for changes in conditions.

Due to the explicit, formal and tangible character of the controls management designs and puts in place in the form of a set of rules, physical constraints and activities, these controls are generally referred to as *hard* controls. However, the dynamic environment with rapidly changing technology, increasing regulatory requirements and globalization requires more than rigorous adherence to policy, procedures and protocols, which may be termed soft controls. Soft controls are the intangible factors in an organization that influence the behaviour of managers and employees. Whereas soft controls are founded in the culture or climate of an organization, the hard controls are more explicit, formal and visible. The control environment includes soft controls like tone-at-the-top, risk-awareness, openness to raise issues and discuss ideas, trust and loyalty, stakeholder focus and enforcement.

To gain an understanding of the entity's internal control, the auditor is required to evaluate the design of controls and determine whether they have been implemented. Evaluating the design of a control involves considering whether the control is capable of effectively preventing, or detecting and correcting, material misstatements. It is especially important to evaluate the design of controls that address significant risks and controls for which substantive procedures alone are not sufficient.

ISA 315 mandates auditors to reassess whether their initial evaluation of material classes of transactions, account balances, or disclosures, previously not considered significant, still holds. This 'stand back' procedure is logical, as auditors might encounter new or differing information during the audit that substantially deviates from the initial risk assessment basis. ISA 315 mentions the example 'that the entity's risk assessment may be based on an expectation that certain controls are operating effectively. In performing tests of those controls, the auditor may obtain audit evidence that they were not operating effectively at relevant times during the audit. Similarly, in performing substantive procedures the auditor may detect misstatements in amounts or frequency greater than is consistent with the auditor's risk assessments.

It is difficult for an auditor to prepare an audit plan if she does not get a preliminary idea of the risks that internal controls may not be operating. One needs to have a certain faith that the data in the accounts and transactions was initiated and processed accurately. It is the controls that give an auditor some assurance that the data is accurate. For example, the auditor has to have assurance that people who input the data were authorized to do so, did not have segregation of duties conflicts and were supervised or reviewed by another party.

7.10   QUESTIONS, EXERCISES AND CASES

QUESTIONS

7.2   **Introduction**

7-1   What are the first two steps in the planning procedures?

7.3   **Understanding Internal Control**

7-2   Define internal control. Discuss the fundamental concepts in the definition: process, people, reasonable assurance, and objectives.

7-3   Describe the four objectives of internal control.

7-4   Why is the auditor interested primarily in controls that relate to reliability of financial reporting, accounting and internal control systems?

7-5   What importance would internal controls have for an audit firm?

7-6   IT controls may generally be grouped into two types. Define these two.

7-7   What things might an auditor consider when evaluating the information system of an entity?

7.4   **Obtaining an understanding of Internal Control Components**

7-8   What are the five interrelated components of internal control? Briefly discuss them.

7.4.1   **Control Environment**

7-9   Define control environment. Why is it important to an entity?

7-10 Can evaluation of the control environment be a key element in determining the nature of the audit work? Why or why not?

7-11 What is meant by 'tone at the top'?

7-12 Muel Kaptein distinguishes seven social-psychological factors which influence people's behavior within organizations. Discuss.

7.4.2   **Risk Assessment**

7-13 What is the difference between management risk assessment and auditor risk assessment?

7-14 Name and discuss one technique that has been developed to identify risk.

7.4.3   **Control Activities**

7-15 Into what five categories do control activities fall?

7-16 Explain the concept of segregation of duties and refer to the acronym 'ARC'.

7.4.4 Information and Communication

7-17 What is the accounting system designed to do? What should be documented about an accounting system as part of the procedures to understand the internal control system?

7.4.5 Monitoring

7-18 Describe the monitoring role of the internal audit department.

7-19 What is meant by the 'three lines of defence'?

7.5 Identifying RMM and Determine Control Deficiencies

7-20 Discuss the four methods of obtaining audit evidence about the design and implementation of relevant controls.

7.6 Stand Back and Reflect

7-21 Why is 'stand back and reflect' a starting point for preparing the audit plan?

PROBLEMS AND EXERCISES

7.3 Understanding Internal Control

7-22 Internal control is geared to the achievement of objectives in one or more separate overlapping categories.
Required:
A.   Define these four categories of objectives.
B.   For each objective give an example of internal control goals for three industries: retail, manufacturing and services.

7-23 Obtain Understanding of Internal Control. Johannes Mullauer, Wirtschaftsprüfer, who has been engaged to audit the financial statements of Ais, GmbH, is about to start obtaining an understanding of the internal control structure and is aware of the inherent limitations that should be considered.
Required:
A.   What are the reasons for establishing objectives of internal control?
B.   What are the reasonable assurances that are intended to be provided by the accounting internal control structure?
C.   When considering the potential effectiveness of any internal control structure, what are the inherent limitations that should be recognized?

7-24 Discuss the following statements:
A.   Information technology benefits an entity's internal control by enabling them to consistently apply predefined business rules and perform complex calculations in processing large volumes of transactions or data; enhance the timeliness, availability and accuracy of information; and facilitate the additional analysis of information.
B.   IT systems enhance the ability to monitor the performance of the entity's activities and its policies and procedures; reduce the risk that controls will be circumvented; and enhance the ability to achieve effective segregation of duties by implementing security controls in applications, databases and operating systems.

7.4 Obtaining an understanding of Internal Control Components

7-25 Components of Internal Control. Internal control consists of five interrelated components. These are derived from the way management runs a business and are integrated with the management process.

Required:

A. Name and define the components of internal control.

B. How do the components of internal control affect each other?

C. Discuss the interrelationship of components using as an example a retail clothing store.

7.4.1 Control Environment

7-26 Assess Internal Control Environment. Using the COSO criteria for assessing internal control environment (Illustration 8.5), describe a company with an effective control environment.

7-27 Control Environment. Hasse Nilsson, Statautoriseret, is in charge of the audit of a new client, US Clothing Store. It is owned by three men, Messrs. Simpson, Andersson and Ding. Only one of the owners, Mr Simpson, is active in the business – the other two live and work in another city. Mr Simpson operated the business as a proprietorship until a few years ago, when he incorporated it and obtained additional capital for store improvements by selling to Ding and Andersson 24 per cent of his equity. In addition to Mr Simpson, the store employs three salesclerks and Miss Tearsson, the cashier-bookkeeper. Miss Tearsson has worked for Mr Simpson for many years. Nilsson and the partner in his firm responsible for the US Clothing Store audit have agreed that one of the first things Nilsson should do when he starts work on the audit is to consider the internal control environment.

Required:

A. Why is it important to consider the internal control enviroanment of even a small company such as US Clothing Store?

B. What particular features of the internal control environment would Nilsson inquire into in the circumstances described above?

7-28 Ambazam, an airline shuttle service operating out of the Tampa, Florida, USA, airport wishes to analyze the necessary controls required for their operation. They pick up arrivals at the airport and deliver people to the airport from hotels in the Tampa area. They operate five shuttle vans and have 10 employees. Their owner, Julio Cruz's, objective is to respond quickly to calls, be courteous to customers, and keep hotel employees, who refer them to hotel guests, happy.

Required:

For each of the seven social-psychological factors which influence people's behaviour within organizations discuss how Mr Cruz could use these factors to set controls that assure employees, customers and hotel employees meet the objectives.

7.4.2 Risk Assessment

7-29 Risk Assessment. OK Yen, Ltd. is a Japanese electronics games and amusements company specializing in pachinko games. Pachinko parlours are a big industry in Japan, whose 18,000 pachinko parlours in 1996 accounted for a quarter of the country's civil sector and are thought to produce Japanese Yen (¥) 30 trillion per year in revenue – more than Japan's auto industry. Customers who play pachinko buy a supply of pinballs costing around ¥4 and cash in the balls they win back for prizes equivalent to ¥2.5 each. Although it is illegal to give cash to winners, the customers may go to nearby shops and sell their prizes for cash. Recently a new form of pachinko has been developed that gives very large prizes to winners but decreases the chances of winning. Although the number of players has decreased over the last four years, the gross sales have doubled. Location of the stores is not crucial, so OK Yen can locate in low-rent areas.

Government authorities have recently given much attention to pachinko gaming. Operations featuring the game have been associated with the yakuza, the Japanese criminal organization. Some people in Japan are concerned that pachinko is really addictive gambling. There are complaints to authorities over children being left to play on busy streets or locked up in parked automobiles while their parents go to play pachinko.

Required:

Following the five-step procedure outlined in the chapter, identify the risks associated with OK Yen's business.

7.4.3 Control Activities

7-30 Separation of Duties. Aurello Pellegrini, Dottore Commercialista (CONSOB), is approached by his client who has just reorganized his medium-sized manufacturing company to make it more structured by giving responsibilities in related areas to one employee. The 'supervisor for customers' is responsible for both collection of accounts receivable and maintenance of accounts receivable records. The 'inventory coordinator' is responsible for purchasing, receiving and storing inventory. The 'payroll agent' handles all payroll matters including personnel records, keeping timecards, preparation of payrolls, and distribution of payroll cheques.

Required:

Consider each of these new positions and discuss the implications of their duties on the internal control system. Discuss what sorts of problems could arise if these positions are created.

7.4.4 Information and Communication

7-31 Information and Communications. The firm of Hayes & Hu, Ltd, personal financial advisers in the Notting Hill area of London, has asked Joseph Smallman, Chartered Accountant (CA), to recommend a computer information system. Hayes & Hu advises individuals on equity investments, manage finances for individuals who are outside the country and develop family budgets.

Required:

A.　What type of inputs (information transactions) are Hayes & Hu likely to make?

B.　What information subsystems are Hayes & Hu likely to need?

C.　What sort of outputs in the form of reports and documents will Hayes & Hu require?

7.4.5 Monitoring

7-32 Monitoring. Monitoring is done in two ways: through ongoing activities and individual evaluations.

Required:
A.   From what sources does ongoing monitoring come? What issues might be considered?
B.   When doing individual evaluations, what should the auditor consider?
C.   What type of reports on monitoring should management receive?

7.5   Identifying RMM and Determine Control Deficiencies

7-33 Control Design. Luxury Auto Leases, Inc. of New Mexico, USA, has offices in Tucumcari, Santa Fe and Albuquerque. Lisa Dockery, the company president, has an office in Santa Fe and visits the other offices periodically for internal audits.

Ms Dockery is concerned about the honesty of her employees. She contacted Back & Front, CPAs, and informed them that she wanted them to recommend a computer system that would prohibit employees from embezzling cash. She also told Back & Front that before starting her own business she managed a nationwide auto leasing company with over 200 offices and was familiar with their accounting and internal control systems. She suggested that Back & Front could base her requested system on the nationwide one.

Required:
A.   How should Back & Front advise Ms Dockery regarding the installation of a system similar to the nationwide one? Explain.
B.   What should Back & Front advise Ms Dockery regarding a system that will absolutely prevent theft? Discuss.
C.   If Back & Front takes Luxury Auto Leasing as an audit client, what procedures should they perform to detect fraud? Would they guarantee that their audit could discover fraud? Why?

7-34 The audit firm of Abdel-Meguid, Okyere and Yildirim (AOY) is planning an audit of Dye Shipper Corporation of Cairo, a television documentary production company. AOY need to assess the control risk of Dye Shipper.

Required:
Describe how Abdel-Meguid, Okyere and Yildirim will systematically assess risk.

CASES

7-35 Internal Control Activities. An example of a lack of internal controls with a disastrous result was the bond trading loss in the New York Office of Daiwa Bank in 1995. Over 11 years 30,000 unauthorized trades were made resulting in a $1.1 billion loss (an average of $400,000 in losses for every trading day). Daiwa allowed Toshihide Iguchi, a bond trader, to authorize sales, have custody of the bond assets and record these transactions.

As a novice trader Iguchi misjudged the bond market, racking up a $200,000 loss. To raise cash to pay Daiwa's brokers, Iguchi would order Bankers Trust New York to sell bonds held in Daiwa's account. The statements from Banker's Trust came to Iguchi who forged duplicates, complete with bond numbers and maturity dates, to make it look as if Banker's Trust still held the bonds he had sold. When he confessed to his misdeeds, Daiwa thought their bond account was $4.6 billion when in fact only $3.5 billion was left.

Inadequate review of internal controls was also to blame. Daiwa's internal auditors had reviewed the New York branch several times since the fraud began, but Banker's Trust was never contacted for confirmation of Daiwa's bank statements. If they had, Iguchi's fraud would have been exposed. Diawa's external auditor never audited the New York branch.

Required:

A. What type of control activities were ignored at Daiwa?

B. For each internal control procedure missing, what damage was caused?

C. What kind of controls could have been instituted that would have prevented the problems at Daiwa?

D. For each of the five internal control activities discussed above, applying each to a bank trading operation, identify a specific error that is likely to be prevented if the procedure exists and is effective.

E. For each of the five internal control activities discussed in this chapter, applying each to a bank trading operation, list a specific intentional or unintentional error that might result from the absence of the control.

7.11 NOTES

1. International Auditing and Assurance Standards Board (IAASB), 2023, International Standard on Auditing 315 (ISA 315) 'Identifying and Assessing the Risks of Material Misstatement', *Handbook of International Quality Control, Auditing, Review, Other Assurance, and Related Services Pronouncements*, 2022 edn, Volume I, International Federation of Accountants, New York., para. 34.

2. Further details are discussed in Sections 12.7 'Opinion on Internal Controls over Financial Reporting' and 14.5 'Assurance reports on ICFR'.

3. Ibid. ISA 315, para. 21, 22, 24, 25 and 26.

4. Ibid. ISA 315, para. 23.

5. Ibid. ISA 315, para. 27.

6. Ibid. ISA 315, para. 34.

7. We refer to chapter 12 for some fraud aspects related to internal controls over financial reporting.

8. 107th US Congress, 2002, 'Sec. 404 Management Assessment of Internal Controls', Sarbanes-Oxley Act of 2002, Public Law 107-204, Senate and House of Representatives of the United States of America in Congress assembled, Washington, DC, 30 July.

9. SEC (2003), 'SEC Implements Internal Control Provisions of Sarbanes-Oxley Act; Adopts Investment Company R&D Safe Harbor', http://www.sec.gov/news/press/2003-66.htm, Washington DC, 27 May.

10. Securities Exchange Act Rules 13a-15(c) and 15d-15(c), 17 CFR, § 240.13a-15(c) and 240.15d-15(c), Securities and Exchange Commission.

11. The 2013 update to the COSO Internal Control Framework helps organizations design and implement internal control in light of the many changes in business and operating environments since the issuance of the original Framework in 1992. The COSO Enterprise Risk Management (ERM) – Integrated Framework (2004) expands on internal control, providing a more robust and extensive focus on the broader subject of enterprise risk management. https://www.coso.org/guidance-erm.

12. In October 2005 the Financial Reporting Council (FRC) issued an updated version of the 1999 guidance with the title 'Internal Control: Guidance for Directors on the Combined Code'. In September 2014 this was superseded by the FRC's Risk Guidance. https://www.icaew.com/technical/corporate-governance/codes-and-reports/turnbull-report

13. Public Company Accounting Oversight Board, 2007, AS 2201: An Audit of Internal Control Over Financial Reporting That Is Integrated with an Audit of Financial Statements, https://pcaobus.org/Standards/Auditing/Pages/AS2201.aspx

14. Committee of Sponsoring Organizations of the Treadway Commission (COSO), 1992, Chapter 1 'Definition, *Internal Control – Integrated Framework*', American Institute of Certified Public Accountants, Jersey City, New Jersey, p. 9. The 2013 update to this Internal Control – Integrated Framework helps organizations design and implement internal control in light of the many changes in business and operating environments since the issuance of the original Framework in 1992. The COSO Enterprise Risk Management (ERM) – Integrated Framework (2004) expands on internal control, providing a more robust and extensive focus on the broader subject of enterprise risk management. While it is not intended to and does not replace the internal control framework, but rather incorporates the internal control framework within it, companies may decide to look to this enterprise risk management framework both to satisfy their internal control needs and to move toward a fuller risk management process. https://www.coso.org/enterprise-risk-management

15. Ibid. ISA 315, appendix 3, para 22.

16. Side letters – agreements made outside the standard company contracts. These otherwise undisclosed agreements may be signed by senior officers, but not approved by the board of directors.

17. Ibid. ISA 315, para. 12m.

18. Ibid. ISA 315, para. 12m.

19. Ibid. ISA 315, paras 21–27. Note the wording and sequence of the Components elements are changed as compared to the COSO report.

20. Ibid. COSo (1992).

21. Ibid. ISA 315, para 12(f).

22. Ibid. ISA 315 (Revised 2019), para A95.

23. Ibid. ISA 315, Appendix 3.

24. All companies traded on the New York Stock Exchange are required to have an audit committee composed of outside (non-executive) directors. The Code of Best Practice of the London Stock Exchange emphasises that the independence and integrity of the board as a whole is enhanced by having non-executive (outside) directors and recommends their use on the audit committee.

25. 107th US Congress, 2002, 'Sec. 301, Public Company Audit Committees', para. 3, Sarbanes-Oxley Act of 2002, Public Law 107–204, Senate and House of Representatives of the United States of America in Congress assembled, Washington, DC, 30 July.

26. The linkage between the control environment and soft controls is integral to the overall effectiveness of an organization's internal control system. The control environment sets the tone of an organization, influencing the consciousness of its people. It is the foundation for all other components of internal control, providing discipline and structure. Soft controls, on the other hand, are less tangible than traditional, hard controls (such as policies, procedures, and checks) and relate more to the culture, values, and behaviors within an organization.

27. Kaptein, Muel (2012), *Why Good People Sometimes Do Bad Things? 52 Reflections of Ethics at Work*: http://papers.ssrn.com/sol3/papers.cfm?abstract_id=2117396.

28. Based on Institute of Internal Auditors (2012), 'Auditing the Control Environment', *IPPF – Practice Guide*, p. 9, April 2011, The Institute of Internal Auditors (IIA) (only accessible for IAA members).

29. The illustration is a combination of: (1) Ibid. COSO, 2013 (see footnote 7); and (2) Ibid. ISA 315 (Revised 2019), appendix 3.

30. From: Internal Control Working Group, 1993, *Internal Control and Financial Reporting: Draft guidance for directors of listed companies registered in the UK in response to the recommendations of the Cadbury Committee*, Institute of Chartered Accountants in England and Wales, London, October, p. 19.

31. Based on the Committee of Sponsoring Organizations of the Treadway Commission (COSO), *1992*, 'Blank Tools – Control Environment', *Internal Control – Evaluation Tools*, American Institute of Certified Public Accountants, Jersey City, New Jersey, pp. 31–32.

32. There is sometimes confusion between 'control activities' and 'control procedures'; ISA and US Generally Accepted Auditing Standards do not define 'control activities' but defined 'control procedures' as the policies and procedures that management installs to meet objectives. The COSO Report uses the term 'control activities' and gives it virtually the same definition. ISA 315 (Revised 2019) though switched to 'control activities'.

33. Ibid. ISA 315, para. A153.

34. Ibid. ISA 315, para. A153-154.

35. Clark, Nicola and David Jolly (2008), 'French Bank Says Rogue Trader Lost $7 Billion', *New York Times*, 25 January:

36. Bank of England (1995), *Report of the Board of Banking Supervision Inquiry into the Circumstances of the Collapse of Barings*, 18 July.

37. Mary Jo White, United States Attorney (1996), *Complaint against Masaxiro Tsuda* (along with Daiwa Bank and Toshihide Iguchi), US Supreme Court Southern District Of New York.

38. Daiwa Bank Ex-trader Fined and Sent to Prison', *The Wall Street Journal*, 17 December 1996, p. B5.

39. Ibid. ISA 315, para. 25.

40. Ibid. ISA 315, para. 12(d).

41. See for additional guidance International Auditing and Assurance Standards Board (IAASB), 2018, International Standard on Auditing 610 (ISA 610) 'Using the Work of Internal Auditors', *Handbook of International Quality Control, Auditing Review, Other Assurance, and Related Services Pronouncements*, 2018 edn, Part I , International Federation of Accountants, New York.

42. https://www.theiia.org/globalassets/documents/resources/the-iias-three-lines-model-an-update-of-the-three-lines-of-defense-july-2020/three-lines-model-updated-english.pdf

43. Ibid. COSO (1992), Chapter 6 'Monitoring'.

44. Based on the Committee of Sponsoring Organizations of the Treadway Commission (COSO), 1992, 'Blank Tools – Control Environment', *Internal Control – Evaluation Tools*, American Institute of Certified Public Accountants, New Jersey, pp. 31–32.

45. Ibid. 315, para. A136 and A177.

46. Derived from (ibid.) ISA 315.

47. Ibid. ISA 3§ 15, para.27 and A182/183.

48. Ibid. ISA 315, para. 36.

49. Ibid. ISA 315, para. A236.

50. International Auditing and Assurance Standards Board (IAASB), 2023, International Standard on Auditing 402 (ISA 402) 'Audit Considerations Relating to an Entity Using a Service Organization', para. A21, *Handbook of International Quality Control, Auditing Review, Other Assurance, and Related Services Pronouncements*, 2022 edn, Volume I, International Federation of Accountants, New York.

51. For US Audit standards on internal control reports from service organisations see: Auditing Standards Board, 1992, Statement of Auditing Standards (SAS) 70 'Reports on the Processing of Transactions by Service Organizations', para. 24, American Institute of Certified

Public Accountants, New York. Content codified as AU-C 402, and reorganized as PCAOB Audit Standard 2601.

52. International Auditing and Assurance Standards Board (IAASB), 2023, International Standard on Assurance Engagements 3402 (ISAE 3402) 'Assurance Reports on Controls at a Service Organization', *Handbook of International Quality Control, Auditing Review, Other Assurance, and Related Services Pronouncements*, 2022 edn, Volume II, International Federation of Accountants, New York.

53. https://www.iaasb.org/publications/isa-315-first-time-implementation-guide

54. Ibid. ISA 315, para. 12(d).

CHAPTER 8

BUILDING AND EXECUTION OF THE AUDIT PLAN AND AUDITOR'S RESPONSE TO ASSESSED RISK

The four phases of the audit:

Acceptance/ continuance	Understanding/ risk analysis	Building/executing audit plan	Evaluating/ completion
Phase 1	Phase 2	Phase 3	Phase 4

8.1   LEARNING OBJECTIVES

After studying this chapter, you should be able to:

1. List audit procedures responsive to assessed risk.
2. Know the definition of evidence in an audit and legal sense.
3. Understand the systematic process of gathering evidence.
4. Describe the meaning of 'sufficient appropriate audit evidence'.
5. Determine which evidence is relevant and which evidence is reliable.
6. Explain what is meant by the nature, timing and extent of substantive procedures.
7. Understand the seven evidence-gathering techniques: inquiry, observation, inspection, re-performance, recalculation, confirmation, and analytical procedures.
8. Discuss evidence-gathering procedures for physical inventory counting and confirmation of accounts receivable.
9. Describe tests of operating effectiveness of internal controls.
10. Characterize and give examples of substantive procedures.
11. Illustrate the main uses of audit sampling.

This chapter 8 is part of Phase III: Building and Execution of the Test Plan. In this chapter we focus on the test plan consisting of tests of controls and substantive procedures.

8.2   THE BASIS OF EVIDENCE

ISA 330 is about the auditor's response to assessed risks[1].

Evidence is anything that can make a person believe that a fact, proposition or assertion is true or false. Audit evidence is information used by the auditor in arriving at the conclusions on which the auditor's opinion is based[2]. Auditors must design and perform audit procedures that are appropriate in the circumstances for the purpose of obtaining sufficient appropriate audit evidence, as they are not expected to address all information that may exist.

Evidence for proof of management assertions is different from evidence in a legal sense. Audit evidence needs only to prove reasonable assurance, whereas legal environments often require thorough documentation and a high standard of proof to ensure fairness and accuracy in resolving disputes or determining guilt or innocence (see illustration 8.1).

ILLUSTRATION 8.1

LEGAL EVIDENCE AND AUDIT EVIDENCE

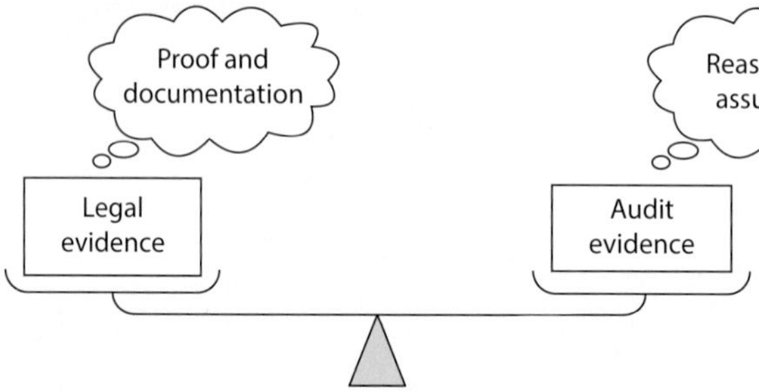

Audit evidence is cumulative in nature, includes audit evidence obtained from a firm's quality control procedures for client acceptance and continuance, from audit procedures performed during the course of the audit and from evidence obtained during previous audits. Audit evidence comprises both information that supports and corroborates management's assertions, and any information that contradicts such assertions. In some cases, the absence of information (for example, management's refusal to provide a requested representation) also constitutes audit evidence.

SOURCES

Information to be used as audit evidence may be obtained or derived from the following sources:
- ▶ Management – responsible for fairness of financial statements – generated internally from the financial reporting system.
- ▶ Management – generated outside the financial reporting system, including from sources external to the entity.
- ▶ Management – obtained from management's specialists.
- ▶ Auditor – obtained from sources external to the entity.
- ▶ Auditor – developed from sources internal or external to the entity.

In making an accounting estimate for an accumulated pension obligation, management may use information that is generated internally by the financial reporting systems, information generated from external sources and information obtained from a management's specialist. An auditor may also obtain information to be used as audit evidence originating from multiple sources. For example, in performing a regression analysis to test completeness of revenue recorded, the auditor may obtain information about size of retail space and sales prices (both management generated) and changes in the Consumer Price Index (an external information source).

Consideration of the sources includes the risk that the information source may not be reliable. In general, the auditor's direct observation is more reliable than management-generated information while outside sources are expected to be more reliable, especially in case of conflict of interest between provider and receiver of information as well as adequate internal controls. Sources of evidence may be available in a hardcopy format or electronically.

AUTOMATED TOOLS AND TECHNIQUES

Automation of (accounting) information and communication systems and development of artificial intelligence (AI), machine learning, robotic process automation (RPA) and blockchain do have great implications for accounting and auditing. Some of the entity's information and accounting data may be available only in electronic form. For example, entities may use electronic data interchange (EDI) or image processing systems.

In EDI, the entity and its customers or suppliers use communication links to transact business electronically. Purchase, shipping, billing, cash receipt and cash disbursement transactions are often consummated entirely by the exchange of electronic messages between the parties. In image processing systems, documents are scanned and converted into electronic images to facilitate storage and reference, and the source documents may not be retained after conversion.

The electronic nature of the accounting documentation usually requires that the auditor use automated tools and techniques, such as audit data analytics that may enable the auditor to aggregate and consider information obtained from multiple sources. Audit data analytics are described as 'the analysis of patterns, identification of anomalies, or extraction of other useful information in data underlying or related to the subject matter of an audit through analysis, modelling, or visualization'[3]. In the near future the use of data produced by the internet of things (IoT) may help develop innovative audit processes[4].

Because accounting data and other information may be available only in electronic form such as purchase orders or invoices it is important that the auditor reviews the client's data retention, recovery and back-up policies while planning the audit to assure all information that is needed is available in time and in appropriate format. Precisely in these circumstances, applying only substantive tests is in general insufficient (see also chapter 7.5).

8.3 FINANCIAL STATEMENT ASSERTIONS

Management is responsible for the fair presentation of financial statements so that they reflect the nature and operations of the company based on the applicable financial reporting framework (IFRS, IAS, GAAP, etc.). Management prepares the financial statements based upon the accounting records and other information, such as minutes of meetings; confirmations from third parties; analysts' reports; comparable data about competitors (benchmarking); and controls manuals. The auditor is likely to use the accounting records and that other information as audit evidence. In representing that the financial statements are in accordance with the applicable financial reporting framework, management implicitly or explicitly makes assertions regarding the recognition, measurement, presentation and disclosure of the various elements of financial statements and related disclosures.

Management makes assertions that can be grouped into three types: (1) assertions about classes of transactions and events for the period under audit; (2) assertions about account balances at the period end; and (3) assertions about presentation and disclosure. Assertions are representations by management, explicit or otherwise, that are embodied in the financial statements, as used by the auditor to consider the different types of potential misstatements that may occur. The standard assertions are occurrence, completeness, accuracy, cut-off, classification, existence, rights and obligations, valuation and allocation, and understandability. The auditor assesses risks of potential misstatements based on these assertions and designs audit procedures to discover sufficient appropriate evidence. In each of the three groups, the assertions are defined differently and sometimes combined. Illustration 8.2 gives the assertions used by the auditor in considering the different types of potential misstatements that may occur which fall into the three categories.[5] Audit evidence comprises both information that supports and corroborates management's assertions, and any information that contradicts such assertions.

8.4 AUDIT PROCEDURES FOR OBTAINING AUDIT EVIDENCE

The auditor performs risk assessment procedures in order to provide a basis for the assessment of risks (as discussed in chapter 6). However, risk assessment procedures by themselves do not provide sufficient appropriate audit evidence on which to base the audit opinion and must be supplemented by performing tests of controls (in this chapter section 8.6.1) and substantive procedures (section 8.6.2), in general a combination of both.

An auditor obtains audit evidence by one or more of the following evidence-gathering techniques and can be used as risk assessment procedures, tests of controls and substantive procedures. See illustration 8.3 for a list, definition and examples of evidence-gathering techniques.

▶ INQUIRY

The most frequently used technique for evidence gathering is inquiry. Inquiry consists of seeking both financial and non-financial information of knowledgeable persons inside or outside the entity. Inquiry of the client is the obtaining of written or oral information from the client in response to specific questions during the audit. Inquiries may range from formal written inquiries, addressed to third parties, to informal oral inquiries, addressed to persons inside the auditee.

Responses to inquiries may provide the auditor with information not previously possessed or with corroborative audit evidence. Also, responses might provide information that differs significantly from other information that the auditor has obtained, for example, information

ILLUSTRATION 8.2

ASSERTIONS USED BY THE AUDITOR[6]

(a) **Assertions about classes of transactions and events, and related disclosures, for the period under audit[7]:**

▶ Occurrence – transactions and events that have been recorded or disclosed have occurred, and such transactions and events pertain to the entity.

▶ Completeness – all transactions and events that should have been recorded have been recorded, and all related disclosures that should have been included in the financial statements have been included.

▶ Accuracy – amounts and other data relating to recorded transactions and events have been recorded appropriately, and related disclosures have been appropriately measured and described.

▶ Cutoff – transactions and events have been recorded in the correct accounting period.

▶ Classification – transactions and events have been recorded in the proper accounts.

▶ Presentation – transactions and events are appropriately aggregated or disaggregated and clearly described, and related disclosures are relevant and understandable in the context of the requirements of the applicable financial reporting framework.

(b) **Assertions about account balances, and related disclosures, at the period end:**

▶ Existence – assets, liabilities and equity interests exist.

▶ Rights and obligations – the entity holds or controls the rights to assets, and liabilities are the obligations of the entity

▶ Completeness – all assets, liabilities and equity interests that should have been recorded have been recorded, and all related disclosures that should have been included in the financial statements have been included.

▶ Accuracy, valuation and allocation – assets, liabilities and equity interests have been included in the financial statements at appropriate amounts and any resulting valuation or allocation adjustments have been appropriately recorded, and related disclosures have been appropriately measured and described.

▶ Classification – assets, liabilities and equity interests have been recorded in the proper accounts.

▶ Presentation – assets, liabilities and equity interests are appropriately aggregated or disaggregated and clearly described, and related disclosures are relevant and understandable in the context of the requirements of the applicable financial reporting framework.

increasing the possibility of management override of controls. In such cases, responses to inquiries provide a basis for the auditor to modify risk assessments and perform additional audit procedures. Evaluating responses to inquiries is an integral part of the inquiry process[8].

Inquiry of company personnel, by itself, does not provide sufficient audit evidence to reduce audit risk to an appropriately low level for a relevant assertion or to support a conclusion about the effectiveness of a control. It cannot be regarded as conclusive because it is not from an independent source and might be biased in the client's favour.[9] Therefore, the auditor must gather evidence to corroborate inquiry evidence by doing

ILLUSTRATION 8.3

AUDIT PROCEDURES (EVIDENCE-GATHERING TECHNIQUES)

Technique	Definition	Examples
Inquiry	Consists of seeking information of knowledgeable persons inside or outside the entity.	Obtaining written or oral information from the client in response to specific questions during the audit.
Observation	Consists of looking at a process or procedure being performed by others.	Observation by the auditor of the counting of inventories by entity's personnel, site visit at the client's facilities.
Inspection	Consists of examining records, documents or tangible assets.	Reviewing sales orders, sales invoices, shipping documents, bank statements, customer return documents, customer complaint letters, etc.
Recalculation	Consists of checking the arithmetical accuracy of source documents and accounting records or performing independent calculations.	Extending sales invoices and inventory, adding journals and subsidiary records, checking the calculation of depreciation expense and prepaid expense.
Reperformance	Consists of independent execution of procedures or controls that were originally performed as part of the entity's internal control.	Use automated tools & techniques to check controls recorded in the database. Re-perform ageing of accounts receivable.
Confirmation	Consists of response to an inquiry to corroborate information contained in the accounting records.	Used to confirm the existence of accounts receivable and accounts payable, verify bank balances with banks, cash surrender value of life insurance, notes payable with lenders or bondholders.
Analytical procedures (see Chapter 9)	Consist of the analysis of significant ratios and trends including the resulting investigation of fluctuations and relationships that are inconsistent with other relevant information or that deviate from predictable amounts.	Calculating trends in sales over the past few years, comparing net profit as a percentage of sales in current year with the percentage of the preceding year, comparing client current ratio to the industry current ratio, and comparing budgets to actual results.

other alternative procedures. For example, the auditor may observe the control procedures (observation) or review related documentation (inspection).

In a famous US court case, *Escott et al.* v *BarChris Const. Corp.* (1968),[10] the court ruled against the auditor because he did not follow up on management answers to inquiries. The court opinion said in part:

> Most important of all, he (the auditor) was too easily satisfied with glib answers (by management) to his inquiries. This is not to say that he should have made a complete audit. But there were enough danger signals in the materials which he did examine to require some further investigation on his part ... It is not always sufficient merely to ask questions.

Illustration 8.4 shows a list of nine dos and don'ts to remember when you're conducting an audit interview, prepared by the Auditor Training Centre of PwC[11].

ILLUSTRATION 8.4

DO'S AND DON'TS WHEN CONDUCTING AN AUDIT INTERVIEW

1 **Greet the person with genuine pleasantness** – don't do the power thing. Shake hands, smile and be nice.

2 **Conduct a mini opening meeting** – explain why you are there and that it's not about them, it's about the system. Put them at ease. Some people will be incredibly nervous and may not have slept the night before – the perception of being audited is much worse than the reality.

3 **Be interested in what they do** – most people spend more than half of their waking day at work, so it's an important part of their life. Some people will have worked there for a very long time and you may be the first person to show any real interest in what it is that they do.

4 **Pay attention** – you may think that you have heard it all before, but everyone has their own take on things. Be engaged, maintain eye contact, smile and nod to show you're listening.

5 **Take good notes** – this does not mean that you need to be constantly writing the whole time as this can be quite intimidating. You do need to write things down, but be open about it and make sure you record sufficiently for any reporting or follow up you may have to do later.

6 **Be transparent** – if you find things that aren't correct or that you may need to follow up on later, tell them. Show the person your notes and explain to them what you are thinking. This will also give you a better understanding of what you need to know.

7 **Don't be a consultant** – don't tell them how you would do it, how good you are, or how you have done it in the past. You are there to audit not to tell them how special you are.

8 **Hold a mini closing meeting** – at the end explain what you have found, confirm that your findings are correct and make sure they understand particularly if there is any possible non-conformity. No one wants a surprise at the closing meeting.

9 **Thank them** – genuinely thank them for their time, remember they still have their job to do and you have just taken up some of their time.

▶ **OBSERVATION**

Observation consists of looking at a process or procedure being performed by others, for example, the observation by the auditor of the counting of inventories by the entity's personnel or observation of internal control procedures that leave no audit trail. Observation provides audit evidence about the performance of a process or procedure but is limited to the point in time at which the observation takes place and by the fact that the act of being observed may affect how the process or procedure is performed.

Observation is mostly visual, but also involves all the other senses. Hearing, touch and smell may also be used in gathering evidence. For example, it is typical for the auditor to do a site visit at the client's facilities. On site visits the auditor can get an idea of the implementation of internal controls, notice what equipment is utilized and what equipment may be collecting dust – or rusting. An auditor with a good knowledge of the industry can tell what equipment and methods are obsolete by observing.

Sufficient evidence is rarely obtained through observation alone. Observation techniques should be followed up by other types of evidence gathering procedures. For example, observation evidence such as a quick visual inspection of a printing press may be corroborated by either a thorough and detailed inspection of the printing press by an auditor's expert mechanic or specialist, or inspection of documents and records relating to the equipment, both of which are evidence gathered by inspection techniques.

OBSERVATION OF PHYSICAL INVENTORY PROCEDURES

A good example of an observation audit procedure is count of physical inventory. ISA 501 discusses the inspection evidence gathering technique for physical inventory counting. It states: 'If inventory is material to the financial statements, the auditor should obtain sufficient appropriate audit evidence regarding its existence and condition of the inventory by attendance at physical inventory counting.'[12]

The attendance by the auditor will enable her to evaluate management's instructions and procedures for recording and controlling the results of the entity's physical inventory counting; observe the performance of management's count procedures; inspect the inventory; perform test counts; and perform audit procedures over the entity's final inventory records to determine whether they accurately reflect actual inventory count results.

ALTERNATIVE INVENTORY PROCEDURES

If unable to attend the physical inventory count on the date planned due to unforeseen circumstances, the auditor should take or observe some physical counts on an alternative date and, when necessary, perform tests of controls of intervening transactions. Where attendance is impractical, due to factors such as the nature and location of the inventory where inventory is held in a location that may pose threats to the safety of the auditor, the auditor should perform alternative audit procedures to obtain sufficient appropriate audit evidence regarding the existence and condition of inventory. For example, documentation of the subsequent sale of specific inventory items acquired or purchased prior to the physical inventory count may provide sufficient evidence. If it is not possible to do so, the auditor must modify the opinion in the auditor's report in accordance with ISA 705.[13]

PLANNING ATTENDANCE AT INVENTORY COUNT

In planning attendance at the physical inventory count or the alternative procedures, the auditor would consider:

- ▶ the risks of material misstatement related to inventory;
- ▶ the nature of the internal control related to inventory;
- ▶ whether adequate procedures are expected to be established and proper instructions issued for physical inventory counting;
- ▶ the timing of physical inventory counting;
- ▶ whether the entity maintains a perpetual inventory system;
- ▶ the locations at which inventory is held, including the materiality of the inventory and the risks of material misstatement at different locations, in deciding at which locations attendance is appropriate.

The auditor would also review management's instructions regarding:[14]

- the application of control procedures (e.g. collection of used stock sheets, accounting for unissued stock sheets and count and re-count procedures);
- accurate identification of the stage of completion of work in progress, of slow-moving, obsolete, or damaged items and items on consignment;[15]
- the procedures used to estimate physical quantities, where applicable, such as may be needed in estimating the physical quantity of a coal pile;
- control over the movement of inventory between areas and the shipping and receipt of inventory before and after the cut-off date.

INVENTORY PROCEDURES IN ADDITION TO OBSERVATION

Inventory counts involve other procedures in addition to observing the inventory take. The auditor will perform test counts. When performing counts, he would test both the completeness and the accuracy of the count records by tracing items selected from those records to the physical inventory and items selected from the physical inventory to the count records. The auditor would also review cut-off procedures including details of the movement of inventory just prior to, during, and after the count so that the accounting for such movements can be checked at a later date. The auditor would test the final inventory listing to assess whether it accurately reflects actual inventory counts. When there is a perpetual inventory system and it is used to determine the period end balance, the auditor would assess the reasons for any significant differences between the physical count and the perpetual inventory records. In case of significant differences, the auditor must perform analytical procedures on the plausibility of the volume/monetary value. After the analysis of differences by the client, the auditor must test its correctness and, if necessary, gather additional audit evidence.

INVENTORY NOT ON COMPANY PREMISES

When inventory under the custody and control of a third party, or consignee, is material to the financial statements, the auditor would obtain direct confirmation from the third party as to the quantities and condition of inventory held on behalf of the entity or perform inspection or other audit procedures appropriate in the circumstances. Depending on how material the inventory is for the entity's operations, the auditor may also consider:

- the integrity and independence of the third party;
- observing, or arranging for another auditor to observe, the physical inventory count;
- obtaining another auditor's report on the adequacy of the third party's accounting and internal control systems for ensuring that inventory is correctly counted and adequately safeguarded;
- inspecting documentation regarding inventory held by third parties, for example, warehouse receipts, or obtaining confirmation from other parties when such inventory has been pledged as collateral.

▶ INSPECTION

Inspection consists of examining records, documents or tangible assets. The objective of inspection of the client's documents and records is to substantiate the information that is or should be included in the financial statements. Examples of evidence gathering by inspection techniques is the review by an auditor of sales orders, sales invoices, shipping documents, bank statements, customer return documents, customer complaint letters, etc. Other examples are the conduct of a thorough mechanical inspection of cash registers and point-of-sales devices and review of electronic records via automated tools and techniques.

Inspection of tangible assets consists of physical examination of the assets. Inspection of tangible assets may provide reliable audit evidence with respect to their existence, but not necessarily as to the entity's rights and obligations or the valuation of the assets. Inspection of individual inventory items ordinarily accompanies the observation of inventory counting.

INSPECTION OF DOCUMENTS

Inspection of records and documents provides audit evidence of varying degrees of reliability depending on their nature, source and the effectiveness of internal controls over their processing:

> ▶ The nature of documents includes quantity of information contained, the difficulty of access to them, and who has custody.
> ▶ The source of the documents may be from inside or outside the firm.
> ▶ The source outside the firm may or may not be independent of the client.
> ▶ The source may be competent or incompetent.
> ▶ The controls over the recording process may be effective or ineffective.

Some documents represent direct audit evidence of an asset's existence, for example, a document constituting a financial instrument such as a stock or bond. Very importantly, inspecting an executed contract may provide audit evidence relevant to the entity's application of accounting principles, such as revenue recognition.

▶ EXTERNAL AND INTERNAL DOCUMENTS

A document's source may be internal or external to the organization. An internal document is one prepared and used within the client's organization and retained without going to an outside party. An external document is one that has been in the hands of someone outside the client's organization who is a party to the transaction being documented. External documents may originate outside the entity and end up in their hands such as insurance policies, vendor's invoices (bills), bank statements and cancelled notes payable. Other external documents originate inside the entity, go to a third party and are then returned to the entity. Cancelled cheques are an example of client to third party and then to client documents.

In the old days external documents were considered fairly reliable evidence, but not so much today. Think of all the (e.g. copying) techniques of falsifying external documents. Moreover, a lot of external documents are frequently provided in a digital form, like contracts, invoices etc. In that case reliability of documents can only be secured by using digital security techniques (e.g. digital signatures). The question is if an auditor is always able to establish if an external document is an 'original' document. Sufficient internal controls are necessary. A lot of external documents can only be relied upon if they have been subject to adequate internal controls.

Internal documents processed under good internal controls are more reliable than those processed under weak controls. Some external documents such as title papers to property, insurance policies and contracts are reliable evidence because they may be easily verified.

The use of documentation to support recorded transactions or amounts is called 'vouching'. The review of how source documents lead to account balances is called 'tracing'. Vouching is an audit process whereby the auditor selects sample items from an account and goes backwards through the accounting system to find the source documentation that supports the item selected (e.g. a sales invoice). For example, to vouch the existence or occurrence of recorded acquisition transactions, the audit procedure would be to track the transactions from the acquisitions journal to supporting vendor's invoices, cancelled cheques or receiving reports.

Tracing tracks transactions in the opposite direction, from source documents to account total balance. Tracing is an audit procedure whereby the auditor selects sample items from basic source documents and proceeds forward through the accounting system to find the final recording of the transaction (e.g., in the general ledger).

▶ RECALCULATION AND REPERFORMANCE

Recalculation consists of checking the arithmetical accuracy of source documents and accounting records or of performing independent calculations. Some common recalculation audit procedures are extending sales invoices and inventory, adding journals and subsidiary records, calculating excise tax expense, and checking the calculation of depreciation expense and prepaid expense. Audit procedures to check the mechanical accuracy of recording include reviews to determine if the same information is entered correctly in point-of-sales records, receiving reports, journals, subsidiary ledgers and

---

ILLUSTRATION 8.5

CHARACTERISTICS OF CONFIRMATION

(a) **Confirmation** is the auditor's receipt of a written or oral response from an independent third party verifying the accuracy of information requested.

(b) **Advantage:** Highly persuasive evidence.

(c) **Disadvantage:** Costly and time-consuming and an inconvenience to those asked to supply them.

Four key characteristics of confirmations

1 Information requested is by the client auditor.
2 Request and response is in writing, sent to the auditor.
3 Response comes from an independent third party.
4 Positive confirmation involves a receipt of information.

Two types of positive confirmations

1 Positive confirmation with the request for information to be supplied by the recipient.
2 Positive confirmation with the information to be confirmed included on the form.

summarized in the general ledger. Computation evidence is relatively reliable because the auditor performs it. Recalculation may be performed through the use of automated tools and techniques (e.g., HighBond Platform, ACL), for instance to check the accuracy of totals in a file.

Reperformance is the auditor's independent execution of procedures or controls that were originally performed as part of the entity's internal control, either manually or through the use of automated tools and techniques, for example, re-performing the ageing of accounts receivable.

▶ CONFIRMATIONS

Confirmation consists of the response to an inquiry of a third party to corroborate information contained in the accounting records. Confirmation is the act of obtaining audit evidence from a third party in support of a fact or condition. Illustration 8.5 gives a summary of the characteristics of confirmation as an evidence-gathering technique.

Confirmation procedures are typically used to confirm the existence of accounts receivable, investments and accounts payable, but they may be used to confirm existence, quantity and condition of inventory held by third parties (e.g., public warehouse consignee) on behalf of the entity. They may be used to verify bank balances with banks; cash surrender value of life insurance or insurance coverage with insurers; notes payable with lenders or bondholders; shares outstanding with stock transfer agents; liabilities with creditors; and contracts terms with customers, suppliers and creditors.

CONFIRMATION OF MANAGEMENT ASSERTIONS

Audit evidence is collected to verify management assertions. External confirmation of an account receivable provides strong evidence regarding the existence of the account as at a certain date. Confirmation also provides evidence regarding the operation of cut-off procedures. Similarly, in the case of goods held on consignment, external confirmation is likely to provide strong evidence to support the existence and the rights and obligations assertions. When auditing the completeness assertion for accounts payable, the auditor needs to obtain evidence that there is no material unrecorded liability. Therefore, sending confirmation requests to an entity's principal suppliers asking them to provide copies of their statements of account directly to the auditor, even if the records show no amount currently owing to them, will usually be effective in detecting unrecorded liabilities.

CONFIRMATION OF ACCOUNTS RECEIVABLE

The confirmation of accounts receivable is typical of the confirmation process. First the auditor either decides to take a random sample of customer accounts or, alternatively, looks through accounts receivable subsidiary ledgers and picks out some customers based on her professional judgement (e.g., customers with very large balances or very small balances, customers that are slow in paying, and/or customers that buy erratically). The auditor then gives this list to the client to prepare a confirmation letter requesting that customers reply directly to the auditor. Then the auditor, not the client, mails these letters. The auditor should check randomly to see if the letters are addressed to the same customers the auditor chose and for the amounts shown on the books.

PARMALAT – MILK SPILLS AFTER SOUR CONFIRMATION

Concept	Importance of confirmations. Responsibility of primary auditor.
Story	Parmalat Finanziaria SpA was a Parma, Italy-based company, whose main operating subsidiary, Parmalat SpA sells dairy products around the world, employed 36,000 people, and has world-wide operations in 30 countries, including the USA. It was Italy's biggest food maker and Italy's eighth largest industrial group with market capitalization of €1.8 billion. On 24 December 2003, Parmalat SpA filed for bankruptcy protection with a court in Parma, Italy, and on 27 December 2003, the court declared Parmalat SpA insolvent (SEC, 2003) with a €14bn ($20bn; £13bn) hole in its accounts in what remains Europe's biggest bankruptcy.

The problems at Parmalat first became apparent in mid-December 2003 when Parmalat failed to meet a €150 million ($184 million) payment to bondholders. This seemed odd because the company showed €4.2 billion in cash on their 30 September balance sheet. Parmalat had raised $8 billion in bonds between 1993 and 2003. Why did they need to keep raising money with their mountain of cash? Their standard reply was that the company was on an acquisition spree and needed cash – and the liquid funds were earning good returns (Edmonson and Cohen, 2004). Now the reckoning had come.

The following week in December, Parmalat executives admitted to their auditor Deloitte that they could not liquidate the €515 million Parmalat claimed it held in Epicurum, a Cayman Islands fund. When Enrico Bondi, an adviser, suggested liquidating the €3.95 billion held by a Cayman Islands subsidiary called Bonlat, the rabbit popped out of the hat. Italian prosecutors say that they discovered that managers simply invented assets to offset as much as €13 billion in liabilities and falsified accounts over a 15-year period (Edmonson and Cohen, 2004).

Bonlat

Parmalat purportedly held the €3.95 billion worth of cash and marketable securities in an account at Bank of America in New York City in the name of Bonlat Financing Corporation ('Bonlat'), a wholly-owned subsidiary incorporated in the Cayman Islands. Bonlat's auditors certified its 2002 financial statements based upon a confirmation that Bonlat held these assets at Bank of America (SEC, 2003).

Confirmation Letter

Grant Thornton, auditor for the Bonlat subsidiary, sent a letter to confirm the balance in the Bonlat account to Bank of America in December 2002. On 6 March 2003, three months later, the auditors received a letter on Bank of America stationery and signed by a senior officer confirming the existence of the account with a balance of €3.95 billion. The letter was mailed, not faxed, to Grant Thornton's offices in Milan (Rigby and Michaels, 2003).

Bank of America Says Letter is a Forgery

On 19 December 2003 the letter certifying that Bank of America held €3.95 billion for Parmalat's offshore unit Bonlat was declared false by the bank in a statement to the US SEC and in a press release. The bank account and the assets did not exist and the purported confirmation had been forged. Agnes Belgrave, the signatory of the letter who worked in Bank of America's

Manhattan offices, denied any involvement in Parmalat's affairs (Betts and Barber, 2004). Although documents concerning the Cayman Island subsidiary had been destroyed, Italian prosecutors found documents and a scanning machine used to forge the bank documents on Bank of America letterhead at DPA, a shell company near Parma.

Parmalat CEO Calisto Tanzi flew out of Italy the day Bank of America announced that the letter showing €3.95 billion was false. He went to Switzerland then Portugal, then an undisclosed country in Central or South America, and finally back to Milan where he was detained by police (Barber, 2003).

The Auditors

In 1999, Parmalat was forced to change its auditor under Italian law, and it replaced Grant Thornton with the Italian unit of Deloitte Touche Tohmatsu. However, Grant Thornton's Italian arm continued to audit at least 20 of Parmalat's units, including Bonlat. Deloitte became increasingly reliant on Grant Thornton for scrutiny of Parmalat's accounts. During its work on the 1999 accounts, other auditors had examined subsidiaries representing 22 per cent of Parmalat's consolidated assets. On the 2002 accounts, Deloitte said other auditors examined subsidiaries representing 49 per cent of consolidated assets (Parker *et al.*, 2004).

A suit filed by US shareholders contends that both Deloitte and Grant Thornton issued materially false reports on Parmalat's 1998–2002 year-end financial statements. Deloitte, which took over as Parmalat's primary auditor, deliberately failed to verify reports from Grant Thornton on assets held by a Parmalat subsidiary. The suit also asserts that on at least eight occasions, Grant Thornton failed to send third-party confirmation request letters in connection with its audits of Parmalat's subsidiaries. Further, it asserts, the firm failed to conduct independent audits on the 17 Parmalat subsidiaries that it was engaged to audit from 1999 to 2003, but rather participated in the falsification of audit confirmation documents (*International Herald Tribune*, 2004).

Italian authorities arrested Lorenzo Penca, chairman of Grant Thornton SpA and Maurizio Bianchi, a partner in the firm's Milan office, on charges that their actions contributed to Parmalat's bankruptcy. They claimed that the two men suggested ways that Parmalat executives could 'falsify the balance sheet' of a subsidiary and then 'falsely certified' the financial statements (Galloni *et al.*, 2004). Prosecutors in Italy have said Penca and Bianchi were behind the plan to create Bonlat and they failed to disclose details of two other offshore Parmalat vehicles in the Netherlands Antilles, according to court documents (US District Court, Southern New York, 2003).

In an academic paper presented at the 2nd International Conference on Corporate Governance on 29 June 2004 Andrea Melis, a researcher from the University of Cagliari, concluded that 'it is not clear whether Grant Thornton sent a second confirmation request given the time lag between the confirmation request and the response. However, they acknowledged that the request to Bank of America was done via the Parmalat chief finance director rather than getting in contact with Bank of America directly. Therefore, it seems reasonable to argue that they could have discovered the fraud if they had acted according to general auditing standards and exhibited the proper degree of professional 'skepticism' in executing their audit procedures.'

| Discussion Questions | ▶ What audit procedures should auditors use in confirming a very material cash balance?
 ▶ If a primary auditor is significantly dependent on the work of another auditor, what reviews and substantive tests should they conduct? |

References   Barber, T., 2003, 'Tanzi Takes a Mystery Tour Amidst the Parmalat Mayhem', *Financial Times*, 30 December, p. 12.

Betts, P. and Barber, T., 2004, 'Parmalat Probe Uncovers Fresh Evidence', *Financial Times*, 2 January, p. 1.

Edmonson, G. and Cohn, L., 2004, 'How Parmalat Went Sour', *Business Week*, 12 January, pp. 46–48.

Galloni, A., Bryan-Low, C. and Ascarelli, S., 2004, 'Top Executives are Arrested at Parmalat Auditor', *Wall Street Journal*, 2 January, A3.

International Herald Tribune, 2004, 'Investors File Lawsuit in Parmalat Inquiry: Officials, Auditors and Lawyers Named', 7 January.

Parker, A., Tessell, T. and Betts, P., 2004, 'Auditors Come Under Growing Scrutiny', *Financial Times*, 3 January, p. 9.

Melis, A., 2004, 'Corporate Governance Failures: To What Extent is Parmalat a Particularly Italian Case?' presented at the 2nd International Conference on Corporate Governance on 29 June 2004.

Rigby, E. and Michaels, A., 2003, 'Parmalat's Auditor 'A Victim of Fraud', *Financial Times*, 27 December, p. 8.

SEC, 2003, Litigation Release No. 18527, Accounting and Auditing Enforcement Release No. 1936, 'SEC Charges Parmalat with Financial Fraud', US Securities and Exchange Commission, 30 December.

US District Court for the Southern District of New York, 2003, 03CU10266 (CPKC) *Securities and Exchange Commission* v *Parmalat Finanziaria, SpA*, 29 December.

POSITIVE AND NEGATIVE CONFIRMATIONS

ISA 505 identifies two forms of confirmations: positive and negative confirmation.[16] The request for *positive confirmation* asks the recipient (debtor, creditor or other third party) to confirm agreement or by asking the recipient to provide written information. A positive confirmation request is a request that the confirming party responds directly to the auditor indicating whether the confirming party agrees or disagrees with the information in the request or provides the requested information. A response to a positive confirmation request is expected to provide reliable audit evidence. The auditor may reduce the risk that a respondent replies to the request without verifying the information by using positive confirmation requests that do not state the amount (or other information) on the confirmation request but asks the respondent to fill in the amount. However, using this type of 'blank' confirmation request may result in lower response rates because additional effort is required of the respondents. The positive form is preferred when inherent or control risk is assessed as high because with the negative form no reply may be due to causes other than agreement with the recorded balance.

It is highly likely that there will be no response to at least a few positive confirmation letters. In that case, an alternative audit procedure is called for, especially if the confirmation is for a significant reason, for instance, confirmation of an investment account that is material (as in the case of Parmalat). An alternative procedure for confirmation of cash is to prepare a reconciliation of the account based on prior investment bank statements and subsequent cash deposits and withdrawals. An alternative procedure for accounts receivable is inspection of after balance sheet date payments received from customers and then tracing them to balances at the end of the year so as to establish existence of the balances.

A *negative confirmation* request asks the respondent to reply only in the event of disagreement with the information provided in the request. However, if there is no response to a negative confirmation request, the auditor cannot be sure that intended third parties have received the confirmation requests and verified that the information contained therein is correct. For this reason, negative confirmation requests ordinarily provide less reliable evidence than the use of positive confirmation requests, and the auditor may consider performing other substantive procedures to supplement the use of negative confirmations.

The auditor must not use negative confirmation requests as the sole substantive audit procedure to address an assessed risk of material misstatement at the assertion level unless all of the following are present:[17]

- ▶ the assessed level of inherent and control risk is low;
- ▶ a large number of small, homogeneous account balances are involved;
- ▶ a substantial number of errors is not expected (exception rate is low);
- ▶ the auditor has no reason to believe that respondents will disregard these requests.

NO RESPONSE TO CONFIRMATION LETTER

In case the auditor does not receive a reply to a positive confirmation request, she ordinarily sends out a second request for confirmation. If the addressee still does not reply to positive confirmation, the auditor should perform alternative audit procedures to obtain relevant and reliable audit evidence. The alternative audit procedures should be such as to provide the evidence about the financial statement assertions that the confirmation request was intended to provide. If the auditor does not obtain such confirmation, the auditor shall determine the implications for the audit and the auditor's opinion.

IF AUDIT CLIENT DOES NOT ALLOW CONFIRMATIONS

When the auditor seeks to confirm certain balances or other information, and management requests that she not do so, the auditor should consider whether there are valid grounds for management's requests and if there is evidence to support the validity of the request. If the auditor agrees to management's request not to seek external confirmation regarding a particular matter, the auditor should apply alternative procedures to obtain sufficient appropriate evidence regarding that matter.

If the auditor concludes that management's refusal to allow the auditor to send a confirmation request is unreasonable, or the auditor is unable to obtain relevant and reliable audit evidence from alternative audit procedures, the auditor shall communicate with those charged with governance. The auditor also shall determine the implications for the audit and the auditor's opinion.[18]

PCAOB AUDIT STANDARD 2310[19]

(New) PCAOB AS 2310, 'The Auditor's Use of Confirmation', strengthens and modernizes the requirements for the confirmation process[20]. The standard and related amendments aim to strengthen the PCAOB's requirements for confirmation use, covering both paper-based and electronic communications. It aligns more closely with risk assessment standards, emphasizing auditors' duties in obtaining reliable audit evidence. Key aspects of the new standard include:

- ▶ Requiring confirmation of cash held by third parties or accessing relevant information directly.
- ▶ Continuing the confirmation requirement for accounts receivable, with provisions for situations where direct access to external sources isn't feasible.
- ▶ Stating that negative confirmation requests alone aren't sufficient audit evidence but can complement other procedures.

▷ Highlighting the auditor's responsibility for the confirmation process, including selecting items, sending requests, and receiving responses.

▷ Specifying scenarios where alternative procedures should be conducted, offering examples for obtaining relevant audit evidence.

8.5 SUFFICIENT APPROPRIATE AUDIT EVIDENCE

According to ISA 500,[21] the objective of the auditor is to design and perform audit procedures in such a way as to enable the auditor to obtain sufficient appropriate audit evidence to be able to draw reasonable conclusions on which to base the auditor's opinion. As explained in ISA 200,[22] reasonable assurance is obtained when the auditor has gathered sufficient appropriate audit evidence to reduce audit risk to an acceptably low level.

▷ SUFFICIENCY

Sufficiency is the measure of the quantity of (the persuasiveness of[23]) audit evidence. Persuasiveness implies the power or ability to persuade based on logic or reason, often depending on the use of inductive or deductive reasoning. Evidence may be persuasive based on the character, credibility or reliability of the source. Unlike legal evidence, audit evidence does not have to be conclusive to be useful.

Ordinarily, the auditor finds it necessary to rely on audit evidence that is persuasive rather than conclusive and will often seek audit evidence from different sources or of a different nature to support the same assertion on which the evidence is based.

Audit evidence is more persuasive when there is consistency between items from different sources or of a different nature. Evidence is usually more persuasive for balance sheet accounts when it is obtained close to the balance sheet date. For income statements, evidence is more persuasive if it is a sample from the entire period. A random sample from the entire period is more persuasive than a sample from the first six months only.

▷ APPROPRIATENESS

Appropriateness is the measure of the quality of audit evidence; that is, evidence's relevance and its reliability in providing support for the conclusions on which the auditor's opinion is based.

The sufficiency and appropriateness of audit evidence are interrelated. Obtaining just more audit evidence, however, may not compensate for its poor quality. The appropriateness of audit evidence needed is affected by the risk of misstatement (the greater the risk, the more audit evidence is required) and also by the quality of the audit evidence (the higher the quality of evidence, the less is required).[24] Illustration 8.6 summarizes the attributes and factors used for determining whether audit evidence is 'sufficient appropriate evidence'.

ISA 330 requires the auditor to conclude whether sufficient appropriate audit evidence has been obtained[25]. The auditor's judgement as to what constitutes sufficient appropriate audit evidence is influenced by factors such as[26]:

▷ the significance of the potential misstatement in the assertion and the likelihood of it having a material effect, individually or aggregated with other potential misstatements, on the financial statements. The more material the item, the greater the required sufficiency and appropriateness of evidence;

ILLUSTRATION 8.6

THE ATTRIBUTES AND FACTORS USED TO EVALUATE INFORMATION TO BE USED AS AUDIT EVIDENCE

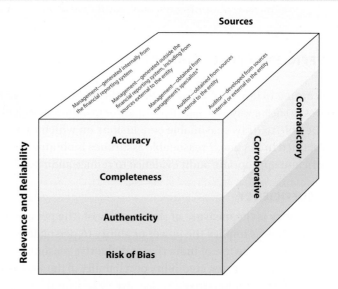

▶ the effectiveness of management's responses and controls to address the risks: strong controls reduce evidence requirements; the experience gained during previous audits with respect to similar potential misstatements: prior experience with the client will indicate how much evidence was taken before and if that was enough or appropriate;

▶ results of audit procedures performed, including whether such audit procedures identified specific instances of fraud or error; source and reliability of the available information; persuasiveness of the audit evidence;

▶ understanding of the entity and its environment, including its internal control.

See illustration 8.7.

When designing and performing audit procedures, the auditor must consider the relevance and reliability of the information to be used as audit evidence. Relevance of evidence is the appropriateness (pertinence) of the evidence to the audit objective being tested. Reliability is the quality of information when it is free from material error and bias and can be depended upon by users to represent faithfully that which it either purports to represent or could reasonably be expected to represent.

▶ RELEVANCE

Relevance deals with the logical connection with, or bearing upon, the purpose of the audit procedure and the assertion under consideration. The relevance of information to be used as audit evidence may be affected by the direction of testing (overstatement or understatement of the account). For example, if the purpose of an audit procedure is to test for overstatement

ILLUSTRATION 8.7

FACTORS EFFECTING SUFFICIENCY AND APPROPRIATENESS OF EVIDENCE

Consideration	Effect on sufficient and appropriate evidence
Materiality of the item being examined.	The more material the item the greater the amount of evidence required.
Effectiveness of management's response to risk.	More effective management responses to risk and controls decreases quality and quantity of evidence required.
Prior audit experience with the client.	Prior audit experience with the client will indicate how much evidence was taken before and if that was enough.
Auditor's assessment of inherent and control risks.	The higher the inherent or control risk, the greater the amount of evidence required.
Reliability of the available information.	The less reliable the source of information, the greater the amount of evidence required.
Whether fraud or error is suspected.	If fraud is suspected, the amount of evidence required increases.

of accounts payable, testing the recorded accounts payable may be a relevant audit procedure. On the other hand, when testing for understatement of accounts payable, testing the recorded accounts payable would not be relevant, but testing such information as subsequent disbursements, unpaid invoices, suppliers' statements and unmatched receiving reports may be relevant.

A given set of audit procedures may provide audit evidence that is relevant to certain assertions, but not others. For example, inspection of documents related to the collection of receivables after the period end may provide audit evidence regarding existence and valuation of sales and the related receivable, but not necessarily cut-off (when the sales occurred). Similarly, obtaining audit evidence regarding a particular assertion, for example the existence of inventory, is not a substitute for obtaining audit evidence regarding another assertion, for example the valuation of that inventory.

▶ **RELIABILITY**

The reliability of evidence depends on the nature and source of the evidence and the circumstances under which it is obtained.[27]

When using information produced by the entity, the auditor must evaluate whether the information is sufficiently reliable for the auditor's purposes, including obtaining audit evidence about the accuracy and completeness of the information; and evaluating whether the information is sufficiently precise and detailed for the auditor's purposes.

The reliability of information to be used as audit evidence, and therefore of the audit evidence itself, is influenced by its source and its nature, and the circumstances under which it is obtained, including the controls over its preparation and maintenance where relevant. Therefore, generalizations about the reliability of various kinds of audit evidence are subject to important exceptions. Even when information to be used as audit evidence is obtained from sources external to the entity, circumstances may exist that could affect its reliability. For example, information obtained from an independent external source may not be reliable if the source is not knowledgeable, or a management's expert may lack objectivity.

While recognizing that exceptions may exist, the following generalizations about the reliability of audit evidence may be useful[28] (see illustration 8.8):

▷ In general, audit evidence from external sources (e.g., external confirmation of cash account received from a bank) is more reliable than evidence generated internally. Evidence obtained directly by the auditor is more reliable than that obtained from the client entity and more reliable than evidence obtained indirectly or by inference (e.g., inquiry about the application of a control).

▷ The reliability of audit evidence that is generated internally is increased when the related controls, including those over its preparation and maintenance, imposed by the entity are effective.

▷ Audit evidence obtained directly by the auditor (for example, observation of the application of a control) is more reliable than audit evidence obtained indirectly or by inference (for example, inquiry about the application of a control).

▷ Audit evidence in documentary form, whether paper, electronic or other medium, is more reliable than evidence obtained orally (for example, a contemporaneously written record of a meeting is more reliable than a subsequent oral representation of the matters discussed).

▷ Audit evidence provided by original documents is more reliable than audit evidence provided by photocopies or facsimiles, or documents that have been filmed, digitized or otherwise transformed into electronic form, the reliability of which may depend on the controls over their preparation and maintenance.

ILLUSTRATION 8.8
RELIABILITY OF AUDIT EVIDENCE

	Least reliable	*Most reliable*
Source relative to entity	Internal (from inside entity)	External (from outside entity)
Source – person: employee or auditor	Employee of company	External auditor
Source – person: employee or third party	Employee of company	Third party
Source: independece of provider	Associated with company	Not associated with company
Source; qualification of provider	Little knowledge of subject	Expert in subject
Source: operation of internal controls	Not in operation	Effective operations

A risk of bias may exist in the development of information itself or due to interpretation of the information by the entity of the auditor.

The auditor's consideration of information to be used as audit evidence may be inhibited by tendencies in judgment that lead to bias and affect professional scepticism, such as the following:

▷ Availability bias, which involves considering information that is easily retrievable as being more likely, more relevant, and more important for a judgement

▷ Confirmation bias, which involves seeking, and treating as more persuasive, information that is consistent with initial beliefs or preferences

▷ Overconfidence bias, which involves overestimating one's own abilities to perform tasks or to make accurate assessments of risk or other judgements and decisions

▷ Anchoring bias, which involves making assessments by starting from an initial numerical value and then adjusting insufficiently away from that initial value in forming a final judgement.

The auditor's considerations of risk of bias (whether by management or the auditor) and whether the information corroborates or contradicts the assertions in the financial statements are specifically intended to bring the issue of professional scepticism into more focus.

In evaluating information to be used as audit evidence, the auditor must consider whether such information corroborates or contradicts the assertions in the financial statements. For example, a signed contract of an investment in tangible assets corroborates information obtained from minutes of a board meeting.

With respect to contradictory information, the auditor must always be professionally sceptical, even when the source of that contradictory information is less reliable than the source of corroborative information. An audit performed in accordance with ISAs rarely involves the authentication of documents, nor is the auditor trained as or expected to be an expert in such authentication. Ordinarily, the auditor may accept records and documents as genuine unless she has reason to believe the contrary. There may be circumstances where the auditor has reason to believe that a document used as evidence may not be authentic or may have been modified without that modification having been disclosed to the auditor. In such a case, the auditor must be professionally sceptical and investigate further. Possible procedures to investigate further may include confirming directly with the third party and using the work of an expert to assess the document's authenticity.

If information to be used as audit evidence has been prepared using the work of a management's expert, the auditor must evaluate the competence, capabilities and objectivity of that expert; obtain an understanding of the work of that expert; and evaluate the appropriateness of that expert's work as audit evidence.

▷ COST/BENEFIT

As an audit is offered in a competitive market[29], sufficient appropriate evidence must be obtained in an efficient manner. The costs of performing audit procedures to gather evidence mainly depend on the hours spent. Hours spent are affected by many client-specific characteristics like complexity of the business model, internal control effectiveness and quality of accounting information systems as well audit (firm, team and auditor) specific characteristics. Hourly fees depend on audit team composition (driven by necessary expertise and experience).

In general, the most expensive evidence-gathering techniques are confirmation and inspection. Confirmation is relatively costly because of the time and outlay required in preparation, mailing, receipt and follow-up. Inspection procedures that require the presence of both the client and auditors, such as an inventory count, are also expensive.

Confirmation of documents is moderately expensive if internal controls are adequate, and documents are easily available. The three relatively least expensive evidence-gathering procedures are observation, analytical procedures and inquiries.

As stated, the matter of difficulty and expense involved is not a valid basis for omitting a necessary procedure.

The overall conclusion about whether sufficient appropriate audit evidence has been obtained to reduce audit risk to an acceptably low level, and thereby enable the auditor to draw reasonable conclusions on which to base the auditor's opinion, is a matter of professional judgment and involves exercising professional scepticism in obtaining and evaluating audit evidence. The auditor's evaluation of whether sufficient appropriate audit evidence has been obtained includes evaluating the following:

- ▶ Whether the assessment of the risks of material misstatement at the relevant assertion level remains appropriate.
- ▶ The nature, timing, and extent of the audit procedures performed.
- ▶ The audit evidence obtained from those procedures in accordance with relevant standards (like ISA 500 and AICPA AU-C sec. 500).

If the auditor has not obtained sufficient appropriate audit evidence as to a material financial statement assertion, she should attempt to obtain further audit evidence. If the auditor is unable to obtain sufficient appropriate audit evidence, she should express a qualified opinion or a disclaimer of opinion.

8.6   RESPONSE TO ASSESSED RISKS

In this section, we explore the development of the audit plan in detail. The plan is formulated based on the assessed risk of material misstatement (RMM), which encompasses the evaluation of inherent risk (IR) and an initial assessment of control risk (CR). This assessment informs the selection and balance of subsequent audit procedures. These procedures are designed to achieve two primary objectives: first, to test the operating effectiveness of internal controls and second, to directly verify the reliability of the data presented in the financial statements through substantive testing.

8.6.1   TESTS OF CONTROLS

As discussed in section 7.8, understanding and identification of risks of material misstatements (RMM) includes evaluating the design and implementation of internal controls. Evaluating the design of controls involves considering whether identified deficiencies can lead to material misstatements due to error or fraud. It is especially important to evaluate the design of controls that address significant risks and controls for which substantive procedures alone are not sufficient.

Tests of controls are audit procedures designed to evaluate the operating effectiveness of internal controls in preventing, or detecting and correcting, material misstatements at the assertion level[30]. If the auditor assumes that the controls are operating effectively (initial low CR), or *substantive procedures* alone would be inadequate to get sufficient evidence (low Detection Risk [DR]), tests of operating effectiveness of controls must be performed.

MATTEL, INC. ORIGINATORS OF 'BILL AND HOLD' TOY WITH ACCOUNTING

Concept	**Sufficient appropriate audit evidence. Mattel employs several accounting tricks that went unnoticed or were not investigated in the audit.**
Story	Mattel, Inc. of El Segundo, California, designs, manufactures and markets various toy products worldwide. Mattel brands include: Barbie dolls and accessories, Hot Wheels, Matchbox, Nickelodeon, Harry Potter, Yu-Gi-Oh!, He-Man, Masters of the Universe, Fisher-Price, Sesame Street, Winnie the Pooh, Blue's Clues, Barney, and View-Master, as well as games and puzzles.

Almost from its founding in 1945, Mattel was very successful, but the company began experiencing serious problems in the early 1970s. Mattel tried several accounting schemes to keep their growth high including a 'bill and hold' program, understatement of inventory reserves, improper amortization of tooling costs, non-payment of royalties, and booking insurance recovery in the wrong period (Knapp, 2001).

Here we will address the sales and accounts receivable 'bill and hold' issues.

Mattel Invents the Term

In order to inflate the company's reported earnings, top executives established the 'bill and hold' program. This was the first instance of the term 'bill and hold' for the practice of billing customers for future sales, recording the sales immediately, and holding on to the inventory – bill and hold. The SEC gave several reasons why the subject sales should not have been recorded in 1971 (SEC, 1981):

▶ The merchandise was not shipped.
▶ The merchandise was not physically segregated from Mattel's inventory.
▶ The customer could cancel the order without penalty.
▶ Mattel retained the risks of ownership.
▶ In many instances, the invoices were prepared without knowledge of the customer.

Covering Their Tracks

To support the bill and hold sales, Mattel prepared bogus sales orders, sales invoices and bills of lading. The bills of lading were signed by the same employees as both themselves and a common carrier and were stamped 'bill and hold' on the face. When the goods were actually sold much later, Mattel's inventory records were full of errors. To resolve the problem, Mattel reversed the sales booked, but this created negative sales for the next period. To fix that problem, Mattel booked a fictitious $11 million sale in their general ledger, but not their accounts receivable subsidiary ledger, creating an unreconciled difference. They reversed another $7 million of the remaining bill and hold sales in fiscal 1972 (SEC, 1981).

The Audit of Sales

Mattel's auditors, Arthur Andersen, sent accounts receivable confirmations. The confirmations were returned with discrepancies in what the customers claimed and what Mattel booked. To resolve the discrepancies, the auditors obtained copies of bills of lading to determine whether goods had actually been shipped. Even though the bills of lading were stamped 'bill and hold', the auditors never asked Mattel to explain the phrase. Furthermore, the bills of lading lacked required routing or delivery instructions. The employee signatures as themselves and common carriers did not get noticed (SEC, 1981).

When the auditors looked at fiscal 1972 they found the $7 million reversing entry that caused that month's general ledger sales to be $7 million less than the sales figure in the corresponding sales invoice register. The staff auditor accepted the explanation of a Mattel employee that the offset to sales was due to 'invoicing errors' uncovered by Mattel employees when comparing computer-prepared invoices to bills of lading. The Andersen senior reviewing the workpapers wrote to the staff person, 'Need a better explanation. This looks like a big problem,' but the problem was investigated no further (Knapp, 2001).

Had Arthur Andersen utilized analytical procedures to evaluate the overall reasonableness of Mattel's monthly sales, they should have discovered that monthly sales varied dramatically from 1970 to 1972. This was a result of errors introduced by the bill and hold scheme and the subsequent reversals.

Discussion Questions	▶ What alternative audit procedures could the Andersen auditors perform when (or if) they found the inconsistencies in confirmations and bills of lading? ▶ Why do you think the staff auditor accepted the explanation of the $7 million discrepancy by the Mattel employee? ▶ Why was it not followed up?
References	Knapp, M., 2001, 'Mattel, Inc', *Contemporary Auditing Real Issues and Cases*, South Western College Publishing, Cincinnati, Ohio, pp. 3–14. SEC, 1981, Accounting Series Release No. 292, 'SEC Charges Mattel, Inc. with Financial Fraud', US Securities and Exchange Commission, 22 June.

Similar to ISA 330, according to PCAOB AS 2301[31], control risk (CR) should be assessed at the maximum level for relevant assertions when controls necessary to sufficiently address the RMM are missing or ineffective. This is also the case when the auditor has not obtained sufficient appropriate evidence to support a control risk assessment below the maximum level.

Designing tests of controls includes identifying conditions that indicate performance of a control or departures from adequate performance.

The presence or absence of those conditions can then be tested by the auditor. When evaluating the operating effectiveness of relevant controls, the auditor must evaluate whether misstatements that have been detected by substantive procedures indicate that controls are not operating effectively. The absence of misstatements detected by substantive procedures, however, does not mean that controls related to the assertion being tested are effective. A material misstatement detected by the auditor's procedures is a strong indicator of the existence of a significant deficiency in internal control.

The concept of effectiveness of the operation of controls recognizes that some deviations in the way controls are applied may occur. Deviations from prescribed controls may be caused by such factors as changes in key personnel, significant seasonal fluctuations in volume of transactions and human error. The detected rate of deviation, particularly compared with the expected rate, may indicate that the control cannot be relied on. If deviations are detected, the auditor should always evaluate the severity of the deficiencies and the effect on the initial assessment of control risk (CR). She could perform tests of other controls related to the same assertion as the ineffective controls, or revise CR and modify the planned substantive procedures as necessary in light of the increased detection risk (DR).

Controls are tested for the particular time, or throughout the period, for which the auditor intends to rely on those controls. Audit evidence pertaining only to a point in time may be sufficient for the auditor's purpose, for example, when testing controls over the entity's physical inventory counting at the period end. If, on the other hand, the auditor intends to rely on a control over a period, tests of the control at relevant times during that period are appropriate. Such tests may include tests of the entity's monitoring of controls.

▶ DESIGNING AND PERFORMING TESTS OF CONTROLS

Tests of controls are performed only on those controls that the auditor has determined are suitably designed to prevent, or detect and correct, a material misstatement in an assertion. In designing and performing tests of controls, the auditor shall obtain more persuasive audit evidence the greater the reliance the auditor places on the effectiveness of a control.

Testing the operating effectiveness of controls is different from obtaining an understanding of, and evaluating the design and implementation of, controls as discussed in chapter 7. However, the same types of audit procedures are used. The auditor may test the operating effectiveness of controls at the same time as evaluating their design and implementation. Although some risk assessment procedures may not have been specifically designed as tests of controls, they may nevertheless provide audit evidence about the operating effectiveness and, consequently, serve as tests of controls. For example, the auditor's risk assessment procedures may have included inquiring about management's use of budgets, observing management's comparison of monthly budgeted and actual expenses, and inspecting reports about the variances between budgeted and actual amounts. These audit procedures provide knowledge about budgeting policies and whether they have been implemented but may also provide audit evidence about the effectiveness of the operation of budgeting policies in preventing or detecting material misstatements in the classification of expenses.

In some cases, the auditor may find it impossible to design effective substantive procedures that by themselves provide sufficient appropriate audit evidence. This may occur when an entity conducts its business using IT and no documentation of transactions outside the IT system is produced or maintained. In such cases, the auditor is required to perform tests of relevant controls.

▶ NATURE AND EXTENT OF TESTS OF CONTROLS

The nature of a particular control influences the type of procedure required to obtain audit evidence about whether the control was operating effectively. For example, if operating effectiveness is evidenced by documentation, the auditor may decide to inspect the documents. For other controls, however, documentation may not be available or relevant. For example, documentation of operation may not exist for some factors such as assignment of authority and responsibility, or for some types of control activities, such as control activities performed by a computer. In such circumstances, audit evidence about operating effectiveness may be obtained through inquiry in combination with other audit procedures such as observation or the use of automated tools and techniques. Illustration 8.9 outlines a test plan linking transactions assessed risks and tests of controls.

LINKING TRANSACTIONS RELATED OBJECTIVES, CONTROLS AND TESTS OF CONTROLS FOR PURCHASES

Transactions related audit objective (purchases)	Initial RMM (only illustrative)	Internal controls (only illustrative)	Test of controls (only illustrative)
Accuracy – recorded transactions are stated at the correct amounts	▶ Invoice is incorrect (price, quantity, address, etc).	▶ Checking price and quantities of invoice with order (contract) by credit administration.	▶ Select a sample of invoices and test (re-performance) if credit administration checked correctness of prices and quantities.
Occurrence – recorded transactions exist	▶ Delivered goods were damaged and returned but no credit note has been received. ▶ Goods are received but were not ordered (payment reminder has been received).	▶ Segregation of duties (authorizing, storing, administer, monitoring). ▶ Approval of order by authorized employee. ▶ Received goods are counted and inspected and compared with order. ▶ Comparison of purchase order, receiving report and invoice before payment (3-way match).	▶ Examine documentation of authorized purchase orders. ▶ Select a sample of payments and inspect reconciliation (price, quantities, authorization, journal entries, etc.) with supporting documentation including receiving report and purchase order.

Inquiry alone is not sufficient to test the operating effectiveness of controls so other audit procedures are performed in combination with inquiry, for instance inquiry combined with inspection or re-performance may provide more assurance. Other audit procedures in combination with inquiry will be performed to obtain audit evidence about the operating effectiveness, including details about how the controls were applied at relevant times during the period under audit; the consistency with which they were applied; and by whom or by what means they were applied. The auditor must also determine whether the controls to be tested depend upon other controls (indirect controls), and, if so, whether it is necessary to obtain audit evidence supporting the effective operation of those indirect controls.

When more persuasive audit evidence is needed regarding the effectiveness of a control, the auditor increases the extent of testing of the control. As well as the degree of reliance on controls, matters the auditor may consider in determining the extent of tests of controls include the frequency of the performance of the control during the period, the expected rate of deviation from a control, the relevance and reliability of the audit evidence, and the extent to which audit evidence is obtained from tests of other controls.

Matters that could affect the necessary extent of testing of a control in relation to the degree of reliance on a control include the following[32]:

- The frequency of the performance of the control by the company during the audit period.
- The length of time during the audit period that the auditor is relying on the operating effectiveness of the control.
- The expected rate of deviation from a control.
- The relevance and reliability of the audit evidence to be obtained regarding the operating effectiveness of the control.
- The extent to which audit evidence is obtained from tests of other controls related to the assertion.
- The nature of the control, including, in particular, whether it is a manual control or an automated control; and
- For an automated control, the effectiveness of relevant information technology general controls.

Because of the inherent consistency of IT processing, it may not be necessary to increase the extent of testing of an automated control. An automated control can be expected to function consistently unless the program (including the tables, files or other permanent data used by the program) is changed. Once the auditor determines that an automated control is functioning as intended (which could be done at the time the control is initially implemented or at some other date), the auditor may consider performing tests to determine that the control continues to function effectively. Such tests might include determining that changes to the program are not made without being subject to the appropriate program change controls and the authorized version of the program is used for processing transactions.

► USING PREVIOUS AUDIT EVIDENCE

In certain circumstances, audit evidence obtained from previous audits may provide audit evidence where the auditor may perform audit procedures to establish its continuing relevance. For example, in a previous audit, the auditor may have determined that an automated control was functioning as intended. The auditor may obtain audit evidence to determine whether changes to the automated control have been made that affect its continued effective functioning through, for example, inquiries of management and the inspection of logs to indicate what controls have been changed.

Changes may affect the relevance of the audit evidence obtained in previous audits such that there may no longer be a basis for continued reliance. For example, changes in a system that enable an entity to receive a new report from the system probably do not affect the relevance of audit evidence from a previous audit; however, a change that causes data to be accumulated or calculated differently does affect it.

The auditor depends on professional judgement in deciding on whether to rely on audit evidence obtained in previous audits for controls that have not changed since they were last tested and are not controls that mitigate a significant risk. However, ISA 330[33] requires controls to be retested *at least once in every third year*. Factors that may decrease the period for retesting a control, or result in not relying on audit evidence obtained in previous audits at all, include the following:

- a deficient control environment;
- deficient monitoring of controls;

- ▸ a significant manual element to the relevant controls;
- ▸ personnel changes that significantly affect the application of the control;
- ▸ changing circumstances that indicate the need for changes in the control;
- ▸ deficient general IT controls.

A small, non-complex company might have less formal documentation regarding the operation of its controls. In those situations, testing controls through inquiry combined with other procedures, such as observation of activities, inspection of less formal documentation, or re-performance of certain controls, might provide sufficient evidence about whether the control is effective.

As financial statements audits and audits of internal control over financial reporting (ICFR) are interrelated in an integrated audit, design the testing of controls to accomplish the objectives of both audits simultaneously[34]:

1 To obtain sufficient evidence to support the auditor's control risk assessments for purposes of the audit of financial statements; and

2 To obtain sufficient evidence to support the auditor's opinion on internal control over financial reporting as of year-end.

In the box below is an example of tests of controls performed by Isle & Oblivian.

Marit Högtträd (Auktoriserad Revisor) is a senior auditor at Isle & Oblivion (I&O) in Stockholm. She remembers decades ago when tests of controls were not taken serious enough, when the auditor cut back on the tests to keep the audit cost down. These were the days when audit firms tried to attract new customers by keeping audit costs very low (audit was considered a competitive commodity). They made up for the audit losses by selling the audit client consulting services. Four things have changed since then: audit ethics and national laws have made it a breach of ethics to offer consulting, bookkeeping or legal services to listed audit clients (except tax preparation); audit standards have required a more extensive review of financial controls in an audit; external oversight has been established and research and experience has shown that control tests are very important to verifying accounting systems and financial statements.

Marit has taken on Boaz AB, a new client, for a financial statement audit. Her initial focus is on evaluating the design and implementation of Boaz's accounting and internal control systems, particularly around accounts payable processes. Evaluating the design of internal controls to determine control deficiencies (preliminary control risk), she notes that Boaz's internal controls are designed to ensure segregation of duties within the accounts payable process. Specifically, controls are in place to prevent a single employee from recording transactions and also handling payments. This is to mitigate the risk of fraud, such as issuing payments for fraudulent claims or creating phony vendor accounts. A supervisor also reviews transactions periodically as an additional layer of control.

Next, in line with the prepared audit plan, Marit conducts tests of controls using various evidence-gathering techniques.

- ▸ She inquires of accounts payable personnel and concludes that computer access for clerks to create new vendors operates as per the design of the control system. However, the supervisor responsible for creating vendor accounts had the ability to authorize payments, which directly violates the principle of segregation of duties and increases the risk of fraudulent payments.
- ▸ Inspection of the accounts payable process revealed a stamp of the controller's signature was found in an unlocked desk drawer. This lapse in physical security measures could allow unauthorized use of the controller's signature for approving fraudulent transactions.

These findings suggest that even though no deficiencies were detected in the design of Boaz's internal controls over accounts payable, the operating effectiveness of these controls was materially weakened by a breach of segregation of duties concerning the supervisor's role and inadequate physical security over the controller's signature stamp.

These weaknesses necessitate additional substantive testing by Marit to assess the extent of any potential financial misstatements due to weakness in operational effectiveness. This may include:

▶ Expanded substantive testing on accounts payable transactions for the period, focusing on fraudulent payments by the supervisor and payments that may have been approved using the unsecured signature stamp
▶ A detailed review of new vendor accounts created during the period to ensure they are legitimate and authorized.

8.6.2   SUBSTANTIVE PROCEDURES

Substantive procedures are responses to the auditor's assessment of the risk of material misstatement. According to the audit risk model (section 6.3)[35], the higher the assessed audit risk (AR), the more likely the extent of the substantive procedures will increase, and the timing of procedures will be performed close to the period audited with the objective of decreasing detection risk (DR) to an acceptable level.

$$DR = \frac{AR}{IR * CR}$$

Irrespective of the assessed risks of material misstatement (IR*CR), the auditor should design and perform substantive procedures for all relevant assertions related to each material class of transactions, account balance and disclosure.[36] Furthermore, if the auditor has determined that an assessed risk of material misstatement at the assertion level is a significant risk, the auditor should perform substantive procedures that are specifically responsive to that risk. For example, if there is a significant risk that management is inflating revenue to meet earnings expectations the auditor may design external confirmations (discussed in a prior section of this chapter) not only to confirm outstanding amounts, but also to confirm the details of the sales agreements, and then follow up those confirmations with inquiries regarding any changes in sales agreements and delivery terms.

▶ NATURE OF SUBSTANTIVE PROCEDURES

Substantive procedures comprise: (1) substantive tests of details (of classes of transactions, account balances and disclosures); and (2) substantive analytical procedures.

These procedures include agreeing the financial statements to the accounting records, examining material adjustments made while preparing them, and other procedures relating to the financial reporting closing process. Substantive analytical procedures (discussed in chapter 9 'Building and Execution of the Test Plan – Analytical Review') are generally more applicable to large volumes of transactions that tend to be predictable over time. Tests of details are ordinarily more appropriate to obtain audit evidence regarding certain financial statement assertions, including existence and valuation.

See illustration 8.10 for audit objectives and related substantive tests.

ILLUSTRATION 8.10

AUDIT OBJECTIVES AND SUBSTANTIVE TESTS

Balance related audit objective – valuation of intangible assets	**Substantive Test of Details (only illustrative)** ▷ Inquiry of management how carrying amounts of intangibles were assesses and of indications of non-recoverability of the carrying amounts. ▷ Inspect and review appropriate documentation. ▷ Test reasonableness of relevant assumptions used by management and compliance with amortization policy and useful lives. ▷ Reperform and recalculate algorithms and check for consistency with prior years. ▷ If necessary, involve an independent expert valuation specialist (ISA 620).
Balance related audit objective – accounts receivable ▷ Accuracy, valuation and allocation – Receivables have been recorded appropriately and any resulting valuation or allocation adjustments have been appropriately recorded.	**Substantive Test of Details (only illustrative)** ▷ Vouch sales invoices to customer orders and shipping documents. ▷ Obtain an aged balance of individual customer accounts and test the aging. ▷ Compare current year write-off to prior year allowance for bad debts. ▷ Recalculate allowance for doubtful debts. ▷ Examine bank receipts after balance sheet date for collections on past due accounts. For large past-due accounts obtain underlying documentation and inquire credit manager about status.
▷ Existence – receivables exist.	▷ Confirmation of a sample of accounts receivables and perform follow-up procedures.
▷ Completeness – receivables that should have been recorded have been recorded.	▷ Perform sales cut-off tests. ▷ Include a sample of zero-balance accounts in the confirmation process.

SUBSTANTIVE TESTS OF DETAILS

Substantive tests of details provide either reasonable assurance of the validity of a general ledger account or identify a misstatement in a class of transactions, balance or disclosure. When testing balances the auditor is concerned with overstatement or understatement of the line item in the financial statement. These tests are used to examine the actual details making up high turnover accounts such as cash, accounts receivable, accounts payable, etc. Tests of balances are important because the auditor's ultimate objective is to express an opinion on financial statements that are made up of account balances.

SUBSTANTIVE TEST OF DETAILS: ACCOUNTS RECEIVABLE = TEST OF REVENUE

From the example above we can see an interesting aspect of a test of balances, which is that the test makes use of the inherent properties of double-entry accounting systems. Accounting transactions involve a double entry. From the auditor's perspective, this means that a test of one side of the transaction simultaneously tests the other side of the transaction. For an example see illustration 8.11.

ILLUSTRATION 8.11

TEST OF ACCOUNTS RECEIVABLE BALANCE

A detailed test of balance may be illustrated as follows. If accounts receivable total €1,500,000 at the end of the year, tests of details may be made of the individual components of the total account. Assume that the accounts receivable control account balance of €1,500,000 is the total of 300 individual customer accounts. As a test of balances, an auditor might decide to confirm a sample of these 300 accounts. Based on an analysis of internal controls, the auditor may decide that the proper sample size should be 100 accounts that should be tested by confirmation. Thus, the auditor tests the detail supporting the account to determine if the line item 'Accounts Receivable' is overstated – i.e. the existence of the accounts has been confirmed. As an additional test, the auditor may examine cash receipts received after year-end, testing for understatement, which provides evidence as to both the existence and measurement of the accounts.

SUBSTANTIVE TEST OF DETAILS: SEARCH FOR UNRECORDED LIABILITIES

A substantive test usually performed on accounts payable is a search for unrecorded liabilities. This test may be part of the closing procedures or done in concert with the confirmation of accounts payable. This test provides evidence as to completeness and some evidence as to valuation.

To search for unrecorded liabilities, the auditor reviews disbursements made by the client for a period after the balance sheet date, sometimes to the date of the completion of field work. Even though a client may not record accounts payable at year-end, vendors will probably pressure the client to pay the accounts payable within a reasonable period of time. Due to this pressure, most unrecorded accounts payable are paid within a reasonable time after the balance sheet date. By reviewing cash disbursements subsequent to the balance sheet date, the auditor has a good idea of the potential population of unrecorded accounts payable.

Procedures to find unrecorded liabilities start with a review of the cash disbursements journal for the period after the balance sheet date. The auditor then vouches a sample of invoices to determine to which period the payment relates. For example, vouching a January electricity payment to an unaccounted December bill will indicate that the payment relates to the period of December, prior to year-end. This would result in an unrecorded liability for which the auditor may propose an adjusting entry, if it is material.

KMART EXECUTIVES MANIPULATE THE CONTRACT PROCESS

Concept	**Side agreements that materially impact a company may be concealed.**

Story	Kmart Corporation is a US discount retailer and a general merchandise retailer. The company operates in the general merchandise retailing industry through 100 Kmart discount stores (reduced from 1,829 stores before the bankruptcy). After a second bankruptcy in 2019, Kmart stores were sold to Transform Holdco.

Just prior to the first bankruptcy, two executives lied to Kmart accounting personnel and concealed a side letter relating to the $42 million payment from one of Kmart's vendors in order to improperly recognize the entire amount in the quarter ended 1 August 2001. Those deceptions caused Kmart to understate losses by the material amount of $0.06 per share, or 32 per cent (Merrick, 2003).

The Securities and Exchange Commission (SEC, 2003) filed civil charges against the two men responsible for this misstatement – Joseph A. Hofmeister and Enio A. Montini Jr. Montini and Hofmeister negotiated a five-year contract for which American Greetings paid Kmart an 'allowance' of $42,350,000 on 20 June 2001. The contract was for, among other things, exclusive rights to sell their product – greetings cards – in Kmart stores. American Greetings was to take over the 847 stores that were formerly supplied by Hallmark, the major competitor of American Greetings, at a rate of $50,000 per store. Under the terms of its 1997 contract with Hallmark, Kmart was obligated to repay a portion of certain prepaid allowances and other costs, and accordingly Kmart paid Hallmark $27,298,210 on or about 4 June 2001.

Accounting Makes a Difference in Bonus

Kmart classified these vendor allowances as a reduction in cost of goods sold in its statement of operations. One of the primary measures of performance for Montini and Hofmeister was contribution to gross margin. Because vendor allowances were generally accounted for as a reduction of cost of goods sold, this could help the two make their gross margin numbers and their bonuses. Montini also received an additional $750,000 forgivable cash loan after the deal was closed.

Secret Negotiations

Montini and Hofmeister conducted their negotiations with American Greetings in secret, excluding from the process key finance and accounting personnel. Since the accounting people had been frozen out of the negotiations, they depended on the two men to give them the details. Montini assured the Finance Divisional VP that there were 'no strings attached' to the $42 million. In fact, American Greetings had insisted that any and all up front monies be covered by a payback provision. American Greetings worried that, given Kmart's shaky financial condition, the retailer might not survive the contract term (SEC, 2003).

Montini had made two agreement letters with American Greetings. One agreement letter appeared to exclude the $42,350,000 from any repayment obligation. A second letter (the side letter) obligated Kmart to pay American Greetings 'liquidated damages' for early termination of the agreement. Montini and Hofmeister provided a copy of the signed 'No Strings Attached' letter, but not the 'Liquidated Damages' letter, to the Finance DVP and Internal Audit.

GAAP, as well as the company's own accounting policies and practices, required that the $42 million be recognized over the term of the agreement. Instead, Kmart improperly recognized the entire $42 million allowance during the quarter ended 1 August 2001; $27 million as an 'offset' to the payment to Hallmark and $15 million in 'incremental' merchandise allowances.

Discussion Questions	▶ What procedures can Kmart's independent auditor use to uncover the side agreement? ▶ What circumstances should have alerted Kmart's management and internal auditors to possible problems?
References	Merrick, A., 2003, 'Leading the News: US Indicts 2 Ex-Executives of Kmart Corp', *Wall Street Journal*, 27 February. SEC, 2003, Litigation Release No. 18000, 'SEC Charges Two Former Kmart Executives with $42 Million Accounting Fraud', US Securities and Exchange Commission, 26 February.

DIRECTION OF TESTING

Testing for overstatement or understatement is called the direction of testing. By coordinating the direction of testing each account balance is simultaneously tested for both overstatement and understatement. For instance, if all liability, equity and revenue balances are tested for understatement and all asset and expense accounts are tested for overstatement, then all account balances in the balance sheet and the income statement will be tested, either directly or indirectly, for both overstatement and understatement.

INTERIM TESTING USING SUBSTANTIVE PROCEDURES

There are several considerations in determining the timing of substantive procedures. In some instances, primarily as a practical matter, substantive procedures may be performed at an interim date. Only using interim testing procedures will increase the risk that misstatements existing at the period end will not be detected. That risk increases the longer the time between interim and period end. If substantive procedures are performed at an interim date, the auditor must cover the remaining period by either performing substantive procedures combined with tests of controls for the intervening period or further substantive procedures only, as long as it will provide a reasonable basis for extending the audit conclusions from the interim date to the period end.[37]

Performing audit procedures at an interim date may assist the auditor in identifying and resolving issues at an early stage of the audit. Ordinarily, the auditor compares and reconciles information concerning the account balances at the period end with the comparable information at the interim date to identify amounts that appear unusual, investigates any such amounts, and performs substantive analytical procedures or tests of details to test the intervening period.

EXTENT OF SUBSTANTIVE PROCEDURES

The greater the risk of material misstatement, the greater the extent of substantive procedures to lower DR to an acceptable level. In planning tests of details of transactions or balances, the extent of testing is ordinarily thought of in terms of the sample size which is affected by the risk of material misstatement (Section 8.7 Sampling). The use of automated tools and techniques may enable more extensive testing of electronic transactions and files. For example, in performing audit procedures, such techniques may be used to test an entire population instead of a sample. Because the risk of material misstatement takes account of internal control, the extent of substantive procedures may be reduced if tests of control show that controls are adequate. Of course, increasing the extent of an audit procedure cannot adequately address an assessed risk of material misstatement unless the evidence to be obtained from the procedure is reliable and relevant. Illustration 8.11 gives examples of audit objectives and substantive tests.

DUAL-PURPOSE TESTS

In some situations, the auditor might perform a substantive test of a transaction concurrently with a test of a control relevant to that transaction (a 'dual-purpose test'). In those situations, the auditor should design the dual-purpose test to achieve the objectives of both the test of the control and the substantive test. When performing such a dual-purpose test, the auditor should evaluate the results of the test in forming conclusions about both the assertion and the effectiveness of the control being tested[38].

8.7 SAMPLING

Audit sampling is the application of audit procedures to less than 100 per cent of items within a population of audit relevance such that all sampling units have a chance of selection in order to provide the auditor with a reasonable basis on which to draw conclusions about the entire population. This enables the auditor to obtain and evaluate audit evidence about some characteristic of the items selected in order to form a conclusion about the population from which the sample is drawn. Audit sampling can use either a statistical or a non-statistical approach.

It is difficult, if not impossible, to audit every source document from sales order to customer payment, purchase order to vendor payment. Sampling is necessary; however, it does not come without risk. Sampling risk is the risk that the auditor's conclusion based on a sample may be different from the conclusion if the entire population were subjected to the same audit procedure. Sampling risk can lead to two types of erroneous conclusions:

1. In the case of a test of controls, that controls are more effective than they actually are, or in the case of a test of details, that a material misstatement does not exist when in fact it does. The auditor is primarily concerned with this type of erroneous conclusion because it affects audit effectiveness and is more likely to lead to an inappropriate audit opinion.

2. In the case of a test of controls, that controls are less effective than they actually are, or in the case of a test of details, that a material misstatement exists when in fact it does not. This type of erroneous conclusion affects audit efficiency as it would usually lead to additional work to establish that initial conclusions were incorrect.

Either a non-statistical or statistical approach to audit sampling can provide sufficient evidential matter. Statistical sampling helps the auditor (a) to design an efficient sample, (b) to measure the sufficiency of the evidential matter obtained, and (c) to evaluate the sample results. By using statistical theory, the auditor can quantify sampling risk to assist her in limiting it to a level she considers acceptable. However, statistical sampling involves additional costs of training auditors, designing individual samples to meet the statistical requirements, and selecting the items to be examined. Because either non-statistical or statistical sampling can provide sufficient evidential matter, the auditor chooses between them after considering their relative cost and effectiveness in the circumstances[39].

Selecting specific items refers to testing all of the items in a population that have a specified characteristic, such as:

- ▶ Key items. The auditor may decide to select specific items within a population because they are important to accomplishing the objective of the audit procedure or exhibit some other characteristic, e.g., items that are suspicious, unusual, or particularly risk-prone or items that have a history of error.
- ▶ All items over a certain amount. The auditor may decide to examine items whose recorded values exceed a certain amount to verify a large proportion of the total amount of the items included in an account.

The application of audit procedures to items that are selected as above mentioned does not constitute audit sampling, and the results of those audit procedures cannot be projected to the entire population.

▶ SAMPLING REQUIREMENTS

To do proper sampling, the auditor must follow certain requirements in sample design, size and selection of items for testing; performing audit procedures; the nature and cause of deviations and misstatements; projecting misstatements; and evaluating results of the sampling.

The sample design requires that the auditor consider the purpose of the audit procedure and the characteristics of the population from which the sample will be drawn. The auditor must determine a sample size sufficient to reduce sampling risk to an acceptably low level. Items for the sample should be selected in such a way that each sampling unit in the population has a chance of selection.

Of course, the auditor must perform audit procedures, appropriate to the purpose, on each item selected. If the audit procedure is not applicable to the selected item, the auditor must perform the procedure on a replacement item. If the auditor is unable to apply the designed audit procedures, or suitable alternative procedures, to a selected item, the auditor shall treat that item as a deviation from the prescribed control, in the case of tests of controls, or a misstatement, in the case of tests of details.

When planning a particular sample for a substantive test of details, the auditor should consider[40]:

- ▶ the relationship of the sample to the relevant audit objective;
- ▶ tolerable misstatement[41];
- ▶ the auditor's allowable risk of incorrect acceptance;
- ▶ characteristics of the population, that is, the items comprising the account balance or class of transactions of interest.

To determine the number of items to be selected in a sample for a particular substantive test of details, the auditor should take into account tolerable misstatement for the population; the allowable risk of incorrect acceptance (based on the assessments of inherent risk, control risk, and the detection risk related to the substantive analytical procedures or other relevant substantive tests); and the characteristics of the population, including the expected size and frequency of misstatements. Illustration 8.12 describes the effects of the factors discussed in the preceding paragraph on sample sizes in a statistical or non-statistical sampling approach[42].

When any deviations or misstatements are found, the auditor investigates the nature and cause and evaluates their possible effect on the audit. In the extremely rare circumstances when the auditor considers a misstatement or deviation discovered in a sample to be an anomaly[43], the auditor must obtain a high degree of certainty that such misstatement or deviation is not representative of the population. This degree of certainty is obtained by performing additional audit procedures to get sufficient appropriate audit evidence that the misstatement or deviation does not affect the remainder of the population.

Once misstatements are found in the sample in tests of details, they should be applied to the population by projecting that it is the same as the sample. For example, if there are two errors per hundred in the sample (2 per cent of the sample is misstated), the auditor would project that there is a 2 per cent misstatement in the whole population from which the sample comes. If the total projected misstatement is less than tolerable misstatement for the account balance or class of transactions, the auditor should consider the risk that such a result might be obtained even though the true monetary misstatement for the population exceeds tolerable misstatement. On the other hand, if the total projected misstatement is close to the tolerable misstatement, the auditor may conclude that there is an unacceptably high risk that the actual misstatements in the population exceed the tolerable misstatement. An auditor uses professional judgment in making such evaluations.

In addition to the evaluation of the frequency and amounts of monetary misstatements, consideration should be given to the qualitative aspects of the misstatements. These include (a) the nature and cause of misstatements, such as whether they are differences in principle or in application, are errors or are caused by fraud, or are due to misunderstanding of instructions or to carelessness, and (b) the possible relationship of the misstatements to other phases of the audit. The discovery of fraud ordinarily requires a broader consideration of possible implications than does the discovery of an error.

If the sample results suggest that the auditor's planning assumptions were incorrect, she should take appropriate action. For example, if monetary misstatements are discovered in a substantive test of details in amounts or frequency that is greater than is consistent with the assessed levels of inherent and control risk, the auditor should alter her risk assessments. The auditor should also consider whether to modify the other audit tests that were designed based upon the inherent and control risk assessments. For example, a large number of misstatements discovered in confirmation of receivables may indicate the need to reconsider the control risk assessment related to the assertions that impacted the design of substantive tests of sales or cash receipts.

The evaluation of the sample should be related to other relevant audit evidence when forming a conclusion about the specific account balance or class of transactions.

Finally, projected misstatement results for all audit sampling applications and all known misstatements from non-sampling applications must be considered in the aggregate along

ILLUSTRATION 8.12

FACTORS INFLUENCING SAMPLE SIZES FOR A SUBSTANTIVE TEST OF DETAILS IN SAMPLE PLANNING[44]

Factor	Conditions leading to Smaller sample size	Larger sample size	Related factor for substantive sample planning
a. Assessment of inherent risk.	Low assessed level of inherent risk.	High assessed level of inherent risk.	Allowable risk of incorrect acceptance.
b. Assessment of control risk.	Low assessed level of control risk.	High assessed level of control risk.	Allowable risk of incorrect acceptance.
c. Assessment of risk for other substantive tests related to the same assertion (including analytical procedures and other relevant substantive tests).	Low assessment of risk associated with other relevant substantive tests.	High assessment of risk associated with other relevant substantive tests.	Allowable risk of incorrect acceptance.
d. Measure of tolerable misstatement for a specific account.	Larger measure of tolerable misstatement.	Smaller measure of tolerable misstatement.	Tolerable misstatement.
e. Expected size and frequency of misstatements.	Smaller misstatements or lower frequency.	Larger misstatements or higher frequency.	Assessment of population characteristics.
f. Number of items in the population.	Virtually no effect on sample size unless population is very small.		

with other relevant audit evidence when the auditor evaluates whether the financial statements taken as a whole may be materially misstated.

When planning a particular audit sample for a test of controls, the auditor should consider:[45]

- the relationship of the sample to the objective of the test of controls;
- the maximum rate of deviations from prescribed controls that would support her planned assessed level of control risk;
- the auditor's allowable risk of assessing control risk too low;
- characteristics of the population, that is, the items comprising the account balance or class of transactions of interest.

The auditor should determine the maximum rate of deviations from the prescribed control that she would be willing to accept without altering her planned assessed level of control risk. This is the tolerable rate. In determining the tolerable rate, the auditor should consider (a) the planned assessed level of control risk, and (b) the degree of assurance desired by the evidential matter in the sample.

For example, if the auditor plans to assess control risk at a low level, and she desires a high degree of assurance from the evidential matter provided by the sample for tests of controls (i.e., not perform other tests of controls for the assertion), she might decide that a tolerable rate of 5 percent or possibly less would be reasonable. If the auditor either plans to assess control risk at a higher level, or she desires assurance from other tests of controls along with that provided by the sample (such as inquiries of appropriate entity personnel or observation of the application of the policy or procedure), the auditor might decide that a tolerable rate of 10 percent or more is reasonable.

To determine the number of items to be selected for a particular sample for a test of controls, the auditor should consider the tolerable rate of deviation from the controls being tested, the likely rate of deviations, and the allowable risk of assessing control risk too low. When circumstances are similar, the effect on sample size of those factors should be similar regardless of whether a statistical or non-statistical approach is used.

The deviation rate in the sample is the auditor's best estimate of the deviation rate in the population from which it was selected. If the estimated deviation rate is less than the tolerable rate for the population, the auditor should consider the risk that such a result might be obtained even though the true deviation rate for the population exceeds the tolerable rate for the population. For example, if the tolerable rate for a population is 5 percent and no deviations are found in a sample of 60 items, the auditor may conclude that there is an acceptably low sampling risk that the true deviation rate in the population exceeds the tolerable rate of 5 percent. On the other hand, if the sample includes, for example, two or more deviations, the auditor may conclude that there is an unacceptably high sampling risk that the rate of deviations in the population exceeds the tolerable rate of 5 percent. An auditor applies professional judgment in making such an evaluation.

In addition to the evaluation of the frequency of deviations from pertinent procedures, consideration should be given to the qualitative aspects of the deviations. These include (a) the nature and cause of the deviations, such as whether they are errors or irregularities or are due to misunderstanding of instructions or to carelessness, and (b) the possible relationship of the deviations to other phases of the audit. The discovery of an irregularity ordinarily requires a broader consideration of possible implications than does the discovery of an error.

If the auditor concludes that the sample results do not support the planned assessed level of control risk for an assertion, she should re-evaluate the nature, timing, and extent of substantive procedures based on a revised consideration of the assessed level of control risk for the relevant financial statement assertions.

The relationships between AR, IR, CR, Analytical Review Risk and Risk of Tests of Detail (TD) are illustrated in table 8.13[46]. It is assumed, for illustrative purposes, that the auditor has chosen an audit risk of 5 percent for an assertion where inherent risk has been assessed at the maximum. It incorporates the premise that no internal control can be expected to be completely effective in detecting aggregate misstatements equal to tolerable misstatement that might occur. The table also illustrates the fact that the risk level for substantive tests of detail for particular assertions is not an isolated decision. Rather, it is a direct consequence of the auditor's assessments of inherent and control risks, and judgments about the effectiveness of analytical procedures and other relevant substantive tests, and it cannot be properly considered out of this context.

ILLUSTRATION 8.13

ALLOWABLE RISK OF INCORRECT ACCEPTANCE (TD) FOR VARIOUS ASSESSMENTS OF CR AND AP; FOR AR = .05 AND IR = 1.0

Auditor's subjective assessment control risk.	Auditor's subjective assessment of risk that analytical procedures and other relevant substantive tests might fail to detect aggregate misstatements equal to tolerable misstatement.			
CR	AP			
	10%	30%	50%	100%
	TD			
10%	*	*	*	50%
30%	*	55%	33%	16%
50%	*	33%	20%	10%
100%	50%	16%	10%	5%

* The allowable level of AR of 5 percent exceeds the product of IR, CR, and AP, and thus, the planned substantive test of details may not be necessary.

Note: The table entries for TD are computed from the illustrated model: TD equals AR/(IR x CR x AP). For example, for IR = 1.0, CR = .50, AP = .30, TD = .05/(1.0 x .50 x .30) or .33 (equals 33%).

8.8 SUMMARY

Evidence is anything that can make a person believe that a fact, proposition or assertion is true or false. Audit evidence is information used by the auditor in arriving at the conclusions on which the auditor's opinion is based. Audit evidence needs only to prove reasonable assurance, whereas in a legal environment there is a more rigorous standard of proof and documentation.

Audit evidence comprises both information that supports and corroborates management's assertions, and any information that contradicts such assertions. In some cases, the absence of information (for example, management's refusal to provide a requested representation) also constitutes audit evidence. Information to be used as audit evidence may be obtained or derived from the following sources: management-generated internally from the financial reporting system; management-generated outside the financial reporting system; Management-obtained from management's specialists; Auditor-obtained from sources external to the entity; and Auditor-developed from sources internal or external to the entity.

In general, the auditor's direct observation is more reliable than management-generated information while outside sources are expected to be more reliable.

Because accounting data and other information may be available only in electronic form such as purchase orders or invoices it is important that the auditor reviews the client's data retention, recovery and back-up policies while planning the audit to assure all information that is needed is available in time and in appropriate format.

Management is responsible for the fair presentation of financial statements so that they reflect the nature and operations of the company based on the applicable financial reporting framework (IFRS, GAAP, etc.). Management prepares the financial statements based upon the accounting records and other information, such as minutes of meetings; confirmations from third parties; analysts' reports; comparable data about competitors (benchmarking); and controls manuals.

Management makes assertions that can be grouped into three groups: (1) assertions about classes of transactions and events for the period under audit; (2) assertions about account balances at the period end; and (3) assertions about presentation and disclosure. The standard assertions are occurrence, completeness, accuracy, cut-off, classification, existence, rights and obligations, valuation and allocation, and understandability.

The auditor performs risk assessment procedures in order to provide a basis for the assessment of risks. However, risk assessment procedures by themselves do not provide sufficient appropriate audit evidence on which to base the audit opinion and must be supplemented by performing tests of controls and substantive procedures or a combination of both.

An auditor obtains audit evidence by one or more of the following evidence-gathering techniques and can be used as risk assessment procedures, tests of controls and substantive procedures: inquiry, observation, inspection, recalculation, reperformance, confirmation, and analytical procedures. The most frequently used technique for evidence gathering is inquiry. Inquiry consists of seeking both financial and non-financial information of knowledgeable persons inside or outside the entity. Inquiry is not sufficient to assess risk. the auditor must gather evidence to corroborate inquiry evidence by doing other alternative procedures.

Observation provides audit evidence about the performance of a process or procedure but is limited to the point in time at which the observation takes place and by the fact that the act of being observed may affect how the process or procedure is performed. A good example of an observation audit procedure is count of physical inventory.

Inspection consists of examining records, documents or tangible assets. The objective of inspection of the client's documents and records is to substantiate the information that is or should be included in the financial statements. A document's source may be internal or external to the organization. Internal documents processed under good internal controls are more reliable than those processed under weak controls. Some external documents such as title papers to property, insurance policies and contracts are reliable evidence because they may be easily verified. The use of documentation to support recorded transactions or amounts is called 'vouching'. The review of how source documents lead to account balances is called 'tracing'.

Recalculation consists of checking the arithmetical accuracy of source documents and accounting records or of performing independent calculations. Some common recalculation audit procedures are extending sales invoices and inventory and adding journals and subsidiary records. Reperformance is the auditor's independent execution of procedures or controls that were originally performed as part of the entity's internal control, either manually or through the use of automated tools and techniques, for example, re-performing the ageing of accounts receivable.

Confirmation consists of the response to an inquiry of a third party to corroborate information contained in the accounting records. Confirmation is the act of obtaining audit evidence from a third party in support of a fact or condition. Confirmation procedures are typically used to confirm the existence of accounts receivable, investments and accounts payable, but they may be used to confirm existence, quantity and condition of inventory held by third parties (e.g. public warehouse consignee) on behalf of the audit client. In conformation procedures the auditor gives a list of the entities to which confirmation letters are to be sent to the client to prepare a confirmation letter requesting that customers reply directly to the auditor. Then the auditor, not the client, mails these letters. ISA 505 identifies two forms of confirmations: positive and negative confirmation. The request for *positive confirmation* asks the recipient (debtor, creditor or other third party) to confirm agreement or by asking the recipient to provide written information. A negative confirmation request asks the respondent to reply only if they disagree with the information provided in the request.

According to ISA 500, the objective of the auditor is to design and perform audit procedures in such a way as to enable the auditor to obtain sufficient appropriate audit evidence to be able to draw reasonable conclusions on which to base the auditor's opinion. As explained in ISA 200, reasonable assurance is obtained when the auditor has obtained sufficient appropriate audit evidence to reduce audit risk (that is, the risk that the auditor expresses an inappropriate opinion when the financial statements are materially misstated) to an acceptably low level. Sufficiency is the measure of the quantity (of the persuasiveness) of audit evidence. The quantity of audit evidence needed is affected by the auditor's assessment of the risks of misstatement (the higher the assessed risks, the more persuasive audit evidence is likely to be required) and also by the quality of such audit evidence (the higher the quality, the less may be required). Appropriateness is the measure of the quality of audit evidence; that is, its relevance and its reliability in providing support for the conclusions on which the auditor's opinion is based.

When designing and performing audit procedures, the auditor must consider the relevance and reliability of the information to be used as audit evidence. Reliability is the quality of information when it is free from material error and bias and can be depended upon by users to represent faithfully that which it either purports to represent or could reasonably be expected to represent. Relevance of evidence is the appropriateness (pertinence) of the evidence to the audit objective being tested. The quantity (relevance and reliability) of audit evidence needed is affected by the risk of misstatement (the greater the risk, the more audit evidence is required) and also by the quality of the audit evidence (the higher the quality of evidence, the less is required).

To meet the objective of obtaining sufficient appropriate audit evidence, the auditor must design and perform audit procedures whose nature, timing and extent are based on, and are responsive to, the assessed risks. The nature of an audit procedure for obtaining evidence refers to its purpose (that is, test of controls or substantive procedure) and its type (that is, inspection, observation, inquiry, confirmation, recalculation, re-performance, or analytical procedure). The nature of the audit procedures is of most importance in responding to the assessed risks. Timing of an audit procedure refers to when it is performed, or the period or date to which the audit evidence applies. The extent of an audit procedure refers to the quantity to be performed, for example, a sample size or the number of observations of a control activity.

Test of controls are audit procedures designed to evaluate the operating effectiveness of controls in preventing, or detecting and correcting, material misstatements at the assertion level. Designing tests of controls to obtain relevant audit evidence includes identifying conditions (characteristics or attributes) that indicate performance of a control, and deviation conditions which indicate departures from adequate performance. The presence or absence of those conditions can then be tested by the auditor.

Substantive procedures are responses to the auditor's assessment of the risk of material misstatement. The higher the assessed audit risk (AR), the more likely the extent of the substantive procedures will increase, and the timing of procedures will be performed close to the period audited with the objective of decreasing detection risk (DR) to an acceptable level. Substantive procedures comprise: (1) tests of details (of classes of transactions, account balances, and disclosures); and (2) substantive analytical procedures. A substantive test usually performed on accounts payable is a search for unrecorded liabilities. This test provides evidence as to completeness and some evidence as to valuation.

The auditor's objective, when using audit sampling, is to provide a reasonable basis for drawing conclusions about the population (e.g., invoices, shipping documents, and other original source material) from which the sample is selected. Audit sampling (sampling) is the application of audit procedures to less than 100 per cent of items within a population of audit relevance such that all sampling units have a chance of selection in order to provide the auditor with a reasonable basis on which to draw conclusions about the entire population. This enables the auditor to obtain and evaluate audit evidence about some characteristic of the items selected in order to form or assist in forming a conclusion concerning the population from which the sample is drawn. Audit sampling can use either a statistical or a non-statistical approach. Sampling risk is the risk that the auditor's conclusion based on a sample may be different from the conclusion if the entire population were subjected to the same audit procedure.

8.9 QUESTIONS, EXERCISES AND CASES

QUESTIONS

8.2 The Basis of Evidence

8-1 Define and discuss the differences between general evidence, audit evidence and legal evidence.

8-2 To meet the objective of obtaining sufficient appropriate audit evidence, what must the auditor do?

8-3 Describe how automation of (accounting) information and communication systems and development of artificial intelligence (AI), machine learning, robotic process automation (RPA) and blockchain will affect accounting and auditing.

8.3 Financial Statement Assertions

8-4 Define management assertions and discuss how they may be grouped? See illustration 8.2.

8.4 Audit Procedures for Obtaining Evidence

8-5 Why should an auditor corroborate evidence for inquiry? Name a famous court case and discuss.

8-6 What alternative procedures can an auditor apply when she is unable to attend a physical inventory?

8-7 Discuss the reliability of external documents as evidence.

8-8 Define and give an example of recalculation and re-performance.

8-9 List the six evidence-gathering techniques in order of reliability. List the six evidence-gathering techniques in order of cost from highest to lowest. Define management assertions and discuss how they may be grouped. See illustration 8.2.

8-10 What are four key characteristics of confirmation?

8-11 Discuss the differences between positive and negative confirmation.

8-12 If a confirmation is not returned to the auditor what alternative procedures can he perform?

8.5 Sufficient Appropriate Audit Evidence

8-13 What factors influence the auditor's judgement as to what constitutes sufficient appropriate audit evidence?

8-14 Given an example of irrelevant audit evidence related to the audit objective completeness of sales.

8-15 Differentiate between the most reliable evidence and the least reliable evidence.

8-16 Why does an auditor prefer persuasive evidence as opposed to conclusive evidence?

8-17 Why should evidence be gathered in an efficient manner?

8.6.1 Tests of Controls

8-18 Explain the difference between assessing CR based on the design of controls and assessing CR based on testing operating effectiveness.

8-19 Define 'test of controls'. What are 'indirect controls'?

8-20 If the auditor hopes to rely on prior audit evidence, evidence is needed in the current audit about what areas?

8-21 Why is it relevant to analyse the root cause of internal control deficiencies?

8.6.2 Substantive Procedures

8-22 What are substantive procedures? Describe the different types of substantive procedures.

8-23 What is the difference between test of details of classes of transactions and test of details of account balances?

8-24 Discuss what is meant by direction of testing.

8-25 A substantive test usually performed on accounts payable is a search for unrecorded liabilities. Discuss this test.

8.7 Sampling

8-26 Define the objective of sampling and audit sampling.

8-27 What should an auditor do when she finds deviations or misstatements when sampling?

PROBLEMS AND EXERCISES

8.2 The Basis of Evidence

8-28 List and define at least ten kinds of electronic evidence that an auditor may review.

8-29 Why is it important that the auditor reviews the client's data retention, recovery and back-up policies while planning the audit?

8-30 Assume you are the auditor of the financial statements of Elzemarie's Coffee Shop located in Marrum. At Elzemarie's request, can you explain why – despite obtaining sufficient appropriate audit evidence – you only express 'reasonable' instead of 'absolute' assurance?

8.3 Financial Statement Assertions

8-31 The following are management assertions (1 through 9) and audit objectives applied to the audit of accounts payable ((a) through (h)).

Management Assertions

1   Existence
2   Rights and obligations
3   Occurrence
4   Completeness
5   Valuation
6   Accuracy
7   Cut-off
8   Understandability
9   Classification

Specific Audit Objectives

(a)   Existing accounts payable are included in the accounts payable balance on the balance sheet date.
(b)   Accounts payable are properly classified.
(c)   Acquisition transactions in the acquisition and payment cycle are recorded in the proper period.
(d)   Accounts payable representing the accounts payable balance on the balance sheet date agree with related subsidiary ledger amounts, and the total is correctly added and agrees with the general ledger.
(e)   Accounts in the acquisition and payment cycle are properly disclosed according to IFRS and IASs.
(f)   Accounts payable representing the accounts payable balance on the balance sheet date are valued at the correct amount.
(g)   Accounts payable exist.
(h)   Any allowances for accounts payable discounts are taken.

Required:

A.   Explain the differences between management assertions, general audit objectives and specific audit objectives, and their relationships to each other.
B.   For each specific audit objective, identify the appropriate management assertion.

8.4 Audit Procedures for Obtaining Audit Evidence

8-32 An auditor obtains audit evidence by one or more of the following evidence-gathering techniques: inquiry, observation, inspection, re-performance, recalculation, confirmation and analytical procedures.

Required:

For each of the evidence-gathering techniques give an example of a substantive test procedure.

8-33 Inquiry, Analytical Procedures and Observation. In the examination of financial statements, auditors must judge the validity of the audit evidence they obtain. For the following questions, assume that the auditors have considered internal control and found it satisfactory.

Required:

A.   In the course of examination, the auditors ask many questions of client officers and employees.

    1   Describe the factors that the auditors should consider in evaluating oral evidence provided by client officers and employees.

    2   Discuss the validity and limitations of oral evidence.

B.   Analytical procedures include the computation of various balance sheet and operating ratios for comparison to prior years and industry averages. Discuss the validity and limitations of ratio analysis as evidential matter.

C.   In connection with an examination of the financial statements of a manufacturing company, the auditors are observing the physical inventory of finished goods, which consists of expensive, highly complex electronic equipment. Discuss the validity and limitations of the audit evidence provided by this procedure.

8-34 Inspection. Discuss what you would accept as satisfactory documentary evidence in support of entries in the following:

A.   Sales journal.

B.   Sales returns register.

C.   Voucher or invoice register.

D.   Payroll register.

E.   Cheque register.

8-35 Attendance at Physical Inventory Counting. A processor of frozen foods carries an inventory of finished products consisting of 50 different types of items valued at approximately $2,000,000. About $750,000 of this value represents inventory stock produced by the company and billed to customers prior to the audit date. This stock is being held for the customers at a monthly rental charge until they request shipment and is not separate from the company's inventory. The company maintains separate perpetual ledgers at the plant office for both stock owned and stock being held for customers. The cost department also maintains a perpetual record of stock owned. The above perpetual records reflect quantities only. The company does not take a complete physical inventory at any time during the year, since the temperature in the cold storage facilities is too low to allow one to spend more than 15 minutes inside at a time. It is not considered practical to move items outside or to defreeze the cold storage facilities for the purpose of taking a physical inventory. Because of these circumstances, it is impractical to test count quantities to the extent of completely counting specific items. The company considers as its inventory valuation at year-end the aggregate of the quantities reflected by the perpetual record of stock owned, maintained at the plant office, priced at the lower of cost or market.

Required:

A.   What are the two principal problems facing the auditor in the audit of the inventory? Discuss briefly.

B.   Outline the audit steps that you would take to enable you to render an unqualified opinion with respect to the inventory. (You may omit consideration of tests of unit prices and clerical accuracy.)

8-36 Accounts Receivable Confirmations – Positive and Negative. In work on accounts receivable, use of confirmations is of great importance.
Required:
A.   What is an audit confirmation?
B.   What characteristics should an audit confirmation possess if an auditor is to consider it as sufficient appropriate audit evidence?
C.   Distinguish between a positive and a negative accounts receivable confirmation.
D.   In confirming a client's accounts receivable, what characteristics should be present in the accounts if the auditor is to use negative confirmations?

8.5   Sufficient Appropriate Audit Evidence

8-37 The auditor finds it necessary to rely on audit evidence that is persuasive rather than conclusive and will often seek audit evidence from different sources or of a different nature to support the same assertion. The reliability of audit evidence is not only important in determining sufficiency (quantity) of the information, but also the appropriateness (quality) of the information. Reliability of audit evidence is influenced by its source and its nature.
Required:
A.   Define these terms: reliability of evidence, persuasiveness of evidence, and relevance of evidence.
B.   Arrange the following people as sources of information from most reliable to least reliable and explain your reasoning:
  1   new company employee,
  2   company employees with five years' experience,
  3   company lawyers,
  4   internal auditors,
  5   external auditors,
  6   auditor's lawyers,
  7   banker,
  8   top management,
  9   board of directors,
  10   company supplier,
  11   company customer.

8-38 Reliability and Cost of Evidence-Gathering Techniques. The financial statements of Utgard Company of Drammen, Norway, a new client, indicate that large amounts of notes payable to banks were paid off during the period under audit. The auditor, Kristinge Korsvold, Statautoriseret Revisor, also notices that one customer's account is much larger than the rest, and therefore decides to examine the evidence supporting this account.
Required:
Evaluate the reliability of each of the following types of evidence supporting these transactions for:
Notes Payable:
A.   Debit entries in the Notes Payable account.

B.   Entries in the cheque register.

C.   Paid cheques.

D.   Notes payable bearing bank perforation stamp PAID and the date of payment.

E.   Statement by client's treasurer that notes had been paid at maturity.

F.   Letter received by auditors directly from bank stating that no indebtedness on part of client existed as of the balance sheet date.

Customer Account:

G.   Computer printout from accounts receivable subsidiary ledger.

H.   Copies of sales invoices in amount of the receivable.

I.   Purchase order received from customer.

J.   Shipping document describing the articles sold.

K.   Letter received by client from customer acknowledging the correctness of the receivable in the amount shown on client's accounting records.

L.   Letter received by auditors directly from customer acknowledging the correctness of the amount shown as receivable on client's accounting records.

8.6.1   Test of Controls

8-39 Tests of Controls. Auditors generally begin tests of controls by interviewing appropriate personnel who either perform or monitor control procedures. During these interviews, the auditors may also examine certain documents and reports used by persons in performing or monitoring control procedures as well as observe personnel performing their duties. Basic Shoes, a shoe manufacturing company in Changchun, China, sells 95 per cent of its product to companies outside China. The company receives orders for shoes by fax and 20 per cent advance payment of the order price. The sales department makes up a sales order and passes it to the manufacturing manager who verifies the order with the cashier's office which receives the advance money. If the cashier okays the order, the manufacturing manager then writes a manufacturing order to produce the goods and orders the necessary raw materials for the warehouse.

The shipping officer receives a copy of the sales order and matches it to the goods manufactured and then ships, forwarding the shipping documents to accounting. Accounting bills the customer after first matching shipping documents to the original sales order. The cashier's office receives the payment from the customer.

Required:

A.   List ten questions that you might ask Basic Shoe's personnel about the sales process.

B.   Discuss which person you would ask each of the questions and why you would ask them.

C.   What documents would you inspect for each question? Why?

D.   Which part of the sales process would you observe? Why?

E.   What control procedures do you believe they might add to ensure that customers do not order goods that they cannot pay for?

8-40 Tests of Controls. Explain what types of control tests an auditor should do in each of the following circumstances and why:

A.   The auditor tests controls that contribute to the reliability of accounting systems and concludes they are effective.

B.   There are control failures, but in identifying and testing alternative controls the auditor finds them to be effective and therefore concludes that the accounting systems are reliable.

C.   The auditor concludes that there are no effective alternative controls that address the transactions and potential errors to which failed controls relate.

D.   The control failures and the absence of effective alternative controls cause the auditor to identify a specific risk.

8.6.2   Substantive Procedures

8-41 Substantive Tests – Analytical Procedures, Balances and Transactions. Substantive tests include (1) tests of the details of transactions, (2) tests of the details of balances, and (3) analytical procedures. Listed below are several specific audit procedures. Identify the type of substantive test – 1, 2, or 3.

A.   Compare recorded travel expense with the budget.

B.   Vouch entries in the cheque register to paid cheques.

C.   Re-compute accrued interest payable.

D.   Calculate inventory turnover ratios by product and compare with prior periods.

E.   Reconcile the year-end bank account.

F.   Discuss uncollectible accounts with the credit manager.

G.   Count office supplies on hand at year-end.

H.   Vouch entries in the sales journal to sales invoices.

I.   Comparison of recorded amount of major disbursements with appropriate invoices.

J.   Comparison of recorded amount of major disbursements with budgeted amounts.

K.   Comparison of returned confirmation forms with individual accounts.

8-42 Detailed tests of Balances. Your client is the Nicholas van Myra Central, a shopping center with 30 store tenants. All leases with the store tenants provide for a fixed rent plus a percentage of sales, net of sales taxes, in excess of a fixed dollar amount computed on an annual basis. Each lease also provides that the landlord may engage a Register Accountant (RA) to audit all records of the tenant for assurance that sales are being properly reported to the landlord.

You have been requested by your client to audit the records of the JaiLai Chinese Ind. Restaurant to determine that the sales, totaling €725,000 for the year ended 31 December 20X4, have been properly reported to the landlord. The restaurant and the shopping centre entered into a five-year lease on 1 January 20X4. The JaiLai offers only table service. No liquor is served. During mealtimes there are four or five waitresses in attendance, who prepare handwritten pre-numbered bills for the customers. Payment is made at a cash register, staffed by the proprietor, as the customer leaves. All sales are for cash.

The proprietor also is the bookkeeper. Complete files are kept of bills and cash register tapes. A daily sales book and general ledger are also maintained.

Required:

List the auditing procedures that you would employ to test the annual sales of the JaiLai Chinese Ind. Restaurant. (Disregard vending machine sales and counter sales of chewing gum and sweets and concentrate on the overall checks that would be appropriate.)

8.7 **Sampling**

8-43 The public accounting firm of Kalinowski, Czajor and Fijalkowska is auditing Whim of Warsaw, a video gaming company. They wish to get a sample of accounts receivable accounts for confirmation. Describe the procedure they would follow when selecting and performing the sampling.

CASES

8-44 Audit Objectives and Financial Statement Accounts. Look at the financial statements of a major public company. Pick three accounts and discuss the financial statement assertions that might be associated with those accounts. For example, the financial statement assertions that might be associated with 'Accrued Product Liability' are valuation, existence, completeness, and presentation and disclosure. Valuation relates to product liability because a judgement (estimate) must be made regarding the expected cost of defective products.

8-45 Substantive Tests: Balances and Transactions. As part of systematic process of gathering and evaluating evidence regarding assertions about economic actions and events, tests of balances and tests of transactions are essential in obtaining audit evidence to detect material misstatements in the financial statements. In the following case, assume that you are an auditor. Before you conduct the actual tests, you are expected to understand the concepts and procedures of tests of balances and transactions.

Required:

A. There are two types of substantive procedures. Identify each.

B. Describe the difference between tests of balances and tests of transactions. Give an example for each test and illustrate them.

C. For tests of balances, what are the major account balances in the balance sheet that needs to be examined? Why are these tests important?

D. For tests of transactions, what are the major accounts that an auditor needs in order to verify transaction amounts and trace transactions to accounts in the financial statements? Why are these tests important?

E. How do inherent properties of double-entry accounting systems relate to the tests of balances? Give examples of double entries that show the simultaneous effect that one transaction has on another.

F. For certain account balances such as assets, auditors prefer to test asset accounts for overstatement. Explain why. Are there any similar preferences for understatement for other accounts? If any, explain why.

G. As an auditor, you are aware of the control risks when design tests of transactions. Explain how these risks might affect the way you design and carry out the procedures.

8-46 Tests of Balances. Swartz Platten, BV, sells chemicals in large, costly returnable containers. Its procedures in accounting for the containers are as follows:

1 When containers are purchased, their cost is charged to 'Inventory – containers on hand'.

2 Containers are billed to customers at cost; full credit is allowed for all containers returned in usable condition. The containers remain the property of Swartz Platten at all times.

3   The cost of containers billed to customers is debited to 'Accounts receivable – containers' and credited to 'Liability for containers billed'. At the same time, the cost of the containers billed is transferred to 'Inventory – containers out' from 'Inventory – containers on hand'. Subsidiary ledgers are maintained for 'Accounts receivable – containers' and 'Inventory – containers out'.

4   When containers are returned in usable condition, the entries in 3 are reversed.

5   A physical inventory of containers on hand is taken at the fiscal year-end.

6   As a partial control over containers in the hands of customers, sales representatives are asked to estimate periodically the number of containers held by each customer. These estimates are checked for reasonableness against the amount shown for the customer in the 'Inventory – containers out' subsidiary ledger.

7   Physical shortages, unusable returned containers, and other inventory adjustments are charged or credited to 'Containers expense – net'. The corresponding adjustments to 'Liability for containers billed' are also charged or credited to 'Containers expense – net'.

8   Containers kept by customers for more than one year are deemed unusable. Roger van Deelgaard had been the auditor of Swartz Platten for many years. He issued an unqualified opinion on the financial statements for the previous fiscal year. Two months before the current year-end, Swartz Platten's accountant requested that van Deelgaard investigate a strange situation which had developed: the balance in the 'Liability for containers billed' had been steadily increasing, to the point where it exceeded the combined balances in 'Inventory – containers out' and 'Inventory – containers on hand'.

Required:

A.   What might have caused the situation described by the company's accountant?

B.   List the procedures van Deelgaard should employ to determine the nature and extent of the misstatement.

8-47   Taxi company eTaxi is a young IT start-up in the Amsterdam area which – after intensive preparation and successful testing – will transport people from A to B starting next 1 January. Key in the service delivery and client experience is the user-friendly app. As a fully digitized company, cash payments are not possible; it's credit cards only for customers. Customers can download the free app in the app stores of Apple and Google. When booking a taxi ride, the client completes the necessary fields in the app; destination, pick up location (both: street, number, postal code), expected pick up time, first name, surname, telephone number, email address and credit card data. Within a minute after submitting the request, the customer receives confirmation about the expected pickup time, the name of the driver and the price. In case no taxi is available directly, an alternative pick up time is proposed. The customer confirms the service, which cannot be cancelled anymore. In case the customer pushes the reject button, the service will be cancelled resulting in the disappearance of the expected service. Which of the 75 available taxis will be selected is driven by a complex algorithm which uses a variety of data including the unique taxi number, the availability of the taxi and its actual location (gps), the destination and pick up point (based on Google Maps), the actual traffic jams of the Country Traffic Information Service and the actual weather (based on the Apple weather app). Once the system has selected the best choice for a taxi, the driver receives an invitation on his iPhone (next to the steering wheel) to pick up the customer. The driver has 10 seconds to accept the invitation by pushing the yes button. If not, the data disappears from this screen and the next-best-located-taxi will get the invitation instead. Once arriving at the destination, the driver pushes the 'arrival' button on his iPhone; the customer is then charged automatically on his credit card. The pdf invoice will be sent automatically to the customer's email address. Directly afterwards, the client gets an online request to rank the driver, and the taxi driver also gets a request to rank the client.

All taxi drivers are entrepreneurs, having a contract with eTaxi including the requirements for the car (owned by the driver) and an eTaxi commission charge (provision) of 25% on each drive. The drivers receive a summary statement weekly including all drives, the sales prices minus the provision. The net amount is paid to the drivers each week.

Behind the app is a self-made cloud-based application which is the cornerstone of the company. All generated customer data are stored in a central data warehouse. The yearly set taxi rates are based on a rate per kilometer, the distance according to Google Maps, and a surcharge of 20% for taxi services between 20:00 and 07:00.

In addition to the managing director, eTaxi has 20 employees, including an in-house lawyer, 3 employees in bookkeeping, a call center employee, an after sales employee and a number of IT specialists. There is a strict segregation of duties between system development, system maintenance and daily operations.

Situation 1

You are the controller of eTaxi and have become enthusiastic about the new opportunities of data analytics for controlling the company. You are preparing to convince the CFO to invest time and money using data analytics.

Required:

Discuss how you are going to use intensively data analytics in your company. Pay attention to:

- ▶ Which kind of data analytics you are envisaging.
- ▶ How you want to use data analytics: preventive/detective, strategic/tactical/operational and as substitute/complementary for manual procedures.
- ▶ Whether you also want to use external data, and for which use.
- ▶ Whether and to what extent you expect the external auditor will be able to rely on your data analytics.

Situation 2

You have been asked to become eTaxi's incoming external auditor. The company gave you an important challenge: make use of the internally used IT system and available data from the data warehouse in your audit approach. Of course, you accept the challenge, remaining realistic about its boundaries in a financial audit.

Required:

Discuss how you are embedding data analytics in your audit approach. Pay attention to:

- ▶ Which kind of data analytics you are envisaging.
- ▶ In which phase of the audit you are going to use data analytics with which objective.
- ▶ Whether you also want to use external data, and for which use.
- ▶ Whether and to what extent you may rely on the data analytics performed by the company.

Situation 3

The partner and manager are discussing the audit approach. Topic at the table: auditing revenues. You both agree on the importance of controlling the revenue recognition in the financial statements.

Required:

Discuss how to set up your audit procedures re revenue recognition with maximum use of data analytics. Pay attention to:

▶ Your understanding of the company's value creating processes and the related risks in the context of revenue recognition.

▶ On which risks data analytics may add to audit evidence.

▶ The attention points/boundaries you observe in the application of these data analytics.

8-48 Champions NV[47]

Champions NV is a national soccer club playing in the top division of the territory soccer league. Its shares are listed at the Amsterdam Stock Exchange. The company has a fiscal year ending 30 June each year and the company is required to publish interim summarized financial statements each quarter. The company is preparing its financial statements in accordance with IFRS as adopted in the EU.

Your audit firm has been the auditor of Champions for six years. You are in the role of senior staff in the audit team preparing some work on behalf of the engagement manager and engagement partner. Assume on each question you aim to convince the manager and partner based on your comprehensive and to-the-point analysis.

Governance is as follows:

▶ An independent supervisory board including an audit committee and a remuneration committee.

▶ Board of directors comprising a CEO and a CFO and CTM (chief soccer matters).

The company has the following departments:

▶ Technical (15 persons)– headed by CTM

▶ Commercial (10 persons) – headed by CEO

▶ Finance (5 persons) – headed by CFO

▶ Operations (25 persons) – headed by CFO

Champions uses two separate applications for the financial administration (off the shelf product, no source code available at Champions) versus the operations (tailormade by an external software supplier). These systems are linked via an interface. During this fiscal year, the Champions had issues with the operations system, resulting in a one-week-offline period.

The stadium is owned by an international brewery. The rental fee is a fixed amount per year. The contract will terminate at 30 June 20X9, during 20X8/20X9 the new contract will be negotiated.

The summarized financial statements of last fiscal year are as follows:

BALANCE SHEET (amounts x € 1.000)					
	30/6/X8	30/6/X7		30/6/X8	30/6/X7
Capitalized transfer fees	89.050	55.761	Equity	158.937	158.873
Tangible fixed assets	20.311	14.390	Long term liabilities	20.323	15.052
Financial fixed assets	46.070	14.390	Short term liabilities	93.064	72.155
Inventory	4.590	2.519			
Receivables	76.172	58.107			
Investment portfolio	23.941	23.326			
Cash & banks	12.190	64.499			
	272.324	**246.080**		**272.324**	**246.080**

PROFIT & LOSS ACCOUNT (amounts x € 1.000)		
	20X7/20X8	20X6/20X7
Revenues	**91.949**	**118.223**
Purchases	7.452	6.994
Wages & Salaries	52.836	55.096
Depreciation fixed assets	3.175	3.180
Other expenses	41.691	44.581
Total expenses	**105.154**	**109.851**
Operating result before transfer fees	**(13.205)**	**8.372**
Amortization transfer fees	(24.979)	(18.082)
Result from player transfers	39.361	78.616
Other	584	310
Result before tax	**1.761**	**67.016**
Corporate tax	(328)	(17.277)
Net result after tax	**1.186**	**49.461**

Transfer fees

When contracting new players, in a number of cases transfer fees have to be paid to the soccer club the player has been played for before joining the Champions. Transfer fees are capitalized at the start and amortized over the remaining contracting period on a straight-line basis. When leaving Champions before the end of the contract, a transfer fee received is considered as realized in the profit & loss account under 'result from player transfers'. Any remaining capitalized transfer fee for this player is then deducted from this result.

Revenues

Champions has 5 regular revenue categories (with percentage of total revenues):
a)   Broadcasting/television rights (25%)
b)   Shirt sponsoring (10%)
c)   Fan shop sales (30%)
d)   Entrance fees (30%)
e)   Drinks during the games (5%)

Ad a) **Broadcasting/television rights**: Champions receives revenues from television rights on a yearly basis based on a contact the soccer league has with the broadcasting company. This revenue per soccer club depends on the ranking in the competition each season. On a monthly basis, Champions receives an advance payment amounting to 1/12 based the revenue on the actual ranking last season. Each year in July after the season, the final revenue is calculated and settled for the amount not yet paid in advance.

Ad c) **The fan shop sales** comprise the sale of mainly shirts, shorts etc. in the fan shop, on the website and to a wholesaler for further distribution to individual sport stores in Netherlands and abroad. All articles are entered in the tailormade operations software as mentioned above.

Once a year in spring, Champions purchases in bulk the articles from one Chinese supplier. All articles are tagged with a bar code. Sales prices in the fan store and on the website are offered based on a pricing list authorized by the CFO. No discounts are given until the end of the playing season (in May).

A contract is signed with a wholesaler, who is the reseller of the goods to individual sport stores. The contract comprises the agreed price per article, the minimum number per category of articles to be purchased by the wholesaler and a bonus incentive correlated with the number of articles sold.

On a monthly basis, an integral inventory count is organized by scanning all articles individually. Any stock count differences are booked in the P&L account as 'inventory difference' under 'Purchases'.

You are auditing the financial statements for the fiscal year ending 30 June 20X9.

Question 1

You are planning the audit of the revenues related to the *fan shop sales* as well as the *television rights*.

▶   Describe per revenue stream:
   a.   The risks of material misstatements specifically related to each of these two revenue streams, including the related assertion(s).
   b.   Your audit response to these risks (controls-based procedures and/or substantive procedures).
   c.   Whether and how you want to include IT aspects in your approach.

Question 2

During the audit, the audit team collected the following findings:
A.   Champion may be accused of non-compliance with law & regulations related to the entrance fees of 2 players 3 years ago. The newspaper of 23 May 20X9 discloses that

these players received a signing fee amounting to 10 million euro per person paid to an offshore Panama based company. Although not yet announced, it is possible that the fiscal authorities may claim these fees are payroll tax liable, resulting in a wage tax payable of 50% of each signing fee added with a 100% fine.

▶ *Consider the impact of above finding and argue why, including the follow up steps to be taken.*

B. On 24 May 20X9, it has been announced that Champion's player The Light got an offer from The OldLady soccer club in Italy, potentially leading to a realized transfer fee of 80 million euro. The settlement of this transfer is contingent on a bank financing arrangement which may not be finalized before the end of June 20X9 (but will be closed before signing of the auditor's report).

Champion's management indicated that the transfer fee will be booked in the 20X8/20X9 as the club already agreed with OldLady, including a disclosure in the financial statements about this transfer.

▶ *Consider the effects of this transfer for your audit procedures, including potential consequences for reporting (auditor's report and report to the supervisory board).*

8.10 NOTES

1. International Auditing and Assurance Standards Board (IAASB), 2023, International Standard on Auditing 330 (ISA 330) 'The Auditor's Responses to Assessed Risks', *Handbook of International Quality Management, Auditing Review, Other Assurance, and Related Services Pronouncements*, 2022 edn, Volume I, International Federation of Accountants, New York.

2. International Auditing and Assurance Standards Board (IAASB), 2023, International Standard on Auditing 500 (ISA 500) 'Audit Evidence', para. 5, *Handbook of International Quality Management, Auditing Review, Other Assurance, and Related Services Pronouncements*, 2022 edn, Volume I, International Federation of Accountants, New York.

3. Audit Data Analytics (ADAs) Can Transform Audits; New AICPA Guide Will Help Auditors Apply ADA Techniques, December 5, 2017, AICPA.

4. The internet of things is the network of devices such as vehicles, machines and home appliances that contain computing power, software, sensors, actuators and connectivity which allow things to connect, interact and exchange data. For example, heavy machinery with sensors that measure vibration, temperature and oil levels can send data to the cloud where it can be analyzed to predict break-downs and schedule preventative maintenance, Ten Improvements in Data Quality Provided by the Internet of Things, Rick Payne, February 5, 2020, IFAC, https://www.ifac.org/knowledge-gateway/preparing-future-ready-professionals/discussion/ten-improvements-data-quality-provided-internet-things?utm_medium=email&utm_source=transactional&utm_campaign=GKG_Latest

5. International Auditing and Assurance Standards Board IAASB. 2023 International Standard on Auditing 315 (revised 2019) Identifying and Assessing the Risks of Material Misstatement. *Handbook of International Quality Management, Auditing, Review, Other Assurance, and Related Services Pronouncements*, 2022 edn, Volume 1, International Federation of Accountants, New York.

6. International Standard on Auditing 315 (Revised 2019) ISA 315 and Conforming and Consequential Amendments to Other International Standards Arising from ISA 315.

7. Ibid. ISA 315.

8.   Ibid. ISA 500.

9.   PCAOB AS 1105: Audit Evidence, para 17, https://pcaobus.org/Standards/Auditing/Pages/
        AS1105.aspx Jeremy Vinson, Byron Pike, Lawrence Chui conclude auditors are subject to
        confirmation bias when judging reasonableness and persuasiveness of the client's expla-
        nation. Alternatively, they find auditors are subject to a recency bias when judging the
        likelihood of material misstatement in the account, which affects their evidence gathering
        choices and is supportive of belief adjustment. Paper, Auditor Inquiry: The Influence of
        Client Message Framing on Auditors' Judgment, SSRN, 2018, https://papers.ssrn.com/sol3/
        papers.cfm?abstract_id=3107164

10.   Escott et al. v BarChris Const. Corp. (1968), United States District Court for the Southern
        District of New York, 283 F, Supp. 643: http://www.casebriefs.com/blog/law/corporations/
        corporations-keyed-to-klein/the-duties-of-officers-directors-and-other-insiders/escott-v-
        barchris-const-corp/

11.   What to do in an audit interview, PwC, Auditor Training, https://www.youtube.com/
        watch?v=TwnQi9f9z_0

12.   International Auditing and Assurance Standards Board (IAASB), 2023, International Stand-
        ards on Auditing 501 (ISA 501) 'Audit Evidence – Specific Considerations for Selected Items',
        para. 4, *Handbook of International Quality Management, Auditing, Review, Other Assurance,
        and Related Services Pronouncements*, 2022 edn, Volume I, International Federation of Ac-
        countants, New York.

13.   International Auditing and Assurance Standards Board (IAASB), 2023, International Stand-
        ards on Auditing 705 (ISA 705) 'Modifications to the Opinion in the Independent Auditor's
        Report', *Handbook of International Quality Management, Auditing, Review, Other Assurance,
        and Related Services Pronouncements*, 2022 edn, Volume I, International Federation of Ac-
        countants, New York.

14.   Ibid. ISA 501.

15.   Consignment is a specialized way of marketing certain types of goods. The consignor deliv-
        ers goods to the consignee, who acts as the consignor's agent in selling the merchandise to
        a third party. The consignee accepts the goods without any liability except to reasonably
        protect them from damage. The consignee receives a commission when the merchandise
        is sold. Goods on consignment are included in the consignor's inventory and excluded
        from the consignee's inventory since the consignor has legal title.

16.   International Auditing and Assurance Standards Board (IAASB), 2023, International Stand-
        ards on Auditing 505 (ISA 505) 'External Confirmations', *Handbook of International Quality
        Management, Auditing, Review, Other Assurance, and Related Services Pronouncements*,
        2022 edn, Volume I, International Federation of Accountants, New York.

17.   Ibid. ISA 501, para. 15.

18.   Ibid. ISA 501.

19.   https://pcaobus.org/oversight/standards/auditing-standards/details/AS2310

20.   The standard will take effect for audits of financial statements for fiscal years ending on or
        after June 15, 2025. https://assets.pcaobus.org/pcaob-dev/docs/default-source/rulemaking/
        docket_028/2023-008_confirmation-adopting-release.pdf

21.   Ibid. ISA 500.

22.   International Auditing and Assurance Standards Board (IAASB), 2023, International
        Standard on Auditing 200 (ISA 200) 'Overall Objectives of the Independent Auditor and
        the Conduct of an Audit in Accordance with International Standards on Auditing', *Hand-
        book of International Quality Management, Auditing Review, Other Assurance, and Related
        Services Pronouncements*, 2022 edn, Volume I, International Federation of Accountants,
        New York.

23. AICPA Statement of Auditing Standards (SAS) 142, 2020 Audit Evidence, para A9 and A10, (AICPA Professional Standards AU-C sec. 500).

24. Ibid. ISA 500.

25. International Auditing and Assurance Standards Board (IAASB), 2023, International Standard on Auditing 330 (ISA 330) 'The Auditor's Responses to Assessed Risks', para. 26, *Handbook of International Quality Management, Auditing Review, Other Assurance, and Related Services Pronouncements*, 2022 edn, Volume I, International Federation of Accountants, New York.

26. Ibid. ISA 330.

27. Public Company Accounting Oversight Board (PCAOB). 2022, Audit Standard 1105, 'Audit Evidence'. PCAOB Washington D.C., 2022.

28. International Auditing and Assurance Standards Board, 2023, International Standards on Auditing 500 (ISA 500), *Handbook of International Quality Management, Auditing Review, Other Assurance, and Related Services Pronouncements*, 2022 edn, Volume I, International Federation of Accountants, New York.

29. The oligopolistic (audit) market is characterized by a certain level of competition. See for example: 'An Empirical Test of Spatial Competition in the Audit Market', Numan, W. and Willekens, M., *Journal of Accounting and Economics*, 53 (1–2), February–April 2012, Pages 450–465, https://doi.org/10.1016/j.jacceco.2011.10.002; 'Competition in the Audit Market: Policy Implications', Gerakos, J. and Syverson, C., *Journal of Accounting Research*, April 2015; Carson, E., Simnett, R., Soo, B.S., Wright, A.M. (2012), 'Changes in Audit Market Competition and the Big N Premium'. *AUDITING: A Journal of Practice & Theory*, August 2012, 31 (3), pp. 47-73. https://doi.org/10.2308/ajpt-10295. Also see https://www.frc.org.uk/news-and-events/news/2023/12/frc-publishes-annual-review-of-competition-in-the-audit-market/

30. Ibid. ISA 500.

31. United States Public Company Accounting Oversight Board (PCAOB), 2022, Audit Standard 2301 (PCAOB (AS 2301): The Auditor's Responses to the Risks of Material Misstatement, https://pcaobus.org/oversight/standards/auditing-standards/details/AS2301

32. PCAOB, Audit Standard 2301 (AS 2301). 2022. The Auditor's Responses to the Risks of Material Misstatement. https://pcaobus.org/Standards/Auditing/Pages/AS2301.aspx

33. Ibid. ISA 330.

34. Ibid. PCAOB, AS 2301, The Auditor's Responses to the Risks of Material Misstatement, para 9c, https://pcaobus.org/Standards/Auditing/Pages/AS2301.aspx, https://pcaobus.org/oversight/standards/auditing-standards/details/AS2301

35. AR = IR * CR * DR

36. International Auditing and Assurance Standards Board (IAASB), 2023, International Standard on Auditing 330 (ISA 330) 'The Auditor's Responses to Assessed Risks', para. 18, Handbook of Inter-national Quality Control, Auditing Review, Other Assurance, and Related Services Pronouncements, 2022 edn, Volume I, International Federation of Accountants, New York. ISA 330.1.

37. Ibid. ISA 330.

38. Ibid. ISA 330.

39. United States Public Company Accounting Oversight Board (PCAOB), 2022, Audit Standard 2315 (AS 2315): Audit Sampling, para 46, https://pcaobus.org/Standards/Auditing/Pages/AS2315.aspx, https://pcaobus.org/oversight/standards/auditing-standards/details/AS2315

40. Ibid, PCAOB AS 2315. 2022. Audit Sampling, https://pcaobus.org/Standards/Auditing/Pages/AS2315.aspx, https://pcaobus.org/oversight/standards/auditing-standards/details/AS2315

41.   Tolerable misstatement for the population to be sampled ordinarily should be less than tolerable misstatement for the account balance or transaction class to allow for the possibility that misstatement in the portion of the account or transaction class not subject to audit sampling, individually or in combination with other misstatements, would cause the financial statements to be materially misstated. PCAOB AS 2315: Audit Sampling, para 18A, https://pcaobus.org/Standards/Auditing/Pages/AS2315.aspx, https://pcaobus.org/oversight/standards/auditing-standards/details/AS2315

42.   Ibid. PCAOB AS 2315: Audit Sampling, appendix 1, Table 1, https://pcaobus.org/oversight/standards/auditing-standards/details/AS2315

43.   Anomaly – a misstatement or deviation that is demonstrably not representative of misstatements or deviations in a population.

44.   International Auditing and Assurance Standards Board (IAASB), 2023, International Standard on Auditing 530 (ISA 530) 'Audit Sampling and Other Means of Testing', Appendix 2, *Handbook of International Quality Management, Auditing Review, Other Assurance, and Related Services Pronouncements*, 2022 edn, Volume I, International Federation of Accountants, New York.

45.   Ibid. PCAOB AS 2315, 2022, Audit Sampling, para 31, https://pcaobus.org/oversight/standards/auditing-standards/details/AS2315

46.   Ibid. PCAOB AS 2315: Audit Sampling, appendix 1, Table 2, 2022, https://pcaobus.org/oversight/standards/auditing-standards/details/AS2315

47.   The case Champions NV is derived from the May 25, 2019 Audit & Assurance exam of the International Executive Master of Auditing, hosted by Maastricht University/Vrije Universiteit Amsterdam, www.iema-edu.org.

CHAPTER 9

ANALYTICAL REVIEW

The four phases of the audit:

Acceptance/ continuance	Understanding/ risk analysis	Building/executing audit plan	Evaluating/ completion
Phase 1	**Phase 2**	**Phase 3**	**Phase 4**

9.1 LEARNING OBJECTIVES

After studying this chapter, you should be able to:

1. Understand the general nature of analytical procedures.
2. Recall the four categories of general analytic procedures.
3. Describe the four diagnostic processes of analytical review.
4. Explain how expectations are developed and what sources are used.
5. Clarify how the effectiveness of an analytical procedure is a function of the nature of the account and the reliability and other characteristics of the data.
6. Calculate the customary ratios that are used during the planning phase to determine accounts that may represent significant risks to the entity of liquidity, solvency, profitability and activity.
7. Understand some indications that the going concern assumption may be questioned.
8. Comprehend why and how analytical procedures may be used at each audit phase.
9. Grasp how analytical procedures are used in substantive procedures.

9.2 ANALYTICAL PROCEDURES DURING DIFFERENT PHASES IN THE AUDIT PROCESS

Analytical procedures are used: (a) to assist the auditor in planning the nature, timing and extent of audit procedures; (b) as substantive testing and procedures; and (c) as an overall review of the financial statements in the final stage of the audit. Illustration 9.1 shows important characteristics of analytical procedures at these three phases.

The auditor must apply analytical procedures at the audit's review stages. Nevertheless, ISA 520 links the analytical procedures performed at the end at the audit with the planning phase: 'The objectives of the of auditor are ... to design and perform analytical procedures near the end of the audit that assist the auditor when forming an overall conclusion as to whether the financial statements are consistent with the auditor's understanding of the entity.'[1]

▶ PLANNING

Analytical procedures performed in the planning stage (Phase II in the Audit Process Model, chapter 6, illustration 6.1) are used to identify unusual changes in the financial statements, or the absence of expected changes, and specific risks. During the planning phase, analytical procedures are usually focused on account balances at the financial statement level and relationships. Application of analytical procedures at the planning stage indicates aspects of the business of which the auditor was unaware and will assist in determining the nature, timing and extent of other audit procedures. Surveys of auditors show that the most extensive use of analytical procedures has been in the planning and completion stages.[2] Risk assessment procedures, according to ISA 315, include analytic procedures.[3]

▶ SUBSTANTIVE TESTING

During the substantive testing stage (Phase III of the Audit Process Model addressed in this chapter) analytical procedures are performed to obtain assurance that financial statement account balances do not contain material misstatements. In substantive testing, analytical procedures focus on underlying factors that affect those account balances through the development of an expectation of how the recorded balance should look.

▶ OVERALL REVIEW

Analytical procedures performed during the overall review (wrap-up) stage (Phase IV of the Audit Process Model, chapter 10, illustration 10.1) are designed to assist the auditor in assessing that all significant fluctuations and other unusual items have been adequately explained and that the overall financial statement presentation makes sense based on the audit results and an understanding of the business.

According to ISA 520, 'The auditor shall design and perform analytical procedures near the end of the audit that assist the auditor when forming an overall conclusion as to whether the financial statements are consistent with the auditor's understanding of the entity.'[4] Analytical procedures at the review stage are intended to corroborate conclusions formed during the audit of individual components of the financial statements. Moreover, they assist in determining the reasonableness of the financial statements. They may also identify areas requiring further procedures.

When performing the analytic procedures, it is important to keep in mind that auditor biases may exist. Two biases are prevalent: automation bias and authority bias. Automation bias: placing weight or undue reliance on output from automated systems or information in digital format, or assuming it is relevant and reliable, without performing appropriate procedures. Authority bias: placing undue reliance on information prepared by an expert or another practitioner, or assuming the information is relevant and reliable, without performing appropriate procedures.

▶ **TESTS OF CONTROLS OVER INFORMATION USED FOR ANALYTICS**

An important consideration in applying analytical procedures is tests of controls over the preparation of information used for analytics. When those controls are effective, the auditor will have more confidence in the reliability of the information and, therefore, in the results of analytical procedures. For non-significant risks, the auditor can perform control tests added with substantive analytics. For significant risks, she cannot stop but needs to add tests of details.

The controls over non-financial information can often be tested in conjunction with tests of accounting-related controls. For example, a company's controls over the processing of sales invoices may include controls over the recording of unit sales; therefore, an auditor could test the controls over the recording of unit sales in conjunction with tests of the controls over the processing of sales invoices.

ILLUSTRATION 9.1

IMPORTANT CHARACTERISTICS OF ANALYTICAL PROCEDURES AT THREE STAGES OF AN AUDIT

Stage of an audit	Required?	Purpose	Comment
Planning	Yes	To assist in planning the nature, timing and extent of other auditing procedures.	Level of aggregation can vary and will have impact on effectiveness.
Substantive testing	No	To obtain evidential matter about particular assertions related to account balances or classes of transactions.	Effectiveness depends upon: ▶ nature of assertion ▶ plausibility and predictability of relations ▶ reliability of data ▶ precision of expectation
Overall review	Yes	To assist in assessing the conclusions reached and in the evaluation of the overall financial statement presentation.	Includes reading financial statements to consider: ▶ accuracy of evidence gathered for unusual or unexpected balances identified during planning or during course of audit ▶ unusual or unexpected balances or relationships previously identified

9.3 THE ANALYTICAL REVIEW PROCESS

Analytical procedures are evaluations of financial information through analysis of plausible relationships among both financial and non-financial data. Analytical procedures also encompass investigation of identified fluctuations or relationships that are inconsistent or unusual or that differ from expected values by a significant amount.[5] Put another way, analytical procedures entail the use of comparisons and relationships to determine whether account balances or other data appear reasonable. Such procedures allow the auditor to answer the question: Do the numbers make sense?

General analytical procedures include trend analysis, ratio analysis, statistical and data mining analysis, and reasonableness tests. *Trend analysis* is the analysis of changes in an account balance over time, for example increases or decreases over time. *Ratio analysis* is the comparison of relationships between financial statement accounts, the comparison of an account with non-financial data, or the comparison of relationships between companies in an industry. Examples include current ratio or gross margin comparison between industry and individual companies. *Reasonableness testing* is the analysis of account balances or changes in account balances within an accounting period in terms of their 'reasonableness' in light of expected relationships between accounts. For example, it is not reasonable if one expects accounts receivable from a given company to be around $100,000, but in one month it is $800,000. *Data mining* is a set of computer-assisted techniques that use sophisticated statistical analysis, including artificial intelligence techniques, to examine large volumes of data with the objective of indicating hidden or unexpected information or patterns. For example, looking at the accounts payable over a period, suddenly there is a big drop in volume.

The process of planning, executing, and drawing conclusions from analytical procedures is called *analytical review*. There are several views, theoretical and practical, of the sub-processes involved in analytical review.

The theoretical view[6] is that the review process consists of four diagnostic processes:

1 mental representation,
2 hypothesis generation,
3 information search,
4 hypothesis evaluation.

Auditors hypothesize causes and related probabilities, gather evidence to test the hypotheses, and ultimately select which hypotheses are most likely to cause the fluctuation.[7]

▶ FOUR-PHASE PROCESS

Here we use a practitioner approach, the four-phase process most common in professional literature.[8] In the auditor standards the following four-step approach is used, taking into account the theoretical view.

▶ phase one – formulate expectations (expectations);
▶ phase two – compare the expected value to the recorded amount (identification);
▶ phase three – investigate possible explanations for a difference between expected and recorded values (investigation);
▶ phase four – evaluate the impact of the differences between expectation and recorded amounts on the audit and the financial statements (evaluation).

Illustration 9.2 shows the four-phase process and its inputs and outputs.

ILLUSTRATION 9.2

FOUR PHASE PROCESS MODEL, INPUTS AND OUTPUTS

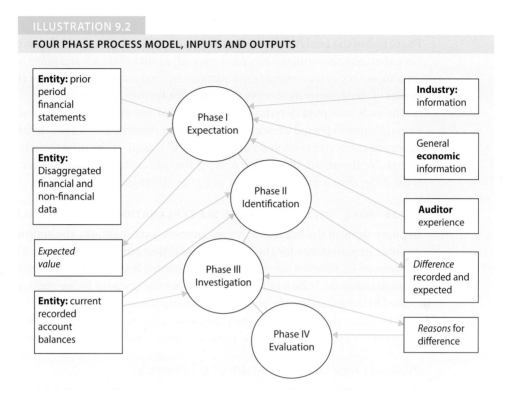

PHASE ONE – FORMULATE EXPECTATIONS

According to ISA 520,[9] the auditor should 'evaluate the reliability of data from which the auditor's expectation of recorded amounts or ratios is developed, taking account of source, comparability, and nature and relevance of information available, and controls over preparation'. In phase one of the analytical review process, the auditor develops expectations of what amounts should appear in financial statement account balances based on prior year financial statements, budgets, industry information and non-financial information. Expectations are the auditor's estimations of recorded accounts or ratios. The auditor develops her expectation in such a way that a significant difference between it and the recorded amount will indicate a misstatement.

Forming an expectation is the most important phase of the analytical procedure process. The closer the auditor's expectation is to the correct balance or relationship, the more effective the procedure will be at identifying potential misstatements.

Expectations are formed from a variety of sources. Research[10] suggests that the use of industrial, economic, or environmental data can improve the predictive ability of analytical procedures. Other resources include industry data, data about similar businesses, and auditor experience. Expectations are also based on the entity's prior financial statements, same store sales, non-financial data, budgets and public reports.

Before determining what analytical procedures to use the auditor must 'determine the suitability of particular substantive analytical procedures for given assertions, taking account of the assessed risks of material misstatement and tests of details, if any, for these assertions'.[11]

PHASE TWO – COMPUTE EXPECTED VALUE

Phase two of the analytical review process (identification) is when the auditor compares her expected value with the recorded amount. Audit efficiency and effectiveness depend on competency in recognizing error patterns in financial data and in hypothesizing likely causes of those patterns to serve as a guide for further testing.

The auditor should determine the amount of any acceptable difference of recorded amounts from expected values. The auditor must consider how large a difference between expected value and recorded amount she will accept. If the difference is less than the acceptable threshold, the auditor accepts the book value without further investigation. If the difference is greater, the next step is to investigate the difference.

PHASE THREE – INVESTIGATE POSSIBLE EXPLANATIONS OF DIFFERENCES

In phase three of the analytical review process (investigation), the auditor investigates possible explanations for the expected/recorded amount difference. The difference between an auditor's expectation and the recorded book value of an account can be due to misstatements, inherent factors that affect the account being audited, and factors related to the reliability of data used to develop the expectation.

The greater the precision of the expectation, the more likely the difference between the auditor's expectation and the recorded value will be due to misstatements.

INQUIRIES AND CORROBORATION OF DIFFERENCES

Where differences between expectation and recorded amounts are found, the first step is usually to ask management for an explanation. However, it is important that the auditor maintains her professional skepticism when considering these answers and it is suggested that the auditor conduct other audit procedures to corroborate these. When analytical procedures are used in the planning phase, corroboration is not immediately required because the purpose of analytical procedures in planning is to chart the work to follow.

PHASE FOUR – EVALUATE THE IMPACT OF THE DIFFERENCES BETWEEN EXPECTATION AND RECORDED AMOUNTS

The final phase (phase four – evaluation) of the analytical review process involves evaluating the impact on the financial statements of the difference between the auditor's expected value and the recorded amount. It is usually not practical to identify factors that explain the exact amount of difference investigated. The auditor attempts to quantify that portion of the difference for which plausible explanations can be obtained and, where appropriate, corroborated. If the amount that cannot be explained is sufficiently small, the auditor may conclude there is no material misstatement. *However, if the amount that cannot be explained exceeds the threshold (determined in phase two), additional substantive procedures are required.*

9.4   FORMULATING EXPECTATIONS

Expectations are developed by identifying plausible relationships that are reasonably expected to exist based on the auditor's understanding of the client and of her industry. These relationships may be determined by comparisons with the following sources:[12]

> financial information for comparable prior periods;
> anticipated results (such as budgets and forecasts, or auditor expectations);
> relationships among elements of financial information within the period;
> similar industry information;
> relationships of financial information with relevant non-financial information.

The auditor can identify account balances that have changed significantly simply by comparing the current client data with prior period data. She may compare the current year's account balances with that of the preceding year; the current trial balance with similar detail for the preceding year; and ratios and percentage relationships between years. She compares current recorded account balances with results expected. For example, company budgets may be compared with actual results for indications of potential misstatements. The auditor may calculate the expected balance for interest expense (notes payable monthly balance times average monthly interest rate) and compare this to recorded interest rates.

One of the standard bases of comparison is between similar companies in the same industry. For example, the auditor compares the gross margin of the industry to the client's gross margin.

Analytical procedures may include consideration of relationships between financial information and relevant non-financial information, such as payroll costs to number of employees. Another example is the revenue of a hotel may be estimated by multiplying the average room rate times the number of rooms times the average occupancy percentage (e.g., $150 average rate X 20 rooms X 60 per cent average occupancy). Similarly, revenues may be calculated for school tuition (average number of students enrolled times the average tuition cost), payroll, and cost of materials sold using non-financial factors.

> ### SOURCES OF INFORMATION AND PRECISION OF EXPECTATIONS

The source of information on which the expectations are based (e.g., prior period statements, forecasts, industry information) determines, in part, the precision with which the auditor predicts an account balance. For example, information from other, similar stores in the same retail chain is more precise than general industry information. Recent years' financial statements are more precise a predictor of this year's balance than older financial statements. Expectations developed at a detailed level generally have a greater chance of detecting misstatement of a given amount than broad comparisons. Monthly amounts will generally be more effective than annual amounts and comparisons by location or line of business usually will be more effective than company-wide comparisons.

> ### NATURE OF ACCOUNT AND CHARACTERISTICS OF DATA

The effectiveness of an analytical procedure is a function of the *nature of the account* and the reliability and other *characteristics of the data*. In determining the nature of the account, we consider whether the balance is based on the number of transactions represented by the balance and the control environment. Subjectively determined balances are more easily manipulated than accumulations of transactions. If the characteristic of the account is that it comprises millions of transactions (e.g., retail revenue), it should be more predictable than those comprising a few transactions (e.g., obsolete inventory). Fixed expenses (e.g., leases) are more predictable than variable expenses (e.g., shipping).

Other data characteristics such as the level of detail (aggregation) on which the auditor can base her expectation and the data's reliability are key characteristics. In general, the more disaggregated the data, the more precise the expectation. For example, the use of monthly instead of annual data tends to improve the precision of the expectation. Preparing an expectation by division is also more precise than an expectation based on consolidated data. Accounting researchers conclude that disaggregated monthly, segment or product line balances are required to implement reliable attention-directing analytical procedures.

The more reliable the source of the data, the more precise the expectation will be. Reliability of data is determined based on the strength of the company's internal control, if the data source is objective or independent, and if data has been subject to auditing procedures or not. Stronger internal control over financial reporting and accounting systems produces more reliable data on financial statements. The use of reliable non-financial data (e.g., store size or occupancy rates) and the use of data that has been subjected to auditing procedures improve the precision of the expectation based on that data.

9.5 GENERAL TYPES OF ANALYTICAL PROCEDURES

The general analytical procedures are trend analysis, ratio analysis, reasonableness tests, statistical and data mining analysis. Determining which type of analytical procedure is appropriate is a matter of professional judgement. A review of audit practice indicates that simple judgmental approaches (such as comparison and ratio analysis) are used more frequently than complex statistical approaches (such as time series modelling or regression analysis).[13] These tests are generally carried out using computer software (i.e., Computer Assisted Audit Technology or CAATs).[14] Trend analysis, ratio analysis and reasonableness tests are discussed in this section.

▶ TREND ANALYSIS

Trend analysis is the analysis of changes in an account balance or ratio over time. Trend analysis could compare last year's account balance to the current unaudited balance or balances in many time periods. Trend analysis works best when the account or relationship is predictable (e.g. rent expense in a stable environment). It is less effective when the audited entity has experienced significant operating or accounting changes. The number of years used in the trend analysis is a function of the stability of operations. The more stable the operations over time, the more predictable the relations and the more appropriate the use of multiple time periods. Trend analysis at an aggregate level (e.g., on a consolidated basis) is relatively imprecise because a material misstatement is often small relative to the aggregate account balance. The most precise trend analysis would be on disaggregated data (e.g., by segment, product or location, and monthly or quarterly rather than annually).

▶ RATIO ANALYSIS

Ratio analysis is the comparison of relationships between financial statement accounts, the comparison of an account with non-financial data, or the comparison of relationships between firms in an industry. Another example of ratio analysis (which is sometimes referred to as common size analysis) is to set all the account balances as either a percentage of total assets or revenue.

Ratio analysis is most appropriate when the relationship between accounts is predictable and stable (e.g., between sales and accounts receivable). Ratio analysis can be more effective than trend analysis because comparisons between the balance sheet and income statement can often reveal unusual fluctuations that an analysis of the individual accounts would not. Like trend analysis, ratio analysis at an aggregate level is relatively imprecise because a material misstatement is often small relative to the natural variations in the ratios.

TYPES OF RATIO ANALYSIS USED IN ANALYTICAL PROCEDURES

There are five types of ratio analysis used in analytical procedures (see illustration 9.3):
1. ratios that compare client and industry data;
2. ratios that compare client data with similar prior period data;
3. ratios that compare client data with client-determined expected results;
4. ratios that compare client data with auditor-determined expected results;
5. ratios that compare client data with expected results using non-financial data.

The Risk Management Association (RMA), Standard & Poor's, Dun & Bradstreet, Ibis World and others publish standard ratios by industry.[15] Similar ratios for both industry and entity may be compared to indicate differences that might affect the auditor's judgement of the nature and extent of audit procedures. The ratios indicate entity liquidity, solvency, profitability and activity. See illustration 9.4 for some standard ratios often used.

▶ REASONABLENESS TESTING

Reasonableness testing is the analysis of account balances or changes in account balances within an accounting period in terms of their 'reasonableness' in light of expected relationships between accounts. This involves the development of an expectation based on financial data, non-financial data, or both. For example, using the number of employees hired and terminated, the timing of pay changes, and the effect of vacation and sick days, the model could predict the change in payroll expense from the previous year to the current balance within a fairly narrow dollar range.

In contrast to both trend and ratio analyses (which implicitly assume stable relationships), reasonableness tests use information to develop an explicit prediction of the account balance. The auditor develops assumptions for each of the key factors (e.g., industry and economic factors) to estimate the account balance. Considering the number of units sold, the unit price by product line, different pricing structures, and an understanding of industry trends during the period could explicitly form a reasonableness test for sales. This contrasts with an implicit trend expectation for sales based on last year's sales. The latter expectation is appropriate only if there were no other factors affecting sales during the current year, which is not the usual situation.

▶ TREND ANALYSIS, RATIO ANALYSIS AND REASONABLENESS TESTS COMPARED

Trend analysis, ratio analysis and reasonableness tests differ as to the number of independent predictive variables considered, use of external data, and statistical precision. Trend analysis is limited to a single predictor, that is, the prior periods' data for that account. Trend analysis, by relying on a single predictor, does not allow the use of potentially relevant operating data, as do the other types of procedures. Because ratio analysis employs two or more related financial or non-financial sources of information, the result is a more precise expectation.

Reasonableness tests and regression analysis further improve the precision of the expectation by allowing potentially as many variables (financial and non-financial) as are relevant for forming the expectation. Reasonableness tests and regression analysis can use external data (e.g., general economic and industry data) directly in forming the expectation. The most statistically precise expectations are formed using statistical and data mining analysis.

ILLUSTRATION 9.3

FIVE TYPES OF RATIO ANALYSIS

Procedures	Examples
Ratios that compare client data with industry.	Standard ratios published by the industry by the Risk Management Association, Standard & Poor's, Dun & Bradstreet and others.
Ratios that compare client data with similar prior period data.	Auditor compares the current year's account balances with that for the preceding year; current trial balances with similar detail for the preceding year; and ratios and percentage relationships between years.
Ratios that compare client data with client-determined expected results.	Client budgets may be compared with actual results for indications of potential misstatements.
Ratios that compare client data with auditor-determined expected results.	Auditor calculates the expected balance for interest expense and compares to recorded interest.
Ratios that compare client data with expected results using non-financial data.	Non-financial data may serve as a basis for expected results and comparison, the revenue of a hotel may be estimated by multiplying average room rate times the number of rooms times the average occupancy percentage.

▶ STANDARD CLIENT AND INDUSTRY RATIOS

At the planning stage of an audit, there are certain customary ratios that are always calculated to determine accounts that may represent significant risks to the entity of liquidity, solvency, profitability and activity. These ratios help to answer some key questions:

- ▷ Is there a possible going concern problem (liquidity ratios)?
- ▷ Is the entity's capital structure sustainable (solvency ratios)?
- ▷ Is gross margin reasonable (profitability)?
- ▷ Could inventory be overstated (activity)?

Illustration 9.4 gives a list of these ratios.

ILLUSTRATION 9.4

STANDARD CLIENT AND INDUSTRY RATIOS

Client and industry standard ratios	Calculation
Liquidity:	
(1) Current ratio	(1) Current assets/Current liabilities
(2) Quick ratio	(2) (Cash + Short-term securities + Accounts receivable)/Current liabilities
Solvency:	
(1) Debt to equity	(1) Long-term debt/Stockholders' equity
(2) Times interest earned	(2) (Net income before interest and taxes)/Interest expense
(3) Debt service coverage	(3) (Net income before interest and depreciation)/Principal and interest payments
Profitability:	
(1) Net profit margin	(1) Net profit/Revenue
(2) Gross margin	(2) (Revenue less cost of goods sold)/Revenue
(3) Return on investment	(3) Net income/Stockholders' equity
(4) Times interest earned	(4) (Net income before interest and taxes)/Interest expense
Activity:	
(1) Receivable turnover	(1) Revenue/Average accounts receivable
(2) Inventory turnover	(2) Cost of goods sold/Average inventory
(3) Asset turnover	(3) Revenue/Total assets

▶ **LIQUIDITY AND GOING CONCERN**

Auditors must determine the possibility that the company is having liquidity problems – that is, is there a possibility that the company may no longer be a *going concern*? ISA 570[16] states that under the going concern assumption, it is assumed that an entity is continuing in business for the foreseeable future (see section 10.8). General purpose financial statements are prepared on a going concern basis, unless management intends to liquidate the entity or to cease operations. When the use of the going concern assumption is appropriate, assets and liabilities are recorded on the basis that the entity will be able to realize its assets and discharge its liabilities in the normal course of business.

Analytical procedures may point to indications of risk that the going concern assumption needs to be questioned. Illustration 9.5 shows the indications of risk that the going concern assumption may be questioned.[17] The significance of the indications in illustration 9.5 can often be mitigated by other factors. For example, the effect of an entity being unable to make its normal debt repayments may be counterbalanced by management's plans to maintain adequate cash flows by alternative means, such as disposal of assets.

ILLUSTRATION 9.5

INDICATIONS THAT THE GOING CONCERN ASSUMPTION MIGHT BE QUESTIONED

The following are examples of events or conditions that, individually or collectively, may cast significant doubt about the going concern assumption. This listing is not all-inclusive nor does the existence of one or more of the items always signify that a material uncertainty exists.

Financial

▶ Net liability or net current liability position.
▶ Fixed-term borrowings approaching maturity without realistic prospects of renewal or repayment, or excessive reliance on short-term borrowing to finance long-term assets.
▶ Indications of withdrawal of financial support by creditors.
▶ Negative operating cash flows indicated by historical or prospective financial statements.
▶ Adverse key financial ratios.
▶ Substantial operating losses or significant deterioration in the value of assets used to generate cash flows.
▶ Arrears or discontinuance of dividends.
▶ Inability to pay creditors on due dates.
▶ Difficulty in complying with the terms of loan agreements.
▶ Change from credit to cash-on-delivery transactions with suppliers.
▶ Inability to obtain financing for essential new product development or other essential investments.

Operating

▶ Management intentions to liquidate the entity or to cease operations.
▶ Loss of key management without replacement.
▶ Loss of a major market, key customer(s), franchise, license or principal supplier(s).
▶ Labor difficulties.
▶ Shortages of important supplies.
▶ Emergence of a highly successful competitor.

Other

▶ Non-compliance with capital requirements or other statutory requirements.
▶ Pending legal proceedings against the entity that may, if successful, result in significant claims.
▶ Changes in law or regulation or government policy expected to adversely affect the entity.
▶ Uninsured or underinsured catastrophes when they occur.

9.6 ANALYTICAL PROCEDURES AS SUBSTANTIVE TESTS

Substantive procedures in the audit are designed to reduce detection risk relating to specific financial statement assertions. Substantive tests include tests of details (either of balances or of transactions) and analytical procedures. Auditors use analytical procedures to identify situations that require increased use of other procedures (i.e., tests of control, substantive audit procedures), but seldom to reduce audit effort.

▶ ANALYTICAL PROCEDURES ADVANTAGES OVER TESTS OF DETAILS

There are several advantages of performing substantive analytical procedures instead of tests of details. One advantage is that the auditor may use her understanding of the client's business obtained during planning procedures. The key factors affecting business may be expected to reflect underlying financial data. Substantive analytical procedures often enable auditors to focus on a few key factors that affect the account balance. Substantive analytical procedures may be more efficient in performing understatement tests. For example, in a test for unrecorded sales, it may be easier to develop an expectation of sales and investigate any significant differences between the expectation and the recorded amount, than to sample statistically a reciprocal population and then perform tests of details.

In planning an audit that uses analytical procedures as substantive procedures, the auditor should:[18]

- ▶ Determine the suitability of particular substantive analytical procedures considering the assessed risks of material misstatement.
- ▶ Evaluate the reliability of data from which the auditor's expectation is developed, taking account of quality of controls, as well as the source, comparability and relevance of the information.
- ▶ Evaluate whether the expectation is sufficiently precise to identify a misstatement that may cause the financial statements to be materially misstated.
- ▶ Determine the amount of any difference of recorded amounts from expected values that is acceptable without further investigation.

▶ DISADVANTAGES OF ANALYTICAL PROCEDURES

Substantive analytical procedures have some disadvantages. They may be more time-consuming initially to design and might be less effective than performing tests of details of balances. Obtaining data used to develop an expectation and ensuring the reliability of that data at a disaggregated level can take a substantial amount of the time otherwise spent performing tests of details. Analytical procedures may be less effective when applied to the financial statements as a whole than when applied to financial information on individual sections of an operation or to financial statements of components of the company.

Substantive analytical procedures will not necessarily deliver the desired results every year. In periods of instability and rapid change, it may be difficult to develop a sufficiently precise expectation of the recorded amount, and it may be more appropriate to apply tests of details. For example, if an economy reaches hyperinflation, it is unlikely that we will be able to develop meaningful expectations efficiently, except in limited circumstances.

▶ CORROBORATION

When analytical procedures serve as substantive tests, the auditor should back up explanations for significant differences by obtaining sufficient audit evidence. For example, re-calculation of invoice extensions (quantity multiplied by price) may be corroborated by interviewing a salesperson about how invoices are filled out. This evidence needs to be of the same quality as the evidence the auditor would expect to obtain to support tests of details.

To corroborate an explanation, one or more of the following techniques may be used:

▶ inquiries of persons outside the client's organization including bankers, suppliers, customers, etc.;

▶ inquiries of independent persons inside the client's organization (e.g., an explanation received from the Chief Financial Officer for an increase in advertising expenditures might be corroborated with the marketing director. It is normally inappropriate to corroborate explanations only by discussion with other accounting department personnel);

▶ evidence obtained from other auditing procedures;

▶ examination of supporting evidence. The auditor may examine supporting documentary evidence of transactions to corroborate explanations. For example, if an increase in the cost of sales in one month was attributed to an unusually large sales contract, the auditor might examine supporting documentation, such as the sales contract and delivery documents such as bills of lading.

▶ SUBSTANTIVE ANALYTICAL PROCEDURES EXAMPLES

Fraudulent payments are often in large amounts. An analytical procedure to detect this is the use of computer-aided audit technology (CAAT) (like a spreadsheet or IDEA program) to stratify the payments by size and then extract all large payments. The auditor may sort the records by type of purchase, since the size of expenditure is related to the typical cost of the product or service.

By analyzing revenue over at least three years, the auditor can detect unexpected trends in revenues. Sales can also be analyzed by type, activity, salesperson, month, or customer. The sales data can be stratified to determine if sales in a certain area or by a certain salesperson are made up of a few large or unusual transactions.

Benford's Law calculations may be done by a CAAT. Benford's Law determines the expected frequency for each digit in any position in a set of random numbers. This means that the chances of any number appearing in a given database are mathematically predictable. Since the expected frequency for each number in the set is known, every number that appears in the database in excess of the expected frequency requires further investigation. For instance, payment amounts authorized by a manager may be consistently just below the maximum allowed for that manager.

▶ PAYROLL

If the auditor suspects fraud in the payroll area, she may do a number of substantive tests to detect a 'ghost employee', an employee who still 'works for the company' even though her employment has been terminated, or excessive overtime charges. Three types of analytical tests can be performed to help detect these kinds of irregularities: duplicate and validity tests, exception testing and recalculations.

Duplicate and validity tests are used to detect a ghost or a terminated employee. A computer assisted audit program can help the auditor check for duplicate social security numbers, names, or, if direct deposit is used, bank account numbers. To find ghost employees, an auditor can also identify employees who take no sick or annual leave, or those who do not have insurance or other deductions taken out of their pay. Additionally, a computer audit technology program can verify that each employee's salary or wage is within the ranges for his or her job description and that tax withholding amounts are reasonable.

FOLLOW-UP IN CASE OF UNEXPECTED DEVIATIONS

When analytical procedures identify significant fluctuations or relationships that are inconsistent with other relevant information or that deviate from predicted amounts, the auditor should investigate and obtain adequate explanations and appropriate corroborative evidence[19]. A comparison of actual results with expected should include considering why there is a difference.

There are primarily two reasons for a significant fluctuation or inconsistency. One is that there is a genuine business reason that was not obvious during planning procedures. The second reason is that there is a misstatement. Work must be done to determine which reason applies.

The investigation of unusual fluctuations and relationships ordinarily begins with management inquiries, followed by corroboration of management responses and determination if additional audit procedures are needed. Management's responses may be backed up by comparing them with the auditor's knowledge of the business and other evidence obtained during the audit.

If a reasonable explanation cannot be obtained, the auditor adds together misstatements that the entity has not corrected. The auditor would then consider whether these aggregated uncorrected items materially misstate the financial statements. If management cannot provide a satisfactory explanation and material misstatement may be possible, other audit procedures should be undertaken.

Upon finding unexpected deviations that exceed the threshold, there may be a need to do some root cause analysis. That root cause analysis may be a reassessment of the effectiveness of controls. If the auditor detects deviations from controls upon which she intends to rely, she must make specific inquiries to understand these matters and their potential consequences. Furthermore, she must determine whether:[20]

- ▷ the tests of controls show an appropriate basis for reliance on the controls;
- ▷ additional tests of controls are necessary; or
- ▷ the potential risks of misstatement need to be addressed using substantive procedures.

ANALYTICAL REVIEW: AN EXAMPLE

Jon Treste, MS, CPA is an audit manager for Isle & Oblivion (I&O). His primary job on the audit is analytical review. Tangent is a long-time client of I&O and Treste is on their audit this year.

Analytical procedures entail the use of comparisons and relationships to determine whether account balances or other data appear reasonable. Identified fluctuations or relationships that are inconsistent or unusual or that differ from expected values by a significant amount require audit consideration. General analytical procedures include trend analysis, ratio analysis, statistical and data mining analysis, and reasonableness tests. Jon Treste starts his analytic analysis by calculating common sized, solvency, turnover and profitability ratios and trends for Tangent's last three years financial statements. See Exhibit A.

EXHIBIT A

Tangent Financials

Exhibit A

Numbers in 1,000	2031	2030	2029
Sales	$68,466	$65,786	$63,435
Credit Card Rev.	$1,399	$1,604	$1,922
Total Revenue	$69,865	$67,390	$65,357
Cost of Sales	$47,860	$45,725	$44,062
Sales, General and Administrative (SG&A) expense	$14,106	$13,469	$13,078
Credit Card Expenses	$446	$860	$1,521
Depreciation & Amort.	$2,131	$2,084	$2,023
EBIT	$5,322	$5,252	$4,673
Nonrecourse Debt Collateralized by Credit Card Receivables	$72	$83	$97
Other Interest Expense	$797	$677	$707
Interest Income	-$3	-$3	-$3
Net Interest Expense	$866	$757	$801
Earnings before Income Taxes	$4,456	$4,495	$3,872
Provision for Income Taxes	$1,527	$1,575	$1,384
Net Earnings	$2,929	$2,920	$2,488
Assets			
Cash & Cash Equiv.	$794	$1,712	$2,200
A/R, Net	$5,927	$6,153	$6,966
Inventory	$7,918	$7,596	$7,179
Other Current	$1,810	$1,752	$2,079
Total Current Assets	$16,449	$17,213	$18,424
PPE			
Land	$6,122	$5,928	$5,793
Buildings	$26,837	$23,081	$22,152
Fixtures and Equipment	$5,141	$4,939	$4,743

Computer Hardware	$2,468	$2,533	$2,575
Construction in Progress	$963	$567	$502
Amortization & Depreciation	-$12,382	-$11,555	-$10,485
Property Plant and Equipment, Net	$29,149	$25,493	$25,280
Other Assets	$1,032	$999	$829
Total Assets	$46,630	$43,705	$44,533
Liabilities and Equity			
Accounts Payable	$6,857	$6,625	$6,511
Accrued Liabilities	$3,644	$3,326	$3,120
Income Taxes Payable	$3,036	$119	$796
Current Portion of Long Term Debt	$750	$0	$900
Total Current Liabilities	$14,287	$10,070	$11,327
Unsecured Debt and Other Borrowings	$13,447	$11,653	$10,643
Nonrecourse Debt Collateralized by Credit Card Receivables	$250	$3,954	$4,475
Deferred Income Taxes	$1,191	$934	$835
Other Noncurrent Liabilities	$1,634	$1,607	$1,906
Total Noncurrent Liabilities	$16,522	$18,148	$17,859
Shareholders' Investment			
Common Stock	$56	$59	$62
Additional Paid in Capital	$3,487	$3,311	$2,919
Retained Earnings	$12,959	$12,698	$12,947
Accumulated Other Comprehensive Loss	-$681	-$581	-$581
Total Shareholders' Investment	$15,821	$15,487	$15,347
Total Liabilities & Shareholders' Investment	$46,630	$43,705	$44,533

Jon calculates the ratios shown in Exhibit B.

EXHIBIT B

Client and industry standard ratios	Calculation

Liquidity:

(1) Current ratio	(1) Current assets/Current liabilities
(2) Quick ratio	(2) (Cash + short-term securities + accounts receivable)/Current liabilities
(3) Working capital	(3) Total current assets – Total current liabilities

Solvency:

(1) Debt to equity	(1) Long-term debt/Stockholders' equity
(2) Times interest earned	(2) (Net income before interest and taxes)/Interest expense
(3) Debt service coverage	(3) (Net income before interest and depreciation)/Principal and interest payments
(4) Debt to assets	(4) (Total Liabilities & shareholders' investment – Total shareholders' investment)/Total assets

Profitability:

(1) Net profit margin	(1) Net profit/Revenue
(2) Gross margin percent	(2) (revenue less cost of goods sold)/Revenue
(3) Return on investment	(3) Net income/Stockholders' equity
(4) Return on assets	(4) Net earnings / ((Total assets current year + Total assets last year)/2)

Activity:

(1) Receivable turnover	(1) Revenue/Average accounts receivable
(2) Inventory turnover	(2) Cost of goods sold/Average inventory
(3) Asset turnover	(3) Revenue/Total assets
(4) Days in inventory	(4) 365/(Inventory turnover ratio)
(5) Days in receivables	(5) 365/(AR turnover ratio)
(6) Accounts payable turn.	(6) (Cost of sales – Inventory last year + Inventory this year)/((Acct payable this year + Acct payable net last year)/2)
(7) Days in payables	(7) 365/Acct payable turnover ratio
(8) Operating cycle	(8) (Days in inventory) + (Days in receivables) – (Days in payables)

These ratios answer certain questions crucial to the audit.

▶ Is there a possible going concern problem (liquidity ratios)?

▶ Is the entity's capital structure sustainable (solvency ratios)?

▶ Is gross margin reasonable (profitability)?

▶ How efficiently is the company using its resources (activity)?

Exhibit C is the result of Treste's calculations of these key **liquidity** ratios for the Tangent audit.

EXHIBIT C		
LIQUIDITY RATIOS		
	2031	**2030**
Current ratio	1.1513	1.7100
Quick ratio	0.4704	0.7800
Quick ratio (incl. other)	0.59711626	0.955014896
Working capital	$2,162	$7,143

Treste's analysis of liquidity ratios indicates that the current ratio, quick ratio and working capital all seem to be weakening from the previous year. Current assets, specifically cash, are the issue. Cash has decreased by 54% from the prior year, whereas other current assets have remained about the same. Treste would like to know what caused this cash decline.

Exhibit D is the result of Treste's calculations of these key **solvency** ratios for the Tangent audit. (Debt service coverage is also used, but we do not calculate it here.)

EXHIBIT D		
SOLVENCY RATIOS		
	2031	**2030**
Debt/Equity	1.95	1.82
Times interest earned	6.15	6.94
Debt/Assets	66.07%	64.56%

Debt and liabilities are increasing. Current liabilities, especially income taxes payable, have increased (income tax 2,450 % increase), Total non-current liabilities have decreased about 9%. Profits do not cover interest in the same multiples as in the prior year, but profit and net earnings are about the same as the prior year. Treste would like to know why income tax has increased so much.

Exhibit E is the result of Treste's calculations of these key **profitability** ratios for the Tangent audit.

PROFITABILITY RATIOS

	2031	2030
Profit margin	4.19%	4.33%
Gross margin %	31.50%	32.15%
Return on investment	18.71%	18.94%
Return on assets	6.48%	6.62%

Net Earnings have decreased only 3% from the prior year. Three components of net profit – cost of sales, SG&A (Sales, general and administrative expense), and depreciation/amortization have increased slightly, but there is a 48% drop in credit card expense. Treste would like to know what is going on with that. The Cost of Sales is almost the same as the previous year. Return on assets and investment is about the same.

Exhibit F is the result of Treste's calculations of these key **activity** ratios for the Tangent audit.

EXHIBIT F

ACTIVITY RATIOS

	2031	2030
A/R turnover	11.57	10.27
Inventory turnover	6.17	6.19
Asset turnover	1.55	1.53
Days in inventory	59.16	58.97
Days in receivables	31.56	35.53
Accounts payable turnover	7.147604213	7.025274056
Days in payables	51.07	51.96
Operating cycle	39.65	42.54

Looking at activity ratios, Jon Treste notices Tangent's accounts receivable turnover is strengthening from last year. Accounts receivable turnover is how many times a year Tangent collects its accounts receivable – the more the better. Days in receivables show they are collecting receivables in about 30 days. The inventory turnover number represents how many times a year they "turn over" their inventory, which is about the same as the prior year. Days in inventory show how many days, on average, Tangent holds inventory until it is sold – less is better. Asset turnover looks like last year. Days in payables is an indicator of the average number of days they hold off until they pay an account payable. The longer one holds accounts payable before payment, the better the cash flow, especially if they have short days in receivables. But other things such as vendor terms and satisfaction with Tangent must be considered. Operating cycle is the average number of days from payment of payable to collection of receivables. The operating cycle is being reduced, which is good.

9.9 SUMMARY

Analytical procedures are used: (a) to assist the auditor in planning the nature, timing and extent of audit procedures; (b) as substantive procedures; and (c) as an overall review of the financial statements in the final stage of the audit. The auditor must apply analytical procedures at the audit's overall review stages. Further, when assessing risk in the planning stage, the auditor must include analytic procedures.

Analytical procedures performed in the planning stage (Phase II in the Audit Process Model) are used to identify unusual changes in the financial statements, or the absence of expected changes, and specific risks. During the planning phase, analytical procedures are usually focused on account balances at the financial statement level and relationships.

During the substantive testing stage (Phase III of the Audit Process Model addressed in this chapter) analytical procedures are performed to obtain assurance that financial statement account balances do not contain material misstatements.

Analytical procedures performed during the overall review (wrap-up) stage (Phase IV of the Audit Process Model) are designed to assist the auditor in assessing that all significant fluctuations and other unusual items have been adequately explained and that the overall financial statement presentation makes sense based on the audit results and an understanding of the business.

An important consideration in applying analytical procedures is tests of controls over the preparation of information used for analytics. When those controls are effective, the auditor will have more confidence in the reliability of the information and, therefore, in the results of analytical procedures. For non-significant risks, the auditor can perform control tests added with substantive analytics. For significant risks, she cannot stop but needs to add tests of details.

Analytical procedures are evaluations of financial information through analysis of plausible relationships among both financial and non-financial data. Analytical procedures also encompass investigation of identified fluctuations or relationships that are inconsistent or unusual or that differ from expected values by a significant amount. Put another way, analytical procedures entail the use of comparisons and relationships to determine whether account balances or other data appear reasonable.

General analytical procedures include trend analysis, ratio analysis, statistical and data mining analysis, and reasonableness tests. Trend analysis is the analysis of changes in an account balance over time. Ratio analysis is the comparison of relationships between financial statement accounts, the comparison of an account with non-financial data, or the comparison of relationships between firms in an industry. Reasonableness testing is the analysis of account balances or changes in account balances within an accounting period in terms of their 'reasonableness' in light of expected relationships between accounts. Data mining is a set of computer-assisted techniques that use sophisticated statistical analysis, including artificial intelligence techniques, to examine large volumes of data with the objective of indicating hidden or unexpected information or patterns.

The process of planning, executing and drawing conclusions from analytical procedures is called analytical review. The four-phase process consists of the following:

1 phase one is to formulate expectations (expectations);
2 phase two is the comparison of the expected value to the recorded amount (identification);
3 phase three requires investigation of possible explanations for a difference between expected and recorded values (investigation);
4 phase four involves evaluation of the impact on the audit and the financial statements of the differences between expectation and recorded amounts (evaluation).

All phases of the analytical review process are important. In phase one the auditor develops expectations of what amounts should appear in financial statement account balances based on prior year financial statements, budgets, industry information and non-financial information. Phase two (identification) is when the auditor compares her expected value with the recorded amount. In phase three (investigation), the auditor investigates possible explanations for the expected/recorded amount difference. The final phase (phase four – evaluation) involves evaluating the impact on the financial statements of the difference between the auditor's expected value and the recorded amount.

Expectations are developed by identifying plausible relationships that are reasonably expected to exist based on the auditor's understanding of the client and of his industry. ISA 520 states that the auditor should 'evaluate the reliability of data from which the auditor's expectation of recorded amounts or ratios is developed, taking account of source, comparability, and nature and relevance of information available, and controls over preparation'.

Determining which type of analytical procedure is appropriate is a matter of professional judgment. A review of audit practice indicates that simple judgmental approaches (such as comparison and ratio analysis) are used more frequently than complex statistical approaches (such as time series modelling or regression analysis. These tests are generally carried out using computer software.

At the planning stage of an audit, there are certain customary ratios that are always calculated to determine accounts that may represent significant risks to the entity of liquidity, solvency, profitability, and activity. These ratios help to answer some key questions: Is there a possible going concern problem (liquidity ratios)? Is the entity's capital structure sustainable (solvency ratios)? Is gross margin reasonable (profitability)? Could inventory be overstated (activity)?

Auditors must determine the possibility that the company is having liquidity problems – that is, is there a possibility that the company may no longer be a *going concern*? ISA 570 states that under the going concern assumption, it is assumed that an entity is continuing in business for the foreseeable future.

Substantive procedures in the audit are designed to reduce detection risk relating to specific financial statement assertions. Substantive tests include tests of details and analytical procedures. Auditors use analytical procedures to identify situations that require increased use of other procedures (i.e., tests of control, substantive audit procedures), but seldom to reduce audit effort.

There are a number of advantages of performing substantive analytical procedures instead of tests of details. They may be more time-consuming initially to design and might be less effective than performing tests of details of balances. Obtaining data used to develop an expectation and ensuring the reliability of that data at a disaggregated level can take a substantial amount of the time otherwise spent performing tests of details. Analytical procedures may be less effective when applied to the financial statements as a whole than when applied to financial information on individual sections of an operation or to financial statements of components of the company.

When analytical procedures identify significant fluctuations or relationships that are inconsistent with other relevant information or that deviate from predicted amounts, the auditor should investigate and obtain adequate explanations and appropriate corroborative evidence. A comparison of actual results with expected should include a consideration of why there is a difference. There are primarily two reasons for a significant fluctuation or inconsistency. One is that there is a genuine business reason that was not obvious during planning procedures. The second reason is that there is a misstatement. Work must be done to determine which reason applies.

9.10 QUESTIONS, EXERCISES AND CASES

QUESTIONS

9.2 Analytical Procedures During Different Phases in the Audit Process

9-1 When should the auditor use analytical procedures? What ISA standard states when they should be used?

9-2 Describe why tests of controls over information used for analytics is important.

9.3 The Analytical Review Process

9-3 Define analytical procedures and give the basic premise for using them.

9-4 Describe the four-step theoretical approach and the four-phase process for analytical review

9.4 Formulating Expectations

9-5 On what sources does an auditor base her expectations? Give examples of how the auditor may use each source.

9-6 Give an example of the nature of an account. Give an example of other characteristics of the data.

9.5 General Types of Analytical Procedures

9-7 What are the five types of ratio analysis used in analytical procedures? Briefly discuss each.

9-8 In assessing going concern, list three financial indicators, three operating indicators and three other indicators.

9.6 Analytical Procedures as Substantive Tests

9-9 Analytical procedure as substantive tests need corroboration of an explanation. What techniques may be used?

9-10 What are some examples of substantive analytical procedures?

9.7 Follow-Up in Case of Unexpected Deviations

9-11 What should an auditor do if she finds significant fluctuations when performing analytical procedures?

9-12 What should an auditor do if they discover unexpected deviations that exceed the threshold set for deviations?

PROBLEMS AND EXERCISES

9.2 Analytical Procedures During Different Phases in the Audit Process

9-13 **Analytical procedures.** Analytical procedures are typically done during the planning phase.

Required:

A.   Define analytical procedures.

B.   Other than during planning, when does an auditor do analytical procedures?

C.   Name five ratios that an auditor could use to do analytical review and briefly describe each.

9.3 The Analytical Review Process

9-14 **Four-Phase Analytical Review Process.** Based on Concept and a Company 9.2 – 'Peregrine Systems – the 37th of December' (see case end of these exercises) discuss what you would imagine each phase of the four-phase analytical review process would involve.

9.4 Formulating Expectations

9-15 **Expectation Sources.** Based on the comparison of a recent year's results from Wal-Mart, Costco, Target and the retail industry, what would your expectations be about Target's revenue growth, gross margin, operating margins and number of employees this year?

	WMT	COST	TGT	Industry
Market Cap	248.07B	17.55B	36.03B	932.18M
Employees	1,400,000	61,800	306,000	10.30K
Rev. Growth	12.20%	9.80%	10.10%	4.50%
Revenue	255.08B	43.87B	46.65B	2.04B
Gross Margin	22.20%	12.45%	31.70%	27.80%
EBITDA	18.50B	1.58B	4.62B	115.53M
Operating Margins	5.35%	2.68%	5.86%	2.16%
Net Income	8.67B	735.45M	1.70B	31.56M
Earnings Per Share	1.972	1.557	1.853	0.82
Price/Earnings Ratio	29.07	24.61	21.33	24.25

Abbreviations:

WMT = Wal-Mart Corp.

COST = Costco Wholesale Corp

TGT = Target Corp

Industry = Supermarkets, Drugstores and Mass Merchandisers

9.5 **General Analytical Procedures**

9-16 Analytical Procedures. At the beginning of the annual audit of Porster, BV, wholesale distributor of Valkenburg, the Netherlands, Lynna Heijn, Registeraccountant, was given a copy of Porster's financial statements as prepared by the company's controller. On reviewing these statements, Heijn noted the following abnormal conditions:

▷ The accounts receivable outstanding at the year-end represent an unusually high number of average days' credit sales.

▷ The inventories on hand at the year-end represent an unusually high proportion of the current assets.

▷ The working capital ratio of the company is almost twice that of the previous year.

▷ The percentage of gross profit on net sales is considerably in excess of that of previous years.

▷ The rate of turnover of inventory is unusually low in comparison with previous years.

Required:

Taking all the above conditions together, what irregularities might Heijn suspect regarding sales and inventories?

9-17 Ratio and Trend Analysis. When an auditor discovers a significant change in a ratio when compared with the prior year's ratio, the auditor considers the possible reasons for the change.

Required:

Give the possible reasons for the following significant changes in ratios:

A. The rate of inventory turnover (ratio of cost of sales to average industry) has decreased from the prior year's rate.

B. The number of days' sales in receivables (ratio of average of daily accounts receivable to sales) has increased over the prior year.

9.6 **Analytical Procedures as Substantive Tests**

9-18 Analytical Procedures. Analytical procedures are extremely useful in the initial audit planning stage.

Required:

A. Explain why analytical procedures are considered substantive tests.

B. Explain how analytical procedures are useful in the initial audit planning stage.

C. Should analytical procedures be applied at any other stages of the audit process? Explain.

D. List several types of comparisons an auditor might make in performing analytical procedures.

9.7 **Follow-Up of Unexpected Deviations**

9-19 Extent of Reliance on Analytical Procedures. The extent of reliance that the auditor places on the results of analytical procedures depends on the materiality of the items involved, other audit procedures performed by the auditor, the accuracy with which expected results can be predicted, and the assessments of inherent and control risks.

Required:

A. Give two examples of circumstances in which the auditor can rely on analytical procedures and two circumstances when reliance on analytical procedures would not be advisable.

B. Explain the relationship between company controls and reliance on analytical procedures.

9-20 Using the references in endnotes to this chapter as a beginning place and accessing journal databases such as ABI Inform, discuss the theoretical view that the review process consists of four diagnostic processes: (1) mental representation, (2) hypothesis generation, (3) information search, and (4) hypothesis evaluation.

9-21 Answer the questions at the end of Concept and a Company 9.1 'Crazy Eddie – His Prices are Insane!'

CONCEPT AND A COMPANY 9.1

'CRAZY EDDIE – HIS PRICES ARE INSANE!'

Concept	Analytical procedures to test inventory.

Story

In 1969, Eddie Antar, a 21-year-old high school dropout from Brooklyn, opened a consumer electronics store with 15 square metres of floor space in New York City. By 1987, Antar's firm, Crazy Eddie, Inc., had 43 retail outlets, sales exceeding $350 million, and outstanding common shares with a collective market value of $600 million.

Shortly after a hostile takeover of the company in November 1987, the firm's new owners discovered that Crazy Eddie's inventory was overstated by more than $65 million. Subsequent investigations by regulatory authorities would demonstrate that Crazy Eddie's profits had been intentionally overstated by Eddie Antar and several subordinates (Belsky and Furman, 1989).

Crazy Like a Fox

Antar acquired the nickname 'Crazy Eddie' because of his unique sales tactic. Whenever a customer would attempt to leave his store without purchasing something, Eddie would block the store's exit, sometimes locking the door until the individual agreed to buy something – anything. To entice a reluctant customer to make a purchase, Antar would lower the price until the customer finally gave in. From 1972, Doctor Jerry was the spokesperson for Crazy Eddie. He made a series of ear-piercing television commercials that featured him screaming 'Crazy Eddie – His prices are insane!' The company promised to refund the difference between the selling price of a product and any lower price for that same item that a customer found within 30 days of the purchase date (Knapp, 2001).

Inventory Overstated

Trouble was that in late 1986 the boom days had ended for the consumer electronics industry. To continue the growth of the company and keep the stock price up, Antar had to do something. Within the first six months after the company went public, Antar ordered a subordinate to overstate inventory by $2 million, resulting in the firm's gross profit being overstated by the same amount. The following year Antar ordered year-end inventory to be overstated by $9 million and accounts payable to be understated by $3 million (Belsky and Furman, 1989). Crazy Eddie employees overstated year-end inventory by preparing inventory count sheets for items that did not exist. To overstate accounts payable, bogus debit memos were prepared and entered in the company's accounting records.

The Audits

Crazy Eddie's auditor was Main Hurdman (later merged with Peat Marwick – now KPMG). Their audits were generally made difficult by management and employee collusion. There were several reported instances in which the auditors requested client documents, only to be told that those documents had been lost or inadvertently destroyed. Upon discovering which sites the auditors would be visiting to perform year-end inventory procedures, Antar would ship sufficient inventory to those stores or warehouses to conceal any shortages. Furthermore, personnel systematically destroyed incriminating documents to conceal inventory shortages from the auditors (Weiss, 1993).

Main Hurdman has been criticised for charging only $85,000 for a complete SEC audit, but millions to install a computerised inventory system. This is even more interesting because Antar ordered his employees to stop using the sophisticated, computer-based inventory system designed by Main Hurdman. Instead, the accounting personnel were required to return to a manual inventory system previously used by the company. The absence of a computer-based inventory system made it much more difficult for the auditors to determine exactly how much inventory the firm had at any point in time (Weiss, 1993).

Crazy Eddie Comparative Income Statements 1984–87

	31 March 87	31 March 86	31 March 85	31 March 84
Net sales	$352,523	$262,268	$136,319	$137,285
Cost of goods sold	−0272,255	−194,371	−103,421	−106,934
Gross profit	80,268	67,897	32,898	30,351
Selling, G&A expense	−61,341	−42,975	−20,508	−22,650
Interest and other income	7,403	3,210	1,211	706
Interest expense	−5,233	−820	−438	−522
Income before taxes	$21,097	$27,312	$13,163	$7,975
Pension contribution	−500	−800	−600	−4,202
Income taxes	−10,001	−13,268	−6,734	
Net income	$10,596	$13,244	$5,829	$3,773
Net income per share	$0.34	$0.48	$0.24	$0.18

Crazy Eddie Comparative Balance Sheets 1984–87

	31 March 87	31 March 86	31 March 85	31 March 84
Current assets				
Cash	$9,347	$13,296	$22,273	$1,375
Short-term investments	121,957	26,840	2,740	2,604
Receivables	10,846	2,246	26,543	23,343
Merchandise inventories	109,072	59,864	645	514
Prepaid expenses	10,639	2,363		
Total current assets	261,861	104,609	52,201	27,836
Restricted cash	26,401	3,356	7,058	5,739
Due from affiliates	6,596	7,172	3,696	1,845
Property, plant and equipment		6,253	1,154	1,149
Construction in process		5,560	1,419	
Other assets				
Total assets	$294,858	$126,950	$65,528	$36,569

Current liabilities				
Accounts payable	$50,022	$51,723	$23,078	$20,106
Notes payable				2,900
Short-term debt	49,571	2,254	423	124
Unearned revenue	3,641	3,696	1,173	764
Accrued expenses	5,593	17,126	8,733	6,078
Total current liabilities	108,827	74,799	33,407	29,972
Long-term debt	8,459	7,701	7,625	46
Convertible subordinated debentures				
Unearned revenue	80,975			
Stockholders' equity	3,337	1,829	635	327
Common stock	313	280	134	50
Additional paid-in capital	57,678	17,668	12,298	574
Retained earnings	35,269	24,673	11,429	5,600
Total stockholders' equity				
Total liabilities and	93,260	42,621	23,861	6,224
stockholders' equity	$294,858	$126,950	$65,528	$36,569

Discussion Questions

Review the Crazy Eddie comparative financial statements and discuss:

▷ What analytical procedures can be performed to determine if inventory is misstated?

▷ What indicators other than financial hinted that there might be problems?

References

Belsky, G. and Furman, P., 1989, 'Calculated Madness: The Rise and Fall of Crazy Eddie Antar', *Cram's New York Business*, 5 June, pp. 21–33.

Knapp, M., 2001, 'Crazy Eddie, Inc.', *Contemporary Auditing Real Issues and Cases*, South Western College Publishing, Cincinnati, Ohio, pp. 71–82.

Weiss, M.I., 1993, 'Auditors: Be Watchdogs, Not Just Bean Counters', *Accounting Today*, 15 November, p. 41.

9-22 Answer the questions at the end of Concept and a Company 9.2 'Peregrine Systems – The 37th of December'.

CONCEPT AND A COMPANY 9.2

PEREGRINE SYSTEMS – THE 37TH OF DECEMBER

Concept

Analytical procedures for revenue tests.

Story

The accounting irregularities that brought down Peregrine Systems, a San Diego, California, maker of software that large companies use to manage their technology resources, included inflated revenues of more than 60 per cent or some $509 million.

Peregrine had reported revenues of $1.34 billion for 2000 and 2001. Of that, $225 million was based on 'non-substantiated transactions' as the company booked revenues when it transferred goods to a software reseller, even when there were no firm commitments in place. Another $70 million of the fictitious revenue was from swap transactions and $100 million came from the premature booking of revenues from long-term instalment contracts. Peregrine had reported another $80 million of revenues that, for a variety of reasons, should not have been recorded until future years and that $34 million of revenues had been based on 'erroneous calculations or unsupported transactions' (Waters, 2003).

An SEC complaint, settled by Peregrine, alleged that the company improperly booked millions of dollars of revenue for purported software licence sales to resellers. These transactions were non-binding sales of Peregrine software with the understanding – reflected in secret side agreements – that the resellers were not obligated to pay Peregrine. Those involved in the scheme called this 'parking' the transaction. Peregrine personnel parked transactions when Peregrine was unable to complete direct sales it was negotiating (or hoping to negotiate) with end-users, but needed revenue to achieve its forecasts (SEC, 2003a).

Peregrine engaged in other deceptive practices to inflate the company's revenue, including entering into reciprocal transactions in which Peregrine essentially paid for its customers' purchases of Peregrine software. Peregrine routinely kept its books open after fiscal quarters ended, and improperly recorded as revenue, for the prior quarter, software transactions that were not consummated until after quarter end. Certain Peregrine officers characterised these transactions as having been completed on 'the 37th of December' (SEC, 2003a).

To conceal the revenue recognition scheme, Peregrine abused the receivable financing process. When Peregrine booked the non-binding contracts, and the customers predictably did not pay, the receivables ballooned on Peregrine's balance sheet. To make it appear that Peregrine was collecting its receivables more quickly than it was, Peregrine 'sold' receivables to banks and then removed them from the company's balance sheet. There were several problems with this. First, Peregrine had given the banks recourse and frequently paid or repurchased unpaid receivables from them. Peregrine should have accounted for the bank transactions as loans and left the receivables on its balance sheet. Secondly, the sold receivables were not valid because the customers were not obligated to pay. Thirdly, several of the sold invoices were fake, including one that purported to reflect a $19.58 million sale (SEC, 2003b).

The SEC complaint also alleged that, as part of the cover up, Peregrine personnel wrote off millions of dollars in uncollectible – primarily sham – receivables, to acquisition-related accounts in Peregrine's financial statements and books and records. These write-offs were improper because they had nothing to do with acquisitions (SEC, 2003a).

Chief Executive Officer Mathew C. Gless, it was alleged in an SEC civil suit, signed false SEC filings and false management representation letters to Peregrine's outside auditors, and responded falsely to an SEC Division of Corporation Finance Comment Letter that inquired about Peregrine's revenue recognition practice. According to the complaint, while Gless was aware of the ongoing fraud, he illegally sold 68,625 shares of Peregrine stock for approximately $4 million, based on material non-public information he possessed about Peregrine's true financial condition (SEC, 2003b).

Peregrine Comparative Balance Sheet 2000–2001 (in 000)

	31 March 01	*31 March 00*
ASSETS		
Cash and cash equivalents	$286,658	$33,511
Accounts receivable, net of allowance for doubtful accounts of $11,511 and $2,179, respectively	180,372	69,940
Other current assets	62,811	22,826
Total current assets	529,841	126,277
Property and equipment, net	82,717	29,537
Goodwill, net of accumulated amortisation of $334,178 and $54,406, respectively	1,192,855	233,504
Other intangible assets, investments and other, net of accumulated amortisation of $24,015 and $1,398, respectively	198,353	134,112

	31 March 01	31 March 00
	$2,003,766	$523,430
LIABILITIES AND STOCKHOLDERS' EQUITY		
Current liabilities:		
Accounts payable	$36,024	$19,850
Accrued expenses	200,886	49,064
Current portion of deferred revenue	86,653	36,779
Current portion of long-term debt	1,731	74
Total current liabilities	325,294	105,767
Deferred revenue, net of current portion	8,299	
Other long-term liabilities	17,197	4,556
Long-term debt, net of current portion	884	1,257
Convertible subordinated notes	262,327	
Total liabilities	614,001	111,580
Stockholders' equity:		
Preferred stock, $0.001 par value, 5,000 shares authorised, no shares issued or outstanding		
Common stock, $0.001 par value, 500,000 shares authorised, 160,359 and 109,501 shares issued and outstanding, respectively	160	110
Additional paid-in capital	2,342,235	480,957
Accumulated deficit	−917,104	−64,863
Unearned portion of deferred compensation	−22,151	−678
Cumulative translation adjustment	−3,950	−666
Treasury stock, at cost	−9,425	−3,010
Total stockholders' equity	1,389,765	411,850

Peregrine Systems Comparative Income Statement 1999–2001 (in 000)

Revenues:	31 March 01	31 March 00	31 March 99
Licences	$354,610	$168,467	$87,362
Services	210,073	84,833	50,701
Total revenues	564,683	253,300	138,063
Costs and expenses:			
Cost of licences	2,582	1,426	1,020
Cost of services	111,165	51,441	31,561
Amortisation of purchased technology	11,844	1,338	50
Sales and marketing	223,966	101,443	50,803
Research and development	61,957	28,517	13,919
General and administrative	48,420	19,871	10,482
Acquisition costs and other	918,156	57,920	43,967
Total costs and expenses	1,378,090	261,956	151,802
Loss from operations before interest (net) and income tax expense	−8,13,407	−8,656	−13,739
Interest income (expense), net	−538	38	664
Loss from operations before income tax expense	−813,945	−8,618	−13,075
Income tax expense	−38,296	−16,452	−10,295
Net loss	−$852,241	−$25,070	−$23,370
Net loss per share basic and diluted:			
Net loss per share	−$6.16	−$0.24	−$0.27
Shares used in computation	138,447	102,332	87,166

Source: US Securities and Exchange Commission, www.sec.gov.

Discussion Question	Review the Peregrine financial statements and determine what analytical procedures could be used to predict the revenue recognition fraud. Are there other indicators that a revenue recognition fraud was under way?
References	SEC, 2003a, Litigation Release No. 18205A, Accounting and Auditing Enforcement Release No. 1808A, 'SEC Charges Peregrine Systems, Inc. with Financial Fraud and Agrees to Partial Settlement', US Securities and Exchange Commission, 30 June. SEC, 2003b, Litigation Release No. 18093, Accounting and Auditing Enforcement Release No. 1759, 'SEC Charges Former Peregrine CFO with Financial Fraud', US Securities and Exchange Commission, 16 April. Waters, R., 2003, 'Irregularities at Peregrine Lifted Revenues 60 Per Cent', *Financial Times*, 3 March, p. 19.

9.11 NOTES

1. International Auditing and Assurance Standards Board (IAASB), 2023, International Standard on Auditing 520 (ISA 520) 'Analytical Procedures', para. 3, *Handbook of International Quality Management, Auditing, Review, Other Assurance, and Related Services Pronouncements*, 2022 edn, Volume I, International Federation of Accountants, New York.
2. See, for example, Booth, P. and Simnett, R. (1991), 'Auditors' Perception of Analytical Review Procedures', *Accounting Research Journal*, Spring, pp. 5–10.
3. International Auditing and Assurance Standards Board (IAASB), 2023, International Standard on Auditing 315 (ISA 315), 'Identifying and Assessing the Risks of Material Misstatement through Understanding the Entity and Its Environment', paragraphs 6 and A14-A17, *Handbook of International Quality Management, Auditing, Review, Other Assurance and Related Services Pronouncements*, 2022 edn, Volume I, International Federation of Accountants, New York.
4. Ibid. ISA 520, para. 3.
5. International Auditing and Assurance Standards Board (IAASB), 2023, International Standards on Auditing 520 (ISA 520) 'Analytical Procedures', para. 4, *Handbook of International Quality Management, Auditing, Review, Other Assurance, and Related Services Pronouncements*, 2022 edn, Volume I, International Federation of Accountants, New York.
6. See Blocher, E. and Cooper, J. (1988), 'A Study of Auditors' Analytical Review Performance', *Auditing: A Journal of Practice and Theory*, Spring, pp. 1–28; and Koonce, L. (1993), 'A Cognitive Characterization of Audit Analytical Review', *Auditing: A Journal of Practice and Theory*, 12 (Supplement), pp. 57–76.
7. Asare, S. and Wright, A. (1997), 'Hypothesis Revision Strategies in Conducting Analytical Procedures', *Accounting, Organizations and Society*, 22, November, pp. 737–55.
8. AICPA, 2017, AICPA Audit Guide to Analytical Procedures, American Institute of Certified Public Accountants, New York.
9. Ibid. ISA 520, para. 5(b).
10. See: (1) Bell, T.B., Marrs, F.O., Solomon, I. and Thomas, H. (1997), *Auditing Organizations Through A Strategic-Systems Lens*, New York, NY: KPMG Peat Marwick LLP; (2) Loebbecke, J.K. and Steinbart, P.J. (1987), 'An Investigation of the Use of Preliminary Analytical Review to Provide Substantive Audit Evidence', *Auditing: A Journal of Practice and Theory*, Spring, pp. 74–89; (3) Wild, J.J. (1987), 'The Prediction Performance of a Structural Model of Accounting Numbers', *Journal of Accounting Research*, 25 (1), pp. 139–60.
11. Ibid. ISA 520, para. 5a.

12. United States Public Company Accounting Oversight Board (PCAOB), 2015, AS 2305, 'Substantive Analytical Procedures', para. 5, Public Company Accounting Oversight Board, https://pcaobus.org/oversight/standards/auditing-standards/details/AS2305

13. Biggs, S.F., Mock, T.J. and Simnett, R. (1999), 'Analytical Procedures: Promise, Problems and Implications for Practice', *Australian Accounting Review*, 9 (1), pp. 42–52.

14. See chapter 13, section 13.2

15. See Standard & Poors, Net Advantage database 2023, McGraw-Hill; Los Angeles; RMA, 2023, Annual Statement Studies: Financial Ratio Benchmarks, Risk Management Association, Philadelphia. https://www.rmahq.org/statementstudies?gmssopc=1

16. International Auditing and Assurance Standards Board (IAASB), 2023, International Standards on Auditing 570 (ISA 570) 'Going Concern', para. 2, *Handbook of International Quality Management, Auditing, Review, Other Assurance, and Related Services Pronouncements*, 2022 edn, Volume I, International Federation of Accountants, New York.

17. Ibid. ISA 570, para. A3.

18. See, for example, Bedard, J. (1989), 'An Archival Investigation of Audit program Planning', *Auditing: A Journal of Practice and Theory*, Fall, pp. 57–71.

19. International Auditing and Assurance Standards Board (IAASB), 2023, International Standard on Auditing 330 (ISA 330) 'The Auditors Responses to Assessed Risks', *Handbook of International Quality Management, Auditing, Review, Other Assurance, and Related Services Pronouncements, 2022 Edn, Volume 1*, International Federation of Accountants, New York.

20. Ibid. ISA 330, para. 17.

CHAPTER 10

EVALUATING AND COMPLETION

The four phases of the audit:

Acceptance/ continuance	Understanding/ risk analysis	Building/executing audit plan	Evaluating/ completion
Phase 1	Phase 2	Phase 3	

10.1 LEARNING OBJECTIVES

After studying this chapter, you should be able to:

1 Reiterate the procedures for the audit completion stage.
2 Understanding specific considerations gathering evidence for selected items.
3 Explain the role of written representations from management.
4 Understand why letters from client legal counsel are necessary and what they contain.
5 Conduct a review for contingent liabilities and commitments.
6 Conduct a review after the balance sheet date for subsequent events and understand what events cause financial statement adjustments.
7 Determine procedures to evaluate going concern issues.
8 Explain the procedures involved in the review of financial statements including disclosures and other information presented with the audited financial statements.
9 Design and perform the wrap-up procedures.

10.2 INTRODUCTION

The audit is not over until the audit report is signed. And even then, it may not be over if facts are discovered after the balance sheet date and before the next report. After the fieldwork is almost complete, a series of procedures are generally carried out to 'complete the audit'. The intent of these procedures is to review the audit work, get certain assurances from the client, uncover any potential problems, check compliance with regulations, and check the consistency of the material that is to be presented to the users of financial statements.

In this text so far, we have followed the standard audit process model through its phases – for client and engagement acceptance/continuance (Phase I), planning through understanding and risk analysis and controls (Phase II), building and execution of the test plan (controls- and substantive procedures) (Phase III). In this chapter, we will discuss evaluation and completion as part 1 of the last phase (IV), while part 2, auditor's reporting, will be discussed in the next chapter.

Some procedures of the evaluation and reporting phase are shown in illustration 10.1.

ILLUSTRATION 10.1

AUDIT PROCESS MODEL – PHASE IV EVALUATION AND COMPLETION

Objective: Complete the audit procedures.

Procedures:

▶ Gathering evidence for selected items.

▶ Written representations.

▶ Perform procedures for discovering contingent liabilities and commitments.

▶ Perform procedures to identify subsequent events.

▶ Perform procedures regarding related party transactions.

▶ Evaluate going concern assumption.

▶ Evaluate misstatements identified during the audit.

▶ Review financial statements and other report material.

▶ Perform wrap-up procedures.

First the auditors must consider gathering evidence for selected items such as inventory, litigation and claims and segment information[1]. Also, the auditors must review financial statements and financial statement disclosures, as well as other information contained in the annual report. Other information that needs to be investigated is the board of directors' report, corporate governance disclosures (where applicable) and all other information in the annual report to shareholders.

Other activities as part of the evaluation and completion phase are wrap-up procedures and report to the audit committee. Wrap-up procedures include:

▶ analytical procedures,

▶ review of working papers,

▶ client approval of adjusting entries.

Prior to the final audit report the auditors will also discuss their findings with the audit committee – amongst other issues irregularities, illegal acts and reportable conditions.

10.3 SPECIFIC CONSIDERATIONS GATHERING EVIDENCE FOR SELECTED ITEMS

With respect to certain aspects of inventory, litigation and claims involving the entity and segment information specific considerations by the auditor in obtaining sufficient appropriate audit evidence is required (ISA 501).[2]

INVENTORY

If inventory is material, the auditor must gather sufficient appropriate audit evidence regarding the existence and condition of inventory. Therefore, the auditor must obtain evidence regarding the:

(a) existence and condition of inventory;

(b) completeness of litigation and claims involving the entity; and

(c) presentation and disclosure of segment information in accordance with the applicable financial reporting framework.

An illustration of required procedures is:

(a) attendance at physical inventory counting, unless impracticable;

  (i) evaluate management's instructions and procedures for recording and controlling the results of the entity's physical inventory counting;

  (ii) observe the performance of management's count procedures;

  (iii) inspect the inventory and perform test counts;

(b) performing audit procedures over the entity's final inventory records to determine whether they accurately reflect actual inventory count results.

If a physical inventory count is conducted at a date other than the date of the financial statements, the auditor must also perform audit procedures to obtain audit evidence about whether changes in inventory between the count date and the date of the financial statements are properly recorded.

LITIGATION AND CLAIMS

To discover litigation, claims and assessments that may have a material effect on the financial statements and thus may be required to be disclosed or accounted for in the financial statements, the auditor relies on both her own field procedures and a letter from the client's legal counsel. The field procedures to discover claims against the client are:

▶ inquiry of management about the policies and procedures adopted for identifying, evaluating and accounting for contingencies; and obtain a description and evaluation of all pending contingencies;

▶ read the corporate meetings' minutes and notes of other appropriate meetings;

▶ read contracts, leases, correspondence and other similar documents;

▶ review guarantees of indebtedness disclosed on bank confirmations;

▶ reviewing legal expense accounts;

▶ inspect other documents for possible client-made guarantees;

▶ determine if there are any side letters.

The auditor will obtain written confirmation from the client that all unasserted claims that require disclosure are disclosed (see next paragraph).

SEGMENT INFORMATION

To obtain sufficient appropriate audit evidence the auditor must:

▷ obtain an understanding of the methods used by management in determining segment information and evaluate whether such methods are likely to result in disclosure in accordance with the applicable financial reporting framework and where appropriate test the application of such methods;

▷ perform appropriate (analytical) procedures.

Other activities as part of the evaluation and completion phase are wrap-up procedures and report to the audit committee. Wrap-up procedures include:

▷ analytical procedures,

▷ review of working papers,

▷ client approval of adjusting entries.

Prior to the final audit report the auditors will also discuss their findings with the audit committee – amongst other issues irregularities, illegal acts and reportable conditions.

10.4 WRITTEN REPRESENTATIONS

Like responses to inquiries, written representations are audit evidence.[3] Although they do not provide sufficient appropriate audit evidence on their own about any of the matters with which they deal. Furthermore, the fact that management has provided reliable written representations does not affect the nature or extent of other audit evidence that the auditor obtains about the fulfilment of management's responsibilities, or about specific assertions. Illustrations of specific written representations are legal letters and management representations letters.

LEGAL LETTER

An important audit procedure that auditors rely on for discovering litigation, claims and assessments that affect the client is a letter from the client's legal counsel called a legal letter or inquiry of client's attorneys. Auditors analyse client legal expenses for the present year and sometimes the prior years. The auditor requires that the client send a standard request letter to every legal adviser. The letter goes to both outside counsel (independent law firms) and inside general counsel (lawyers that are employees of the client). The standard letter from the client's attorney is prepared on the client's letterhead and signed by one of the client company's management. The desired date of the letter from the attorney is close to the date of the auditor's report.

A sample request for such a legal letter (or inquiry of client's attorney letter) from the client is shown in illustration 10.2.

MANAGEMENT REPRESENTATION LETTER

International Standard on Auditing 580 states[4] that the auditor should obtain evidence that management acknowledges its responsibility for the fair representation of the financial statements in accordance with the relevant financial reporting framework and has

ILLUSTRATION 10.2
LEGAL LETTER

Legal Letter

From: Sports888
Via Giuseppe Garibaldi 421
Como, Italia
26 January, 20XX

To: Strelitz Rechtsanwälte & Partner
Trompstrasse 5G
Dresden 01067
Deutschland

Dear Mrs Santvoort LLM,

Our auditors, Rudi Pietro Dottore Commercialista (RPDC), are now engaged in an audit of our financial statements as of 31 December 20XX and for the year then ended. In connection with the audit, management has furnished RPDC with information concerning certain contingencies involving matters with respect to which you have been engaged and to which you have devoted substantive attention on behalf of the Company. These contingencies individually represent a maximum potential loss exposure in excess of $430,000.

Pending or Threatened Litigation, Claims and Assessments
We have furnished our auditors with the following information in relation to the only pending or threatened litigation, claim or assessment your firm is handling on our behalf and to which you have devoted substantive attention in the form of legal consultation or representation:
1 Description of the nature of the case – antitrust complaint filed against the company by the German Department of Justice for discriminatory pricing policies.
2 Process of case to date – case is in the discovery phase.
3 Response to the case – management intends to contest the case vigorously.
4 Evaluation of the likelihood of an unfavourable outcome and an estimate, if one can be made, of the amount or range of potential loss – management believes that the probability of an unfavourable outcome is remote. No estimate of loss can be made.

Please furnish to RPRC such explanation, if any, that you consider necessary to supplement the foregoing information, including an explanation of those matters as to which your views may differ from those stated and an identification of the omission of any pending or threatened litigation, claim or assessment, or a statement that the list of such matters is complete.

Unasserted Claims and Assessments
We understand that whenever, in the course of performing legal services for us with respect to a matter recognised to involve an unasserted possible claim or assessment that may call for financial statement disclosure, if you have formed a professional conclusion that we must disclose or consider disclosure concerning such possible claim or assessment, as a matter of

professional responsibility to us, you will so advise us and will consult with us concerning the question of such disclosure and the applicable requirements of International Financial Reporting Standard IAS 37. Please specifically confirm to RPRC that our understanding is correct. We will be representing to RPRC that there are no unasserted possible claims or assessments that you have advised are probable of assertion and must be disclosed in accordance with International Financial Reporting Standard IAS 37 in the financial statements currently under audit.

Other Matters

Your response should include matters that existed at 31 December 20XX and for the period from that date to the date of your response. Please make your response effective as of 8 February 20XX, and specifically identify the nature of, and reasons, for any limitation on your response. Also, please furnish RPDC with the amount of any unpaid fees due you as of 31 December 20XX for services rendered through that date. Please mail your reply directly to Rudi Pietro Dottore Commercialista, Via Patari 33, Milano, Italia. A stamped, addressed envelope is enclosed for your convenience. Also, please furnish us a copy of your reply.

Sincerely,

Wenke P. Tromp, CEO

approved the financial statements. One of the audit procedures in the evaluation and completion cycle is to gather a representation letter from management. This letter should be addressed to the auditor.[5]

ILLUSTRATION 10.3

MANAGEMENT REPRESENTATION LETTER[6]

The following illustrative letter includes written representations that are required by ISA 580 and other ISAs in effect for audits of financial statements. It is assumed in this illustration that the applicable financial reporting framework is International Financial Reporting Standards; the requirement of ISA 570 to obtain a written representation is not relevant; and that there are no exceptions to the requested written representations. If there were exceptions, the representations would need to be modified to reflect the exceptions. Representations by management will vary from one entity to another and from one period to the next.

(a) (Entity's Letterhead)

(b) To Auditor… …

(c) (date)

(d) Subject: Representation in connection with the financial statements 201X

(e) Dear (addressee),

(f) This representation letter is provided in connection with your audit of the financial statements 20XX of Company XYZ for the purpose of expressing an opinion as to whether the financial statements give a true and fair view of the financial position of XYZ as at December 31, 20XX and of the result for the year then ended in accordance with Part 9 of Book 2 of the Dutch Civil Code. We have made appropriate inquiries of management and officers of the entity with the relevant knowledge and experience, as we considered necessary and relevant for the purpose of appropriately informing ourselves. Accordingly, we confirm, to the best of our knowledge and belief, the following representations:

Financial Statements

1   We acknowledge our responsibility for the preparation and fair presentation of the financial statements and for the preparation of the management board report, both in accordance with Part 9 of Book 2 of the Dutch Civil Code. We have fulfilled our responsibilities, as set out in the terms of the audit engagement dated [insert date], for the preparation of the financial statements including its fair presentation.

2   All transactions have been recorded in the accounting records and are reflected in the financial statements.

3   Significant assumptions used by us in making accounting estimates, including those measured at fair value and… (name of elements with accounting estimates), are reasonable.

4   All events subsequent to the date of the financial statements and for which Part 9 of Book 2 of the Dutch Civil Code requires adjustment or disclosure have been adjusted or disclosed.

5   The effects of uncorrected misstatements are immaterial, both individually and in the aggregate, to the financial statements as a whole. A list of the uncorrected misstatements is attached to the representation letter.

6   [The auditor shall obtain a specific written representation regarding any restatement made to correct a material misstatement in prior period financial statements that affect the comparative information.] The restatement of the comparative information of 20XX-1 as a result of the adjustment of a material misstatement in the prior period financial statements has been appropriately recorded and disclosed in accordance with the requirements of Part 9 of Book 2 of the Dutch Civil Code.

7   [The auditor shall also obtain a specific written representation if events or conditions have been identified that may cast significant doubt on the entity's ability to continue as a going concern.]The financial statement discloses all information of which we are aware that is deemed relevant for our assessment with respect to the entity's ability to continue as a going concern. This includes all relevant key events and circumstances, mitigating factors and our plans for future action. We intend to execute these plans and consider these to be feasible. We confirm that the attached schedule contains our plans for future action relevant to the entity's ability as a going concern, which is the base for our assessment that the entity will be able to continue as a going concern [overview of plans].

Information Provided

8   We have provided you with:
   – Access to all information of which we are aware that is relevant to the preparation of the financial statements such as records, supporting documentation and other matters including all minutes of the General Meetings, Supervisory Board/Audit Committee (or similar body) and the Board of Directors, namely those held on [Data], respectively, and when applicable, summaries of actions of meetings held after period end for which minutes have not yet been prepared, namely those held on [Date].
   – Additional information that you have requested from us for the purpose of the audit; and
   – Unrestricted access to persons within the entity from whom you determined it necessary to obtain audit evidence as part of the audit of the financial statements.

Fraud and compliance with law and regulation

9 The term fraud refers to an intentional act by one or more individuals among management, those charged with governance, employees, or third parties, involving the use of deception to obtain an unjust or illegal advantage. Fraud also includes misstatements resulting from misappropriation of assets, including pledging of assets without proper authorization. Fraudulent financial reporting involves intentional misstatements or omissions of amounts or disclosures in the financial statements to deceive financial statement users.

10 We acknowledge responsibility for the design and implementation of internal control to prevent and detect fraud.

11 We have disclosed to you the results of our assessment of the risk that the financial statements may be materially misstated as a result of fraud.

12 We have disclosed to you all information in relation to suspected fraud, allegation of fraud or fraud affecting the entity involving:
  – Management;
  – Employees who have significant roles in internal control; or
  – Others where the fraud could have a material effect on the financial statements.

13 We have disclosed to you all information in relation to any suspected fraud, allegations of fraud, or fraud, affecting the entity's financial statements communicated by employees, former employees, analysts, regulators or others.

14 We have disclosed to you all known instances of non-compliance or suspected noncompliance with laws and regulations whose effects should be considered when preparing financial statements.

Related parties

15 We have disclosed to you the identity of the entity's related parties and all the related party relationships and transactions of which we are aware.

16 Related party relationships and transactions have been appropriately accounted for and disclosed in accordance with the requirements of Part 9 of Book 2 of the Dutch Civil Code.

Claims and litigations

17 We have disclosed to you all known actual or possible litigation and claims whose effects should be considered when preparing the financial statements and have appropriately accounted for and/or disclosed these in the financial statements in accordance with Part 9 of Book 2 of the Dutch Civil Code. [Other representations which the auditor considers necessary.]

Additional representation [if deemed relevant]

18 Presentation and disclosure of fair value measurements are in accordance with Part 9 of Book 2 of the Dutch Civil Code. The amounts disclosed represent our best estimate of fair value of assets and liabilities required to be disclosed by these standards. The measurement methods and significant assumptions used in determining fair value have been

applied in a consistent way, are reasonable and such assumptions appropriately reflect our intent and ability to carry out specific courses of action on behalf of the entity where relevant to the fair value measurements or disclosures.

19 We have no plans or intentions that may materially alter the carrying value or classification of assets and liabilities reflected in the financial statements.

20 We believe that the carrying amounts of all fixed assets will be recoverable.

21 Information regarding financial risks exposure and our financial risk management objectives and policies has been adequately disclosed in the financial statements.

22 The entity has economic title to all assets. There are no rights of distrait or mortgage rights on the entity's assets, except for those that are disclosed in [Note X] to the financial statements.

23 We have properly recorded or disclosed in the financial statements the capital stock repurchase options and agreements, and capital stock reserved for options, warrants, conversions and other requirements.

24 We have requested the legal advisors who perform services for us to provide you with all required information and have requested them to disclose to you any matters you may request in this respect.

(g) Yours Sincerely,

(h) Company XYZ

(i) [Senior Executive Officer]

(j) [Senior Financial Officer]

(k) Optional cc: Audit Committee

(l) Enclosure: Schedule of uncorrected financial statement misstatements

The letter should contain the information requested by the auditor, be appropriately dated as near as practicable to, but not after, the date of the auditor's report on the financial statements and signed. The members of management who have primary responsibility for the entity and its financial aspects, usually the chief executive officer and the chief financial officer, both sign the letter.

In instances when other sufficient appropriate audit evidence cannot reasonably be expected to exist, the auditor should obtain written representations from management on matters material to the financial statements. She may document in her working papers evidence of management's representations by summarizing oral discussions with management and by obtaining written representations from management.

Matters that are ordinarily included in a management representation letter are shown in illustration 10.3. When these representations relate to matters that are material to the financial statements, the auditor must seek corroborative audit evidence, evaluate whether the representations made by management appear reasonable and consistent with other audit evidence, and consider whether the individuals making the representations are competent to do so.

UNIVERSAL HEALTH SERVICES AND KPMG – 'I AM NEITHER A CERTIFIED PUBLIC ACCOUNTANT NOR A SECURITIES LAWYER

Concept	Management representation letter and responsibility for financial statements.
Story	Universal Health Services, Inc. (UHS) is an American Fortune 500 company[that provides hospital and healthcare services It offers operating acute care and behavioural health hospitals, ambulatory surgery and radiation centres in the USA, Puerto Rico and France.

In February 2003, UHS's CFO Kirk Gorman, a company veteran of 16 years, was asked to resign at the urging of its auditor, KPMG LLP. KPMG were doing their first audit for the company, having just replaced the predecessor auditor Arthur Andersen. According to UHS, there was a dispute related to Gorman's theoretical views about the split of duties and responsibilities between the CFO and the auditor (Gallaro, 2003).

Gorman wrote a letter to the Philadelphia office of KPMG explaining that, while he was willing to sign the management representation letter (attesting that the financial statements he submitted for audit were, to the best of his knowledge, accurate), he was relying on KPMG to ensure that the accounting treatment was in accordance with GAAP (Leone, 2003). He asked if KPMG would be willing to sign a similar statement vouching for the accuracy of its work (*Corporate Finance*, 2003). Furthermore, the letter released by UHS stated that 'I do review and analyse the financial statements and disclosures in our 10-Q and 10-K filings, but I can't personally verify that all of our accounts are in accordance with GAAP.' Because he was 'neither a certified public accountant nor a securities lawyer' that lead him to 'rely upon KPMG to ensure that our financial statements ... are in compliance with [generally accepted accounting principles] and securities regulations' (UHS, 2002).

In a letter dated 10 February (UHS, 2003), Gorman sought to clarify his position. He wrote that he had not intended to leave the impression that he doubted the veracity of the company's financial statements or that he wanted to shift responsibility for the statements' accuracy to KPMG (Gallaro, 2003).

Nevertheless, KPMG went to the UHS board and argued that it couldn't approve the company's financial statements as long as Gorman remained CFO. Due to 'philosophical differences', the company asked Gorman to resign.

Discussion Questions	▶ Who is responsible for the financial statements and why is that the case?
	▶ Should an auditor sign a statement vouching for the accuracy of his work? Why?

References Corporate Finance, 2003, 'Auditors Turn up the Heat on CFOs', *Corporate Finance*, London, March, p.1.
Gallaro, V., 2003, 'Executive Reservations', *Modern Healthcare*, Chicago, 24 February, Vol. 33, Issue 8, p.12.
Leone, M., 2003, 'New Certification and Internal Control Requirements are Heaping New Hazards on Finance Chiefs. Here's How Some are Coping', CFO.com, Boston, 9 May, p. 1.
UHS, 2002, 'Letter to KPMG from Gorman', www.uhs.com, dated 12 December.

If management refuses to provide representations that the auditor considers necessary, this will be considered a limitation on scope. It is also a scope limitation if management has provided an oral representation but refuses to confirm it in writing. This scope limitation would mean that the auditor should express a qualified opinion or a disclaimer of opinion.

If management does not provide one or more of the requested written representations, the auditor must first discuss the matter with management. Next, the auditor will re-evaluate the integrity of management and evaluate the effect that this may have on the reliability of representations (oral or written) and audit evidence in general. Finally, the auditor should take appropriate actions, including determining the possible effect on the opinion in the auditor's report.

10.5   REVIEW FOR CONTINGENT LIABILITIES AND COMMITMENTS

A contingent liability is a potential future obligation to an outside party for an unknown amount resulting from the outcome of a past event, for example an adverse tax court decision, lawsuit, and notes receivable discounted. Footnote disclosure is ordinarily required if there are probable losses. Three conditions are required for a contingent liability to exist:

1 There is a potential future payment to an outside party or potential future assets impairment.
2 There is an uncertainty about the amount of payment or asset impairment.
3 The outcome will be resolved by some future event.

Audit procedures that test for contingencies are not just done in the last days of the audit, but from the beginning. Income tax disputes, investigations by government or industry authorities, and the amount of unused bank lines of credit are generally known from the start of the audit. Procedures such as reviews of contracts, correspondence, credit agreements and inquiries of management should point out possible contingencies.

One audit procedure for finding contingencies is the legal letter already discussed where the auditor analyses legal expenses and statements from legal counsel and obtains a letter from each major lawyer as to the status of pending litigation. Three other common procedures are to: review working papers; examine letters of credit to confirm used and unused balances; and evaluation of known contingent liabilities.

Contingencies that are of concern to the auditor, among others, are: pending litigation for patent infringement, product liability or other actions; guarantees of obligations of others; product warranties; income tax disputes; and notes receivable discounted.

Similar to contingent liabilities are commitments. Commitments are agreements that the entity will hold to a fixed set of conditions, such as the purchase or sale of merchandise at a stated price, at a future date, regardless of what happens to profits or to the economy as a whole. Examples are commitments to purchase raw materials, lease premises, royalty agreements, licensing agreements and agreements to sell merchandise or services at a fixed price. There may be commitments to employees in the form of profit sharing, stock options, health benefits and pension plans.

All material commitments are ordinarily either described together in a separate footnote or combined in a footnote related to contingencies.

10.6 REVIEW FOR DISCOVERY OF SUBSEQUENT EVENTS

Discovery of subsequent facts and events may be essential to a correct opinion. The auditor must consider events up to the date of the auditor's report and between the balance sheet date and the issuance of the statements. Discovery of such facts after the financial statements' issuance are not generally as crucial but sometimes require further analysis, discussion with management and legal advice. Review for subsequent events is the auditing procedures performed by auditors to identify and evaluate subsequent events. Subsequent events are events occurring between the date of the financial statements and the date of the auditor's report, and facts that become known to the auditor after the date of the auditor's report. (See Concept and Company 10.2.) Under International Standard on Auditing (ISA) 560 the auditor should consider the effect of subsequent events on the financial statements and on the auditor's report.

TYPES OF EVENTS AFTER THE BALANCE SHEET DATE

International Financial Reporting Standard IAS 10 deals with the treatment of financial statement of events, favourable and unfavourable, occurring after period end. It identifies two types of events:[7]

1 those that provide evidence of conditions that existed at the end of the reporting period (adjusting events after the reporting period); and

2 those that are indicative of conditions that arose after the reporting period (non-adjusting events after the reporting period).

The first type requires adjustment to the financial statements and the second type, if material, requires disclosure.

EVENTS RELATING TO CONDITIONS THAT EXISTED AT PERIOD END

Events relating to assets and liabilities conditions that existed at period end may require adjustment of the financial statements. For example, adjustments may be made for a loss on a trade receivable account that is confirmed by the bankruptcy of a customer that occurs after the balance sheet date. Other examples of these events that require adjustment of financial statements are:

▶ settlement of litigation at an amount different from the amount recorded on the books;
▶ disposal of equipment not being used in operations at a price below current book value;
▶ sale of investments at a price below recorded cost.

EVENTS NOT AFFECTING CONDITIONS AT PERIOD END

Events that fall into the second category, i.e., those that do not affect the condition of assets or liabilities at the balance sheet date but are of such importance that non-disclosure would affect the ability of the users of the financial statements to make proper evaluations and decisions, should be disclosed. Examples of these types of events are:

▶ a decline in the market value of securities held for temporary investment or resale;
▶ issuance of bonds or equity securities;
▶ a decline in the market value of inventory as a consequence of government action barring further sale of a product;
▶ an uninsured loss of inventories as a result of fire.

CONCEPT AND A COMPANY 10.2

ARABIAN AMERICAN DEVELOPMENT COMPANY (NOW TRECORA RESOURCES) – THE UNDISCLOSED EVENT

Concept	**Subsequent events and disclosure**

Story	Arabian, a Delaware corporation based in Dallas, Texas, is in the business of refining petrochemical products and developing mining operations in Saudi Arabia and the USA. Arabian maintains an office in Jeddah, Saudi Arabia, to manage its Saudi Arabian operations. Hatem El-Khalidi, age 78, a US citizen and resident of Jeddah, Saudi Arabia, helped found Arabian in 1967. Arabian and El-Khalidi, violated SEC rules which required Arabian to include in annual and quarterly reports any material information that might be necessary to make those reports not misleading. They failed to disclose a material lease that had a high probability of expiring, affecting severely the company's total assets.

In 1993, Arabian obtained a 30-year lease from the Saudi Arabian government to mine zinc, lead and gold in the Al Masane area of Saudi Arabia. The Al Masane lease is Arabian's largest asset, accounting for approximately $36 million (65 per cent) of Arabian's $56 million in total assets. The lease agreement requires Arabian to build the mine, and begin mining operations, pursuant to a work schedule, and if Arabian fails to comply with the work schedule, the Saudi government may have the right to terminate the lease (SEC, 2003).

In the late 1990s the economic crisis in Southeast Asia caused a sharp drop in mineral prices, making it uneconomical for Arabian to comply with the work schedule required by the lease. In May 2000, the Ministry for Petroleum and Mineral Resources of Saudi Arabia, an agency of the Saudi Arabian government, notified Arabian, via correspondence sent to El-Khalidi in Saudi Arabia, that Arabian must implement the Al Masane Project, as required by the lease agreement. If Arabian failed to do so, the Ministry would begin procedures to terminate the lease (SEC, 2003).

Ignoring this correspondence, in April 2002, El-Khalidi signed a management representation letter with Grant Thornton, Arabian's outside auditor, representing, among other things: (1) that Arabian has complied with all aspects of contractual agreements that would have a material effect on the company's financial statements in the event of non-compliance; (2) that no events have occurred which would impair the company's ability to recover its investment in the Al Masane Project and other interests in Saudi Arabia; and (3) there is no impairment of the company's investment in the Al Masane Project (SEC, 2003).

In late November 2002, El-Khalidi disclosed to Arabian's Treasurer that the Saudi government was threatening to terminate the Al Masane lease. The Treasurer promptly informed Arabian's other officers and directors and, on 23 December 2002, Arabian filed a Form 8-K with the SEC that publicly disclosed for the first time that the Saudi government was threatening to terminate Arabian's lease. The Treasurer also informed Grant Thornton, which subsequently withdrew its audit reports for Arabian's 2000 and 2001 financial statements and resigned as Arabian's outside auditor (SEC, 2003).

Discussion Questions	▷ Why should the problems with the mining lease be disclosed, even though it had no current impact on Arabian?
	▷ After Grant Thornton learnt of the lease problem, what were their options in relation to their prior audit opinions?
	▷ Why do you think Grant Thornton resigned as auditor?

References	All material from SEC, 2003, Litigation Release No. 48638, Accounting and Auditing Enforcement Release No. 1898, 'In the Matter of Arabian American Development Company and Hatem El-Khalidi', US Security and Exchange Commission, 16 October.

EVENTS UP TO THE DATE OF THE AUDITOR'S REPORT

The auditor should perform procedures designed to obtain sufficient appropriate audit evidence that all events up to the date of the auditor's report that may require adjustment of, or disclosure in, the financial statements have been identified. Some of these procedures are described in illustration 10.4. When the auditor becomes aware of events which materially affect the financial statements, the auditor should consider whether such events are properly accounted for and adequately disclosed in the financial statements.

ILLUSTRATION 10.4

AUDIT PROCEDURES TO IDENTIFY EVENTS THAT MAY REQUIRE ADJUSTMENT OF, OR DISCLOSURE IN, THE FINANCIAL STATEMENTS

The nature of procedures performed in a subsequent events review depends on many variables, such as the nature of transactions and events and the availability of data and reports. However the following procedures are typical of a subsequent events review:

▶ Enquiring into management's procedures/systems for the identification of subsequent events;
▶ Inspection of minutes of board meetings;
▶ Reviewing accounting records including budgets, forecasts and quarterly information;
▶ Enquiring of directors if they are aware of any subsequent events that require reflection in the year-end account;
▶ Obtaining from management a letter of representation that all subsequent events have been considered in the preparation of the financial statements;
▶ Inspection of invoices and correspondence with legal advisors;
▶ Gathering relevant publicly available information (general, industry and company);
▶ Enquiring status with regards to reported provisions and contingencies; and
▶ Regular audit procedures in order to verify year-end balances:
  ▶ checking after date receipts from receivables;
  ▶ inspecting the cash book for payments/receipts that were not accrued for at the year-end; and
  ▶ checking suppliers' invoices received in the new period.

FACTS WHICH BECOME KNOWN TO THE AUDITOR AFTER THE DATE OF THE AUDITOR'S REPORT BUT BEFORE THE DATE THE FINANCIAL STATEMENTS ARE ISSUED

The auditor has no obligation to perform any audit procedures or make any inquiry regarding the financial statements after the date of the auditor's report. However, if, after the date of the auditor's report but before the date the financial statements are issued, a fact becomes known to the auditor that, had it been known to the auditor at the date of the auditor's report, may have caused the auditor to amend the auditor's report, the auditor should discuss the matter with management and those charged with governance. She should determine if the financial statements need amendment; and inquire how management intends to address the matter in the financial statements.

When management amends the financial statements, the auditor would carry out the procedures necessary in the circumstances and would provide management with a new report on the amended financial statements dated not earlier than the date the amended financial statements are signed or approved. The procedures outlined in illustration 10.4 would be extended to the date of the new auditor's report.

When management does not amend the financial statements in circumstances where the auditor believes they need to be amended and the auditor's report has not been released, the auditor should express either a qualified or an adverse opinion. If the auditor's report has been released to the entity's governance body, she would notify those persons not to issue financial statements and the auditor's report. If the financial statements are subsequently issued to the regulators or public, the auditor needs to take action to prevent reliance on that auditor's report.

DISCOVERY OF FACTS AFTER THE FINANCIAL STATEMENTS HAVE BEEN ISSUED

After the financial statements have been issued the auditor has no obligation to make any inquiry regarding such financial statements. If, however, after the statements have been issued, the auditor becomes aware of a fact which existed at the date of the auditor's report and which, if known then, may have caused the auditor to amend the auditor's report, the auditor should discuss it with management and consider revision of the financial statements. The new or amended auditor's report should include an emphasis of a matter paragraph or other matter paragraph referring to a note to the financial statements that more extensively discusses the reason for the revision of the previously issued financial statements and to the earlier report issued by the auditor.

10.7 RELATED PARTIES

Parties are considered to be related if one party has the ability to control the other party or exercise significant influence over the other party in making financial and operational decisions. A *related party transaction* is a transfer of resources or obligations between related parties, regardless of whether a price is charged.

In the normal course of business there may be many related party transactions. In most circumstances, they may carry no higher risk of material misstatement of the financial statements than similar transactions with unrelated parties. However, the nature of related party relationships and transactions may, in some circumstances, contribute to higher risks of material misstatements than transactions with unrelated parties. Some examples of these risk-increasing circumstances are:

> ▶ Related parties may operate through an extensive and complex range of relationships and structures, with a corresponding increase in the complexity of related party transactions.
> ▶ Information systems may be ineffective at identifying or summarising transactions and outstanding balances between an entity and its related parties.
> ▶ Related party transactions may not be conducted under normal market terms and conditions; for example, some related party transactions may be conducted with no exchange of consideration.

Two aspects of related party transactions of which an auditor must be aware are adequate disclosure of related party transactions and the possibility that the existence of related parties increases the risk of management fraud. International Financial Reporting Standards (IAS 24)[8] and other financial reporting frameworks require disclosure of the nature and volume of transactions with related parties. There are many legitimate reasons for significant transactions with related parties but the risk for an auditor is that management will conceal transactions between related parties causing the disclosures to be misstated, i.e., the related party disclosures are not complete.

Even if the applicable financial reporting framework establishes minimal or no related party requirements, the auditor nevertheless needs to obtain an understanding of the entity's related party relationships and transactions. This understanding should be sufficient to form a conclusion as to whether the financial statements achieve fair presentation (for fair presentation frameworks) or are not misleading (for compliance frameworks). In addition, an understanding of the entity's related party relationships and transactions is relevant to the auditor's evaluation of whether one or more fraud risk factors are present because fraud may be more easily committed through related parties.

Owing to the inherent limitations of an audit, there is an unavoidable risk that some material misstatements of the financial statements may not be detected. In the context of related parties, the potential effects of limitations on the auditor's ability to detect material misstatements are greater because, for example, management may be unaware of the existence of all related party relationships and transactions, or related party relationships may present a greater opportunity for collusion, concealment or manipulation by management.

PROCEDURES TO DISCOVER RELATED PARTY TRANSACTIONS

Because of the possibility of related party transactions, the auditor should perform audit procedures designed to obtain sufficient appropriate audit evidence regarding the identification and disclosure by management of related parties and the effect of related party transactions. However, an audit cannot be expected to detect all related party transactions. Audit procedures must identify circumstances that increase the risk of misstatement or that indicate material misstatement regarding related parties has occurred. If these circumstances exist, the auditor should perform modified, extended or additional procedures. Illustration 10.5 shows examples of circumstances and may indicate the existence of previously unidentified related parties. The next 'Concept and a Company' presents related party questions related to Adelphia Communications.

ILLUSTRATION 10.5

CIRCUMSTANCES THAT MAY INDICATE UNIDENTIFIED RELATED PARTIES

During the course of the audit, the auditor needs to be alert for transactions that appear unusual in the circumstances and may indicate the existence of previously unidentified related parties. Examples include:

▶ Transactions which have abnormal terms of trade, such as unusual prices, interest rates, guarantees and repayment terms.

▶ Transactions which lack an apparent logical business reason for their occurrence.

- Transactions in which substance differs from form.
- Transactions processed in an unusual manner.
- High-volume or significant transactions with certain customers or suppliers as compared with others.
- Unrecorded transactions such as the receipt or provision of management services at no charge.

UNDERSTANDING THE ENTITY'S RELATED PARTY RELATIONSHIPS AND TRANSACTIONS

The engagement team discussion required by ISA 315[9] and ISA 240[10] includes specific consideration of the susceptibility of the financial statements to material misstatement due to fraud or error that could result from the entity's related party relationships and transactions.

To acquire and understanding, the auditor will inquire of management regarding:

- The identity of the entity's related parties, including changes from the prior period.
- The nature of the relationships between the entity and these related parties.
- Whether the entity entered into any transactions with these related parties during the period and, if so, the type and purpose of the transactions.
- The controls, if any, that management has established to:
  - identify, account for and disclose related party relationships and transactions in accordance with the applicable financial reporting framework;
  - authorize and approve significant transactions and arrangements with related parties; and authorize and approve significant transactions and arrangements outside the normal course of business.

CONCEPT AND A COMPANY 10.3

RELATED PARTY QUESTIONS RELATED TO ADELPHIA COMMUNICATIONS

Concept	**Related parties and unrecorded liabilities.**
Story	Adelphia Communications, when it was the sixth largest cable television provider in the USA, was the subject of a Securities and Exchange Commission (SEC) and federal grand jury investigation into its finances as its accounting practices were questioned. The company was founded and managed by John Rigas and his family.

Adelphia had fraudulently excluded from the Company's annual and quarterly consolidated financial statements portions of its bank debt, totalling approximately $2.3 billion in undisclosed, off-balance-sheet bank debt as of 31 December 2001, by systematically recording those liabilities on the books of unconsolidated affiliates, which were controlled by the Rigas family (Rigas Entities). They included in those financial statements a footnote disclosure implicitly misrepresenting that such portions had been included on Adelphia's balance sheet (SEC, 2002). Adelphia and its executives created sham transactions backed by fictitious documents to give the false appearance that Adelphia had actually repaid debts, when, in truth, it had simply shifted them to unconsolidated Rigas-controlled entities.

Since at least 1998, Adelphia used fraudulent misrepresentations and omissions of material fact to conceal rampant self-dealing by the Rigases, the family which founded and ran Adelphia, including use of Adelphia funds to: pay for vacation properties and New York City apartments; develop a golf course mostly owned by the Rigases; and purchase over $772 million of Adelphia shares of common stock and over $563 million of Adelphia notes for the Rigases' own benefit (SEC, 2002).

In addition to Adelphia's own business operations, it also managed and maintained virtually every aspect of the Rigas Entities that owned and operated cable television systems, including maintaining their books and records on a general ledger system shared with Adelphia and its subsidiaries. Rigas Entities did not reimburse or otherwise compensate Adelphia for these services.

Adelphia and the Rigas Entities, including those that are in businesses unrelated to cable systems, participated jointly in a cash management system operated by Adelphia (the 'Adelphia CMS'). Adelphia, its subsidiaries, and Rigas Entities all deposited some or all of their cash generated or otherwise obtained from their operations, borrowings and other sources in the Adelphia CMS, withdrew cash from the Adelphia CMS to be used for their expenses, capital expenditures, repayments of debt and other uses, and engaged in transfers of funds with other participants in the Adelphia CMS. This resulted in the commingling of funds among the Adelphia CMS participants, including Adelphia subsidiaries and Rigas Entities, and created numerous related party payables and receivables among Adelphia, its subsidiaries and Rigas Entities (SEC, 2002).

To conceal that the Rigases were engaged in rampant self-dealing at Adelphia's expense, Adelphia misrepresented or concealed a number of significant transactions by which the Rigases used Adelphia resources with no reimbursement or other compensation to Adelphia. The defendants engaged in these practices to afford Adelphia continued access to commercial credit and the capital markets.

In November 2002, Adelphia Corporation filed suit against its former auditor, Deloitte & Touche, claiming the firm was partly responsible for the alleged fraud that cost company shareholders billions of dollars. 'If Deloitte had acted consistently with its professional responsibilities as Adelphia's outside auditor, these losses could have been preventable,' according to the complaint. The complaint alleges that some of the Rigas family's (which controlled Adelphia) acts of self-dealing were apparent to Deloitte on the books and records which Deloitte reviewed and that Deloitte knew or should have known of such acts! During its 2000 audit, for which an unqualified audit opinion was given, Deloitte asked the Rigases to disclose the full amount of the loans, which totalled $1.45 billion at the time but later amounted to more than $3 billion. The Rigases refused, and Deloitte never disclosed this issue or any disagreement to the audit committee. Adelphia's cash management system had a pool of corporate funds that the Rigases used as their personal bank account. The complaint alleges that Deloitte knew about the system and didn't report it to the audit committee (Frank, 2002).

Discussion Questions	▶ What audit procedures could the auditor undertake to detect the Adelphia related party transactions?
	▶ What kind of control environment encourages related party transactions?
	▶ At what point would the auditor report related party dealings to the board of directors?

References   Frank, R., 2002, 'The Economy: Adelphia Sues Deloitte & Touche, Accusing Former Auditor of Fraud', *Wall Street Journal* (Eastern edn), New York, NY, 7 November, p. A2.

SEC, 2002, *Litigation Release* No. 17837, Accounting Auditing Enforcement Release No. 1664, '*Securities And Exchange Commission v Adelphia Communications Corporation, John J. Rigas, Timothy J. Rigas, Michael J. Rigas, James P. Rigas, James R. Brown, and Michael C. Mulcahey*', US Securities and Exchange Commission, 14 November.

REVIEW MANAGEMENT AND BOARD FOR RELATED PARTIES

The auditor should review information provided by the directors and management identifying related party transactions while being alert for other material related party transactions. She should review management information identifying the names of all known related parties. The auditor may perform the following procedures to determine completeness of this information:

- ▶ review prior year working papers for names of known related parties;
- ▶ review the entity's procedures for identification of related parties;
- ▶ inquire as to the affiliation of directors and officers with other entities;
- ▶ review shareholder records to determine the names of principal shareholders or, if appropriate, obtain a listing of principal shareholders from the share register;
- ▶ review minutes of the meetings of shareholders and the board of directors and other relevant statutory records such as the register of directors' interests;
- ▶ inquire of other auditors currently involved in the audit, or predecessor auditors, as to their knowledge of additional related parties;
- ▶ review the entity's income tax returns and other information supplied to the regulatory agencies.

During the audit, the auditor should remain alert for arrangements that management has not disclosed that may indicate the existence of related party relationships or transactions. In particular, the auditor must inspect bank and legal confirmations and minutes of shareholders or governance bodies for indications of the existence of related party transactions.

In case the auditor identifies significant related party transactions outside the entity's normal course of business he must inspect the underlying contracts or agreements and evaluate whether the business rationale (or lack of rationale) for the transactions suggests that they may have been entered into to engage in fraudulent financial reporting or to conceal misappropriation (theft) of assets. When considering the contracts, the auditor must also determine if the terms of the transactions are consistent with management's explanations and that the transactions have been appropriately authorised, approved and disclosed.

In forming an opinion on the financial statements in accordance with ISA 700,[11] the auditor must evaluate whether the identified related party relationships and transactions have been appropriately accounted for and disclosed. Further, she should consider whether the effects of the related party relationships and transactions prevent the financial statements from achieving fair presentation or make them misleading.

The auditor shall communicate with those charged with governance significant matters arising during the audit in connection with the entity's related parties (unless all of those charged with governance are involved in managing the entity). The auditor shall include in the audit documentation the names of the identified related parties and the nature of the related party relationships.

10.8   EVALUATION OF GOING CONCERN ASSUMPTION

Financial statements are prepared on a going concern basis, unless management either intends to liquidate the entity or to cease operations or has no realistic alternative but to do so. When the use of the going concern assumption is appropriate, assets and liabilities are recorded on the basis that the entity will be able to realize its assets and discharge its liabilities in the normal course of business.

Reporting on going-concern-related uncertainties remains one of the most challenging issues faced by external auditors. Even though professional standards do not hold external auditors responsible for predicting future events, if an auditor refrains from issuing a going concern audit opinion (sections 10.8 and 11.5) and the client company subsequently fails (i.e., a 'type II' reporting error), the costs to the auditor in terms of increased litigation and loss of reputation are often substantial[12].

Since the going concern assumption is a fundamental principle in the preparation of financial statements, management must assess the entity's ability to continue as a going concern even if the financial reporting framework does not include an explicit requirement to do so. Management's assessment involves making a judgment, at a particular point in time, about inherently uncertain future outcomes of events or conditions.

The auditor's responsibility is to obtain sufficient appropriate audit evidence about the appropriateness of management's use of the going concern assumption and to conclude whether there is a material uncertainty about the entity's ability to continue as a going concern. As the auditor cannot predict future events or conditions, the absence of any reference to going concern uncertainty in an auditor's report cannot be viewed as a guarantee as to the entity's ability to continue as a going concern.

When performing risk assessment procedures, the auditor must consider whether there are events or conditions that may cast significant doubt on the entity's ability to continue as a going concern. The auditor will discuss the assessment with management and determine whether management has identified events or conditions that may cast significant doubt on the entity's ability to continue as a going concern and, if so, management's plans to address them.

If such events or conditions have been identified, the auditor must obtain sufficient appropriate audit evidence to determine whether or not a material uncertainty exists through performing additional audit procedures, including consideration of mitigating factors. These procedures must include:

(a) Where management has not yet performed an assessment of the entity's ability to continue as a going concern, requesting management to make its assessment.

(b) Evaluating management's plans for future actions in relation to its going concern assessment, whether the outcome of these plans is likely to improve the situation and whether management's plans are feasible.

(c) Where the entity has prepared a cash flow forecast, and analysis of the forecast is a significant factor in considering the future outcome of events or conditions in the evaluation of management's plans for future action:

   (i) Evaluating the reliability of the underlying data generated to prepare the forecast; and

   (ii) Determining whether there is adequate support for the assumptions underlying the forecast.

(d) Considering whether any additional facts or information have become available since the date on which management made its assessment.

(e) Requesting written representations from management and, where appropriate, those charged with governance, regarding their plans for future action and the feasibility of these plans.

If the auditor concludes that the use of the going concern assumption is appropriate in the circumstances but a material uncertainty exists, the auditor must determine whether the financial statements:

(a) Clearly describe the events or conditions that may cast significant doubt on the entity's ability to continue as a going concern and management's plans to deal with these events or conditions; and

(b) Disclose clearly that there is a material uncertainty related to events or conditions that may cast significant doubt on the entity's ability to continue as a going concern and, therefore, that it may be unable to realize its assets and discharge its liabilities in the normal course of business.

If adequate disclosure is made in the financial statements, the auditor shall express an unmodified opinion and include an Emphasis of Matter paragraph in the auditor's report (chapter 11) to:[13]

(a) highlight the existence of a material uncertainty relating to the event or condition that may cast significant doubt on the entity's ability to continue as a going concern; and

(b) draw attention to the note in the financial statements that discloses the matters.

10.9 EVALUATION OF MISSTATEMENTS IDENTIFIED DURING THE AUDIT

It is the auditor's responsibility when forming an opinion on the financial statements to conclude whether reasonable assurance has been obtained about whether the financial statements as a whole are free from material misstatement. The auditor's conclusion takes into account her evaluation of uncorrected *misstatements*. Therefore, the objective of the auditor is to evaluate the effect of identified misstatements on the audit and the effect of *uncorrected misstatements* on the financial statements.

The auditor must accumulate misstatements identified during the audit, other than those that are clearly trivial. Findings during the audit may require the auditor to consider whether the overall audit strategy and audit plan need to be revised. For instance, the audit plan may have to be revised if the nature of identified misstatements and their circumstances indicate that other misstatements may exist that, when added to misstatements accumulated during the audit, could be material.

EVALUATING AUDIT FINDINGS FOR MATERIAL MISSTATEMENTS

When the audit tests for each item in the financial statements are completed, the staff auditor doing the work will sign off completion of steps in the audit programme, identify monetary misstatements in the financial statements, and propose adjustment to the financial statements. Monetary misstatements are misstatements that cause a distortion of the financial statements. Monetary misstatements may result from mistakes in processing transactions (such as mistakes in quantities, prices or computations), mistakes in the selection of accounting principles, and mistakes in facts or judgements about accounting estimates.

MISSTATEMENT WORKSHEET

To assist the auditor in evaluating the effect of misstatements accumulated during the audit and in communicating misstatements to management and those charged with governance, it may be useful to distinguish between factual misstatements, judgmental misstatements and projected misstatements:

- ▶ *Factual misstatements* are misstatements about which there is no doubt.
- ▶ *Judgmental misstatements* are differences arising from the judgements of management concerning accounting estimates that the auditor considers unreasonable, or the selection or application of accounting policies that the auditor considers inappropriate.
- ▶ *Projected misstatements* are the auditor's best estimate of misstatements in populations, involving the projection of misstatements identified in audit samples to the entire populations from which the samples were drawn. Guidance on the determination of projected misstatements and evaluation of the results is set out in ISA 530.

The most practical way to consider whether the financial statements are materially misstated at the conclusion of the audit is to use a worksheet that determines the combined effect of uncorrected misstatements, individually or in aggregate, on important totals or subtotals in the financial statements.[14] The evaluation of uncorrected misstatements includes evaluation of the effects of uncorrected misstatements detected in prior years and misstatements detected in the current year that relate to prior years.

In the combined effect worksheet procedure, a worksheet summarizing the results of sampling on each account balance is combined with a worksheet giving the results of audit tests that did not use sampling.

As a result of the interaction of quantitative and qualitative considerations in materiality judgments, uncorrected misstatements of relatively small amounts could have a material effect on the financial statements. For example, an illegal payment of an otherwise immaterial amount could be material if there is a reasonable possibility that it could lead to a material contingent liability or a material loss of revenue. Also, a misstatement made intentionally could be material for qualitative reasons, even if relatively small in amount.[15]

At the auditor's request, management (and where appropriate those charged with governance) must include in the written representation whether they believe the uncorrected misstatements are immaterial. In general, the auditor discusses with those charged with governance the reasons for, and the implications of, a failure to correct misstatements, having regard to the size and nature of the misstatement judged in the surrounding circumstances, and possible implications in relation to future financial statements.

REVIEW LAWS AND REGULATION

All countries have laws that apply to businesses operating there. The auditor should know the laws that apply to their client, review the criteria required to comply with that statute, and test for the client company's compliance. Any non-compliance with laws and regulations is discussed in chapter 12. Many governing security market authorities[16] review financial statements of publicly traded companies because they meet certain high-risk criteria. Therefore, it is wise for the auditor to understand the criteria that will set the client apart for review and determine if any problems may occur. For example, the US Securities and Exchange Commission (SEC) reviews a publicly traded company if the following factors are evident:

- ▶ companies that have issued material restatements of financial results;
- ▶ companies that experience significant volatility in their stock price as compared to other companies;
- ▶ companies with the largest market capitalization;
- ▶ emerging companies with disparities in price to earnings ratios;
- ▶ companies whose operations significantly affect any material sector of the economy;
- ▶ any other factors that the SEC may consider relevant.

COMMUNICATION AND CORRECTION OF MISSTATEMENTS

The auditor is required to communicate with those charged with governance the responsibilities of the auditor, an overview of the scope of the audit, significant findings from the audit, and compliance with ethics.

Generally, if misstatements are found, the auditor asks management to correct them. If management corrects the misstatements that were detected, the auditor must still perform additional audit procedures to determine whether misstatements remain. If management refuses to correct some or all of the misstatements communicated by the auditor, the auditor should consider management's reasons for not making the corrections.

The auditor must determine whether uncorrected misstatements are material, individually or in aggregate. In making this determination, the auditor should consider the size and nature of the misstatements and the circumstances of their occurrence. She should also consider the effect of uncorrected misstatements related to prior periods on the relevant account balances or disclosures, and the financial statements as a whole.

In addition to management, the auditor is required to communicate with those charged with governance (usually the board of directors) any uncorrected misstatements and the effect that they have on the opinion in the auditor's report. The auditor's communication will identify material uncorrected misstatements individually and request that uncorrected misstatements be corrected. The auditor also communicates the effect of uncorrected misstatements related to prior periods.

The auditor must request a written representation from management and, where appropriate, those charged with governance whether they believe the effects of uncorrected misstatements are immaterial to the financial statements. A summary of such items shall be included in or attached to the written representation.

In their work paper documentation, the auditors must include:

▷ sufficient documentation to enable an experienced auditor to understand the audit procedures undertaken;

▷ the nature, timing and extent of the audit procedures performed;

▷ discussion of significant matters with management including when and with whom; and

▷ how the auditor addressed any inconsistencies with the auditor's conclusion.

10.10 REVIEW OF FINANCIAL STATEMENTS AND OTHER INFORMATION

FINANCIAL STATEMENT DISCLOSURE CHECKLIST

An important consideration in completing the audit is determination of whether the disclosures in the financial statements are adequate. Adequate disclosure includes consideration of all the financial statements, including related footnotes.

Many audit firms use a financial statement disclosure checklist to remind the auditor of common disclosure problems encountered on audits and also to facilitate the final review of the entire audit. Illustration 10.6 shows a partial financial statement disclosure checklist. Of course, in any given audit some aspects of the engagement require much greater expertise in accounting than can be obtained from such a checklist.

ILLUSTRATION 10.6

FINANCIAL STATEMENT DISCLOSURE CHECKLIST: INVENTORY

1 Are the following disclosures included in the financial statements or notes?
   (a) The accounting policies adopted in measuring inventories, including the cost formula used.
   (b) The total carrying amount of inventories and the carrying amount in classifications.
   (c) The carrying amount of inventories carried at net realisable value.
   (d) The amount of any reversal of any write-down that is recognised as income in the period.
   (e) The circumstances or events that led to the reversal or write-down of inventories.
   (f) The carrying amount of inventories pledged as security for liabilities.
2 Do the financial statements disclose either:
   (a) the cost of inventories recognised as an expense during the period; or
   (b) the operating costs, applicable to revenues, recognised as an expense during the period, classified by their nature

THE AUDITOR'S RESPONSIBILITIES FOR OTHER INFORMATION

The final review of the financial statements involves procedures to determine if disclosures of financial statements and other required disclosures (for corporate governance, management reports, etc.) are adequate. The auditor has a responsibility for all information that appears with the audited financial statements, so therefore the auditor must also see if there are any inconsistencies between this other information and the audited financial statements.[17]

Under the Sarbanes-Oxley Act (SOX)[18], auditors have the responsibility of considering certain financial statement disclosures connected with the financial statements[19] and must attest to, and report on, the assessment made by the management (section 14.5). Companies must also disclose all material correcting adjustments and off-balance sheet transactions. As explained in section 5.3, understanding corporate governance plays an important role in planning the audit and assessing the risk of a material misstatement due to fraud or error (RMM), but is also important for effectively reviewing corporate governance statements and disclosures. This information can be disclosed separately or as part of the documents containing the financial statements. In the latter case, auditor should act in accordance with ISA 720 (Other Information) and relevant national law and regulation. But as discussed in chapter 14, auditors can also be engaged to provide assurance on corporate governance related information such as internal control statements as required by Sarbanes-Oxley Act (SOX).

ISA 720 states that the auditor should read the other information (in documents containing audited financial statements) to identify material inconsistencies with the audited financial statements. The auditor reads this information because the credibility of the audited financial statements may be undermined by material inconsistencies between the audited financial statements and other information. 'Other information', on which the auditor may have no obligation to report but which he must check for material inconsistencies, includes several documents such as an annual report, a report by management or the board of directors on operations, financial summary or highlights, employment data, planned capital expenditures, financial ratios, names of officers and directors, selected quarterly data, and documents used in securities offerings and documents accompanying audited financial statements and the auditor's report on those documents. The auditor's responsibilities (i.e., the work effort) includes reading the other information for consistency with the audited financial statements and considering the other information for consistency with the auditor's understanding of the entity and the environment.

MATERIAL INCONSISTENCY

A material inconsistency exists when other information contradicts information contained in the audited financial statements. A material inconsistency may raise doubts about the audit conclusions drawn from audit evidence obtained and, possibly, about the basis for the auditor's opinion on the financial statements.

If the auditor identifies a material inconsistency on reading the other information, she should determine whether the audited financial statements or the other information needs to be amended. If an amendment is necessary in the other information and the entity refuses to make the amendment, the auditor should consider including in the auditor's report an emphasis of matter paragraph describing the material inconsistency or taking other action. If an amendment is necessary for the audited financial statements and the entity (management and the board) refuses to allow it, the auditor must address the material misstatement in the auditor's report.[20]

MATERIAL MISSTATEMENT OF FACT

If the auditor becomes aware that the other information appears to include a material misstatement of fact, she should discuss the matter with the company's management. A material misstatement of fact in other information exists when such information, not related to matters appearing in the audited financial statements, is incorrectly stated or presented. If the auditor still considers there is an apparent misstatement of fact, she should request that management consult with a qualified third party, such as the entity's legal counsel, and should consider the advice received. If management still refuses to correct the misstatement, the auditor should take appropriate action that includes discussing the issue with the board of directors. If the material misstatement is not adjusted, the auditor must report the misstatement in the auditor's opinion.[21]

10.11 WRAP-UP PROCEDURES

Wrap-up procedures are those procedures done at the end of an audit that generally cannot be performed before the other audit work is complete. Wrap-up procedures include: supervisory review, final analytical procedures (discussed in chapter 9 'Phase III: Building and Execution of the Test Plan – Analytical Review'), working paper review, evaluating audit findings for material misstatements, client approval of adjusting journal entries and review of laws and regulation.

SUPERVISORY REVIEW

Wrap-up procedures start with the in-charge (senior) auditor reviewing the work of the staff auditor. In turn, the manager and partner in charge of the audit review the work submitted by the in-charge auditor. Often, for larger audits, an additional review of the engagement is performed by a manager or partner not working on the engagement to provide an objective assessment of compliance with firm standards (and SOX where applicable). For auditing firms with multiple offices, it is common practice for review teams to visit the various offices periodically and review selected engagements. See chapter 13 for Group Audits.

Before signing off on the audit work, the in-charge or senior auditor must make sure that all phases of the work have been concluded in accordance with the audit planning memorandum, that applicable audit procedures have been satisfactorily completed, the audit objectives have been satisfied, that all is done in line with ISAs and that the working papers reflect conclusions supporting the audit opinion.

Illustration 10.7 summarizes the wrap-up procedures normally undertaken.

ILLUSTRATION 10.7

TYPICAL WRAP-UP PROCEDURES

Supervisory review
- ▶ in charge reviews work of staff auditor
- ▶ manager reviews work of in charge
- ▶ partner reviews manager's work

Do analytical procedures
- ▶ review of trends and important ratios
- ▶ review of unexpected audit findings

Review working papers
- ▶ reviewed by an independent member of the audit firm
- ▶ reviewed for results of audit tests
- ▶ reviewed for sufficiency of evidence
- ▶ make a completing-the-engagement checklist
- ▶ make an unadjusted error worksheet

Evaluate audit findings for material misstatement
- ▶ sign off completion of steps in audit programme
- ▶ identify monetary misstatements in financial statements
- ▶ propose adjustments to financial statements

Client approval of adjusting entries
- ▶ proposed the manager approves adjusting entries
- ▶ obtain client approval for all proposed adjusting and reclassification journal entries

Review laws and regulations
- ▶ review recent changes in statutes and regulations
- ▶ test compliance with regulations

RESOLUTION OF REVIEW QUESTIONS

Resolution of review questions raised by the manager and partner will usually require more extensive documentation and explanation in the working papers. This phase of the review will usually involve a completion of a firm checklist to determine that all reporting standards have been complied with. Illustration 10.8 is a review checklist.

WORKING PAPER REVIEW

The 'in-charge' or 'senior' auditor will obtain the agreement of the manager that the fieldwork is complete before leaving the client's premises. This will usually involve the manager spending the last day or two of the fieldwork at the client's offices reviewing the working papers to determine that the audit programs are complete and that sufficient evidence has been obtained to support the opinion.

ILLUSTRATION 10.8

REVIEW CHECKLIST

Client _____

Closing Date _____   Yes   No

Comments

I General Questions
1   Have you reviewed work paper files?
2   Are you satisfied that:
   (a)   The judgements and conclusions reached are supported by documented evidence?
   (b)   The work paper files contain no unresolved statements that are prejudicial to the interests of the firm?
   (c)   Appropriate changes in the next examination, if any, have been summarised?
3   Do the work papers include adequate documentation as to:
   (a)   Changes in accounting policies?
   (b)   Conformity with generally accepted accounting principles or another comprehensive basis of accounting, if appropriate?
   (c)   Appropriate changes in the next examination, if any, have been summarised?
4   Have you reviewed the audit conclusion on all material Items in the financial statements?
5   Based on your review and your knowledge of the client, do the financial statements fairly present the company's financial position, results of its operations and cash flow?
6   Is the work performed consistent with the arrangements made with the client?
7   Does the work performed comply with the firm's quality control policies in all material respects?
8   Has the computer-assisted audit techniques-related documentation been reviewed by a qualified computer specialist
9   Have required job evaluation forms been completed?

II Financial Statements
1   Is the name of the company exact?
2   Are the dates of the balance sheet and period covered by statements of income, stockholders' equity and cash flow exa
3   Are all material facts that are necessary to make the financial statements not misleading adequately disclosed?
4   Have all material and/or extraordinary subsequent events been evaluated and properly treated and/or disclosed?
5   Is there adequate footnote disclosure? Do the footnotes clearly communicate the facts?
6   Do the financial statements maintain a uniform manner of format, capitalisation, headings and appearance in general within themselves?
7   Are you satisfied that other information contained agrees with the financial statements and auditor's report?

III The Audit Report

1   Is the audit report addressed to the proper party?
2   Is the audit report properly worded?
3   Is an explanatory paragraph included in our opinion when the financial statements are inconsistent?
4   Is the date of our report proper?
5   Is any date in the footnotes that requires special mention, with respect to the date of our report, appropriately reflected in the date of our report (e.g. dual dating)?
6   Is the option on the supplementary financial information proper and supported by auditor examination?
7   Are disclosures in the opinion, financial statements and notes to financial statements adequate?

IV Client Relations

1   Have we performed the engagement in accordance with the arrangement (including any request by the client for extra services)?
2   Are you satisfied that the audit did not disclose any suspicions of irregularities or illegal acts?
3   Are you satisfied that the client is a going concern?
4   Have arrangements been made:
    (a)   For the client's review and approval of the proposed adjustments?
    (b)   For the client to review a draft of the report?
    (c)   To communicate reportable conditions and material weaknesses in the internal control structure?
5   Have suggestions been summarised for a management letter?
6   Are we satisfied that no unusual client problem was noted during the audit?

V Report Production

1   Are instructions as to processing specific, including the type of report, client number, numbers of copies required, due date, delivery instruction (when and how)?
2   Does the report style and appearance conform appropriately with the standards we have established for all reports?
3   Is the language of the report simple and concise?

Working papers (*or work papers*) are a record of the auditor's planning; nature, timing and extent of the auditing procedures performed; results of such procedures; and the conclusions drawn from the evidence obtained.

Working papers may be in the form of data stored on paper, film, electronic, other media, on servers or in the cloud. They should contain sufficient information to enable an experienced auditor having no previous connection with the audit to ascertain from them the evidence that supports the auditors' significant conclusions and judgments. Working papers serve two main functions: to aid in the conduct and supervision of the audit and as primary support for the auditor's opinion, especially the representation that the audit was conducted in accordance with ISAs.[22]

Working papers are a physical aid in recording the results of audit tests. For example, when a sample is taken, the items sampled must be recorded and computations must be made. Since supervisors who usually perform none of the audit tests make final decisions concerning the audit opinion, the working papers serve as a basis for evaluating the evidence given. After the opinion has been given, working papers are the only physical proof that the auditor has that an adequate audit was conducted because original documents and accounting records remain with the client.

The working papers are reviewed for sufficiency of evidence. Evidence recorded in the working papers should be both relevant and valid. Relevance is largely a matter of the relationship between the evidential matter and the financial statement assertion involved. For example, if the assertion concerns existence of an asset, the reviewer should find that the auditor selected items included in the account balance and physically examined and confirmed those items.

ENGAGEMENT QUALITY REVIEW

Someone who did not take part in the audit reviews the working papers. This is called an *engagement quality review*.[23] At the completion of the audit, work papers may be reviewed by an independent member of the audit firm who has not participated in the audit for four basic reasons:

1 to evaluate the performance of inexperienced personnel;
2 to make sure that the audit meets the audit firm's standard of performance;
3 to counteract the bias that frequently enters the auditor's judgement;
4 to comply with audit regulation such as the Sarbanes-Oxley Act.

As also mentioned in chapter 2.11, in accordance with ISA 220.36[24], the engagement quality control reviewer must evaluate the significant judgments made by the engagement team, and the conclusions reached. This evaluation involves:

(a) discussion of significant matters;
(b) review of the financial statements and the proposed auditor's report;
(c) review of selected audit documentation relating to the significant judgments the engagement team made and the conclusions it reached; and
(d) evaluation of the conclusions reached in formulating the auditor's report and consideration of whether the proposed auditor's report is appropriate.

10.12 SUMMARY

The audit is not over until the audit report is signed. And even then, it may not be over if facts are discovered after the balance sheet date and before the next report. After the fieldwork is almost complete, a series of procedures are generally carried out to 'complete the audit'. In this chapter the evaluation and finalization phase (Phase 4) is described.

At this phase, the auditors must review financial statements, financial statement disclosures, and other information in the annual report. Other information that needs to be investigated is the board of directors' report, corporate governance disclosures (where applicable) and all other information in the annual report to shareholders. Other activities as part of the evaluation and completion phase are wrap-up procedures and report to the audit committee. Prior to the final audit report the auditors will also discuss their findings with the audit committee – amongst other issues irregularities, illegal acts and reportable conditions

Specific considerations need to be made for a number of selected items when it comes to gathering audit evidence. This concerns in particular inventory, litigation and claims and segment information. In this phase, written confirmations must also be obtained from the management and from external lawyers.

The auditor must obtain evidence regarding the existence and condition of inventory; completeness of litigation and claims involving the entity; and presentation and disclosure of segment information in accordance with the applicable financial reporting framework. The required procedures may include attendance at physical inventory counting; evaluation of management's instructions and procedures for recording, controlling the physical inventory count, observation of the performance of management's count procedures and inspection of the inventory and perform test counts; and performing audit procedures over the entity's final inventory records to determine whether they accurately reflect actual inventory count.

A review of contingent liabilities and commitments is also part of the evaluation and completion phase. Such liabilities and commitments must after all be explained in the notes to the financial statements. Evaluating the going concern opinion is also a procedure that must be performed by the auditor. If there is a serious uncertainty about the going concern, this must be explained in the notes and the auditor will refer to this in the auditor's report.

Written representations and legal letters are audit evidence. ISA 580 states that the auditor should obtain evidence that management acknowledges its responsibility for the fair representation of the financial statements in accordance with the relevant financial reporting framework and has approved the financial statements. One of the audit procedures in the evaluation and completion cycle is to gather a representation letter from management. An important audit procedure that auditors rely on for discovering litigation, claims and assessments that affect the client is a letter from the client's legal counsel called a legal letter or inquiry of client's attorneys. Auditors analyze client legal expense for the present year and sometimes the prior years. The auditor requires that the client send a standard request letter to every legal adviser.

A contingent liability is a potential future obligation to an outside party for an unknown amount resulting from the outcome of a past event, for example an adverse tax court decision, lawsuit, and notes receivable discounted. Footnote disclosure is ordinarily required if there are probable losses.

The auditor must consider events up to the date of the auditor's report and between the balance sheet date and the issuance of the statements. Discovery of such facts after the financial statements' issuance are not generally as crucial but sometimes require further analysis, discussion with management and legal advice. Review for subsequent events is the auditing procedures performed by auditors to identify and evaluate subsequent events. Subsequent events are events occurring between the date of the financial statements and the date of the auditor's report, and facts that become known to the auditor after the date of the auditor's report.

Parties are considered to be related if one party has the ability to control the other party or exercise significant influence over the other party in making financial and operational decisions. A *related party transaction* is a transfer of resources or obligations between related parties, regardless of whether a price is charged. Two aspects of related party transactions of which an auditor must be aware are adequate disclosure of related party transactions and the possibility that the existence of related parties increases the risk of management fraud. The engagement team discussion required by ISA 315 and ISA 240 includes specific consideration of the susceptibility of the financial statements to material misstatement due to fraud or error that could result from the entity's related party relationships and transactions.

Reporting on going-concern-related uncertainties remains one of the most challenging issues faced by external auditors. Even though professional standards do not hold external auditors responsible for predicting future events, if an auditor refrains from issuing a going concern audit opinion and the client company subsequently fails, the costs to the auditor in terms of increased litigation and loss of reputation are often substantial. When performing risk assessment procedures, the auditor must consider whether there are events or conditions that may cast significant doubt on the entity's ability to continue as a going concern.

It is the auditor's responsibility when forming an opinion on the financial statements to conclude whether reasonable assurance has been obtained about whether the financial statements as a whole are free from material misstatement. The auditor's conclusion takes into account her evaluation of uncorrected *misstatements*. Therefore, the objective of the auditor is to evaluate the effect of identified misstatements on the audit; and the effect of *uncorrected misstatements* on the financial statements. Generally, if misstatements are found, the auditor asks management to correct them. If management corrects those, the auditor must still perform additional audit procedures to determine whether misstatements remain. If management refuses to correct some or all of the misstatements communicated by the auditor, the auditor should consider management's reasons for not making the corrections.

The final review of the financial statements involves procedures to determine if disclosures of financial statements and other required disclosures (for corporate governance, management reports, etc.) are adequate. The auditor has a responsibility for all information that appears with the audited financial statements, so therefore the auditor must also see if there are any inconsistencies between this other information and the audited financial statements.

Together with the audited financial statements, other information is usually made public. Examples include the management report, corporate governance information and CSR information. The auditor will have to determine on the basis of the knowledge obtained during the financial statement audit that this other information is adequate and is consistent with the financial statements.

During this fourth phase of the audit 'wrap up activities' are carried out, such as supervisory review, quality assurance review, working paper review and audit findings are evaluated and communicated with management and those charged with governance. Wrap-up procedures start with the in-charge (senior) auditor reviewing the work of the staff auditor. In turn, the manager and partner in charge of the audit review the work submitted by the in-charge auditor. The manager will review the working papers to determine that the audit programs are complete and that sufficient evidence has been obtained to support the opinion. *Working papers* (*work papers*) are a record of the auditor's planning; nature, timing and extent of the auditing procedures performed; results of such procedures; and the conclusions drawn from the evidence obtained. Furthermore, someone who did not take part in the audit reviews the working papers. This is called an *engagement quality review*.

10.13 QUESTIONS, EXERCISES AND CASES

QUESTIONS

10.2 Introduction

10-1 What are the general procedures for completing the audit as shown in the standard audit process model?

10.3 Specific Considerations Gathering Evidence for Selected Items

10-2 Which audit procedures are required regarding the existence and condition of inventory?

10-3 List the procedures to discover claims against your audit client.

10-4 Give some examples of 'Segment Information' and motivate why evaluation of audit evidence is important.

10.4 Written Representations

10-5 What should be included in the letter from client's legal counsel?

10-6 What kind of evidence does ISA 580 suggest that the auditor get from management? Where might an auditor find evidence to fulfil this requirement?

10.5 Review for Contingent Liabilities and Commitments

10-7 What is a contingent liability? What three conditions must be met for a contingent liability to exist?

10-8 What are commitments?

10.6 Review for Discovery of Subsequent Events

10-9 What is a review for discovery of subsequent events? What should an auditor do if she becomes aware of facts that existed at the date of the auditor's report after the financial statements have been issued?

10-10 If the auditor becomes aware of a fact that may materially affect the financial statements after the date of the auditor's report but before the financial statements have been issued, what should an auditor do and how may this affect the financial statements? What if a material fact is discovered after the financial statements have been issued?

10.7 Related Party Transactions

10-11 Discuss circumstances involving related parties that contribute to higher risks of material misstatements than transactions with unrelated parties.

10-12 Because of the possibility of related party transactions, the auditor should perform audit procedures designed to obtain sufficient appropriate audit evidence regarding the identification and disclosure by management of related parties and the effect of related party transactions. Name the procedures an auditor may perform regarding related party information provided by management.

10.8 Evaluation of Going Concern Assumption

10-13 What are some indications that the continuance of the company as a going concern may be questionable?

10-14 What procedures should an auditor perform when events or conditions have been identified which may cast significant doubt on the entity's ability to continue as a going concern?

10.9 Evaluation of Misstatements Identified During the Audit (ISA 450)

10-15 Can you outline the key steps auditors should follow according to International Standard on Auditing 450 when evaluating misstatements discovered during an audit process? Additionally, how do auditors distinguish between material and immaterial misstatements, and what actions should they take in response to each category?

10-16 In what ways does International Standard on Auditing 450 provide guidance to auditors on assessing the implications of misstatements identified during an audit, particularly regarding their nature, cause, and potential impact on the fairness and reliability of financial statements?

10-17 What are monetary misstatements? What mistakes can cause a monetary misstatement?

10.10 Review of Financial Statements and Other Information

10-18 When reviewing for adequate disclosure, what does an auditor look for? Give some examples.

10-19 When does a material inconsistency exist in information other than the financial statements? What other information must an auditor review for material inconsistencies? What should an auditor do if a material inconsistency is found?

10.11 Wrap-up Procedures

10-20 What are wrap-up procedures? Give some examples.

10-21 What must the audit supervisor do before she can consider the audit work complete?

10-22 What are monetary misstatements? What mistakes can cause a monetary misstatement?

PROBLEMS AND EXERCISES

10.3 Specific Considerations Gathering Evidence for Selected Items

10-23 **Attendance at Physical Inventory Counting**. A processor of frozen foods carries an inventory of finished products consisting of 50 different types of items valued at approximately $2,000,000. About $750,000 of this value represents stock produced by the company and billed to customers prior to the audit date. This inventory stock is being held for the customers at a monthly rental charge until they request shipment and is not separate from the company's inventory.

The company maintains separate perpetual ledgers at the plant office for both stock owned and stock being held for customers. The cost department also maintains a perpetual record of stock owned. The above perpetual records reflect quantities only.

The company does not take a complete physical inventory at any time during the year, since the temperature in the cold storage facilities is too low to allow one to spend more than 15 minutes inside at a time. It is not considered practical to move items outside or to defreeze the cold storage facilities for the purpose of taking a physical inventory. Because of these circumstances, it is impractical to test count quantities to the extent of completely counting specific items. The company considers as its inventory valuation at year-end the aggregate of the quantities reflected by the perpetual record of stock owned, maintained at the plant office, priced at the lower of cost or market.

Required:

A. What are the two principal problems facing the auditor in the audit of the inventory? Discuss briefly.

B. Outline the audit steps that you would take to enable you to render an unqualified opinion with respect to the inventory. (You may omit consideration of tests of unit prices and clerical accuracy.)

10.4 Written Representations

10-24 Inquiry of Client's Attorney. Morgan LeFay, AS, of Horsens, Denmark, auditor Jan Ogier, Statsautoriseret Revisor, determines that LeFay has paid legal fees to four different law firms during the year under audit. Ogier requests standard attorney letters as of the balance sheet date from each of the four law firms.

Jan Ogier receives the following responses:

1 One attorney furnished the following opinion: 'It is our opinion that, based on a complete investigation of the facts known to us, no liability will be established against LeFay in the suits referred to in your letter of inquiry.'

2 Attorney number two states that there may be a potentially material lawsuit against the client but refuses to comment further to protect the legal rights of the client.

3 By the last day of field work, Ogier has not received any letter from the third attorney.

4 The letter from the fourth attorney writes that their firm deals exclusively in registering song copyrights and cannot comment on LeFay lawsuits or any other legal affairs.

Required:

A. Discuss the adequacy of the attorney's response in each of the four cases. What procedures should Ogier take in response to each letter?

B. What impact will each of these letters have on Ogier's audit report? Explain.

C. Should you refer to the attorney's opinion in your audit report or disclosures?

10-25 Management Representation Letter. Robert Dingle, president of Alcmena Manufacturing, Ltd., of Perth, Australia, and the company external auditor Deny H. Lawrence, Chartered Accountant (CA), reviewed matters that were supposed to be included in a written representation letter. Upon receipt of the following client representation letter, Lawrence contacted Dingle to state that it was incomplete. The letter Lawrence received is given below.

To D.H. Lawrence, CA

In connection with your audit of the balance sheet of Alcmena Manufacturing as of 31 December 20X2, and the related statements of income, retained earnings, and cash flows for the year then ended, for the purpose of expressing an opinion as to whether the financial statements present fairly, in all material respects, the financial position, results of operations, and cash flows of Alcmena Manufacturing in conformity with generally accepted accounting principles, we confirm, to the best of our knowledge and belief, the following representations made to you during your audit. There were no:

▶ Plans or intentions that may materially affect the carrying value or classification of assets and liabilities.

▶ Communications from regulatory agencies concerning noncompliance with, or deficiencies in, financial reporting practices.

▶ Agreements to repurchase assets previously sold.

▶ Violations or possible violations of laws or regulations whose effects should be considered for disclosure in the financial statements or as a basis for recording a loss contingency.

▶ Unasserted claims or assessments that our lawyer has advised are probable of assertion and must be disclosed in accordance with International Accounting Standards No.10.

▶ Capital stock repurchase options or agreements or capital stock reserved for options, warrants, conversions, or other requirements.

▶ Compensating balance or other arrangements involving restrictions on cash balances.

R. Dingle, President

Alcmena Manufacturing Ltd.

14 March 20X3

Required:

Identify the other matters that Dingle's representation letter should specifically confirm.

10.6 Review for Discovery of Subsequent Events

10-26 Subsequent Facts and Events. The following unrelated events occurred after the balance sheet date but before the audit report was prepared:

1 The granting of a retrospective pay increase to selected employees.

2 Receipt of a letter from the tax authorities stating that additional income tax is due for a prior year.

3 Filing of an antitrust suit by the federal government.

4 Declaration of a stock dividend.

5 Sale of a fixed asset at a substantial profit.

Required:

A. Define 'review for discovery of subsequent events' and 'subsequent events'.

B. Identify what procedure to identify events the auditor might have used to bring each of these items to the auditor's attention. (Hint: See illustration 10.8.)

C. Discuss the auditor's responsibility to recognise each of these in connection with the audit report.

10-27 Subsequent Facts and Events. In connection with their audit of the financial statements of Swan Mfg. Corporation of Ayutthay, Thailand, for the year ended 31 December 20X4, Virameteekul, Kanchana & Banharn, Chartered Accountants (CA) review of subsequent events disclosed the following items:

1 3 January 20X5: The government approved a plan for the construction of an express highway. The plan will result in the expropriation of a portion of the land owned

by Swan Mfg. Corporation. Construction will begin in late 20X5. No estimate of the condemnation award is available.

2 4 January 20X5: The funds for Baht 1,000,000 loan to the corporation made by the company president, Somsak Na Lan, on 15 July 20X4, were obtained by him from a loan on his personal life insurance policy. The loan was recorded in the account 'loan from officers'. Mr Somsak's source of the funds was not disclosed in the company records.

   (i) The corporation pays the premiums on the life insurance policy, and Mrs Somsak, wife of the president, is the beneficiary.

3 January 20X5: The mineral content of a shipment of ore, en route on 31 December 20X4, was determined to be 72 per cent. The shipment was recorded at year-end at an estimated content of 50 per cent by a debit to raw material inventory and a credit to accounts payable in the amount of Baht 824,000. The final liability to the vendor is based on the actual mineral content of the shipment.

4 31 January 20X5: As a result of reduced sales, production was curtailed in mid-January and some workers were laid off. On 5 February 20X5, all the remaining workers went on strike. To date the strike is unsettled.

Required:

Assume that the items described above came to your attention prior to completion of your audit work on 15 February 20X5. For each item:

A. Give the audit procedures, if any, that would have brought the item to your attention. Indicate other sources of information that may have revealed the item.

B. Discuss the disclosure that you would recommend for the item, listing all details that you would suggest should be disclosed. Indicate those items or details, if any, that should not be disclosed. Give your reasons for recommending or not recommending disclosure of the items or details.

10.7 Related Party Transactions

10-28 D'orsay Dore, SA is being audited by Stolowy & Oxibar, Expert Comptables. During the course of the audit Stolowy & Oxibar discover D'orsay Dore sold inventory to Parisienne de Fedora for 90-day terms, three times the typical payment period required, and the payments went directly to the president of D'orsay Dore, not to the accounting department which was the usual practice. Industriel Cuir supplies over 40 per cent of the raw materials D'orsay purchases whereas no other supplier provides more than 5 per cent of raw materials. D'orsay management says that they do so much business with Industriel Cuir because they provide D'orsay management assistance at no charge.

D'orsay's business is greatest in the last month before the fiscal year end when they book 30 per cent of their sales, some years in the last week before closing. D'orsay Dore has provided Stolowy & Oxibar with a management representation letter that states that there are no related party transactions.

Required:

A. Should Stolowy & Oxibar take D'orsay Dore's word when Dore says there are no related parties? Why?

B. List the circumstances at D'orsay Dore that may indicate the existence of unidentified related parties.

C. What audit procedures should Stolowy & Oxibar perform to investigate the possibility of related parties?

10.8 Evaluation of Going Concern Assumption

10–29 Going Concern. When an auditor finds the ability of a company to continue as a going concern is questionable, the auditor will use certain audit procedures to obtain further evidence. Jocques Entremont, Expert Comptable, the external auditor for Japonaiseries SA, a company which retails Japanese art and woodcuts in Boulogne, France, suspects that there is a going concern problem.

Required:

A. List the procedures the auditor would perform.

B. Write the auditor's opinion if disclosure of the problem is considered adequate.

C. Write the auditor's opinion if adequate disclosure is not made.

10-30 Going Concern. In evaluating management's assessment of the entity's ability to continue as a going concern, the auditor must cover the same period as that used by management to make its assessment as required by the applicable financial reporting framework, or by law or regulation if it specifies a longer period. If management's assessment of the entity's ability to continue as a going concern covers less than twelve months from the date of the financial statements the auditor must request management to extend its assessment period to at least twelve months from that date.

Required:

A. Why should the auditor cover the same period as by management?

B. When should the assessment period be longer than twelve months?

10.9 Evaluation of Misstatements Identified During the Audit

10-31 Seth Automobile Ltd is a publicly traded company operating in the manufacturing sector. It has been audited by Hugo Talltree, a partner of a reputable Scottish audit firm, BEAM Auditors Inc., for several years. This year, during the audit process, significant misstatements were identified by the audit team. The auditors must now evaluate these misstatements in accordance with International Standard on Auditing (ISA) 450 to determine their impact on the financial statements. During the audit of the financial statements of Seth Automobile, the audit team identified several misstatements in the financial statements. These misstatements included errors in revenue recognition, incorrect valuation of inventory, and understatement of liabilities. The audit team gathered evidence through various audit procedures, including substantive testing and analytical procedures, to assess the accuracy of the financial statements.

Question:

How should Hugo Talltree evaluate misstatements identified during the audit process, in accordance with International Standard on Auditing (ISA) 450, to determine their impact on the financial statements?

10.10 Review of Financial Statements and Other Information

10-32 Board of Directors Disclosures. The board of directors of Celestial City Corporation of Taejon, Korea, is issuing a corporate governance report. In this audit year Celestial City lost 1,280,000,000 South Korean Won (won) due to a weakness in their internal controls in the treasury department which represents 10 per cent of their current assets. The controller's assistant, Dongsung Young, a Certified Public Accountant (CPA), is asked to write the first draft of the internal control portion of the report.

Required:

Pretend that you are Mr. Young and write a draft of the internal controls portion of Celestial City Corporation's corporate governance report. Since Celestial City is publicly traded on the American Stock Exchange and a Depository Receipt, use the SEC requirements for the report. See 'Final Rule: Management's Report on Internal Control Over Financial Reporting and Certification of Disclosure in Exchange Act Periodic Reports'.

10.11 Wrap-up Procedures

10-33 Working Paper Review. Berins & Trichet, Reviseurs d'Entreprises, of Brussels, Belgium has a policy of having their audit papers reviewed by both the partner in charge and an independent reviewer.

Required:

A. Define 'working paper'.

B. Describe the difference between a regular working paper review and an independent review.

C. What items does the regular reviewer examine? The independent reviewer?

10-34 Engagement Quality Review. Charalambos Viachoutsicos is assigned the responsibility of setting up a quality review programme at his St Petersburg, Russia, audit firm, Levenchuk.

Required:

A. What should the verification procedures include? Who should perform the procedures?

B. What type of documentation is required?

C. What should be covered in the report on the quality review programme?

D. What organisational authority is required for the personnel who carry out the quality audit?

E. What qualifications should the personnel have?

CASES

10-35 SEC Regulation, Tax and Working Papers. Marshall and Wyatt, CPAs, have been for several years the independent auditors of Interstate LDC Land Development Corporation of New Orleans, Louisiana. During these years, Interstate LDC prepared and filed its own annual income tax returns.

During 20X3, Interstate LDC requested Marshall and Wyatt to audit all the necessary financial statements of the corporation to be submitted to the US Securities and Exchange Commission (SEC) in connection with a multi-state public offering of one million shares of Interstate Land Development Corporation common stock. This public offering came under the provisions of the US Securities Act of 1933. The audit was performed carefully and the financial statements were fairly presented for the respective periods. These financial statements were included in the registration statement filed with the SEC.

While the registration statement was being processed by the SEC, but before the effective date, the US taxing authority, the Internal Revenue Service (IRS), obtained a federal court subpoena directing Marshall and Wyatt to turn over all of its working papers relating to Interstate LDC for the years 20X0–X2. Marshall and Wyatt initially refused to comply for two reasons. First, Marshall and Wyatt did not prepare Interstate LDC's tax returns. Second, Marshall and Wyatt claimed that the working papers were confidential matters subject to the privileged communications rule. Subsequently, however, Marshall and Wyatt did relinquish the subpoenaed working papers. Upon receiving the subpoena, Wyatt called Dan Dunkirk, the chairman of Interstate LDC's board of directors, and asked him about the IRS investigation. Dunkirk responded, 'I'm sure the IRS people are on a 'fishing expedition' and that they will not find any material deficiencies.'

A few days later Chairman Dunkirk received a written memorandum from the IRS stating that Interstate LDC had underpaid its taxes during the period under review. The memorandum revealed that Interstate LDC was being assessed $800,000, including penalties and interest for the three years. Dunkirk forwarded a copy of this memorandum to Marshall and Wyatt.

This $800,000 assessment was material relative to the financial statements as of 31 December 20X3. The amount for each year individually, exclusive of penalty and interest, was not material relative to each respective year.

Required:

A. In general terms, discuss the extent to which a US CPA firm's potential liability to third parties is increased in an SEC registration audit.

B. Discuss the implications of the IRS investigation, if any, relative to Marshall and Wyatt's audit of Interstate LDC's 20X3 financial statements. Discuss any additional investigative procedures that the auditors should undertake or any audit judgments that should be made as result of this investigation.

C. Can Marshall and Wyatt validly refuse to surrender the subpoenaed working papers to the IRS? Explain.

10-36 Going Concern. Financial Statements Going Concern Examples (derived from www.ifrssystem.com)

A. Letter of support from Cogny SpA (parent company). As at 30 June 20XX the Cogny Group SpA (consolidated) had a net asset deficiency of $15,444,521 which included related party loans of $6,221,923 However, the financial statements have been prepared on a going concern basis as Cogny SpA (ultimate parent company) has pledged its continuing support for a minimum of 12 months from the date of issuing these financial statements.

B. The consolidated financial statements of Tobacco Inc. have been prepared on a going concern basis. For the year ended 30 June 20XX, the consolidated entity incurred a loss from continuing operations after tax of $3,626,833 (20XX-1: $7,444,333,121). In the same period Tobacco Inc. had operating cash outflows of 33,121,122 (2017: $26,244,369). A cash flow forecast for the next 12 months prepared by management has indicated that the consolidated entity will have sufficient cash assets to be able to meet its debts as and when they are due. No adjustments have been made relating to recoverability and classification of recorded asset amounts and classification of liabilities that might be necessary should the consolidated entity not continue as a going concern.

Required:

For both situations (A. Letter of Support and B. Cash Flow Forecast) describe the procedures to gather sufficient and appropriate audit evidence about the going concern assumptions.

10.14 NOTES

1. IFRS 8 Operating Segments requires particular classes of entities (essentially those with publicly traded securities) to disclose information about their operating segments, products and services, the geographical areas in which they operate, and their major customers. Information is based on internal management reports, both in the identification of operating segments and measurement of disclosed segment information.

2. International Auditing and Assurance Standards Board (IAASB), 2023, International Standard on Auditing 501 (ISA 501) 'Audit Evidence – Specific Considerations for Selected Items, *Handbook of International Quality Control, Auditing Review, Other Assurance, and Related Services Pronouncements*, 2022 edn, Part I, International Federation of Accountants, New York.

3. International Auditing and Assurance Standards Board (IAASB), 2023, International Standard on Auditing 505 (ISA 505) 'External Confirmations', *Handbook of International Quality Control, Auditing Review, Other Assurance, and Related Services Pronouncements*, 2022 edn, Part I, International Federation of Accountants, New York.

4. Ibid. ISA 580.6.

5. Ibid. ISA 580, para. 15.

6. Example representation letter for the audit of financial statements, appendix 2, ISA 580.

7. International Accounting Standards Board (IASB), 2023, International Financial Reporting Standards IAS 10 'Events After the Balance Sheet Date', IASB, London, https://www.ifrs.org/issued-standards/list-of-standards/ias-10-events-after-the-reporting-period/#:~:text=IAS%2010%20prescribes%3A,events%20after%20the%20reporting%20period.

8. International Accounting Standards Board (IASB), 2013, International Financial Reporting Standards IAS 24 'Related Party Transaction Disclosures'. https://www.ifrs.org/issued-standards/list-of-standards/ias-24-related-party-disclosures/.

9. International Auditing and Assurance Standards Board (IAASB), 2023, International Standards on Auditing 315 (ISA 315) 'Identifying and Assessing the Risks of Material Misstatement through Understanding the Entity and Its Environment', para. 17-18, *Handbook of International Quality Control, Auditing, Review, Other Assurance, and Related Services Pronouncements*, 2022 edn, Part I, International Federation of Accountants, New York.

10. International Auditing and Assurance Standards Board (IAASB), 2023, International Standard on Auditing 240 (ISA 240) 'The Auditor's Responsibilities Relating to Fraud in an Audit of Financial Statements', para. 16, *Handbook of International Quality Management, Auditing, Review, Other Assurance, and Related Services Pronouncements*, 2022 edn, Volume I, International Federation of Accountants, New York.

11. International Auditing and Assurance Standards Board (IAASB), 2023, International Standards on Auditing 700 (ISA 700) ' Forming an Opinion and Reporting on Financial Statements', paras 10–15, *Handbook of International Quality Control, Auditing, Review, Other Assurance, and Related Services Pronouncements*, 2022 edn, Part I, International Federation of Accountants, New York.

12. For an overview of academic literature, we refer to Geiger, Gold, Wallage, A Review of Global Research and Future Research Opportunities, Routledge, London, 2021.

13. International Auditing and Assurance Standards Board (IAASB), 2023, International Standard on Auditing 570 (ISA 570) 'going Concern', para 19, *Handbook of International Quality Control, Auditing Review, Other Assurance, and Related Services Pronouncements*, 2022 edn, Part I, International Federation of Accountants, New York.

14. Immaterial is sometimes described as 'clearly trivial'. Matters that are clearly trivial will be inconsequential, whether taken individually or in aggregate and whether judged by any criteria of size, nature, or circumstances. When there is any uncertainty about whether one or more items are clearly trivial, the matter is not considered trivial.

15. The auditor cannot assume that an instance of error or fraud is an isolated occurrence. Therefore, the auditor should evaluate the nature and effects of the individual misstatements accumulated during the audit on the assessed risks of material misstatement. PCAOB, AS 2810.19.

16. Examples are the Securities and Exchange Committee (SEC) in the US, the Financial Reporting Council in the UK, the Authority Financial Markets in the Netherlands, Bundesanstalt für Finanzdienstleistungsaufsicht (Bafin) in Germany, China Securities Regulatory Commission (CSRC), The Autorité des marchés financiers, France, Commissione Nazionale per le Società e la Borsa (CONSOB), Italy, The Federal Commission on Securities Market (FCSM) of Russia.

17. Ibid. ISA 720, para. 11.

18. Sarbanes–Oxley Act of 2002, https://www.congress.gov/bill/107th-congress/house-bill/3763

19. Public Company Accounting Oversight Board (PCAOB), 2018, Audit Standard 2201 (AS 2201) An Audit of Internal Control over Financial Reporting That Is Integrated with An Audit of Financial Statements.

20. International Auditing and Assurance Standards Board (IAASB), 2023, International Standard on Auditing 720 (ISA 720) 'The Auditors Responsibility Relating to Other Information', para. 16-17, *Handbook of International Quality Control, Auditing Review, Other Assurance, and Related Services Pronouncements*, 2022 edn, Part I, International Federation of Accountants, New York.

21. Ibid.

22. International Auditing and Assurance Standards Board (IAASB), 2023, International Standard on Auditing 230 (ISA 230) 'Audit Documentation', para. 2, *Handbook of International Quality Control, Auditing Review, Other Assurance, and Related Services Pronouncements*, 2022 edn, Part I, International Federation of Accountants, New York.

23. ISA 220.12b. Engagement quality control review – A process designed to provide an objective evaluation, on or before the date of the auditor's report, of the significant judgments the engagement team made and the conclusions it reached in formulating the auditor's report. The engagement quality control review process is for audits of financial statements of listed entities and those other audit engagements, if any, for which the firm has determined an engagement quality control review is required. Also see PCAOB, AS 1220.

24. International Auditing and Assurance Standards Board (IAASB), 2023, International Standard on Auditing 220 (ISA 220) "Quality Control for an Audit of Financial Statements, para. 36, *Handbook of International Quality Control, Auditing Review, Other Assurance, and Related Services Pronouncements*, 2022 edn, Part I, International Federation of Accountants, New York.

CHAPTER 11

REPORTING

The four phases of the audit:

Acceptance/ continuance	Understanding/ risk analysis	Building/executing audit plan	Evaluating/ completion
Phase 1	Phase 2	Phase 3	Phase 4

11.1 LEARNING OBJECTIVES

After studying this chapter, you should be able to:

1. Grasp who has responsibility for the financial statements and why.
2. Understand the basic elements of the auditor's report: contents and form.
3. Explain the contents and importance of the unmodified audit opinion.
4. Distinguish between the different types of opinions given in audit reports on financial statements.
5. Describe the circumstances under which the auditor will modify an opinion.
6. Explain importance and content of key audit matters.
7. Provide circumstances in which the unmodified opinion requires an emphasis of a matter paragraph.
8. Discuss the audit matters of governance interest arising from the audit of financial statements that the auditor must communicate to those charged with governance of an entity.
9. Give details contained in the long-form audit report.
10. List the general content of a management letter.
11. Motivate why an auditor attends a meeting of the shareholders of a company.

11.2 INTRODUCTION

A standard auditor's report takes no more than a few pages. Because of its brevity those not knowledgeable in auditing may view it as constituting little more than a necessary legal formality, lacking in substance. However, it may surprise that the auditor's report requires great care, and it is the consummation of a rigorous and lengthy process. As illustration of such a long process being reduced to a few words, a study in the USA[1] in the 1990s found that in one given year a global audit firm's five largest clients required average audit work of 128,000 hours per client. This resulted in audit reports of only 175 words or less. One might conclude that to get so many hours into so few words, auditors must be poets. More likely, this brevity is out of concern for the users of financial statements. The authors of that same study suggest that the anxious investor does not want to muddle through a length catalogue of work done and detailed findings (imagine how long that would be after 128,000 hours of work) when the final message is 'It is OK'.

During the financial crisis of 2007/2008, societal trust in financial markets and its key players like bankers and auditors declined sharply. To regain societal trust in the auditor's report, the International Auditing and Assurance Standards Board (IAASB), the US Public Company Accounting Oversight Board (PCAOB) and others developed a lengthier and more detailed auditor's report. ISA 700, 'Forming an Opinion and Reporting on Financial Statements' promotes consistency in the auditor's report as it promotes credibility in the global marketplace by making more readily identifiable those audits that have been conducted in accordance with globally recognized standards.

In the United States, the PCAOB has issued a similar standard (AS 3101) entitled 'The Auditor's Report on an Audit of Financial Statements When the Auditor Expresses an Unqualified Opinion'.

You will find the Auditor's Report on the Audit of the Financial Statements of Facebook Inc. 2022 as an example (illustration 11.1).

ILLUSTRATION 11.1

AUDITOR'S REPORT META PLATFORMS, INC., 2022
Report of Independent Registered Public Accounting Firm
To the Stockholders and the Board of Directors of Meta Platforms, Inc.

Opinion on the Financial Statements
We have audited the accompanying consolidated balance sheets of Meta Platforms, Inc. (the Company) as of December 31, 2022 and 2021, the related consolidated statements of income, comprehensive income, stockholders' equity and cash flows for each of the three years in the period ended December 31, 2022, and the related notes (collectively referred to as the 'consolidated financial statements'). In our opinion, the consolidated financial statements present fairly, in all material respects, the financial position of the Company at December 31, 2022 and 2021, and the results of its operations and its cash flows for each of the three years in the period ended December 31, 2022, in conformity with U.S. generally accepted accounting principles. We also have audited, in accordance with the standards of the Public Company Accounting Oversight Board (United States) (PCAOB), the Company's internal control over financial reporting as of December 31, 2022, based on criteria established in Internal Control – Integrated Framework issued by the Committee of Sponsoring Organizations of the Treadway Commission (2013 framework), and our report dated February 1, 2023, expressed an unqualified opinion thereon.

Basis for Opinion

These financial statements are the responsibility of the Company's management. Our responsibility is to express an opinion on the Company's financial statements based on our audits. We are a public accounting firm registered with the PCAOB and are required to be independent with respect to the Company in accordance with the U.S. federal securities laws and the applicable rules and regulations of the Securities and Exchange Commission and the PCAOB. We conducted our audits in accordance with the standards of the PCAOB. Those standards require that we plan and perform the audit to obtain reasonable assurance about whether the financial statements are free of material misstatement, whether due to error or fraud. Our audits included performing procedures to assess the risks of material misstatement of the financial statements, whether due to error or fraud, and performing procedures that respond to those risks. Such procedures included examining, on a test basis, evidence regarding the amounts and disclosures in the financial statements. Our audits also included evaluating the accounting principles used and significant estimates made by management, as well as evaluating the overall presentation of the financial statements. We believe that our audits provide a reasonable basis for our opinion.

Critical Audit Matters

The critical audit matters communicated below are matters arising from the current period audit of the financial statements that were communicated or required to be communicated to the Audit & Risk Oversight Committee and that: (1) relate to accounts or disclosures that are material to the financial statements and (2) involved our especially challenging, subjective or complex judgments. The communication of critical audit matters does not alter in any way our opinion on the consolidated financial statements, taken as a whole, and we are not, by communicating the critical audit matters below, providing separate opinions on the critical audit matters or on the accounts or disclosures to which they relate.

Loss Contingencies

Description of the Matter

As described in Note 13 to the consolidated financial statements, the Company is party to various legal proceedings, claims, and regulatory or government inquiries and investigations. The Company accrues a liability when it believes a loss is probable and the amount can be reasonably estimated. In addition, the Company believes it is reasonably possible that it will incur a loss in some of these cases, actions or inquiries described above. When applicable, the Company discloses an estimate of the amount of loss or range of possible loss that may be incurred. However, for certain other matters, the Company discloses that the amount of such losses or a range of possible losses cannot be reasonably estimated at this time. Auditing the Company's accounting for, and disclosure of, these loss contingencies was especially challenging due to the significant judgment required to evaluate management's assessments of the likelihood of a loss, and their estimate of the potential amount or range of such losses.

How We Addressed the Matter in Our Audit

We obtained an understanding, evaluated the design and tested the operating effectiveness of controls over the identification and evaluation of these matters, including controls relating to the

Company's assessment of the likelihood that a loss will be realized and their ability to reasonably estimate the potential range of possible losses. To test the Company's assessment of the probability of incurrence of a loss, whether the loss was reasonably estimable, and the conclusion and disclosure regarding any range of possible losses, including when the Company believes it cannot be reasonably estimated at this time, we read the minutes or a summary of the meetings of the committees of the board of directors, read the proceedings, claims, and regulatory, or government inquiries and investigations, or summaries as we deemed appropriate, requested and received internal and external legal counsel confirmation letters, met with internal and external legal counsel to discuss the nature of the various matters, and obtained representations from management. We also evaluated the appropriateness of the related disclosures included in Note 13 to the consolidated financial statements.

Uncertain Tax Positions
Description of the Matter
As discussed in Note 16 to the consolidated financial statements, the Company has received certain notices from the Internal Revenue Service (IRS) related to transfer pricing agreements with the Company's foreign subsidiaries for certain periods examined. The IRS has stated that it will also apply its position to tax years subsequent to those examined. If the IRS prevails in its position, it could result in an additional federal tax liability, plus interest and any penalties asserted. The Company uses judgment to (1) determine whether a tax position's technical merits are more-likely-than-not to be sustained and (2) measure the amount of tax benefit that qualifies for recognition. Auditing the Company's accounting for, and disclosure of, these uncertain tax positions was especially challenging due to the significant judgment required to assess management's evaluation of technical merits and the measurement of the tax position based on interpretations of tax laws and legal rulings.

How We Addressed the Matter in Our Audit
We obtained an understanding, evaluated the design and tested the operating effectiveness of controls over the Company's process to assess the technical merits of tax positions related to these transfer pricing agreements and to measure the benefit of those tax positions. As part of our audit procedures over the Company's accounting for these positions, we involved our tax professionals to assist with our assessment of the technical merits of the Company's tax positions. This included assessing the Company's correspondence with the relevant tax authorities, evaluating income tax opinions or other third-party advice obtained by the Company, and requesting and receiving confirmation letters from third-party advisors. We also used our knowledge of, and experience with, the application of international and local income tax laws by the relevant income tax authorities to evaluate the Company's accounting for those tax positions. We analyzed the Company's assumptions and data used to determine the amount of the federal tax liability recognized and tested the mathematical accuracy of the underlying data and calculations. We also evaluated the appropriateness of the related disclosures included in Note 16 to the consolidated financial statements in relation to these matters.
/s/ Ernst & Young LLP
We have served as the Company's auditor since 2007.
San Mateo, California February 1, 2023

To further improve the value of the audit report, ISA 701 requires auditor's reports since 2016 to include so-called *Key Audit Matters* (KAMs)[2]. The purpose of communicating KAMs is to enhance the communicative value of the auditor's report by providing greater transparency about the audit that was performed. Instead of KAM, PCAOB standard AS3101 requires audit reports since 2019 to include *Critical Audit Matters* (CAM)[3]. A CAM is defined as any matter arising from the audit of the financial statements that was communicated or required to be communicated to the audit committee and that:

▶ relates to accounts or disclosures that are material to the financial statements; and

▶ involved especially challenging, subjective, or complex auditor judgment.

KAMs will be discussed in further detail in section 11.4 of this chapter. An example of such an Auditor's Report is included in illustration 11.1.

▶ **MANAGEMENT RESPONSIBILITY FOR FINANCIAL STATEMENTS**

Up until 2002, corporate officers of publicly traded companies in the US were not held liable for misstated financial statements unless fraud could be proven. In other words, the officers knew it was misstated and that was their intent. All that changed with the Sarbanes-Oxley Act of 2002 (SOX) which since requires[4] the CEO and CFO to sign a certification in each annual or quarterly report filed or submitted to the US Securities and Exchange Commission (SEC). This applies also to officers of corporations headquartered outside the USA whose company's stock is traded on US stock exchanges. In several European countries ilaw requires that all members of the board of directors (or, in a two-tier system, the executive board and the supervisory board) sign the financial statements, thereby demonstrating that their responsibility for these statements is a joint one rather than only that of the CEO and CFO. However, this does not detract from the principle that the responsibility for the financial statements and the internal controls rests with those charged with governance, which is the key issue in the Sarbanes-Oxley Act.

An example of a certification by Facebook's Chairman and Chief Executive Officer Mark Zuckerberg that was submitted in the 10-K report to the SEC for 2022 (illustration 11.2[5]).

ILLUSTRATION 11.2

CERTIFICATION OF PERIODIC REPORT UNDER SECTION 302 OF THE SOX ACT OF 2002.

I, Mark Zuckerberg, certify that:

1. I have reviewed this annual report on Form 10-K of Facebook, Inc.;

2. Based on my knowledge, this report does not contain any untrue statement of a material fact or omit to state a material fact necessary to make the statements made, in light of the circumstances under which such statements were made, not misleading with respect to the period covered by this report;

3. Based on my knowledge, the financial statements, and other financial information included in this report, fairly present in all material respects the financial condition, results of operations and cash flows of the registrant as of, and for, the periods presented in this report;

4. The registrant's other certifying officer and I are responsible for establishing and maintaining disclosure controls and procedures (as defined in Exchange Act Rules 13a-15(e) and 15d-

15(e)) and internal control over financial reporting (as defined in Exchange Act Rules 13a-15(f) and 15d-15(f)) for the registrant and have:

a) Designed such disclosure controls and procedures, or caused such disclosure controls and procedures to be designed under our supervision, to ensure that material information relating to the registrant, including its consolidated subsidiaries, is made known to us by others within those entities, particularly during the period in which this report is being prepared;

b) Designed such internal control over financial reporting, or caused such internal control over financial reporting to be designed under our supervision, to provide reasonable assurance regarding the reliability of financial reporting and the preparation of financial statements for external purposes in accordance with generally accepted accounting principles;

c) Evaluated the effectiveness of the registrant's disclosure controls and procedures and presented in this report our conclusions about the effectiveness of the disclosure controls and procedures, as of the end of the period covered by this report based on such evaluation; and

d) Disclosed in this report any change in the registrant's internal control over financial reporting that occurred during the registrant's most recent fiscal quarter (the registrant's fourth fiscal quarter in the case of an annual report) that has materially affected, or is reasonably likely to materially affect, the registrant's internal control over financial reporting; and

5. The registrant's other certifying officer and I have disclosed, based on our most recent evaluation of internal control over financial reporting, to the registrant's auditors and the audit committee of the registrant's board of directors (or persons performing the equivalent functions):

a) All significant deficiencies and material weaknesses in the design or operation of internal control over financial reporting which are reasonably likely to adversely affect the registrant's ability to record, process, summarize and report financial information; and

b) Any fraud, whether or not material, that involves management or other employees who have a significant role in the registrant's internal control over financial reporting.

date: February 1, 2023

/s/ MARK ZUCKERBERG

Mark Zuckerberg, Chairman and Chief Executive Officer

(Principal executive officer)

11.3 BASIC ELEMENTS OF THE AUDITOR'S REPORT

According to ISA 700, the auditor must evaluate whether the financial statements are prepared, in all material respects, in accordance with the requirements of the applicable financial reporting framework. This evaluation includes consideration of the qualitative aspects of the entity's accounting practices, including indicators of possible bias in management's judgment. The auditor's report should contain a clear written expression of opinion on the financial statements taken as a whole.

The auditor's report must include the following basic elements that are discussed in more detail in this section:

- ▶ A title, e.g. 'Independent Auditor's Report'
- ▶ An addressee
- ▶ Auditor's Opinion
- ▶ Basis for Opinion
- ▶ Going Concern
- ▶ Key Audit Matters
- ▶ Responsibility of management for the preparation of the financial statements
- ▶ Auditor's responsibility to express an opinion on the financial statements and the scope of the audit
- ▶ Name of the Engagement Partner
- ▶ The auditor's signature
- ▶ The date of the auditor's report
- ▶ The auditor's address

TITLE

The auditor's report should have an appropriate title that helps the reader to identify it and easily distinguish it from other reports, such as that of management. ISA 700 requires 'Independent Auditor's Report' to distinguish the auditor's report from reports that might be issued by others[6].

IESBA's Code of Ethics for Professional Accountants (see chapter 3 'Ethics') stresses the great importance of auditor independence both in fact and appearance. PCAOB auditing standards also require an auditor's report to include as title 'Report of Independent Registered Public Accounting Firm'[7].

ADDRESSEE

The report should be addressed as required by the circumstances of the engagement and the local regulations. The report is usually addressed either to the shareholders or supervisory board or the board of directors of the entity whose financial statements have been audited. Historically, in some countries, such as the Netherlands, auditor's reports were not addressed at all because the reports are meant to be used by (the anonymous) public at large.

To minimize the risk of claims and liabilities from stakeholders, UK auditors explicitly state that 'the auditor's report has only been prepared for the parent Company's members as a body in accordance with the Companies Act 2006 and for no other purpose[8]. Auditors do not, in giving the report, accept or assume responsibility for any other purpose or to any other person to whom the report is shown or into whose hands it may come save where expressly agreed by their prior consent in writing.'

OPINION

The Opinion section of the auditor's report must:

(a) Identify the entity whose financial statements have been audited;

(b) State that the financial statements have been audited;

(c) Identify the title of each statement comprising the financial statements;

(d) Refer to the notes, including the summary of significant accounting policies; and

(e) Specify the date of, or period covered by, each financial statement comprising the financial statements.

When expressing an unqualified opinion on financial statements prepared in accordance with a fair presentation framework like IFRS, the auditor's opinion includes one of the following phrases:

(a) In our opinion, the accompanying financial statements present fairly, in all material respects, [...] in accordance with IFRS; or

(b) In our opinion, the accompanying financial statements give a true and fair view of [...] in accordance with IFRS.

BASIS FOR OPINION

The auditor's report must confirm that the audit was conducted in accordance with ISAs and must include a statement that the auditor is independent of the entity in accordance with the relevant ethical requirements. The auditor's report must also state whether the auditor believes that the audit evidence obtained is sufficient and appropriate to provide a basis for the opinion on the financial statements. When she modifies the opinion, she will amend the heading 'Basis for Opinion' to 'Basis for Qualified Opinion,' 'Basis for Adverse Opinion,' or 'Basis for Disclaimer of Opinion' and include a description of the matter giving rise to the modification[9].

MANAGEMENT'S RESPONSIBILITY FOR THE FINANCIAL STATEMENTS

The auditor's report must describe management's responsibility for the preparation of the financial statements. The description shall include an explanation that management is responsible for the preparation of the financial statements in accordance with the applicable financial reporting framework, and for internal control to enable the preparation of financial statements that are free from material misstatement, whether due to fraud or error. Where the financial statements are prepared in accordance with a fair presentation framework, the explanation of management's responsibility for the financial statements in the auditor's report shall refer to 'the preparation and fair presentation of these financial statements' or 'the preparation of financial statements that give a true and fair view', as appropriate in the circumstances.

AUDITOR'S RESPONSIBILITY

The auditor's report must state that the responsibility of the auditor is to express an opinion on the financial statements based on the audit conducted in accordance with International Standards on Auditing. The auditor's report explains that ISAs require that the auditor comply with ethical requirements and that the auditor plan and perform the audit to obtain reasonable assurance about whether the financial statements are free from material misstatement.

The auditor's report includes under 'auditor's responsibility' the scope of an audit by stating that:

▷ An audit involves performing procedures to obtain audit evidence about the amounts and disclosures in the financial statements.

▷ The procedures selected depend on the auditor's judgement, including the assessment of the risks of material misstatement of the financial statements, whether due to fraud or error. In making those risk assessments, the auditor considers internal control relevant to the entity's preparation of the financial statements in order to design audit procedures that are appropriate in the circumstances. But consideration of internal controls is not for the purpose of expressing an opinion on the effectiveness of the entity's internal control. In circumstances where the auditor also has a responsibility to express an opinion on the effectiveness of internal control in conjunction with the audit of the financial statements, the auditor shall omit the phrase that the auditor's consideration of internal control is not for the purpose of expressing an opinion on the effectiveness of internal control.

▷ An audit also includes evaluating the appropriateness of the accounting policies used and the reasonableness of accounting estimates made by management, as well as the overall presentation of the financial statements.

REPORT ON OTHER INFORMATION IN THE ANNUAL REPORT

In most countries, in addition to the financial statements, the management report and other information must be included in the annual report.

Auditors have a professional responsibility to evaluate this other information accompanying the audited financial statements to ensure that no materially misleading information is included[10]. More precisely, auditors are required to read the other information and assess whether it is consistent with the information in the audited financial statements or whether it contains one or more significant misstatements of fact based on knowledge obtained while conducting the audit.

There are two reasons for this: the auditor may discover on the basis of her knowledge that there are matters in the management report or other information that are materially incorrect. For example, she could conclude that during her audit she identified an important fraud or continuity risk that is not mentioned in the risk section with the most important risks. If she identifies a material deviation, she will ask the Board of Directors to adjust it. If the Board does not want to do that, the auditor will adjust her statement.

The other information in the management report may also lead the auditor to conclude that she has missed something in the audit of the financial statements. In that case, she may have to perform additional audit procedures.

If the auditor addresses other reporting responsibilities in the auditor's report on the financial statements that are in addition to the auditor's responsibility under the ISAs to report on the financial statements, these other reporting responsibilities shall be addressed in a separate section in the auditor's report that shall be subtitled 'Report on Other Legal and Regulatory Requirements', or otherwise as appropriate to the content of the section. Finally, in accordance with Article 10 of Regulation (EU) 537/2014, the other reporting responsibilities section of auditor reports of financial statements of Private Industrial Enterprises (PIEs) must include by whom the auditor has been appointed, the date of appointment and period of total uninterrupted engagement of the audit unit including previous extensions and reappointments. See illustrations 11.3 and 11.4 for sample reporting of other information.

OTHER INFORMATION PARAGRAPH DERIVED FROM INDEPENDENT AUDITOR'S REPORT SIEMENS ANNUAL REPORT, 2022[11]

Other information

The Supervisory Board is responsible for the Report of the Supervisory Board in the Annual Report 2022 within the meaning of ISA [DE] 720 (Revised). Management and the Supervisory Board are responsible for the declaration pursuant to Sec. 161 AktG ['Aktiengesetz': German Stock Corporation Act] on the Corporate Governance Code, which is part of the Corporate Governance Statement, and for the Compensation Report. In all other respects, management is responsible for the other information. The other information comprises the last paragraph of chapter 1 beginning with 'Disclosures in accordance with EU taxonomy' of the group management report, the sections '8.5.1 Internal Control System (ICS) and ERM' and '8.5.2 Compliance Management System (CMS)' in chapter 8.5 of the combined management report as well as the content of the Corporate Governance Statement.

In addition, the other information comprises parts to be included in the Annual Report, of which we received a version prior to issuing this auditor's report, in particular:

▶ the Responsibility Statement (to the Consolidated Financial Statements and the Group Management Report),
▶ the Responsibility Statement (to the Annual Financial Statements and the Management Report),
▶ the Five-Year Summary,
▶ the Compensation Report,
▶ the Report of the Supervisory Board,
▶ notes and forward-looking statements,

but not the consolidated financial statements and the annual financial statements, not the disclosures of the combined management report whose content is audited and not our auditor's reports as well as not our auditor's report on a limited assurance engagement on the disclosures in accordance with EU Taxonomy thereon.

Our opinions on the consolidated financial statements and on the group management report do not cover the other information, and consequently we do not express an opinion or any other form of assurance conclusion thereon.

In connection with our audit, our responsibility is to read the other information and, in so doing, to consider whether the other information

▶ is materially inconsistent with the consolidated financial statements, with the group management report or our knowledge obtained in the audit, or
▶ otherwise appears to be materially misstated.

If, based on the work we have performed, we conclude that there is a material misstatement of this other information, we are required to report that fact. We have nothing to report in this regard.

ILLUSTRATION 11.4

OTHER INFORMATION PARAGRAPH DERIVED FROM INDEPENDENT AUDITOR'S REPORT SERABI GOLD, 2022[12]

Other information

The other information comprises the information included in the annual report, other than the financial statements and our auditor's report thereon. The directors are responsible for the other information contained within the annual report. Our opinion on the group and parent company financial statements does not cover the other information and, except to the extent otherwise explicitly stated in our report, we do not express any form of assurance conclusion thereon. Our responsibility is to read the other information and, in doing so, consider whether the other information is materially inconsistent with the financial statements or our knowledge obtained in the course of the audit, or otherwise appears to be materially misstated. If we identify such material inconsistencies or apparent material misstatements, we are required to determine whether this gives rise to a material misstatement in the financial statements themselves. If, based on the work we have performed, we conclude that there is a material misstatement of this other information, we are required to report that fact.
We have nothing to report in this regard.

Opinions on other matters prescribed by the Companies Act 2006

In our opinion, based on the work undertaken in the course of the audit:

▶ the information given in the strategic report and the directors' report for the financial year for which the financial statements are prepared is consistent with the financial statements; and

▶ the strategic report and the directors' report have been prepared in accordance with applicable legal requirements.

Matters on which we are required to report by exception

In the light of the knowledge and understanding of the group and the parent company and their environment obtained in the course of the audit, we have not identified material misstatements in the strategic report or the directors' report. We have nothing to report in respect of the following matters in relation to which the Companies Act 2006 requires us to report to you if, in our opinion:

▶ adequate accounting records have not been kept by the parent company, or returns adequate for our audit have not been received from branches not visited by us; or

▶ the parent company financial statements are not in agreement with the accounting records and returns or

▶ certain disclosures of directors' remuneration specified by law are not made; or

▶ we have not received all the information and explanations we require for our audit.

NAME AND SIGNATURE OF THE AUDITOR AND DATE OF THE REPORT

The report should be signed in the name of the audit firm, or the personal name of the auditor, or both as appropriate for the particular jurisdiction. The auditor's report is ordinarily signed in the name of the firm because the firm assumes responsibility for the audit. According to ISA 700 it is currently not required that the personal name of the auditor be signed. Inclusion of the name in a reference is sufficient. In some cases, law or regulation may allow for the use of electronic signatures in the auditor's report. According to PCAOB requirements, the name of the engagement partner must be disclosed as well as for other accounting firms participating in the audit[13]:

- ▶ 5% or greater participation: The name, city and state (or, if outside the United States, the city and country), and the percentage of total audit hours attributable to each other accounting firm whose participation in the audit was at least 5% of total audit hours.
- ▶ Less than 5% participation: The number of other accounting firms that participated in the audit whose individual participation was less than 5% of total audit hours, and the aggregate percentage of total audit hours of such firms.

The auditor must not date the report earlier than the date on which she has obtained sufficient appropriate audit evidence. This informs the reader that the auditor has considered the effect on the financial statements and on the report of events or transactions about which the auditor became aware and that occurred up to that date. The auditor should not date the report earlier than the date on which the financial statements are signed or approved by management.

AUDITOR'S ADDRESS

The report should name a specific location, which is usually the city in which the auditor maintains an office that serves the client audited. PCAOB's Auditing Standard No.3101 (S-X Rule 2-02(a) also requires that an auditor include the city and state (or city and country, in the case of non-local auditors) from which the auditor's report has been issued. Note: in some countries it is not required that the audit report give the specific address for the auditor. See illustration 11.5.

ILLUSTRATION 11.5

AUDITOR'S NAME AND ADDRESS IN AUDITORS' REPORTS 2022 OF CHOPPIES, KOFOLA AND INFOSYS

Mazars

Mazars
Certified Auditors
Practicing member: Shashikumar Velambath
Membership number: CAP 022 2023

Date: 21 September 2023
Gaborone

For DELOITTE HASKINS & SELLS LLP
Chartered Accountants
(Firm's Registration No. 117366W/W-100018)

Sanjiv V. Pilgaonkar
Partner
(Membership No.039826)
UDIN : 23039826BGXRYR4513

Place: Bengaluru
Date: April 13, 2023

Statutory Auditor Responsible for the Engagement

Blanka Dvořáková is the statutory auditor responsible for the audit of the separate and consolidated financial statements of Kofola ČeskoSlovensko a.s. as at 31 December 2022, based on which this independent auditor's report has been prepared.

Prague

13 April 2023

Unsigned version

Blanka Dvořáková

KPMG Česká republika Audit, s.r.o.

Partner Registration number 712031

▶ **OTHER FORMATS OF THE AUDITOR'S REPORT**

An auditor may be required to conduct an audit in accordance with the auditing standards of a specific jurisdiction (the 'national auditing standards') but may additionally have complied with the ISAs in the conduct of the audit. If this is the case, the auditor's report may refer to International Standards on Auditing in addition to the national auditing standards. However, the auditor shall make reference to ISAs and the national standards only if there is no conflict between the requirements of the two sets of standards that would lead the auditor to form a different opinion, or not to include an Emphasis of Matter paragraph that, in the particular circumstances, is required by ISAs. Furthermore, the auditor's report must still include each of the elements required by the ISA format when he uses the layout or wording specified by the national auditing standards. When the auditor's report refers to both the national auditing standards and International Standards on Auditing, the auditor's report must identify the jurisdiction of origin of the national auditing standards.

If the company audited is traded on a US stock exchange, PCAOB's Auditing Standard No. 3101 requires that in a report the auditor must refer to the standards of the 'Public Company Accounting Oversight Board'.

In the UK and the Netherlands, auditors of financial statements of PIEs must explain the materiality as applied in the audit and the manner in which it is determined in a separate section in the auditor's report. We refer to two examples included in illustration 11.6.

DISCLOSURE OF MATERIALITY IN THE AUDITOR'S REPORT 2022 OF MULTITUDE[14], MORRISONS SUPERMARKETS LTD[15] AND SERABI GOLD[16]

Materiality

The scope of our audit was influenced by our application of materiality. An audit is designed to obtain reasonable assurance whether the financial statements are free from material misstatement. Misstatements may arise due to fraud or error. They are considered material if individually or in aggregate, they could reasonably be expected to influence the economic decisions of users taken on the basis of the financial statements.

Based on our professional judgement, we determined certain quantitative tresholds for materiality, including the overall group materiality for the consolidated financial statements as set out in the table below. These, together with qualitative considerations, helped us to determine the scope of our audit and the nature, timing and extent of our audit procedures and to evaluate the effect of misstatements on the financial statements as a whole.

Overall group materiality How we determined it Rationale for the materiality benchmark applied	€ 1,6 million (previous year € 1,6 million) Total revenue We chose total revenue as the benchmark because, in our view, it best reflects the extent of the business operations and the growth rate of the group and it is a generally accepted benchmark.

Materiality Morrisons

▷ Overall Group materiality: £23,500,000 (prior period: £15,000,000) based on 2.5% of EBITDA before exceptionals, supply chain disruption and excluding McColl's.

▷ Overall Company materiality: £21,000,000 (prior period: £13,500,000) based on the Company allocation of Group materiality.

▷ Performance materiality: £17,500,000 (prior period: £11,250,000) (Group) and £15,500,000 (prior period: £10,125,000) (Company).

Materiality Serabi Gold

Our application of materiality

We apply the concept of materiality both in planning and performing our audit, and in evaluating the effect of misstatements. At the planning stage materiality is used to determine the financial statement areas that are included within the scope of our audit.

Materiality for the group financial statements as a whole was $881,000 with performance materiality set at $528,000, being 60% of group materiality. Materiality for the financial statements as a whole was based upon 1.5% of the group's revenues. In determining materiality, we considered the Key Performance Indicators ('KPIs') used in the Annual Report and Accounts.

We consider revenue to be the primary measure used by the shareholders in assessing the performance of the group, driving profitability within the group and revenue is expected to provide a more stable measure year on year. The percentage applied to this benchmark has been selected to bring into scope all significant classes of transactions, account balances and disclosures relevant for the shareholders, and also to ensure that matters that would have a significant impact on the reported profit were appropriately considered. In determining performance materiality, the significant judgements made were in respect of the prior year's identified fraud investigation and the fact that 2022 represented the first year of our appointment as auditors to the group.

We agreed with the audit committee that we would report all individual audit differences identified for the group during the course of our audit in excess of $44,000 together with any other audit misstatements below that threshold that we believe warranted reporting on qualitative grounds. Materiality applied to the company's financial statements was $735,000 with performance materiality set at $441,000, being 60% of the company materiality. The benchmark for materiality of the company was 0.6% of the company's gross assets.

The significant judgements used by us in determining this were that total assets are the primary measure used by the shareholders in assessing the performance of the company. The percentage applied to this benchmark has been selected to bring into scope all significant classes of transactions, account balances and disclosures relevant for the shareholders, and also to ensure that matters that would have a significant impact on the reported profit were appropriately considered. In determining performance materiality, the significant judgements made were in respect of the prior year's identified fraud investigation and the fact that 2022 represented the first year of our appointment as auditors to the company.

We agreed with the Audit Committee that we would report all individual audit differences identified for the company during the course of our audit in excess of $36,000 together with any other audit misstatements below that threshold that we believe warranted reporting on qualitative grounds.

For audits of financial statements of PIEs in the UK and the Netherlands, the auditor is also required to disclose in a separate section 'Scope of the group audit' how the audit of group entities, where applicable, was organized and performed. See illustration 11.7.

AUDIT SCOPE FROM AUDITOR'S REPORTS 2022 OF ROLLS ROYCE[17] AND POST.NL[18]

Our audit approach

Overview

Audit scope

▶ Following our assessment of the risks of material misstatement of the financial statements, including the impact of climate change, we subjected 33 individual components (including three joint ventures) to full scope audits for group purposes, which following an element of sub-consolidation, equates to 16 group reporting opinions. In addition, nine components performed targeted specified procedures.

▶ In addition, the group engagement team audited the company and other centralised functions including those covering the group treasury operations, corporate costs, corporate taxation, post-retirement benefits, and certain goodwill and intangible asset impairment assessments. The group engagement team performed audit procedures over the group consolidation and financial statements disclosures and performed group level analytical procedures over out of scope components.

▶ The components on which full scope audits, targeted specified procedures and centralised work was performed accounted for 98% of revenue, 79% of loss before tax from continuing operations and 90% of total assets.

▶ Central audit testing was performed where appropriate for reporting components in group audit scope who are supported by the group's Finance Service Centres (FSCs).

▶ As part of the group audit supervision process, the group engagement team has performed 16 file reviews, which included meetings on approach and conclusions with the component teams and review of their audit files and final deliverables. In person site visits to components in the UK, Germany and US were also performed.

Scope of the group audit

PostNL is at the head of a group of components. The financial information of this group is included in the financial statements of PostNL. Because we are ultimately responsible for the auditor's report, we are also responsible for directing, supervising and performing the group audit. In this respect we have determined the nature and extent of the audit procedures to be carried out for components reporting for group audit purposes. Our group audit mainly focused on significant components within the segments Parcels and Mail in the Netherlands and PostNL Other (including finance and real-estate components). Based on their significance and/or our risk assessment we performed scope an audit of the complete reporting package or audit of specific items on the 23 group entities within those segments.

For the entities in scope, except for Spring Hong Kong, the group engagement team performed the audit procedures. This resulted in a coverage of 87% of total revenue and 91% of total assets. The remaining 13% of total revenue and 9% of total assets is represented by a significant number of components ('remaining components'), none of which individually represent more than 2% of total revenue and 3% of total assets.

For these remaining components we performed central procedures among others analytical procedures to validate our assessment that there are no risks of material misstatement within these components

11.4 KEY AUDIT MATTERS (KAMS)

As mentioned in the introduction of this chapter, the purpose of communicating KAMs (CAMs in the US) is to enhance the communicative value of the auditor's report by providing greater transparency about the audit that was performed. KAMs are those matters that, in the auditors' professional judgement, were of most significance in the audit of the financial statements and include the most significant assessed risks of material misstatement identified by the auditors, including those which had the greatest effect on: the overall audit strategy; the allocation of resources in the audit; and directing the efforts of the engagement team[19]. These matters, and any comments made on the results of audit procedures on them, are addressed in the context of the audit of the financial statements as a whole, and the auditor does not provide a separate opinion on these matters.

From the matters communicated with those charged with governance and those matters that required significant auditor attention, the following issues must be considered:

(a) Areas of higher assessed risk of material misstatement, or significant risks identified in accordance with ISA 315.

(b) Significant auditor judgments relating to areas in the financial statements that involved significant management judgment, including accounting estimates that have been identified as having high estimation uncertainty.

(c) The effect on the audit of significant events or transactions that occurred during the period.

The description of each key audit matter in the Key Audit Matters should refer to the related disclosure(s), if any, in the financial statements and must address:

(a) Why the matter was considered to be one of most significance in the audit and therefore determined to be a key audit matter; and

(b) How the matter was addressed in the audit.

The auditor must communicate the selected KAMs with those charged with governance.

The matters that required significant auditor attention and the rationale for the auditor's determination as to whether or not each of these matters is a key audit matter should be documented.

KAMs can be distinguished into *entity specific* and *general* matters. 'Entity specific' means that the issue is explicitly linked to the company, while reading KAMs as a general matter could apply to any company. Another distinction is KAMs on *entity level* and KAMs on *account level*. An example of the first category could be a major Denial of Service (DOS) attack while an example of the latter could be the amortization of goodwill.

Illustration 11.8 shows examples of KAMS of respectively Choppies Ltd[20], Post.nl[21] and CAM of ASML[22].

KAMS OF RESPECTIVELY CHOPPIES LTD, POST.NL AND CAM OF ASML

CHOPPIES LTD

Matter #02	**Accuracy and Completeness of Related Party Transactions**
Description of Key Audit Matter	The Group has undertaken transactions with numerous related parties. These include sales of goods to related parties, as well as purchase of goods from related parties. We have identified accuracy and completeness of the related party transactions as a key audit matter due to the significance of related party transactions; the risk that transactions are entered into on a non-arm's length basis, and the risk that such transactions remain undisclosed.

The disclosure associated with related parties is set out in the financial statements on the following notes:

▶ Accounting policy note 1.7 – Financial Instruments (IFRS 9) – Amounts due from related parties

▶ Note 37 – Related Parties

How we addressed the Key Audit Matter

Our procedures relating to related party relationships, transactions and balances included, amongst others:

- ▶ We inquired from management and those charged with governance, and performed other risk assessment procedures considered appropriate, to obtain an understanding of the controls, if any, established to identify, account for, and disclose related party relationships and transactions in the financial statements;
- ▶ We maintained alertness for related party information when reviewing records and other supporting documents during the fieldwork phase of the audit.

We reviewed an extensive list of business documents and compiled a list of related parties and related party transactions independently.

Our procedures relating to related party relationships, transactions and balances included, amongst others:

- ▶ We inquired from management and those charged with governance, and performed other risk assessment procedures considered appropriate, to obtain an understanding of the controls, if any, established to identify, account for, and disclose related party relationships and transactions in the financial statements;
- ▶ We maintained alertness for related party information when reviewing records and other supporting documents during the fieldwork phase of the audit.

We reviewed an extensive list of business documents and compiled a list of related parties and related party transactions independently.

POSTNL

Description

Revenue related accruals (terminal dues)

As disclosed in note 3.1.4 to the financial statements, PostNL has outstanding accrued liability positions with international postal operators for services provided for or received totalling €181 million (2021: €204 million). Terminal dues is significant to our audit due to the amounts and judgement involved.

Our response

We have:

- ▶ evaluated the process and models used by management in its estimate and performed walkthroughs of the revenue classes of transactions and evaluated the design and implementation of the relevant controls;
- ▶ performed retrospective review of estimates made by management in the past;

Our observation

We consider that management's assumptions related to terminal dues positions are within the reasonable range. Furthermore we assessed that the disclosures are appropriate.

This position involves a certain level of management judgement in calculating positions, where negotiations with the counterparties on prices and volume are not yet finalized as per balanced sheet date. This results in assumptions being used by management in determination of the accrued terminal dues which can have an impact on operating revenues. The actual settled amounts may differ from management's estimate as a result of negotiations. Further reference is made to the accounting policy around revenue related accruals in note 1.4. This both relates to prices and quantities, which are considered the main significant assumptions of the estimate. Considering this process is sensitive for management override of controls, this is considered a risk of fraud.

- inquired with management regarding developments in mail volumes, development in terminal dues and progress of settlement negotiations and performed analytical procedures on terminal due positions and development of mail volumes and evaluated whether the assumptions are reasonable;
- performed test of details to verify accuracy of prices and quantities as a basis for the terminal dues by reconciliation to supporting documentation including contractual agreements and performed test of details on manual adjustments;
- assessed the appropriateness of the accounting policies and the adequacy of the financial statements disclosures in note 3.1.4 in the financial statements.

ASML

Critical Audit Matter

The critical audit matter communicated below is a matter arising from the current period audit of the consolidated financial statements that was communicated or required to be communicated to the audit committee and that: (1) relates to accounts or disclosures that are material to the consolidated financial statements and (2) involved our especially challenging, subjective, or complex judgments. The communication of a critical audit matter does not alter in any way our opinion on the consolidated financial statements, taken as a whole, and we are not, by communicating the critical audit matter below, providing a separate opinion on the critical audit matter or on the accounts or disclosures to which it relates.

Revenue recognition – Identification of distinct performance obligations and allocation of the total contract consideration

As disclosed in note 2 to the consolidated financial statements, net system sales was EUR 15,430.3 million for the year ended December 31, 2022. Sales of systems are usually entered into with customers under Volume Purchase Agreements (VPAs). These VPAs contain multiple performance obligations, for example delivery of goods, installation, warranty and training. Once these performance obligations are identified, the total contract consideration, including discounts, offer of free goods or services and credits that can be used towards future purchases, is allocated to the performance obligations. We identified revenue recognition, and specifically the identification of performance obligations in certain VPAs as well as the allocation of the total contract consideration, including discounts, offer of free goods or services and credits that can be used towards future purchases, as a critical audit matter since it is inherently judgmental, and complex. As a result, evaluating the Company's judgments regarding the identified performance obligations, notably the estimate of the number of systems to be delivered, and the allocation of the total contract consideration to these performance obligations required a high degree of auditor judgment. The following are the primary procedures we performed to address this critical audit matter. We evaluated the design and tested the operating effectiveness of certain internal controls related to the critical audit matter. This includes controls related to VPA assessments for the identification of performance obligations and the allocation of the total contract consideration to these performance obligations, and the correct application to individual sales transactions. We evaluated the identification of performance obligations and the allocation of the total contract consideration by inspecting a selection of VPAs and the related documentation, performing inquiries with relevant operational functions in the Company, and performing sensitivity analyses, to assess the impact of the estimated number of systems to be delivered on the allocation. Furthermore, we tested a selection of recognized sales transactions under VPAs and performed a retrospective review of prior period estimates to assess management's ability to estimate the number of systems to be delivered. Finally, we checked the accuracy of the Company's model used to allocate the contract consideration to the identified performance obligations.

11.5 EMPHASIS OF MATTER PARAGRAPH AND OTHER MATTER PARAGRAPH[23]

The auditor, having formed an opinion on the financial statements, sometimes must draw the financial statement users' attention to a matter, although appropriately presented or disclosed in the financial statements, that is of such importance that it is fundamental to users' understanding of the financial statements. Also, attention may be drawn to any other matter that is relevant to users. This part of the opinion is called an *Emphasis of a Matter paragraph*. This paragraph refers to 'a matter appropriately presented or disclosed in the financial statements,' while an *Other Matter paragraph* refers to 'a matter other than those presented or disclosed in the financial statements.' Ordinarily, an auditor might write an emphasis of a matter paragraph:

▶ If there is a significant uncertainty which may affect the financial statements, the resolution of which is dependent upon future events. Examples of uncertainties that might be emphasized include: the existence of related party transactions, important accounting matters occurring subsequent to the balance sheet date, matters affecting the comparability of financial statements with those of previous years (e.g. change in accounting methods), and litigation, long-term contracts, recoverability of asset values, losses on discontinued operations. Illustration 11.9 provides an example.

▶ An auditor is required to include an emphasis of a matter paragraph to highlight a material matter regarding a going concern problem. Illustration 11.10 shows an emphasis of matter paragraph relating to going concern; also see ISA 570 'Going Concern'.

DERIVED FROM INDEPENDENT AUDITORS' REPORT TO THE MEMBERS OF REC LIMITED, MUMBAI, 2023[24]

Emphasis of matter

We draw attention to Note No. 47.1.3 to the standalone Ind AS Financial Statements regarding the provision of impairment allowance in respect of its loan assets and Letters of Comfort. In this regard, we have relied upon the basis of determination of impairment allowance in so far as it relates to technical aspects/parameters considered by independent agency and management judgement for ascertaining impairment allowance as management overlay.

Our opinion is not modified in respect of above matter.

FROM AUDITOR REPORT REGARDING ANNUAL REPORT 2022 OF EMERGING TOWNS & CITIES SINGAPORE LTD.[25]

Report on the Audit of the Financial Statements

Disclaimer of Opinion

We were engaged to audit the financial statements of Emerging Towns & Cities Singapore Ltd. (the 'Company') and its subsidiaries (the 'Group'), which comprise the consolidated statement of financial position of the Group and the statement of financial position of the Company as at 31 December 2022, and the consolidated statement of profit or loss and other comprehensive income, consolidated statement of changes in equity and consolidated statement of cash flows for the year then ended, and notes to the financial statements, including a summary of significant accounting policies. We do not express an opinion on the accompanying consolidated financial statements of the Group and the statement of financial position of the Company. Because of the significance of the matters described in the Basis for Disclaimer of Opinion section of our report, we have not been able to obtain sufficient appropriate audit evidence to provide a basis for an audit opinion on these financial statements.

Basis for Disclaimer of Opinion

Use of going concern assumption

The Group and the Company had net current liabilities of $8,085,000 and $1,908,000, respectively, as at 31 December 2022. In addition, for the financial year ended 31 December 2022, the Group incurred a net loss of $42,471,000. As disclosed in Note 16(i) to the financial statements, the Group did not meet a financial covenant and did not make full payment for a facility fee that was due in respect of its bank loan during the financial year ended 31 December 2022, resulting in the loan being repayable on demand. Consequently, the bank loan of $53,556,000 had been wholly classified as current as at 31 December 2022. The Group had borrowings amounting to $59,301,000 due for repayment within the next 12 months or on demand, with cash and bank balances of $4,011,000 as at 31 December 2022. The Group's working capital primarily comprises development properties in Myanmar. The challenging conditions and events which have an adverse impact on the property market in Myanmar continue to affect the realisation of the Group's development properties, resulting in a significant strain on its cash flows. The conditions and events above give rise to material uncertainties on the ability of the Group and the Company to continue as going concern. Management has prepared the financial statements on a going concern basis based on the assumptions disclosed in Note 2(a) to the financial statements. However, based on the information available to us, we have not been able to obtain sufficient appropriate audit evidence to satisfy ourselves whether the use of the going concern assumption in preparing these financial statements is appropriate in view of the factors described above. If the Group and the Company were unable to continue in operational existence, the Group and the Company may be unable to discharge their liabilities in the normal course of business, and adjustments may have to be made to reflect the situation that assets may need to be realised other than in the normal course of business and at amounts which could differ significantly from the amounts at which they are currently recorded in the statements of financial position. In addition, the Group and the Company may need to reclassify non-current assets and non-current liabilities as current assets and current liabilities, respectively. No such adjustments have been made to the financial statements.

▶ **GOING CONCERN OPINION (EMPHASIS OF MATTER)**

As already mentioned in section 10.8, the going concern assumption is one of the fundamental assumptions underlying preparation of financial statements. An enterprise is normally viewed as a going concern, that is, as continuing in operation for the foreseeable future. ISA 570 establishes standards and provides guidance on the auditor's responsibilities regarding the appropriateness of the going concern assumption as a basis for preparing financial statements. When a question arises regarding the appropriateness of the going concern assumption, the auditor should gather sufficient appropriate audit evidence to attempt to resolve, to the auditor's satisfaction, the question regarding the entity's ability to continue in operation for the foreseeable future.

If adequate disclosure is made in the financial statements, the auditor must express an unmodified opinion and include an Emphasis of Matter paragraph in the auditor's report to highlight the existence of a material uncertainty relating to the event or condition that may cast significant doubt on the entity's ability to continue as a going concern and draw attention to the note in the financial statements that discloses the event or condition. Such an emphasis of matter paragraph must refer to adequate disclosures in the financial statements:

(a) highlight the existence of a material uncertainty relating to the event or condition that may cast significant doubt on the entity's ability to continue as a going concern; and

(b) draw attention to the note in the financial statements that discloses the matters.

In the UK and the Netherlands are obliged to report about the going concern assumption as used by management preparing the financial statements (illustration 11.11).

ILLUSTRATION 11.11

REPORT ABOUT THE GOING CONCERN ASSUMPTION DERIVED FROM AUDITOR'S REPORT OF POST.NL 2022[26]

Audit response to going concern – no significant going concern risks identified

The Board of Management has performed its going concern assessment and has not identified any going concern risks. To assess the Board of Management's assessment, we have performed, among other things, the following procedures:

> ► we considered whether the Board of Management's assessment of the going concern risks includes all relevant information of which we are aware as a result of our audit;
>
> ► we analysed the Company's financial position as at year-end and compared it to the previous financial year in terms of indicators that could identify going concern risks and considered whether the deteriorated macroeconomic environment indicate a going concern risk. The outcome of our risk assessment procedures did not give reason to perform additional audit procedures on management's going concern assessment.

The Other Matter paragraph is a paragraph included in the auditor's report that refers to a matter other than those presented or disclosed in the financial statements that, in the auditor's judgement, is relevant to users' understanding of the audit, the auditor's responsibilities or the auditor's report. An example would be a paragraph restricting the use of an auditor's report in case of special purpose financial statements (illustration 11.12).

ILLUSTRATION 11.12

OTHER MATTER PARAGRAPH DERIVED FROM AUDITOR'S REPORT OF PADENGA HOLDINGS LTD, 2022[27]

Other matter – comparative information

The consolidated financial statements of the Group as at and for the year ended 31 December 2021, excluding the adjustments described in note 32 to the restated consolidated financial statements, were audited by another auditor who expressed a qualified opinion on those consolidated financial statements on 28 April 2022 as a result of non-compliance with the requirements of IAS 21 – *The effects of Changes in Foreign Exchange Rates*, IFRS 3 – *Business Combinations* and IAS 8 – *Accounting Policies, Changes in Accounting Estimates and Errors*.

As part of our audit of the consolidated financial statements as at and for the year ended 31 December 2022, we audited the adjustments described in note 32 that were applied to restate the comparative review, or apply any procedures to the consolidated financial statements for the year ended 31 December 2021, other than with respect to the adjustments described in note 32 to the consolidated financial statements. Accordingly we do not express an opinion or any other form of assurance on those respective consolidated financial statements taken as a whole. However, in our opinion, the adjustments described in note 32 to the consolidated financial statements are appropriate and have been properly applied.

11.6 TYPE OF AUDIT REPORT

In order to form that opinion, the auditor shall conclude as to whether she has obtained reasonable assurance about whether the financial statements as a whole are free from material misstatement, whether due to fraud or error. That conclusion takes into account whether sufficient appropriate audit evidence has been obtained, if uncorrected misstatements are material, individually or in aggregate and certain evaluations as to correspondence of financial statements to the requirements of the applicable financial reporting framework. Evaluation of the compliance to the reporting framework includes consideration of the qualitative aspects of the entity's accounting practices, including indicators of possible bias in management's judgements. In particular, the auditor must evaluate:

- ▶ whether the financial statements adequately disclose the significant accounting policies selected and they are consistent and appropriate
- ▶ accounting estimates made by management are reasonable;
- ▶ information presented in the financial statements is relevant, reliable, comparable and understandable;
- ▶ disclosures to enable the intended users to understand the effect of material transactions and events on the information conveyed in the financial statements; and
- ▶ terminology used in the financial statements, including the title of each financial statement, is appropriate.

When the financial statements are prepared in accordance with a fair presentation framework, the evaluation above will also include whether the financial statements achieve fair presentation. The auditor's fairness evaluation includes consideration of the overall presentation, structure and content of the financial statements; and whether the financial statements and related notes represent the underlying transactions and events achieve fair presentation.

If the auditor concludes, based on the audit evidence, that the financial statements as a whole are not free from material misstatement, or she is unable to obtain sufficient appropriate audit evidence, she must modify the opinion in the auditor's report by expressing a qualified, adverse or disclaimer of opinion.

▶ MODIFIED OPINIONS

As the user's understanding will be better if the form and content of each type of audit opinion is uniform. ISA 705, 'Modifications to the Opinion in the Independent Auditor's Report', includes suggested wording to express a qualified, adverse or disclaimer of opinion.

The table below illustrates how the auditor's judgement about the nature of the matter giving rise to the modification, and the pervasiveness of its effects or possible effects on the financial statements, affects the type of opinion to be expressed.

Auditor's judgement about the pervasiveness of the effects or possible effects on the financial statements		
Nature of matter giving rise to the modification	Material but not pervasive	Material and pervasive
Financial statements are materially misstated	Qualified opinion	Adverse opinion
Inability to obtain sufficient appropriate audit evidence	Qualified opinion	Disclaimer of opinion

The key concepts to consider are materiality and pervasiveness. Information is material if its omission or misstatement could influence the economic decisions of users taken on the basis of the financial statements. Materiality depends on the size of the item or error judged in the particular circumstances of its omission or misstatement. Thus, materiality provides a threshold or cut-off point rather than being a primary qualitative characteristic which information must have if it is to be useful. *Pervasive* is a term used to describe the effects on the financial statements of misstatements or the possible effects on the financial statements of misstatements that are undetected due to an inability to obtain sufficient appropriate audit evidence. Pervasive effects on the financial statements are those that, in the auditor's judgement:

- ▶ are not confined to specific elements, accounts or items of the financial statements;
- ▶ if so confined, represent or could represent a substantial proportion of the financial statements; or
- ▶ in relation to disclosures, are fundamental to users' understanding of the financial statements.

▶ FORM AND CONTENT OF THE AUDITOR'S REPORT WHEN THE OPINION IS MODIFIED

When the auditor modifies the opinion on the financial statements, she will include a paragraph in the auditor's report that provides a description of the basis for the modification. This paragraph is placed immediately before the opinion paragraph in the auditor's report under the heading 'Basis for Qualified Opinion', 'Basis for Adverse Opinion' or 'Basis for Disclaimer of Opinion', as appropriate. The auditor includes in the basis for modification paragraph a description and quantification of the financial effects of the misstatement. If it is not practical to quantify the financial effects, the auditor shall state that in the basis for modification paragraph. If the modification results from an inability to obtain sufficient appropriate audit evidence, the auditor shall include in the basis for modification paragraph the reasons for that inability.

If there is a material misstatement of the financial statements that relates to narrative disclosures, an explanation of how the disclosures are misstated should be included in the basis for modification paragraph. If a material misstatement relates to the non-disclosure of information required to be disclosed, the auditor shall discuss the non-disclosure with those charged with governance; describe in the basis for modification paragraph the nature of the omitted information; and include the omitted disclosures to the extent that they are quantifiable.

When the auditor modifies the audit opinion, she uses the heading 'Qualified Opinion', 'Adverse Opinion' or 'Disclaimer of Opinion', as appropriate, for the opinion paragraph.

- ▶ When the auditor expresses a *qualified opinion*, the auditor states in the opinion paragraph that, in the auditor's opinion, except for the effects of the matter(s) described in the Basis for Qualified Opinion paragraph, the financial statements present fairly, in all material respects (or give a true and fair view) in accordance with the applicable financial reporting framework when reporting in accordance with a fair presentation framework; or in accordance with the applicable financial reporting framework when reporting in accordance with a compliance framework.
- ▶ When the modification arises from an inability to obtain sufficient appropriate audit evidence and the auditor concludes that the possible effects on the financial statements of undetected misstatements, if any, could be material but not pervasive.

In that case she uses the corresponding phrase 'except for the possible effects of the matter(s) ...' for the modified opinion.

When the auditor expresses an *adverse opinion*, the auditor will state in the opinion paragraph that, in the auditor's opinion, because of the significance of the matter(s) described in the Basis for Adverse Opinion paragraph the financial statements do not present fairly (or give a true and fair view) in accordance with the applicable financial reporting framework when reporting in accordance with a fair presentation framework; or in accordance with the applicable financial reporting framework when reporting in accordance with a compliance framework.

When the auditor *disclaims an opinion* due to an inability to obtain sufficient appropriate audit evidence, the auditor states in the opinion paragraph that because of the significance (material and pervasive) of the matter(s) described in the Basis for Disclaimer of Opinion paragraph, the auditor has not been able to obtain sufficient appropriate audit evidence to provide a basis for an audit opinion; and, accordingly, the auditor does not express an opinion on the financial statements as a whole.

▶ QUALIFIED OPINION

According to ISA 705 the auditor issues a qualified opinion when[28]:
- ▶ having obtained sufficient appropriate audit evidence, the auditor concludes that misstatements, individually or in the aggregate, are material, but not pervasive, to the financial statements; or
- ▶ the auditor is unable to obtain sufficient appropriate audit evidence on which to base the opinion, but the auditor concludes that the possible effects on the financial statements of undetected misstatements, if any, could be material but not pervasive.

In case of misstatements, the auditor may disagree with management regarding:
- ▶ the acceptability of the accounting policies selected;
- ▶ the method of policy application, including the adequacy of valuations and disclosures in the financial statements; or
- ▶ the compliance of the financial statements with relevant regulations and statutory requirements.

If any of these disagreements are material, the auditor should express a qualified opinion. If the effect of the disagreement is so material and pervasive to the financial statements that she concludes that a qualification would not be adequate to disclose the misleading or incomplete nature of the financial statements, an adverse opinion should be expressed.

In case of *scope limitations*, auditors are unable for any reason to obtain the information and explanations considered necessary for the audit. Scope may be limited by the inability to carry out a procedure the auditors consider necessary and the absence of proper accounting records. The client, for example, may sometimes impose a limitation on the scope of the auditor's work when the terms of the engagement specify that the auditor will not carry out an audit procedure that the auditor believes is necessary.

Scope limitations may also be caused by circumstances beyond control of either the client or the auditor. When restrictions are due to conditions beyond the client's control, a modified opinion is more likely than a disclaimer. Such a scope limitation may be imposed by circumstances, for example, when the timing of the auditor's appointment makes it difficult to observe the counting of physical inventories. It may also arise when the accounting records are inadequate or when the auditor is unable to carry out a necessary audit procedure. In these circumstances, the auditor should attempt to carry out reasonable alternative procedures to obtain sufficient audit evidence to support an unmodified opinion.

An example of the wording of a qualified report is given in illustration 11.13[29]. This illustration is a qualified opinion report based on inability to obtain sufficient appropriate audit evidence[30].

ILLUSTRATION 11.13

EXAMPLE OF A QUALIFIED OPINION

Convenience translation into English of independent auditor's report originally issued in Turkish on the board of directors' annual report

To the General Assembly of Türkiye Cumhuriyeti Ziraat Bankası A.Ş.

1. Qualified Opinion

We have audited the annual report of Türkiye Cumhuriyeti Ziraat Bankası A.Ş. (the 'Bank'), and its consolidated subsidiaries (collectively referred as the 'Group') of for the accounting period of 1 January 2022 – 31 December 2022.

In our opinion, except for the matter described in the Basis for Qualified Opinion section below, the financial information and the analysis made by the Board of Directors by using the information included in the audited financial statements regarding the Bank's and Group's position in the Board of Directors' Annual Report are consistent and presented fairly, in all material respects, with the audited full set unconsolidated and consolidated financial statements and with the information obtained in the course of independent audit.

2. Basis for Qualified Opinion

As expressed in Basis for Qualified Opinion section of our auditor's report dated 17 February 2023 on the full set unconsolidated financial statements of the Bank for the period between 1 January 2022 – 31 December 2022; unconsolidated financial statements include of a free provision amounting to TL 28.300.000 thousand which consist of TL 3.710.000 thousand provided in prior periods and TL 24.590.000 thousand recognized in the current year by the Bank management which is not within the requirements of BRSA Accounting and Financial Reporting Legislation.

As expressed in Basis for Qualified Opinion section of our auditor's report dated 17 February 2023 on the full set consolidated financial statements of the Group for the period between 1 January 2022 – 31 December 2022; consolidated financial statements include of a free provision amounting to TL 29.304.000 thousand which consist of TL 3.730.000 thousand provided in prior periods, TL 25.574.000 thousand recognized in the current year by the Group management which is not within the requirements of BRSA Accounting and Financial Reporting Legislation

Our audit was conducted in accordance with the 'Regulation on independent Audit of Banks' published by the BRSA on the Official Gazette No.29314 dated 2 April 2015 and the

Standards on Independent Auditing (the 'SIA') that are part of Turkish Standards on Auditing issued by the Public Oversight Accounting and Auditing Standards Authority (the 'POA'). Our responsibilities under these standards are further described in the 'Auditor's Responsibilities for the Audit of the Consolidated Financial Statements' section of our report. We hereby declare that we are independent of the Group in accordance with the Ethical Rules for Independent Auditors (including International Independence Standards) (the 'Ethical Rules') and the ethical requirements regarding independent audit in regulations issued by POA that are relevant to our audit of the financial statements. We have also fulfilled our other ethical responsibilities in accordance with the Ethical Rules and regulations. We believe that the audit evidence we have obtained during the independent audit provides a sufficient and appropriate basis for our qualified opinion.

▶ ADVERSE OPINION

The auditor shall express an adverse opinion when the auditor, having obtained sufficient appropriate audit evidence, concludes that misstatements, individually or in the aggregate, are both material and pervasive to the financial statements. An adverse opinion is issued when the effect of a disagreement is so material and pervasive to the financial statements that the auditor concludes that a qualification of his report is not adequate to disclose the misleading or incomplete nature of the financial statements. An example of the wording of (basis for) adverse opinion for materially misstated financial statements (due to the non-consolidation of a subsidiary) is given in illustration 11.14[31].

ILLUSTRATION 11.14

EXAMPLE OF AN ADVERSE OPINION
INDEPENDENT AUDITOR'S REPORT

To the Members of Jharkhand Bijli Vitran Nigam Limited

Report on the Audit of Consolidated Ind AS Financial Statements

Adverse Opinion
We have audited the accompanying Consolidated Ind AS financial Statement of Jharkhand Bijli Vitran Nigam Limited ('the Company'), **Regd. Office: Engineering Building, H.E.C, Dhurwa, Ranchi-834004 (CIN: U40108JH2013SGC001702) (PAN: AADCJ3148A)** and its subsidiary and joint venture which comprise the Consolidated Balance Sheet as at 31st March 2022, the Consolidated Statement of Profit & Loss Account (including the Statement of Other Comprehensive Income), the Consolidated Statement of Cash Flows and the Consolidated Statement of Changes in Equity for the year then ended and notes to the consolidated financial statement including summary of significant accounting policies and other explanatory information.

In our opinion and to the best of our information and according to the explanations given to us, because of the significance of matters described in the Basis of Adverse opinion section of our report and based on the consideration of report of other auditors on separate financial statements and other information of joint operations, subsidiaries and joint ventures the aforesaid consolidated Ind AS financial statements give the information required hby the Companies Act, 2013 ('the Act') in the manner so required and does not give true and fair view in conformity with the Indian accounting standards prescribed under section 133 of the act read with Companies (Indian Accounting Standards) Rule, 2015, as amended (Ind AS) and other accounting principles generally accepted in India, of the consolidated state of affairs of the Group as at 31st March 2022 and its Loss, total consolidated comprehensive Loss, its consolidated cash flows and the consolidated changes in equity for the year ended on that date.

Basis of Adverse Opinion

We conducted our audit of the consolidated Ind AS financial statements in accordance with Standards on Auditing (Sas) specified under section 143(10) of the Act. Our responsibilities under those Standards are further described in the 'Auditor's Responsibilities for the Audit of the consolidated Ind AS Financial Statements' section of our report. We are independent of the Company in accordance with the 'Code of Ethics' issued by the Institute of Chartered Accountants of India (ICAI) together with the ethical requirements that are relevant to our audit of the consolidated financial statements under the provisions of the Companies Act, 2013 and the rules thereunder, and we have fulfilled our other ethical responsibilities in accordance with these requirements and the ICAI's Code of Ethics. We believe that the audit evidence we have obtained is sufficient and appropriate to provide a basis for our adverse opinion on the consolidated Ind AS financial statements.

We draw attention to the matters described in **Annexure 'A'** the effect of which, individually or in aggregate, are material and pervasive to the Consolidated Ind AS financial statement and matters where we are unable to obtain sufficient and appropriate audit evidence. The effects of matters described in said Annexure 'A' which could be reasonably determined are quantified and given therein. Our opinion is adverse in respect of these matters.

It is obvious from reading the opinion paragraph that an adverse opinion report is likely to have a very negative effect on the readers of the report and the related financial statements; therefore, such reports are issued only after all attempts to persuade the client to adjust the financial statements have failed[32]. The only other option available to the auditor in this situation is withdrawal from the engagement.

▶ DISCLAIMER OF OPINION

The auditor will disclaim an opinion when she is unable to obtain sufficient appropriate audit evidence on which to base the opinion, and she concludes that the possible effects on the financial statements of undetected misstatements could be both material and pervasive. The auditor would also disclaim an opinion when, in extremely rare circumstances involving multiple uncertainties, the auditor concludes that, notwithstanding having obtained sufficient appropriate audit evidence regarding each of the individual uncertainties, it is not possible to form an opinion on the financial statements due to the potential interaction of the uncertainties and their possible cumulative effect on the financial statements. See illustration 11.15[33].

ILLUSTRATION 11.15

EXAMPLE OF DISCLAIMER OF OPINION

Independent Auditors' Report

Secretary of the Army and
Inspector General of the Department of Defense:

Report on the Audit of the Consolidated Financial Statements

Disclaimer of Opinion

We were engaged to audit the consolidated financial statements of the United States (U.S.) Department of the Army (Army) General Fund (GF), which comprise the consolidated balance sheets as of September 30, 2023 and 2022, and the related consolidated statements of net costs, consolidated statements of changes in net position, and combined statements of budgetary resources for the years then ended, and the related notes to the consolidated financial statements (collectively, the consolidated financial statements).

We do not express an opinion on the accompanying consolidated financial statements of the Army GF. Because of the significance of the matters described in the Basis for Disclaimer of Opinion section of our report, we have not been able to obtain sufficient appropriate audit evidence to provide a basis for an audit opinion on the consolidated financial statements.

Basis for Disclaimer of Opinion

Management did not provide sufficient appropriate evidential matter to support the amounts in the consolidated financial statements due to inadequate processes, controls, and records to support transactions and account balances. As a result, we were unable to determine whether any adjustments were necessary related to the consolidated financial statements. Additionally, management revalued a significant portion of general equipment during fiscal year 2020, using standard purchase price prior to the application of depreciation which is not in accordance with U.S. generally accepted accounting principles.

ISA 210 states that when the limitation in terms of a proposed engagement is such that the auditor believes that she would need to issue an auditor's report containing a disclaimer of opinion, she would ordinarily not accept the audit engagement unless required to do so by statute or law[34]. A statutory auditor should not accept an audit engagement when the limitation infringes on his statutory duties.

If, *after* accepting the engagement, the auditor becomes aware that management has imposed a limitation on the scope of the audit that the auditor considers likely to result in the need to express a qualified opinion or to disclaim an opinion on the financial statements the auditor must request that management remove the limitation. If management refuses to remove the limitation, the auditor must communicate the matter to those charged with governance and determine whether it is possible to perform alternative procedures to obtain sufficient appropriate audit evidence.

If the auditor concludes that the possible effects on the financial statements of undetected misstatements could be both material and pervasive, she must withdraw from the audit. If withdrawal from the audit before issuing the auditor's report is not practicable or possible, the auditor should disclaim an opinion on the financial statements[35]. Before withdrawing, the auditor will communicate to those charged with governance any matters regarding misstatements identified. When the auditor disclaims an opinion due to an inability to obtain sufficient appropriate audit evidence, she must amend the introductory paragraph of the auditor's report to state that the auditor was engaged to audit the financial statements[36].

▶ **REFERENCE TO EXPERT**

When expressing an unmodified (unqualified) opinion, the auditor generally should not refer to the work of an expert in her report because such a reference might be misunderstood to be a qualification of the auditor's opinion or a division of responsibility. If the auditor, as a result of the other auditor's or expert's work, issues an opinion other than unmodified, she may in some circumstances describe the work of the expert. Making use of an expert is further discussed in section 13.3.

11.7 OPINION ON INTERNAL CONTROLS OVER FINANCIAL REPORTING

In the US, auditors of listed companies must audit management assertions about Internal Control over Financial Reporting as required by Sarbanes-Oxley Act Section 404 (also see section 14.5).

PCAOB AS 2201 (An Audit of Internal Control Over Financial Reporting That Is Integrated with An Audit of Financial Statements) establishes requirements and provides direction that applies when an auditor is engaged to perform an audit of management's assessment of the effectiveness of internal control over financial reporting that is integrated with an audit of the financial statements[37].

Effective internal control over financial reporting provides reasonable assurance regarding the reliability of financial reporting and the preparation of financial statements for external purposes. If one or more material weaknesses exist, the company's internal control over financial reporting cannot be considered effective.

According to PCAOB AS 2201, the audit of internal control over financial reporting must be integrated with the audit of the financial statements. The objectives of the audits are not identical, however, and the auditor must plan and perform the work to achieve the objectives of both audits. The following example expresses an unqualified opinion on both internal control over financial reporting and the financial statements (illustration 11.16).[38]

ILLUSTRATION 11.16

REPORT OF INDEPENDENT REGISTERED PUBLIC ACCOUNTING FIRM

To the Shareholders and the Board of Directors of Walmart Inc.

Opinion on Internal Control over Financial Reporting

We have audited Walmart Inc.'s internal control over financial reporting as of January 31, 2023, based on criteria established in Internal Control – Integrated Framework issued by the Committee of Sponsoring Organizations of the Treadway Commission (2013 framework) (the COSO criteria). In our opinion, Walmart Inc. (the Company) maintained, in all material respects, effective internal control over financial reporting as of January 31, 2023, based on the COSO criteria.

We also have audited, in accordance with the standards of the Public Company Accounting Oversight Board (United States) (PCAOB), the consolidated balance sheets of Walmart Inc. as of January 31, 2023 and 2022, the related consolidated statements of income, comprehensive income, shareholders' equity and cash flows for each of the three years in the period ended January 31, 2-23, and the related notes and our report dated March 17, 2023 expressed an unqualified opinion thereon.

Basis for Opinion

The Company's management is responsible for maintaining effective internal control over financial reporting and for its assessment of the effectiveness of internal control over financial reporting included in the accompanying Report on Itnernal Control over Fianncial Reporting. Our responsibility is to express an opinion on the company's internal control over financial reporting based on our audit. We are a public accounting firm registered with the PCAOB and are required to be independent with respect to the Company in accordance with the U.S. federal securities laws and the applicable rules and regulations of the Securities and Exchange Commission and the PCAOB.

We conducted our audit in accordance with the standards of the PCAOB. Those standards require that we plan and perform the audit to obtain reasonable assurance about whether effective internal control over financial reporting was maintained in all material respects.

Our audit included obtaining an understanding of internal control over financial reporting, assessing the risk that a material weakness exists, testing and evaluating the design and operating effectiveness of internal control based on the assessed risk, and performing such other procedures as we considered necessary in the circumstances. We believe that our audit provides a reasonable basis for our opinion.

Definition and Limitations of Internal Control over Financial Reporting

A company's internal control over financial reporting is a process designed to provide reasonable assurance regarding the reliability of financial reporting and the preparation of financial statements for external purposes in accordance with generally accepted accounting principles. A company's internal control over financial reporting includes those policies and procedures that (1) pertain to the maintenance of records that, in reasonable detail, accurately and fairly reflect the transactions and dispositions of the assets of the company; (2) provide reasonable assurance that transactions are recorded as necessary to permit preparation of financial statements in accordance with generally accepted accounting principles, and that receipts and expenditures of the company are being made only in accordance with authoriza-

COMMUNICATIONS WITH THOSE CHARGED WITH GOVERNANCE

tions of management and directors of the company; and (3) provide reasonable assurance regarding prevention or timely detection of unauthorized acquisition, use, or disposition of the company's assets that could have a material effect on the financial statements.

Because of its inherent limitations, internal control over financial reporting may not prevent or detect misstatements. Also, projections of any evaluation of effectiveness to future periods are subject to the risk that controls may become inadequate because of changes in conditions, or that the degree of compliance with the policies or procedures may deteriorate.

/s/ Ernst & Young LLP

Rogers, Arkansas
March 17, 2023

11.8 COMMUNICATIONS WITH THOSE CHARGED WITH GOVERNANCE

The auditors are required to communicate their audit findings to the management and board of directors of a corporation. This is not only given in the ISA standards[39], but also required by law in some countries[40]. Audit matters of governance interest to be communicated by the auditor to the board or audit committee ordinarily include: material weaknesses in internal control, non-compliance with laws and regulations, fraud involving management, questions regarding management integrity, and other matters.

▶ **COMMUNICATIONS WITH THE AUDIT COMMITTEE**

As explained in section 5.3, 'Governance' is the term used to describe the role of persons entrusted with the supervision, control and direction of an entity. Those persons are the ones responsible for financial reporting and for ensuring that the company achieves its objectives. Those charged with corporate governance are usually the Board of Directors, Supervisory Board, or the Audit Committee.

The *audit committee* is a body formed by a company's board of directors to allow the board to focus on issues affecting external reporting and, in some cases, internal control. In general, the board of directors is composed of outside (non-employee) directors. The audit committee selects and appraises the performance of the auditing firm. It develops a professional relationship with the external auditing firm to ensure that accounting and control matters are properly discussed. Besides evaluating external auditor's reports, the committee may evaluate internal audit reports, review management representations, and get involved with public disclosure of corporate activities. ISA 260 'Communication with Those Charged with Governance' applies to communications between the external auditor and the audit committee.

This ISA states that effective two-way communication is important in assisting the auditor and those charged with governance in understanding matters related to the audit in context, and in developing a constructive working relationship. Communication is important for the auditor in obtaining information relevant to the audit from those charged with governance. (For example, those charged with governance may assist the

TYCO INTERNATIONAL LTD – MANAGEMENT'S PIGGY BANK

Concept	Financial statement disclosure, corporate governance and loans.

Story	Tyco was a US company composed of two major business segments: security solutions and fire protection. On September 9, 2016 Johnson Controls merged with Tyco, and all businesses of Tyco and Johnson Controls was combined under Tyco International plc, renamed Johnson Controls International plc.

In 2002, three former top executives of Tyco (former CEOs Dennis Kozlowski, Mark Swartz and the chief legal officer Mark Belnick) were sued by the SEC. Kozlowski and Swartz granted themselves hundreds of millions of dollars in secret low-interest and interest-free loans from Tyco that they used for personal expenses. They later caused Tyco to forgive tens of millions of dollars they owed the company, without disclosure to investors as required by the federal securities laws (SEC, 2002). Kozlowski and Swartz engaged in numerous highly profitable related party transactions with Tyco and awarded themselves lavish perquisites – without disclosing either the transactions or perquisites to Tyco shareholders (US District Court, 2002).

'Messrs. Kozlowski and Swartz … treated Tyco as their private bank, taking out hundreds of millions of dollars of loans in compensation without ever telling investors,' said Stephen M. Cutler, the SEC's Director of Enforcement (SEC, 2002).

But Not What He Told Them

At the same time that Kozlowski and Swartz engaged in their massive covert fraudulent use of corporate funds, Kozlowski regularly assured investors that at Tyco 'nothing was hidden behind the scenes', that Tyco's disclosures were 'exceptional' and that Tyco's management 'prided itself on having sharp focus with creating shareholder value'. Similarly, Swartz regularly assured investors that 'Tyco's disclosure practice remains second to none' (US District Court, 2002).

KELP and Relocation Loans

Most of Kozlowski's and Swartz's improper Tyco loans were taken through abuse of Tyco's Key Employee Corporate Loan Program (the 'KELP'). A disclosure description of the plan, as filed with the SEC, explicitly described its narrow purpose (US District Court 2002):

[U]nder the Program, loan proceeds may be used for the payment of federal income taxes due upon the vesting of Company common stock from time to time under the 1983 Restricted Stock Ownership Plans for Key Employees, and to refinance other existing outstanding loans for such purpose.

Kozlowski and Swartz bestowed upon themselves hundreds of millions of dollars in KELP loans which they used for purposes not legitimately authorized by the KELP. From 1997 to 2002, Kozlowski took an aggregate of approximately $270 million charged as KELP loans – even though he only used $29 million of that to cover taxes from the vesting of his Tyco stock. The rest was used for impermissible and unauthorized purposes. For example, with his KELP loans, Kozlowski amassed millions of dollars in fine art, yachts and estate jewelry, as well as an apartment on Park Avenue and a palatial estate in Nantucket. He also used the KELP to fund his personal investments and business ventures (US District Court, 2002).

Kozlowski and Swartz also abused Tyco's relocation loan program to enrich themselves. When Tyco moved its corporate offices from New Hampshire to New York City, an interest-free loan program was established. It was designed to assist Tyco employees who were required to relocate from New Hampshire to New York. Kozlowski used approximately $21 million of 'relocation' loans for various other purposes, including the purchase of prestigious properties in New Hampshire, Nantucket and Connecticut. Kozlowski even used approximately $7 million of Tyco's funds to purchase a Park Avenue apartment for his wife from whom he had been separated for many years and whom he subsequently divorced (US District Court, 2002).

Kozlowski and Swartz did not stop there. Instead, they oversaw and authorized transactions by which tens of millions of dollars of their KELP loans and relocation loans were forgiven and written off Tyco's books. They also directed the acceleration of the vesting of Tyco common stock for their benefit (US District Court, 2002).

They Deserve Bonuses

In December 2000, Kozlowski and Swartz engineered another program whereby Tyco paid them bonuses comprised of cash, Tyco common stock, and/or forgiveness of relocation loans. From that program, Kozlowski received 148,000 shares of Tyco common stock, a cash bonus of $700,000, and $16 million in relocation loan forgiveness. Swartz received 74,000 shares of Tyco common stock, a cash bonus of $350,000, and $8 million in relocation loan forgiveness. None of these payments were disclosed as part of Kozlowski's and Swartz's executive compensation in Tyco's annual reports (US District Court, 2002).

The Auditor

In 2003, the SEC sued Richard P. Scalzo, CPA, the PricewaterhouseCoopers LLP (PwC) audit engagement partner for Tyco from 1997 through 2001 (SEC, 2003a).

The SEC alleged that Scalzo received 'multiple and repeated facts' regarding the lack of integrity of Tyco's senior management, but he did not take appropriate audit steps in the face of this information. The SEC maintained that those facts were sufficient to obligate Scalzo to re-evaluate the risk assessment of the Tyco audits and to perform additional audit procedures, including further audit testing of certain items (most notably, certain executive benefits, executive compensation, and related party transactions). He did not perform these procedures (SEC, 2003a).

Red Flags and Post Period Adjustments

In the 30 September 1997 audit, factual red flags appeared in the audit working papers. The working papers contained 26 pages of reports prepared by the company, listing the activity in the various KELP accounts of Tyco employees. Three of those 26 pages listed the KELP account activity for L. Dennis Kozlowski. Most of the line items for the Kozlowski account also include a brief description, and 18 carry descriptions that are immediately recognizable as not being for the payment of taxes on the vesting of restricted stock. For example, one item reads 'WINE CELLAR', another reads 'NEW ENG WINE', another 'BMW REG/TAX', another 'ANGIE KOZLOWS', and 13 read either 'WALDORF', 'WALDORF RENT', 'WALDORF EXPEN', 'WALDORF RENT A' or WALDORF RENT S' (SEC, 2003b).

In the 30 September 1998 audit, the audit team noticed a series of transactions in which three Tyco executives exercised Tyco stock options, by borrowing from the KELP, and then sold the shares back to the company the next business day through an offshore Tyco subsidiary. Tyco then wrote a cheque to the executives, representing a net settlement of the transactions. After consulting with PwC national partners, the PwC audit team came to the conclusion that Tyco should include a compensation charge of approximately $40 million (SEC, 2003b).

Faced with the reality of having to book an unanticipated $40 million compensation charge, Tyco suddenly arrived at $40 million in additional, contemporaneous, post-period adjustments which had the effect of negating the impact of the $40 million charge. The $40 million in credits raised significant issues – $7.8 million resulted from Tyco reversing a previous 'fourth quarter charge for restricted stock expense for certain executives no longer required'. The rationale advanced for that reversal was that the executives had decided to forego the corresponding bonuses in the fourth quarter.

The company's treatment for certain executive bonuses provided evidence of problems. For example, Tyco made an initial public offering (IPO) of its previously wholly-owned subsidiary, TyCom Ltd. Because of the IPO's success, Kozlowski decided to grant $96 million in bonuses to Tyco officers and employees. Tyco accounted for the bonuses as: (1) a TyCom offering expense, (2) a credit for previous over-accruals of general and administrative expense, and (3) a contra-accrual for federal income taxes. None of it was booked as compensation expense.

Discussion Questions	▷ What tests should an auditor perform to find evidence concerning misstatement of executive compensation expense?
	▷ Are public statements by the CEO to investors considered a disclosure that requires the attention of the auditor?
	▷ If the Sarbanes–Oxley Act, Section 402 Enhanced Conflict Provisions was in effect in 2001, would that have made a difference to the disclosure requirements?

References   SEC, 2002, Press Release 2002-135, 'SEC Sues Former Tyco CEO Kozlowski, Two Others for Fraud', Securities and Exchange Commission, 12 September.

SEC, 2003a, Press Release 2003-95, 'Former Tyco Auditor Permanently Barred from Practicing before the Commission,' Securities and Exchange Commission, 13 August.

SEC, 2003b, Securities Exchange Act of 1934 Release No. 48328. Accounting And Auditing Enforcement Release No. 1839, 'In the Matter of Richard P. Scalzo, CPA', Securities and Exchange Commission, 13 August.

United States District Court Southern District of New York, 2002, 'Securities and Exchange Commission v. L. Dennis Kozlowski, Mark H. Swartz, and Mark A. Belnick', Securities and Exchange Commission, 12 September.

auditor in understanding the entity and its environment, in identifying appropriate sources of audit evidence, and in providing information about specific transactions or events.)

The audit committee also has the responsibility for hiring an independent auditor. The auditor must communicate important findings to the Board. Auditors may attend board of directors' meetings to discuss accounting and auditing matters. Some matters that might be discussed are the accounting system, internal controls, and impacts of changes in accounting standards, and disclosure. Discussion with the Board is essential for matters that cannot be successfully resolved with the executive officers. According to PCAOB Standard AS 1301: Communications with Audit Committees, the objectives of the auditor are to[41]:

▷ Communicate to the audit committee the responsibilities of the auditor in relation to the audit and establish an understanding of the terms of the audit engagement with the audit committee;

▷ Obtain information from the audit committee relevant to the audit;

▷ Communicate to the audit committee an overview of the overall audit strategy and timing of the audit; and

▷ Provide the audit committee with timely observations arising from the audit that are significant to the financial reporting process.

Audit matters of governance interest to be communicated by the auditor to the board or audit committee ordinarily include:

▷ material weaknesses in internal control;

▷ non-compliance with laws and regulations;

▷ fraud involving management;

▷ questions regarding management integrity;

▷ the general approach and overall scope of the audit;

▷ the selection of, or changes in, significant accounting policies and practices that have a material effect on the financial statements;

▷ the potential effect on the financial statements of any significant risks and exposures, such as pending litigation, that requires disclosure in the financial statements;

▷ significant audit adjustments to the accounting records;

▷ material uncertainties related to the entity's ability to continue as a going concern;

▷ disagreements with management about matters that could be significant to the entity's financial statements or the auditor's report (these communications include consideration of whether the matter has, or has not, been resolved and the significance of the matter);

▷ expected modifications to the auditor's report.

▷ **COMMUNICATIONS OF DEFICIENCIES IN INTERNAL CONTROL**

ISA 265[42] discusses the auditor's communications to management and those charged with governance when the auditor has identified internal control deficiencies in an audit of financial statements[43]. A deficiency in internal control exists when: (1) a control is designed, implemented or operated in such a way that it is unable to prevent, or detect and correct, misstatements in the financial statements on a timely basis; or (2) a control necessary to prevent, or detect and correct, misstatements in the financial statements on a timely basis is missing. A significant deficiency in internal control is a deficiency or combination of deficiencies in internal control that, in the auditor's professional judgement, is of sufficient importance to merit the attention of those charged with governance[44]. The auditor is required to obtain an understanding of internal control relevant to the audit when identifying and assessing the risks of material misstatement.

The auditor must communicate to management at an appropriate level of responsibility on a timely basis and in writing, significant deficiencies in internal control and any other deficiencies in internal control identified during the audit that have not been communicated to management by other parties and that, in the auditor's professional judgement, are of sufficient importance to merit management's attention.

The auditor is required to include in the written communication of significant deficiencies in internal control:

▷ A description of the deficiencies and an explanation of their potential effects.

▷ Sufficient information to enable those charged with governance and management to understand the context of the communication. In particular, the auditor shall explain that:

▷ the purpose of the audit was for the auditor to express an opinion on the financial statements;

▷ the audit included consideration of internal control relevant to the preparation of the financial statements in order to design audit procedures that are appropriate in the circumstances, but not for the purpose of expressing an opinion on the effectiveness of internal control; and

▷ the matters being reported are limited to those deficiencies that the auditor has identified during the audit and that the auditor has concluded are of sufficient importance to merit being reported to those charged with governance.

▶ REPORTABLE CONDITIONS

Major internal control problems (material weakness or reportable conditions) should be reported to management, and where necessary, the board of directors. In deciding whether a matter is a reportable condition, the auditor considers factors such as the size of the company and its ownership characteristics, the organizational structure, and the complexity and diversity of company activities. For example, an internal control structure deficiency that is a reportable condition for a large sophisticated financial institution may not be a reportable condition for a small manufacturing concern.

The reportable conditions are generally communicated in a separate letter, the so- called management letter. The management letter (discussed later in this chapter in Section 11.10) also includes suggestions for improvement of internal controls focused on financial, compliance and operational processes.

11.9 EXTENDED AUDITOR'S REPORT

In many countries it is customary for the auditor to prepare a long-form (extended) report to the entity's board of directors in addition to the publicly published short-form report discussed in this chapter. The topics covered in the report may vary as there are no standards, but a typical long-form report will include:

▷ an overview of the audit engagement;

▷ an analysis of the financial statements;

▷ a discussion of risk management and internal control;

▷ various optional topics subject to the circumstances;

▷ auditor independence and quality control;

▷ fees.

In the overview, the long-form report will discuss nature, scope, organization, level of materiality, new audit work and work with other auditors and experts.

▶ **DISCUSSION OF FINANCIAL ISSUES**

Highlights of the financial statements are discussed. Accounting issues need to be clarified. Several issues may require judgement in accounting such as provisions, accruals and contingent liabilities. Changes in client, national, and international accounting policies are explained in terms of their impact on the financial statements. acquisitions and divestments and their effect on the accounts should be covered. The financial position of the company for possible financing or refinancing and the related debt covenant ratios and defaults are gone into.

Other financial statement topics such as disagreement or discussion with management and future client developments are reviewed. Management and auditors may disagree on certain financial statement issues, so the long-form report must address these. Future client development affecting the annual report may include a discussion of future uncertainties and subsequent events.

▶ **RISK DISCUSSION**

Risk management and internal controls are ever more important to the board of directors. A discussion of risk in the long-form report may include:
- ▶ major operational and financial risks;
- ▶ effectiveness of the client's risk management;
- ▶ quality of internal reporting and management accounting;
- ▶ frauds and irregularities;
- ▶ ethics compliance and special areas such as treasury, new business and quality control.

Internal control topics unveiled might include strengths and weaknesses of internal controls, recommendations for improving controls, information technology and internal audit department.

Risk management is an important topic for board members. Of course, the audit client is interested in major operational and financial risks, so they are reviewed at least in so far as they are related to the audit. The effectiveness of the client's risk management and quality of internal reporting and management accounting are meaningful to the board. Of crucial importance is the discussion of any frauds and irregularities suspected by the auditor or uncovered in the audit. Industry ethics affect the moral and legal position of the client so a discussion of compliance with ethics standards is very important. Popular areas for quality management are treasury effectiveness, new business development and quality control.

▶ **OTHER TOPICS DISCUSSED**

There may be topics not typically addressed that the auditor may feel warrant discussion because of the circumstances of the company, the economy, or the audit. These topics may include tax, pension, treasury function, impact of world economic changes, and audit-related requirements.

Audit-related areas that might be discussed include special advisory projects on the financial statements, risk control, insurance coverage, and pension arrangements. Other areas related to the audit that may be reviewed are tax compliance work and constancy projects such as cost benchmarking, information technology and logistics.

Furthermore, it is required by law in some countries that the auditors describe how their independence has been warranted, and what quality control procedures they have applied to deliver a high-quality audit report. Also, overviews of audit fees compared to budget, and of other fees, have to be presented.

11.10   MANAGEMENT LETTER

The management letter identifies issues not required to be disclosed in the auditor's report but represent the auditor's concerns and suggestions noted during the audit. The management letter is the auditor's letter addressed to the client. It contains the public accountant's conclusions regarding the company's accounting policies and procedures, internal controls and operating policies. An evaluation is made of the present system, pointing out problems.

Recommendations for improvement are cited. Also included is a discussion of any problem which may require immediate action to correct. The management letter is designed to point out the problems but also offer recommendations/solutions and provide any special approach that might benefit the enterprise.

There is no format or requirements for management letters given in the ISAs or most other national standards. The audit firm may develop a format and typical contents for their own organization over time. Some may choose to incorporate just the communications required under ISA 240 'The Auditor's Responsibilities Relating to Fraud in an Audit of Financial Statements', ISA 250 'Consideration of Laws and Regulations in an Audit of Financial Statements', ISA 260 'Communication with Those Charged with Governance' and ISA 265 'Communicating Deficiencies in Internal Control to Those Charged with Governance and Management'. Other firms have adopted alternative language that they prefer. In certain cases, due to an audit client's specific circumstances, additional or modified wording may be used. When communicating material that is not required by standards and statute, the auditor must be sure that there is no conflict with the general purpose of communication set forth by ISAs.

11.11   GENERAL MEETING OF SHAREHOLDERS

In countries like India, Australia[45], UK, Hong Kong and the Netherlands, the statutory auditors must be present at the Annual General Meeting of Shareholders. During the meeting management answers questions about the audited financial statements raised by shareholders. Auditors can be asked to answer any queries shareholders may have about the audit. According to the UK Companies Act of 2006, SEC 502, a company's auditor is entitled[46]:

  ▸ to receive all notices of, and other communications relating to, any general meeting which a member of the company is entitled to receive,
  ▸ to attend any general meetings of the company, and
  ▸ to be heard at any general meeting which she attends on any part of the business of the meeting which concerns her as auditor.

According to Guidelines of The Royal Netherlands Institute of Chartered Accountants (NBA) the starting point for answering questions is that it is the responsibility of the board to inform the shareholders about matters that concern the company, including the content of the financial statements and the quality of the internal control system[47]. The auditor limits herself to answering questions about her audit procedures and her auditor's report. Given the (societal) role of the auditor, she can also be asked about her work on the management report, the report of the supervisory board, other information and – if applicable – with regard to the CSR report. Questions regarding the report of the auditor to the supervisory board and the management letter should be addressed to the chairman of the meeting and be answered by representatives of the company. When answering questions, the auditor should of course provide relevant and specific information but prevent disclosure of price-sensitive information and should not respond to questions outside the annual meeting as the ethical principal of confidentiality is always applicable. When the auditor breaches the confidentiality obligation with permission of the chair of the annual meeting, she must still consider the interests of all involved parties, third parties, and also the public interest in the decision-making process. Requesting permission from the chair of the meeting is a result of this consideration.

11.12 SUMMARY

A standard auditor's report is relatively brief, in general occupying no more than one or two pages. This is a paradox because the audit report requires great care and is the consummation of a rigorous and lengthy audit process.

In general, management must take responsibility for the companies' financial report. For example, the US Sarbanes-Oxley Act of 2002 requires that the principal executive officer or officers and the principal financial officer or officers of any firm, foreign or domestic, that is publicly traded, certify certain conditions in each annual or quarterly report filed or submitted to the US Securities and Exchange Commission (SEC). In several European countries law requires that all members of the board of directors (or, in a two-tier system, the executive board and the supervisory board) sign the financial statements, thereby demonstrating that their responsibility for these statements is a joint one rather than only that of the CEO and CFO.

The unmodified auditor's report, under ISA 700, should include the following basic elements: title, addressee, opinion paragraph containing an expression of opinion on the financial statements, basis for opinion, Key Audit Matters, a description of the responsibility of management for the preparation of the financial statements, a description of the auditor's responsibility to express an opinion on the financial statements and the scope of the audit, a report on other reporting responsibilities, name of the engagement partner, auditor's signature the auditor's address and the date of the report.

The auditor's report should have an appropriate title that helps the reader to identify it and easily distinguish it. ISA 700 requires 'Independent Auditor's Report' to distinguish the auditor's report from reports that might be issued by others. The report is usually addressed either to the shareholders or supervisory board or the board of directors of the entity whose financial statements have been audited.

When expressing an unqualified (unmodified) opinion on financial statements prepared in accordance with a fair presentation framework like IFRS, the auditor's opinion includes one of the following phrases:

▶ In our opinion, the accompanying financial statements present fairly, in all material respects, […] in accordance with IFRS; or

▶ In our opinion, the accompanying financial statements give a true and fair view of […] in accordance with IFRS.

The auditor's report must state that the responsibility of the auditor is to express an opinion on the financial statements based on the audit conducted in accordance with International Standards on Auditing (ISA) or the national auditing standards of that jurisdiction. The auditor's report explains that ISAs require that the auditor comply with ethical requirements and that the auditor plan and perform the audit to obtain reasonable assurance about whether the financial statements are free from material misstatement.

Auditors have a professional responsibility to evaluate this other information accompanying the audited financial statements to ensure that no materially misleading information is included10. More precisely, auditors are required to read the other information and assess whether it is consistent with the information in the audited financial statements or whether it contains one or more significant misstatements of fact based on knowledge obtained while conducting the audit.

The purpose of communicating Key Audit Matters (KAMs) is to enhance the communicative value of the auditor's report by providing greater transparency about the audit that was performed. KAMs are those matters that, in the auditor's professional judgement, were of most significance in the audit of the financial statements and include the most significant assessed risks of material misstatement identified by the auditor, including those which had the greatest effect on the overall audit strategy; the allocation of resources in the audit; and directing the efforts of the engagement team. These matters, and any comments made on the results of the auditor's procedures, are addressed in the context of the audit of the financial statements as a whole, and in forming the opinion thereon. The auditor does not provide a separate opinion on KAMs.

The auditor, having formed an opinion on the financial statements, sometimes must draw the financial statement users' attention to a matter, although appropriately presented or disclosed in the financial statements, that is of such importance that it is fundamental to users' understanding of the financial statements; or any other matter that is relevant to users' understanding of the audit, the auditor's responsibilities, or the auditor's report. This part of the opinion is called an emphasis of a matter paragraph. The addition of an emphasis of matter paragraph does not affect the auditor's opinion (see ISA 706).

An auditor must write an emphasis of matter paragraph if there is a significant uncertainty that may affect the financial statements, the resolution of which is dependent upon future events. An auditor is required to include an emphasis of a matter paragraph to highlight a material matter regarding a going concern problem. Other situations which might require emphasis are the existence of related party transactions, important accounting matters occurring subsequent to the balance sheet date, litigation, long-term contracts, and losses on discontinued operations.

In order to form that opinion, the auditor shall conclude as to whether she has obtained reasonable assurance about whether the financial statements as a whole are free from material misstatement, whether due to fraud or error. If the auditor concludes, based on the audit evidence, that the financial statements as a whole are not free from material misstatement, or she is unable to obtain sufficient appropriate audit evidence, she must modify the opinion in the auditor's report by expressing a qualified, adverse or disclaimer of opinion.

The auditor's unmodified report is expressed when the auditor concludes that the financial statements are prepared, in all material respects, in accordance with the identified financial reporting framework.

When the auditor modifies the opinion on the financial statements, she will include a paragraph in the auditor's report that provides a description of the basis for the modification. This paragraph is placed immediately before the opinion paragraph in the auditor's report under the heading 'Basis for Qualified Opinion', 'Basis for Adverse Opinion' or 'Basis for Disclaimer of Opinion', as appropriate. The auditor includes in the basis for modification paragraph a description and quantification of the financial effects of the misstatement.

The auditor expresses a qualified opinion when:

▷ having obtained sufficient appropriate audit evidence, the auditor concludes that misstatements, individually or in the aggregate, are material, but not pervasive, to the financial statements; or

▷ the auditor is unable to obtain sufficient appropriate audit evidence on which to base the opinion, but the auditor concludes that the possible effects on the financial statements of undetected misstatements, if any, could be material but not pervasive.

The auditor expresses an adverse opinion when the auditor, having obtained sufficient appropriate audit evidence, concludes that misstatements, individually or in the aggregate, are both material and pervasive to the financial statements.

The auditor will disclaim an opinion when she is unable to obtain sufficient appropriate audit evidence on which to base the opinion, and she concludes that the possible effects on the financial statements of undetected misstatements could be both material and pervasive.

The auditors are required to communicate their audit findings to the management or board of directors of a corporation. This is not only given in the ISA standards, but also required by law in some countries. The auditor should communicate audit matters of governance interest arising from the audit of financial statements with those charged with governance of an entity. 'Governance' is the term used to describe the role of persons entrusted with the supervision, control and direction of an entity. Those persons are the ones responsible for financial reporting and for ensuring that the company achieves its objectives. Those charged with corporate governance are usually the board of directors or supervisory board or the audit committee.

In many countries it is customary for the auditor to prepare an extended auditor's report in addition to the published short-form report to the entity's board of directors in addition to the publicly published short-form report discussed in this chapter. The topics covered in the report may vary as there are no standards, but a typical extended report will include: an overview of the audit engagement, an analysis of the financial statements, a discussion of risk management and internal control, various optional topics subject to the circumstances, and fees.

The management letter identifies issues not required to be disclosed in the auditor's report but represent the auditor's concerns and suggestions noted during the audit. The management letter is the auditor's letter addressed to the client. It contains the public accountant's conclusions regarding the company's accounting policies and procedures, internal controls and operating policies.

In the US, auditors of listed companies must audit management assertions about Internal Control over Financial Reporting as required by Sarbanes-Oxley Act Section 404. PCAOB Audit Standard 2201 establishes requirements and provides direction that applies when an auditor is engaged to perform an audit of management's assessment of the effectiveness of internal control over financial reporting that is integrated with an audit of the financial statements.

In countries like India, Australia, UK and the Netherlands, the statutory auditors should be present at the Annual General Meeting of Shareholders. During this meeting management answers questions about the audited financial statements raised by shareholders. Auditors can be asked to answer any queries shareholders may have about the audit.

11.13 QUESTIONS, EXERCISES AND CASES

QUESTIONS

11.2 Introduction

11-1 How long should an audit report be? Can all-important information be conveyed in a standard length?

11-2 What must the chief executive officer or officers and chief financial officer or certify in each annual or quarterly report filed or submitted to the US Securities and Exchange Commission (SEC) according to the Sarbanes-Oxley Act of 2002 (SOX)?

11.3 Basic Elements of the Auditor's Report

11-3 What elements make up an auditor's report? Briefly discuss each.

11-4 What are the phrases used to express the auditor's opinion that the financial statements have been prepared according to local legislation, rules issued by professional bodies, etc.?

11-5 Why must an auditor's report be dated?

11.4 Key Audit Matters

11-6 What is the objective of including KAMs in the Auditor's report?

11-7 Why should KAMs refer to related disclosure(s) in the financial statements?

11.5 Emphasis of Matter Paragraph

11-8 Define emphasis of a matter paragraph. In what circumstances would an auditor write an emphasis of a matter paragraph?

11-9 If the going concern questions are not resolved, the auditor must adequately disclose in her report the principal conditions that raise doubt about the entity's ability to continue in operation in the foreseeable future. What are the characteristics of this disclosure?

11.6 **Type of Audit Report**

11-10 There are the four different opinions an auditor can issue. Briefly discuss each and the requirements to give that opinion.

11-11 When does an auditor express a qualified opinion? Discuss the terms 'material' and 'pervasive'.

11-12 When is an adverse opinion given? How is the wording of an adverse opinion different from that of an unqualified (unmodified) opinion?

11-13 When is a disclaimer of opinion issued? How is the wording of a disclaimer of opinion different from that of an unmodified opinion?

11-14 Explain the circumstances where the auditor may not be able to express an unmodified opinion.

11-15 Define limitations of scope. under what circumstances do scope limitations arise? give some examples of scope limitations. what should an auditor do if a limitation on scope is imposed by circumstances beyond the client's control?

11.7 **Opinion on Internal Controls over Financial Reporting**

11-16 Why is an auditor's opinion on internal controls required since the issuance of the Sarbanes-Oxley Act in 2002?

11-17 Why does PCAOB standard AS 2201 refer to an integrated audit?

11.8 **Communications with those Charged with Governance**

11-18 Define governance, audit committee and non-executive directors.

11-19 What audit matters of governance interest would ordinarily be communicated by the auditor to the board of directors or audit committee?

11-20 Why is effective two-way communication important in assisting the auditor and those charged with governance in understanding matters related to the audit?

11-21 What kind of findings would you directly report to the audit committee without discussing in advance with the executive board?

11.9 **Extended Auditor's Report**

11-22 What topics are included in a typical 'long-form' (extended) report by the auditors? Briefly discuss each topic.

11.10 **Management Letter**

11-23 What is the purpose of the management letter and what does it usually contain?

11.11 **General Meeting of Shareholders**

11-24 Why should the auditor avoid answering questions during the general meeting about the financial statements?

11-25 How should the auditor deal with the ethical requirement of confidentiality during a general meeting of shareholders?

11.3 Basic Elements of the Auditor's Report

11-26 When fieldwork was finished on 31 December 20x0, the following unqualified auditor's report was given by Eldridge and Lloyd, Chartered Accountants (CAs), of Surrey, England:

Auditor's report

We have audited the accompanying financial statements.

In our opinion, the financial statements correctly show the account balances and comply with the Companies Acts 1948 to 1981.

Eldridge and Lloyd, Charted Accountants

Required:

A. List the basic elements that should appear in an unmodified (unqualified) auditor's report.

B. List and explain the deficiencies and omissions in the Eldridge and Lloyd auditor's report.

11-27 Form of the Audit report. The most common type of audit report is the standard unqualified report.

Required:

Review the standard wording of the ISA 700 audit report and illustration 11.1, the unmodified (unqualified) report of Meta Inc.

A. List the differences, paragraph-by-paragraph, between the two reports.

B. List the similarities, paragraph-by-paragraph, between the two reports.

11.4 Key Audit Matters

11-28 Why should KAMs be rather company specific? Discuss and illustrate.

11-29 Do you think a KAM could be repeated for several years? Discuss and illustrate.

11-30 Provide an example of both an entity-level- KAM and an account-level- KAM.

11-31 In extremely rare circumstances the auditor can determine that a matter should not be communicated as KAM. Can you provide an example?

11-32 Discuss the following KAM included in the unqualified Audit report of Canary Holdings Limited 202x.

During the 202x financial year, the financial director of Canary Holdings Limited resigned as at 31 May 202x. The financial manager of Canary Holdings Limited had also resigned during the period. A new financial manager has been appointed. Based on the fact that key financial staff members had left the company there is an increased risk of misstatement due to the potential impact of this on the functioning of the controls and record keeping of the company. During the current financial year, the entity did not have a full-time appointed executive financial director. The entity, however, engaged in consultation with the national regulator of financial markets regarding the employment of a part time executive financial director and this was permitted in terms of section 325 (a) of the Listing requirements which does allow the financial director to be employed on a part time basis in special circumstances. The entity had also employed a suitably qualified financial manager within a reasonable time frame. Our procedures in relation to the changes of staff in the financial department included: – the testing of controls around the revenue, Purchases and Payroll cycles. Based on the testing we had performed there were no major exceptions or changes identified within the control functions other than a change in personnel performing such controls. Because of time and budget constrains we were not able to perform additional substantive testing. We confirmed substantively that the company had complied with government requirements.

11.5 Emphasis of a Matter Paragraph

11-33 Ordinarily, an auditor might write an emphasis of a matter paragraph (1) if there is a significant uncertainty which may affect the financial statements, the resolution of which is dependent upon future events; (2) to highlight a material matter regarding a going concern problem, and (3) other matters. Write an emphasis of a matter paragraph for each of these three circumstances.

11-34 Going Concern. In the audit of Cerberus, SA, of Bydgoszcz, Poland, Merek Olzewski, Certified Public Accountant (CPA), found indications that Cerberus may have going concern problems.

Required:

A. List three financial, two operating and two other indications that Olzewski might have found that show Cerberus may have going concern problems.

B. Because the going concern assumption is in question, what additional audit procedures would Olzewski undertake?

11.6 Type of Audit Report

11-35 Unmodified (Unqualified) Audit Report. upon completion of all fieldwork on 23 September 20x1, the following audit report was rendered by Feather Dlouhy, Auditor, to the directors of Rabochaya Raum Company of Docesky, the Czech Republic.

To the directors of the Rabochaya Raum Company:

We have examined the balance sheet and the related statement of income and retained earnings of the Rabochaya Raum Company as of 31 July 20x1. In accordance with your instructions, a complete audit was conducted.

In many respects, this was an unusual year for the Rabochaya Raum Company. The weakening of the economy in the early part of the year and the strike of plant employees in the summer of 20x1 led to a decline in sales and net income. After making several tests of sales records, nothing came to our attention that would indicate that sales have not been properly recorded.

In our opinion, with the explanation given above, and with the exception of some minor errors that are considered immaterial, the aforementioned financial statements present fairly the financial position of the Rabochaya Raum Company at 31 July 20x1, and the results of its operations for the year then ended, in conformity with pronouncements of International Accounting standards Committee applied consistently throughout the period.

Feather Dlouhy, Auditor 23 September 20x1

Required:

List and explain the deficiencies and omissions in the auditor's report. Organise your answer sheet by section (opinion, management's responsibility, auditor's responsibility etcetera) of the auditor's report.

11-36 Adverse Audit Opinion. Bheda Bhasya, Ltd, a company from Ahmadabad, India, without consulting its Chartered Accountant (CA), has changed its accounting so that it is not in accordance with International financial reporting standards (IFRS). During the regular audit engagement, the CA discovers that the statements based on the accounts are so grossly misleading that they might be considered fraudulent.

Required:

A. Discuss the specific action to be taken by the CA.

B. What type of opinion would the CA issue? Why?

In this situation what obligation does the CA have to a new auditor if he is replaced? discuss briefly.

11-37 Modification of Unqualified Opinion. Jorge Leyva, Licenciado en Contaduría Público, has completed the examination of the financial statements of medina Construcción of Caracas, Venezuela, for the year ended 31 July 20x4. Leyva also examined and reported on the medina financial statements for the prior year. Leyva's report is as follows: derived from Auditor's report to Board of directors of medina Construcción.

Opinion

We have audited the accompanying balance sheet of medina Construcción as of 31 December 20x3, and the related statements of income and retained earnings for the year then ended. These financial statements are the responsibility of the Company's management.

In our opinion, the financial statements referred to above present fairly, in all material respects, the financial position of Medina Construcción as of 31 December 20x3, and the results of its operations for the year then ended in conformity with International Accounting standards and comply with Venezuela's national law, applied on a basis consistent with that of the preceding year.

Basis for Opinion

We conducted our audit in accordance with International Standards on Auditing and approved Auditing standards of the Federación de Collegios de Contadores Publicos. Those standards require that we plan and perform the audit to obtain reasonable assurance about whether the financial statements are free of material misstatement. An audit includes examining, on a test basis, evidence supporting the amounts and disclosures in the financial statements. An audit also includes assessing the accounting principles used and significant estimates made by management, as well as evaluating the overall financial statement presentation. We believe that our audit provides a reasonable basis for our opinion.

Jorge Leyva, LCP 13 November 20x4

International Centre 456 Alhambra Calabozo, Venezuela

Other information:

1 Medina is presenting comparative financial statements.

2 During 20x3, Medina changed its method of accounting for long-term construction contracts and properly reflected the effect of the change in the current year's financial statements and restated the prior year's financial statements. Leyva is satisfied with Medina's justification for making the change. The change is discussed in footnote number 8 to the report.

3 Leyva was unable to perform normal accounts receivable confirmation procedures, but alternate procedures were used to satisfy Leyva as to the validity of the receivables.

4 Medina Construcción is the defendant in a litigation, the outcome of which is highly uncertain. If the case is settled in favour of the plaintiff, Medina will be required to pay a substantial amount of cash, which might require the sale of certain fixed assets. The litigation and the possible effects have been properly disclosed in footnote number 11 to the report.

5 Medina issued debenture bonds payable on 31 January 20x6, in Venezuela Bolivars (VB), for the amount of VB 1,000,000,000. The funds obtained from the issuance were used to finance the expansion of plant facilities. The debenture agreement restricts the payment of future cash dividends to earnings after 31 December 20x6. medina declined to disclose this essential data in the footnotes to the financial statements.

Required:

Consider all facts given and rewrite the auditor's report in acceptable and complete format incorporating any necessary departures from the standard unqualified report. Explain any items included in 'other Information' that need not be part of the auditor's report.

11-38 Limitation on Scope. Lorts Corporation of Maastricht, The Netherlands (whose fiscal year will end 31 December 20x3), informs you on 18 December 20x3 that it has a serious shortage of working capital because of heavy operating losses incurred since 1 October 20x3. Application has been made to a bank for a loan, and the bank's loan officer has requested financial statements.

The management of Lorts Corporation requests a meeting with you. You try to imagine the following independent sets of circumstances.

1 Lorts asks that you save time by auditing the financial statements prepared by Lorts' chief accountant as of 30 September 20x3. The scope of your audit would not be limited by Lorts in any way.

2 Lorts asks that you conduct an audit as of 15 December 20x3. The scope of your audit would not be limited by Lorts in any way.

3 Lorts asks that you conduct an audit as of 31 December 20x3 and render a report by 16 January. To save time and reduce the cost of the audit, it is requested that your examination not include confirmation of accounts receivable or observation of the taking of inventory.

4 Lorts asks that you prepare financial statements as of 15 December 20x3 from the books and records of the company without audit. The statements are to be submitted on plain paper without your name being associated in any way with them. The reason for your preparing the statements is your familiarity with proper form for financial statements.

Required:

Indicate the type of opinion you would render under each of the above set of circumstances. Give reasons for your decision.

11-39 Disagreement with Management. Emiko Lamiva, Certified Public Accountant (CPA), audited the Satsuma Company's earthquake insurance policies. All routine audit procedures with regard to the earthquake insurance register have been completed (i.e. vouching, footing, examination of cancelled cheques, computation of insurance expense and repayment, tracing of expense charges to appropriate expense accounts, etc.).

After the insurance review, Lamiva came to the conclusion that the insurance coverage against loss by earthquake is inadequate and that, if loss occurs, the company may have insufficient assets to liquidate its debts. After a discussion with Lamiva, management refuses to increase the amount of insurance coverage.

Required:

A. What mention will Lamiva make of this condition and contingency in his standard report? Why?

B. What effect will this condition and contingency have upon the audit opinion? Give reasons for your position.

11-40 **Uncertainty Concerning Future Events**. Vilma Castro, Contador Público Autorizado, has completed fieldwork for her examination of the Wigwam Winche Company of Panama City, Panama, for the year ended 31 December 20x1, and now is in the process of determining whether to modify her report. Presented below are two independent, unrelated situations which have arisen.

Situation 1

In September, 20x1, a lawsuit was filed against Wigwam to have the court order it to install pollution-control equipment in one of its older plants. Wigwam's legal counsel has informed Castro that it is not possible to forecast the outcome of this litigation. However, wigwam's management has informed Castro that the cost of the pollution-control equipment is not economically feasible and that the plant will be closed if the case is lost. In addition, Castro has been told by management that the plant and its production equipment would have only minimal resale values and that the production that would be lost could not be recovered at other plants.

Situation 2

During 20x1, Wigwam purchased a franchise amounting to 20 per cent of its assets for the exclusive right to produce and sell a newly patented product in the north-eastern USA. There has been no production in marketable quantities of the product anywhere to date. Neither the franchiser nor any franchisee had conducted any market research with respect to the product.

In deciding the type of report or modification, if any, Castro will submit, take into account such considerations as follows:

1 uncertainty of outcome.
2 likelihood of error.
3 expertise of the auditor.
4 pervasive impact on the financial statements.
5 inherent importance of the item.

Required:

Discuss Castro's type of report decision for each situation in terms of the above and other appropriate considerations. Assume each situation is adequately disclosed in the notes to the financial statements. Each situation should be considered independently. In discussing each situation, ignore the other.

11.7 **Opinion on Internal Control over Financial Reporting**

11-41 Do you think an adverse opinion on internal control over financial reporting could be combined with an unqualified opinion on the financial statements? Same question in the case of an adverse opinion on the financial statements and unqualified on internal control over financial reporting? Discuss and illustrate.

11.8   Communications with those Charged with Governance

11-42   Nordtek, A/S, a manufacturer of fine skiing equipment based in Skien, Norway, has retained the firm of Berzins, Dybtsyna and Kaarboe (BDK) as their auditors. BDK have found significant deficiencies in internal control which they are required to report to Nordtek's audit committee. During the audit BDK discovered that Nordtek does not have manuals of policies and procedures for monitoring and reporting on internal controls. The board has no code of business ethics. New employees undergo minimal background checks and knowledge testing. The company has no employee training program.

Eight of the ten members of the board of directors are not independent of the company and none of the audit committee members are independent (non-executive) directors. There are no board committees for executive remuneration, government relations and investment review. Management does not have a budgeting process. They have no internal audit department. Employees never switch tasks. The internal controls have never been tested for effectiveness. Nordtek's inventory storerooms were unlocked and there were no checks on those who entered or left the premises.

Required:

Write a written communication to the Audit Committee explaining the deficiencies based on the requirements for such a report described in ISA 265.

11.9   Extended Auditor's Report

11-43   Pick a listed company from the SEC website www.sec.gov, search for the 10K, review risk factors, Controls and Procedures, Changes in and disagreements with Accountants on Accounting and financial disclosure, management's discussion and Analysis of Financial Condition and results of operations, the financial statements, auditor's fees, and disclosure notes. Imagine that you are the auditor for the most recent 10K. Write up a long-form audit report for that listed company.

11.10   Management Letter

11-44   An unqualified audit opinion has been issued for Hans Werner Musik Ag financial statements for 202x. Discuss the following text from the Management Letter sent to the management Board of Hans Werner Musik Ag dated February 28, 202x: 'When checking the tax position as per year end, we found that the adjusted tax rates were not taken into account. The reason for the error is that your bookkeeping department has not implemented the new percentage in the relevant spreadsheet program. This means that the tax position liability per year end is overstated with an amount of euro 352,000. As discussed earlier, we conduct our audit with a materiality of euro 250,000. You have indicated that the draft financial statements have already been provided to the bank, and you prefer to adjust the annual statement in the next financial year. As we discussed already, the adjustment should formally be processed in this year's financial statements. However, to prevent you having to renegotiate a recent loan agreement, we accept your considerations. For future years we advise you to have your controller assess the tax position calculated by the accounting department annually.'

Required:

Discuss how this text derived from the management Letter addressed to the management Board of Hans Werner Musik Ag relates to the audit opinion issued?

11.11 General Meeting of Shareholders

11-45 You are present as financial statement auditor at the shareholders' meeting of your client Boender Materiales de Construcción SRL. A shareholder asks a question about the condition of the management board's pension plan. The CFO gives an incorrect answer as he does not mention an improvement in conditions that has been agreed but not disclosed in the financial statements. Shocked by this unexpected answer you give a sign to the chair of the meeting (chair of the board) that you wish to speak. She ignores your signal. What are you going to do?

CASE

11-46 Material misstatements or omissions in Audit reports. Auditors are required to report internal control weaknesses to management. The auditors, however, have no responsibility to report internal control weaknesses in the audit report and failing to do so does not constitute a material misstatement or omission.

Required:

A. Using the library, Lexis-Nexis or internet, find the case of James g. Monroe and Penelope E. Monroe v Gary C. Hughes: Thomas r. Hudson and Deloitte & Touche (1994 US App. Lexis 18003). Summarize the case.

B. List the reasons why the auditing firm was not found guilty of issuing an audit report with a material misstatement or omission.

11.14 NOTES

1. In Woolf, Emile (1997), *Auditing Today*, 6th edn, Hertfordshire, UK: Prentice Hall.
2. Communicating Key Audit Matters in the Independent Auditor's Report, ISA 701. https://iaasa.ie/publications/isa-ireland-701/#:~:text=International%20Standard%20on%20Auditing%20%28Ireland%29%20701%20deals%20with,and%20the%20form%20and%20content%20of%20such%20communication
3. AS 3101: The Auditor's Report on an Audit of Financial Statements When the Auditor Expresses an Unqualified Opinion, PCAOB, https://pcaobus.org/oversight/standards/auditing-standards/details/AS3101. The determination of CAMs is based on the facts and circumstances of each audit. PCAOB AS 3101 is principles-based and does not specify any matters that would always constitute CAMs.
4. US Public Company Accounting Oversight Board (PCAOB), 2007, Auditing Standard No. 5, 'An Audit of Internal Control over Financial Reporting that is Integrated with an Audit of Financial Statements', para. 85, Public Company Accounting Oversight Board, June, 2007. Current AS 2201: An Audit of Internal Control Over Financial Reporting That Is Integrated with An Audit of Financial Statements. https://pcaobus.org/oversight/standards/auditing-standards/details/AS2201
5. US SEC Form 10K, Meta Platforms Inc, 2022, Exhibit 31.1. https://d18rn0p25nwr6d.cloudfront.net/CIK-0001326801/3fc942c1-0c26-42be-a884-09a7e0eefad2.html

6. International Auditing and Assurance Standards Board (IAASB), 2023, International Standard on Auditing 700 (ISA 700) 'Forming and Reporting on Financial Statements', para. 21, Handbook of International Quality Control, Auditing, Review, Other Assurance, and Related Services Pronouncements, 2022 Edition Volume I, IAASB, New York.

7. US Public Company Accounting Oversight Board (PCAOB), PCAOB Audit Standard 3101 (AS 3101), 'The Auditor's Report on an Audit of Financial Statements When the Auditor Expresses an Unqualified Opinion', para 9g, requires a statement that the auditor is a public accounting firm registered with the PCAOB (United States) and is required to be independent with respect to the company in accordance with the US federal securities laws and the applicable rules and regulations of the SEC and the PCAOB.

8. Companies Act 2006, UK Public General Acts 2006, c. 46 Part 16, Chapter 3, http://www. legislation.gov.uk/ukpga/2006/46/part/16/chapter/3/2013-04-30.

9. International Auditing and Assurance Standards Board (IAASB), 2023, International Standard on Auditing 705 (ISA 705) 'Modifications to the opinion in the independent auditor's report', para. 20, Handbook of International Quality Control, Auditing, Review, Other Assurance, and Related Services Pronouncements, 2022 Edition Volume I, IAASB, New York.

10. International Auditing and Assurance Standards Board (IAASB), 2023, International Standard on Auditing 720 (ISA 720) 'The Auditor's Responsibilities Relating to Other Information', Handbook of International Quality Control, Auditing Review, Other Assurance, and Related Services Pronouncements, 2022 edn, Volume I, International Federation of Accountants, New York.

11. https://assets.new.siemens.com/siemens/assets/api/uuid:19bbc110-8533-46e4-a27e-ec128d1d1434/Annual-Financial-Report-FY2022.pdf

12. https://serabigold.wpenginepowered.com/wp-content/uploads/2023/05/2022-Full-Annual-Report-v_FINAL.pdf

13. https://pcaobus.org/oversight/standards/auditing-standards/details/AS-3101-09A

14. https://www.multitude.com/~/media/Files/M/Multitude/reports-and-presentations/2022/auditors-report-2022.pdf

15. https://www.morrisons-corporate.com/globalassets/corporatesite/about-us/biographies/final-annual-report.pdf

16. https://www.serabigold.com/investor-centre/annual-reports/

17. https://www.rolls-royce.com/~/media/Files/R/Rolls-Royce/documents/annual-report/2023/2022-annual-report.pdf

18. https://annualreport.postnl.nl/2022/performance-statements/other-information/independent-auditor-s-report

19. Defined according to International Auditing and Assurance Standards Board (IAASB), 2023, International Standard on Auditing 701 (ISA 701) 'Communicating Key Audit Matters In The Independent Auditor's Report', *Handbook of International Quality Control, Auditing Review, Other Assurance, and Related Services Pronouncements*, 2022 edn, Volume I, International Federation of Accountants, New York.

20. CHOPPIES ENTERPRISES LIMITED (Registration number BW00001142508) Consolidated and Separate Annual Financial Statements for the year ended 30 June 2023, page 7. https://choppiesgroup.com/pdf/integrated-reports/integrated-reports-2023.pdf

21. https://annualreport.postnl.nl/2022/performance-statements/other-information/independent-auditor-s-report

22. https://www.asml.com/en/investors/annual-report/2022

23. ISA 706, Emphasis of Matter Paragraphs and Other Matter Paragraphs in the Independent Auditor's Report.

24. https://recindia.nic.in/uploads/files/25-Independent-Auditor-Report-SFS-FY-2022-23.pdf

25. https://investor.etcsingapore.com/newsroom/20230405_174434_1Co_EZS3P32K0IRTW4S6.1.pdf

26. https://annualreport.postnl.nl/

27. https://www.vfex.exchange/wp-content/uploads/2023/05/PHL.vx-2022-FY-Results-Audit-Report.pdf

28. Ibid. ISA 705, para. 7.

29. Ibid. ISA 705, Appendix: Illustrations of Auditor's Reports with Modifications to the Opinion.

30. https://www.ziraatbank.com.tr/SitePages/InteraktifRaporlar/2022/en/m-3-7.html

31. https://jbvnl.co.in/upload/98QVEH.Consolidated%20Financial%20Statement%20along%20with%20audit%20report%202021-22.pdf

32. Mazars signed off on its audit of H2O's 2022 accounts in December. The financial statements were then originally posted to the Luxembourg Trade and Company Register in January with two pages of the audit opinion missing. After the FT asked H2O and Mazars about the discrepancy, a corrected version of the accounts containing the full audit letter was posted to the corporate register in the last week of February' March 3, 2024, FT, H2O's auditor warns accounts 'do not give a true and fair view, Robert Smith and Cynthia O'Murchu, https://www.ft.com/content/e75ea758-5144-4ad1-b9f3-41847007bb6e

33. https://www.asafm.army.mil/portals/72/Documents/Audit/fy23afr.pdf

34. International Auditing and Assurance Standards Board (IAASB), 2023, International Standard on Auditing 210 (ISA 210) 'Agreeing the Terms of Audit Engagements', para. 7, *Handbook of International Quality Control, Auditing Review, Other Assurance, and Related Services Pronouncements*, 2022 edn, Volume I, International Federation of Accountants, New York.

35. Ibid. ISA 705, para. 13.

36. Ibid. ISA 705, para. 28.

37. US Public Company Accounting Oversight Board (PCAOB), PCAOB Audit Standard 2201 (AS 2201), 'An Audit of Internal Control Over Financial Reporting That Is Integrated with An Audit of Financial Statements', https://pcaobus.org/oversight/standards/auditing-standards/details/AS2201

38. https://s201.q4cdn.com/262069030/files/doc_financials/2023/ar/Walmart-10K-Reports-Optimized.pdf

39. Ibid. ISA 705, para. 30.

40. For instance, in the USA, the Sarbanes–Oxley Act requires auditors to report directly to the audit committee of the board of directors.

41. US Public Company Accounting Oversight Board (PCAOB), PCAOB Audit Standard 1301 (AS 1301): 'Communications with Audit Committees'. https://pcaobus.org/oversight/standards/auditing-standards/details/AS1301

42. International Auditing and Assurance Standards Board (IAASB), 2023, International Standard on Auditing 265 (ISA 265), 'Communicating Deficiencies in Internal Control to Those Charged with Governance and Management, *Handbook of International Quality Control, Auditing Review, Other Assurance, and Related Services Pronouncements*, 2022 edn, Volume I, International Federation of Accountants, New York.

43. Similar to PCAOB Standard AS 1305: 'Communications About Control Deficiencies in an Audit of Financial Statements'. https://pcaobus.org/oversight/standards/auditing-standards/details/AS1301

44. Material weakness is a deficiency, or a combination of deficiencies, in internal control over financial reporting, such that there is a reasonable possibility that a material misstatement of the company's annual or interim financial statements will not be prevented or detected on a timely basis. PCAOB AS 1305: Communications About Control Deficiencies in an Au-

dit of Financial Statements, https://pcaobus.org/oversight/standards/auditing-standards/details/AS1305

45. For an example of guidance we refer to https://www.auasb.gov.au/media/5hndnis1/gs10_09-21.pdf

46. Where the auditor is a firm, the right to attend or be heard at a meeting is exercisable by an individual authorized by the firm in writing to act as its representative at the meeting.

47. NBA practice note 1118. The performance of the external auditor in the general meeting of listed companies, NBA (The Royal Netherlands Institute of Chartered Accountants. https://www.nba.nl/siteassets/wet--en-regelgeving/nba-handreikingen/1118/nba-handreiking-1118-definitief-20230227.pdf

SPECIFIC SUBJECTS AND THEMES

CHAPTER 12

FRAUD AND OTHER CONSIDERATIONS OF LAW AND REGULATION IN AN AUDIT

12.1 LEARNING OBJECTIVES

After studying this chapter, you should be able to:

1. Describe what is fraud.
2. Understand the difference between financial statement fraud and misappropriation of assets.
3. Discuss the 'fraud triangle' factors that may lead to fraud.
4. Be able to describe anti-fraud measures.
5. Identify responses to fraud assessment.
6. Sketch responsibilities of management and financial statement auditor.
7. Understand audit planning and fraud risk assessment and types of audit procedures.
8. Describe communication related to fraud with management, board and third parties.
9. Understand the concepts of compliance with law and regulation and specifically bribery, corruption and money laundering.

12.2 INTRODUCTION

Many books and papers have been written about fraud and irregularities as they both have a negative societal impact because of great financial losses as well as loss of trust in institutions and markets. Today it is expected that organizations lose approximately 5% of their annual revenues to fraud (ACFE, 2022[1]). To place this estimate in context, if the 5% loss estimate were applied to the 2021 estimated Gross World Product of USD 94.5 trillion, it would result in a projected total global fraud loss of nearly USD 4,7 trillion.

It won't be a surprise that from the origins of the audit profession, detection of fraud has been a major issue. Notorious high-profile fraud cases like McKesson Robbins Case

(US, 1938), Pincoff (Netherlands, 1879[2]) and Hatry Group (UK, 1929[3]), stimulated the demand for independent audits[4].

During the nineteenth century and at the beginning of the twentieth century, fraud detection was seen as a key part of financial statement audits. The decline in the importance of fraud as an audit objective started in the UK towards the end of the nineteenth century. This is reflected in the judgement in the Kingston Cotton Mill Case (1896). Auditors do not approach their work with the foregone conclusion that something is wrong; however, once something unexpected is discovered, the auditor should investigate. Is the possible error or defalcation so material as to affect the auditor's opinion on the accounts? It is said that 'an auditor is a watchdog but not a bloodhound'.

In the Irish Woollen Co. Ltd. v Tyson and Others (1900) case, it was held that an auditor is liable for any damages sustained by a company by reason of falsification which might have been discovered by the exercise of reasonable care and skill in the performance of the audit. Auditors are not required to detect all frauds, but it is the auditors' duty to exercise reasonable care and skill in the conduct of their work.[5] According to current professional audit standards, the auditor must maintain professional scepticism throughout the audit, recognizing the possibility that a material misstatement due to fraud could exist, notwithstanding the auditor's past experience of the honesty and integrity of the entity's management and those charged with governance[6] (ISA 240.13).

The Association of Certified Fraud Examiners (ACFE, 2022[7]) studied 2,110 cases of occupational fraud across 133 nations. In addition to exploring its impact, the report looks at various fraud detection measures and their effect on the duration of the fraud and the size of loss incurred. Illustration 12.1 sketches some findings.

A typical perpetrator of fraud tends to be between the ages of 36 and 55, working with the victim organization for more than six years and holding an executive position in operations, finance or general management (KPMG, 2016[8]). Seventy three percent (73%) of occupational fraud perpetrators were male. This is consistent with our prior studies, all of which found a significant gender disparity in terms of occupational fraud frequency. The gap in median loss between men and women in this study was much smaller than in our previous research. Median losses caused by men (USD 125,000) were only 25% higher than median losses caused by women (USD 100,000)[9].

Some other general perpetrator characteristics are[10]:

▶ Has education beyond high school;
▶ Is likely to be married;
▶ Is member of a mosque, temple, or church;
▶ Ranges in age from teens to over 60;
▶ Is socially conforming;
▶ Has an employment tenure from 1 to 20 years;
▶ Has no arrest record;
▶ Usually acts alone;
▶ Unfortunately, a fraudster looks like most everybody else!

ILLUSTRATION 12.1

FRAUD DETECTION MEASURES AND THEIR EFFECT ON THE DURATION OF THE FRAUD AND THE SIZE OF LOSS (ACFE, 2022)

1. Occupational fraud resulted in $3,6B in total losses in 2021 (2110 cases).

The report identifies three categories of fraud: asset misappropriation, corruption, and financial statement fraud. Asset misappropriation was the most common type of fraud and occurred 86% of the time. However, financial statement fraud led to much greater median losses – $593K versus $100K median loss in asset misappropriation. Of all asset misappropriation cases, billing fraud presents highest risk followed by altering checks and payments both leading to the greatest median losses.

2. Fraud cases resulted in losses greater than $1M or more in 21% of cases.

Most companies either lose a relatively small sum (less than $200K) or a significantly larger amount. The differences are extreme. In 21% of cases, businesses incurred more than $1M in losses. Of the 2,110 fraud cases examined, the median loss was $117K.

3. 42% of fraud cases were detected by a 'tip'.

Early detection is key when it comes to limiting the losses associated with occupational fraud. According to the study, most of the fraud detection (42%) comes from tips, which far surpasses the second highest detection source, internal audit (16%).

Tips can come from anyone, but generally they come from within the company. In ACFE's report, 55% of tips were received internally whereas 35% were from an outside source and 16% anonymous. Hotlines go hand-in-hand with tips as an effective way to detect fraud. Of the companies analyzed, those with an accessible hotline detected fraud cases 47% of the time, compared to a 31% success rate for companies without hotlines. Fraud losses were at organizations without hotlines two times higher.

4. 85% of fraudsters displayed at least one behavioral red flag of fraud.

The ability to commit fraud is a skill, and the ACFE data suggests that the longer a person works for a company, the better they become at fraud. Detection activities should take place throughout an employee's tenure. Only 4% of fraudsters had a history of criminal fraud. This is important information, as a pre-hire background check is likely insufficient on its own in preventing fraud. These first-time offenders require active and effective detection efforts to continuously protect the organization.

- ▸ Six behavioural tendencies shared among fraudsters can be identified:
- ▸ Living beyond means.
- ▸ Unusual close association with vendor/ customer.
- ▸ Control issues, unwillingness to share duties.
- ▸ Bullying or intimidation.
- ▸ Irritability, suspiciousness, or defensiveness.
- ▸ Recent divorce or family problems.

5. Data monitoring and analysis combined with surprise audits reduce fraud loss.

Surprise audits and data monitoring are a powerful combination according to ACFE's 2022 findings. Together, these contributed to significant reductions in fraud loss. When in place, proactive data monitoring and surprise audits got fraud cases under control in approximately half the time. Compared to cases where these controls were not in place, it reduced fraud losses by more than half.

Despite their effectiveness, neither proactive data analysis nor surprise audits tops the list for commonly used fraud control measures.

6. Weak internal security was responsible for almost half of the fraud instances.

Nearly half of the cases occurred due to lack of internal controls (29%) or override of existing controls (20%). Of the victim companies 75% increased management review procedures and 64% increased use of proactive data-monitoring/ analysis while 54% increased surprise audits.

7. Fraudsters who had been employed for more than 10 years stole three times as much.

Fraudsters with long tenure (more than 10 years) to those with moderate-to-low tenure (5 years or less). The less-tenured fraudsters were more than twice as likely to have been previously fired of punished for fraud-related conduct.

8. Collusion between two perpetrators doubles the loss.

Long-tenured fraudsters are more likely to collude. Collusion is common in occupational fraud: 49% of cases investigated involved more than one fraudster. holds. Schemes with three or more perpetrators escalate faster than those with just one or two perpetrators. Likewise, schemes committed by an owner/executive have a velocity nearly three times that of schemes committed by employees and manager-level individuals. These findings emphasize how those in the highest positions can damage the company much more quickly than those in lower-level positions.

12.3   RESPONSIBILITIES OF THE BOARD

The primary responsibility for the prevention and detection of fraud rests with both management of the entity and those charged with governance of the entity and management. It is important that management place a strong emphasis on fraud prevention, which may reduce opportunities for fraud to take place, and fraud deterrence, which could persuade individuals not to commit fraud because of the likelihood of detection and punishment. Fraud prevention also involves a commitment to creating a culture of honesty and ethical behaviour which can be reinforced by an active oversight by those charged with governance.

Oversight by those charged with governance includes considering the potential for override of controls or other inappropriate influence over the financial reporting process, such as efforts by management to manipulate earnings to influence the perceptions of analysts as to the entity's performance and profitability. According to good corporate governance, the audit committee should undertake preparatory work for the supervisory board's decision-making regarding the supervision of the integrity and quality of the company's financial reporting and the effectiveness of the company's internal risk management and control systems (Dutch Corporate Governance Code, 2022[11], 1.5.1 and UK Corporate Governance Code, 2022[12]).

12.4 AUDITOR'S RESPONSIBILITY

The Audit Standard on fraud, ISA 240 'The Auditor's Responsibilities Relating to Fraud in an Audit of Financial Statements', deals with the auditor's responsibilities relating to fraud. Specifically, it expands on how ISA 315 (on assessing material risks) and ISA 330 (on auditor response to risk) are to be applied in relation to risks of material misstatement due to fraud. Because of the significant financial impact and moral and legal condemnation of fraud, most countries historically have issued specific laws and regulation to prevent and detect fraud and other irregularities like fraudulent reporting, misappropriation of assets, money laundering, financing of terrorism and corruption. Most important for an auditor is fraud in a financial audit context. The auditor may identify fraud or suspected fraud when performing audit procedures. Suspected fraud may also be identified when allegations of fraud come to the auditor's attention during the audit[13].

Unfortunately, in practice financial statement auditors are not always capable of detecting fraud. As described in ISA 200.2 the potential effects of inherent limitations are particularly significant if financial misstatement results from fraud. The risk of not detecting fraud is higher than the risk of not detecting error because fraud may involve sophisticated and carefully organized schemes designed to conceal it (such as forgery, deliberate failure to record transactions). Concealment of fraud from collusion may be even harder to detect. Perpetrators may be familiar with accounting procedures. Collusion may cause the auditor to believe audit evidence is persuasive when it is false. Furthermore, because management is frequently in a position to manipulate accounting records or override controls, the risk of the auditor not detecting management fraud is greater than for employee fraud. However, the inherent limitations of an audit are not a justification for the auditor to be satisfied with less than persuasive audit evidence[14].

Because of its impact, the average businessperson expects that fraud should 'always' be detected by the financial statement auditor. Although they have expertise, auditors are in general not 'fraud experts' as expertise and experience of an individual auditor with respect to fraud is generally limited[15]. Financial statement auditors are not forensic accountants who are specifically trained and engaged to detect fraud. Not being able to detect fraud in a financial statement audit, is one of the major factors of the 'audit-expectation gap' which is the gap between what the general public expects as discussed in section 1.6.[16]

12.5 FRAUD DEFINED

The ISA Glossary of Terms defines fraud as 'an intentional act by one or more individuals among management, those charged with governance, employees, or third parties, involving the use of deception to obtain an unjust or illegal advantage.' Many aspects of being an auditor require a close look-out for fraud.

Professional scepticism requires that the auditor be alert to conditions which may indicate possible misstatement due to fraud. The auditor employs risk assessment procedures to uncover material misstatement, whether due to fraud or error, at the financial statement and assertion levels. And, of course, one must be mindful of fraud when giving an opinion.

According to ISA 320, misstatements, including omissions, are material if they, individually or in aggregate, could be expected to influence the economic decisions of users taken based on the financial statements. Judgments about materiality are made in light of surrounding circumstances and are affected by the size or nature of a misstatement, or a combination of both. Because of its nature, misstatements due to fraud can reasonably be expected to influence the economic decisions of users more than due to error.

THE AUDITOR'S ROLE AND MODEL WITH RESPECT TO FRAUD[17]

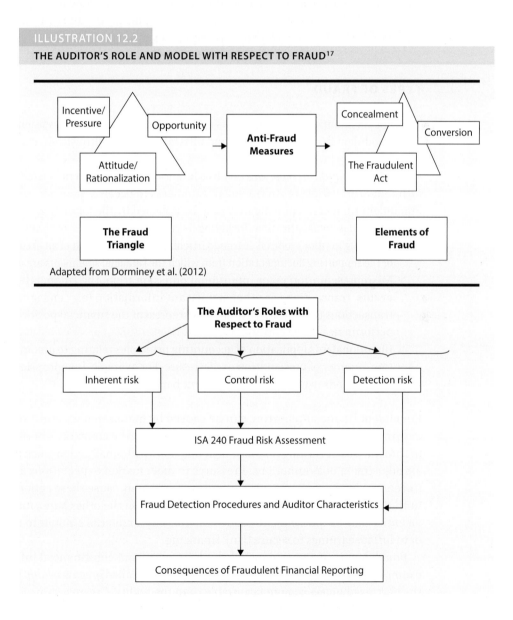

Adapted from Dorminey et al. (2012)

With regards to fraud, the objectives of the auditor are:[18]
- ▶ to identify and assess the risks of material misstatement of the financial statements due to fraud;
- ▶ to obtain sufficient appropriate audit evidence regarding the assessed risks of material misstatement due to fraud, through designing and implementing appropriate responses;
- ▶ to respond appropriately to fraud or suspected fraud identified during the audit; and
- ▶ to communicate and report about matters related to fraud.

Over the years, a great deal of academic research has been done into the phenomenon of fraud and the role of the auditor (Trompeter et al, 2014)[19]. Illustration 12.2 shows a synthesis of fraud-related research (Trompeter et al, 2013).

12.6 TYPES OF FRAUD

Two types of intentional misstatements are relevant to the auditor: misstatements resulting from fraudulent financial reporting and misstatements resulting from misappropriation of assets.

Fraudulent financial reporting involves intentional misstatements including omissions of amounts or disclosures in financial statements to deceive financial statement users. Fraudulent financial reporting may be accomplished by the following:
- ▶ Manipulation, falsification (including forgery), or alteration of accounting records (e.g. recording fictitious journal entries, particularly close to the end of an accounting period) or the supporting documentation from which the financial statements are prepared.
- ▶ Misrepresentation in, or intentional omission from, the financial statements of events, transactions or other significant information (e.g., engaging in complex transactions that are structured to misrepresent the financial position or financial performance of the entity).
- ▶ Intentional misapplication of accounting principles relating to amounts, classification, manner of presentation or disclosure. For example, inappropriately adjusting assumptions used to estimate account balances.

Fraudulent financial reporting can be caused by management's effort to manipulate earnings to deceive financial statement users as to the company's performance and profitability. Such earnings management may start with small actions such as inappropriate adjustment of assumptions. Pressures to meet market expectations and the desire (incentive) to maximize executive compensation may cause these actions to increase until they result in fraudulent financial reporting. On the other hand, management of an entity may be motivated to reduce earnings by a material amount to minimize tax or to inflate earnings to secure bank financing.

Fraudulent reporting can include both financial and non-financial information. An example of fraudulent non-financial reporting is so-called *greenwashing*. In such a case the portrayed image is more favourable than the reality. Greenwashing is discussed in further detail in chapter 15.

Misappropriation of assets involves the theft of an entity's assets and is often perpetrated by employees in relatively small and immaterial amounts. However, it can also involve management who are usually more able to disguise or conceal misappropriations in ways that are difficult to detect. Misappropriation of assets is often accompanied by false records or documents to conceal the fact that the assets are missing or have been pledged without proper authorization. Misappropriation of assets can be accomplished in a variety of ways including:

▶ Embezzling receipts (for example, misappropriating collections on accounts receivable or diverting receipts in respect of written-off accounts to personal bank accounts).

▶ Stealing physical assets or intellectual property (for example, stealing inventory for personal use or for sale, stealing scrap for resale, colluding with a competitor by disclosing technological data in return for payment).

▶ Causing an entity to pay for goods and services not received (for example, payments to fictitious vendors, or kickbacks paid by vendors to the entity's purchasing agents in return for inflating prices, and payments to fictitious employees).

▶ Using an entity's assets for personal use (for example, using the entity's assets as collateral for a personal loan or a loan to a related party).

LEHMAN BROTHERS SCANDAL (2008)

▶ *Company: Global financial services firm.*

▶ *What happened: Hid over $50 billion in loans disguised as sales.*

▶ *Main players: Lehman executives and the company's auditors, Ernst & Young.*

▶ *How they did it: Allegedly sold toxic assets to Cayman Island banks with the understanding that they would be bought back eventually. Created the impression Lehman had $50 billion more cash and $50 billion less in toxic assets than it really did.*

▶ *How they got caught: Went bankrupt.*

▶ *Penalties: Forced into the largest bankruptcy in U.S. history. SEC didn't prosecute due to lack of evidence.*

▶ *Fun fact: In 2007 Lehman Brothers was ranked the #1 'Most Admired Securities Firm' by Fortune Magazine.*

Although the auditor may suspect or, in rare cases, identify the occurrence of fraud, the auditor does not make legal determinations of whether fraud has occurred because this conclusion is reserved for the judge.

12.7 FRAUD TRIANGLE AND ANTI-FRAUD MEASURES

To understand the risk of fraud, auditors often refer to the 'Fraud Triangle', first identified by sociologist Donald Cressey.[20] Fraud involves *incentive or pressure* to commit fraud, a perceived *opportunity* to do so and some *rationalization* of the act. These three 'points' of the Fraud Triangle are factors which are present for fraud (illustration 12.3):

Motivation/ incentive/pressure. Pressure, such as a financial need, is the 'motive' for committing the fraud. Individuals may be under pressure to misappropriate assets because of a gambling problem or because the individuals are living beyond their means. Fraudulent financial reporting may be committed because management is under pressure, from sources outside or inside the entity, to achieve an expected (and perhaps unrealistic) earnings target – particularly since the consequences to management for failing to meet

FRAUD TRIANGLE

financial goals can be significant. A motive, in the fraud context, is some kind of pressure a person experiences and believes to be unshareable with friends and confidants:

▶ Actual or perceived need for money (economic motive).
▶ 'Habitual criminal' who steals for the sake of stealing (psychotic motive).
▶ Committing fraud for personal prestige (egocentric motive).
▶ Cause is morally superior, justified in making others victims (ideological motive).

Opportunity. The person committing the fraud sees an internal control weakness and believes internal control can be overridden, for example, because the individual is in a position of trust or has knowledge of specific weaknesses in internal control. The individual, believing no one will notice if funds are taken, begins the fraud with a small amount of money. If no one notices, the amount will usually grow larger. An opportunity is an open door for solving the unshareable problem by violating a trust. Examples are:

▶ Weak internal controls.
▶ Circumvention of internal controls.
▶ The greater the position, the greater the trust and exposure to unprotected assets.

Rationalization/attitude/culture. The person committing the fraud frequently rationalizes the fraud. Rationalizations may include, 'I'll pay the money back', 'They will never miss the funds' or 'They don't pay me enough'. When people do things that are contrary to their personal beliefs – outside their normal behaviour – they provide an argument to make the action seem like it is in line with their moral and ethical beliefs. Some of the most frequent rationalizations are:

▶ I need it more than the other person.
▶ I'm borrowing the money and will pay it back.
▶ Everybody does it.
▶ The company is big and will never miss it.

▷ Nobody will get hurt.
▷ I am underpaid, so this is due compensation.
▷ I need to maintain a lifestyle and image.

In any organization, the risk of fraud can be reduced. Even otherwise honest individuals can commit fraud in an environment that imposes sufficient pressure on them, so it is difficult to predict or reduce their personal pressures. Rationalization seems to come naturally to most people. However, internal control procedures can particularly diminish the 'opportunity' point of the Fraud Triangle.

On January 7, 2009, B. Ramalinga Raju – founder and chairman of Satyam Computer Services, one of India's largest and most respected software and IT services companies – admitted that he had committed India's biggest corporate fraud, having manipulated the company's income statements, cash flows and balance sheet for more than 7 years.

The $1.47 billion fraud on the Satyam (meaning truth, in Sanskrit) balance sheet included over-stated revenues and profits, acts that were perpetrated by the founder and his brother, the company's CEO, to attract more business and avoid any possible hostile takeover. "It was like riding a tiger, not knowing how to get off without being eaten," Mr. Raju wrote in his confession statement (Bashin, 2013[21]).

CYBER-FRAUD RISKS

As administrative and communication systems, along with IT applications, become more automated, the risk of cybercrime escalates. This automation makes processes faster and more efficient but also opens up new vulnerabilities that cybercriminals can exploit. To mitigate these risks, it's essential to continually update and secure internal control systems. These systems are crucial for identifying, assessing, and managing the threats to digital assets and sensitive information.

EXAMPLES OF CYBERATTACKS THAT HAVE BECOME MORE PREVALENT WITH ADVANCES IN TECHNOLOGY INCLUDE:

1   **Phishing**: This involves tricking individuals into revealing personal information, such as passwords and credit card numbers, by pretending to be a legitimate entity in digital communications.
2   **Ransomware**: Malicious software that encrypts the victim's data, with the attacker demanding payment for the decryption key.
3   **Denial-of-Service (DoS)**: An attack meant to shut down a machine or network, making it inaccessible to its intended users by overwhelming it with a flood of internet traffic.
4   **Man-in-the-Middle (MitM)**: An attacker intercepts communication between two parties to steal or manipulate the information being exchanged.
5   **SQL Injection**: A technique where malicious SQL statements are inserted into an entry field for execution (e.g., to dump the database contents to the attacker).
6   **Cross-Site Scripting (XSS)**: A vulnerability that allows attackers to inject malicious scripts into webpages viewed by other users, potentially stealing data or impersonating the user.
7   **Zero-Day Exploits**: Attacks that take advantage of security vulnerabilities on the same day they become known, before a patch or solution is implemented.
8   **DNS Spoofing**: Redirecting the traffic of a website to another fraudulent website by corrupting the DNS (Domain Name System) resolution process.

To combat these threats, companies must take anti-fraud measures and employ a robust cybersecurity strategy that includes regular updates to security measures, employee training on recognizing and responding to cyber threats, and the implementation of advanced technologies such as encryption, firewalls, and intrusion detection systems.

CONCEPT AND A COMPANY 12.2

ZZZZ BEST – HOW TO FOOL THE AUDITORS

Concept	I had to fool accountants and auditors into believing those numbers were real before I could perpetrate the fraud,' Barry Minkow (ACFE, 2002).
Story	ZZZZ Best began operations in the fall of 1982 as a door-to-door carpet cleaning business operating out of the Reseda, California, garage of 16-year-old Barry Minkow. In the three-year period from 1984 to 1987, net income grew from less than $200,000 to more than $5 million on revenue of $50 million. In the spring of 1987, ZZZZ Best had a market value of $200 million. By the end of 1987 the company was in bankruptcy and the assets were auctioned off for only $64,000 (Knapp, 2004). The company for almost its entire history was a fraud.

ZZZZ Best had a legitimate carpet-cleaning business that accounted for 20 per cent of reported revenue and a phoney building restoration business which was 80 per cent of revenue. To create loans for the company, ZZZZ Best management made fraudulent invoices, set up cheque accounts for front companies, created fraudulent vendors, wrote cheques for phoney expenses, and kept the money circulating by cheque kiting at several banks (Knapp, 2004).

False Documents

Thousands of company cheques in the company written by hand, in large numbers, and often payable to cash were made out to different people or firms but paid into the same account. The same money – obtained from ZZZZ Best investors and lenders – kept going around and around from ZZZZ Best to phoney vendors and customers and back to ZZZZ Best. The purpose of all these movement was to make ZZZZ Best look like a legitimate business (Akst and Berton, 1988).

'Accounts receivable are a wonderful thing,' Barry Minkow said, 'They are a tool used by a fraudster like me to ask to borrow money and to show earnings' (ACFE, 2002). He would create an invoice from a phoney customer, write a cheque to ZZZZ Best from the front company's cheque account, and deposit it to the company account. 'One way you cannot dispute a receivable is if it has been paid ... I was a paperwork manufacturing machine,' he said (ACFE, 2002).

Convincing the Auditors

To avoid the auditors finding anything, Minkow employed a number of tricks besides false documentation. He steered the auditors to examine the legitimate carpet cleaning business instead of the non-existent building restoration business. 'The restoration business was 80 per cent of the revenue, but I made sure that the auditors did 80 per cent of due diligence in the carpet cleaning business,' he said. He also intimidated the auditors, ingratiated himself to the auditors, and in one instance created a completely false audit environment.

Auditing is a very competitive business. 'Competition is what you leverage,' Minkow said. 'I can't remember how many times [I said] "Larry, I just know Coopers and Lybrand would love this account." Does he want to go back to his clients and managers and say that he lost the ZZZZ Best account because he wanted to be petty? No, he does not want to lose the ZZZZ Best account, and I leveraged that to the hilt, too' (ACFE, 2002).

Minkow's charm and entrepreneurial spirit caused the media to tout him as an example of what America's youth could obtain if they applied themselves. As a guest on the The Oprah Winfrey Show on US network television in April 1987 he encouraged his peers to adopt his personal motto, 'The sky is the limit' (Knapp, 2004). He ingratiated himself by having dinner with the auditors and their wives. He felt that if the wives liked him and the auditor wanted to be hard on Minkow, the wives would say, 'but he is such a nice kid.' Minkow said, 'The final touch was "Well, the kid is on Wall Street. If there was something wrong, someone would have found out by now"' (ACFE, 2002).

Classic Tricks

Minkow's tricks to mislead the accountants doing audit procedures are classic. They included phoney confirmations, financial statements manipulated to reflect industry standards, false documentation and, in one instance, creation of an entire false audit environment.

Minkow paid an insurance claims adjuster from a legitimate company to confirm over the telephone to banks and any other interested third parties that ZZZZ Best was the recipient of insurance restoration contracts. ZZZZ Best's first external auditor, George Greenspan, maintained that he performed analytical procedures comparing the company to the industry, confirmed the existence of contracts, and obtained and reviewed copies of key documents. Greenspan, however, did not inspect any restoration sites (US Congress, 1988).

Ernst & Whinney (E&W) took over as ZZZZ Best's auditor in 1986. E&W repeatedly insisted on visiting several of the largest of the contract sites, so that finally Minkow agreed to a visit. E&W wanted to visit a large site in Sacramento, California, for which ZZZZ Best claimed to have a multi-million dollar contract.

Minkow sent two associates to Sacramento to find a large building under construction or renovation that would be a plausible site for a restoration contract. Posing as leasing agents, they convinced the supervisor of the construction site to provide keys to the building one weekend on the pretext that a possible future tenant wanted to tour the building. Before E&W visited the site, placards were placed on the walls indicating that ZZZZ Best was the contractor for building renovation. The building's security officer was paid to greet the visitors and demonstrate that he was aware in advance of the auditor's visit (US Congress, 1988).

Another site visit by E&W required that ZZZZ Best lease a partially completed building and hire subcontractors to do a large amount of work on the site. In total ZZZZ Best spent several million dollars just to deceive its auditors (US Congress, 1988).

ZZZZ Best required that E&W sign a confidentiality agreement before the visits were made on the pretext that the insurance company required it. The agreement required that E&W not disclose the location of the building and not 'make any follow-up telephone calls to any contractors, insurance companies, building owner or other individuals' (Knapp, 2004).

Minkow and 10 other ZZZZ Best insiders were indicted by a Los Angeles federal grand jury in January 1988 on 54 counts of racketeering, securities fraud, money laundering, embezzlement, mail fraud, tax evasion and bank fraud. On 27 March 1989 Minkow was sentenced to 25 years in prison. He was also placed on five years' probation and ordered to pay $26 million in restitution.

After being released from jail, Minkow became a preacher and a fraud investigator, and spoke at schools about ethics. This all came to an end in 2011, when he admitted to helping deliberately drive down the stock price of homebuilder Lennar and was ordered back to prison.

Discussion Questions	▶ What procedures should an auditor carry out to determine the validity of a significant source of company revenue? ▶ What actions of Minkow and the company's audit history would have caused an auditor to become suspicious? ▶ How does signing a confidentiality agreement affect auditor substantive procedures?
References	ACFE, 2002, 'Cooking the Books' video, Introduction to Higher Education, Association of Certified Fraud Auditors, Austin, Texas, 12 February. Akst, D. and Berton, L., 1988, 'Accountants Who Specialise in Detecting Fraud Find Themselves in Great Demand', *The Wall Street Journal*, 26 February. Knapp, M, 2004, 'ZZZZ Best Company, Inc', *Contemporary Auditing Real Issues and Cases*, South-Western College Publishing, pp. 41–56. US Congress, House, Subcommittee on Oversight and Investigation of the Committee on Energy and Commerce, 1988, 100th Congress, *Hearing 100-115*, 'Failure of ZZZZ Best Co', US Government Printing Office, Washington, DC, 27 Jvanuary to 1 February. http://en.wikipedia.org/wiki/Barry_Minkow#Conviction_and_prison

ANTI-FRAUD MEASURES

To prevent and detect fraud, the company board should develop and introduce a robust system of anti-fraud controls as a powerful deterrent. From the ACFE study,[22] the following anti-fraud mechanisms were present at the victim organization at the time the fraud occurred. As illustrated below, 82% of the organizations had a code of conduct and underwent external financial statement audits, while 77% had internal audit departments, and 74% had company management certify the financial statements. On the other end of the spectrum, 25% of organizations had policies requiring job rotation or mandatory vacation, and only 15% provided rewards for whistle-blowers. See illustration 12.4.

Interestingly, illustration 12.5 below shows that the leading detection methods are tips, internal audit, and management review. Collectively, these three detection methods were cited in 70% of the cases in the ACFE 2022 study. Also, more than half of all tips (55%) were provided by employees of the victim organizations. Meanwhile, nearly one-third (31%) of the tips that led to fraud detection came from people outside the organization: customers, vendors, and competitors.

Additionally, 16% of tips came from an anonymous source, demonstrating that a significant portion of those who reported fraud did not want their identities known. Whistleblowers often have a fear of being identified or retaliated against, which is why it is important that they be able to make reports anonymously.

Based on the COSO principles of enterprise risk management as published by COSO in 2017, Fraud Risk Management Guide (COSO 2023[23]) has been developed to give organizations the information necessary to design a plan specific to the risks for that entity. There is no 'onesize-fits-all approach' to managing fraud risk. But with the organization can create a custom-fitted program tailored to its specific needs. A Fraud Risk Management Program will further strengthen fraud deterrence

ILLUSTRATION 12.4

WHAT ANTI-FRAUD CONTROLS ARE MOST COMMON?[24]

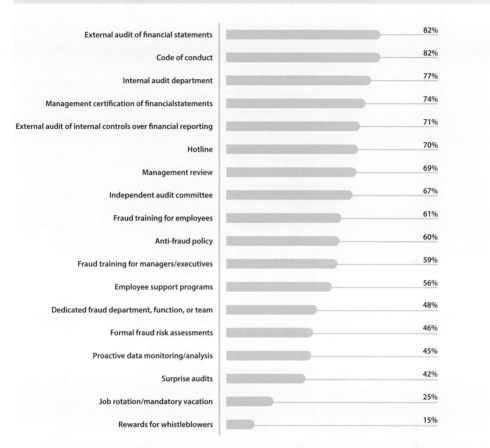

External audit of financial statements	82%
Code of conduct	82%
Internal audit department	77%
Management certification of financial statements	74%
External audit of internal controls over financial reporting	71%
Hotline	70%
Management review	69%
Independent audit committee	67%
Fraud training for employees	61%
Anti-fraud policy	60%
Fraud training for managers/executives	59%
Employee support programs	56%
Dedicated fraud department, function, or team	48%
Formal fraud risk assessments	46%
Proactive data monitoring/analysis	45%
Surprise audits	42%
Job rotation/mandatory vacation	25%
Rewards for whistleblowers	15%

by making it known that potential fraud perpetrators face a significant likelihood of getting caught and being punished. See illustration 12.6 diagram illustrating the risk management process.

Deterrence is also supported and enhanced by the knowledge throughout the organization that:

1 Those charged with governance have made a commitment to comprehensive fraud risk management.
2 Periodic fraud risk assessments are being conducted and updated as risks change, or new information becomes known.
3 Fraud preventive and detective control activities, including data analytics – overt and covert – are being conducted.
4 Suspected frauds are investigated quickly.
5 Fraud reporting mechanisms are in place.
6 Discovered frauds are remediated thoroughly.
7 Wrongdoing has been appropriately disciplined.
8 The entire Fraud Risk Management Program is being constantly monitored.

ILLUSTRATION 12.5

HOW IS OCCUPATIONAL FRAUD INITIALLY DETECTED?[25]

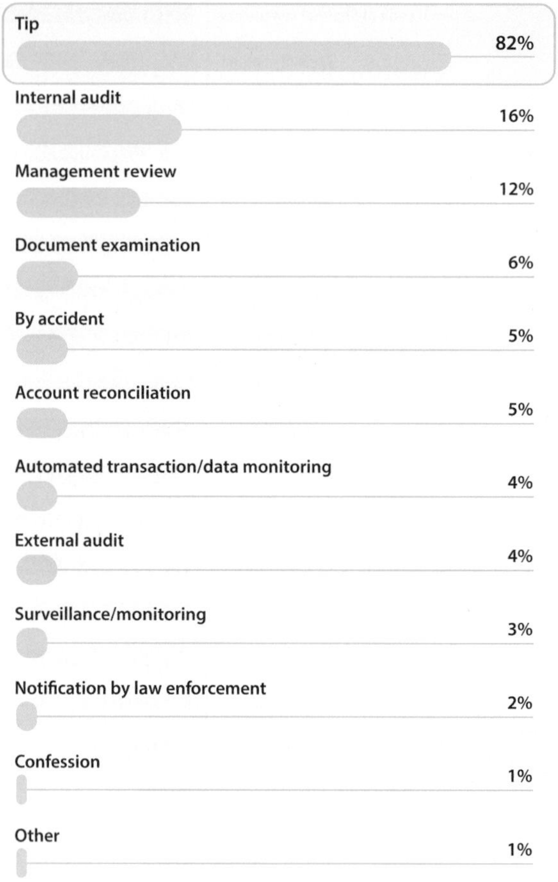

Tip	82%
Internal audit	16%
Management review	12%
Document examination	6%
By accident	5%
Account reconciliation	5%
Automated transaction/data monitoring	4%
External audit	4%
Surveillance/monitoring	3%
Notification by law enforcement	2%
Confession	1%
Other	1%

12.8 AUDIT PLANNING AND FRAUD RISK ASSESSMENT

When considering fraud or suspected fraud during an audit, the auditor should be mindful of the need for professional scepticism, discuss the possibility of fraud with the engagement team, perform certain risk assessment procedures, identify the risks of material misstatement due to fraud, respond to those assessed risks and evaluate the audit evidence gathered.[26]

We have discussed professional scepticism in chapter 4. The auditor must maintain professional scepticism throughout the audit, recognizing the possibility that a material misstatement due to fraud could exist. Although the auditor cannot be expected to disregard past experience of the honesty and integrity of the entity's management and those charged with governance, the auditor's professional scepticism is very important in considering the risks of material misstatement due to fraud resulting from changes in circumstances.

ONGOING, COMPREHENSIVE FRAUD RISK MANAGEMENT PROCESS[27]

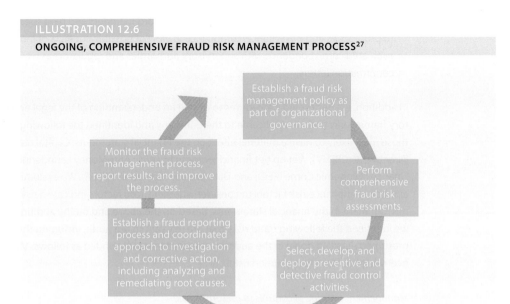

An audit performed in accordance with ISAs rarely involves the authentication of documents, nor is the auditor trained as, or expected to be, an expert in such authentication. If the auditor believes that a document may not be authentic or that terms in a document have been secretly modified or where responses to inquiries of management are inconsistent, the auditor must investigate the inconsistencies.

Below we illustrate the audit scope in relation to fraud and non-compliance with laws and regulations as disclosed in KPMG's Independent Auditor's Report 2022 of Leaseplan Corporation NV (illustration 12.7).

DERIVED FROM KPMG'S INDEPENDENT AUDITOR'S REPORT 2022 OF LEASEPLAN CORPORATION NV[28]

Audit response to the risk of fraud and non-compliance with laws and regulations

In chapter 'Risk Management' of the annual report, the management board describes its procedures in respect of the risk of fraud and non-compliance with laws and regulations. As part of our audit, we have gained insights into the Company and its business environment, and environment and assessed the design and implementation of the Company's risk management in relation to fraud and non-compliance. Our procedures included, among other things, assessing the Company's code of conduct, whistleblowing procedures and its procedures to investigate indications of possible fraud and non-compliance. Furthermore, we performed relevant inquiries with management, those charged with governance and other relevant functions, such as Internal Audit, Legal Counsel and Compliance. As part of our audit procedures, we:

▶ assessed other positions held by management board members and paid special attention to procedures and governance/compliance in view of possible conflicts of interest;

▶ evaluated correspondence with supervisory authorities and regulators as well as legal confirmation letters.

In addition, we performed procedures to obtain an understanding of the legal and regulatory frameworks that are applicable to the Company and identified the following areas as those most likely to have a material effect on the financial statements: Capital requirement Directive IV (CRD IV); Wet op het financieel toezicht (Wft); Anti-Money Laundering (AML)/ Financial Economic Crime (FEC); and Data privacy regulation (GDPR). We evaluated the fraud and non-compliance risk factors to consider whether those factors indicate a risk of material misstatement in the financial statements. Based on the above and on the auditing standards, we identified the following fraud risks that are relevant to our audit, including the relevant presumed risks laid down in the auditing standards, and responded as follows: Management override of controls (a presumed risk).

Management override of controls (a presumed risk)
Risk: Management is in a unique position to manipulate accounting records and prepare fraudulent financial statements by overriding controls that otherwise appear to be operating effectively such as estimates related to the valuation of operating lease assets and the revenue.

Responses: We evaluated the design and the implementation and, where considered appropriate, tested the operating effectiveness of internal controls that mitigate fraud and non-compliance risks, such as processes related to journal entries and estimates related to the valuation of operating lease assets and the revenue recognition for service income. We performed a data analysis of high-risk journal entries that are indicative of management override of control and evaluated key estimates and judgments for bias by the Company's management, including retrospective reviews of prior years' estimates with respect to the valuation of operating lease assets, the revenue recognition for service income and the impact of the expected merger with ALD. Where we identified instances of unexpected journal entries or other risks through our data analytics, we performed additional audit procedures to address each identified risk, including testing of transactions back to source information. We incorporated elements of unpredictability in our audit, including potential bias by the Company's management in relation to the expected merger with ALD.

Revenue recognition for service income (a presumed risk)
Risk: We assess the accounting of revenue for service income as a complex and judgmental area, which gives management the opportunity to manipulate the recognized revenue for service income, which has a potential impact on the results of the company.

Response: Our audit procedures did not reveal indications and/or reasonable suspicion of fraud and noncompliance that could have a material effect on amounts recognized or disclosures provided in the financial statements. We refer to key audit matter 'Revenue recognition for service income'. Our audit procedures did not reveal indications and/or reasonable suspicion of fraud and non-compliance that could have a material effect on amounts recognised or disclosures provided in the financial statements.

RISK ASSESSMENT PROCEDURES

By applying ISA 315.13 the auditor obtains audit evidence that provides an appropriate basis for the:

(a) identification and assessment of risks of material misstatement due to fraud at the financial statement and assertion levels, considering fraud risk factors; and

(b) design of further audit procedures in accordance with ISA 330.

Risk assessment procedures that may indicate fraud include inquiries of management regarding:

▶ Management's assessment of the risk that the financial statements may be materially misstated due to fraud, including the nature, extent and frequency of such assessments.

▶ Management's process for identifying and responding to the risks of fraud, including any specific risks of fraud that has been brought to management's attention, and classes of transactions, account balances or disclosures for which a risk of fraud is likely to exist.

▶ Any management communication to those charged with governance regarding the risks of fraud in the entity and any communication to employees regarding management views on business practices and ethical behaviour.

▶ Whether management has knowledge of any actual, suspected or alleged fraud affecting the entity.

Internal auditors and the board of directors might also offer insight. The auditor should make inquiries of internal auditors to determine whether they have knowledge of any actual, suspected or alleged fraud, and to obtain their views about the risks of fraud. Examples of others within the entity to which the auditor may direct inquiries about the existence or suspicion of fraud include:

▶ Operating personnel not directly involved in the financial reporting process.

▶ Employees with different levels of authority.

▶ Employees involved in initiating, processing or recording complex or unusual transactions and those who supervise or monitor such employees.

▶ In-house legal counsel.

▶ Chief ethics officer or equivalent person.

▶ The person or persons charged with dealing with allegations of fraud.

The auditor shall obtain an understanding of how those charged with governance exercise oversight of management's processes for identifying and responding to the risks of fraud. The auditor must ask those charged with governance if they have knowledge of any actual, suspected or alleged fraud. These inquiries are made in part to corroborate the responses to the inquiries of management.

The auditor must understand whether the information obtained from the other risk assessment procedures (for instance, unusual or unexpected relationships identified when performing analytical procedures) indicates that one or more fraud risk factors are present. She may identify an unexpected relationship when the entity's valuation of investment in government bonds remained stable, whereas the interest rates of central banks increased to counter inflation and which, in turn, led to a depreciation in market values of government bonds.

Finally, the auditor considers whether the audit evidence obtained from the risk assessment procedures and related activities indicates that one or more fraud risk factors (Fraud Triangle, illustration 12.3) are present. The significance of fraud risk factors varies widely. Accordingly, the determination as to whether fraud risk factors, individually or in combination, indicate that there are risks of material misstatement due to fraud is a matter of professional judgment.

According to ISA 315.20 the auditor needs to obtain an understanding of the entity and Its environment, the applicable financial reporting framework and the entity's system of internal control. Entity's structure, location, industry or accounting policies may lead to an increased susceptibility to misstatement due to management bias or other fraud risk factors. Based on the auditor's understanding and evaluation of each of the components of the entity's system of internal control (chapter 7), the auditor determines whether there are deficiencies in internal control identified that are relevant to the prevention or detection of fraud[29].

DISCUSSION WITH ENGAGEMENT TEAM

ISA 315.17 requires a discussion among the engagement team members and a determination by the engagement partner of which matters should be communicated to those team members not involved in this discussion. This discussion shall place particular emphasis on how and where the entity's financial statements may be susceptible to material misstatement due to fraud, including how fraud might occur, setting aside beliefs that the management and those charged with governance are honest and have integrity. According to ISA 240.16 the discussion among team members may include such matters as an exchange of ideas among engagement team members about how and where they believe the entity's financial statements may be susceptible to material misstatement due to fraud, how management could perpetrate and conceal fraudulent financial reporting, and how assets of the entity could be misappropriated.

Issues that may be included are considerations of[30]:

▷ Circumstances that might be indicative of earnings management and the practices that might be followed by management to manage earnings that could lead to fraudulent financial reporting.
▷ The known external and internal factors affecting the entity that may create an incentive or pressure for management or others to commit fraud, provide the opportunity for fraud to be perpetrated, and indicate a culture or environment that enables management or others to rationalize committing fraud.
▷ Management's involvement in overseeing employees with access to cash or other assets susceptible to misappropriation.
▷ Any unusual or unexplained changes in behaviour or lifestyle of management or employees which have come to the attention of the engagement team.
▷ Importance of maintaining a proper state of mind throughout the audit regarding the potential for material misstatement due to fraud.
▷ The types of circumstances that, if encountered, might indicate the possibility of fraud.

> ▶ How an element of unpredictability will be incorporated into the nature, timing and extent of the audit procedures to be performed.

> ▶ Audit procedures that might be selected to respond to the susceptibility of the entity's financial statement to material misstatement due to fraud and whether certain types of audit procedures are more effective than others.

> ▶ Allegations of fraud that have come to the auditor's attention.

> ▶ The risk of management override of controls.

IDENTIFICATION AND ASSESSMENT OF THE RISKS OF MATERIAL MISSTATEMENT DUE TO FRAUD

ISA 315.28 requires that the auditor identifies and assesses the risks of material misstatement (RMM) due to fraud at the financial statement level, and at the assertion level for classes of transactions, account balances and disclosures. Assessed risks of material misstatement due to fraud are always to be treated as significant risks. To the extent not already done so, she identifies controls that address such risks, evaluates whether they have been designed effectively and determines whether they have been implemented. Revenue recognition manipulation is a frequent basis for fraud, so the auditor must evaluate which types of revenue, revenue transactions or assertions give rise to fraud risks. Examples are an overstatement of revenues because of premature revenue recognition or recording fictitious revenues or understating revenues through shifting revenues to a later period. Where the auditor concludes that the presumption is not applicable in the circumstances and, accordingly, has not identified revenue recognition as a risk due to fraud, this should be documented.

Management is in a unique position to perpetrate fraud because of management's ability to manipulate accounting records and prepare fraudulent financial statements by overriding internal controls. Due to the unpredictable way in which such an override could occur, it is a risk of material misstatement due to fraud and thus a significant risk.

Fraud can be committed by management overriding controls using such techniques as (ISA 240.A4):

> ▶ Recording fictitious journal entries, particularly close to the end of an accounting period, to manipulate operating results or achieve other objectives.

> ▶ Inappropriately adjusting assumptions and changing judgments used to estimate account balances.

> ▶ Omitting, advancing or delaying recognition in the financial statements of events and transactions that have occurred during the reporting period.

> ▶ Concealing, or not disclosing, facts that could affect the amounts recorded in the financial statements.

> ▶ Engaging in complex transactions that are structured to misrepresent the financial position or financial performance of the entity.

> ▶ Altering records and terms related to significant and unusual transactions.

Assessing the RMM due to cyber-fraud, the auditor evaluates how cyber-fraud could impact financial reporting and identifies specific risks related to the entity's IT systems. She also gains insights into the design and effectiveness of cybersecurity policies, procedures, and technologies that prevent, detect, and respond to cyber threats. Identifying and responding to fraud risks, especially those stemming from cyber incidents, is a critical component of an auditor's responsibilities. This process involves two main steps: identifying the specific risks of fraud that could arise from cyber incidents and then designing audit procedures tailored to address those identified risks. By specifically identifying risks of fraud from cyber incidents and designing targeted audit procedures, auditors can provide more effective oversight and contribute to the integrity and reliability of financial reporting.

12.9 RESPONSES TO FRAUD RISK ASSESSMENT

The auditor shall design and perform audit procedures in response to the assessed risks of material misstatement due to fraud in a manner that is not biased towards obtaining audit evidence that corroborates management's assertions or towards excluding audit evidence that may contradict such assertions[31].

In determining overall responses to address the assessed risks of fraud at the financial statement level, the auditor must:

▶ Assign and supervise audit staff taking into account the knowledge, skill and ability of each staff member. This can be done by assigning to the audit additional individuals with specialized skills and knowledge, such as forensic and IT experts, or by assigning more experienced individuals to the engagement.
▶ Evaluate whether the company's accounting policies, especially those related to subjective measurements and complex transactions, may indicate fraudulent financial reporting resulting from management of earnings,
▶ Incorporate an element of unpredictability in the selection of the nature, timing and extent of audit procedures.

In accordance with ISA 330, the auditor designs and performs further audit procedures whose nature, timing and extent are responsive to the assessed risks of material misstatement due to fraud. The following are examples of responses:

▶ Visiting locations or performing certain tests on a surprise or unannounced basis. For example, observing inventory at locations where auditor attendance has not been previously announced or counting cash at a particular date on a surprise basis.
▶ Altering the audit approach in the current year. For example, contacting major customers and suppliers orally in addition to sending written confirmation, sending confirmation requests to a specific party within an organization, or seeking more or different information.
▶ Performing a detailed review of the entity's quarter-end or year-end adjusting entries and investigating any that appear unusual as to nature or amount.
▶ Conducting interviews of personnel involved in areas where a risk of material misstatement due to fraud has been identified, to obtain their insights about the risk and whether, or how, controls address the risk.
▶ Applying automated tools and techniques, such as data mining to test for anomalies in a population.

Examples of responses to the auditor's assessment of the risk of material misstatements due to misappropriation of assets are as follows:

▶ Counting cash or securities at or near year-end.

▶ Confirming directly with customers the account activity (including credit memo and sales return activity as well as dates payments were made) for the period under audit.

▶ Analysing recoveries of written-off accounts.

▶ Analysing inventory shortages by location or product type.

▶ Comparing key inventory ratios to industry norm.

▶ Reviewing supporting documentation for reductions to the perpetual inventory records.

Irrespective of the auditor's assessment of the risks of management override of controls, the auditor must design and perform audit procedures to:

▶ Review journal entries or any adjustments made at the end of a reporting period and test journal entries throughout the audit period.

▶ Review accounting estimates for biases and evaluate whether they represent a risk of material misstatement due to fraud. In performing this review, the auditor must evaluate whether management accounting estimates indicate a possible bias and perform a retrospective review of management judgements and assumptions related to significant accounting estimates made the prior year. If estimates or prior year statements show bias, the auditor must re-evaluate the accounting estimates.

▶ For significant transactions that are outside the normal course of business for the entity, or appear to be unusual, the auditor must evaluate whether the business rationale (or the lack thereof) for the transactions suggests they have been entered into for the purpose of fraudulent financial reporting or to conceal misappropriation of assets. Examples are transactions that involve non-consolidated related parties, have not been properly reviewed or approved by those charged with governance of the entity.

To effectively identify and respond to cyber-fraud risks, the auditor may take a comprehensive approach that includes:

▶ Tailored audit procedures designed around specific risks, like evaluating recovery strategies for ransomware threats.

▶ Utilizing data analytics to detect unusual activities indicating cyber-fraud.

▶ Enhanced inquiry and observation by deeply probing cybersecurity practices and responses to incidents.

▶ Adjusting audit methods as new threats emerge or information changes, ensuring audits stay effective against cyber-fraud.

▶ FRAUD OR SUSPECTED FRAUD

When fraud or suspected fraud is identified, the engagement partner is required to:

▶ Understand the matter by inquiring about the matter with appropriate levels of management and those charged with governance. Also, the entity's process to investigate the matter should be evaluated. An assessment of potential control deficiencies related to the identified fraud or suspected fraud is imperative[32].

▷ Based on this understanding, the auditor determines whether additional risk assessment procedures are necessary. Additionally, she considers any legal, regulatory, or ethical responsibilities related to non-compliance and evaluates the impact on other engagements, including those from previous years[33].

▷ If a misstatement due to fraud is identified, the auditor determines the materiality of the misstatement and assesses its implications on other aspects of the audit.

▷ If the financial statements are materially misstated due to fraud, the auditor evaluates the implications for the audit and her opinion in accordance with ISA 705, which deals with modifications to the opinion in the independent auditor's report. In more complex situations, seeking advice from legal counsel is advisable.[34]

▷ If the auditor is unable to conclude on material misstatements, the implications for the audit or the auditor's opinion are to be considered (ISA 705).[35]

This structured approach ensures that auditors handle the challenging task of fraud detection and response with diligence, maintaining the integrity and reliability of the audit process.

▶ EVALUATION OF AUDIT EVIDENCE AND DOCUMENTATION

Once procedures to determine fraud are complete the auditor must evaluate the audit evidence gathered, especially results of analytical procedures and misstatements possibly due to fraud.

The auditor must evaluate if analytical procedures performed near the end of the audit indicate a previously unrecognized risk of material misstatement due to fraud. If a misstatement is found and it is indicative of fraud, the auditor must determine if the findings affect other aspects of the audit, particularly the reliability of management representations. An instance of fraud is unlikely to be an isolated occurrence.

If the auditor identifies a misstatement in which management (particularly senior management) is involved, the auditor shall re-evaluate the initial assessment of the risks of material misstatement due to fraud. They may then modify the nature, timing and extent of audit procedures to respond. The auditor shall also consider whether circumstances or conditions indicate possible collusion involving employees, management or third parties when reconsidering the reliability of evidence previously obtained.

Fraud related procedures must be documented in the audit work papers describing the entity and its environment, assessed risks of material misstatements at the financial statement level and assertion level, including significant risks, responses to assessed risks (ISA 330[36]), and communications to management and the governance organization.[37]

▶ DISCONTINUANCE OF THE ENGAGEMENT

If there is a misstatement resulting from fraud or suspected fraud, this might bring into question whether the auditor should continue performing the audit. Before she acts, the auditor should determine the professional and legal responsibilities applicable in the circumstances, including whether there is a requirement for her to report to management, those charged with governance, or regulatory authorities. Further, the auditor must consider whether it is appropriate to withdraw from the engagement. Before the auditor withdraws from the engagement, she should discuss the possibility of, and the reasons for, withdrawal with management and those charged with governance. There may be professional or legal requirements to report withdrawal from the engagement to the person or the persons who made the audit appointment or regulatory authorities.

▶ **WRITTEN REPRESENTATIONS OF MANAGEMENT**

Regardless of whether fraud is suspected, the written representations from management (see chapter 10, 'Evaluation and Completion') should require management to acknowledge their responsibility to prevent, detect and disclose any fraud. The auditor must obtain written representations from management stating that management acknowledges their responsibility for the design, implementation and maintenance of internal controls to prevent and detect fraud. Management also states that they have disclosed to the auditor their knowledge of fraud, suspected fraud or allegations of fraud involving management or employees who have significant roles in internal control.

12.10 COMMUNICATION RELATED TO FRAUD WITH MANAGEMENT, BOARD AND THIRD PARTIES

As required by ISA 240, the auditor should communicate with management and those charged with governance matters related to fraud at appropriate times throughout the audit engagement. Management should be informed about any material weaknesses in internal control related to the prevention or detection of fraud and error and the auditor should be satisfied that those charged with governance have been informed of any material weaknesses that either have been brought to the auditor's attention by management or have been identified by the auditor during the audit.

If the auditor has identified a fraud or has obtained information that indicates that a fraud may exist, it is her duty to communicate these matters to management. This is so even if the matter might be considered inconsequential (for example, a minor defalcation by an employee at a low level in the entity's organization).

Ordinarily, the appropriate level of management to report to is at least one level above the persons who appear to be involved with the suspected fraud. Due to the nature and sensitivity of fraud involving senior management, or fraud that results in a material misstatement in the financial statements, the auditor reports such matters to those charged with governance on a timely basis in writing.

Other matters related to fraud to be discussed with those charged with governance of the entity may include, for example:
- ▶ The auditor's evaluation of the entity's control environment, including questions regarding the competence and integrity of management.
- ▶ Actions by management that may be indicative of fraudulent financial reporting, such as management's selection and application of accounting policies that may be indicative of management's effort to manage earnings in order to deceive financial

statement users by influencing their perceptions as to the entity's performance and profitability.

As explained in chapter 11 ('Reporting (Phase 4, Part 2)'), auditor's opinion should include 'Key Audit Matters'. Fraud can (and will often be) such a matter. Illustration 12.8 gives an example.

Users of the annual accounts, like investors, supervisory bodies, and banks, have been wondering for some time which work the auditor performs regarding fraud when auditing the financial statements. Investors and other interested users of annual accounts also have an increasing need for transparency in both the annual accounts and the board/management report on, for example, company-specific insights and long-term perspectives. In order to fulfil this need, auditors in the Netherlands are required to report on (their work performed on) fraud and going concern in their auditor's report as of the audit year of 2022[38]. Not in general terms, but specifically with respect to the client, with a focus on the identified risks, the work performed, and, if possible and relevant, the outcomes of this work. In other words, the report for the user of the annual accounts will be more tailored[39]. Illustration of structure of the fraud section (for an example see illustration 12.6):

  ▶ The fraud risk factors relevant to the auditor and the identified fraud risks will be listed. Management override is always a fraud risk. In addition, a fraud risk related to turnover reporting will often be included.
  ▶ A description of the audit work performed by the auditor to mitigate these risks, addressing the specific circumstances of the organisation.
  ▶ (Optional) A description of the specific findings if the circumstances and outcomes of the work require.

Although the auditor's professional duty to maintain the confidentiality of client information may preclude such reporting, the auditor's legal responsibilities may override the duty of confidentiality. If the auditor has identified or suspects a fraud, she must determine whether there is a responsibility to report it to third parties outside the entity (such as Regulatory and Enforcement Authorities). In some countries, the auditor of a financial institution has a statutory duty to report the occurrence of fraud to supervisory authorities.

Also, in some countries the auditor has a duty to report misstatements to authorities in those cases where management and those charged with governance fail to take corrective action. The auditor may consider it advisable to obtain legal advice to determine the appropriate course of action in the circumstances, the purpose of which is to ascertain the steps necessary in considering the public interest aspects of identified fraud.

If the auditor concludes it is impossible to continue performing the audit due to a misstatement resulting from fraud or suspected fraud, withdrawal from the engagement must be seriously considered. If the auditor withdraws, she should:

  ▶ discuss with those charged with governance the auditor's withdrawal from the engagement and the reasons for the withdrawal;
  ▶ consider whether there is a professional or legal requirement to report to regulatory authorities, the auditor's withdrawal from the engagement and the reasons for the withdrawal.

ILLUSTRATION 12.8

KEY AUDIT MATTER ANNUAL REPORT 2018 SBM OFFSHORE NV

Key audit matter
Settlement agreements reached in Brazil
Notes 4.3.1, 4.3.26 and 4.3.28 to the consolidated financial statements
On 26 July 2018, the Company signed a leniency agreement with the Brazilian Ministry of
Transparency and the Comptroller's General Office ('CGU'), the General Counsel for the Repub-
lic ('AGU') and Petrobras. In addition, the Company has signed an agreement with the Brazilian
Federal Prosecutor's Office ('MPF'). The Agreements mean that the Company has reached a
final settlement with the MPF over alleged improper sales practices before 2012, in addition
to that with the other Brazilian Authorities and Petrobras. Following the approval of the Fifth
Chamber on 18 December 2018, the MPF has made a court filing to terminate the improbity
lawsuit filed by the MPF in 2017. The agreement provides for the payment of an additional
fine by SBM Offshore of BRL 200 million (USD 48 million as at 31 December 2018), to be paid in
instalments. Considering the significance of the settlements and the appropriate disclosure of
rights and obligations in the financial statements regarding the settlements, we considered
this a key audit matter.

Our audit work and observations
We have discussed the settlements between the Company, the Brazilian authorities and
Petrobras with the Management Board. We have examined the settlement agreements,
vouched payments to bank statements, have obtained lawyers' letters and held discussions
with the Company's Brazilian and Dutch external lawyers. We assessed whether the fines and
compensation for damages as set out in the settlement agreements are appropriately recognised in the financial statements. We have assessed the adequacy of the related disclosures
in note 4.3.1, 4.3.26 and 4.3.28. Our audit procedures did not indicate material findings with
respect to the settlements, as recorded, and the contingent liability relating to the closure of
the improbity lawsuit, as disclosed in the financial statements.
https://2018.annualreport.sbmoffshore.com/xmlpages/resources/TXP/sbm_fr_2018/pdf/
SBM_Annual_Report_2018_Financial_Statements.pdf

Current (2023) proposed changes in ISA 240 aim to establish consistency in auditing
practices and induce behavioural shifts among auditors[40]. Seven key modifications, as
identified by the IAASB Fraud Task Force, focus on critical areas, including

> ▶ clarifying auditor responsibilities in fraud detection,
> ▶ reinforcing the application of professional scepticism,
> ▶ improving communication with management and governance entities,
> ▶ enhancing risk identification and assessment processes,
> ▶ addressing fraud or suspected fraud,
> ▶ promoting transparency in auditor reports, and
> ▶ emphasizing thorough documentation practices (illustration 12.9).

These changes seek to bolster the effectiveness of audits and adapt to evolving challenges
in the business environment.

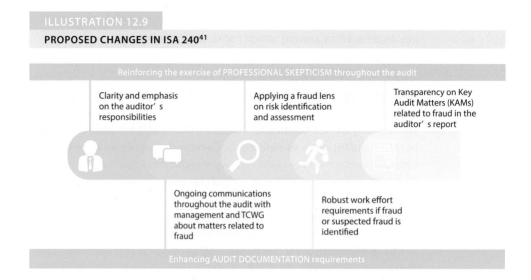

12.11 COMPLIANCE WITH LAW AND REGULATION, CORRUPTION AND MONEY LAUNDERING

ISA 250 deals with the auditor's responsibility to consider laws and regulations in an audit of financial statements and distinguishes the auditor's responsibilities in relation to compliance with two different categories of laws and regulations.[42] The provisions of those laws and regulations generally recognized to have a direct effect on the determination of material amounts and disclosures in the financial statements such as tax and pension laws and regulations. The audit must obtain sufficient and appropriate audit evidence regarding compliance with the provisions of those laws and regulations generally recognized to have a direct effect on the determination of material amounts and disclosures in the financial statements.

Other laws and regulations include those that do have an indirect effect on the determination of the amounts and disclosures in the financial statements, as compliance with which may be fundamental to the operating aspects of the business, to avoid material penalties (for example, compliance with the terms of an operating license, compliance with regulatory solvency requirements, or compliance with environmental regulations). Non-compliance with such laws and regulations may therefore have a material effect on the financial statements and may even threaten a going concern.

The auditor must perform the following procedure to help identify instances of non-compliance with other laws and regulations that may have a material effect on the financial statements:

▶ Inquiring of management and, where appropriate, those charged with governance, as to whether the entity is in compliance with such laws and regulations; and

▶ Inspecting correspondence, if any, with the relevant licensing or regulatory authorities.

▶ The auditor must of course remain alert for instances of non-compliance.

▷ Obtain written representation that all known instances of non-compliance or suspected non-compliance with laws and regulations whose effects should be considered when preparing financial statements have been disclosed to the auditor.

Identifying non-compliance with laws and regulations can influence other aspects of the audit. For example, the integrity of management or employees in reporting compliance with regulations may affect valuation of accounting estimates. When the auditor concludes, based on information obtained and, if necessary, consultation with legal counsel, that an illegal act has or is likely to have occurred, the auditor should consider the effect on the financial statements as well as the implications for other aspects of the audit.

Also, if the client does not comply with laws and regulations, for example by cooperating in corruption investigations, this may result in a material misstatement in the financial statements. In the case of corruption, this can lead to fines and damage claims for which a provision must be made in the annual accounts or adequate explanations must be included.

The auditor should consider the implications of noncompliance with law or regulations in relation to other aspects of the audit, particularly the reliability of representations of management. The implications of particular illegal acts will depend on the relationship of the perpetration and concealment, if any, of the illegal act to specific control procedures and the level of management or employees involved. Such non-compliance must be communicated to those charged with governance, such as the audit committee.

If the auditor concludes that the non-compliance has a material effect on the financial statements and has not been adequately reflected in the financial statements, the auditor shall express a qualified opinion or an adverse opinion on the financial statements.

If the auditor is precluded by management or those charged with governance from obtaining sufficient appropriate audit evidence to evaluate whether non-compliance that may be material to the financial statements has, or is likely to have, occurred, the auditor shall express a qualified opinion or disclaim an opinion on the financial statements on the basis of a limitation on the scope. Non-compliance could also lead to a 'Key Audit Matter' and therefore disclosed in the auditor's opinion.

Fraud, bribery, corruption and money laundering are all examples of non-compliance with laws and regulation and can have direct as well as indirect impact on financial statements.

Dutch bank ING has agreed to pay €775m in penalties for compliance failures that allowed companies – including a Curacao lingerie company and Russian mobile phone operator – to allegedly launder hundreds of millions of euros and pay bribes over six years.

The bank's failings were unearthed after the Dutch prosecutor probed wrongdoing at four companies that had accounts at ING, including $55m in bribes paid to the daughter of Uzbekistan's president by a unit of Russian mobile operator VimpelCom.

The other ING clients it investigated included a Curacao-based women's underwear company that allegedly laundered €150m, a Suriname one-man building materials group that is accused of laundering €9m, and a fruit and vegetable importation front company for money laundering.

Martin Arnold, *Financial Times*, September 4, 2018.[43]

Audit documentation must include identified or suspected non-compliance with laws and regulations and the results of discussion with management and, where applicable, those charged with governance and other parties outside the entity.

BRIBERY AND CORRUPTION

The word corruption was first used by Aristotle and later by Cicero who added the terms bribe and abandonment of good habits. 'Bribery' is offering corrupt payments in exchange for obtaining a favour while 'Extortion' is asking for a corrupt payment in exchange for providing a service.

In general corruption is described as an action to:
- ▶ secretly provide
- ▶ a good or a service to a third party
- ▶ so that he or she can influence certain actions which
- ▶ benefit the corrupt, a third party, or both
- ▶ in which the corrupt agent has authority

Corruption involves acts that are related to making a gift or a promise to persuade the other person (including a civil servant but also a party under private law) to do or not do something. With so-called 'facilitation payments' it concerns payments of smaller amounts to speed up actions. Corruption is often also related to issues of conflict of interest (mixing of business and private interests). In many (very) low wages and income countries, extortion and bribery are a supplement to income. In a sense, these forms of corruption are institutionalized.

The following forms of corruption are common in practice:
- ▶ Kick-back payments to private individuals as part of the purchasing process.
- ▶ Providing goods or services to individuals in private. Well-known examples of goods are 'free' vacations, expensive watches, jewellery and art. Types of services offered include maintenance work on the private home, travel and client entertainment.
- ▶ Corruption can also take the form of making goods available, for example the use of a (holiday) apartment or car.
- ▶ Payments for the use of 'intermediaries' to obtain contracts.

Corruption is becoming increasingly common in the form of commitments for future benefits. These deferred payments are in line with the pattern of 'for what, hear what' and 'I take care of you now, you take care of me later'.

Efforts to combat corruption have, among other things, led to the worldwide Convention on Combating Bribery of Foreign Public Officials in International Business Transactions. This treaty was established through the Organization for Economic Cooperation and Development (OECD). Pursuant to this treaty is Dutch legislation which has been tightened since 2001 (including Article 177 of the Criminal Code). Dutch companies are also increasingly dealing with (extraterritorial) legislation, such as the US Foreign Corrupt Practices Act (US FCPA)[44] and the UK Bribery Act. In addition, public opinion on corruption has changed: society has become more critical of corruption.

Based on responses from national experts, Transparency International's classification of foreign bribery enforcement in OECD Anti-Bribery Convention countries is as follows (2022 index listed in order of their share of world exports, illustration 12.10):[45]

ILLUSTRATION 12.10

CORRUPTION PERCEPTION INDEX 2022, TRANSPARENCY INTERNATIONAL

So called kickbacks differ from other forms of corruption, such as diversion of assets, as in embezzlement, because of the collusion between two parties.

In December 2016, Brazillian engineering giant Odebrecht and its subsidiary, Braksem, admitted bribery to the tune of £553m, in which the US Department of Justice called 'the largest foreign bribery case in history'. Odebrecht paid off politicians, political parties, officials, lawyers, and bankers to secure lucrative contracts in Brazil and abroad – covering 12 nations in total. Remarkably, they even created a special department to manage its dodgy deals, named the Division of Structured Operations, leaving prosecutors speechless. In April of the following year, Odebrecht was formally fined $2.6bn (approx. £2bn) by a US judge. The ripple effects have been far-reaching, with the scandal implicating a staggering number of Brazil's senators and governors, as well as forcing the resignation of the president and the imprisonment of Ecuador's vice-president.[46]

The US Foreign Corrupt Practices Act (FCPA[47]) criminalizes bribing foreign (non-US) government officials. In addition, this law sets requirements for internal control and the administrative transparent processing of transactions. 'Facilitation payments' are not punishable, provided that the strict FCPA conditions are met.

The provisions of the FCPA apply to both US individuals and companies operating worldwide, as well as to non-US individuals and companies with US-listed securities. In addition, the provisions may apply to actions that take place in or via US banking or communication facilities including e-mail, for example when two non-US companies conduct a mutual transaction through a US bank. This is the so-called extraterritorial effect.

Thus, placing a telephone call or sending an e-mail, text message, or fax from, to, or through the United States involves interstate commerce as does sending a wire transfer from or to a U.S. bank or otherwise using the U.S. banking system, or traveling across state borders or internationally to or from the United States.[48]

Examples of transactions to be alert to (increased) risks of corruption transactions:[49]

▶ of a relatively large size
▶ with the intervention of third parties
▶ that have been concluded on the basis of a success fee
▶ where the performance (goods or service) is difficult to value
▶ where use is made of personal networks
▶ where decision-making is in the hands of a limited number of people
▶ that use cash
▶ the settlement of which takes place in an unusual or inexplicable manner
▶ without (visible) compensation

It is the auditor's responsibility to evaluate corruption risks during the risk analysis and, if necessary, to arrange her audit work accordingly. When auditing an annual account, the auditor will not normally find clear records of the above forms of corruption in the administration. However, evidence of corruption does appear in the administration. These indications of corruption often manifest themselves in transactions that the auditor may encounter during her audit work. Based on the client-specific circumstances that the auditor has identified, she will assess, based on ISA 315, 240 and 250, whether those circumstances lead to risks of material misstatement at the financial statement level and allegations of corruption.

▶ Gaining insight into the design and existence of the client's internal control with regard to corruption risks;
▶ Gaining insight the functioning of the client's internal control with regard to corruption risks;
▶ Obtain audit evidence based on substantive audit procedures;
▶ Request written confirmations.

In the event of evidence of corruption, as well as evidence of fraud, the auditor will perform additional procedures to determine the nature and extent of potential violations and its consequences. In case of (indications of) corruption the auditor must act in accordance with ISA 240/250 and other relevant laws and regulations.

Illustration 12.11 includes examples of red flags linked with suggested audit procedures.

ILLUSTRATION 12.11

EXTERNAL AUDITORS' GUIDE FOR DETECTING BRIBERY

Types of Bribery	Red Flags	Suggested Audit Procedures
Kickbacks	The difference in price between the materials that were contracted and those that were actually delivered	Inquire of management
Bid-rigging	A particular contractor repeatedly wins the contract	Auditors sould investigate what actually happens for bidders participating in the various bids. They should also interview key employees and management about the reason behind this.
Kickbacks and Bid-rigging	An employee of the company who has close relationships with the supplier	The auditor could compare the disclosed names and addresses of employees with the vendors list to reveal if a vendor company is owned or run by an employee of the company
Bid-rigging	Cases when low-bid awards are frequently followed by change orders or amendments that significantly increase payments to the vendor	Inquire of management
Kickbacks	Unusual or unexplained fluctuation in payables, expenses or disbursements	The auditor should inspect supporting documents for such transactions and ensure that management confirms payables balances on an interim basis
Kickbacks	The purchase of inferior-quality inventory or merchandise with very near expiration date	Management inquiry. The auditor should also ask for a technical report showing the reason for buying these goods
Kickbacks	Unusually high price contracts for goods or services purchased by the company	The auditor should review the contracts and bids for any trends in prices. A comparison with industry norms was also suggested. Management should also be advised to monitor price trends
Kickbacks	Improper or unauthorized payment for goods or services	The auditor should review the contracts to highlight any unauthorized or improper authorization
Bid-rigging	The existence of very large, unexplained price differences among bidders	Management inquiry could highlight the reason behind this unexplained price differences
Kickbacks	The prices of the company's suppliers are higher than market rate	Compare the market rate with the company's pricing policy
Kickbacks	Poor credit ratings and the company's inability to pay its debt on due dates	Management inquiry and a review of credit policy
Bid-rigging	When qualified bidders fail to submit contract proposals or fewer bidders than expected respond to a request for proposals	Review bidding contracts and inquire of management
Kickbacks	Budget overruns either because of overcharges or excessive quantities purchased or both	The auditor should scrutinize larger budget overruns and should inquire of management about large differences between actual and budgeted amounts. Actual expenditures (incomplete sentence), compared to prior years

Source: Kaseem, R. and A.W. Higson, 2016. 'Detecting Bribery: A Guide for External Auditors, Insights from the Audit Profession in Egypt'. *Journal of Emerging Trends in Economics and Management Sciences*, 7 (2), pp. 97–105.

MONEY LAUNDERING

Money laundering is the act of concealing the transformation of profits from illegal activities and corruption into ostensibly 'legitimate' assets. The dilemma of illicit activities is accounting for the origin of the proceeds of such activities without raising the suspicion of law enforcement agencies. Illustration 12.12 sketches how cash generated by illicit activities can be used to acquire legitimate assets.

The following conduct, when committed intentionally, must be regarded as money laundering (EU Directive):[50]

(a) the conversion or transfer of property, knowing that such property is derived from criminal activity or from an act of participation in such activity, for the purpose of concealing or disguising the illicit origin of the property or of assisting any person who is involved in the commission of such an activity to evade the legal consequences of that person's action;

(b) the concealment or disguise of the true nature, source, location, disposition, movement, rights with respect to, or ownership of, property, knowing that such property is derived from criminal activity or from an act of participation in such an activity;

(c) the acquisition, possession or use of property, knowing, at the time of receipt, that such property was derived from criminal activity or from an act of participation in

ILLUSTRATION 12.12

SKETCHES HOW CASH GENERATED BY ILLICIT ACTIVITIES CAN BE USED TO ACQUIRE LEGITIMATE ASSETS

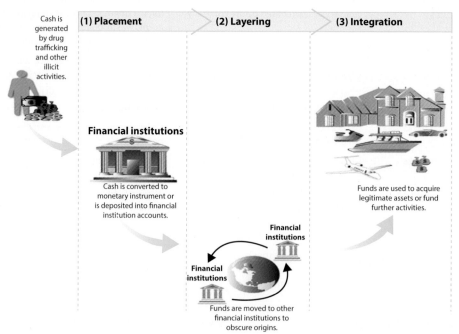

Source: Financial Crimes Enforcement Network, *FinCEN Related Series: An Assessment of Narcotics Related Money Laundering.* July 1992. | GAO -17-684

such an activity; (d) participation in, association to commit, attempts to commit and aiding, abetting, facilitating and counselling the commission of any of the actions referred to in points (a), (b) and (c).

Of course, the risk of money laundering differs per region as culture, legal system and economic development are specific to countries. According to the Basle AML Index examples of high-risk money laundering countries (2023) are Haiti, Chad, Myanmar, Republic of Congo, Mozambique, Gabon, Guinea-Bissau, Venezuela and Laos.[51]

Former Pakistani President Asif Ali Zardari was arrested after his bail application was rejected in connection with a high-profile money laundering case that saw vast sums of money allegedly siphoned out of the country. Zardari, the husband of assassinated ex-Prime Minister Benazir Bhutto, served as president from 2008 until 2013. He has long been the subject of corruption allegations and is widely known in Pakistan as 'Mr Ten Percent', which later became hundred percent. After coming into the government, he started taking 10% of all major contract investments before he would approve the contract.[52]

EU Anti-Money Laundering (AML) laws aim to prevent money laundering and enhance financial transparency. Key aspects include risk assessment, customer due diligence, record-keeping, reporting obligations, supervision, beneficial ownership registers, scrutiny of high-risk jurisdictions, and penalties for non-compliance. Businesses must stay updated on directives to ensure effective compliance.

As the auditor's role is essential in maintaining the integrity of financial systems and preventing illicit financial activities, they play a role in ensuring compliance with EU AML regulation and identifying potential risks. Financial statement auditors play a crucial role in detecting and preventing money laundering by implementing various procedures during their audit processes. Illustration 12.13 sketches some procedures auditors could apply to assist in detecting money laundering.

By combining these methods, financial statement auditors can enhance their ability to detect and prevent money laundering activities within the organizations they audit.

All European Union member states have established Financial Intelligence Units (FIUs) as part of their efforts to combat money laundering and terrorist financing. Each FIU operates as an independent agency or unit within the respective national jurisdiction. These units serve as central authorities responsible for receiving, analysing, and disseminating financial intelligence related to suspicious transactions. According to the Dutch AML and Anti-Terrorist Financing Act,[53] the auditor has a reporting obligation with regard to unusual transactions: 'Transactions where the reporting party has reason to assume that they may be related to money laundering or terrorist financing.'[54] Whether a transaction is unusual in nature depends on the facts and circumstances. If there is corruption, there will generally also be an unusual transaction: there is often a benefit from a crime. Unusual transactions must be reported to the Financial Intelligence Unit-the Netherlands (FIU-the Netherlands). In the event of evidence of corruption, as well as evidence of fraud, the auditor will perform additional procedures to determine the nature and extent of potential violations and its consequences. In case of (indications of) money laundering the auditor must act in accordance with ISA 240/250 and other relevant law and regulation.

PROCEDURES TO DETECT MONEY LAUNDERING[55]

▶ *Understanding the Business and its Environment*

Auditors need to have a deep understanding of the client's business, industry, and the economic environment in which it operates. This knowledge helps in identifying unusual transactions or activities that may indicate money laundering.

▶ *Risk Assessment*

Conducting a comprehensive risk assessment is essential. Auditors should identify and assess the risks related to money laundering specific to the industry and client.

▶ *Client Due Diligence*

Auditors need to perform due diligence on their clients, understanding their ownership structure, business relationships, and the nature of their operations. This can help identify any potential red flags related to money laundering.

▶ *Transaction Analysis*

Auditors should analyse transactions to identify any inconsistencies or unusual patterns. Large or complex transactions without a clear business purpose may raise suspicions and warrant further investigation.

▶ *Internal Controls Review*

Evaluating and testing the effectiveness of internal controls is crucial. Weak controls can provide opportunities for money laundering activities. Auditors should ensure that controls are in place to prevent and detect suspicious transactions.

▶ *Training and Awareness*

Training audit team members to be vigilant about money laundering risks can be beneficial.

▶ *Data Analytics*

Using data analytics tools can help auditors analyse large volumes of financial data quickly. Unusual patterns or anomalies in the data may indicate potential money laundering activities.

▶ *Continuous Monitoring*

Money laundering risks evolve over time, so auditors should implement continuous monitoring procedures. Regularly updating risk assessments and staying informed about industry trends are crucial aspects of this approach.

In what is a record fine for an Australian operator in 2022, regulators fined Sydney's The Star Casino 100 million Australian dollars (AUD) for failing to prevent money laundering activity from taking place on the casino's premises. It was the maximum fine possible. The Star also lost its license as a result of the regulatory investigation. This fine comes on the back of increased pressure on the wider Australian casino industry due to reports of financial crime.[56]

12.12 SUMMARY

From the origins of the audit profession, detection of fraud has been a major issue. Notorious high-profile fraud cases like McKesson Robbins Case (US, 1938), Pincoff (Netherlands, 18792) and Hatry Group (UK, 19293), stimulated the demand for independent audits. Fraud results in large financial losses and loss of trust in institutions and markets. Although the importance of fraud as an audit objective declined towards the end of the nineteenth century, in the current era detection of fraud is perceived as one of the most important audit objectives.

A typical perpetrator of fraud tends to be between the ages of 36 and 55, working with the victim organization for more than six years and holding an executive position in operations, finance or general management. Seventy three percent (73%) of occupational fraud perpetrators were male. Median losses caused by men (USD 125,000) were only 25% higher than median losses caused by women (USD 100,000).

The primary responsibility for the prevention and detection of fraud rests with both management of the entity and those charged with governance of the entity and management. Fraud prevention involves a commitment to creating a culture of honesty and ethical behaviour which can be reinforced by an active oversight by those charged with governance.

Because of its impact, the average businessperson expects that fraud should 'always' be detected by the financial statement auditor. Although they have expertise, auditors are in general not 'fraud experts' as expertise and experience of an individual auditor with respect to fraud is generally limited. Financial statement auditors are not forensic accountants who are specifically trained and engaged to detect fraud. Because of these reasons, fraud detection is one of the major factors of the expectation gap.

In the context of the audit, fraud is defined as an intentional act by one or more individuals among management, those charged with governance, employees, or third parties, involving the use of deception to obtain an unjust or illegal advantage. Types of fraud are fraudulent financial reporting and misstatements due to misappropriation of assets. *Fraudulent financial reporting* involves intentional misstatements including omissions of amounts or disclosures in financial statements to deceive financial statement users. *Misappropriation of assets* involves the theft of an entity's assets and is often perpetrated by employees in relatively small and immaterial amounts.

To understand the risk of fraud, auditors often refer to the 'Fraud Triangle'. According to the 'Fraud Triangle', fraud involves incentives or pressure to commit fraud, a perceived opportunity to do so and some rationalization of the act.

According to a cited study, the leading fraud detection methods are tips, internal audit, and management review. Collectively, these three detection methods were cited in 70% of the cases. Also, more than half of all tips (55%) were provided by employees of the victim organizations. Meanwhile, nearly one-third (31%) of the tips that led to fraud detection came from people outside the organization: customers, vendors, and competitors.

When considering fraud, the auditor must be mindful of the need for professional scepticism, discuss the possibility of fraud with the engagement team, perform certain risk assessment procedures, identify the risks of material misstatement due to fraud, respond to those assessed risks and evaluate the audit evidence gathered. Management is in a unique position to perpetrate fraud because of management's ability to manipulate accounting records and prepare fraudulent financial statements by overriding internal controls.

ISA 315.17 requires a discussion among the engagement team members and a determination by the engagement partner of which matters should be communicated to those team members not involved in this discussion. This discussion shall place particular emphasis on how and where the entity's financial statements may be susceptible to material misstatement due to fraud, including how fraud might occur, setting aside beliefs that the management and those charged with governance are honest and have integrity.

The auditor will design and perform audit procedures in response to the assessed risks of material misstatement due to fraud in a manner that is not biased towards obtaining audit evidence that corroborate management's assertions or towards excluding audit evidence that may contradict such assertions. In accordance with ISA 330, the auditor designs and performs further audit procedures whose nature, timing and extent are responsive to the assessed risks of material misstatement due to fraud.

Irrespective of the auditor's assessment of the risks of management override of controls, the auditor must design and perform audit procedures to:

- ▶ Review journal entries or any adjustments made at the end of a reporting period
- ▶ Review accounting estimates for biases and evaluate whether they represent a risk of material misstatement due to fraud.
- ▶ For significant transactions that are outside the normal course of business for the entity, or appear to be unusual, the auditor must evaluate whether the business rationale (or the lack thereof) for the transactions suggests they have been entered into for the purpose of fraudulent financial reporting or to conceal misappropriation of assets.

If a misstatement is found and it is indicative of fraud, the auditor must determine if the findings affect other aspects of the audit, particularly the reliability of management representations. An instance of fraud is unlikely to be an isolated occurrence. If the auditor identifies a misstatement in which management (in particular, senior management) is involved, the auditor shall re-evaluate the initial assessment of the risks which may require modification the nature, timing and extent of their audit procedures. The auditor shall also consider whether circumstances or conditions indicate possible collusion involving employees, management or third parties when reconsidering the reliability of evidence previously obtained.

If the auditor has identified a fraud or has obtained information that indicates that a fraud may exist, this must be communicated to management. Due to the nature and sensitivity of fraud involving senior management, or fraud that results in a material misstatement in the financial statements, the auditor reports such matters to those charged with governance.

If the auditor has identified or suspects a fraud, she must determine whether there is a responsibility to report it to third parties outside the entity (such as Regulatory and Enforcement Authorities).

Non-compliance with laws and regulations by the client can be distinguished in two different categories. The first includes provisions of those laws and regulations generally recognized to have a direct effect on the determination of material amounts and disclosures in the financial statements such as tax and pension laws and regulations. The other category provisions do not have a direct effect on the determination of the amounts and disclosures in the financial statements, but compliance may be fundamental to the operating aspects of the business, to an entity's ability to continue its business, or may have a material effect on the financial statements. The auditor must perform sufficient and appropriate procedures to help identify instances of non-compliance with other laws and regulations that may have a material effect on the financial statements.

Corruption is an action to secretly provide a good or a service to a third party so that they can influence certain actions which benefit the corrupt, a third party, or both in which the corrupt agent has authority. 'Bribery' is offering corrupt payments in exchange for obtaining a favor while 'Extortion' is asking for a corrupt payment in exchange for providing a service. 'Money laundering' is the act of concealing the transformation of profits from illegal activities and corruption into ostensibly 'legitimate' assets. In the event of (indications of) corruption or money laundering, the auditor will perform additional procedures to determine the nature and extent of potential violations and their consequences.

Money laundering is the act of concealing the transformation of profits from illegal activities and corruption into ostensibly 'legitimate' assets. The dilemma of illicit activities is accounting for the origin of the proceeds of such activities without raising the suspicion of law enforcement agencies.

12.13 QUESTIONS, EXERCISES AND CASES

QUESTIONS

12.2 Introduction

12-1 How important for the auditor was fraud detection in the 19th and early 20th century? Why was that the case?

12-2 Summarize some of the characteristics of a fraudster. Do you think you could become a fraudster during your life? Could your best friend be? Motivate.

12.3 Responsibilities of the Board

12-3 Who holds the primary responsibility for the prevention and detection of fraud? Why is that important?

12-4 What components does governance oversight include in addressing fraud?

12.4 Auditor's Responsibility

12-5 Define the auditor's responsibility for preventing and detecting fraud.

12.5 Fraud Defined

12-6 With regards to fraud, what are the objectives of the auditor?

12.6 Types of Fraud

12-7 Explain the different types of fraud and what they impact.

12-8 Describe the difference between financial statement fraud and misappropriation of assets.

12.7 Fraud Triangle and Anti-fraud Measures

12-9 Sketch the so-called fraud triangle and for each element give an example.

12-10 Why is a bad corporate culture a predictor of fraud?

12-11 Describe anti-fraud controls management could implement.

12.8 **Audit Planning and Fraud Risk Assessment**

12-12 Describe some fraud risk assessment procedures.

12-13 Identify techniques that management can use to commit fraud by overriding controls.

12.9 **Responses to Fraud Risk Assessment**

12-14 Give four examples of further audit procedures whose nature, timing and extent are responsive to the assessed risks of material misstatement due to fraud.

12-15 Give three examples of responses to the auditor's assessment of the risk of material misstatements due to misappropriation of assets.

12-16 Why is management fraud in general more difficult to detect than employee fraud?

12-17 Discuss why misstatement due to fraud or suspected fraud could lead to discontinuance of the engagement.

12-18 Why must auditors obtain a written representation by management in which they confirm they are responsible for preventing and detecting fraud?

12.10 **Communication Related to Fraud with Management, Board and Third Parties**

12-19 Ordinarily, what is the appropriate level of management to report to when the auditor suspects fraud?

12-20 Explain why, though the auditor's professional duty is to maintain the confidentiality of client information, they may in certain instances report to third parties.

12.11 **Compliance with Law and Regulation, Corruption and Money Laundering**

12-21 Describe why non-compliance with laws and regulations could directly and indirectly have an effect on the financial statements

12-22 Explain the concept of corruption and why the auditor should assess the corruption risk in the context of the financial statement audit.

12-23 Explain the concept of money laundering and why the auditor should assess the risk of money laundering in the context of the financial statement audit.

PROBLEMS AND EXERCISES

12.2 **Introduction**

12-24 Choose one of the fraud cases listed in section 12.2 Introduction. Research the case and discuss what fraud detection measures could have been done to reduce the duration and size of the fraud in the early stages.

12.6, 12.7 **Types of Fraud and Anti-Fraud Measures**

12-25 In a California smart phone app company an employee discovered a flaw in the accounting system. The accounts payable clerk found she was able to change the names of vendors in the computer system to her name. She would create false invoices and create a cheque for the false invoice. The name on the cheque was changed to the name of the employee. After the cheque was printed, the name in the system could then be changed back to the appropriate vendor. The cheque register would show only the name of the vendor. The fraudulent employee had authorization to sign cheques under $2,000. By writing small cheques, she was able to defraud the company of $90,000. An employee of another department was looking through the vendor list on her computer after the fraudulent employee had changed the vendor's name to his name. A few entries later, the vendor's name changed again. She wondered how this switch could occur and asked her supervisor. Soon after, the fraudulent employee was caught.

Required:

A. What kind of fraud is being committed – financial statement or misappropriation of assets? Discuss.

B. Discuss four safeguards that might have prevented this fraud.

12.7, 12.8, 12.9 **Fraud Triangle, Audit Planning and Risk, Responses to Risk Assessment**

12-26 Assume Joe Pasz has been the audit engagement partner of the fast-growing IHHI group of companies for seven years. IHHI is owned by Brian Farry, a dominant entrepreneur, who is also the CEO. Up to now Joe assessed fraud risk as relatively low. Recently Joe discussed fraud risk with Brian who, as usual, assessed fraud risk within the company as almost zero because of his own monitoring role, the wonderful tone-at-the-top and the existence of a code of conduct. Because of the aggressive growth of the company, the staff turnover rate is rather high. Only recently the CFO left the company. He was succeeded by a niece of Brian. During the planning meeting with the engagement team Joe wants to discuss and assess fraud risk. Joe starts the discussion sharing your view that fraud risk is rather low as in previous years. For the second year you are the audit manager on the job and Joe asks you to share your thoughts.

A. How do you assess fraud risk? Answer Joe and discuss your reasoning. Illustrate with use of the fraud triangle.

CASES

12.9, 12.10 **Fraud Risk Assessment and Responses**

12-27 Olympus. The Olympus financial scandal exploded in late 2011 when then president and CEO Michael Woodford came forward with information exposing fraudulent accounting practices in the organization. Woodford had only served as CEO for two weeks when he revealed the financial malfeasance. The fraud is one of the most significant corporate corruption scandals in the history of Japan. In 2000, accounting standards in Japan changed significantly after the failure of Yamaguchi Securities in 1997. The new accounting standards required losses on certain assets to be noted at the end of each accounting period. Rather than comply with the standards and disclose mounting losses, Olympus constructed a complicated system of hiding its bad assets. The company began selling bad assets for exorbitant prices to newly created entities under its control without recognizing losses from the sales. The Olympus fraud shows that tone-at-the-top matters. Woodford wrote letters to the board about his concerns and was subsequently fired. This exemplified the company's unethical culture. C-level executives must act according to the principles expected of employees at all levels and across the enterprise.

Required:

A. Discuss – with hindsight – if the auditor of Olympus missed indications of fraud. Motivate your answer.

B. Why must C-level executives act according to the principles expected of employees at all levels and across the enterprise?

12.5, 12.8, 12.9 **Fraud Defined, Fraud Risk Assessment and Responses**

12-28 **Gupta scandal.** Brothers Ajay, Atul and Rajesh (aka Tony) Gupta moved to South Africa from Uttar Pradesh in 1993 and set up Sahara Computers, with the group expanding to mining, air travel, energy, technology and media. The family became extremely close to Jacob Zuma, serving as the fourth President of South Africa, leading to accusations of 'state capture' and widespread corruption, but the empire began to crumble in 2018, with one Gupta business after another filing for administration. On 14th February 2018 Jacob Zuma resigned and on the same day the Gupta brothers disappeared, believed to have fled the country to Dubai. On 16th February 2018, Ajay Gupta was declared a fugitive from justice by the South African authorities after failing to hand himself over. The collapse happened in February 2018, although controversies date as far back as 2013 when a Gupta family plane bearing guests for a Sun City wedding landed at Waterkloof Air Base near Pretoria, a military base usually used by visiting heads of state.

Required:

A. Explain why civil servants and politicians are prone to bribery and prone to be bribed.

B. Assume a significant bribe was transferred via Gupta's bank account to a South African politician. How could the financial statement auditor have detected this transaction? And in case of a cash payment?

C. Could the landing of a Gupta family plane bearing guests for a Sun City wedding at Waterkloof Air Base near Pretoria, a military base usually used by visiting heads of state, have been an indication of bribery? Do you think the financial statement auditor missed or misinterpreted this indication? Motivate.

12.8, 12.11 **Audit Planning and Fraud Risk Assessment, Compliance With Law And Regulation, Corruption And Money Laundering**

12-29 **Laundry services.** Al Pone owns a lucrative illegal drug distribution ring. The cash gains are too great to conceal from US Internal Revenue Service (IRS) without raising their suspicions. So, Al begins plowing the funds into several legitimate neighborhood laundry services owned by his eldest son Cap. Cap's laundry services look like a normal laundry service, complete with regular customers. But it's actually a front for Al's primary economic activity which he can't list on his tax returns or bank account applications. He routes most of the money he makes by selling drugs through the laundry services, spending it on laundry equipment, luxury buildings, expensive cars, marketing, supplies, services and staff (most family members receive nice bonuses). Once on the laundry services' balance sheet, the illicit funds mix with legitimate gains from paying customers. It's difficult or impossible to determine whether a given expense involves legit or illicit funds. To the public, Al is running a successful laundry service and feels safe extracting income from it, even though much of it comes from an activity that would normally land him in prison.

Required:

A. Assume Cap Pone is asking you to become his financial statement auditor. What would be your requirements regarding the design (and operating effectiveness) of internal controls over financial reporting?

B. How could the auditor of Cap's laundry services detect the money laundry activities as set up by Al?

12.4, 12.8, 12.9   Auditor Responsibilities, Audit Planning and Fraud Risk and Responses

12-30 The Wirecard Scandal: An Audit Case Study

In June 2020, Wirecard AG, once hailed as one of Germany's most successful fintech companies, filed for insolvency after revealing a $2.1 billion hole in its balance sheet. The scandal raised questions about the efficacy of financial audits, particularly regarding the role of Ernst & Young (EY), Wirecard's auditor. EY had signed off on Wirecard's financial statements for years, giving investors a false sense of security. To be able to answer the following questions, take note of publicly available information about Wirecard (for example take note of https://www.ft.com/wirecard).

Required:

A. What were the red flags in Wirecard's financial statements that should have prompted closer scrutiny from auditors like EY?

B. Discuss the responsibilities and obligations of auditors, such as EY, in ensuring the accuracy and reliability of financial statements.

C. How did Wirecard manage to deceive auditors, regulators, and investors for so long, and what could have been done differently to prevent such a massive fraud?

D. Analyse the potential conflicts of interest that may have influenced EY's auditing practices in the case of Wirecard. How can auditors maintain independence and objectivity when auditing clients?

E. Reflecting on the aftermath of the Wirecard scandal, what reforms or improvements should be implemented in the auditing profession to prevent similar incidents in the future?

12.6, 12.9   Types of Fraud, Responses to Fraud Risk Assessment

12-31 COGA Sondheim Inc., an agricultural supply company, undergoes annual audits conducted by Isle and Oblivion (I&O), an external audit firm. The company's CFO, Caleb Airmak, orchestrates a fraud scheme involving inventory manipulation to embezzle funds.

Fraudulent Activities:

1 False Inventory Adjustments: Caleb Airmak overstated the ending inventory by falsifying inventory records, inflating both quantity and value of products.

2 Collusion with Warehouse Manager: Airmak colludes with the warehouse manager to provide false information about inventory quantity and condition, aiding in concealing the fraud.

3 Bogus Purchase Transactions: Fictitious purchase transactions are created by Airmak to support inflated inventory figures. Payments are made to fake vendors under Airmak's control.

Required:

Discuss the fraudulent activities involving inventory manipulation at COGA Sondheim Inc. orchestrated by Caleb Airmak, the CFO. Explain how an auditor can detect such fraudulent practices during the audit process. Include in your discussion the specific audit procedures and techniques that can be employed to uncover misappropriation of assets in financial statements.

12.14 NOTES

1.   The Association of Certified Fraud Examiners (ACFE) performs a bi-annual report. Its 2022 Report to the Nations can be found at https://legacy.acfe.com/report-to-the-nations/2022/?_ga=2.162510268.1016213299.1706031048-716276921.1706031048

2.   Pincoff established a trading company (Rotterdamsche Handelsvereeniging), a public-private venture for dealing with Africa. The company was unsuccessful and Pincoff decided to hide the losses. He funneled funds from the company to his failing African business. In 1879 his fraud was exposed, and he fled the country.

3.   Central to Hatry's fraud was the 1923 collapse of the Commercial Corporation of London. However, his ambitions could not be contained, and by 1929 he owned a string of financial businesses, including a successful brokerage that issued bonds for local towns, undercutting established firms, and several investment trusts. Due to a bad investment in a photo-booth company, which he tried to prop up, Hatry succumbed to the temptation to forge municipal bonds that his brokerage was underwriting and used them to raise additional cash. (https://moneyweek.com/508563/great-frauds-in-history-clarence-hatry/).

4.   Great Swindles of the 19th Century, Notorious Swindles and Frauds Marked the 1800, By Robert J. McNamara, Updated on May 17, 2019, Also see for example https://www.businessinsider.nl/fraud-financial-scandals-notable-and-expensive-2018-4?international=true&r=US. https://money.usnews.com/investing/articles/biggest-corporate-frauds-in-history as well as https://en.wikipedia.org/wiki/List_of_fraudsters

5.   Higson, Andrew, 'Developments in Auditing and Assurance' (chapter 5). In: *Corporate Financial Reporting: Theory & Practice*, DOI: http://dx.doi.org/10.4135/9781446220863.n5, http://sk.sagepub.com/books/corporate-financial-reporting/n5.xml

6.   Ibid. ISA 240, para. 13.

7.   Ibid. note 1.

8.   Global Profiles of the Fraudster. KPMG, 2016 https://assets.kpmg.com/content/dam/kpmg/pdf/2016/05/profile-of-a-fraudster-infographic.pdf

9.   Ibid. note 1, p.51.

10.   Ibid. note 6.

11.   Dutch Corporate Governance Code 2022, https://www.mccg.nl/publicaties/codes/2022/12/20/dutch-corporate-governance-code-2022.

12.   https://www.grantthornton.co.uk/insights/the-corporate-governance-code-and-financial-services/

13.   Proposed ISA 240 (Revised), IAASB Agenda 2A, December 2023, https://www.iaasb.org/consultations-projects/fraud

14.   International Auditing and Assurance Standards Board (IAASB), 2023, International Standard on Auditing 200 (ISA 200) Overall Objective of the Independent Auditor, and the Conduct of an Audit in Accordance with International Standards on Auditing, para. A54, *Handbook of International Quality Management, Auditing, Review, Other Assurance, and Related Services Pronouncements*, 2022 edn, Volume I, International Federation of Accountants, New York.

15.   They may lack adequate training in fraud and investigative methodologies compared with forensic auditors. Also time and budgetary constraints could play a role and financial statement auditors may have relatively infrequent experience of fraud in their career due to the low base-rate of fraud detection. (Mui, G.Y., Defining Auditor Expertise in Fraud Detection, Journal of Forensic and Investigative Acccounting, Vol. 10: Issue 2, 2018.)

16. Ruhnke, Klaus and Schmidt, Martin (2014), 'The Audit Expectation Gap: Existence, Causes, and the Impact of Changes', *Journal Accounting and Business Research*, 44(5); Hassink, H., Bollen, L.H., Meuwissen, R.H.G. and Vries, M.J.de (2009), 'Corporate Fraud and the Audit Expectations Gap: A Study among Business Managers', *Journal of International Accounting, Auditing and Taxation*, 18(2), pp. 85–100. Addressing Information Needs to Reduce the Audit Expectation Gap: Evidence from Dutch Bankers, Audited Companies and Auditors, June 2015, International Journal of Auditing 19(3).

17. Derived from: Trompeter, G., Carpenter, T., Jones, K., Desai, K and Riley, R. (2013), 'A Synthesis of Fraud-related Research'. *Auditing: A Journal of Practice & Theory* 32 (Supplement 1), pp. 287–321.

18. International Auditing and Assurance Standards Board (IAASB), 2023, International Standard on Auditing 240 (ISA 240) 'The Auditor's Responsibilities Relating to Fraud in an Audit of Financial Statements', para. 11, *Handbook of International Quality Management, Auditing, Review, Other Assurance, and Related Services Pronouncements*, 2022 edn, Volume I, International Federation of Accountants, New York.

19. Trompeter, G., Carpenter, T., Jones, K. and Riley, R., 'What We Learn about Fraud from Other Disciplines', *Accounting Horizons American Accounting Association*, 28(4). DOI: 10.2308/acch-50816, 2014, pp. 769–804.

20. Cressey, Donald (1973), *Other People's Money: A Study in the Social Psychology of Embezzlement*, Montclair, NJ: Patterson Smith, p. 30.

21. Bashin, M. (2013), 'Corporate Accounting Scandal at Satyam: A Case Study of India's Enron', *European Journal of Business and Social Sciences*, 1(12), pp. 25–47.

22. Ibid. note 1.

23. https://www.acfe.com/-/media/files/acfe/pdfs/fraud-risk-tools/coso-fraud-risk-management-guide-second-edition-executive-summary.ashx

24. Ibid. note 1, Figure 22, p34.

25. Ibid. note 1, ACFE, 2022, Figure 10, p22.

26. International Auditing and Assurance Standards Board (IAASB), 2023, International Standard on Auditing 315 (ISA 315) 'Identifying and Assessing the Risks of Material Misstatement through Understanding the Entity and Its Environment', *Handbook of International Quality Management Auditing Review, Other Assurance, and Related Services Pronouncements*, 2022 edn, Volume I, International Federation of Accountants, New York. Although experimental research indicates that explicit integration of fraud risk in RMM assessment can affect auditor judgments by helping auditors acquire and retain more fraud related information with which to build a more coherent story of fraud. (Popova, Velina K. (2018), 'Integration of Fraud Risk in the Risk of Material Misstatement and the Effect on Auditors Planning Decisions'. *Journal of Forensic Accounting Research*, 3(1), pp. A52–A79).

27. Fraud Risk Management Guide, 2nd edition, Executive Summary, March 2023, COSO/ACFE, Page 12, Figure 1.

28. https://www.leaseplan.com/-/media/leaseplan-digital/nl/public-pages/documents/footer/leaseplan-2022-annual-report.pdf?rev=65bc76373fb04d8eae376b6cfd275bc3 p214

29. Ibid. ISA 315 para. 26.

30. Ibid. ISA 240, para. 11.

31. Ibid. ISA 240, para. 13.

32. ISA 240.54, Agenda-Item 2-A, December IAASB meeting IAASB Main Agenda (December 2023), Proposed ISA 240 (Revised), Issues Paper.

33. Ibid. footnote 31.

34. Ibid. footnote 31.

35. Ibid. footnote 31.

36. International Auditing and Assurance Standards Board (IAASB), 2023, International Standard on Auditing 330 (ISA 330) 'The Auditor's Responses to Assessed Risks', para 28, *Handbook of International Quality Management, Auditing, Review, Other Assurance, and Related Services Pronouncements*, 2022 edn, Volume I, International Federation of Accountants, New York.

37. International Auditing and Assurance Standards Board (IAASB), 2023, International Standard on Auditing 230 (ISA 230) 'Audit Documentation', para. 10, *Handbook of International Quality Management, Auditing, Review, Other Assurance, and Related Services Pronouncements*, 2022 edn, Volume I, International Federation of Accountants, New York.

38. Audits of organisations with a public interest (PIEs) are already required to report on fraud as of the audit year of 2021.

39. https://www.nba.nl/siteassets/themas/thema-fraude-en-witwassen/brochures/2022022-nba-brochure-continuiteits-en-fraudeparagraaf-engels.pdf

40. IAASB Main Agenda (December 2023), Agenda Item 2, Proposed ISA 240 (Revised), Issues Paper. It is recommended that you consult the latest publications from the IAASB for the most current and accurate information on these revisions.

41. IAASB Main Agenda (December 2023) Agenda Item 2, Prepared by: IAASB Staff Page 1 of 44 Proposed ISA 240 (Revised), The Auditor's Responsibilities Relating to Fraud in an Audit of Financial Statements – Issues Paper. https://www.iaasb.org/publications/proposed-international-standard-auditing-240-revised-auditor-s-responsibilities-relating-fraud-audit

42. United States Public Company Accounting Oversight Board (PCAOB) standards use the term illegal acts instead of non-compliance with law and regulation to refer to violations of laws or governmental regulations. According to PCAOB standard 2405 Illegal Acts by Clients are acts attributable to the entity whose financial statements are under audit or acts by management or employees acting on behalf of the entity. Illegal acts by clients do not include personal misconduct by the entity's personnel unrelated to their business activities. Generally, the further removed an illegal act is from the events and transactions ordinarily reflected in financial statements, the less likely the auditor is to become aware of the act or to recognize its possible illegality.

43. https://www.ft.com/content/f3e64e3e-b02b-11e8-99ca-68cf89602132.

44. A provision, known as the Foreign Extortion Prevention Act (FEPA), has been signed in December 2023 broadening the scope and reach of U.S. antibribery laws in a way policy supporters say will fight corruption, which the Biden administration has said is one of its top national security priorities. The FEPA complements the Foreign Corrupt Practices Act, a longstanding U.S. antibribery law that prohibits the paying of bribes to foreign officials to win or keep business. Under FEPA, violators would be fined no more than $250,000 or three times the value of the bribe; imprisoned for no more than 15 years, or both. The WSJ, January 3, 2024, Morning Risk Report: U.S. Prosecutors Can Charge Foreign Officials With Bribery Under New Provision, by David Smagalla.

45. https://www.transparency.org/en/

46. https://www.icij.org/investigations/bribery-division/bribery-division-what-is-odebrecht-who-is-involved/

47. https://www.justice.gov/sites/default/files/criminal-fraud/legacy/2012/11/14/fcpa-english.pdf or https://www.justice.gov/criminal/criminal-fraud/statutes-regulations

48. Source: US DOJ – A Resource Guide to the US Foreign Corrupt Practices Act, November 2012, p. 11.

49. Nederlandse Beroepsorganisatie van Accountants, Practice Note 1137 Corruption, procedures of the auditor, December 22, 2016, https://www.nba.nl/siteassets/wet--en-regelgev-

ing/nba-handreikingen/1137/nba-practice-note-1137-corruption-procedures-for-auditors. pdf

50. Council Directive 2015/849 on prevention of the use of the financial system for the purpose of money laundering or terrorist financing. https://eur-lex.europa.eu/legal-content/EN/TXT/PDF/?uri=CELEX:32015L0849&from=EN.

51. https://index.baselgovernance.org/ranking

52. https://www.aljazeera.com/news/2019/6/11/pakistan-ex-president-zardari-arrested-over-corruption-charges

53. https://www.dnb.nl/en/sector-information/open-book-supervision/laws-and-eu-regulations/anti-money-laundering-and-anti-terrorist-financing-act/introduction-wwft/

54. For reporting unusual transactions to the FIU there are several subjective indicators and one objective indicator. A subjective indicator is a transaction for which the auditor has reason to believe that it might be related to money laundering or terrorism financing. The objective indicator is a transaction to the sum of €10,000 or more, paid to or through the entity in cash, cheques payable to bearer, a prepaid instrument of payment (prepaid card) or similar means of payment. https://www.fiu-nederland.nl/en/meldergroep/4

55. See for example: A Lawyer's Guide to Detecting and Preventing Money Laundering A collaborative publication of the International Bar Association, the American Bar Association and the Council of Bars and Law Societies of Europe October 2014.

56. https://www.reuters.com/business/australia-casino-firm-star-be-fined-62-mln-following-inquiry-sydney-morning-2022-10-16/

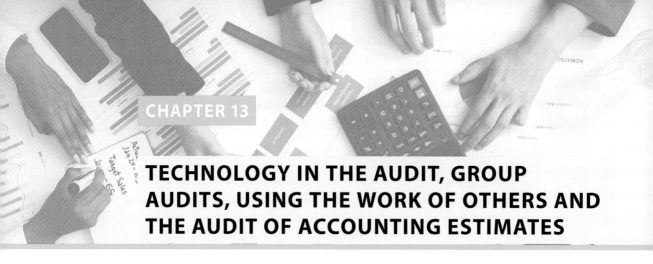

TECHNOLOGY IN THE AUDIT, GROUP AUDITS, USING THE WORK OF OTHERS AND THE AUDIT OF ACCOUNTING ESTIMATES

13.1 LEARNING OBJECTIVES

After studying this chapter, you should be able to:

1 Understand contribution of automated tools & techniques to audit quality.
2 Sketch challenges the auditor may face when using automated tools & techniques in the audit.
3 Explain what a group engagement partner for a Group Audit is responsible for.
4 Understand what a component is.
5 Comprehend the matters to be considered in obtaining an understanding of the consolidation process.
6 Learn examples of conditions or events that may indicate risks of material misstatement of the group financial statements.
7 Comprehend the relationship between the component auditor and the group engagement partner.
8 Determine the scope of work and reporting requirements of the component auditor.
9 Understand auditor's responsibilities using the work of experts.
10 Explain differences between using the work of external and management's experts.
11 Sketch audit considerations relating to an auditee using a service organization.
12 Discuss the key concepts in audit of estimates.

This chapter discusses four specific topics: technology in the audit, group audits, using the work of others and the audit of accounting estimates.

13.2 TECHNOLOGY IN THE AUDIT

The pervasiveness of technology in society has expanded tremendously in the last decade. Technology has established a central role in business processes. Whereas business models in the past were based on people driving business recording into IT systems, now new technology drives business models. As a result, technology is driving business, leading to a blue ocean of data collected from different sources and embedding algorithms, artificial intelligence and blockchain, and business models have been revolutionized with great speed. So now it is becoming more and more not people driving business but technology driving business affecting people.

Where computers take over procedures that can be done more effectively, efficiently, and more cheaply than with human intervention, people are still involved and have to navigate in this new world. This is also relevant for auditors. Therefore, we introduced automated tools & techniques, as the overarching notion of 'auditing with IT' reflecting the revised ISA 315 and highlighted the pervasiveness of the client's IT environment covering 'auditing of IT'. In the following section we bring automated tools & techniques into the broader perspective of auditing concepts, reflecting the IAASB initiatives, which started with the publication of 'Exploring the Growing Use of Technology in the Audit, with a Focus on Data Analytics'[1].

▶ EVOLVING HISTORY RELATED TO ELECTRONIC DATA

Where auditing originally used simple computer-assisted audit techniques, current process mining techniques and the use of big data are expected to significantly change the audit production process. Although these techniques are all based on seeking patterns in data, traditional Computer Assisted Audit Techniques (CAAT)[2] testing was limited to general ledger and sub-ledger only. With process mining, logistical patterns based on the operational processes are added, combining audit evidence from different internal sources under segregated duties. Adding big data outside the company may further enhance the corroborative evidence combining internal and external sources.

When the size of electronic data usage and the depth of data usage grow, it is expected the design of the audit approach will change accordingly. For example: testing a full population with data analytics may replace testing a sample. Or assessing the proper use of a three-way match between purchase order, goods receipt and purchase invoice on the full population of purchase invoices using process mining including embedded audit hypotheses for the three-way match, may replace a manual test of control repeated during the year.

▶ CONTRIBUTION TO AUDIT QUALITY

According to IAASB[3], the quality of a financial statement audit can be enhanced by the use of data analytics. IAASB specifically highlights the following:

> ▶ The application of professional scepticism and professional judgment is improved when the auditor has a robust understanding of the entity and its environment. In an increasingly complex and high-volume data environment, the use of technology and data analytics offers opportunities for the auditor to obtain a more effective

and robust understanding of the entity and its environment, enhancing the quality of the auditor's risk assessment and response.

▶ Enhancing the auditor's ability to gather audit evidence from the analysis of larger populations, including enabling better risk-based selections from those populations for further testing by the auditor.

▶ Broader and deeper auditor insight of the entity and its environment, which provides the entity being audited with additional valuable information to inform its own risk assessment and business operations.

As a result, auditors embracing technology in their audit may find new ways of enhancing audit quality, 'where the audit can be bigger, better, faster and stronger and having a broader audit scope with continuance assurance and assurance over non-financial information'[4].

▶ DATA ANALYTICS IN THE ISAS

The attention for the use of electronic data in the International Standards on Auditing (ISAs) had been quite limited until 2019[5]. ISA 330 includes a few references to CAATs as an alternative for audit evidence derived from other sources. For instance, CAATs can be useful to select sample transactions from key electronic files to sort transactions with specific characteristics, or to test an entire population instead of a sample[6]. Furthermore, CAATs are mentioned in combination with testing of controls[7].

▶ WAY FORWARD IN DATA ANALYTICS

Based on the publication 'Exploring the Growing Use of Technology in the Audit, with a Focus on Data Analytics'[8] and the responses to this paper, IAASB made some key statements related to data analytics:

▶ The ISAs do not prohibit, nor stimulate, the use of data analytics.[9] However, the examples in the standard's application material might demonstrate more advanced technological applications in auditing.

▶ Data analytics is not a new audit procedure but a technology-based technique of main audit procedures throughout the audit.

As a result, IAASB decided to embed automated tools & techniques in upcoming revisions of audit standards rather than raising an audit standard focusing on automated tools & techniques only. See illustration 13.1.

While the benefits are clear, there are also attention points that auditors need to be aware of in using data analytics. IAASB[10] refers to a number of examples (also see illustration 13.2):

▶ Overwhelming volumes of available data may reduce focus on audit effectiveness. Auditors need to have a clear understanding of the data they are analysing, particularly the relevance of the data to the audit. Analysis of data that is not relevant to the audit, is not well controlled, is unreliable, or the source of which (internal or external) is not well understood could have negative consequences for audit quality. While the analysis of relevant and reliable data provides valuable insights to the auditor, it will not provide everything the auditor needs to know.

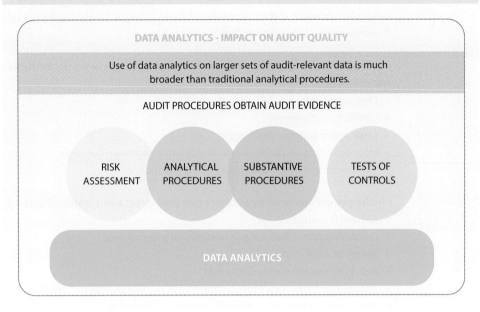

ILLUSTRATION 13.1

DATA ANALYTICS AS A MODERN TECHNIQUE FOR TRADITIONAL AUDIT PROCEDURES[11]

- ▶ Need to exercise professional judgement. Due to the need for the auditor to exercise professional judgments in relation to accounting and auditing, as well as issues related to data completeness and validity, being able to test 100% of a population does not imply that the auditor is able to provide something more than a reasonable assurance opinion or that the meaning of 'reasonable assurance' changes.

- ▶ There's more in life than data when auditing financial statements. In the financial statements of the majority of entities, there are significant amounts and disclosures that are accounting estimates (or that are based on accounting estimates) or that contain qualitative information. Professional judgement is necessary to assess the reasonableness of the entity's estimated value and disclosures of those items. While the data analytics technology of today is able to unlock valuable insights for the auditor to consider, its use in a financial statement audit will not replace the need for professional judgement and professional scepticism.

- ▶ Overconfidence. The risk of overconfidence when auditors lack a clear understanding of the uses and limitations of technology. For instance: reliability of the source data when testing a full population says something about accuracy, not automatically about the completeness or cut-off assertions.

▶ **ARTIFICIAL INTELLIGENCE (AI)**

As mentioned in section 1.7, Future of Auditing, the impact of Artificial Intelligence (AI) on financial statement auditors is transformative, introducing efficiencies,

ILLUSTRATION 13.2

CHALLENGES WHEN USING DATA ANALYTICS IN THE AUDIT[12]

Despite its optimism about the potential for enhancing audit quality, IAASB highlights challenges when using data analytics in the audit:

Challenges posed by environmental factors and circumstances in the business environment

▷ Data acquisition
▷ Conceptual challenges
▷ Legal and regulatory challenges
▷ How regulators and audit oversight authorities maintain oversight
▷ The investment in re-training and re-skilling auditors

Challenges encountered by auditors that may affect audit standard setting

▷ General IT Controls
▷ Considering the relevance and reliability of external data
▷ Nature of audit evidence
▷ Risk and response nature of the ISAs
▷ Nature of audit evidence responding to risk via data analytics
▷ Appropriate level of work effort for exceptions identified
▷ Risk measurement
▷ Applying documentation requirements when applying data analytics
▷ Importance of audit firms establishing quality control processes around tooling

improving accuracy, and influencing the overall audit process. AI represents the science of instructing programs and machines to execute tasks traditionally reliant on human intelligence. Within AI, two primary categories emerge: Narrow AI and General AI. Also termed weak AI, Narrow AI comprises systems tailored to excel in specific tasks, like chess or medical diagnoses. However, these capabilities remain confined to their designated tasks. Contrarily, General AI, or strong AI, embodies human-level intelligence, facilitating knowledge transfer across various domains. Presently, General AI remains largely theoretical, existing mostly within science fiction narratives.

APPLICATION IN AUDIT

In auditing, AI holds immense potential, particularly in refining audit scope and planning. By harnessing AI capabilities, auditors can expedite procedures responsive to actual risk, thereby enhancing efficiency and effectiveness. For instance, AI revolutionizes journal entry testing by enabling auditors to prioritize high-risk items early in the audit cycle. By incorporating AI algorithms and conducting full population testing, auditors can conduct journal entry testing during initial risk assessments. Consequently, auditors gain the ability to scrutinize high-risk transactions promptly, potentially reassessing significant balances or transaction classes to tailor procedures more adeptly to residual risk.

ADVANCED AI APPLICATIONS

The most promising applications of AI extend to various domains, including:

- ▶ Computer Vision: Employed in self-driving cars, drones, retail, agriculture, and healthcare, computer vision facilitates pattern detection and analysis.
- ▶ Natural Language Processing (NLP): Ubiquitous in daily interactions, NLP aids in understanding and generating spoken or written language, enhancing communication and data analysis.
- ▶ Natural Language Generation (NLG): NLG transforms visualized data into coherent narratives, facilitating data comprehension and report generation.
- ▶ Analyzing Big Data: With the proliferation of data from IoT, social media, and cloud computing, organizations harness AI for descriptive, diagnostic, predictive, and prescriptive analytics, empowering decision-making processes and innovation.

AI's integration in audit processes enables auditors to navigate complex datasets effectively, refine risk assessment, and adapt audit procedures to evolving risks. Thus, AI emerges as a transformative tool enhancing audit quality and responsiveness to dynamic business environments[13].

ADVANTAGES OF AI IN FINANCIAL STATEMENT AUDITING:

- ▶ Enhanced Efficiency: AI automates repetitive tasks, enabling auditors to focus on high-value activities, thereby enhancing overall audit efficiency.
- ▶ Improved Accuracy: AI algorithms can analyze large datasets with precision, reducing the likelihood of errors compared to manual processes.
- ▶ Enhanced Risk Assessment: AI aids in identifying high-risk areas and transactions promptly, allowing auditors to allocate resources effectively and prioritize audit procedures accordingly.
- ▶ Timely Insights: AI facilitates real-time data analysis, enabling auditors to obtain insights promptly and make informed decisions throughout the audit process.

DISADVANTAGES OF AI IN FINANCIAL STATEMENT AUDITING:

- ▶ Complexity: Implementing AI systems requires specialized expertise and resources, leading to increased complexity in audit processes and potential challenges in integration.
- ▶ Cost: Developing and maintaining AI infrastructure can be costly, especially for smaller audit firms, potentially limiting access to advanced technologies.
- ▶ Data Security Concerns: AI relies heavily on data, raising concerns about data privacy and security, particularly regarding sensitive financial information.
- ▶ Overreliance on Technology: Excessive reliance on AI tools may lead to complacency among auditors, potentially overlooking nuanced issues that require human judgment.

In summary, while AI offers significant benefits in terms of efficiency, accuracy, and risk assessment in financial statement auditing, it also presents challenges related to complexity, cost, data security, and the potential for overreliance on technology. Successful implementation of AI in auditing requires careful consideration of these factors to maximize its effectiveness and mitigate risks.

As notified in illustration 13.2, it's not always easy to apply innovative solutions in the audit. Whereas illustration 13.2 focuses on practical and conceptual issues when applying data analytics, in essence these issues may also be applicable when applying AI in the audit.

13.3 GROUP AUDITS

In the context of accounting, a component is an entity or business activity whose financial information is included in the group financial statements. ISA 600 (revised)[14] and PCAOB Audit Standard 1205 deal with special considerations that apply to group audits, in particular those that involve components[15]. IAASB summarized how the new standard reflects changes based on key public interest issues. See illustration 13.3.

ILLUSTRATION 13.3

KEY PUBLIC INTEREST ISSUES[16] IN ISA 600 (REVISED)

ISA 600 (Revised) enhancements (amongst others):
- ▶ Significant component removed.
- ▶ Reflecting the various ways business can be organised, including share service centres, branches and divisions and non-controlled entities.
- ▶ Reflecting risk assessment procedures in ISA 315 starting with risk assessment procedures at consolidated level with a deep dive to components.
- ▶ Adaptability and scalability by focusing on identifying, assessing, and responding to risks of material misstatement.
- ▶ Encouraging proactive management of quality throughout the group audit engagement, including the dynamics between group auditor and component auditor.
- ▶ Fostering an appropriately independent and challenging sceptical mindset of the auditor.
- ▶ Reinforcing the need for robust communication and interactions during the audit.

ISA 600 (Revised) replaces the concept of a 'significant component' with a focus on assessing risks of material misstatement at the assertion level in group financial statements linked to various components. It broadens the definition of 'component' to include branches, divisions, and other organizational units, offering greater flexibility. This change eliminates the requirement for full audits on previously designated significant components, directing auditors to concentrate on risks at the assertion level. Auditors now adapt their approach to testing by evaluating balances across components and choosing the appropriate level – group, sub-group, or individual component – based on the specific risks and characteristics of significant accounts. A component could be a head office, parent, division, location, business unit, branch, subsidiary, activity, shared service centre, joint venture, associated company, or other entity whose financial information is included in the group financial statements. Determining what is a component will require professional judgement and is guided by: the structure of the group, the flow of the financial information and the audit approach.

A component auditor is the auditor who, at the request of the group engagement team, performs work on the financial information related to a component. The component auditor is part of the engagement team[17,18].

The revised ISA mirrors ISA 315 (see chapters 6 and 7) as it relates to identifying and assessing the risks of material misstatement of the group financial statements, which in turn drives an approach to scoping a group audit that is focused on responding to such group risk assessment.

The group audit team focuses on determining in-scope components based on the relationship of the assessed risks of material misstatement in the group financial statements to the financial information of the components. Based on an understanding of the group, its components, and their environment the group engagement team identifies components that may entail substantial risks of material misstatement in the group's financial statements. The scope of work will be targeted to the significant accounts and relevant assertions for the group financial statements. The revised ISA emphasizes that the determination of group scoping needs to be reflective of the assessed risks of material misstatements of the group financial statements. The size of the component is not an upfront consideration, therefore there is no distinction between significant and non-significant components (which was defined in the previous ISA 600 applicable until 2023).

The group engagement partner[19] is responsible for the direction, supervision and performance of the audit engagement and the auditor's report. Ordinarily, she takes sole responsibility for the audit opinion on the group financial statements and for compliance with the requirements of this ISA and therefore should be sufficiently and appropriately involved throughout the group audit engagement. In the case where the group auditor decides to take sole responsibility for the audit opinion on the group financial statements, she should not refer to the other auditor in the auditor's report on the group financial statements[20].

When she considers whether she can act as group auditor, there are two scenarios. In one scenario, she might have completed almost all of the audit work already, with only a minor portion remaining. Alternatively, significant parts of the audit could have been carried out by other auditors. In evaluating whether the group auditor will be able to be sufficiently and appropriately involved in the work of the component auditor, she may obtain an understanding of whether the component auditor is subject to any restrictions that limit communication with the group auditor, including with regard to sharing audit documentation with the group auditor. The group auditor may also obtain an understanding about whether audit evidence related to components located in a different jurisdiction may be in a different language and may need to be translated for use by the group auditor.[21]

She must determine whether sufficient appropriate audit evidence can reasonably be expected to be obtained about the consolidation process and the financial information of the components. To do this, the group team shall obtain an understanding of the group, its components and their environments to identify components that are likely to be significant and implement audit procedures to address potential material misstatements in the group financial statements. This involves using professional judgment to select specific components for audit work based on factors such as the group's characteristics, its operating environment, and practical considerations like the centralization of audit procedures, shared service centres, and common information systems and internal controls.

The group engagement partner is responsible for directing, supervising, and reviewing the work of component auditors. This involves focusing on areas with higher assessed risks or significant risks in the group financial statements and areas requiring substantial judgment.

She must evaluate the component auditors to determine if the group engagement team should also be involved in their work to obtain sufficient audit evidence.

Furthermore, it is essential for her to establish communication with component auditors, clearly outlining their responsibilities, ethical requirements, expectations, and emphasizing the importance of timely communication throughout the entire group audit process.

As in any audit, the engagement team should demonstrate professional scepticism through their actions and communications. This involves highlighting the importance of every team member maintaining professional scepticism and taking specific steps to address any impediments that could hinder its proper exercise.

In the case of a new engagement, the group's understanding to be audited may be obtained from group management and from the previous auditor, component management or component auditors. Important matters to be considered are[22]:

> ▶ The structure of the group (consolidated company).
> ▶ Significance of the (business activities) of the components.
> ▶ The use of service organizations.
> ▶ A description of group-wide controls.
> ▶ The complexity of the consolidation process.
> ▶ Component auditors not being part of the network of the group auditor.
> ▶ Having unrestricted access to relevant persons and information.
> ▶ Ability to perform work on the financial information of the components.

When dealing with a continuing engagement the focus will be on changes in the above matters.

If the group engagement partner determines that group management cannot provide the audit team with access to information or unrestricted access to individuals within the group due to external restrictions, she must consider the potential impact on the group audit. If the limitations are imposed by group management and it becomes impossible to obtain sufficient and appropriate audit evidence, leading to a potential disclaimer of opinion on the group financial statements, she has two options:

> ▶ for an initial engagement, not accept the engagement or, for a recurring engagement, withdraw from it if withdrawal is permitted by applicable law; or
> ▶ if declining the engagement or withdrawal is not possible, and after performing the audit to the extent feasible, issue a disclaimer of opinion on the group financial statements[23].

▶ UNDERSTANDING THE GROUP BEING AUDITED, ITS COMPONENTS AND THEIR ENVIRONMENTS

To be able to identify and assess the RMMs the group engagement team must enhance its understanding of the group auditee, its components and their environments, including group-wide controls obtained during the acceptance or continuance stage. The group team must also understand the consolidation process, including the instructions issued by group management to components.

Matters to be considered are:

- Industry, regulatory and other external factors.
- The applicable financial reporting framework.
- The nature of the entity.
- Objectives and strategies and related business risks.
- Measurement and review of the entity's performance.
- Instructions issued by group management to components: accounting manual, reporting package and a timetable.
- Identification and assessment of risks of fraud: the key members of the engagement team (may include component auditors) are required to discuss the susceptibility of an entity to material misstatement of the financial statements due to fraud or error, specifically emphasizing the risks due to fraud.

Information instrumental in recognizing RMM in the group's financial statements due to fraud may encompass the following:

- Evaluation by group management of the potential risks leading to material misstatement in the group financial statements as a result of fraud.
- Scrutiny of group management's processes for identifying and addressing fraud risks within the group, encompassing any specific fraud risks identified by group management. This evaluation extends to account balances, classes of transactions, or disclosures where a risk of fraud is deemed likely.
- Determination of specific components that may be susceptible to fraud risks.
- Assessment of how those overseeing the governance of the group oversee group management's processes for recognizing and managing fraud risks within the group. This includes an examination of the controls implemented by group management to alleviate these risks.
- Review of responses from those overseeing the governance of the group, group management, relevant individuals in the internal audit function, and, if deemed appropriate, component management, component auditors, and others. This is in response to inquiries from the group engagement team about any knowledge they may have regarding actual, suspected, or alleged fraud impacting a component or the group.

The previous matters to be considered possess a more generic character. Matters specific to a group, including the consolidation process, are:

- Group-wide controls: regular meetings between group management and component management, monitoring of components' operations and their financial results, group management's risk assessment process, intra- group transactions, process for financial information received from components, control activities within the IT environment, internal audit, code of conduct and arrangements for assigning authority and responsibility to component management.
- Consolidation process: matters relating to the applicable reporting framework, matters relating to the consolidation process and matters relating to consolidation adjustments.

The group engagement team obtains an understanding that is sufficient to confirm or revise its initial identification of components relevant for the group audit, and next to assess the risks of material misstatement of the group financial statements. In applying ISA 315 (chapter 6), the audit team is required to discuss the application of the applicable financial reporting framework and the susceptibility of the group's financial statements to material misstatements. These discussions may include the component auditors and provide an excellent opportunity to share knowledge of the components and the business risks of the group and its components. External and internal pressures that may create an incentive, opportunity, or indicate a culture for fraud are assessed including the risk that management may override controls. Furthermore, they will consider how differences in accounting policies are identified and adjusted, discuss identified fraud and share information that may indicate non-compliance with laws or regulations.

The discussion within the engagement team offers an opportunity to:

▶ Share knowledge about the components and their operational environments, particularly highlighting centralized activities.

▶ Exchange information on business risks, assessing how inherent risk factors might impact the susceptibility to misstatements in transactions, account balances, and disclosures.

▶ Exchange ideas on potential areas of susceptibility to material misstatement in the group financial statements due to fraud or error, with particular emphasis on fraud considerations as required by ISA 240.

▶ Identify management policies that may be biased or designed to manipulate earnings for potential fraudulent financial reporting.

▶ Consider both external and internal factors influencing the group that might create incentives or pressures for fraud, provide opportunities for fraud, or indicate a culture conducive to fraud.

▶ Evaluate the risk of management overriding controls.

▶ Discuss any identified fraud or information indicating the existence of fraud.

▶ Identify RMMs in components where there may be obstacles to exercising professional scepticism.

▶ Evaluate the consistency of accounting policies across components for group financial statements and address differences as required by the applicable financial reporting framework.

▶ Share information about risks of material misstatement in a component that may be relevant to other components.

▶ Share information indicating potential non-compliance with national laws or regulations, such as bribery payments and improper transfer pricing practices.

▶ Discuss events or conditions, identified by group or component management or the engagement team, that could raise significant doubts about the group's ability to continue as a going concern.

▶ Discuss related party relationships or transactions identified by management, and any other related parties known to the engagement team.

Examples of conditions or events that may indicate RMMs of the group financial statements are:

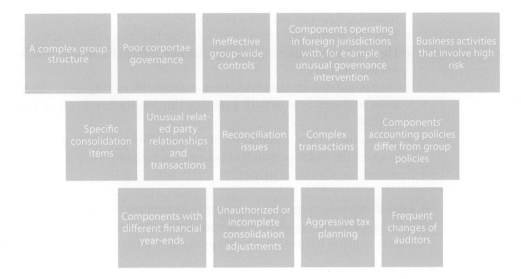

▶ **UNDERSTANDING THE COMPONENT AUDITOR**

If the group engagement team plans to request a component auditor to perform work on the financial information of a component, the group engagement team must obtain an understanding of the following[24]:

> ▶ Determine that component auditors have the appropriate competence and capabilities, including sufficient time, to perform the assigned procedures at the component. If a component auditor does not meet the independence requirements or the group engagement team has serious concerns about the component auditor's ethical requirements, the group engagement team shall obtain sufficient appropriate evidence without the component's auditor involvement.
> ▶ Results of the monitoring and remediation process of external inspections related to the component auditor.

In addition, the group engagement team considers factors such as:

> ▶ The significance of the component, its materiality and the identified significant risks.
> ▶ The level of work to be requested of the component auditor.
> ▶ The complexity of the component.
> ▶ Whether the component auditor is part of the network of the group auditor.

The group engagement team can explore various methods to learn about the component auditor, particularly during the initial year of collaboration. Examples include:

> ▶ They can review the results of quality management monitoring activities, including those carried out by the network, if both the group engagement team and the component auditor belong to a firm or network with common monitoring policies.

▶ They may visit the component auditor to discuss specific matters about, for example, communications between regulatory authorities and entities or business units related to financial reporting matters.

▶ They can ask the component auditor to confirm these matters in writing.

▶ The team may request the component auditor to fill out questionnaires about relevant matters.

▶ They might discuss the component auditor with colleagues in the group engagement partner's firm or with a reliable third-party familiar with the component auditor.

▶ Alternatively, they can obtain confirmations from the professional body or bodies to which the component auditor belongs, the authorities that license the component auditor, or other third parties.

In subsequent years, the group engagement team's understanding of the component auditor may be based on their past experience working together. They may ask the component auditor to confirm if there have been any changes related to the matters listed above.

▶ **MATERIALITY**

In the context of a group audit materiality levels are established for both the group financial statements as a whole and for the financial information of the components. The group engagement team shall determine the following:

▶ Materiality for the group financial statements when establishing the overall group audit strategy.

▶ The materiality level (amount) to be applied when there are particular transactions, balances or disclosures for which misstatements of any larger amounts could be expected to influence the economic decisions of users[25].

▶ The performance materiality: to reduce to an appropriate level the probability that the total of uncorrected and undetected misstatements in the financial information exceeds overall materiality.

▶ The threshold above which misstatements cannot be regarded as clearly trivial to the group financial statements.

Specifically related to the components: the group engagement team shall determine the following[26]:

▶ Component performance materiality, which shall be lower than group performance materiality.

▶ The threshold above which misstatements identified in the component financial information are to be communicated to the group auditor.

For those components where component auditors perform audit or review work for the group audit, the group engagement team determines the overall materiality, the performance materiality and the amount applicable to group reporting. The group auditor communicates the levels to the component auditors or confirms approval of the levels to the component auditors. Professional judgement is to be applied in establishing the overall materiality for a component.

Component materiality need not be an arithmetical portion of the materiality for the group financial statements as a whole and consequently the aggregate of component materiality for the different components may exceed the materiality for the group financial statements as a whole[27]. Component performance materiality needs to be established at an amount lower than component overall materiality. Research indicates that in practice a haircut between 25 per cent to 50 per cent is to be applied[28].

RESPONDING TO ASSESSED RISKS

The auditor must develop and implement responses to address identified risks of material misstatement in the financial statements. The group engagement team is responsible for determining the tasks to be carried out by either the group- or component auditors on the financial information of the components. Also, the group engagement team is tasked with deciding the extent of its involvement in the component auditors' work.

When a component auditor conducts audit procedures, the group engagement team must participate in the risk assessment. The extent of their involvement depends on their understanding of the component auditor but should, at a minimum, include:

- Discussing significant business activities of the component with the component auditor or management.
- Assessing the component's vulnerability to material misstatements in financial information due to fraud or error with the component auditor.
- Reviewing the component auditor's documentation regarding significant risks of material misstatement in the group financial statements. This documentation may be in the form of a memorandum reflecting the component auditor's conclusions on these risks.

If significant risks of material misstatement in the group financial statements are identified in a component audited by a component auditor, the group engagement team will assess the need for additional audit procedures. The decision to be involved in these procedures will be based on the group engagement team's understanding of the component auditor.

If the consolidation process or examination of component financial information relies on the assumption of effective group-wide controls or if substantive procedures alone are insufficient for obtaining appropriate audit evidence at the assertion level, the group engagement team must either conduct or request the component auditor to conduct tests to verify the operating effectiveness of those controls.

DETERMINING THE TYPE OF WORK WITH RESPECT TO COMPONENTS

As ISA 600 (Revised) is scalable, there is no one-size-fits-all approach for allocating work to component auditors as the overall risk assessment at group level drives the work to be done on specific components. In general, there are some alternatives.

- An audit of the financial information of the component using component materiality (full scope).
- An audit of one or more account balances, classes of transactions or disclosures (specific scope).
- Specified procedures relating to likely significant risks of material misstatement of the group financial statements.

▶ **CONSOLIDATION**

The group auditor is required to obtain an understanding of the consolidation process, including the instructions issued by group management to components[29]. The consolidation process includes: the recognition, measurement, presentation and disclosure of the financial information of the components in the group financial statements by way of consolidation, proportionate consolidation, or the equity or cost methods of accounting. Also, part of the consolidation process is the aggregation in combined financial statements of the financial information of components that have no parent but are under common control.

The group engagement team obtains an understanding of group-wide controls and the consolidation process, including the instructions issued by group management to components. If group-wide controls are not operating effectively, or if substantive procedures alone cannot provide sufficient appropriate audit evidence, the group engagement team or the component auditor tests the operating effectiveness of the group-wide controls. The group engagement team must evaluate the appropriateness, completeness and accuracy of consolidation adjustments and reclassifications.

If the financial information of a component has not been prepared in accordance with the same accounting policies applied to the group financial statements, the group engagement team evaluates whether the financial information of the component has been appropriately adjusted to the accounting policies of the group entity. The group engagement team also determines if the financial information identified in the component auditor's communication is the same as in the group financial statements.

▶ **GROUP AUDITOR AND COMPONENT AUDITOR COMMUNICATION**

The group engagement team sets out the work to be performed, the use to be made of that work and the form and content of the communication with the group engagement team. See Appendix 13.1 provides an example of the content of group audit instructions.

Based on the information received the group auditor must evaluate the component auditor's communication and adequacy of their work. The group engagement team discusses significant matters arising from that evaluation with the component auditor, component management or group management. They determine whether it is necessary to review other relevant parts of component auditor's documentation. If the group engagement team concludes that the work of the component auditor is insufficient, they determine additional procedures to be performed and whether they are to be performed by the component auditor or by the group engagement team.

The group engagement team must evaluate whether sufficient appropriate evidence has been obtained from the audit procedures performed on the consolidation process and the work performed by the group engagement team and the component auditors as a whole on which to base the group audit opinion. The group engagement partner must evaluate the effect on the group audit opinion of any uncorrected misstatements and any instances where there has been an inability to obtain sufficient appropriate audit evidence.

The communication by the component auditor must include the information shown in illustration 13.4.

ILLUSTRATION 13.4

INFORMATION REQUIRED IN GROUP AUDITOR COMMUNICATION TO THE COMPONENT AUDITOR

The group auditor is required to seek communication from the component auditor regarding various aspects relevant to the group audit conclusion. This communication should cover:

▶ Identification of the financial information subjected to the component auditor's audit procedures;

▶ Confirmation of the completion of requested work by the component auditor;

▶ Adherence to ethical requirements, including independence, related to the group audit engagement;

▶ Disclosure of instances of non-compliance with laws or regulations;

▶ Reporting both corrected and uncorrected misstatements in the component financial information, exceeding the threshold communicated by the group auditor;

▶ Indications of potential management bias;

▶ Description of any identified deficiencies in the internal control system during audit procedures;

▶ Reporting on fraud or suspected fraud involving component management, employees with significant roles in the component's internal control system, or others leading to material misstatements in the component financial information;

▶ Disclosure of other significant matters communicated or expected to be communicated to component management or governance bodies;

▶ Any additional matters pertinent to the group audit, or as deemed appropriate by the component auditor, including exceptions noted in written representations requested from component management;

▶ Presentation of the component auditor's overall findings or conclusions.

▶ **GROUP AUDITOR COMMUNICATION WITH MANAGEMENT AND THOSE CHARGED WITH GOVERNANCE**

Another important element in a group audit is the communication with group management and those charged with governance. The group engagement team shall determine which internal control deficiencies will be communicated with group management. Fraud issues must be communicated on a timely basis to the appropriate level of group management.

The following matters must be communicated by the group engagement team to those charged with governance of the group[30]:

▶ An overview of the work to be performed at the components of the group and the nature of the group auditor's planned involvement in the work to be performed by component auditors.

▶ Instances when the group auditor's review of the work of a component auditor gave rise to a concern about the quality of that component auditor's work, and how the group auditor addressed the concern.

▶ Any limitations on the scope of the group audit, for example, significant matters related to restrictions on access to people or information.

▶ Fraud or suspected fraud involving group management, component management, employees who have significant roles in the group's system of internal control or others when the fraud resulted in a material misstatement of the group financial statements.

► SUBSEQUENT EVENTS

Subsequent events are events occurring between the date of the financial statements and the date of the auditor's report, and facts that become known to the auditor after the date of the auditor's report. In performing subsequent event procedures, the component auditor needs to gain an understanding of the controls and procedures component management and group management have in place that affect the component. Normally the group engagement team will ask the component auditor to perform the relevant procedures. The aforementioned procedures are only required when performing an audit of the financial information of a component. For all other types of work, the component auditor must inform the group engagement team if they become aware of any events.

► GROUP AUDIT REPORTING

The group engagement partner must evaluate the effect on the group audit opinion of any uncorrected misstatements and inability to obtain sufficient appropriate audit evidence. This evaluation allows her to determine whether the group financial statements as a whole are materially misstated.

When the group auditor is unable to obtain sufficient appropriate audit evidence due to restrictions on access to information or people, the group auditor may:

▶ Communicate the restrictions to the group auditor's firm to assist the group auditor in determining an appropriate course of action. For example, the group auditor's firm may communicate with group management about the restrictions and encourage group management to communicate with regulators. This may be useful when restrictions affect multiple audits in the jurisdiction or by the same firm, for example, because of war, civil unrest or outbreaks of disease in a major economy.

▶ Be required by law or regulation to communicate with regulators, listing authorities, or others, about the restrictions.

Restrictions on access may have other implications for the group audit. For example, if restrictions are imposed by group management, the group auditor may need to reconsider the reliability of group management's responses to the group auditor's inquiries and whether the restrictions call into question group management's integrity.

When the group audit opinion is modified because the group engagement team was unable to obtain sufficient appropriate audit evidence in relation to the financial information of one or more components, the auditor's report on the group financial statements describes the reasons for that without referring to the component auditor (unless such a reference is necessary for an adequate explanation of the circumstances)[31].

Where access to information is restricted by circumstances, the group engagement team may still be able to obtain sufficient appropriate audit evidence; however, this becomes less likely as the component's significance increases. Although the group engagement team may in this situation be able to obtain sufficient appropriate audit evidence, the reason for the restriction may affect the group audit opinion. For example, it may affect the reliability of group management's responses and representations to the group engagement team. If the component is significant, the group engagement team will not comply with the requirements of ISA 600. Further guidance about the effect on the auditor's opinion is available in ISA 705[32].

▶ DOCUMENTATION

In addition to documentation required by ISA 230[33] and other ISAs, the group engagement team shall include in the audit documentation the following matters[34]:

(a) Significant matters related to restrictions on access to people or information within the group that were considered before deciding to accept or continue the engagement, or that arose subsequent to acceptance or continuance, and how such matters were addressed.

(b) The basis for the group auditor's determination of components for purposes of planning and performing the group audit.

(c) The basis for the determination of component performance materiality, and the threshold for communicating misstatements in the component financial information to the group auditor.

(d) The basis for the group auditor's determination that component auditors have the appropriate competence and capabilities, including sufficient time, to perform the assigned audit procedures at the components.

(e) Key elements of the understanding of the group's system of internal control.

(f) The nature, timing and extent of the group auditor's direction and supervision of component auditors and the review of their work, including, as applicable, the group auditor's review of additional component auditor audit documentation.

(g) Matters related to communications with component auditors, including:
  - ▶ Matters, if any, related to fraud, related parties or going concern communicated
  - ▶ Matters relevant to the group auditor's conclusion with regard to the group audit, in accordance with paragraph 45, including how the group auditor has addressed significant matters discussed with component auditors, component management or group management.

(h) The group auditor's evaluation of, and response to, findings or conclusions of the component auditors about matters that could have a material effect on the group financial statements.

Examples of important issues in the group audit to be documented encompass:
- ▶ Addressing significant issues related to access restrictions within the group, assessed before accepting or continuing the engagement, and detailing how such issues were handled.
- ▶ Outlining the rationale behind the group auditor's selection of components for planning and executing the group audit.
- ▶ Explaining the basis for determining component performance materiality and the threshold for reporting misstatements in component financial information to the group auditor.
- ▶ Describing the basis for the group auditor's assessment that component auditors possess the necessary competence, capabilities, and time for assigned audit procedures.
- ▶ Highlighting key elements of understanding the group's internal control system.

▶ Summarizing the nature, timing, and extent of the group auditor's guidance, supervision of component auditors, and the review of their work, including any additional review of component auditor audit documentation.

▶ Addressing matters in communication with component auditors, including those related to fraud, related parties, or going concern. Additionally, covering matters relevant to the group auditor's conclusion on the group audit, including the handling of significant issues discussed with component auditors, component management, or group management.

▶ Discussing the group auditor's evaluation and response to findings or conclusions by component auditors regarding matters that could materially affect the group financial statement.

> Disposition of matters raised by the component auditor(s), materiality levels used for group purposes and the evaluation of the adequacy of the component auditor's work are part of the documentation.

13.4 USING THE WORK OF OTHERS AND CONSIDERING CLIENT USE OF SERVICE ORGANISATIONS

In the course of an audit engagement an auditor may rely on the work of the company's internal auditors, and in some cases, they may hire an expert external to their firm to provide expertise[35] necessary for the audit but not available at the audit firm. The auditor may also find it necessary to review the work of any outsourced services which may impact the financial statement.

▶ USING THE WORK OF AN AUDITOR'S EXPERT

The auditor's education and experience enable her to be knowledgeable about business matters in general, but she is not expected to have the expertise of a person trained for another profession such as an actuary or engineer. If the auditor requires special expertise, the auditor should consider hiring an expert to assist in gathering the necessary evidence[36]. ISA 620.46 defines an expert as an 'individual or organization possessing expertise in a field other than accounting or auditing, whose work in that field is used by the auditor to assist the auditor in obtaining sufficient appropriate audit evidence.' Situations where an auditor might use an expert are valuations of certain types of assets (land and building, complex financial instruments, works of art, precious stones, intangibles etc.), determination of physical condition of assets (e.g. estimation of oil and gas reserves), actuarial valuation, value of contracts in progress, specific IT expertise (e.g. in the audit of a telecommunications company), and legal opinions.

Further, ISA 620 only refers to experts outside the field of accounting and auditing. The standard clarifies that tax and IT knowledge are expected to be within the field of accounting and auditing. As a result, the use of IT auditors in the audit is to be considered as a member of the audit engagement team which is covered in ISA 220 (Quality Control for an Audit of Financial Statements). It is arguable that specialized tax and IT knowledge such as international transfer pricing and IT security respectively is outside the field of accounting and auditing. As a result, the auditor may use them in line with ISA 620[37].

AHOLD – RAPID GLOBAL EXPANSION AND THE GROUP AUDIT

Concept	Difficulties of a group audit.

Story

In 2003, Koninklijke Ahold N.V. (Royal Ahold), a 115-year-old Netherlands company, had 9,000 stores in 27 countries that served 40 million customers a week, and owned or had interest in about 9,000 supermarkets as well as discount and speciality stores in some 25 countries in Asia, Europe and the Americas. In February 2003, Ahold revealed improperly booked profit of approximately $1.12 billion (Sams, 2003).

Ahold's auditor, Deloitte & Touche (DT), discovered the company's accounting irregularities as part of its 2002 year-end audit. As a result of the discovery, Ahold had to restate its audited financial statements for 2001 which had been given an unqualified audit opinion (Weil, 2003). Speaking at the company's annual meeting, Henry de Ruiter, in his last official engagement as Ahold chairman, said that Ahold's supervisory and executive boards felt responsible for the 'horrendous' events. He added that Ahold would not replace DT, saying there was no evidence the auditor knew of the fraud prior to its discovery (Bickerton and Watkins, 2003).

Irregularities involving improper booking of vendor allowances were discovered in US subsidiaries US Foodservice and Tops Markets. The company's Disco subsidiary engaged transactions that were illegal and improperly accounted for. Unauthorized side letters (supplements to contracts) created errors of consolidation regarding joint ventures in Sweden/Norway, Brazil, Guatemala and Argentina (Mirabella, 2003).

Ahold's executive and supervisory boards ordered an investigation by a forensic team from PricewaterhouseCoopers (PwC). For the period 1 April 2000 (the effective date of Ahold's acquisition of US Foodservice) to 28 December 2002, (the end of Ahold's 2002 fiscal year), PwC has identified total overstatements of pre-tax earnings of approximately $880 million. Of this amount, approximately $110 million relates to fiscal year 2000, approximately $260 million relates to fiscal year 2001, and approximately $510 million relates to fiscal year 2002. In addition, PwC identified approximately $90 million of adjustments required to be made to the opening balances for US Foodservice at the date of its acquisition. This consists of a reclassification of such amount from current assets to goodwill primarily as a result of required write-offs of vendor receivables (NACS, 2003).

The forensic accounting work at Albert Heijn, Stop & Shop, Santa Isabel in Chile, Ahold's operations in Poland and the Czech Republic, and the ICA Ahold Scandinavian joint venture found no evidence of financial fraud (NACS, 2003).

The main problem in the US was improper booking of vendor allowances. The allowances are a broad industry term that covers everything from vendor payments for prime shelf space in a store, to rebates awarded to retailers who hit sales targets for suppliers' products. These payments were allegedly booked too high and were, in some cases, booked without the manufacturers' permission. Subsidiaries were also faulted for booking vendor allowances as revenue, when, in most cases, they should be booked as a reduction in the cost of sales. Ahold says that Tops was principally to blame for $29 million in overstated income. Another of its US subsidiaries, US Foodservice, overstated its pre-tax income by $880 million over three years (Glenn, 2003).

Cees van der Hoeven, Ahold's Chief Executive, took the retailer on a worldwide buying spree, from Chile to Thailand, running up net debts of around €13 billion. Ahold began its buying spree in 1976 when it acquired a Spanish supermarket and the Bi-Lo chain in the American South. In 1996, it bought Stop & Shop for $2.9 billion and added dozens of chains in Latin America, Europe and Asia. It tried to buy Pathmark Stores in 1999, but that deal was blocked by the US Federal Trade Commission. Ahold subsequently turned to food service for growth, acquiring US Foodservice for $3.6 billion in 2000 (Knowledge@Wharton, 2004). Also, in 2000, Ahold acquired PYAO Monarch for $2.57 billion and paid $75 million for Peapod.

Ahold's broad strategy was to buy regional supermarket retailers and gain economies of scale and savings through consolidation of back-office and buying operations. Other chains sought to do the same thing, modelling themselves on the successful expansion of chain drugstores. However, grocery stores are more complicated than drugstores and depend to a greater extent on regional suppliers and marketing (Knowledge@Wharton, 2004).

Discussion Questions	▷ Discuss ways that a buying spree like that of Mr Van der Hoeven can create problems for the group auditor. ▷ What pressures may be applied to the management of newly acquired divisions that would encourage misstatement of income? ▷ What special audit procedures should be applied to an audit of an acquisitive company?

References	Bickerton, I. and Watkins, M., 2003, 'Ahold Says Up to 10 people to Blame for Fraud', *Financial Times*, London, 27 November, p.15. Glynn, M., 2003, 'Vendor Rebates to Retailers Are Under the Microscope', *Buffalo News*, Buffalo, NY, 1 June, p. B.9. Knowledge@Wharton, 2004, 'Royal Ahold's Royal Hold Up', http://knowledge.wharton.upenn.edu/, 12 March. Mirabella, L., 2003, 'Dutch Grocery Chain Raided', *Cincinnati Post*, Cincinnati, Ohio, 8 July, p. C.9.0. NACS 2003, 'Ahold Releases Results of US Foodservice Forensic Accounting Investigation', *Daily News*, National Association of Convince Stores, 9 May. Sams, R., 2003, 'Ahold Accounting Probes Reveal More Irregularities', *Washington Business Journal*, 1 July. Weil, J., 2003, 'Deloitte's Work for Ahold Raises Questions on Auditing', *Wall Street Journal* (Eastern edition), New York, NY, 25 February, p. A.10.

In using an expert, the objective of the auditor is to determine whether to use the auditor's expert in the first place and, if using the expert's work, to determine whether that work is adequate. The auditor must evaluate whether the auditor's expert has the necessary competence, capabilities and objectivity. A broad range of circumstances may threaten objectivity, for example, self-interest threats, advocacy threats, familiarity threats, self-review threats, and intimidation threats. Safeguards may eliminate or reduce such threats (see chapter 3). Interests and relationships that it may be relevant to discuss with the auditor's expert include financial interests, business and personal relationships.

Evaluating the work of the auditor's expert means reviewing the relevance and reasonableness of their findings and its consistency with other audit evidence. If that expert's work involves use of significant assumptions and methods, the auditor must evaluate the reasonableness of that approach.

▷ AUDITOR'S EXPERT AGREEMENT AND REPORTS

The auditor must agree with the auditor's expert, in writing when appropriate, on the following matters: the nature, scope and objectives of that expert's work; the respective roles and responsibilities of the auditor and that expert; the nature, timing and extent of communication between the auditor and that expert. The auditor and expert must also agree on the form of any report to be provided by that expert and the need for the auditor's expert to observe confidentiality requirements.

As explained in section 11.6, the type of opinion determines if an auditor may or may not refer to the work of an auditor's expert. When issuing an unqualified (unmodified) auditor's report, the auditor should ordinarily not refer to the work of the expert. Such a reference might be misunderstood to be a qualification of the auditor's opinion or division of responsibility, neither of which is intended. If, as a result of the work of an expert, the auditor decides to issue a modified auditor's report, in some circumstances when explaining the nature of the modification it may be appropriate to refer to the expert by name and the extent of his involvement. This disclosure requires the permission of the expert.

▶ USING MANAGEMENT'S EXPERT

Whereas ISA 620 only refers to using the work of auditor's experts, the client may also use experts, the so-called 'management's experts' as covered in ISA 500.8. The auditor uses the same due process when using a management's expert compared with using an auditor's expert. As the management's expert is hired by the client, the auditor is specifically skeptical of this expert's relative independent position from management. For instance, a hired in-house lawyer is, despite her professional standards, still part of the company. As a result, the auditor must build in additional corroborative procedures compared with using an auditor's expert.

▶ USING THE WORK OF THE AUDITEE'S INTERNAL AUDITORS

ISA 610[38] 'Using the Work of Internal Auditors' deals with the external auditor's responsibilities relating to the internal audit function when the external auditor has determined that the internal audit function is likely to be relevant to the audit. The internal audit function is an appraisal activity established or provided as a service to the entity. Its functions include, amongst other things, examining, evaluating and monitoring the adequacy and effectiveness of internal control. Irrespective of the degree of autonomy and objectivity of the auditee's internal auditors, they are not independent of the auditee as is required of the external auditor[39]. Internal auditors are those individuals who perform the activities of the internal audit function. Internal auditors may belong to an internal audit department or equivalent function[40]. Again, the external auditor has sole responsibility for the audit opinion expressed, and that responsibility is not reduced by the external auditor's use of the work of the internal auditors.

The external auditor must determine the adequacy, and the planned effect, of the work of the internal auditors on the nature, timing or extent of her audit procedures. To determine whether the work of the internal auditors is adequate, the external auditor must evaluate the objectivity of the internal audit function, the technical competence of the internal auditors, whether the internal auditors use due professional care, and whether communication between the internal auditors and the external auditor is likely to be effective. In determining the planned effect of the internal auditors' work on the audit procedures, the external auditor must consider the nature and scope of specific work performed by the internal auditors, the related assessed risks of material misstatement, and the degree of subjectivity involved in the evaluation of the audit evidence gathered by the internal auditors.

To determine the adequacy of specific work performed by the internal auditors, the external auditor must evaluate whether the work was performed by internal auditors having adequate technical training and proficiency and was properly supervised, reviewed and documented. Was there adequate audit evidence obtained to enable the internal auditors to draw reasonable conclusions? Were the conclusions reached appropriate and were any reports prepared by the internal auditors consistent with the results of the work performed? If there were any exceptions or unusual matters disclosed by the internal auditors, were they properly resolved?

If the external auditor uses specific work of the internal auditors, the external auditor must include in the audit documentation the conclusions reached regarding the evaluation of the adequacy of the work of the internal auditors and the audit procedures performed by the external auditor on that work.

▶ AUDIT CONSIDERATIONS RELATING TO AN AUDITEE USING A SERVICE ORGANIZATION

ISA 402[41] 'Audit Considerations Relating to an Entity Using a Service Organization' discusses the external auditor's responsibility to obtain sufficient appropriate audit evidence when an auditee uses the services of one or more service organizations. Specifically, it expands on how the auditor applies ISA 315 and ISA 330 in obtaining an understanding of the auditee sufficient to identify and assess the risks of material misstatement. It also helps in designing and performing further audit procedures responsive to those risks. A service organization is a third-party organization (or segment of a third-party organization) that provides services to user entities that are part of those entities' information systems relevant to financial reporting.

Many entities outsource aspects of their business to organizations that provide services ranging from performing a specific task to replacing an entity's entire business units or functions. Services provided by a service organization are relevant to the audit of financial statements when those services are part of the entity's information system. A service organization's services are part of a user entity's information system if these services affect any of the following:

- ▶ The classes of transactions in the auditee's operations that are significant to their financial statements.
- ▶ The procedures, within both information technology (IT) and manual systems, by which the entity's transactions are initiated, recorded, processed, corrected, transferred to the general ledger and reported in the financial statements.
- ▶ The related accounting records supporting information and specific accounts in the user entity's financial statements.
- ▶ The financial reporting process used to prepare the user entity's financial statements, including significant accounting estimates and disclosures.
- ▶ Controls surrounding journal entries, including non-standard journal entries used to record non-recurring, unusual transactions or adjustments.

▶ **OBTAINING AN UNDERSTANDING OF THE USE OF SERVICES OF SERVICE ORGANIZATIONS**

To obtain an understanding of the auditee based on ISA 315[42] the auditor must obtain an understanding of how that entity uses the services of a service organization in its operations, including understanding the nature of the services provided by the service organization and their significance; the nature and materiality of the transactions, accounts or financial reporting processes affected by the service organization; and the nature of the relationship between the auditee and the service organization (including contractual agreements). Also, in accordance with ISA 315[43] the auditor evaluates the design and implementation of relevant controls.

If the auditor is unable to obtain the data they need from the auditee, the auditor must obtain that understanding by one or more of the following procedures: obtaining a Type 1 or Type 2 ISAE 3402 report; contacting the service organization, through the auditee, to obtain specific information; visiting the service organization and performing procedures to provide information about the relevant controls at the service organization; or using another auditor to perform procedures that will provide the necessary controls information at the service organization.

Type 1 and Type 2 reports may be critical to understanding the service organization. The Type 1 report, described as 'a report on the description and design of controls at a service organization'[44] encompasses: (a) a description by management of the service organization, the service organization's system,[45] control objectives and related controls and (b) a report by the service auditor[46] conveying her opinion of the service organization's system, control objectives and related controls and the suitability of the design of the controls to achieve the specified control objectives.

The Type 2 report, called 'report on the description, design, and operating effectiveness of controls at a service organization',[47] encompasses: (a) management's description of the service organization, the service organization's system, control objectives and related controls, their design and implementation and, in some cases, their operating effectiveness throughout a specified period; (b) a report by the service auditor conveying her opinion on the description of the service organization's system, control objectives and related controls, the suitability of the design of the controls to achieve the specified control objectives, and the operating effectiveness of the controls; and (c) a description of the service auditor's tests of the controls and the results thereof.

The auditor must consider the sufficiency and appropriateness of the audit evidence provided by a Type 1 or Type 2 report. If the auditor plans to use a Type 1 or Type 2 report as audit evidence to support an understanding of controls at the service organization, she should make sure it is for a date or for a period that is appropriate and determine whether controls identified by the service organization are relevant to the auditee's business.

Sometimes a service organization may use its own service organization, called a subservice organization, to provide services to the auditee. A subservice organization is a service organization used by another service organization to perform some of the services provided to user entities[48] (the auditee) that are part of those user entities' information systems relevant to financial reporting. If the service organization user's auditor plans to use a Type 1 or a Type 2 report that excludes the services provided by a subservice organization and those services are relevant to the audit of the user entity's financial statements, the auditor must get a report on the subservice organization or carry out her own investigation.

Section 14.5 provides further information about an ISAE 3402 report.

13.5 AUDIT OF ACCOUNTING ESTIMATES

Some financial statement items cannot be measured precisely but can only be estimated. These items are accounting estimates. An *accounting estimate* approximates a monetary amount in the absence of a precise means of measurement. This term is used for an amount measured at fair value where there is estimation uncertainty, as well as for other amounts that require estimation. Estimate audit standards are ISA 540 'Auditing Accounting Estimates, Including Fair Value Accounting Estimates, and Related Disclosures'[49] (also PCAOB AS 2501 and AS 2502). See illustration 13.6 which describes the key points of ISA 540.

The nature and reliability of information available to management to support the making of an accounting estimate varies widely, which thereby affects the degree of estimation uncertainty associated with accounting estimates. The degree of estimation uncertainty affects the risks of material misstatement of accounting estimates, including their susceptibility to unintentional or intentional management bias. The measurement objective of accounting estimates can vary. The measurement objective for some accounting estimates is to forecast the outcome of transactions. The measurement objective is different for other accounting estimates, including many fair value accounting[50] estimates, and is expressed in terms of the value of a current transaction or financial statement item. This type of measurement is based on conditions prevalent at the measurement date, such as estimated market price for a particular type of asset or liability.

▶ **ACCOUNTING ESTIMATE RISK ASSESSMENT PROCEDURES**

In order to provide a basis for the identification and assessment of the risks for accounting estimates, the auditor must understand how management identifies accounting estimates that are needed and how these estimates are made.[51] To determine how management identifies those transactions that require accounting estimates, the auditor must ask management what changes in circumstances give rise to new (or revised prior) accounting estimates.

▶ **ACCOUNTING ESTIMATE RESPONSES TO ASSESSED RISKS**

Based on the assessed risks of material misstatement, the auditor must determine whether management has appropriately applied the requirements of the financial reporting framework and whether the methods for making the accounting estimates have been applied consistently. She must also determine whether changes from the prior period in accounting estimates or in the estimation method are appropriate in the circumstances.

The auditor shall test how management made the accounting estimate and the data on which it is based. Further, she must make her own point estimate to compare to management's estimates. The auditor makes a point estimate or a range to evaluate

ILLUSTRATION 13.5

ISA 540 (REVISED) AUDITING ESTIMATES

IAASB issued a revised ISA 540[52] which, according to IAASB[53] has the following key enhancements:

Definitions

The IAASB has made the following key enhancements to ISA 540 (Revised) with regard to the definitions:

▶ Explicitly recognized the **spectrum of inherent risk** building on existing concepts in ISA 200, ISA 315 (Revised), and ISA 330, to drive scalability.

▶ Introduced the concept of **inherent risk factors**, including not only estimation uncertainty but also complexity, subjectivity and others.

▶ Enhanced **risk assessment** procedures relating to obtaining an understanding of the entity and its environment, including the entity's internal control.

▶ Introduced a **separate assessment of inherent risk and control risk** for accounting estimates.

▶ Emphasized the importance of the auditor's decisions about **controls** relating to accounting estimates by highlighting relevant requirements in ISA 315 (Revised) and ISA 330.

▶ Introduced **objectives-based work effort** requirements directed to methods (including specifically when complex modelling is involved), data and assumptions, to design and perform further audit procedures to respond to assessed risks of material misstatement.

▶ Enhanced the **'stand back'** requirement, by adding an evaluation of the audit evidence obtained regarding the accounting estimates, including both corroborative and contradictory audit evidence.

▶ Enhanced **disclosure** requirements to obtain audit evidence about whether the related disclosures are 'reasonable'.

▶ Included a new requirement to consider matters regarding accounting estimates when **communicating with those charged with governance.**

▶ New and enhanced **application material**.

▶ With respect to **external information sources**, conforming and consequential amendments to the definitions, requirements and application material in ISA 500.

What are inherent risk factors?

Inherent risk factors are characteristics of conditions and events that may affect the susceptibility of an assertion to misstatement, before consideration of controls.

Which inherent risk factors should the auditor take into account?

In the identification and assessment of the risks of material misstatement, extant ISA 540 focused on estimation uncertainty. ISA 540 (Revised) acknowledges that there may be other inherent risk factors and requires the auditor to take into account:

▶ *Estimation Uncertainty* Estimation uncertainty is the susceptibility to an inherent lack of precision in the measurement of an accounting estimate.

▶ *Complexity* Complexity refers to the complexity inherent in the process of making an accounting estimate, such as when multiple data sets or assumptions are required.

> *Subjectivity* Subjectivity arises from inherent limitations in the knowledge or data reasonably available about valuation attributes.

How have the procedures to obtain audit evidence changed?

As in extant ISA 540, the auditor's response to assessed risks include one or more **testing strategies**:

▶ Obtaining audit evidence from events occurring up to the date of the auditor's report;

▶ Testing how management made the accounting estimate; or

▶ Developing an auditor's point estimate or range.

For these testing strategies, the IAASB introduced **objective-based requirements,** directed to methods (including models), assumptions and data. The objective-based requirements allow scalability in the nature, timing and extent of the procedures performed, recognizing that the higher the assessed risks of material misstatement, the more persuasive the audit evidence needs to be.

The auditor must also determine how management makes accounting estimates including:

▶ the method and model used in making the accounting estimate;

▶ relevant controls;

▶ whether management has used an expert;

▶ the assumptions underlying the accounting estimates;

▶ whether there has been, or ought to have been, a change from the prior period in the methods for making the accounting estimates, and if so, why; and

▶ whether and, if so, how, management has assessed the effect of estimation uncertainty.

The auditor must review the outcome of accounting estimates included in the prior period financial statements, or their subsequent re-estimation for the current period.

In identifying and assessing the risks of material misstatement, the auditor must evaluate the degree of estimation uncertainty associated with an accounting estimate. Do any of those accounting estimates having high estimation uncertainty give rise to significant risks?

management's point estimate. If the auditor uses assumptions or methods that differ from management's, the auditor evaluates any significant differences from management's point estimate. The auditor must identify whether there are indicators of possible management bias.

▶ **WRITTEN REPRESENTATIONS AND DOCUMENTATION**

The auditor must obtain written representations from management and, where appropriate, those charged with governance, saying that they believe significant assumptions used in making their accounting estimates are reasonable.

The auditor must include in the audit documentation the basis for the auditor's conclusions about the reasonableness of accounting estimates and their disclosure that give rise to significant risks; and indicators of possible management bias, if any.

13.6   AUDITING OF ACCOUNTING ESTIMATES: AN EXAMPLE

Some people believe that we accountants can measure financial items precisely. That is not always possible as some items can only be estimated. An accounting estimate is an approximation of a monetary amount in the absence of a precise means of measurement. This term is used for an amount measured at fair value under estimation uncertainty. All audits require accounting estimates for some of the work, for instance calculation of expenses like depreciation and amortization or asset valuations such as long-term contracts, good will and pension funds.

Valentine M. Smith, CA, is an audit manager at Isle & Oblivion (I&O). He has the greatest expertise in accounting estimates of the accounting team auditing El-Five, plc, an elevated rail transportation company. Most of their massive infrastructure projects are long-term (more than a year). Their business requires estimates of future costs. About 70% of their sales are work-in-progress and they are dependent on percentage of completion payments.

▶ INFORMATION FORMING A BASIS OF UNDERSTANDING FOR ACCOUNTING ESTIMATES

Audit manager Smith is concerned with inherent risk factors in the estimating process such as estimation uncertainty, complexity, subjectivity, and control environment, among other considerations. In order to provide a basis for the identification and assessment of the risks for accounting estimates, Valentine Smith has to determine how management identifies what accounting estimates are needed and how these estimates are made. First, he asks management what changes in El-Five circumstances give rise to new (or revised prior) accounting estimates. Smith asks management to discuss the complexity inherent in the process of making an accounting estimate, such as when multiple data sets or assumptions are required. Smith is especially keen on learning about any subjective decisions required, such as determination of interest rates used or assumptions about future timelines for work completed, expenses and asset acquisition.

Before proceeding with testing, Smith inquired how management makes accounting estimates including: the method and model used in making the accounting estimate; whether management has used an expert; and the assumptions underlying the accounting estimates. Smith also asks whether there has been, or ought to have been, a change from the prior period in the methods for making the accounting estimates, and if so, why; and whether and, if so, how, management has assessed the effect of estimation uncertainty.

▶ TESTING FOR RISKS IN ACCOUNTING ESTIMATES

Valentine Smith reviews the estimates to see if they meet International Financial Reporting Standards (IFRS) and whether the methods for making the accounting estimates have been applied consistently. He considers whether changes from the prior period in accounting estimates or in the estimation method are appropriate in the circumstances. Smith tested how management made the accounting estimate and the data on which it is based. As part of the testing process Smith makes an independent point estimate to compare to management's estimates and evaluates any significant differences from management's point estimate. Is there any possible management bias?

13.7   SUMMARY

The pervasiveness of technology in society has expanded tremendously in the last decade. Technology has established a central role in business processes. Where auditing originally used simple computer assisted audit techniques, current process mining techniques and the use of big data are expected to significantly change the audit production process.

IAASB highlights that audit quality can be enhanced using data analytics in the various stages of the audit. Despite the fact that the benefits are clear, there are also attention points that auditors need to be aware of in using data analyses, including the overwhelming volumes of available data, the need to exercise professional judgement, other areas in the financial statements that are not captured with data analytics, and overconfidence when auditors lack a clear understanding of the uses and limitations of technology.

ISA 600 (and PCAOB Audit Standard 1205) deals with special considerations that apply to group audits, particularly those involving component auditors. A component auditor is the auditor who, at the request of the group engagement team, performs work on the financial information related to a component. A component is an entity or business activity whose financial information is included in the group financial statements. However, component auditors may perform work on the financial information of the components and are responsible for their work.

The group engagement partner is responsible for the direction, supervision and performance of the audit engagement and the auditor's report. The group engagement partner must evaluate the component auditors who perform work on the financial information of the components. The group engagement team considers certain matters such as: Industry, regulatory and other external factors; The applicable financial reporting framework; client objectives and strategies and related business risks; instructions issued by group management to components; accounting manual, reporting package and a timetable; and identification and assessment of risks of fraud.

A component could be a head office, parent, division, location, business unit, branch, subsidiary, activity, shared service centre, joint venture, associated company, or other entity whose financial information is included in the group financial statements. Determining what is a component will require professional judgement. In the context of a group audit materiality levels are established for both the group financial statements as a whole and for the financial information of the components.

An important consideration when executing a group audit is the *scope of the component audit*. The scope of an audit refers to the audit procedures deemed necessary in the circumstances to achieve the audit's objective. The scope may be full scope, specific scope, limited scope or no scope. *Full scope* involves performing a full audit of the component's financial statements. A *specific scope* involves audit procedures in those areas where significant risks were identified. Those areas can be one or more account balances, classes of transactions or disclosures relating to the likely significant risks. A *limited scope* involves a review of the component entity's financial statements. This minimum level of scoping is called *no scope*, as it does not contain specific audit procedures at the level of the component.

The group engagement team sets out the work to be performed, the use to be made of that work and the form and content of the communication with the group engagement team. In conformity with the ISA 600 standard the component auditor communicates matters relevant to the group engagement team's conclusion on the group audit.

Another important element in a group audit is the communication with group management and those charged with governance. The group engagement team shall determine which internal control deficiencies will be communicated with group management. Fraud issues must be communicated on a timely basis to the appropriate level of group management.

The group auditor is required to obtain an understanding of the consolidation process, including the instructions issued by group management to components. The *consolidation process* includes: the recognition, measurement, presentation and disclosure of the financial information of the components in the group financial statements by way of consolidation, proportionate consolidation, or the equity or cost methods of accounting. The group engagement partner must evaluate the effect on the group audit opinion of any uncorrected misstatements and inability to obtain sufficient appropriate audit evidence. This evaluation allows her to determine whether the group financial statements as a whole are materially misstated.

An accounting estimate is an approximation of a monetary amount in the absence of a precise means of measurement. This term is used for an amount measured at fair value where there is estimation uncertainty, as well as for other amounts that require estimation. Estimate audit standards are ISA 540 'Auditing Accounting Estimates, Including Fair Value Accounting Estimates, and Related Disclosures' (also PCAOB AS 2501 and AS 2502).

In order to provide a basis for the identification and assessment of the risks for accounting estimates, the auditor must understand how management identifies accounting estimates that are needed and how these estimates are made. To determine how management identifies those transactions that require accounting estimates, the auditor must ask management what changes in circumstances may give rise to new (or revised prior) accounting estimates. The auditor also must determine how management makes accounting estimates.

ISA 620 'Using the Work of an Auditor's Expert' deals with the auditor's responsibilities relating to the work of an auditor's expert when that work is used to assist the auditor in obtaining sufficient appropriate audit evidence. An auditor's expert is an individual or organisation possessing expertise in a field other than accounting or auditing, whose work in that field is used by the auditor to assist the auditor in obtaining sufficient appropriate audit evidence.

The internal audit function is an appraisal activity established or provided as a service to the auditee. Its functions include, amongst other things, examining, evaluating and monitoring the adequacy and effectiveness of internal control. Irrespective of the degree of autonomy and objectivity of the auditee's internal auditors, they are not independent of the auditee as is required of the external auditor. Internal auditors are those individuals who perform the activities of the internal audit function. Internal auditors may belong to an internal audit department or equivalent function.

A service organisation is a third-party organisation (or segment of a third-party organisation) that provides services to user entities that are part of those entities' information systems relevant to financial reporting. If the auditor is unable to obtain the data they need from the auditee, the auditor must obtain that understanding by one or more of the following procedures: obtaining a Type 1 or Type 2 ISAE 3402 report; contacting or visiting the service organization and performing procedures to provide information about the relevant controls at the service organization; or using another auditor to perform procedures that will provide the necessary controls information at the service organization.

The auditor shall test how management made the accounting estimate and the data on which it is based. Further, she must make her own point estimate to compare to management's estimates. The auditor must obtain written representations from management and, where appropriate, those charged with governance, saying that they believe significant assumptions used in making their accounting estimates are reasonable.

13.8 QUESTIONS, EXERCISES AND CASES

QUESTIONS

13.2 Technology in the Audit

13-1 What are automated tools & techniques and how does an auditor use them? (Review chapter 7.)

13-2 How can the quality of a financial statement audit be enhanced by the use of data analytics?

13-3 What are examples of attention points that auditors need to be aware of in using data analytics?

13.3 Group Audit

13-4 What matters should an auditor consider concerning a new group audit client which can be obtained from group management?

13-5 What matters must be considered when understanding the group entity and its environment?

13-6 If the group engagement team plans to request a component auditor to perform work on the financial information of a component, what must the group engagement team understand about the component auditor?

13-7 What is meant by 'scope of an audit'? What are the considerations when determining the scope of the component audit?

13-8 What information must the group auditor communicate to the component auditor? What information must the component auditor communicate to the group auditor?

13-9 What should the group and component audit team understand about consolidation?

13-10 In addition to documentation required by ISA 230 and other ISAs, the group engagement team must include which other matters in the audit documentation?

13.4 Using the Work of Others

13-11 Define auditor's expert. What must the auditor consider when evaluating the work of an auditor's expert?

13-12 Describe the similarities and differences between using an auditor's expert, a management expert and a team member with specialised knowledge.

13-13 Type 1 and Type 2 internal control reports from service organizations may be critical to understanding the service organization. Discuss the difference between Type 1 and Type 2 reports.

13.5 Audit of Accounting Estimates

13-14 What issues arise in auditing accounting estimates?

13-15 What must the auditor ascertain about the methods management uses to make accounting estimates and the data they rely on?

PROBLEMS AND EXERCISES

13.2 Technology in the Audit

13-16 Using ACL or idea software perform the following procedures:

Required:

A. Open the accounts receivable file then (1) determine the number (count) of customers. (2) find the customers who owe more than $5,000. (3) perform Benford analysis.

B. Open the inventory file then (1) Count the number of inventory items. (2) determine the most expensive and least expensive item. (3) find which products have a sales price less than the unit price.

13.3 Group Audit

13-17 Newtight is a Japanese manufacturer of high technology adhesives traded on the Tokyo Nikkei stock exchange. The Kobe audit firm of Noda, Haider, and Itabashi, CPAs, is doing a group audit on the company.

Newtight has 14 subsidiaries located in 10 different countries. They own 100 per cent of four subsidiaries, 50 per cent of 5 and 10 per cent of the last five. The most important subsidiaries are Newtight USA in Compton, California, owned 100 per cent and Euro-Newtight of Brussels owned 10 per cent with the rest owned by the government of Belgium. They use service organizations for payroll and collection of receivables. The company has only three internal auditors for all their operations. Management believes they know everything that happens in the organization and all important decisions are made by the CEO. There are no group-wide controls. Management believes that each component division will handle internals their own way. The accounts of the full company are consolidated one month after the end of the fiscal year by their accounting department. Currency exchange rates are determined by using the best rate for the prior year. One of the 50 per cent owned subsidiaries is located in Nigeria and another one is in Syria.

Management has warned the audit firm of Noda, Haider and Itabashi, CPAs, that they will have very limited access to top executives and the chief executive of each of the divisions to protect company industrial secrets.

Required:

Write a memo describing an understanding of Newtight based on important matters to be considered.

13-18 Describe a company that would have a high risk of material misstatement of the group financial statements. Make sure it reflects a complex group structure; poor corporate governance; ineffective group-wide controls; has components operating in foreign jurisdictions with unusual governance intervention; and conducts business activities that involve high risk. The company should have unusual related party relationships and transactions, reconciliation issues and complex transactions. The group company and the component companies have important differences: the components' accounting policies differ from group policies and components with different financial year-ends.

The board of directors encouraged aggressive tax planning and made frequent changes of auditors.

13-19 The Taipei, Taiwan, audit firm of Hung, Pan and Wu is being considered as a component auditor to audit the manufacturing component of Forever Teen clothing company, a Munich, Germany, based firm. Forever Teen's auditors are Claassen, Sohn, Schanz and Kupper, Wirtschaftsprüfers (CSSK). What questions would CSSK ask of Hung, Pan and Wu to determine if they are qualified to be component auditors?

13-20 The Tel Aviv, Israel, firm of Levi, Bar-Hava, Kama and Segal, CPAs, are the auditors for ZoomZa Optical Devices, a manufacturer of high technology scopes and viewing devices. They have a manufacturing plant in Guangzhou, China, which will be audited by Rui, Li and Chen, CPAs. The group auditors Levi, Bar-Hava, Kama and Segal, CPAs consider the component manufacturing plant in Guangzhou as 'not significant' and want to select the type of work to be performed by Rui, Li and Chen. What considerations would affect the decisions of Levi, Bar-Hava, Kama and Segal, CPAs?

13-21 Sweetheart Junkyard, a Sao Paulo based worldwide online dating site for individuals who feel they have been unlucky in love, has hired Chiquento Da Silva, Aquino, Franco de Lima and Coda (CAFC) as their group auditor. CAFC proposes a financial statement audit of Sweetheart Junkyard and the main subsidiaries SJ Euro and SJ USA. Three other subsidiaries – SJ China, SJ Asia and SJ South America – will get a review. CAFC will work with a different component auditor for each of the locations. The subsidiary SJ Asia audit by Wu and Wang, CPAs, was not up to the quality standards of CAFC because they offered no safeguards against self-interest and self-review threats. The group auditors, CAFC, will not do an internal control audit and will limit their management letter comments. There is a suspected employee fraud involving accounts payable at the SJ Euro location.
Required:
Write a communication to the board of directors explaining the audit of Sweetheart Junkyard.

13-22 Siffre Industries of Port Elizabeth, South Africa, has several subsidiaries which are consolidated into the Siffre Industries financial statements. Empire Manufacturing is a manufacturing subsidiary that is one of the components that is being consolidated into Siffre's financial statement. Empire Manufacturing's largest customer, Turley Distributing, has gone bankrupt one month after the balance sheet date. Siffre is being audited by Hoogenboom, Coetzee and Schmulian (HCS).
Required:
A. Discuss the consolidation process.
B. Discuss how the work on subsequent events should be handled.
C. If Siffre refuses to revise their financial statements and disclosures because of the subsequent event, how will this affect the opinion of audit firm HCS?

13.4 Using the Work of Others

13-23 This exercise aims to familiarize you with the role of internal auditors in the financial statement auditing process and enhance your understanding of how external auditors interact with internal audit functions.
A. Provide a brief overview of the roles of internal auditors and external auditors in the context of financial statement auditing.

B. Explain the importance of collaboration and coordination between internal and external auditors for effective audit processes.

C. Present a hypothetical case study involving a company undergoing a financial statement audit. Describe the company's industry, size, operations, and any relevant audit considerations and introduce the internal audit department within the company and outline its responsibilities, scope, and recent activities.

D. Identify Areas of Collaboration and identify specific areas where collaboration between the external audit team and the internal audit department could enhance audit effectiveness and efficiency. Consider areas such as risk assessment, internal controls evaluation, substantive testing, and fraud detection. Explain how internal audit findings may impact the external audit approach, including risk assessment and testing strategies.

13.5 Audit of Accounting Estimates

13-24 The public accounting firm of Rodriguez, Chen and Veenstra, Charted Accountants, is auditing the Windsor, Canada, company Gold Mountain which sells gold and precious metals on their website GoldMountain.com. Gold Mountain's holdings include derivative gold contracts, gold certificates and physical deposits of gold bullion. All their holdings must be valued to the market equivalent. What responses to the assessed risk of material misstatement caused by the estimates must Rodriguez, Chen and Veenstra undertake?

13-25 Future Focus Investments of Odense, Denmark, is being audited by the public accounting firm of Loft, Blasev and Graversen. Future Focus's primary investments are in virtual currencies such as Bitcoin. Future Focus makes a great deal of estimates in how their investments are valued. In the year under audit Bitcoin's value on a Tokyo-based exchange varied from DKK (Danish Krone) 54,891 in March to DKK 71,431 in April. Discuss the procedures Loft, Blasev and Graversen would undertake to audit the company's estimates of the Danish Krone value of the investments.

CASES

13-26 Group Audit of TransGlobal Logistics Inc.

TransGlobal Logistics Inc. (TGL) is a multinational transportation company providing freight and logistics services worldwide. Headquartered in the United States, TGL operates subsidiaries and affiliates in various countries, including Brazil. The company's operations involve transporting goods via air, sea, and land, serving a diverse range of industries. As part of the annual audit engagement for TransGlobal Logistics Inc., your audit firm has been appointed as the group auditor. The audit scope includes the examination of financial statements of TGL and its subsidiaries, in compliance with International Standards on Auditing (ISA). One of the subsidiaries, TGL Brazil, is a significant component of the group's operations, contributing substantially to its revenue.

During the audit process, the component auditor responsible for auditing TGL Brazil, a local audit firm based in São Paulo, identified a potential indication of bribery involving certain transactions and payments made by TGL Brazil to government officials and third-party agents in Brazil. The component auditor has provided a report highlighting the findings related to this indication of bribery.

Required:

A. Describe the factors that the group auditor should consider when planning the audit of TGL, taking into account the multinational nature of its operations and the significance of TGL Brazil.

B. Outline the audit procedures that the group auditor should perform to obtain sufficient appropriate audit evidence regarding the financial statements of TGL Brazil, considering the indication of bribery reported by the component auditor.

C. Discuss the specific considerations for assessing the risk of material misstatement related to bribery and corruption in the audit of TGL Brazil.

D. Explain the reporting requirements under ISA 600 regarding the group auditor's responsibilities for the work of the component auditor, including the reporting of significant findings such as indications of bribery.

E. Discuss the implications of the indication of bribery in Brazil on the group auditor's opinion and reporting in the consolidated financial statements of TransGlobal Logistics Inc.

F. Analyse the ethical issues and responsibilities of the audit firm in responding to the indication of bribery identified in the audit of TGL Brazil.

13-27 You are partner of a group audit team and asked your manager to prepare the audit instructions. You both discussed the rationale: Group audit instructions typically provide guidance and procedures for auditors when conducting audits of a group of companies. The manager is aware that the contents of group audit instructions may vary based on the specific requirements and circumstances[54]. The manager suggested using Chat GPT for a general outline of what it might include, before tailoring it to the client circumstances. Below you see the table of content of the instructions your manager gave to you for your review.

Required:

Review the content using ISA 600 requirement as reference. What is your overall view? Did you also encounter mistakes? Are important things missing?'

OUTLINE GROUP AUDIT INSTRUCTIONS

1. **Introduction**
   ▶ Overview of the group structure.
   ▶ Purpose and objectives of the group audit.

2. **Scope of the Audit**
   ▶ Definition of the group and its components.
   ▶ Inclusion and exclusion criteria for entities in the group audit.
   ▶ Explanation of materiality thresholds.

3. **Responsibilities**
   ▶ Clarification of the responsibilities of the group auditor and component auditors.
   ▶ Coordination and communication protocols between group and component auditors.
   ▶ Procedures for addressing potential conflicts of interest.

OUTLINE GROUP AUDIT INSTRUCTIONS

4. Group Risk Assessment
▷ Identification and assessment of significant risks at the group level.
▷ Consideration of the risk of material misstatement due to fraud.
▷ Evaluation of the group's internal control environment.

5. Materiality and Performance Materiality
▷ Determination of materiality thresholds for the group and individual components.
▷ Guidelines on establishing performance materiality.

6. Audit Planning
▷ Detailed planning procedures for the group audit.
▷ Allocation of resources and responsibilities among audit team members.
▷ Timing and coordination of audit work at the group and component levels.

7. Audit Procedures
▷ Detailed audit procedures for group-level financial statement items.
▷ Consideration of the audit work performed by component auditors.
▷ Special considerations for significant components.

8. Consolidation Process
▷ Examination of the consolidation process, including elimination of intercompany transactions and balances.
▷ Review of accounting policies and adjustments made during consolidation.

9. Communication and Reporting
▷ Requirements for communication between group and component auditors.
▷ Reporting obligations, including the form and content of the audit report.
▷ Considerations for group-wide and component materiality.

10. Documentation
▷ Standards for documenting audit evidence and conclusions.
▷ Retention and access requirements for audit documentation.

11. Quality Control
▷ Procedures for ensuring the quality of the audit process.
▷ Review processes and quality control checks.

12. Ethical Considerations
▷ Guidance on handling ethical issues and conflicts of interest.
▷ Compliance with professional standards and regulations.

13-28 You are audit manager of a component team who is expected to report to the group audit team. The group auditor sent you a template for reporting to the group auditor. You looked at it and wondered whether the template was logical and/or could be simplified. You challenged your senior whether she might come up with a better template. If so, you are willing to have a conversation with your group auditor on how to report. The senior used Chat GPT and came back with the following 'example of a group audit review checklist to be filled in by the component auditor'.
Required:
Review the content using ISA 600 requirement as reference. What is your overall view? Did you encounter any omissions?

'EXAMPLE OF A GROUP AUDIT REVIEW CHECKLIST TO BE FILLED IN BY THE COMPONENT AUDITOR'

Auditor Information

[ ] Auditor's Name:

[ ] Component Being Audited:

[ ] Audit Period:

Planning and Risk Assessment

[ ] Have you identified and documented the key activities of the component?

[ ] Have risks associated with the component been assessed and documented?

[ ] Have you coordinated with the group audit team on risk assessment and planning?

Internal Control System

[ ] Have you evaluated the design of the internal control system relevant to the audit?

[ ] Have you tested the operating effectiveness of these controls?

Audit Evidence

[ ] Have you obtained sufficient and appropriate audit evidence?

[ ] Have significant findings been discussed with the relevant parties?

[ ] Have you evaluated the implications of the findings on the audit?

Group Reporting

[ ] Have you reported critical matters to the group auditors in a timely fashion?

[ ] Have you complied with the group audit instructions?

Financial Information

[ ] Have you reviewed the financial information of the component for accuracy and completeness?

[ ] Have you ensured that the financial information is in accordance with the group's accounting policies?

Communication

[ ] Have you communicated appropriately with the component's management and those charged with governance?

[ ] Have you received all necessary information from the component's management?

Conclusion and Reporting

[ ] Have you concluded on the work performed and its impact on the group audit?

[ ] Have you prepared a report detailing your findings, conclusions, and any recommendations?

Sign-off

[ ] Auditor's Signature:

[ ] Date:

13.9   NOTES

1. International Auditing and Assurance Standards Board (IAASB), 2016. Exploring the Growing Use of Technology in the Audit, with a Focus on Data Analytics, IAASB Data Analytics Working Group. https://www.ifac.org/system/files/publications/files/IAASB-Data-Analytics-WG-Publication-Aug-25-2016-for-comms-9.1.16.pdf.

2. Computer Assisted Audit Techniques (CAAT) has been used until 2019, when IAASB introduced the new term Automated Tools & Techniques (AT&T). The more generic term is data analytics.

3. Ibid. IAASB (2016), p. 7.

4. See Peter Eimers, 2017. New Way to Rome. Animation visualizing the potential of data analytics in auditing https://www.youtube.com/watch?v=17OTj5cbIEY.

5. In 2019 the ISA 315 (Revised 2019) was published where automated tools & techniques were embedded in the application material throughout the standard. See chapter 7, illustration 7.7.

6. International Auditing and Assurance Standards Board (IAASB), 2023, International Standards on Auditing 330 (ISA 330) 'The Auditor's Responses to Assessed Risks', para. A16, Handbook of International Quality Control, Auditing, Review, Other Assurance, and Related Services Pronouncements, 2022 edn, Part I, International Federation of Accountants, New York.

7. Ibid. ISA 330, para. A27.

8. Ibid. IAASB (2016).

9. Ibid. IAASB (2016), p. 8.

10. Derived from IAASB (2016), p. 8, with adapted headings by the authors.

11. Ibid. IAASB (2016), p. 7.

12. Ibid. IAASB (2016), pp. 11–14.

13. Chartered Professional Accountants of Canada: A CPA's Introduction to AI: From Algorithms to Deep Learning, What You Need to Know, 2019 https://us.aicpa.org/content/dam/aicpa/interestareas/frc/assuranceadvisoryservices/downloadabledocuments/56175896-cpas-introduction-to-ai-from-algorithms.pdf

14. International Auditing and Assurance Standards Board (IAASB), 2023, International Standards on Auditing 600 Revised (ISA 600 Revised) 'Special Considerations – Audits of Group Financial Statements (Including the Work of Component Auditors)', *Handbook of International Quality Management, Auditing, Review, Other Assurance, and Related Services Pronouncements*, 2022 edn, Volume I, International Federation of Accountants, New York.

15. AS 1205 offers guidance to independent auditors on key professional judgments when deciding whether to be the principal auditor and use reports from other auditors who examined specific components in financial statements. The guidance emphasizes that auditors should base their decisions on professional considerations and not suggest that a report referencing another auditor is less reputable than one without such a reference. The focus is on the auditor's judgment regarding the appropriateness of serving as the principal auditor without personally auditing certain aspects of the client's financial information.

16. International Auditing and Assurance Standards Board (IAASB), 2022, Basis for Conclusions: ISA 600 (Revised), Specific Considerations – Audits of Group Financial Statements (including the Work of Component Auditors), https://www.iaasb.org/publications/international-standard-auditing-600-revised-special-considerations-audits-group-financial-statements

17. Ibid. ISA 600, para. 14c.

18. ISA 600 (Revised) adapted as necessary in the circumstances, may also be useful in an audit of financial statements other than a group audit when the engagement team includes individuals from another firm. For example, this ISA may be useful when involving such an individual to attend a physical inventory count, inspect property, plant and equipment, or perform audit procedures at a shared service center at a remote location. (ISA 600 (Revised), para 3).

19. Group engagement partner – the partner or other person in the firm who is responsible for the group audit engagement and its performance, and for the auditor's report on the group financial statements that is issued on behalf of the firm. Where joint auditors conduct the group audit, the joint engagement partners and their engagement teams collectively constitute the group engagement partner and the group engagement team.

20. However, if national standards allow division of responsibility between the group and component auditors, the group auditor may choose to share responsibility. National standards differ as to whether division of responsibility between the group auditor and a component auditor is allowed.

21.	Ibid. ISA 600 (Revised), para. A57.

22.	Ibid. ISA 600 (Revised), para A32.

23.	Ibid. ISA 600 (Revised), para 21.

24.	Ibid. ISA 600 (Revised). para 26 and 27.

25.	This and the next two bullet points are consistent with ISA 320. IAASB, 2023, International Standards on Auditing 320 (ISA 320) 'Materiality in Planning and Performing an Audit', *Handbook of International Quality Management, Auditing, Review, Other Assurance, and Related Services Pronouncements*, 2022 edn, Volume I, International Federation of Accountants, New York.

26.	Ibid. ISA 600 (Revised), Para. 35.

27.	If a component is audited due to legal or regulatory requirements, and the group engagement team uses that audit evidence, they must ensure that materiality for the component financial statements and performance materiality at the component level meet ISA requirements.

28.	In his PhD thesis and article, Trevor Stewart introduces a model with which materiality for components (GUAM model) can be determined: Stewart, Trevor (2013), 'A Bayesian Audit Assurance Model with Application to the Component Materiality Problem in Group Audits', PhD thesis, Vrije Universiteit Amsterdam; and 'Group Audits, Group-Level Controls, and Component Materiality: How Much Auditing Is Enough?', 2013, *Accounting Review*, March.

29.	Ibid. ISA 600 (Revised), para. 38.

30.	Ibid. ISA 600 (Revised), para. 57.

31.	ISA 600 (Revised), para. A45 and ISA 705.20. Under US auditing standards group auditors have the option to share responsibility with the component auditor in the audit opinion. PCAOB AS 1205.03. https://pcaobus.org/oversight/standards/auditing-standards/details/AS1205

32.	International Auditing and Assurance Standards Board (IAASB), 2023, International Standards on Auditing 705 (ISA 705) 'Modifications to the Opinion in the Independent Auditor's Report', *Handbook of International Quality Management, Auditing, Review, Other Assurance, and Related Services Pronouncements*, 2022 edn, Volume I, International Federation of Accountants, New York.

33.	International Auditing and Assurance Standards Board (IAASB), 2023, International Standards on Auditing 230 (ISA 230) 'Audit Documentation', paras 8–11 and A6, *Handbook of International Quality Management, Auditing, Review, Other Assurance, and Related Services Pronouncements*, 2022 edn, Volume I, International Federation of Accountants, New York.

34.	Ibid. ISA 600 (Revised), para. 59.

35.	According to ISA.620-6b 'expertise' includes skills, knowledge and experience in a particular field.

36.	International Auditing and Assurance Standards Board (IAASB), 2023, International Standard on Auditing 620 (ISA 620) 'Using the Work of an Auditor's Expert', Handbook of International Quality Management, Auditing, Review, Other Assurance, and Related Services Pronouncements, 2022 edn, Volume I, International Federation of Accountants, New York.

37.	Ibid. ISA 620.A2.

38.	International Auditing and Assurance Standards Board (IAASB), 2023, International Standard on Auditing 610 (ISA 610) 'Using the Work of Internal Auditors', Handbook of International Quality Control, Auditing, Review, Other Assurance, and Related Services Pronouncements, 2022 edn, Volume I, International Federation of Accountants, New York.

39.	Ibid. ISA 610.11.

40.	Ibid. ISA 610.13.

41. International Auditing and Assurance Standards Board (IAASB), 2023, International Standard on Auditing 402 (ISA 402) 'Audit Considerations Relating to an Entity Using a Service Organization', *Handbook of International Quality Management, Auditing, Review, Other Assurance, and Related Services Pronouncements*, 2022 edn, Volume I, International Federation of Accountants, New York.

42. Ibid ISA 402.1.

43. Ibid. ISA 315.A177.

44. Report on the description and design of controls at a service organisation (referred to in this ISA as a Type 1 report) – a report that comprises: '(1) A description, prepared by management of the service organization, of the service organization's system, control objectives and related controls that have been designed and implemented as at a specified date; and (2) A report by the service auditor with the objective of conveying reasonable assurance that includes the service auditor's opinion on the description of the service organization's system, control objectives and related controls and the suitability of the design of the controls to achieve the specified control objectives' – as defined in ISA 402, para. 8.

45. Service organization's system – the policies and procedures designed, implemented and maintained by the service organization to provide user entities with the services covered by the service auditor's report.

46. Service auditor – an auditor who, at the request of the service organization, provides an assurance report on the controls of a service organization.

47. Report on the description, design and operating effectiveness of controls at a service organization (referred to in this ISA as a Type 2 report) – a report that comprises: '(1) A description, prepared by management of the service organization, of the service organization's system, control objectives and related controls, their design and implementation as at a specified date or throughout a specified period and, in some cases, their operating effectiveness throughout a specified period; and (2) A report by the service auditor with the objective of conveying reasonable assurance that includes: (a) The service auditor's opinion on the description of the service organization's system, control objectives and related controls, the suitability of the design of the controls to achieve the specified control objectives, and the operating effectiveness of the controls; and (b) A description of the service auditor's tests of the controls and the results thereof' – as defined in ISA 402, para. 8.

48. User entity – an entity that uses a service organization and whose financial statements are being audited.

49. International Auditing and Assurance Standards Board (IAASB), 2023, International Standards on Auditing 540 (ISA 540) 'Auditing Accounting Estimates, Including Fair Value Accounting Estimates, and Related Disclosures', para 8, *Handbook of International Quality Management, Auditing, Review, Other Assurance, and Related Services Pronouncements*, 2022 edn, Volume I, International Federation of Accountants, New York.

50. Ibid, International Standards on Auditing 230 (ISA 230) 'Audit Documentation', 2023 *Handbook of International Quality Management, Auditing, Review, Other Assurance, and Related Services Pronouncements*, 2022 edn, Volume I, International Federation of Accountants, New York.

51. International Auditing and Assurance Standards Board (IAASB), 2023, International Standards on Auditing 540 (ISA 540) 'Auditing Accounting Estimates, Including Fair Value Accounting Estimates, and Related Disclosures', paras 10–11, *Handbook of International Quality Management, Auditing, Review, Other Assurance, and Related Services Pronouncements*, 2022 edn, Volume I, International Federation of Accountants, New York.

52. Ibid. 2023 International Standards on Auditing 540 (Revised) (ISA 540 Revised) 'Auditing Accounting Estimates and Related disclosures'.

53.   International Auditing and Assurance Standards Board (IAASB), 2023, ISA 540 (Revised) and Related Conforming and Consequential Amendments, https://www.ifac.org/system/files/publications/files/ISA-540-At-a-Glance.pdf

54.   It's important to note that the specific content and details of group audit instructions may vary depending on the applicable auditing standards, regulatory requirements, and the complexity of the group structure being audited. Auditing firms often tailor these instructions to suit the unique characteristics of each audit engagement.

CHAPTER 14

OTHER ASSURANCE AND RELATED SERVICES

14.1   LEARNING OBJECTIVES

After studying this chapter, you should be able to:

1. Explain what an assurance engagement entails.
2. Identify the assurance and non-assurance services normally performed by auditors.
3. Describe the five elements exhibited by all assurance engagements.
4. Know the various subject matters that can be covered in an assurance engagement.
5. Distinguish between the different suitable criteria applicable to an assurance service.
6. Understand characteristics of a review engagement.
7. Describe the key users of reports on prospective financial information.
8. Explain the audit of internal control over financial reporting standards.
9. Give the distinguishing characteristics of sustainability reports.
10. Define agreed-upon procedures and compilation engagements.

14.2   THE CONCEPTS

Auditors offer many more services than just the audit of historical financial information. Except for consulting services, the work that auditors do for their clients falls under the guidance of engagement standards set by the International Auditing and Assurance Standards Board (IAASB). All auditor services have as their basis the *IESBA Code of Ethics* and *International Standards on Quality Management* (ISQM)[1].

Some engagement standards are based on the 'International Framework for Assurance Engagements' (assurance engagements), and others fall under Related Services. Four sets of standards (ISAs, ISREs, ISAEs) share the assurance engagement framework and one set of standards (ISRS) refers to related services. ISAs, ISAEs, ISREs and ISRSs are collectively referred to as the IAASB's Engagement Standards (illustration 14.1).

International Standards on Auditing (ISAs) describe the main concepts applicable to financial statement audit and special area engagements. International Standards for Review Engagements (ISREs) are to be applied in the review of historical financial information.

PRONOUNCEMENTS ISSUED BY THE IAASB AND THEIR RELATIONSHIP TO EACH OTHER AND THE IESBA CODE[2]

International Standards on Assurance Engagements (ISAE) 3000 'Assurance Engagements Other than Audits or Reviews of Historical Financial Information' describes concepts applicable to assurance services whose subject matter is not related to historical financial information. International Standard on Sustainability Assurance (ISSA) 5000 is still in exposure draft and is discussed in further detail in chapter 15. Engagements covered by International Standards on Related Services (ISRSs) applied to two related services: agreed-upon procedures (ISRS 4400) and compilation engagements (ISRS 4410).

Examples of engagements not governed by Standards of IAASB are consulting services, tax compliance or tax consulting, engagements in which a practitioner is engaged to testify as an expert witness in accounting, services related to merger and acquisitions, bookkeeping services, legal and IT services as well as other professional services.

ATTESTATION AND DIRECT ENGAGEMENTS

Assurance engagements include both attestation and direct engagements. In an attestation engagement a party other than the practitioner (auditor)[3] measures or evaluates the underlying subject matter against the criteria and presents the resulting subject matter information in a report or statement. In such an 'assertion based' engagement, for example an audit of the financial statements, the auditor's conclusion addresses whether the subject matter information is free from material misstatement. However, in a direct engagement it is the auditor who measures or evaluates the underlying subject matter against the applicable criteria and presents the resulting subject matter in an assurance report. In other words, the auditor's conclusion addresses the reported outcome of the measurement or evaluation of the underlying subject matter against the criteria.

REASONABLE AND LIMITED ASSURANCE ENGAGEMENTS

Under International Framework for Assurance Engagements, there are two types of assurance engagement: a *reasonable assurance engagement* and a *limited assurance engagement*. The objective of a reasonable assurance engagement is a reduction in assurance engagement risk to an acceptably low level in the circumstances of the engagement as the basis for a positive form of expression of the practitioner's conclusion. The objective of a limited assurance engagement is a reduction in assurance engagement risk to a level that is acceptable in the circumstances of the engagement, but where that risk is greater than for a reasonable assurance engagement, as the basis for a negative form of expression of the practitioner's conclusion. In a limited assurance engagement, the level of assurance the practitioner aims to attain cannot be precisely quantified[4]. Whether this level of assurance is meaningful relies on the professional judgement of the practitioner, considering the specific context of the engagement. In such engagements, the procedures carried out differ in nature and scope compared to those in reasonable assurance engagements. However, they are meticulously planned to provide a level of assurance that carries significance. To be deemed meaningful, the assurance obtained by the practitioner should substantially enhance the confidence of intended users regarding the sustainability information, going beyond minor significance. Several factors come into play when determining what constitutes meaningful assurance in a given engagement:

▷ *Characteristics of Sustainability Matters and Applicable Criteria.*
The nature of the sustainability matters and the criteria applied are essential considerations.

▷ *Guidance from Relevant Parties.*
Instructions or indications from the relevant parties may specify necessary procedures or aspects to focus on within the scope of the assurance engagement. However, the practitioner may deem additional procedures necessary to gather appropriate evidence for meaningful assurance.

▷ *Accepted Industry Practices.*
Any established practices within the field of assurance engagements for sustainability information should be taken into account.

▷ *Information Needs of Intended Users.*
The assurance required depends on the potential impact on intended users if they were to receive an incorrect conclusion in cases of material misstatement. The greater the consequences, the higher the level of assurance needed to make it meaningful.

▷ *Expectation for Timely and Cost-Effective Assurance.*
Intended users may anticipate that the practitioner will deliver the limited assurance conclusion swiftly and cost-effectively. However, in some instances, the significance of the consequences may necessitate a reasonable assurance engagement for meaningful assurance. In summary, achieving meaningful assurance in limited assurance engagements involves a delicate balance of professional judgment, tailored procedures, and consideration of various contextual factors.

ENGAGEMENT ACCEPTANCE

As under the ISAEs assurance can be provided regarding a wide range of subject matter, an adequate engagements acceptance process is essential. At the phase of engagement acceptance, the auditor should verify that all five elements of an assurance engagement can be applied to the specific engagement, before signing an engagement letter. The five elements are a three-party relationship, an underlying subject matter, criteria, evidence and an assurance report.

When the client requests the auditor to change the engagement to a non-assurance engagement or from a reasonable assurance engagement to a limited assurance engagement, the auditor should not agree to a change without reasonable justification. A change in circumstances that affects the intended users' requirements, or a misunderstanding concerning the nature of the engagement, ordinarily will justify a request for a change in the engagement. If such a change is made, the auditor does not disregard evidence that was obtained prior to the change.

The assurance engagement calls for planning, gathering evidence and reporting. The extent of planning, the sufficiency of evidence, acceptable engagement risk, and the level of assurance of the opinion will depend on the type of assurance engagement. An assurance engagement based on historical financial information requires more intensive planning and evidence gathering than a related services engagement. The auditor should reduce assurance engagement risk to an acceptably low level in the case of a historical financial information engagement. It is also possible to conduct an assurance engagement that provides a reasonable level of assurance on a subject matter other than historical financial information (e.g. the subject matter of a sustainability report or internal control report).

14.3 ELEMENTS OF AN ASSURANCE ENGAGEMENT

Following the IAASB Assurance Framework,[5] 'assurance engagements' are engagements in which a practitioner expresses a conclusion designed to enhance the degree of confidence of the intended users[6] (other than the responsible party)[7] about the outcome of the evaluation or measurement of a subject matter[8] against criteria.[9]

The assurance framework uses the term 'subject matter information' to mean the outcome of the evaluation or measurement of a subject matter. It is the subject matter information about which the practitioner gathers evidence to provide a reasonable basis for expressing a conclusion in an assurance report. Subject matter could be financial statements, statistical information, non-financial performance indicators, capacity of a facility, etc. The subject matter could also be systems and processes (e.g. internal controls, environment, IT systems) or behaviour (e.g. corporate governance, compliance with regulation, human resource practices). The assurance engagement evaluates whether the subject matter conforms to suitable criteria that will meet the needs of an intended user. For example, an assertion about the effectiveness of internal control (outcome) results from applying a framework for evaluating the effectiveness of internal control, such as COSO[10] or CoCo[11] (criteria) to internal control (subject matter)).

FIVE ELEMENTS EXHIBITED BY ALL ASSURANCE ENGAGEMENTS

The International Framework for Assurance Engagements describes five elements[12] that all assurance engagements exhibit:

1 a three-party relationship involving a practitioner, a responsible party, and the intended users;

2 an appropriate subject matter;

3 suitable criteria;

4 sufficient appropriate evidence; and

5 a written assurance report in the form appropriate to a reasonable assurance engagement or a limited assurance engagement.

Illustration 14.2 is a context data flow diagram of the relations between the five elements during an engagement process.[13]

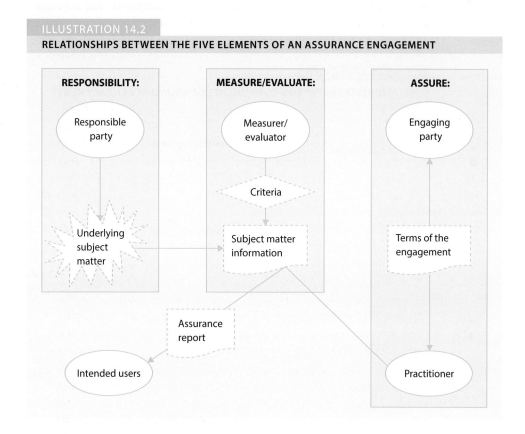

ILLUSTRATION 14.2

RELATIONSHIPS BETWEEN THE FIVE ELEMENTS OF AN ASSURANCE ENGAGEMENT

THREE-PARTY RELATIONSHIP – PRACTITIONER, RESPONSIBLE PARTY AND USER

Assurance engagements always involve three separate parties: a practitioner, a responsible party, and the intended users. The practitioner e.g. auditor (accountant or expert) gathers evidence to provide a conclusion to the intended users about whether a subject matter (e.g. financial statements) conforms, in all material respects, to identified criteria.

The responsible party is the person (or persons) – usually management or the board of directors – who in a direct reporting engagement is responsible for the subject matter. In an assertion-based engagement, the responsible party is responsible for the subject matter information (the assertion) and may be responsible for the subject matter.

The responsible party may or may not be the party who engages the auditor (the engaging party). The responsible party ordinarily provides the auditor with a written representation that evaluates or measures the subject matter against the identified criteria.

The intended users are the person, persons or class of persons for whom the auditor prepares the assurance report. The responsible party can be one of the intended users, but not the only one. Whenever practical, the assurance report is addressed to all the intended users. Also, whenever practical, intended users are involved with the auditor and the responsible party in determining the requirements of the engagement. However, the auditor is responsible for determining the nature, timing and extent of procedures and is required to pursue any matter she becomes aware of that leads her to believe that a material modification should be made to the subject matter information.

As you can see from illustration 14.3, the responsible party selects criteria (e.g. the tax

ILLUSTRATION 14.3

RELATIONSHIPS BETWEEN 5 COMPONENTS OF ASSURANCE ENGAGEMENTS

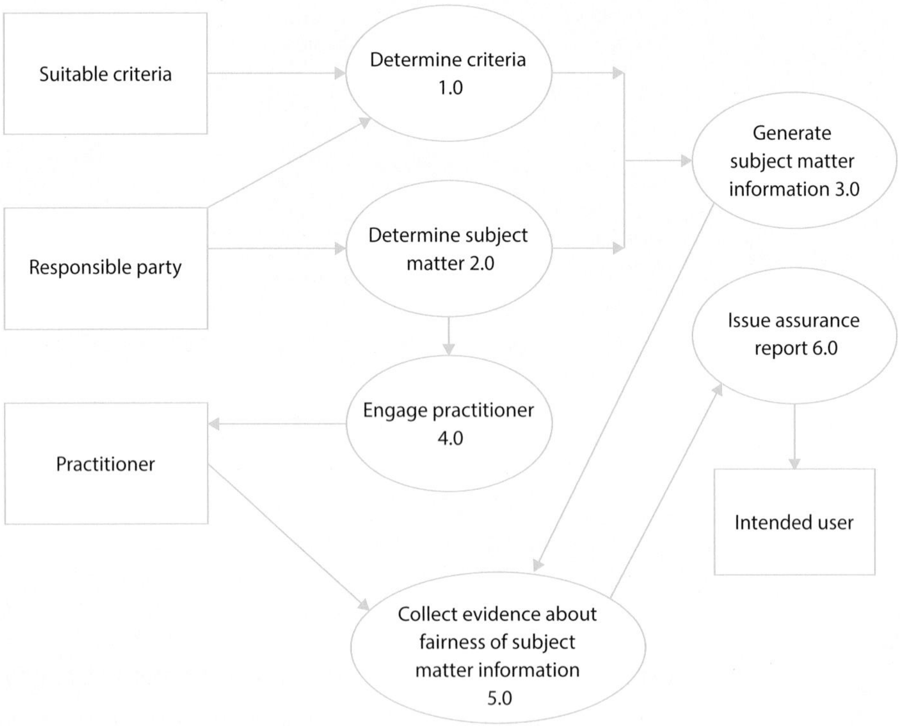

code), determines the subject matter (financial statements) and engages the practitioner (auditor). The subject matter and criteria taken together generate the subject matter information. For example, the tax code criteria and financial statements subject matter combine to make the company income tax returns. In an audit, the criteria could be IFRS, the subject matter is financial performance and position of the company, and subject matter information would be the income statement and balance sheet. In preparing internal control assurances, the criteria could be the COSO criteria, subject matter internal controls, and the subject matter information could be a measure of effectiveness of internal control.

The practitioner determines if the criteria are suitable, collects evidence about the subject matter information and issues an assurance report. For example, the auditor determines if the proper income tax codes are being used, evaluates the income tax information provided by the company by seeking evidence that the information is complete and all transactions from which the data were derived exist. Put another way – a responsible party measures, the auditor, re-measures.

SUBJECT MATTER

The subject matter, and subject matter information, of an assurance engagement can take many forms, such as:

- ▷ Financial performance or conditions (for example, historical or prospective financial position, financial performance and cash flows) for which the subject matter information may be the recognition, measurement, presentation and disclosure represented in financial statements.
- ▷ Non-financial performance or conditions (for example, sustainability performance of an entity) for which the subject matter information may be key indicators of efficiency and effectiveness.
- ▷ Physical characteristics (for example, capacity of a facility) for which the subject matter information may be a specifications document.
- ▷ Systems and processes (for example, an entity's internal control or IT system) for which the subject matter information may be a statement of effectiveness.
- ▷ Behaviour (for example, corporate governance, compliance with regulation, human resource practices) for which the subject matter information may be a statement of compliance or a statement of effectiveness.
- ▷ Governance (for example, information about the composition and performance of the board, strategy, compliance with governance codes).

The subject matter must be identifiable and capable of consistent evaluation or measurement against identified, suitable criteria. It must also be in a form that can be subjected to procedures for gathering evidence to support that evaluation or measurement.

SUITABLE CRITERIA

Suitable criteria are the benchmarks (standards, objectives, or set of rules) used to evaluate evidence or measure the subject matter of an assurance engagement. For example, in the preparation of financial statements, the suitable criteria may be International Financial Reporting Standards (IFRS), US Generally Accepted Accounting Principles (US GAAP), or national standards. When reporting on sustainability aspects of the company an auditor might use the Global Reporting Initiative, European Sustainability Reporting Standards (ESRS) or IFRS-Sustainability Standards (more information in chapter 15).

Several standards may guide the report, depending on the assurance service. When using accounting criteria to report on internal control, the criteria may be an established internal control framework, such as the COSO report criteria, or individual control objectives specifically designed for the engagement. When reporting on compliance, the criteria may be the applicable law, regulation or contract, or an agreed level of performance (for instance, the number of times a company's board of directors is expected to meet in a year). Without the frame of reference provided by suitable criteria, any conclusion is open to individual interpretation and misunderstanding.

THE CHARACTERISTICS FOR ASSESSING SUITABLE CRITERIA

An auditor cannot evaluate or measure a subject matter on the basis of her own expectations, judgments and individual experience. That would not constitute suitable criteria. The characteristics for assessing whether criteria are suitable are as follows:[14]

- ▶ *Relevance*: relevant criteria contribute to conclusions that meet the objectives of the engagement and assist decision making by the intended users.
- ▶ *Completeness*: criteria are sufficiently complete when relevant factors that could affect the conclusions in the context of the engagement objectives are not omitted. Complete criteria include, where relevant, benchmarks for presentation and disclosure of the subject matter.
- ▶ *Reliability*: reliable criteria result in reasonably consistent evaluation or measurement including, where relevant, presentation and disclosure of the subject matter, when used in similar circumstances by similarly qualified practitioners.
- ▶ *Neutrality*: neutral criteria that contribute to conclusions are free from bias.
- ▶ *Understandability*: understandable criteria are clear and comprehensive and are not subject to significantly different interpretation.

CRITERIA ESTABLISHED OR SPECIFICALLY DEVELOPED

Criteria can be either established or specifically developed. Established criteria are those embodied in laws or regulations, or issued by recognised bodies of experts that follow due process. Specifically developed criteria are those identified for the purpose of the engagement, and which are consistent with the engagement objective. Examples of specifically developed criteria are criteria generally understood by the intended users (e.g. the criterion for measuring time in hours and minutes is generally understood); or criteria available only to specific intended users (e.g. the terms of a contract, or criteria issued by an industry association that are available only to those in the industry). Criteria need to be available to the intended users to allow them to understand how the subject matter has been evaluated or measured.

EVIDENCE

The auditor plans and performs an assurance engagement with an attitude of professional scepticism to obtain sufficient appropriate evidence about whether the subject matter information is free of material misstatement. The practitioner considers materiality, assurance engagement risk, and the quantity and quality of available evidence when planning and performing the engagement, in particular when determining the nature, timing and extent of evidence-gathering procedures.

SUFFICIENCY, APPROPRIATENESS, RELIABILITY OF EVIDENCE AND MATERIALITY

Sufficiency is the measure of the quantity of evidence. Appropriateness is the measure of the quality of evidence; that is, its relevance and its reliability. The quantity of evidence needed is affected by the risk of the subject matter information being materially misstated (the greater the risk, the more evidence is likely to be required) and also by the quality

A 'CLEAN AUDIT' FOR HEALTHSOUTH

Concept	What is an assurance service? What is an audit-related service?

Story   Ernst & Young (E&Y) were the independent auditors of HealthSouth (now called Encompass Health Corp.) between 2000 and 2002. They also conducted janitorial inspections of the company's facilities. These inspections were called 'pristine audits.' E&Y advised HealthSouth to classify the payments for 'pristine audits' as 'audit-related fees'.

HealthSouth, headquartered in Birmingham, Alabama, USA during this period was the largest provider of outpatient surgery, diagnostic and rehabilitative healthcare services in the USA with approximately 1,800 worldwide facilities in the USA, Australia, Puerto Rico and the UK. Today Encompass Health Corp is the leading owner and operator of inpatient rehabilitation hospitals in the USA. Its former CEO, Richard M. Scrushy, was under an 85-count federal indictment, accused of conspiracy, securities fraud, mail and wire fraud, and money laundering (SEC, 2003).

A US government indictment charged that between 1996 and 2002 HealthSouth managers, at the insistence of Scrushy, inflated profits by $2.74 billion. Scrushy certified the Health-South financial statements when he knew that they were materially false and misleading. On 4 November 2003, he became the first CEO of a major company to be indicted for violating the Sarbanes–Oxley Act, which holds executives personally accountable for their companies' financial reporting (*Business Week*, 2003).

Six months elapsed from the start of the SEC's investigation to the filing of its fraud suit against Scrushy in March 2003. It took just seven weeks, from 19 March to 5 May, for the US Justice Department to accumulate 11 guilty pleas from Scrushy aides. All five CFOs in the company's history have admitted to cooking the books (Helyar, 2003).

Pristine Audits

Scrushy devised a facilities inspection program called 'Pristine Audits' and hired E&Y to do the work. The primary purpose of the inspections was to check the cleanliness and physical appearance of HealthSouth's surgical and rehabilitation facilities. Under the program, E&Y made unannounced visits to each facility once a year, using dozens of junior-level accountants who were trained for the inspections at HealthSouth's headquarters. For the most part E&Y used audit personnel who were not members of the HealthSouth audit-engagement team to conduct the pristine audits.

The accountants carried out the reviews using as criteria a 50-point checklist designed by Mr Scrushy. The checklist included procedures such as seeing if magazines in waiting rooms were orderly, the toilets and ceilings were free of stains, and the trash receptacles all had liners. Other items on the checklist included: check the walls, furniture, floors and whirlpool areas for stains; check that the heating and cooling vents 'are free of dust accumulation'; that the 'floors are free of trash'; and that the 'overall appearance is sanitary'. A small portion of the checklist pertained to money matters, though none of it pertained to accounting. Assignments included checking if petty-cash drawers were secure and company equipment was properly tagged. The checklists did not cover insurance-billing procedures or the quality of the medical treatment (Weil, 2003a).

Describing the pristine audits, Mr Scrushy told an investor group: 'We believe one of the reasons that we have done so well has to do with the fact that we do audit all of our facilities, 100 per cent, annually. And we use an outside audit firm, our auditors, Ernst & Young. They visit all our facilities, 100 per cent.' On its website, HealthSouth said the pristine audit 'administered independently by Ernst & Young LLP ... ensures that all of our patients enjoy a truly pristine experience during their time at HealthSouth. The average score was 98 per cent, with more than half of our facilities scoring a perfect 100 per cent.'

In 2002 E&Y ended their relationship with HealthSouth, and HealthSouth discontinued the pristine audits.

E&Y Fees Charged HealthSouth

HealthSouth's April 2001 proxy (form DEF14A), filed with the SEC, said the company paid E&Y $1.03 million to audit its 2000 financial statements and $2.65 million of 'all other fees'. The proxy said the other fees included $2.58 million of 'audit-related fees', and $66,107 of 'non-audit-related fees'. In its April 2002 proxy, HealthSouth said it paid E&Y $1.16 million for its 2001 audit and $2.51 million for 'all other fees'. The proxy said the other fees included $2.39 million for 'audit-related fees' and $121,580 for 'non-audit-related fees'.

Neither proxy described in any detail the audit-related or non-audit-related services for which E&Y was paid. Andrew Brimmer, a HealthSouth spokesman, was quoted as saying the 'audit-related-fee' figures for each year included about $1.3 million for the pristine audits. Mr Brimmer said HealthSouth paid E&Y $5.4 million for 2002, including $1.1 million for financial-statement audit services and $1.4 million for the pristine audits (Weil, 2003a).

Pristine Audits as 'Audit-Related Fees'

A March 2002 E&Y report to HealthSouth's Board of Directors included an attachment that summarized E&Y's fees and provided a suggested 'Proxy Disclosure Format'. The attachment classified the pristine audits as 'audit-related services' and the fees for them as 'audit-related fees' (Weil, 2003a).

David Howarth, a spokesman for E&Y is quoted as saying: 'The audit-related category is not limited to services related to the financial statement audit per se. At the time of HealthSouth's disclosures, there were no SEC rules that defined audit-related services. Describing operational audit procedures as audit-related services was reasonable.' Howarth claimed that SEC ruled that audit-related fees would include assurance services traditionally performed by the independent auditor, including 'internal-control reviews'. He maintained the pristine audit was an internal control review. 'Under the new SEC rules adopted in response to the Sarbanes-Oxley Act, these (internal control review) fees are specifically mentioned as ones that should be included in audit-related fees' (Weil, 2003b).

After the Weil (2003b) article appeared, Scott A. Taub, the Deputy Chief Accountant of the SEC wrote a letter to E&Y partner Ed Caulson. Taub wrote: 'The Commission's current rules state that registrants are to 'disclose, under the caption *Audit-Related Fees*, the aggregate fees billed in each of the last two fiscal years for assurance and related services by the principal accountant that are reasonably related to the performance of the audit or review of the registrant's financial statements. It is clear from a reading of the release text and related rules that the Commission's intent is that only fees for services that are reasonably related to the performance of an audit or review of the financial statements and that traditionally have been performed by the independent accountant should be classified as audit-related' (emphasis added) (Taub, 2003).

Discussion Questions	▷ What criteria would the pristine audits have to meet to be considered an audit engagement? ▷ What criteria would the pristine audits have to meet to be considered 'audit-related'? ▷ Can the pristine audits be considered an assurance service? How does the pristine audit meet the five criteria required to qualify an engagement as an assurance service?

References	*Business Week*, 2003, 'Sarbanes-Oxley's First', p. 52, 17 November. Helyar, J., 2003, 'The Insatiable King Richard; He Started as a Nobody. He Became a Hotshot CEO. He tried to be a Country Star. Then it All Came Crashing Down. The Bizarre Rise and Fall of HealthSouth's Richard Scrushy', *Fortune*, p. 76. 7 July. SEC, 2003, Litigation Release 18044, 'SEC Charges HealthSouth Corp. CEO Richard Scrushy with $1.4 Billion Accounting Fraud', US Security and Exchange Commission, 20 March. Taub, S., 2003, *Letter to Ed Coulson, Partner Ernst & Young*, Office of Chief Accountant, US Security and Exchange Commission, 8 July. Weil, J., 2003a, 'What Ernst Did for HealthSouth – Proxy Document Says Company Performed Janitorial Inspections Misclassified as Audit-Related', *Wall Street Journal*, 11 June. Weil, J., 2003b, 'HealthSouth and Ernst Renew Flap Over Fee Disclosures', *Wall Street Journal*, 1 July.

of such evidence (the higher the quality, the less may be required). The reliability of evidence is influenced by its source and by its nature and is dependent on the individual circumstances under which it is obtained (which is discussed in chapter 9).[15]

Ordinarily, available evidence will be persuasive rather than conclusive. The quantity or quality of evidence available is affected by:

▷ The characteristics of the subject matter. For example, when the subject matter is future oriented, less objective evidence might be expected to exist than when the subject matter is historical.

▷ Circumstances of the engagement other than the characteristics of the subject matter, when evidence that could reasonably be expected to exist is not available because of, for example, the timing of the practitioner's appointment, an entity's document retention policy, or a restriction imposed by the responsible party.

Persuasiveness of evidence will in general be less in case of limited assurance compared with a reasonable assurance engagement. However, if the practitioner becomes aware of signals that there may be a material misstatement, additional procedures are necessary when conducting limited assurance engagements to gather further evidence. Obtaining more evidence may not compensate for its poor quality. As in other assurance engagements, in gathering reasonable assurance, relying solely on inquiries generally falls short of offering sufficient appropriate evidence. Also, substantive testing under certain circumstances does not provide sufficient evidence and internal control must be relied on.

Materiality is relevant when the practitioner determines the nature, timing and extent of evidence-gathering procedures, and when assessing whether the subject matter information is free of misstatement. Materiality is considered in the context of quantitative and qualitative factors, such as relative magnitude and the nature and extent of the effect of these factors on the evaluation of the subject matter. The concept of materiality as well as the way it is assessed can differ as per subject matter.[16] For example, is reporting eight instead of nine fatalities in a Health Safety and Environmental Report of one of the large Oil & Gas Companies a 'material' misstatement? The concept of double materiality has been introduced for sustainability reporting (see section 15.3). Materiality assessment is not affected by the level of assurance. This means that, for the same intended users and purpose, materiality for reasonable engagements is the same as for limited assurance engagements.

PLANNING

Effective planning is not only a fundamental requirement for a financial audit (chapter 6) but for all assurance and audit related services, ensuring a targeted focus on crucial areas, facilitating timely issue identification, and establishing a well-organized approach to managing the engagement. This involves strategically allocating tasks within the engagement team, streamlining direction, supervision, and review processes.

Central to the planning process is the inclusive involvement of essential team members, fostering active participation in collaborative discussions. The nature, timing, and extent of planned procedures are evaluated within the context of an overarching strategy that guides the engagement's scope, timing, and direction. This strategy is then detailed into an engagement plan, rationalizing decisions on procedures. Information gathered during the acceptance and continuance process aids in planning, and coordination with other practitioners and subject matter experts is considered.

Professional judgement is exercised by the practitioner in planning and conducting assurance procedures for evidence. Understanding how the entity organizes sustainability information for reporting is crucial in planning the assurance task, taking into account factors such as criteria, reporting objectives, policies, and boundaries.

While the practitioner may discuss planning elements with the entity for coordination, the overall responsibility for the engagement strategy and plan rests with her. These discussions, although common, do not diminish her ultimate responsibility for the engagement.

FRAUD OR NON-COMPLIANCE WITH LAWS AND REGULATION

In responding to identified or suspected fraud or non-compliance with laws and regulation, some appropriate actions that the practitioner may take include:

- ▸ Discussing the matter with the entity.
- ▸ Requesting the entity to consult with an appropriately qualified third party, such as legal counsel or a regulator.
- ▸ Reviewing correspondence with relevant licensing or regulatory authorities.
- ▸ Considering how the matter affects other aspects of the engagement, including risk assessments and the reliability of written representations from the entity.
- ▸ Seeking legal advice regarding potential courses of action.
- ▸ Communicating with third parties, such as regulators.
- ▸ Potentially withholding the assurance report.
- ▸ Possibly withdrawing from the engagement.

DOCUMENTATION

The practitioner is responsible for creating timely assurance engagement documentation. This documentation should serve as a comprehensive record, offering sufficient and appropriate information and enable an experienced assurance practitioner, who has no prior involvement with the engagement, to understand:

▷ The nature, timing and extent of the procedures performed to comply with ISAE 3000 and other applicable legal and regulatory requirements.
▷ The results of the procedures performed, and the evidence obtained; and
▷ Significant matters arising during the assurance engagement, the conclusions reached thereon, and significant professional judgments made in reaching those conclusions.

The assurance engagement documentation also includes[17]:
▷ Discussions of significant matters with management, those charged with governance and others, including the nature of the significant matters discussed, and when and with whom the discussions took place.
▷ If the practitioner identifies information that is inconsistent with the practitioner's final conclusion regarding a significant matter, how the practitioner addressed the inconsistency.
▷ Issues identified with respect to compliance with relevant ethical requirements and how they were resolved.
▷ Conclusions on compliance with independence requirements that apply to the assurance engagement, and any relevant discussions with the firm that support these conclusions.
▷ Conclusions reached regarding the acceptance and continuance of client relationships and assurance engagements, including with respect to the preconditions for an assurance engagement; and
▷ The nature and scope of, and conclusions resulting from, consultations undertaken during the course of the assurance engagement.
▷ Team discussions and significant decisions. This should encompass the discussions held among the engagement team and the significant decisions that were reached during the course of the engagement.
▷ Key understanding, inquiries, and discussions. This includes the practitioner's understanding of the subject matter, relevant risks, and the approach taken to address those risks.

ASSURANCE REPORT

The practitioner provides a written report containing a conclusion that conveys the assurance obtained from the subject matter information. ISAs, ISREs and ISAEs establish basic elements for assurance reports. Also, the auditor considers other reporting responsibilities, including communicating with those charged with governance when appropriate.

In an attestation engagement, the practitioner's conclusion can be worded either:
▷ in terms of the responsible party's assertion (for example: 'In our opinion the responsible party's assertion that internal control is effective, in all material respects, based on XYZ criteria, is fairly stated'); or
▷ directly in terms of the subject matter and the criteria (for example: 'In our opinion internal control is effective, in all material respects, based on XYZ criteria').

The standard elements of the report include the title, addressee, the identification of the subject matter information, identification of the criteria, identification of the responsible party and their responsibilities, the practitioner's responsibilities, a statement that the engagement was performed in accordance with ISAEs, summary of the work performed, practitioner's conclusion, assurance report date, practitioner's name and specific location, and, if appropriate, a description of any significant inherent limitations, or a statement restricting the use to certain intended users. Illustration 14.4 gives the basic elements of the assurance report.

COMPONENTS OF AN ASSURANCE REPORT

Addressee — Title

Identification of responsible party — Description of the subject matter

Statement that engagement is performed in accordance with International Standards of Assurance Engagements

Summary of work undertaken — Identification of criteria

Conclusion

Report date

Practitioner and address

RESPONSIBLE PARTY

The report also includes a statement to identify the responsible party and to describe the responsible parties and the practitioner's responsibilities: this informs the intended users that the responsible party is responsible for the subject matter in the case of a direct reporting engagement, or the subject matter information in the case of an assertion-based engagement, and that the practitioner's role is to independently express a conclusion about the subject matter information. Where there is a subject matter specific ISAE, that ISAE may require that the assurance report refers specifically to being performed in accordance with that specific ISAE.

SUBJECT MATTER

In the body of the report is a description of the subject matter, for example, identification of the subject matter and explanation of the subject matter characteristics. An identification and description of the subject matter information and the subject matter includes, for example:

 ▶ The point in time or period of time to which the evaluation or measurement of the subject matter relates.
 ▶ The name of the entity or component of the entity (such as a subsidiary company or transactions in the sales cycle) to which the subject matter relates.

▶ An explanation of those characteristics of the subject matter or the subject matter information of which the intended users should be aware, and how such characteristics may influence the precision of the evaluation of the subject matter against the identified criteria. For example:

▶ The degree to which the subject matter information is qualitative versus quantitative, objective versus subjective, or historical versus prospective.

▶ Changes in the subject matter or other engagement circumstances that affect the comparability of the subject matter information from one period to the next. When the practitioner's conclusion is worded in terms of the responsible party's assertion, that assertion is appended to the assurance report, reproduced in the assurance report or referenced therein to a source that is available to the intended users.

IDENTIFICATION OF THE CRITERIA

Criteria by which the evidence is measured or evaluated can be either established or specifically developed. To illustrate, IFRS are established criteria for the preparation and presentation of financial statements in the private sector, but specific users may decide to specify some other comprehensive basis of accounting (OCBOA) such as cash accounting, rules of a regulatory authority, or income tax basis that meets their specific information. When users of the report have agreed to criteria other than established criteria, then the assurance report states that it is only for the use of identified users and for the purposes they have specified.

The assurance report identifies the criteria so the intended users can understand the basis for the auditor's conclusion. Disclosure of the source of the criteria, measurement methods used, and significant interpretations made are important for that understanding. The auditor may consider disclosing the source of the criteria (e.g. laws, regulations, recognised bodies of experts, measurement methods used, and any significant interpretations made in applying the criteria).

A SUMMARY OF THE WORK PERFORMED

The summary will help the intended users understand the nature of the assurance conveyed by the assurance report. ISA 700 'Forming an Opinion and Reporting on Financial Statements' and ISRE 2400 'Engagements to Review Financial Statements' provide a guide to the appropriate type of summary. Where no specific ISAE provides guidance on evidence-gathering procedures for a particular subject matter, the summary might include a more detailed description of the work performed.

Because in a limited assurance engagement an appreciation of the nature, timing and extent of evidence-gathering procedures performed is essential to understanding the assurance conveyed by a conclusion expressed in the negative form, the limited assurance summary is more detailed than for a reasonable assurance engagement and identifies the limitations on the nature, timing and extent of evidence-gathering procedures. The summary for a limited assurance engagements states that the evidence-gathering procedures are more limited than for a reasonable assurance engagement, and therefore less assurance is obtained than in a reasonable assurance engagement.

SPECIAL STATEMENTS

A description of any significant, inherent limitation associated with the evaluation or measurement of the subject matter against the criteria is necessary in the assurance report. For example, in an assurance report related to the effectiveness of internal control, it may be appropriate to note that the historic evaluation of effectiveness is not relevant to future periods due to the risk that internal control may become inadequate because of changes in conditions, or that the degree of compliance with policies or procedures may deteriorate.

When the criteria used to evaluate or measure the subject matter are available only to specific intended users, or are relevant only to a specific purpose, a statement is made restricting the use of the assurance report to those intended users or that purpose. Furthermore, when the assurance report is intended only for specific intended users or a specific purpose this would be stated in the assurance report.

PRACTITIONER'S CONCLUSION

The practitioner's conclusion is expressed in positive form, negative form or as a reservation or denial of conclusion.[18]

In the case of an audit of financial statements or Sarbanes-Oxley internal control engagement, the opinion must be expressed in the positive form. The practitioner's conclusion may, for example, be worded as follows: 'In our opinion internal control is effective, in all material respects, based on XYZ criteria' or 'In our opinion the responsible party's assertion that internal control is effective, in all material respects, based on XYZ criteria, is fairly stated.'

In the case of a review of financial statements, the conclusion should be expressed in the negative form. For example, 'Based on our work described in this report, nothing has come to our attention that causes us to believe that internal control is not effective, in all material respects, based on XYZ criteria' or 'Based on our work described in this report, nothing has come to our attention that causes us to believe that the responsible party's assertion that internal control is effective, in all material respects, based on XYZ criteria, is not fairly stated.'

The conclusion should clearly express a reservation in circumstances where some or all aspects of the subject matter do not conform, in all material respects, to the identified criteria; or the auditor is unable to obtain sufficient appropriate evidence.

When the subject matter information is made up of a number of different aspects, separate conclusions may be provided on each aspect. The conclusion should inform the intended user of the context to which the conclusion applies.

MODIFIED CONCLUSIONS

The practitioner should not express an unqualified conclusion when the following circumstances exist and, the effect of the matter is or may be material:

▶ There is a limitation on the scope of the practitioner's work, that is, either circumstances or the responsible party imposes restrictions that prevent her from obtaining sufficient appropriate audit evidence.

▶ In those cases where the practitioner's conclusion is worded in terms of the responsible party's assertion which is not fairly stated; and the subject matter information is materially misstated, the practitioner should express a qualified or adverse conclusion; or when it is discovered, after the engagement has been accepted, that the criteria are unsuitable, or the subject matter is not appropriate for an assurance engagement.

The practitioner should express a qualified conclusion when the effect of a matter is not as material or pervasive as to require an adverse conclusion or a disclaimer of conclusion. A qualified conclusion is expressed as being 'except for' the effects of the matter to which the qualification relates.

COMMUNICATIONS WITH THE AUDIT COMMITTEE

The practitioner communicates relevant matters arising from the assurance engagement with those charged with governance (such as the audit committee). Relevant matters of governance interest include only information that has come to the attention of the auditor as a result of performing the assurance engagement. She is not required to design procedures for the specific purpose of identifying matters of governance interest.

A practitioner who, before the completion of an assurance engagement, is requested to change the engagement to a non-assurance engagement or from an audit-level engagement to a review-level engagement should consider if that is appropriate. She should not agree to a change where there is no reasonable justification for the change. Examples of a reasonable basis for requesting a change in the engagement are a change in circumstances that affects the intended users' requirements or a misunderstanding concerning the nature of the engagement.

14.4 HIGHLIGHTS OF VARIOUS KINDS OF ASSURANCE ENGAGEMENTS

Standard auditor's reports are based on financial statements 'taken as a whole'. However, sometimes the practitioner (auditor) may have a request for a financial statement based on historical financial information, but which is not based on the financial statements as a whole or on IFRS or the requisite national accounting standard.

An auditor may be called upon to report on components of the financial statements, such as when a bank requests an audit of the accounts receivable (a component of the balance sheet) in anticipation of financing. Sometimes there are audits that give an opinion on compliance with legal agreements required of a company. For instance, a subcontractor may ask for an audit to give comfort to a main contractor. Management or the board of directors may request a summarised financial statement. Small businesses are generally not required to comply with IFRS or a national standard. Small businesses may want to have financial statements based on the cash basis, an income tax basis, or a basis required by regulatory agencies.

SPECIAL AREA ENGAGEMENTS

Auditors refer to this type of work described above as 'Special Area Engagements' and it may include any of the following:

> ▶ Reports on Financial Statements Prepared in Accordance with the Special Purpose Framework (ISA 800), such as reports based on a tax basis of accounting, the cash

receipts and disbursements basis of accounting, the financial reporting provisions established by a regulator or the financial reporting provisions of a contract.

▶ Reports on Audits of Single Financial Statements and Specific Elements, Accounts or Items of Financial Statement (ISA 805).

▶ Reports on Summarised Financial Statements (ISA 810).

REPORTS ON FINANCIAL STATEMENTS PREPARED IN ACCORDANCE WITH THE SPECIAL PURPOSE FRAMEWORK (ISA 800)[19]

The Special Purpose Framework is a financial reporting framework designed to meet the financial information needs of specific users and relates to a complete set of special purpose financial statements, including related notes. The financial reporting framework may be a fair presentation framework or a compliance framework.

Examples of special purpose frameworks are:

▶ A tax basis of accounting for a set of financial statements that accompany an entity's tax return.

▶ The cash receipts and disbursements basis of accounting for cash flow.

▶ Information that an entity may be requested to prepare for creditors.

▶ The financial reporting provisions established by a regulator to meet the requirements of that regulator.

▶ The financial reporting provisions of a contract, such as a bond indenture, a loan agreement, or a project grant.

The auditor's report on special purpose financial statements must describe the purpose for which the financial statements are prepared and, if necessary, the intended users, or refer to a note in the special purpose financial statements that contains that information. If management has a choice of financial reporting frameworks in the preparation of such financial statements, the report explains management's responsibility for the financial statements and shall also make reference to management's responsibility for determining the financial reporting framework used is acceptable in the circumstances.

The auditor's report on special purpose financial statements shall include an emphasis of matter paragraph alerting users of the auditor's report that the financial statements are prepared in accordance with a special purpose framework and that, as a result, the financial statements may not be suitable for another purpose.

The auditor's report on financial statements prepared in accordance with the Special Purpose Framework should include a statement that indicates the basis of accounting used. The opinion paragraph of the report should state whether the financial statements are prepared, in all material respects, in accordance with the identified basis of accounting.

REPORTS ON AUDITS OF SINGLE FINANCIAL STATEMENTS AND SPECIFIC ELEMENTS, ACCOUNTS OR ITEMS OF A FINANCIAL STATEMENT (ISA 805)[20]

The auditor may be requested to express an opinion on one or more elements of financial statements (for example, accounts receivable, inventory, an employee's bonus calculation, or a provision for income taxes). This type of engagement may be done as a separate engagement or in conjunction with an audit of the entity's financial statements. However, this type of engagement does not result in a report on the financial statements taken as a whole and, accordingly, the auditor would express an opinion only as to whether that specific element audited is prepared in accordance with the accounting standards.

The auditor's report on an element of financial statements should include a statement that indicates what the basis of accounting is for the element is presented or refers to an agreement that specifies the basis.

The opinion should state whether the element is prepared, in all material respects, in accordance with the identified basis of accounting.

When an adverse opinion or disclaimer of opinion on the entire financial statements has been expressed, the auditor should report on elements of the financial statements only if those elements are not so extensive as to constitute a major portion of the financial statements. To do otherwise may overshadow the report on the entire financial statements.

REPORTS ON SUMMARISED FINANCIAL STATEMENTS (ISA 810)[21]

Some financial statement users may only be interested in the highlights of a company's financial position. Therefore, a company may only require statements summarising its annual audited financial statements. An auditor should only take an engagement to report on summarised financial statements if she has expressed an audit opinion on the financial statements from which the summary is made.

Summarised financial statements are much less detailed than annual audited financial statements. Therefore, the summarised nature of the information reported needs to be clearly indicated. The report must caution the reader that summarised financial statements should be read in conjunction with the company's most recent audited financial statements.

REVIEW OF FINANCIAL STATEMENTS

An Engagements to Review Financial Statements (International Standards for Review Engagements (ISRE) 2000–2699[22]) is similar to an audit of financial statements in the way it requires terms of an engagement, planning, consideration of work performed by others, documentation, and paying attention to subsequent events.[23] These concerns are discussed throughout this book, especially chapter 6 on planning, and chapter 10 which considers completing the audit. Where reviews of financial statements differ most from a financial statement audit is that in a review report engagement only limited procedures are performed. (inquiry of management and analytical procedures and procedures addressing specific circumstances[24]). According to ISRE 2400.48. the practitioner's inquiries of management and others within the entity, as appropriate, shall include the following:

(a) How management makes the significant accounting estimates required under the applicable financial reporting framework;

(b) The identification of related parties and related party transactions, including the purpose of those transactions;

(c) Whether there are significant, unusual or complex transactions, events or matters that have affected or may affect the entity's financial statements, including significant:
- changes in the entity's business activities or operations;
- changes to the terms of contracts that materially affect the entity's financial statements, including terms of finance and debt contracts or covenants;
- journal entries or other adjustments to the financial statements;

> ▶ transactions occurring or recognized near the end of the reporting period;
> ▶ uncorrected misstatements identified during previous engagements; and
> ▶ effects or possible implications for the entity of transactions or relationships with related parties;

(d) The existence of any actual, suspected or alleged fraud or illegal acts affecting the entity and non-compliance with provisions of laws and regulations that are generally recognized to have a direct effect on the determination of material amounts and disclosures in the financial statements, such as tax and pension laws and regulations;

(e) Whether management has identified and addressed events occurring between the date of the financial statements and the date of the practitioner's report that require adjustment of, or disclosure in, the financial statements;

(f) The basis for management's assessment of the entity's ability to continue as a going concern;

(g) Whether there are events or conditions that appear to cast doubt on the entity's ability to continue as a going concern;

(h) Material commitments, contractual obligations or contingencies that have affected or may affect the entity's financial statements, including disclosures; and

(i) Material non-monetary transactions or transactions for no consideration in the financial reporting period under consideration.

The objective of a review of financial statements is to enable an auditor to state (based on procedures that are not as extensive as would be required in a full financial statement audit) 'nothing has come to the auditor's attention that causes the auditor to believe that the financial statements do not give a true and fair view (or are not presented fairly, in all material respects) in accordance with [an identified financial reporting framework].' This way of expressing an opinion is called negative assurance.

REVIEW PROCEDURES

Sufficient appropriate evidence for a financial statement review is limited to inquiry, analytical procedures, limited inspection and, in certain cases only, additional evidence gathering procedures. Inquiry consists of seeking information of knowledgeable persons inside or outside the entity. Analytical procedures (discussed in chapter 9) consist of the analysis of significant ratios and trends including the resulting investigation of fluctuations and relationships that are inconsistent with other relevant information or deviate from predictable amounts. Inspection (discussed in chapter 8), which consists of examining records, documents, or tangible assets, is carried out on a limited basis.

A review engagement, unlike a full financial statement audit, usually does not involve collecting evidence about the design and operation of internal control or obtaining evidence to back up the findings from inquiries or analytical procedures (i.e. corroborating evidence). Review engagements do generally not employ the evidence gathering techniques used in a financial statement audit such as observation, confirmation, recalculation, re-performance or extensive inspection. If the auditor is unable to form a conclusion on the financial statements due to inability to obtain sufficient appropriate evidence, the auditor must qualify or disclaim the conclusion.

REVIEW REPORT OF FINANCIAL STATEMENTS

The report on a review of financial statements should contain the following basic elements, ordinarily in the following layout (see illustration 14.5 for a sample unqualified review report):[25]

- ▶ Title.
- ▶ Addressee.
- ▶ Opening or introductory paragraph.
- ▶ A description of the responsibility of management for the preparation of the financial statements.
- ▶ A description of the auditor's responsibility to express a conclusion on the financial statements.
- ▶ A description of a review of financial statements and its limitations.
- ▶ A paragraph under the heading 'Conclusions' that contains the conclusion as well as a reference to the applicable financial reporting framework.
- ▶ A reference to the auditor's obligation to comply with relevant ethical requirements.
- ▶ Date of the report.
- ▶ Auditor's address.
- ▶ Auditor's signature.

ILLUSTRATION 14.5

UNQUALIFIED REVIEW REPORT ON THE FINANCIAL STATEMENTS

INDEPENDENT PRACTITIONER'S REVIEW REPORT

[Appropriate Addressee]

Report on the Financial Statements
We have reviewed the accompanying financial statements of ABC Company, which comprise the statement of financial position as at December 31, 20X1, and the statement of comprehensive income, statement of changes in equity and statement of cash flows for the year then ended, and a summary of significant accounting policies and other explanatory information.

Management's Responsibility for the Financial Statements
Management is responsible for the preparation and fair presentation of these financial statements in accordance with the International Financial Reporting Standard for Small and Medium-sized Entities, and for such internal control as management determines is necessary to enable the preparation of financial statements that are free from material misstatement, whether due to fraud or error.

Practitioner's Responsibility
Our responsibility is to express a conclusion on the accompanying financial statements. We conducted our review in accordance with International Standard on Review Engagements (ISRE) 2400 (Revised), Engagements to Review Historical Financial Statements. ISRE 2400 (Revised) requires us to conclude whether anything has come to our attention that causes us to believe that the financial statements, taken as a whole, are not prepared in all material respects in ac-

cordance with the applicable financial reporting framework. This Standard also requires us to comply with relevant ethical requirements.

A review of financial statements in accordance with ISRE 2400 (Revised) is a limited assurance engagement. The practitioner performs procedures, primarily consisting of making inquiries of management and others within the entity, as appropriate, and applying analytical procedures, and evaluates the evidence obtained.

The procedures performed in a review are substantially less than those performed in an audit conducted in accordance with International Standards on Auditing. Accordingly, we do not express an audit opinion on these financial statements.

Conclusion

Based on our review, nothing has come to our attention that causes us to believe that these financial statements do not present fairly, in all material respects, (or do not give a true and fair view of) the financial position of ABC Company as at December 31, 20X1, and (of) its financial performance and cash flows for the year then ended, in accordance with the International Financial Reporting Standard for Small and Medium-sized Entities.

Report on Other Legal and Regulatory Requirements

[Form and content of this section of the practitioner's report will vary depending on the natureof the practitioner's other reporting responsibilities.]

[Practitioner's signature]

[Date of the practitioner's report]

[Practitioner's address]

14.5 ASSURANCE ENGAGEMENTS OTHER THAN AUDITS OR REVIEWS OF HISTORICAL FINANCIAL INFORMATION

The International Standards on Assurance Engagements ISAEs 3000-3399 establish basic principles and essential procedures for the performance of all assurance engagements. ISAEs 3400-3699 provide subject specific principles and procedures for engagements on subject matters other than historical financial information standards.

The subject specific matters currently covered by IAASB's pronouncements are:
- ISAE 3400 The Examination of Prospective Financial Information.
- ISAE 3402 Assurance Reports on Controls at a Service Organization.
- ISAE 3410 Assurance Engagements on Greenhouse Gas Statements.
- ISAE 3420 Assurance Engagements to Report on the Compilation of Pro Forma Financial Information Included in a Prospectus.

THE EXAMINATION OF PROSPECTIVE FINANCIAL INFORMATION (ISAE 3400)[26]

'Prospective financial information' means financial information based on assumptions about events that may occur in the future. Prospective financial information can be in the form of a forecast, a projection or a combination of both. A 'forecast' is prospective financial information prepared on the basis of management's assumptions as to future events (best-estimate assumptions). A 'projection' means prospective financial information prepared on the basis of hypothetical assumptions about future events and management actions which may or may not take place, such as a possible merger of two companies. A projection is a 'what-if' scenario.

A report on an examination of prospective financial information may take several forms. It may be a prospectus to provide potential investors with information about future expectations. The report may take the form of an annual report to provide information to shareholders, regulatory bodies, and other interested parties. It might be a report to lenders of cash flow forecasts.

PROSPECTIVE FINANCIAL INFORMATION OFFERS MODERATE LEVEL OF ASSURANCE

Reporting on prospective financial information is highly subjective. Prospective financial information relates to events and actions that have not yet occurred and may not occur. While evidence may be available to support the assumptions, the evidence is future oriented and, therefore, speculative in nature. This means that this evidence does not offer the same level of assurance as historical financial information. The auditor is, therefore, not in a position to express an opinion as to whether the results shown in the prospective financial information will be achieved.

It's feasible, however, to gather evidence regarding whether the forward-looking information adheres to the relevant criteria, based on the assumptions employed by the entity. This evidence includes:

- ▶ In the case of forecasts, there is a reasonable basis for the assumptions used in preparing the sustainability information; or
- ▶ In the case of hypothetical assumptions, such assumptions are consistent with the purpose of the information.

In some circumstances, the evidence available may support a range of possible outcomes with the disclosure falling within that range.

Example of evidence for forward-looking information

When disclosures relate to future strategy, a target, or other intentions of an entity, the practitioner may focus evidence- gathering activities on whether management or those charged with governance have an intention to follow that strategy, the target or intention exists, or there is a reasonable basis for the intended strategy or target (e.g., the practitioner may obtain evidence to support that the entity has the ability to carry out its intent, or is implementing controls over source data and the assumptions on which the strategy is based.

Given the types of evidence available, it may be difficult for the auditor to obtain a level of satisfaction sufficient to provide a positive expression of opinion. The auditor can generally only provide a moderate level of assurance.

REPORT ON EXAMINATION OF PROSPECTIVE FINANCIAL INFORMATION

The report by an auditor on an examination of prospective financial information differs from the reports on historical financial information in that it contains the following:[27]

- ▶ identification of the prospective financial information;

▶ a statement that management is responsible for the prospective financial information including the assumptions on which it is based;

▶ when applicable, a reference to the purpose and/or restricted distribution of the prospective financial information;

▶ a statement of negative assurance as to whether the assumptions provide a reasonable basis for the prospective financial information;

▶ an opinion as to whether the prospective financial information is properly prepared on the basis of the assumptions and is presented in accordance with the relevant financial reporting framework;

▶ appropriate caveats concerning the achievability of the results indicated by the prospective financial information.

The warnings in the report on prospective financial statements should be clear. They would state that actual results are likely to be different from the prospective financial information since anticipated events frequently do not occur as expected and the variation could be material. In the case of a projection, the caveat would be that 'the prospective financial information has been prepared for [state purpose], using a set of assumptions that include hypothetical assumptions about future events and management's actions that are not necessarily expected to occur.'

INTERNAL CONTROLS OVER FINANCIAL REPORTING (ICFR) ASSURANCE ENGAGEMENTS

Currently, various standards for internal control reporting exist. Most common is reporting according to SOX 404, which is required for all companies that trade on the stock exchanges in the USA including companies headquartered outside the USA[28]. In some countries like Japan and Canada similar requirements apply for listed companies[29]. As SOX is most common worldwide, we focus on SOX as an example of Internal Control Reporting.

The Sarbanes-Oxley Act of 2002 (SOX) requires certification of internal control by the Chief Executive Officer (CEO) and Chief Financial Officer (CFO) of all companies that trade on the stock exchanges in the USA including companies headquartered outside the USA.

The rules on internal control reporting published by the SEC[30] require a company's annual report to include an internal control report of management that contains[31]:

▶ A statement of management's responsibility for establishing and maintaining adequate internal control over financial reporting for the company.

▶ A statement identifying the framework used by management to evaluate the effectiveness of the company's internal control over financial reporting.

▶ Management's assessment of the effectiveness of the company's internal control over financial reporting, including a statement as to whether or not the company's internal control over financial reporting is effective[32]. The assessment must include disclosure of any 'material weaknesses' in the company's internal control over financial reporting identified by management.

▶ A statement that the registered public accounting firm that audited the financial statements included in the annual report has issued an attestation report on management's assessment of the registrant's internal control over financial reporting.

SOX requires that the company's auditor give an opinion on management's report on internal control (we discuss this auditor's report in section 11.7)[33]. The US Public Company Accounting Oversight Board (PCAOB) established an internal control audit standard (AS 2201) required by US publicly traded companies[34]. See illustration 11.16 for a sample integrated auditor's opinion on internal control over financial reporting and financial statements.

ILLUSTRATION 14.6

ISAE 3402 REPORT

Independent auditor's assurance report on the description of controls, their design and operating effectiveness regarding the A-online accounting system (OAS) for the period 1 December 202X to 30 November 202Y

To Management of Fleur Company a/s

Scope
We have been engaged to report on Mystique A-online accounting system description in Section Y of the general IT controls supporting processing customers' transactions throughout the period 1 December 202X to 30 November 202Y (the description) and on the design and operation of controls related to the control objectives stated in the description. The general IT controls included in this report have been tested at Fleur Company a/s covering the global A-online solution.

Fleur Company a/s' responsibility
Fleur Company a/s is responsible for: preparing the description and accompanying statement in Section W, including the completeness, accuracy and method of presentation of the description and the statement; providing the services covered by the description; stating the control objectives; and designing, implementing and effectively operating controls to achieve the stated control objectives.

Our independence and quality control
We have complied with the independence and other ethical requirements of the Code of Ethics for Professional Accountants issued by the International Ethics Standards Board for Accountants. We apply International Standard on Quality Management, ISQM1 and accordingly maintain a comprehensive system of quality control including documented policies and procedures regarding compliance with ethical requirements, professional standards and applicable legal and regulatory requirements.

Auditor's responsibility
Our responsibility is to express an opinion on Fleur Company a/s' description and on the design and operation of controls related to the control objectives stated in that description based on our procedures. We conducted our engagement in accordance with International Standard on Assurance Engagements 3402, 'Assurance Reports on Controls at a Service Organizations' in order to obtain reasonable assurance for our opinion. That standard requires that we plan and

perform our procedures to obtain reasonable assurance about whether, in all material respects, the description is fairly presented and the controls are suitably designed and operating effectively. An assurance engagement to report on the description, design and operating effectiveness of controls at a service organiszation involves performing procedures to obtain evidence about the disclosures in the service organization's description of its system and the design and operating effectiveness of controls. The procedures selected depend on the service auditor's judgement, including the assessment that the description is not fairly presented, and that controls are not suitably designed or operating effectively. Our procedures including testing the operating effectiveness of those controls that we consider necessary to provide reasonable assurance that the control objectives stated in the description were achieved. An assurance engagement of this type also includes evaluating the overall presentation of the description, the suitability of the control objectives stated therein, and the suitability of the criteria specified by Fleur Company a/s and described in Section W.

We believe that the evidence we have obtained is sufficient and appropriate to provide a basis for our opinion.

Limitations of controls at a service organization

Fleur Company a/s' description is prepared to meet the common needs of a broad range of customers and their auditors and may not, therefore, include every aspect of the system that each individual customer may consider important in its own particular environment. Also, because of their nature, controls at a service organization may not prevent or detect all errors or omissions in processing or reporting transactions. Also, the projection of any evaluation of effectiveness to future periods is subject to the risk and that controls at a service organization may become inadequate or fail.

Opinion

Our opinion has been formed on the basis of the matters outlined in this report. The criteria we used in forming our opinion were those described in Section Y. In our opinion, in all material respects:

(a) the description fairly presents the general IT controls supporting the economic online accounting system as designed and implemented throughout the period from 1 December 202X to 30 November 202Y; and

(b) the controls related to the control objectives stated in the description were suitably designed throughout the period from 1 December 202X to 30 November 202Y; and

(c) the controls tested, which were those necessary to provide reasonable assurance that the control objectives stated in the description were achieved, operated effectively throughout the period from 1 December 202X to 30 November 202Y.

Description of tests of controls

The specific controls tested and the nature, timing and result of those tests are listed in Section Z.

Intended users and purpose

This report and the description of tests of controls in Section Z are intended only for Fleur Company a/ s' customers and their auditors, who have a sufficient understanding to consider it, along with other information, including information about controls operated by Fleur Company a/ s' customers themselves, when obtaining an understanding of customers' information systems relevant to financial reporting.

Kolding, 7 March 202Z
Wilhelmina Fuvius
Statsautoriseret Revisionspartnerselskab

ASSURANCE REPORTS ON CONTROLS AT A SERVICE ORGANIZATION (ISAE 3402)

Various companies (user entities) use service organizations for specific services, for example payroll services. As these user entities would like to rely on controls of services organizations, the IAASB came with a standard to audit the controls at a service organization that is likely to be relevant to user entities' internal control as it relates to financial reporting. This standard is the counterpart of ISA 402 'Audit Considerations Relating to an Entity Using a Service Organization'.[35]

The objectives of the service auditor are to obtain reasonable assurance about whether, in all material respects, based on suitable criteria:

▶ The service organization's description of its system fairly presents the system as designed and implemented throughout the specified period (or in the case of a type 1 report, as at a specified date).

▶ The controls related to the control objectives stated in the service organization's description of its system were suitably designed throughout the specified period (or in the case of a type 1 report, as at a specified date).

▶ Where included in the scope of the engagement, the controls operated effectively to provide reasonable assurance that the control objectives stated in the service organization's description of its system were achieved throughout the specified period.

And these matters would be reported in accordance with the service auditor's findings.[36]

Some of the considerations are similar to those of a financial statement audit, which are discussed throughout this book. The primary considerations of an assurance report on controls at service organizations that differ from an audit of financial statements are the subject matter and reporting (type 1 or 2). We refer to chapter 6, section 6.7 'Obtaining an Understanding of the Use of Services of Service Organizations'.

TYPE OF REPORT

According to ISAE 3402 two types of reports are applicable related to control reporting of service organizations:

▶ a type 1 report, a report on the description and design of controls at a service organization;

▶ a type 2 report, a report on the description, design and operating effectiveness of controls at a service organization.

To be able to verify the effectiveness of the operating controls of the service organization, user entities need to request a type 2 report from the service organization.

SUSTAINABILITY ASSURANCE ENGAGEMENTS

The verification of sustainability reports providing assertions regarding economic, environmental and social performance has become a mature assurance service. Important drivers of this demand are:

▶ the legal requirement to report on environmental issues in several countries.

▶ required as part of an emission trading scheme.

▶ voluntary sustainability reporting to inform stakeholders.

Besides separate sustainability reports, integrated reporting is becoming common practice. Integrated reporting is a process that results in communication, most visibly a periodic 'integrated report', about value creation over time[37]. An integrated report is a concise communication about how an organization's strategy, governance, performance and prospects lead to the creation of value over the short, medium and long term. In many countries local stock exchanges have introduced a range of sustainability reporting requirements for listed companies, such as in China (Shanghai/Shenzen), South Africa (Johannesburg) and Brazil (Bovespa). In the EU companies have to issue a sustainability report in accordance with the CSRD from 2024 onwards and practitioners have to provide (limited) assurance.

In chapter 15 sustainability assurance engagements are discussed in further detail.

ASSURANCE ENGAGEMENTS ON GREENHOUSE GAS STATEMENTS

The Greenhouse Gas Protocol (GHG Protocol) is the most widely used international accounting tool to understand, quantify, and manage greenhouse gas emissions. The GHG Protocol is a partnership between the World Resources Institute (WRI) and the World Business Council for Sustainable Development (WBCSD). The GHG Protocol is working with businesses, governments, and environmental groups around the world to build a new generation of credible and effective programmes for tackling climate change. The Corporate Standard classifies a company's direct and indirect GHG emissions into three 'scopes,' and requires that companies account for and report all scope 1 emissions (i.e., direct emissions from owned or controlled sources) and all scope 2 emissions (i.e., indirect emissions from the generation of purchased energy consumed by the reporting company). The Corporate Standard gives companies flexibility in whether and how to account for scope 3 emissions (i.e., all other indirect emissions that occur in a company's value chain). Illustration 14.7 gives an overview of GHG Protocol scopes and emissions across the value chain.

ISAE 3410 deals with assurance engagements to report on an entity's greenhouse gas (GHG) statement. The objectives of the practitioner are:

▶ To obtain reasonable or limited assurance, as appropriate, about whether the GHG statement is free from material misstatement, whether due to fraud or error, thereby enabling the practitioner to express a conclusion conveying that level of assurance.

▶ To report, in accordance with the practitioner's findings, about whether:

▶ in the case of a reasonable assurance engagement, the GHG statement is prepared, in all material respects, in accordance with the applicable criteria; or

▶ in the case of a limited assurance engagement, anything has come to the practitioner's attention that causes the practitioner to believe, on the basis of the

ILLUSTRATION 14.7

OVERVIEW OF GHG PROTOCOL SCOPES AND EMISSIONS ACROSS THE VALUE CHAIN[38]

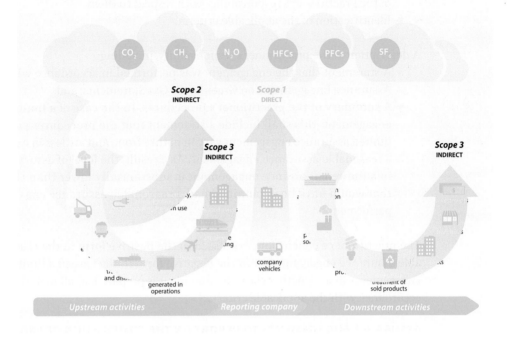

procedures performed and evidence obtained, that the GHG statement is not prepared, in all material respects, in accordance with the applicable criteria; and

▷ To communicate as otherwise required by this ISAE, in accordance with the practitioner's findings.[39]

Some of the considerations are similar to those of a financial statement audit, which are discussed throughout this book. The primary considerations of an assurance report that differ from an audit of financial statements are the choice in level of assurance (limited versus reasonable assurance), engagement acceptance, subject matter and reporting.

REPORTING ON GREENHOUSE GAS STATEMENT

The report by an auditor on greenhouse gas differs from the reports on historical financial information in that it contains the following:

▷ Identification of the GHG statement, including the period(s) it covers, and, if any information in that statement is not covered by the practitioner's conclusion, clear identification of the information subject to assurance as well as the excluded information, together with a statement that the practitioner has not performed any procedures with respect to the excluded information and, therefore, that no conclusion on it is expressed.

▷ A statement that GHG quantification is subject to inherent uncertainty.

> ▶ If the GHG statement includes emissions deductions that are covered by the practitioner's conclusion, identification of those emissions deductions, and a statement of the practitioner's responsibility with respect to them.
> ▶ Identification of the applicable criteria.

A description of the practitioner's responsibility, including:

> ▶ A statement that the engagement was performed in accordance with ISAE 3410, Assurance Engagements on Greenhouse Gas Statements; and
> ▶ A summary of the practitioner's procedures. In the case of a limited assurance engagement, this shall include a statement that the procedures performed in a limited assurance engagement vary in nature from, and are less in extent than for, a reasonable assurance engagement. As a result, the level of assurance obtained in a limited assurance engagement is substantially lower than the assurance that would have been obtained had a reasonable assurance engagement been performed.

The practitioner's conclusion, expressed in the positive form in the case of a reasonable assurance engagement or in the negative form in the case of a limited assurance engagement, about whether the GHG statement is prepared, in all material respects, in accordance with the applicable criteria.[40]

ASSURANCE ENGAGEMENTS TO REPORT ON THE COMPILATION OF PRO FORMA FINANCIAL INFORMATION INCLUDED IN A PROSPECTUS (ISAE 3420)

The ISAE 3420 'Assurance Engagement to Report on the Compilation of Pro Forma Financial Information Included in a Prospectus' deals with reasonable assurance engagements undertaken by a practitioner to report on the responsible party's compilation of pro forma financial information included in a prospectus.[41]

14.6 RELATED SERVICES

Besides assurance engagements, auditors can be engaged for non-assurance engagements. A related service engagement is generally an examination of historical financial statements to develop a conclusion based on the criteria, but no audit opinion. In some instances, this kind of engagement could also be linked to information other than historical financial statements. The IAASB covers two types of non-assurance engagements as Related Services: engagements to perform agreed-upon procedures regarding financial information (ISRS 4400) and compilation engagements (ISRS 4410).

A report issued by an auditor in connection with an engagement that does not exhibit all of the elements described in the Assurance Framework should specifically state it does not express assurance.

Furthermore, it does not purport to enhance the degree of confidence intended users can have with a conclusion of an opinion. So as not to confuse users, a report that is not an assurance report avoids, for example:

> ▶ Implying compliance with Assurance Standards.

▶ Inappropriately using the words 'assurance,' 'audit' or 'review.'
▶ Including a statement that could reasonably be mistaken for a conclusion based on sufficient appropriate evidence that is designed to enhance the degree of confidence of intended users about the outcome of the measurement or evaluation of an underlying subject matter against criteria.

Also, the auditor and the responsible party may agree to apply the principles of the Assurance Framework to an engagement when there are no intended users other than the responsible party but where all other requirements of relevant Assurance Standards are met. In such cases, the assurance report includes a statement restricting the use of the report to the responsible party[42].

ENGAGEMENTS TO PERFORM AGREED-UPON PROCEDURES REGARDING FINANCIAL INFORMATION (ISRS 4400)[43]

An agreed-upon procedures engagement is an engagement in which a practitioner is engaged to carry out procedures to which the practitioner and the engaging party (and if relevant other parties have agreed and to communicate the procedures performed and the related factual results[44] in an agreed-upon procedures report.

Agreed-upon procedures are not considered an assurance engagement. While the intended user of the report may derive some assurance from the report of the factual results, the engagement is not intended to provide, nor does the auditor express, a conclusion that provides a level of assurance. Rather, the intended user assesses the procedures and results and draws his own conclusions[45] (see illustration 14.8, 'Agreed-upon procedures').

Examples of financial and non-financial subject matters on which an agreed-upon procedures may be performed include[46]:
▶ Financial subject matters relating to:
  ▶ The entity's financial statements or specific classes of transactions, account balances or disclosures within the financial statements.
  ▶ Eligibility of expenditures claimed from a funding program.
  ▶ Revenues for determining royalties, rent or franchise fees based on a percentage of revenues.
  ▶ Capital adequacy ratios for regulatory authorities.
▶ Non-financial subject matters relating to:
  ▶ Numbers of passengers reported to a civil aviation authority.
  ▶ Observation of destruction of fake or defective goods reported to a regulatory authority.
  ▶ Datta generating processes for lottery draws reported to a regulatory authority.
  ▶ Volume of greenhouse gas emissions reported to a regulatory authority.

OBJECTIVE

The objective of an agreed-upon procedures engagement is for the auditor to carry out procedures of an audit nature to which the auditor, the company, and some third party have agreed and to report on factual results of the performed agreed-upon procedures. The report is restricted to those parties that have agreed to the procedures since others, unaware of the reasons for the procedures, may misinterpret the results.

INDEPENDENCE NOT REQUIRED

Independence is not a requirement for agreed-upon procedures engagements; however, the terms or objectives of an engagement or national standards may require the auditor to comply with the independence requirements of IESBA Code of Ethics. Where the auditor is not independent, a statement to that effect would be made in the report of factual results.[47]

PROFESSIONAL JUDGEMENT

Also, in agreed-upon engagements, the practitioner exercises professional judgment throughout the engagement, including in accepting, conducting and reporting on the engagement, taking into account the circumstances of the engagement.

MATTERS TO BE AGREED

The auditor should ensure that all involved parties have a clear understanding regarding the agreed procedures and the conditions of the engagement. Matters to be agreed between auditor and management include the:[48]

- ▷ Nature of the engagement including the fact that no assurance will be expressed on the procedures performed.
- ▷ Identification of the financial information to which the agreed-upon procedures will be applied.
- ▷ Nature, timing and extent of the specific procedures to be applied.
- ▷ Anticipated form of the report of factual results.
- ▷ Limitations on distribution of the report of factual results. When such limitation would be in conflict with the legal requirements, if any, the auditor would not accept the engagement.

PROCEDURES PERFORMED

An engagement to perform agreed-upon procedures may involve the auditor in performing certain procedures on subject matter information like financial data (e.g. accounts payable, accounts receivable, purchases from related parties, and sales and profits of a segment of an entity), a financial statement (e.g. a balance sheet) or even a complete set of financial statements.

The procedures applied in an engagement to perform agreed-upon procedures may include: inquiry and analysis, recalculate, comparison and other clerical accuracy checks, observation, inspection and obtaining confirmations (these are discussed in chapter 8).

AGREED-UPON PROCEDURES REPORT

The report on an agreed-upon procedures engagement needs to describe the purpose and the agreed-upon procedures of the engagement in sufficient detail to enable the reader to understand the nature and the extent of the work performed. The report of factual results should contain,[49] among other things, a description of the auditor's factual results including sufficient details of errors and exceptions found and a statement that the report is restricted to those parties that have agreed to the procedures to be performed. Agreed-upon procedures should not be unclear or misleading and descriptions of actions could include for example confirm, agree, compare, trace, inspect, observe, inquire instead of audit, review, assurance, conclusion that could imply expression of an assurance opinion or conclusion.[50]

Illustration 14.8 contains an example of a report of factual results issued in connection with an engagement to perform agreed-upon procedures regarding financial information.[51]

ILLUSTRATION 14.8

AGREED-UPON PROCEDURES REPORT ON PROCUREMENT OF [XYZ] PRODUCTS[52]

To [Addressee]

Purpose of this Agreed-Upon Procedures Report
Our report is solely for the purpose of assisting [Engaging Party] in determining whether its procurement of [xyz] products is compliant with its procurement policies and may not be suitable for another purpose.

Responsibilities of the Engaging Party and the Responsible Party
[Engaging Party] has acknowledged that the agreed-upon procedures are appropriate for the purpose of the engagement. [Responsible Party], as identified by [Engaging Party], is responsible for the subject matter on which the agreed-upon procedures are performed.

Practitioner's Responsibilities
We have conducted the agreed-upon procedures engagement in accordance with the International Standard on Related Services (ISRS) 4400, Agreed-Upon Procedures Engagements. An agreed-upon procedures engagement involves our performing the procedures that have been agreed with [Engaging Party], and reporting the findings, which are the factual results of the agreed-upon procedures performed. We make no representation regarding the appropriateness of the agreed-upon procedures. This agreed-upon procedures engagement is not an assurance engagement. Accordingly, we do not express an opinion or an assurance conclusion.

Had we performed additional procedures, other matters might have come to our attention that would have been reported.

Professional Ethics and Quality Management
We have complied with the ethical requirements in [describe the relevant ethical requirements]. For the purpose of this engagement, there are no independence requirements with which we are required to comply. Our firm applies International Standard on Quality Management 1, which requires the firm to design, implement and operate a system of quality management including policies or procedures regarding compliance with ethical requirements, professional standards and applicable legal and regulatory requirements.

Procedures and Findings
We have performed the procedures described below, which were agreed upon with [Engaging Party], on the procurement of [xyz] products.

Procedures		Findings
1	Obtain from management of [Responsible Party] a listing of all contracts signed between [January 1, 20X1] and [December 31, 20X1] for [xyz] products ('listing') and identify all contracts valued at over $25,000.	We obtained from management a listing of all contracts fo [xyz] products which were signed between [January 1, 20X1] and [December 31, 20X1]. Of the 125 contracts on the listing, we identified 37 contracts valued at over $25,000.
2	For each identified contract valued at over $25,000 on the listing, compare the contract to the records of bidding and determine whether the contract was subject to bidding by at least 2 contractors from [Responsible Party]'s 'Pre-qualified Contractors List.'	We inspected the records of bidding related to the 37 contractts valued at over $25,000. We found that all of the 37 contracts were subject to bidding by at least 3 contractors from the [Responsible Party]'s 'Pre-qualified Contractors List.'
3	For each identified contract valued at over $25,000 on the listing, compare the amount payable per the signed contract to the amount ultimately paid by [Responsible Party] to the contractor and determine whether the amount ultimately paid is within $100 of the agreed amount in the contract.	We obtained the signed contracts for the 37 contracts valued at over $25,000 on the listing and compared the amounts payable in the contracts to the amounts ultimately paid by [Responsible Party] to the contractor. We found that the amounts ultimately paid were within $100 of the agreed amounts in all of the 37 contracts with no exceptions noted.

[Practitioner's signature] [Date of practitioner's report]
[Practitioner's address]

ENGAGEMENTS TO COMPILE FINANCIAL INFORMATION (ISRS 4410)[53]

The objective of a compilation engagement is for the professional accountant to use accounting expertise, as opposed to auditing expertise, to collect, classify and summarise financial information. This ordinarily entails reducing detailed data to a manageable and understandable form without a requirement to test the assertions underlying that information. The procedures employed do not enable the practitioner to express any assurance on the financial information.

INDEPENDENCE

Unlike assurance engagements, independence is not a requirement for a compilation engagement. However, national ethical codes or laws or regulations may specify requirements or disclosure rules pertaining to independence.[54]

UNDERSTANDING TERMS OF THE ENGAGEMENT

The professional accountant should ensure that there is a clear understanding between the client and the professional accountant regarding the terms of the engagement. Matters to be considered, among other things, include:[55]

- ▶ The intended use and distribution of the financial information, and any restrictions on either its use or its distribution where applicable.
- ▶ Identification of the applicable financial reporting framework.
- ▶ The objective and scope of the compilation engagement.
- ▶ The responsibilities of the practitioner, including the requirement to comply with relevant ethical requirements.
- ▶ The responsibilities of management.
- ▶ The expected form and content of the practitioner's report.

COMPILATION PROCEDURES

A compilation engagement would ordinarily include the preparation of financial statements (which may or may not be a complete set of financial statements) but may also include the collection, classification and summarisation of other financial information.

The practitioner should read the compiled information and consider whether it appears to be appropriate in form and free from obvious material misstatements. If this compiled information does not satisfy the accountant, he should bring it to the attention of management and request for additional or corrected information.

In principle, the practitioner is not required to: assess internal controls; verify any matters or explanations; or make any inquiries of management to assess the reliability and completeness of the information provided.

REPORTING ON A COMPILATION ENGAGEMENT

Reports on compilation engagements should contain, among other requirements:[56]

- ▶ A statement that the practitioner has compiled the financial information based on information provided by management.
- ▶ A description of the responsibilities of management, or those charged with governance as appropriate, in relation to the compilation engagement, and in relation to the financial information.
- ▶ A description of the practitioner's responsibilities in compiling the financial information, including that the engagement was performed in accordance with this ISRS, and that the practitioner has complied with relevant ethical requirements.
- ▶ Explanations that:
  - ▶ since a compilation engagement is not an assurance engagement, the practitioner is not required to verify the accuracy or completeness of the information provided by management for the compilation; and
  - ▶ accordingly, the practitioner does not express an audit opinion or a review conclusion on whether the financial information is prepared in accordance with the applicable financial reporting framework.

The financial information compiled by the practitioner should contain a reference such as 'Unaudited', 'Compiled without Audit or Review' or 'Refer to Compilation Report' on each page of the financial information or on the front of the complete set of financial statements.

Illustration 14.9 includes an example of a standard compilation report on financial statements prepared in accordance with accounting principles generally accepted in the United States of America (SSARS 9080, AICPA, 2016)[57].

ILLUSTRATION 14.9

COMPILATION REPORT [APPROPRIATE SALUTATION]

I (we) have compiled the accompanying balance sheet of XYZ Company as of December 31, 20XX, and the related statements of income, retained earnings, and cash flows for the year then ended. I (we) have not audited or reviewed the accompanying financial statements and, accordingly, do not express an opinion or provide any assurance about whether the financial statements are in accordance with accounting principles generally accepted in the United States of America. Management (owners) is (are) responsible for the preparation and fair presentation of the financial statements in accordance with accounting principles generally accepted in the United States of America and for designing, implementing, and maintaining internal control relevant to the preparation and fair presentation of the financial statements. My (our) responsibility is to conduct the compilation in accordance with Statements on Standards for Accounting and Review Services issued by the American Institute of Certified Public Accountants. The objective of a compilation is to assist management in presenting financial information in the form of financial statements without undertaking to obtain or provide any assurance that there are no material modifications that should be made to the financial statements.

[Signature of accounting firm or accountant, as appropriate]
[Date]

14.7 SUMMARY

Auditor services are work that an audit firm performs for their clients. Except for consulting services, the work that auditors do is under the guidance of engagement standards set by the International Auditing and Assurance Standards Board (IAASB). All auditor services standards have as their basis the IESBA Code of Ethics and International Standards on Quality Management (ISQM).

The sets of standards based on the assurance framework are ISA and ISAE. International Standards on Auditing 200 (ISA 200) 'Overall Objectives of The Independent Auditor and the Conduct of an Audit in Accordance with International Standards on Auditing' describes the main concepts applicable to audit and special purpose engagements. International Standards on Assurance Engagements 3000 (ISAE 3000) 'Assurance Engagements on Subject Matters Other than Historical Financial Information' describes concepts applicable to assurance services whose subject matter is not related to historical financial information. Engagements covered by International Standards on Related Services (ISRS) are based on the 'Related Services'. Standards under this framework are applied currently to two related services: engagements to perform agreed-upon procedures regarding financial information (ISRS 4400) and compilations (ISRS 4410).

There are two levels of assurance engagements: a reasonable assurance engagement and a limited assurance engagement. The objective of a reasonable assurance engagement is a reduction in assurance engagement risk to an acceptably low level based on the circumstances of the engagement as the basis for a positive form of expression of the practitioner's conclusion. The objective of a limited assurance engagement is a reduction in assurance engagement risk to a level that is acceptable in the circumstances of the engagement, but where that risk is greater than for a reasonable assurance engagement, as the basis for a negative form of expression of the practitioner's conclusion.

The International Framework for Assurance Engagements describes five elements that all assurance engagements exhibit: (1) a three-party relationship involving a practitioner, a responsible party and the intended users; (2) an appropriate subject matter; (3) suitable criteria; (4) sufficient appropriate evidence; and (5) a written assurance report in the form appropriate to a reasonable assurance engagement or a limited assurance engagement.

Sometimes the auditor may have a request for a financial statement audit based on historical financial information, but which is not based on the financial statements as a whole or on IFRS or the requisite national standard. Examples are:

- Reports on Financial Statements Prepared in Accordance with the Special Purpose Framework (ISA 800), such as:
  - a tax basis of accounting for a set of financial statements that accompany an entity's tax return;
  - the cash receipts and disbursements basis of accounting for cash flow information that an entity may be requested to prepare for creditors;
  - the financial reporting provisions established by a regulator to meet the requirements of that regulator; or
  - the financial reporting provisions of a contract, such as a bond indenture, a loan agreement or a project grant.
- Reports on Audits of Single Financial Statements and Specific Elements, Accounts or Items of a Financial Statement (ISA 805).
- Reports on Summarised Financial Statements (ISA 810).

A review of financial statements is similar to an audit of financial statements in the way it requires terms of an engagement, planning, consideration of work performed by others, documentation, and paying attention to subsequent events (ISRE 2000-2699). Where reviews of financial statements differ most from a financial statement audit is that in a review report engagement only limited procedures are performed (primarily inquiry of management and analytical procedures). The objective of a review of financial statements is to enable an auditor to state (based on procedures that are not as extensive as would be required in a full financial statement audit) 'nothing has come to the auditor's attention that causes the auditor to believe that the financial statements do not give a true and fair view (or are not presented fairly, in all material respects) in accordance with [an identified financial reporting framework].' This way of expressing a conclusion is called negative assurance.

The International Standard on Assurance Engagements (ISAE) 3000 establishes basic principles and essential procedures for professional accountants in public practice for the performance of assurance engagements on subject matters other than historical financial information. Assurance engagements other than historical financial information have two main components: (1) topics that apply to all assurance engagements (ISAEs 3000-3399) and (2) subject specific standards (ISAEs 3400-3699). The subject matter currently covered by IAASB's pronouncements are:

▶ ISAE 3400 The Examination of Prospective Financial Information.
▶ ISAE 3402 Assurance Reports on Controls at a Service Organization.
▶ ISAE 3410 Assurance Engagements on Greenhouse Gas Statements.
▶ ISAE 3420 Assurance Engagements to Report on the Compilation of Pro Forma Financial Information Included in a Prospectus.

Related Services are agreed-upon procedures on financial information (ISRS 4400) and compilation engagements (ISRS 4410). For related services involving either agreed upon procedures or compilation the practitioner does not express any assurance on the financial information. An agreed-upon procedures engagement is an engagement in which the party engaging the professional accountant or the intended user determines the procedures to be performed and the professional accountant provides a report of factual findings as a result of undertaking those procedures.

A compilation engagement would ordinarily include the preparation of financial statements (which may or may not be a complete set of financial statements) but may also include the collection, classification and summarisation of other financial information. The objective of a compilation engagement is for the practitioner to use accounting expertise, as opposed to auditing expertise, to collect, classify, and summarise financial information. This ordinarily entails reducing detailed data to a manageable and understandable form without a requirement to test the assertions underlying that information. In both Related Services the practitioner does not express any assurance on the financial information.

14.8   **QUESTIONS, EXERCISES AND CASES**

14.2   **The Concepts**

14-1   What are auditor services? List the major categories (except for consulting) of auditor's services.

14-2   Which assurance services have historical financial information as subject matter? Discuss the differences between these assurance engagements.

14.3   **Elements of an Assurance Engagement**

14-3   What is an assurance engagement? Name the five elements exhibited by all assurance engagements.

14-4   Define subject matter and subject matter information. Give some examples of common subject matter in assurance and related service engagements.

14-5   Discuss the difference between a reasonable assurance and a limited assurance engagement.

14-6   Are the criteria given in the assurance report always based on established criteria? Explain.

14.4   **Highlights of various kinds of Assurance Engagements**

14-7   Sometimes the practitioner (auditor) may have a request to provide assurance on specific components of the financial statements. Give an example. For such an engagement, can the auditor use the same materiality level as for the audit of the financial statements 'taken as a whole'? Discuss.

14-8   The auditor's report on special purpose financial statements shall include an emphasis of matter paragraph. Why is this necessary?

14-9   What are the basic elements required being included in the assurance report according to International Standards for Review Engagements 2400?

14.5   **Assurance Engagements Other than Audits or Reviews of Historical Financial Information**

14-10   Describe what is meant by 'prospective financial information'. Give some examples of when a prospective financial information report might be used.

14-11   What must auditors cover in their internal control report under the PCAOB standards?

14-12   Various companies use service organisations for specific services, for example payroll services. As these user entities would like to rely on controls of services organizations, the IAASB came with a standard to audit the controls at a service organization that is likely to be relevant to user entities' internal control as it relates to financial reporting. According to ISAE 3402 two types of reports are applicable related to control reporting of service organizations. Briefly describe the types of reports.

14.6   **Related Services**

14-13   Do accountants who offer related services have to be independent? Justify your answer.

14-14   In an agreed-upon procedures engagement, what matters generally have to be agreed between auditor and management?

14-15 Do you think users won't derive any assurance from a compilation report? Discuss the motivation for your answer.

PROBLEMS AND EXERCISES

14.2 The Concepts

14-16 Halmtorvet, a Copenhagen, Denmark, company that manufactures security devices, has contacted Christian Jespersen, Statautoriseret Revisor, to submit a proposal to do a financial statement audit. Halmtorvet was a bit taken aback when they saw the cost of the financial statement audit, even though the fees were about average for an audit of a company Halmtorvet's size. Halmtorvet's board of directors determined that the company could not afford to pay that price.

Required:

A. Discuss the alternatives to having a financial statement audit.

B. What should Halmtorvet consider when choosing the assurance service?

14.3 Elements of an Assurance Engagement

14-17 Jacqueline Corporation offers a unique service to telecommunication companies in South America. For a fee they will review the telecom's telephone transactions for calls from outside their country that might originate illegally from inside their country.

Required:

Use the five elements exhibited by all assurance engagements to prove that Jacqueline's work is an assurance engagement.

14-18 Discuss the differences between assurance conclusions expressed in the positive (reasonable assurance) form versus the negative (limited assurance) form. Give examples of assurance engagements that generally use the positive form and others that use the negative form.

14-19 Primo Promo, an advertising and public relations firm headquartered in Ljubljana, Slovenia, owned by Arnold Rikli III, wishes an assurance report in accordance with ISAEs on the prospective financial impact on local towns resulting from tourist attendance at castles such as Bled, Polhov Gradec, Brisra and other locations. The report will be used to solicit new advertising business in the local towns. Primo Promo have retained the public accounting firm of Cankarja, Kugy and Ormoz, Public Auditors, located in Piran, Slovenia. Cankarja, Kugy and Ormoz found, after examining local, Slovenian and international statistics that the castle tourist business should increase 23 per cent over the next ten years.

Required:

Write the assurance opinion for this audit.

14.4 Highlights of various kinds of Assurance Engagements

14-20 List the types of special area engagement and give some examples of each.

14-21 Using illustrations 14.1 through 14.3, compare the following three reports:

1 A report on financial statements prepared in accordance with the special purpose framework: a statement of provisions of a contract.

2 A Report on an element of a financial statement: schedule of the liability for 'incurred but not reported' claims in an insurance portfolio.

3 A report on summarized financial statement.

Required:

Make a comparison on the following three paragraphs (A-C):

A. Using the introductory paragraph as the basis of comparison.

B. Using the auditor's responsibility paragraph as the basis of comparison.

C. using the opinion paragraph as the basis of comparison.

14-22 Da Xing Fan, CPA, is engaged by the management of Ky-lin, a non-public company, to review the company's financial statements for the year ended 28 February 20XX.

Required:

A. Discuss the content of the report on a review of financial statements.

B. Summarise Fan's responsibilities if she finds the financial statements contain a material departure from IFRS.

14.5 Assurance Engagements Other than Audits or Reviews of Historical Financial Information

14-23 Haruspex is a new consulting company. They specialise in analysis of the market and process of producing sellable products from industrial waste. They have asked Sophia Coronis to prepare an examination of prospective financial information report based on the prospective company financial statements for the first two years. This will be presented to Apollo Bank as part of a loan request.

Required:

A. What type of report would Coronis prepare – a forecast or a projection?

B. Draft the report for Apollo Bank.

14-24 Diamond Jousts, a UK Limited Company, is traded on the American Stock Exchange as American Depository Receipts (ADRs). They hire Lancelot, Elaine and Guinevere, Chartered Accountants, to prepare an internal control report to meet Sarbanes-Oxley requirements.

Required:

A. What should the report of management contain?

B. Draft an unqualified opinion on management's assessment of the effectiveness of internal control for the CA firm. (See illustration 14.6 for an example.)

14.6 Other Related Services

14-25 The following list describes seven situations Certified Accountants may encounter, or contentions they may have to deal with, in their association with and preparation of *unaudited* financial statements. Briefly discuss the extent of the certified account-ant's responsibilities and, if appropriate, the actions they should take to minimize any misunderstandings.

1 Armando Almonza, CPA, was engaged by telephone to perform accounting work including the compilation of financial statements. The client believes that Almonza has been engaged to audit the financial statements and will examine the records accordingly.

2 A group of investors who own a farm that is managed by an independent agent engage An Nguyen, CPA, to compile quarterly unaudited financial statements for them.

3 In comparing the trial balance with the general ledger, Thynie Pukprayura, CPA, finds an account labelled 'Audit Fees' in which the client has accumulated his CPA firm's

quarterly billings for accounting services including the compilation of quarterly unaudited financial statements.

4   Unaudited financial statements for a public company were accompanied by the following letter of transmittal from Franz Ravel, Expert Comptable:

5   To determine appropriate account classification, Jose Torres, CP Titulado, examined a number of the client's invoices. He noted in his working papers that some invoices were missing, but did nothing further because it was felt that the invoices did not affect the unaudited financial statements he was compiling. When the client subsequently discovered that invoices were missing, he contended that the Torres should not have ignored the missing invoices when compiling the financial statements and had a responsibility to at least inform him that they were missing.

6   Omar El Qasaria, CA, compiled a draft of unaudited financial statements from the client's records. While reviewing this draft with his client, El Qasaria learnt that the land and building were recorded at appraisal value.

7   Tomoko Nakagawa, CPA, is engaged to compile the financial statements of a non-public company. During the engagement, Nakagawa learns of several items for which IFRS would require adjustments of the statements and note disclosure. The controller agrees to make the recommended adjustments to the statements, but says that she is not going to add the notes because the statements are unaudited.

CASES

14-26 Scott London, an ex-KPMG partner in Los Angeles, has been charged in a federal complaint with one count of conspiracy to commit securities fraud through insider trading. The complaint alleges that London provided confidential information about KPMG clients to Bryan Shaw, a close friend, over a period of several years and that Shaw used this information to make highly profitable securities trades that generated more than $1 million in illegal proceeds.

In some cases, London called Shaw two to three days before press releases of KPMG clients were issued and read Shaw the details that would soon be made public. London also tipped Shaw off to mergers and even strategized with Shaw on how to conceal his trading so that the two would not be caught.

From late 2010 and continuing until March 2013, London secretly passed 'highly sensitive and confidential information' to Shaw regarding forthcoming earnings announcements by certain KPMG clients, including Herbalife, Skechers, and Deckers Outdoor Corp., before that financial information was disclosed to the public. In exchange, Shaw gave London tens of thousands of dollars in cash, typically instructing London to meet him on a side street near Shaw's business in order to give him bags containing $100 bills wrapped in $10,000 bundles. (Reference: Walter Hamilton and Andrea Chang, 2013, 'Details emerge in case against ex-KPMG auditor Scott London', *Los Angeles Times*, 11 April). KPMG said it plans to reassess its internal safeguards.

Required:

Using the details in the Scott London story, answer these questions:

A. If KPMG contracted another Big Four firm to reassess its internal safeguards, what type of auditor service would this be? What IAASB framework would the outside auditors use?

B. If the audit service to reassess internal safeguards by another Big Four firm is an assurance service: (1) Who would be the practitioner, responsible party and intended user? (2) What would be the subject matter and subject matter information? (3) What criteria should be used? (4) What would constitute sufficient appropriate evidence?

C. What quality control procedure could KPMG put in place to assure that the risk of insider information coming from partners would be reduced to a reasonably low level?

14-27 Champions NV[58]

Champions NV is a national soccer club playing in the top division of the territory soccer league. Its shares are listed on the Amsterdam Stock Exchange. The company has a fiscal year ending 30 June each year and the company is required to publish interim summarized financial statements each quarter. The company is preparing its financial statements in accordance with IFRS as adopted in the EU.

Your audit firm has been the auditor of Champions for six years. You are in the role of senior staff in the audit team preparing some work on behalf of the engagement manager and engagement partner. Assume on each question you aim to convince the manager and partner based on your comprehensive and to-the-point analysis.

Governance is as follows:
▶ An independent supervisory board including an audit committee and a remuneration committee.
▶ Board of directors comprising a CEO and a CFO and CTM (chief soccer matters).

The company has the following departments:
▶ Technical (15 persons)– headed by CTM
▶ Commercial (10 persons) – headed by CEO
▶ Finance (5 persons) – headed by CFO
▶ Operations (25 persons) – headed by CFO

Champions uses two separate applications for the financial administration (off the shelf product- no source code available at Champions) versus the operations (tailormade by an external software supplier). These systems are linked via an interface. During this fiscal year, the Champions had issues with the operations system, resulting in a one-week-offline period.

The stadium is owned by an international brewery. The rental fee is a fixed amount per year. The contract will terminate at 30 June 20X9; during 20X8/20X9 the new contract will be negotiated.

The summarized financial statements of last fiscal year are as follows:

BALANCE SHEET (amounts x € 1.000)					
	30/6/X8	30/6/X7		30/6/X8	30/6/X7
Capitalized transfer fees	89.050	55.761	Equity	158.937	158.873
Tangible fixed assets	20.311	14.390	Long term liabilities	20.323	15.052
Financial fixed assets	46.070	14.390	Short term liabilities	93.064	72.155
Inventory	4.590	2.519			
Receivables	76.172	58.107			
Investment portfolio	23.941	23.326			
Cash & banks	12.190	64.499			
	272.324	**246.080**		**272.324**	**246.080**

PROFIT & LOSS ACCOUNT (amounts x € 1.000)		
	20X7/20X8	20X6/20X7
Revenues	**91.949**	**118.223**
Purchases	7.452	6.994
Wages & Salaries	52.836	55.096
Depreciation fixed assets	3.175	3.180
Other expenses	41.691	44.581
Total expenses	**105.154**	**109.851**

Operating result before transfer fees	**(13.205)**	**8.372**
Amortization transfer fees	(24.979)	(18.082)
Result from player transfers	39.361	78.616
Other	584	310
Result before tax	**1.761**	**67.016**
Corporate tax	(328)	(17.277)
Net result after tax	**1.186**	**49.461**

Transfer fees

When contracting new players, in a number of cases transfer fees have to be paid to the soccer club the player has played for before joining Champions. Transfer fees are capitalized at the start and amortized over the remaining contracting period on a straight-line basis. When leaving Champions before the end of the contract, a transfer fee received is considered as realized in the profit & loss account under 'result from player transfers'. Any remaining capitalized transfer fee for this player is then deducted from this result.

Revenues

Champions has 5 regular revenue categories (with percentage of total revenues):

1 Broadcasting/television rights (25%)
2 Shirt sponsoring (10%)

3 Fan shop sales (30%)
4 Entrance fees (30%)
5 Drinks during the games (5%)

Ad a) **Broadcasting/television rights**: Champions receives revenues from television rights on a yearly basis based on a contact the soccer league has with the broadcasting company. This revenue per soccer club is depending on the ranking in the competition each season. On a monthly basis, Champions receives an advance payment amounting 1/12th based on the revenue on the actual ranking last season. Each year in July after the season, the final revenue is calculated and settled for the amount not yet paid in advance.

Ad c) **The fan shop sales** comprise the sale of mainly shirts, shorts etc. in the fan shop, on the website and to a wholesaler for further distribution to individual sport stores in Netherlands and abroad. All articles are entered in the tailormade operations software as mentioned above.

Once a year in spring, Champions purchases in bulk the articles from one Chinese supplier. All articles are tagged with a bar code. Sales prices in the fan store and on the website are offered based on a pricing list authorized by the CFO. No discounts are given until the end of the playing season (in May).

A contract is signed with a wholesaler, who is the reseller of the goods to individual sport stores. The contract comprises the agreed price per article, the minimum number per category of articles to be purchased by the wholesaler and a bonus incentive correlated with the number of articles sold.

On a monthly basis, an integral inventory count is organized by scanning all articles individually. Any stock count differences are booked in the P&L account as 'inventory difference' under 'Purchases'.

QUESTION

The CEO is quite excited about the new contract due to the commercial effects of the contract but needs the approval by the supervisory board. The supervisory board is in the position whether or not to agree with the new rental contract. Unfortunately, the controller has a burn out and is not able to prepare the in-depth calculations.

Therefore, the CFO asks your engagement partner whether they may use your services. Based on a brainwave he comes to you and asks you to reflect on the following potential services:

A. Preparing the in-depth calculations instead of the controller
B. Advising about the financial consequences of the new contract on request of the supervisory board
C. Performing specified calculations on forecasted volumes, including analysis based on historical figures for the benefit of the CFO and/or supervisory board.
D. Formulating an opinion how to classify the barter transaction in the P&L.
E. Provide an assurance report on a yearly basis confirming the actual volume of drinks to be reported to the owner of the stadium.

Taking into account you are the context of this engagement (described in this whole exam), respond to your partner:

(a) Indicate which services A-B-C-D are allowed under the IESBA Code of Ethics and if yes under which conditions and argue why.

(b) In case of an assurance report under E:
- ▶ Whether and how you can leverage on the audit procedures already performed in the context of the audit of the financial statements
- ▶ Which additional considerations you have before accepting this additional assurance engagement setting the right conditions for such engagement.
- ▶ Describe the headlines of your approach including risk analysis and main testing procedures.

14.9 NOTES

1. International Auditing and Assurance Standards Board (IAASB), 2023, International Standard on Quality Management (ISQM) 1, 'International Standard on Quality Management (ISQM) 1. Quality Management for Firms that Perform Audits or Reviews of Financial Statements, or Other Assurance or Related Services Engagements, Handbook of International Quality Control, Auditing Review, Other Assurance, and Related Services Pronouncements, 2022 edn, Volume I International Federation of Accountants, New York.

2. Derived from IAASB, adapted by the authors incorporating (ED) ISSA 5000 and visualizing services not governed by the standards of IAASB. Sources: Handbook of International Quality Management, Auditing, Review, Other Assurance and Related Services Pronouncements 2022 Edition Volume I, International Federation of Accountants (IFAC). New York., volume I, page 5 combined with volume III, page 57.

3. IAASB uses the word 'practitioner' for the broader range of accountants in public practice: not all of them are (financial) auditors. We sometimes use auditor or (professional) accountant instead of a practitioner.

4. But the level of assurance is obviously more than 50% to have rational value!

5. Ibid. International Framework for Assurance Engagements.

6. The intended users are the person, persons or class of persons for whom the practitioner prepares the assurance report. The responsible party can be one of the intended users, but not the only one.

7. The responsible party is the person (or persons) who: (a) in a direct reporting engagement, is responsible for the subject matter; or (b) in an assertion-based engagement, is responsible for the subject matter information (the assertion) and may be responsible for the subject matter.

8. The subject matter of an assurance engagement is the topic about which the assurance engagement is conducted. Subject matter could be financial statements, statistical information, non-financial performance indicators, capacity of a facility, etc.

9. Criteria are the benchmarks used to evaluate or measure the subject matter including, where relevant, benchmarks for presentation and disclosure. Criteria can be formal or less formal. There can be different criteria for the same subject matter. Suitable criteria are required for reasonably consistent evaluation or measurement of a subject matter within the context of professional judgement.

10. 'Internal Control – Integrated Framework', 1992, 2013 (revised) The Committee of Sponsoring Organizations of the Treadway Commission.

11. 'Guidance on Assessing Control – The CoCo Principles', 1995, Criteria of Control Board, The Canadian Institute of Chartered Accountants.

12. Ibid. International Framework for Assurance Engagements para. 26.

13. Ibid. International Framework for Assurance Engagements, Appendix 3.

14. International Auditing and Assurance Standards Board (IAASB), 2023, International Standards on Assurance Engagements 3000 (ISAE 3000), 'Assurance Engagements Other than Audits or Reviews of Historical Financial Information', paragraph 24, Handbook of International Quality Control, Auditing Review, Other Assurance, and Related Services Pronouncements, 2022 edn, Volume III, International Federation of Accountants, New York.

15. Evidence includes both information contained in relevant information systems, if any, and other information. (i) Sufficiency of evidence is the measure of the quantity of evidence. (ii) Appropriateness of evidence is the measure of the quality of evidence. For purposes of the ISAEs: (Ref: ISAE 3000 Para. A147–A154).

16. Materiality in sustainability reporting is not limited to those sustainability topics that have a significant financial impact. See paragraph 15.3.1 Double Materiality.

17. ibid. ISAE 3000 para.79-93.

18. In an auditor's report, the auditor provides an *opinion* on the financial statements with reasonable assurance, while he provides a *conclusion* with limited assurance in a review report.

19. International Auditing and Assurance Standards Board (IAASB), 2023, 'International Framework for Assurance Engagements', ISA 800 'Special Considerations – Audits of Financial Statements Prepared in Accordance With Special Purpose Frameworks', Handbook of International Quality Control, Auditing Review, Other Assurance, and Related Services Pronouncements, 2022 edn, Volume I, International Federation of Accountants, New York.

20. Ibid. ISA 805.

21. Ibid. ISA 810.

22. This ISRE is to be applied, adapted as necessary, to reviews of other historical financial information. Limited assurance engagements other than reviews of historical financial information are performed under ISAE 3000 (section 14.3).

23. Subsequent events – events occurring between the date of the financial statements and the date of the auditor's report, and facts that become known to the auditor after the date of the auditor's report.

24. The requirements of this ISRE relating to designing and performing inquiry and analytical procedures, and procedures addressing specific circumstances, are designed to enable the practitioner to achieve the objectives specified in this ISRE. The circumstances of review engagements vary widely and, accordingly, there may be circumstances where the practitioner may consider it effective or efficient to design and perform other procedures. For example, if in the course of obtaining an understanding of the entity, the practitioner becomes aware of a significant contract the practitioner may choose to read the contract. ISRE 2400.A81.

25. International Auditing and Assurance Standards Board (IAASB), 2023, International Standards on Review Engagements 2400' (ISRE 2400) 'Engagements to Review Historical Information', para 86, Handbook of International Quality Control, Auditing Review, Other Assurance, and Related Services Pronouncements, 2022 edn, Volume II, International Federation of Accountants, New York.

26. International Auditing and Assurance Standards Board (IAASB), 2023, International Standards on Review Engagements 3400', (ISAE 3400), ' The Examination of Prospective Financial Information', Handbook of International Quality Control, Auditing Review, Other

Assurance, and Related Services Pronouncements, 2022 edn, Volume II, International Federation of Accountants, New York.

27.   Ibid. ISAE 3400 The Examination of Prospective Financial Information, para 27.

28.   The Securities and Exchange Commission voted March 12, 2020 to exempt smaller public companies with less than $100 million in annual revenue from the requirement for an attestation of their internal control over financial reporting by an outside auditor.

29.   Financial Instruments and Exchange Act, promulgated on June 14, 2006, is the main statute codifying securities law and regulating securities companies in Japan. The Keeping the Promise for a Strong Economy Act (Budget Measures), 2002, also known as Bill 198, was an Ontario legislative bill effective April 7, 2003, which provides for regulation of securities issued in the province of Ontario. Corporate Law Economic Reform Program (Audit Reform & Corporate Disclosure) Act 2004, commonly called CLERP 9, modified the Corporations Act 2001 (Commonwealth) which governs corporate law in Australia.

30.   US Securities and Exchange Commission (SEC), 2003, Release. No. 33-8238, Section II.A(1), 'Final Rule: Management's Reports on Internal Control Over Financial Reporting and Certification of Disclosure in Exchange Act Periodic Reports', SEC, 5 June.

31.   Ibid. US Securities and Exchange Commission (SEC), 2003, Release. No. 33-8238.

32.   Management must state whether or not the company's internal control over financial reporting is effective. A negative assurance statement indicating that nothing has come to management's attention to suggest that the company's internal control over financial reporting is not effective will not be acceptable.

33.   US Securities and Exchange Commission (SEC), 2008, Release Nos. 33-8238; 34-47986; IC-26068; File Nos. S7-40-02; S7-06-03, 'Final Rule: Management's Report on Internal Control Over Financial Reporting and Certification of Disclosure in Exchange Act Periodic Reports, https://www.sec.gov/rules/final/33-8238.htm

34.   United States Public Company Accounting Oversight Board (PCAOB), 2018, Audit Standard 2201 (AS 2201) 'An Audit of Internal Control Over Financial Reporting That Is Integrated with An Audit of Financial Statements'. https://pcaobus.org/oversight/standards/auditing-standards/details/AS2201

35.   International Auditing and Assurance Standards Board (IAASB), 2023, International Standards for Assurance Engagements 3402 (ISAE 3042), 'Assurance Reports on Controls at a Service Organisation', Handbook of International Quality Control, Auditing Review, Other Assurance, and Related Services Pronouncements, 2022 edn, Volume II, International Federation of Accountants, New York.

36.   Ibid. ISAE 3402.

37.   Sustainability reporting for large public companies around the world has become the norm. Si2's research this year (2018) found that 78 percent of the S&P 500 issued a sustainability report for the most recent reporting period, most with environmental and social performance metrics. https://corpgov.law.harvard.edu/2018/12/03/state-of-integrated-and-sustainability-reporting-2018/

38.   Source is https://www.wri.org/initiatives/greenhouse-gas-protocol

39.   International Auditing and Assurance Standards Board (IAASB), 2023, International Standards on Assurance Engagements 3410, (ISAE 3410), 'Assurance Engagements on Green House Gas Statements', Handbook of International Quality Control, Auditing Review, Other Assurance, and Related Services Pronouncements, 2022 edn, Volume II, International Federation of Accountants, New York.

40.   Ibid. ISAE 3410, paragraph 13.

41.   Ibid. ISAE 3420 para.1.k

42. According to ISAE 3000 paragraph 8, the following engagements are not considered assurance engagements in terms of the ISAEs: (a) Engagements to testify in legal proceedings regarding accounting, auditing, taxation or other matters; and (b) Engagements that include professional opinions, views or wording from which a user may derive some assurance, if all of the following apply:
    1. Those opinions, views or wording are merely incidental to the overall engagement;
    2. Any written report issued is expressly restricted for use by only the intended users specified in the report;
    3. Under a written understanding with the specified intended users, the engagement is not intended to be an assurance engagement; and
    4. The engagement is not represented as an assurance engagement in the professional accountant's report.

43. International Auditing and Assurance Standards Board (IAASB), 2023, 'International Standards on Related Services 4400 (ISRS 4400) 'Engagements to Perform Agreed-Upon Procedures Regarding Financial Information', Handbook of International Quality Control, Auditing Review, Other Assurance, and Related Services Pronouncements, 2022 edn, Volume II, International Federation of Accountants, New York.

44. Factual findings are capable of being objectively verified, meaning that different practitioners perform the same procedures are expected to arrive at equivalent results. Findings exclude the expression of an opinion or a conclusion. (ISRS 4400.A12.)

45. However, if, in the judgement of the professional accountant, the procedures agreed to be performed are appropriate to support the expression of a conclusion that provides a level of assurance on the subject matter, then that engagement becomes an assurance engagement governed by the International Standards on Assurance Engagements and the Assurance Framework.

46. ISRS 4400.A2.

47. International Auditing and Assurance Standards Board (IAASB), 2023, International Standards on Related Services 4400 (ISRS 4400), 'Engagements to Perform Agreed-Upon Procedures Regarding Financial Information', para 30, Handbook of International Quality Control, Auditing Review, Other Assurance, and Related Services Pronouncements, 2022 edn, Volume II, International Federation of Accountants, New York.

48. Ibid. ISRS 4400.

49. Ibid., ISRS 4400, para 30.

50. Ibid. ISRS 4400, para. A32-33.

51. Ibid. ISRS 4400, Appendix 2. Also, the scope of agreed-upon procedures could be on both financial and non-financial subject matters.

52. For purposes of this illustrative agreed-upon procedures report, the following circumstances are assumed.
    1. The engaging party is the addressee and the only intended user. The engaging party is not the responsible party. For example, the regulator is the engaging party and intended user, and the entity overseen by the regulator is the responsible party.
    2. No exceptions were found.
    3. The practitioner did not engage a practitioner's expert to perform any of the agreed-upon procedures.
    4. There is no restriction on the use or distribution of the report.
    5. There are no independence requirements with which the practitioner is required to comply.
    6. A quantitative threshold of $100 for reporting exceptions in Procedure 3 has been agreed with the engaging party.

53. Ibid. ISRS 4410.
54. Ibid. ISRS 4410, para A21.
55. Ibid. ISRS 4410, para 24.
56. Ibid. ISRS 4410, para 40.
57. AR Section 9080 Compilation of Financial Statements: Accounting and Review Services Interpretations of Section 80, AICPA, 2016.
58. The case Champions NV is derived from the May 25, 2019 Audit & Assurance exam of the International Executive Master of Auditing, hosted by Maastricht University/Vrije Universiteit Amsterdam, www.iema-edu.org

SUSTAINABILITY ASSURANCE ENGAGEMENTS

This chapter includes a comprehensive overview of the sustainability journey including developments related to reporting and assurance. As a result, this chapter is readable on a stand-alone base.
The following table of contents is your guide.

15.1   LEARNING OBJECTIVES

After studying this chapter, you should be able to:

1   Understand the importance of sustainability information.
2   Explain the development of sustainability and related concepts!
3   Be familiar with current developments in sustainability reporting.
4   Identify and discuss most important relevant laws and regulations in the field of sustainability.
5   Explain the auditor's responsibilities in sustainability assurance in comparison to auditing financial statements.
6   Understand and apply sustainability assurance standards.
7   Understand and discuss the phases of the sustainability assurance process.
8   Be familiar with internal controls over sustainability reporting.
9   Describe the different concepts of reasonable and limited sustainability assurance engagements.
10   Understand and prepare a sustainability assurance report.

15.2   SETTING THE SCENE

15.2.1   INTRODUCTION

During the 1970s, there was a strong emphasis on the social aspects of sustainability. However, as we entered the 1990s, the focus gradually shifted towards actively combatting environmental pollution. As time has passed, there has been a steadily increasing recognition of the critical need to address climate change and its wide-ranging societal consequences.

Main drivers of increased recognition are:

▶ **Stakeholder Expectations**
Customers, investors, employees, and other stakeholders increasingly expect organizations to be more transparent and accountable for their environmental, social, and governance (ESG) impacts[1]. They want to know that companies are actively contributing to society and the environment in a positive and sustainable manner and that a chemical company does not dispose of toxic waste in rivers and seas or that clothing is not made by children in Bangladesh.

▶ **Global Sustainability Agreements**[2]
International agreements and initiatives, such as the United Nations Sustainable Development Goals (SDGs) and the Paris Agreement on climate change, have set clear targets for sustainability and carbon emissions reduction[3]. These agreements provide a framework for organizations to align their practices and reporting with broader global objectives.

▶ **Legal Requirements**
Governments and regulatory bodies in various countries have introduced laws and regulations that mandate or encourage organizations to report on their sustainability

performance. Compliance with these requirements is becoming a legal obligation for many companies because violation of the rules leads to high fines and loss of reputation and (shareholders)value.

▷ **Investor Priorities**
Institutional investors, asset managers, and pension funds have integrated sustainability considerations into their investment decisions. They recognize that sustainable practices and responsible business conduct can lead to better long-term financial performance and are better positioned for sustainable growth.

▷ **Risk Management**
Companies are increasingly recognizing that sustainability related issues, such as climate change, resource scarcity, labour practices, and supply chain management, pose significant risks to their operations and reputation. Sustainability reporting helps them identify and mitigate these risks.

▷ **Reputation and Brand Value**
Positive sustainability performance can enhance a company's reputation and brand value. Conversely, negative incidents related to ESG issues can result in reputational damage and impact consumer loyalty. For example, if a company is found to be involved in environmental pollution, it can lead to public outrage and a decline in customer trust, which may ultimately affect its bottom line.

▷ **Comparative Analysis**
Sustainability reporting allows stakeholders to compare the performance of different organizations in terms of their environmental and social impacts. This transparency encourages healthy competition and motivates companies to improve their practices.

▷ **Long-term Business Resilience**
Embracing sustainability practices and reporting enables organizations to build resilience and adapt to increasingly rapidly evolving market conditions and societal expectations and be prepared for the financial and physical and transition risks from climate change.

In response to these drivers, many companies have started voluntarily reporting on their sustainability efforts and progress. Moreover, as sustainability becomes increasingly integrated into corporate strategies and business models, it is likely that more regulations and requirements related to sustainability reporting will emerge to address global challenges such as climate change, social inequality, and environmental degradation.

It won't surprise that the accountants' profession as gatekeepers of society play an important role in these developments[4]. Reflecting on the G20's theme of One Earth, One Family, One Future, the International Federation of Accountants (IFAC) confirmed its commitment to drive sustainable development and demonstrating leadership as a truly global and inclusive profession.

15.2.2   **THEORETICAL PERSPECTIVE**

From a theoretical perspective the development of sustainability reporting and assurance can be explained by both agency and stakeholder theory (see chapter 1). Both theories explain the market for both financial and sustainability information and assurance. However, traditionally, financial reporting has been primarily focused on shareholders, whereas sustainability reporting is designed to address the interests of a broader range of stakeholders.

Also, signalling theory can be used to explain the growth in (voluntary) sustainability reporting. As illustrated in illustration 15.1 the assumption is that one party (the sender) credibly conveys information about itself to another party (the receiver)[5].

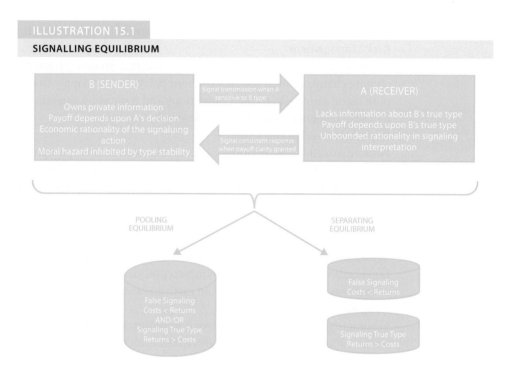

ILLUSTRATION 15.1

SIGNALLING EQUILIBRIUM

To summarize the theories from a sustainability perspective:

- ▶ *Agency theory* focuses on the relationship between principals (shareholders) and agents (company management). In the context of sustainability reporting, shareholders are the principals who seek to align the interests of management with their own. As concerns about sustainability issues have grown, shareholders have demanded more transparency and accountability from companies. Sustainability reporting serves as a mechanism to reduce information asymmetry (where one party has better information than the other) between principals and agents, enabling shareholders to monitor management's performance and decision-making in areas related to sustainability. Assurance provides independent verification of the reported information, adding credibility and reducing the agency costs associated with 'sustainability' information asymmetry.
- ▶ *Stakeholder theory* posits that organizations have a responsibility to consider the interests of all stakeholders, not just shareholders. As stakeholders, including customers, employees, communities, and regulators, become increasingly concerned about the environmental and social impacts of businesses, companies are motivated to respond to these concerns through sustainability reporting. By disclosing their

sustainability performance, organizations demonstrate their commitment to addressing stakeholder interests and building trust with their various stakeholders. Assurance provides independent verification of the reported information, adding credibility and reducing the (stakeholder) costs associated with 'sustainability' information asymmetry[6].

▶ *Signalling theory* proposes that companies use voluntary disclosures, such as sustainability reports, as signals to convey favourable information about their qualities or performance to stakeholders. By voluntarily disclosing positive sustainability practices and outcomes, companies signal their commitment to responsible business practices, environmental stewardship, and social well-being. This signalling can help companies attract investors, customers, and employees who align with their values. Assurance of sustainability information further enhances the credibility of these signals, reducing the perception of greenwashing and strengthening stakeholder trust.

Driven by shareholders, stakeholders, law and regulation, markets, public opinion and press, more and more company boards now see the advantages of transparency, leading to a growing trend of integrating sustainability into their strategies and sharing it in comprehensive reports. The interaction of agency theory, stakeholder theory, and signalling theory is key in understanding sustainability reporting and assurance as a phenomenon[7].

15.2.3 A JOURNEY TOWARDS SUSTAINABILITY

During the mid-1980s, Royal Dutch Shell (Shell) found itself embroiled in sustainability debates when it became entangled in the apartheid system in South Africa. NGOs initiated a disinvestment campaign, urging the South African Government to dismantle the discriminatory system. As a commodity, oil was not available in South Africa, and Shell's involvement in helping the country bypass the oil embargo drew sharp criticism from anti-apartheid groups. This led to an international campaign against Shell, with anti-apartheid campaigners picketing Shell garages and calling for a boycott of Shell products.

In 1995, another public concern arose when the British government supported Shell's application to dispose of 'The Brent Spar,' an oil platform, in deep Atlantic waters. However, Greenpeace organized a global media campaign against this plan, which gained widespread public opposition and triggered a boycott of Shell service stations. Despite claiming that disposing of Brent Spar at sea was the safest option environmentally and in terms of industrial health and safety, Shell eventually abandoned the plan in response to public pressure.

In the same period, execution of activist Ken Saro-Wiwa by Nigeria's military regime also had quite an impact on Shell's reputation. In 2009 a $15.5 million settlement ended a lawsuit. According to a lawyer, the settlement was a message to Shell and other multinationals that operate in developing countries. 'You can't commit human rights violations as a part of doing business.'

These challenging issues motivated Shell, along with other companies, to begin reporting on their progress in contributing to sustainable development starting from 1997[8].

The Shell report 1998, titled 'Profits and Principles – does there have to be a choice?' addressed various critical aspects:

- ▶ Values and Principles.
- ▶ Communication with Stakeholders through 'Tell Shell Reply Cards'.
- ▶ Issues and Dilemmas faced by the company.
- ▶ A Road Map outlining the sustainable path forward, covering reporting, standards and systems, external verification/assurance, continuous improvements, targets, and internal and external engagement.

ILLUSTRATION 15.2

THE SHELL REPORT – 1998[9]

To increase societal trust in Shell's sustainability activities, the company's board asked their financial statement auditors (KPMG and Price Waterhouse; joint auditors) to check the integrity of the data generated by management systems and to provide assurance on specific sustainability information in the 1998 report.

Shell motivated engaging traditional auditors[10] because of their professional skills, their infrastructure which exists in over 100 countries in which the company operates, and their familiarity with its management systems. Also, financial reports have been subject to rigorous audit processes for decades based on increasingly sophisticated control and audit mechanisms.

However, Shell explicitly noted that they had to resolve how assurance could best be achieved and mentioned a number of possibilities, including:

- ▶ The use of the traditional auditors who are developing their expertise in this area.
- ▶ The use of new firms who specialize in this form of assurance.
- ▶ Inviting non-governmental and other organizations to review specific areas of Shell's activities; or a mixture of the three.

By using colour and symbols in the verification report 2002, the independent auditors explain which information and to what extent, has been verified (illustration 15.3).

ILLUSTRATION 15.3

REPORT OF THE INDEPENDENT AUDITORS 2002

Assurance Report
To: Royal Dutch Petroleum Company and The "Shell" Transport and Trading Company, p.l.c.

Introduction
We have been asked to provide assurance over selected data, graphs and statements of the Royal Dutch/Shell Group of Companies reported in this year's Shell Report. We have marked these statements with the symbols below. This Report is the responsibility of management. Our responsibility is to express an opinion on the data, graphs and statements indicated, based on work referred to above in "Message from the Independent Auditors".

In our opinion:
⊕ The data and graphs (together with the notes), properly reflect the performance of the reporting entities for each parameter (SE – for portfolio as at 31 December 2001) marked with this symbol.

◉ The statements marked with this symbol are supported by underlying evidence.

In addition the data for each parameter marked ⊕ are properly aggregated at Group level.

Basis of opinion
There are no generally accepted international environmental, social and economic reporting standards. This engagement was conducted in accordance with the International Standards for Assurance Engagements. Therefore, we planned and carried out our work to provide reasonable, rather than absolute, assurance on the reliability of the data and statements marked with the symbols ⊕ and ◉ and on the accuracy of the Group level aggregation process for data marked ⊕ . We believe our work provides a reasonable basis for our opinion.

Assurance work performed
In forming our opinion, we carried out the work summarised above in "Message from the Independent Auditors." We used a multi-disciplinary team, comprising financial auditors and environmental and social specialists. We also examined the whole Report to confirm consistency of the information reported with our findings.

44 The Shell Report

Considerations and limitations
It is important to read the data and statements in the context of the reporting policies and limitations on page 45 and the notes to the graphs. Environmental and social data are subject to many more inherent limitations than financial data given both their nature and the methods used for determining, calculating or estimating such data.

We have not provided assurance over all contents of this report, nor have we undertaken work to confirm that all relevant issues are included.

We have not carried out any work on data reported in respect of future projections and targets. Where we have not provided assurance over previous years' data it is clearly shown.

We have not carried out any work to provide assurance over the completeness and accuracy of the underlying data for the parameters aggregated at Group level, and marked with ⊕.

It is also important that, in order to obtain a thorough understanding of the financial results and financial position of the Group, the reader should consult the Royal Dutch/ Shell Group of Companies Financial Statements for the year ended 31 December 2002.

5 March 2003

KPMG Accountants N.V.   The Hague

PricewaterhouseCoopers LLP   London

KPMG

PRICEWATERHOUSECOOPERS

15.3   SUSTAINABILITY REPORTING

As mentioned earlier, there is a growing trend of sustainability reporting. Nowadays 96% of the G250 companies[11] report on sustainability matters, 64% of these companies acknowledge climate change as a risk to their business and 49% acknowledge social elements as a risk to their business, with Western Europe as the leading region.[12]

In determining the information to be reported, sustainability matters are considered and selected to be disclosed by management. Such a disclosure represents specific information and can be in various forms (e.g., narrative descriptions or other qualitative information, tables with key performance indicators or other quantitative information) and may be limited to a single paragraph or table or may span multiple pages in a separate sustainability report, part of the entity's annual report or some other reporting mechanism.

'Sustainability' is often synonymous with terms like Corporate Social Responsibility (CSR), Triple Bottom Line (people, planet, profit) and Environmental, Social and Governance (ESG). Although these labels carry similar meanings, they differ in their scope. It encompasses the following components:

▶ The **E** (environmental) component of ESG information covers how a company deals with risks and opportunities related to climate, natural resource scarcity, pollution, waste, and other environmental factors. It examines the organization's impact on living and non-living natural systems, including ecosystems, land, air, and water[13].

▶ The **S** (social) component includes information concerning the company's values and business relationships, including its impact on the social systems within which it operates. Social performance is assessed through an analysis of the organization's impact on stakeholders at the local, national, and global levels. Examples of significant topics include occupational health and safety, employee satisfaction, and human rights.

▶ The **G** (governance) component of ESG encompasses information about a company's corporate governance. This can include details about the board of directors' structure and diversity, executive compensation, responsiveness during critical events, corporate resiliency, policies on lobbying, political contributions, bribery, corruption, and internal controls over financial and non-financial reporting (disclosures).

Of course, sustainability may also have an economic dimension. This relates to the organization's impact on the economic circumstances of its stakeholders and economic systems at local, national, and global levels.

15.3.1 **DOUBLE MATERIALITY[14]**

The concept of double materiality requires companies to report relevant information from both an 'inside-out' and 'outside-in' perspective (illustration 15.4[15]).

ILLUSTRATION 15.4

DOUBLE MATERIALITY

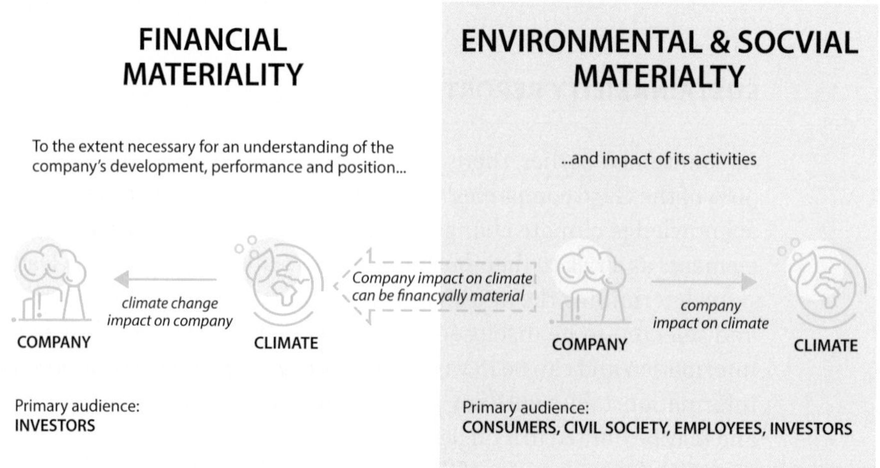

FINANCIAL MATERIALITY

To the extent necessary for an understanding of the company's development, performance and position...

climate change impact on company

COMPANY ← CLIMATE

Company impact on climate can be financyally material

Primary audience:
INVESTORS

ENVIRONMENTAL & SOCVIAL MATERIALTY

...and impact of its activities

company impact on climate

COMPANY → CLIMATE

Primary audience:
CONSUMERS, CIVIL SOCIETY, EMPLOYEES, INVESTORS

When a company determines which topics in its reports have or can have an effect on its financial performance, this is called *financial materiality (outside-in)*.

Companies must report this information because it allows users of the sustainability report to understand how sustainability matters influence the company itself. This includes disclosing how external sustainability factors, such as environmental or social issues (per user group), impact the company's decision making, operations, performance, and long-term prospects). An example of an outside-in effect is a company that is responsible for regularly releasing a large volume of pollutants into a river. There could be indirect impacts on the company itself, through loss of revenue from customers unhappy with the company's attitude towards damaging the environment as well as direct impacts such as the cost of clean-up or fines from authorities.

However, there may also be impacts on the environment, and perhaps on local communities using the river for fishing or a water supply. Such an effect the company has on the economy, environment, or society, is called *impact materiality (inside-out)*[16]*.* This information allows users of the sustainability report to understand how the company's actions and decisions affect various sustainability aspects. This is important for a wider group of people who are interested in how the company affects the world, not just those who provide debt or equity.

Stakeholder engagement activities are therefore an important part of a preparer identifying reporting topics. An open dialogue with stakeholders may give better results than passive interaction or asking them to comment on an existing list of reporting topics, however there may be a need to adequately inform stakeholders about the entity and its activities to enable them to engage effectively with the process.

In illustration 15.5, we depict the materiality assessment process derived from Barry Callebaut AG, a Swiss-Belgian cocoa processor and chocolate manufacturer. The company was created in 1996 through the merging of the French company Cacao Barry and the Belgian chocolate producer Callebaut. It is currently based in Zürich, Switzerland, and operates in over 30 countries worldwide. Its customers include multinational and national branded consumer goods manufacturers and artisanal users of chocolate (chocolatiers, pastry chefs, bakeries, and caterers).

ILLUSTRATION 15.5

DOUBLE MATERIALITY ASSESSMENT BARRY CALLEBAUT AG

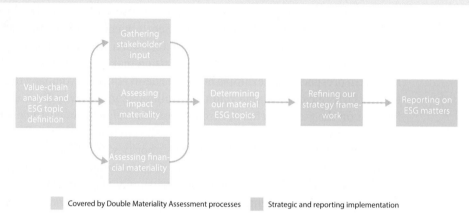

Barry Callebaut conducted thorough sustainability assessments following international standards and best practices. For the 2023 assessment, they partnered with an ESG consultancy, for unbiased expertise. Aligning with EU CSRD regulation, they structured their double materiality analysis as follows[17]:

▶ **Value Chain Analysis and ESG Topic Definition**
Identifying ESG touchpoints in our processes, Barry Callebaut formed an ESG topic framework. The illustration below sketches the company's value chain:

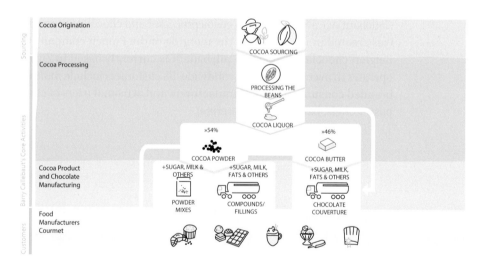

▶ **Gathering Stakeholder Perspectives**
Prioritizing stakeholder inclusion, the company conducted surveys and interviews to capture diverse opinions.

▶ **Sustainability Materiality Assessment**
Analysing operations' impacts on people and the environment. The illustration below sketches Barry Callebaut's impact assessment categories:

▶ **Financial Materiality Assessment**

Identifying ESG risks and opportunities and evaluating their financial impact. The illustration below sketches Barry Callebaut's financial materiality assessment:

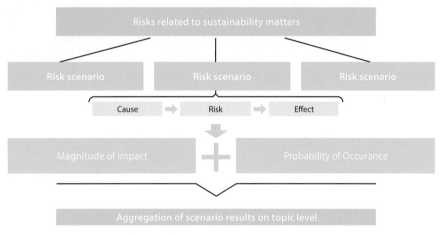

Combining these assessments, the company constructed a sustainability materiality matrix to focus on key topics for maximum impact. Such a scatterplot presents the results of their analysis of topics that would be of 'interest to intended users' and that would have an 'impact'. The positioning of reporting topics may be influenced by considering both the likelihood that a reporting topic occurs and the magnitude of their significance. Illustration 15.6 illustrates the materiality matrix of Barry Callebaut AG.

ILLUSTRATION 15.6

MATERIALITY MATRIX OF BARRY CALLEBAUT AG[18]

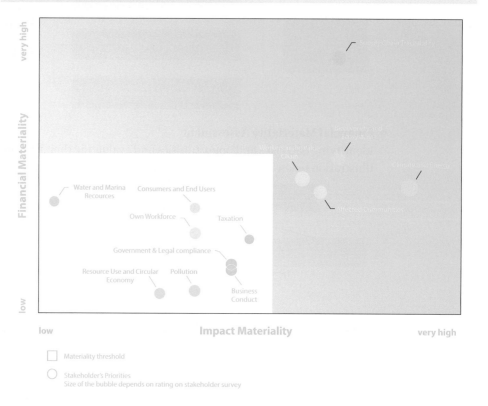

15.3.2 MISSTATEMENTS DUE TO FRAUD AND ERROR

As in the preparation of the financial statements, management can make mistakes in sustainability reporting. If it is the case that these misstatements are intentional, involving the use of deception to obtain an unjust or illegal advantage, it is fraud. Misstatements in sustainability information due to fraud may result from intentional[19]:

▶ Manipulation, falsification, or alteration of information or supporting documentation from which the sustainability information is prepared.

▶ Misrepresentation in, or omission from, the sustainability information.

In sustainable information, there is a risk that the portrayed image is intentionally more favourable than the reality and that is called 'greenwashing'. Fraudulent reporting risk increases as rewards become more dependent on sustainability KPIs/goals. The opportunity for fraud exists because administrative systems and internal controls have not yet reached the level of financial information, and there are still few hard standards, comparisons, and historical data available. A possible form of rationalization arises by focusing on how positively automation of the production process contributes to the financial results, thereby downplaying potential negative consequences for employment. Examples of violations of laws and regulations include intentional pollutions or as a result of intentional gross negligence or laundering the proceeds of ESG-related crimes. What applies to financial information also applies to non-financial information. We refer to chapter 12 for more information on fraudulent financial reporting. Illustration 15.7 sketches some challenges in identifying sustainability fraud risks.

CHALLENGES IN IDENTIFYING FRAUD RISKS[20]

Limited Standardization: The lack of standardized ESG reporting frameworks makes it challenging to establish consistent criteria for evaluating and comparing data.	**Incomplete Data:** Incomplete or unreliable ESG data, coupled with a lack of historical and industry-specific information, hinders the ability to detect anomalies or irregularities.	**Subjectivity in Reporting:** ESG reporting often involves subjective reporting often involves subjective assessments, making it difficult to objectively measure and identify objectively measure and identify fraudulent activities.	**Greenwashing:** Companies may engage in greenwashing, where they exaggerate or falsely claim their environmental and social responsibility efforts, making it challenging to discern genuine ESG practices.
Complex Supply Chains: Multifaceted and global supply chains increase the complexity of assessing and monitoring ESG practices throughout the entire value chain.	**Lack of Oversight:** Insufficient regulatory oversight and enforcement contribute to a higher risk of fraudulent ESG reporting going undetected.	**Limited Legal Precedents:** The relatively young nature of ESG reporting means there are few legal precedents or established frameworks for addressing fraudulent activities, creating uncertainties in legal consequences.	**Interconnected Risks:** ESG fraud risks are often interconnected with financial, reputational, and operational risks, making it challenging to isolate and address them effectively.
	Inadequate Internal Controls: Companies may lack effective internal controls specifically designed to detect and prevent ESG related fraud, leaving gaps in risk-mitigation.	**Varied Stakeholder Expectations:** Diverse stakeholder expectations regarding ESG performance make it challenging for companies to prioritize and address all relevant concerns, potentially leaving room for manipulation	

In case of greenwashing, stakeholders, such as consumers, often feel misled because companies claim to offer environmentally friendly products that are not as environmentally friendly as advertised. When a company compares its product to a more environmentally damaging alternative rather than addressing its own shortcomings, it might be attempting to distract from its own practices. This form of greenwashing, often termed 'comparative greenwashing,' involves highlighting a product's relative benefits in comparison to a worse option rather than addressing the product's own environmental impact. For instance, an automobile manufacturer might boast about its electric vehicle's lower emissions compared to a gas-guzzling SUV while conveniently overlooking other aspects, such as resource-intensive battery production or limited recycling options[21]. In illustration 15.18 we give some further examples of material misstatements due to fraud.

15.3.3 ACCOUNTING INFORMATION SYSTEMS AND INTERNAL CONTROL OVER SUSTAINABILITY REPORTING (ICSR)

Comparing the effectiveness of internal controls over financial reporting (ICFR) and internal controls over sustainability reporting (ICSR) involves considering the nature, purpose, and regulatory environment of each type of reporting. Here are some reasons why internal controls over financial reporting may be perceived as more effective than those over sustainability reporting:

▶ Regulatory Framework
  ▶ Financial reporting is often subject to strict regulatory frameworks, such as the Generally Accepted Accounting Principles (GAAP) or International Financial Reporting Standards (IFRS). These standards provide clear guidelines and requirements, making it easier to establish and enforce internal controls over financial reporting.
  ▶ In contrast, sustainability reporting still lacks a universally accepted and standardized framework (see section 15.4).
▶ Quantifiable Metrics
  ▶ Financial reporting primarily deals with quantifiable and measurable metrics, such as revenues, expenses, and profit margins. The precision and clarity of these metrics make it easier to design and implement effective internal controls.
  ▶ Sustainability reporting often involves qualitative and non-financial metrics, which can be more subjective and challenging to measure. This makes it harder to establish robust internal controls over the collection and reporting of such data.
▶ Maturity of Practice
  ▶ Financial reporting has a longer history and more mature practices compared to sustainability reporting as it is based upon double entry bookkeeping since the 15th century and is embedded in sophisticated IT systems (like SAP). The longer-established norms and practices contribute to a more robust internal control environment.
  ▶ Sustainability reporting is a relatively new practice, and organizations may still be developing and refining internal controls as the field evolves.

It's essential to note that both financial reporting and sustainability reporting play crucial roles in providing a comprehensive view of an organization's performance. As sustainability reporting continues to evolve, efforts are being made to enhance standardization and establish clearer frameworks, which may contribute to the improvement of internal controls over sustainability reporting in the future.

The narrative of Shell, as depicted in section 15.2, provides an insightful overview of the historical evolution of sustainability reporting. Looking ahead, the landscape of sustainability reporting is poised for significant transformation with the integration of Information Technology (IT) and Artificial Intelligence (AI). Anticipating a substantial influence, it is foreseeable that generative AI will emerge as a pivotal player in shaping the future of sustainability reporting. An application of AI, developed by Maria Tymtsias, could look like this[22]:

Peer and Industry Assessment

▶ Deploy AI to assess competitors' sustainability practices. Gain insights into relevant industry trends and position your ESG strategy accordingly.

▶ Utilize AI for in-depth analysis of peers' sustainability topics, ensuring your approach stays competitive and relevant.

Double Materiality Assessment

▶ Engage ChatGPT for an extensive list of material topics relevant to your sector, alongside a report on unique risks and overlooked areas.

▶ Provide a list of stakeholders and receive a custom engagement plan that aligns with stakeholder engagement standards like GRI. ESRS.

▶ Get AI assistance in developing double materiality assessment workshops, from question formulation to strategic implementation.

▶ Employ ChatGPT for creating stakeholder questionnaires and utilize AI for efficient note-taking and analysis during workshops to not overlook raised points.

ESRS Data Points Mapping and Collection

▶ Post-assessment, utilize GPT to identify crucial ESRS data points.

▶ Input existing data for AI to write a compelling narrative for identified data points.

▶ Receive AI-driven advice on essential uncollected data and effective collection methodologies.

Sustainability Strategy Creation

▶ Utilize AI to craft a solid ESG strategy, integrating insights from your materiality assessment and KPIs.

Disclosure Validation

▶ Rely on GPT to verify the relevancy and correct application of your sustainability disclosures.

▶ Employ AI for a comprehensive review, ensuring thoroughness and accuracy.

Report Creation

▶ Request GPT's input on the structure of your sustainability report, referencing existing exemplars.

▶ Have AI generate content for each section, grounded in your materiality assessment, policies, strategies, and data points.

▶ Utilize AI to maintain report objectivity and avoid greenwashing.

15.4 SUSTAINABILITY REPORTING GOALS, REGULATIONS AND STANDARDS

Various initiatives and guidelines, such as the Organization for Economic Co-operation and Development (OECD) Guidelines for Multinational Enterprises and the UN Global Compact further promote sustainable development goals for responsible business practices and reporting illustration 15.8[23].

ILLUSTRATION 15.8

UN SUSTAINABLE DEVELOPMENT GOALS

Sustainability reporting requirements have become prevalent worldwide, with many countries and stock exchanges implementing regulations to promote transparency and accountability in environmental, social, and governance (ESG) matters. Examples of countries with specific sustainability reporting requirements include the USA, Canada, and Australia's Corporations Acts, which mandate companies preparing a Director's Report to provide details of performance concerning environmental regulations. Similarly, local stock exchanges in countries like China (Shanghai/Shenzhen), South Africa (Johannesburg), and Brazil (Bovespa) have introduced sustainability reporting requirements for listed companies and often refer to sustainability reporting standards. In the next paragraph the most important reporting standards are briefly discussed.

15.4.1 INTEGRATED REPORTING COUNCIL (IIRC)

The International Integrated Reporting Council (IIRC) is a global coalition of regulators, investors, companies, standard setters, the accounting profession, and NGOs. It promotes sustainability through integrated reporting, which combines financial and non-financial information to provide a comprehensive view of an organization's performance. Integrated reporting aims to enhance transparency, accountability, and decision-making by considering the organization's broader societal and environmental impacts alongside its financial results. An integrated report provides comprehensive insights into how an organization's strategy, governance, performance, and future prospects contribute to value creation over the short, medium, and long term (illustration 15.9).[24] Integrated reporting facilitates a more holistic understanding of how an organization operates and creates value.

ILLUSTRATION 15.9

VALUE CREATION PROCESS[25]

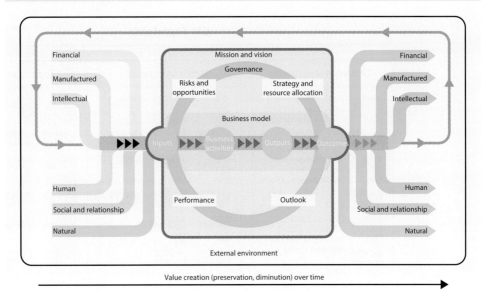

Value creation (preservation, diminution) over time

15.4.2 GLOBAL REPORTING INITIATIVE (GRI)

Many large corporations follow the Global Reporting Initiative (GRI) standards for environmental and social reporting[26]. These guidelines are designed to help organizations report on the economic, environmental, and social aspects of their activities, products, and services. The reports serve various purposes, including benchmarking sustainability performance against laws, norms, codes, and voluntary initiatives, as well as demonstrating the organization's influence and response to expectations about sustainable development.

The GRI standards are modular and provide a comprehensive view of an organization's material topics, their related impacts, and how they are managed[27]. The Universal Standards cover reporting on human rights and environmental due diligence, applicable to all organizations. They include[28]:

▶ Foundation 2021 (GRI 1) explains the purpose of the GRI Standards, critical concepts, and how to use them. It also emphasizes principles such as accuracy, balance, and verifiability that underpin high-quality reporting.

▶ General Disclosures 2021 (GRI 2) contains disclosures related to the organization's structure, reporting practices, activities, workers, governance, strategy, policies, practices, and stakeholder engagement.

▶ Material Topics 2021 (GRI 3) outlines the steps for determining an organization's most relevant topics and describes how the Sector Standards are used in this process. The Topic Standards provide disclosures for reporting information on various topics, such as waste, occupational health and safety, and tax. Each standard includes an overview of the topic and specific disclosures on how the organization manages its associated impacts.

ILLUSTRATION 15.10

OVERVIEW OF GRI STANDARDS[29]

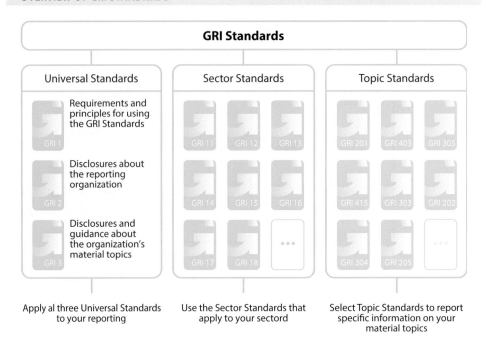

While GRI recommends reporting in accordance with all GRI Standards, organizations may choose to report only specific information for certain purposes, such as regulatory compliance. In such cases, reports must include a GRI content index, making reported information traceable.

15.4.3 INTERNATIONAL SUSTAINABILILTY STANDARDS BOARD (ISSB)

Recognizing the need for standardized sustainability reporting, the International Financial Reporting Standards (IFRS) Foundation established the International Sustainability Standards Board (ISSB) to develop sustainability standards. These standards aim to meet the information needs of investors and other capital market participants, enabling them to make informed decisions regarding sustainability-related risks and opportunities of companies.

▶ IFRS-S

The ISSB has issued IFRS S1 General Requirements for Disclosure of Sustainability-related Financial Information and IFRS S2 Climate-related Disclosures[30]. IFRS S1 provides a set of disclosure requirements for companies to communicate sustainability-related risks and opportunities they face over the short, medium, and long term to investors[32]. IFRS S2 outlines specific climate-related disclosures.

An entity that prepares sustainability-related financial disclosures in accordance with the ISSB Standards must always apply IFRS S1. IFRS S1 identifies the essential

ILLUSTRATION 15.11

SUMMARY IFRS S1 AND S2[31]

	IFRS S1: General Sustainability Disclosures	IFRS S2: CLimate-Related Disclosures
Objective	Information about **significant sustainability-related risks and opportunities**. Disclosures should be useful to the primary users of general purpose financial reporting in making decisions related to providing resources to the entity.	Information about **climate-related risks and opportunities**. Disclosures should assist users in understanding the use of resources and evaluating strategies, businesses model, and operational adaption abilities
Key Disclosure Topics	• *Governance*–Processes, controls, and procedure to monitor and manage **sustainability-related** risks and opportunities. • *Strategy*–Approach for adressing **sustainability-related** risks and opportunities that could affect business model and strategy over the short, medium and long term. • *Risk management*–processes to identify, assess, and manage **sustainability-related** risks • *Metrics and targets*–Information used to assess, manage, and monitor **sustainability-related** risks and opportunities.	• *Governance*–Processes, controls, and procedure to monitor and manage **climate-related** risks and opportunities. • *Strategy*–Approach for adressing **climate-related** risks and opportunities that could affect business model and strategy over the short, medium and long term. • *Risk management*–processes to identify, assess, and manage **climate-related** risks • *Metrics and targets*–Information used to assess, manage, and monitor **climate-related** risks and opportunities.

elements of a complete set of sustainability-related disclosures and sets out the qualitative characteristics of useful sustainability-related financial information. That is, an entity will apply IFRS S1 in preparing and reporting sustainability-related financial disclosures for the full 'universe' of sustainability-related information and disclosures are linked to single materiality (financial). IFRS S2 further specifies the information an entity is required to disclose about climate-related risks and opportunities including emissions scopes 1, 2 and 3.

IFRS S1 and IFRS S2 must always be applied together.

The IFRS-S standards are converging with other international standards and frameworks. It is expected that the European standards discussed in the following paragraph will align as much as possible with the international standards.

15.4.4 EU CORPORATE SUSTAINABILITY DIRECTIVE (CSRD)[33]

The EU Corporate Sustainability Reporting Directive (CSRD) was adopted in 2023, introducing strengthened rules to report social and environmental information within the European Union. This directive aims to provide comprehensive and standardized reporting on sustainability matters, ensuring that relevant information is disclosed

ILLUSTRATION 15.12

OVERVIEW OF ESRS AND GENERAL PRINCIPLES[35]

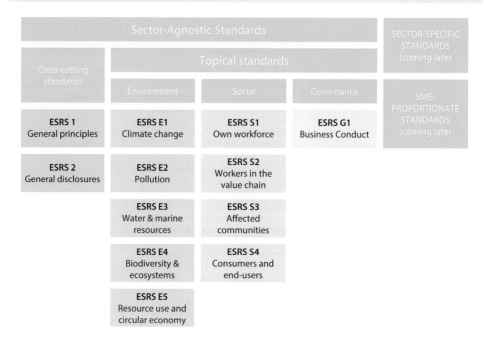

ESRS 1: General Principles

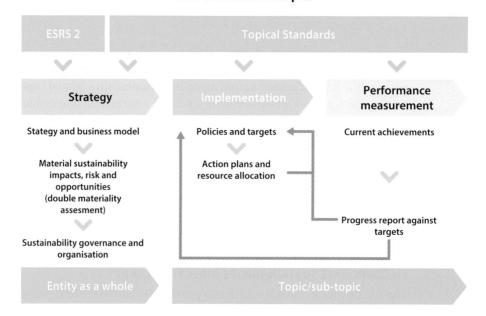

consistently across various entities, facilitating better comparability and understanding of their sustainability performance.

Under the CSRD, in-scope companies[36] are required to disclose a wide range of sustainability-related information. This information includes:

- ▶ a description of the company's business model, strategy and sustainability risks and opportunities;
- ▶ ESG-related targets and annual progress on meeting these targets;
- ▶ separate sustainability statements included in the company's management reports, containing sector-agnostic, sector-specific and company-specific information, in accordance with European Sustainability Reporting Standards (ESRS);
- ▶ sustainability matters that affect the company and the impact of the company on sustainability matters (the so called 'double materiality' perspective).
- ▶ greenhouse gas emissions targets;
- ▶ policies in relation to sustainability (including incentive schemes linked to sustainability matters);
- ▶ EU taxonomy alignment data; and
- ▶ due diligence processes implemented by the company in relation to sustainability matters and the actual and potential adverse impacts of the company's operations and value chain.

Sustainability information is presented in Sustainability Statements, which are part of the company's management report. These reporting areas are covered by so-called cross-cutting and topical standards, providing comprehensive and relevant information for stakeholders.

▶ **ESRS**

On 31 July 2023 the European Commission adopted the Delegated Act on the first set of European Sustainability Reporting Standards (ESRS).

Cross-cutting standards (ESRS 1 and 2) address disclosures that are essential for understanding the relationship between sustainability matters and the company's strategy, business model, governance, organization, and materiality assessment[34]. Following the concept of double materiality, companies are required to identify both their material sustainability-related impacts (inside-out) and the external risks and opportunities (outside-in).

Topical standards (E, S, and G) focus on specific sustainability topics or subtopics related to the environment (required emissions scopes 1, 2 and 3), social, and governance aspects. These standards set disclosure requirements for sustainability impacts, risks, and opportunities that are considered material for all entities, regardless of their sectors. The topical standards complement the cross-cutting standards and cover the following information to be reported:

- ▶ The policies, targets, actions, and action plans, as well as the resources adopted by the entity concerning a particular sustainability topic or subtopic.
- ▶ Corresponding performance measurement metrics for each sustainability topic or subtopic. These targets and metrics align with the TCFD (Task Force on Climate-related Financial Disclosures) and ISSB (International Sustainability Standards Board) 'targets and metrics reporting' pillar.

In the sustainability report, the company is encouraged to link retrospective (historical) and forward-looking (future-oriented) information. This linkage helps stakeholders comprehend the company's historical performance and how it aligns with its sustainability goals and future plans.

▶ DUE DILIGENCE

Sustainability due diligence is an essential process for companies today. It's about thoroughly examining and managing the negative effects a company might have on the environment and society due to its operations. This involves companies being transparent about the problems they find within their operations and supply chains, and the steps they're taking to fix these issues. Engaging with stakeholders – like customers, employees, and local communities – is a key part of this process, helping companies to spot potential problems, understand risks, and find ways to reduce harm.

The Corporate Sustainability Reporting Directive (CSRD) marks a significant change in how companies approach sustainability. Unlike previous rules that focused mainly on a company's direct environmental impact, the CSRD emphasizes the importance of looking at the whole supply chain[37]. This makes sense because the majority of a company's environmental and social risks actually come from its supply chain. With CSRD, companies are now required to take responsibility for their suppliers, ensuring they meet high environmental, social, and ethical standards.

The goal of supply chain due diligence under CSRD isn't just to check boxes; it's about fundamentally changing how companies think about and act on their responsibilities. It involves a detailed evaluation of suppliers to minimize harm and ensure that companies comply with laws, which in turn protects the company's reputation. CSRD brings transparency and due diligence to the forefront, setting new standards for reporting on environmental, social, and governance (ESG) issues. This means companies have to disclose more about their supply chain risks and how they're addressing them. This shift aims to streamline reporting, increase accountability, and extend the focus to the full value chain, pushing companies towards greater transparency and responsibility[38]. The task of collecting enough relevant information within the supply chain presents a significant challenge for companies and their auditors. They must evaluate this information meticulously to ensure it can be accurately reflected in the sustainability report. This process is crucial for creating a comprehensive and transparent account of a company's sustainability practices.

15.4.5 SECURITIES AND EXCHANGE COMMISSION (US)

The SEC is adopting amendments that require registrants to provide certain climate-related information in their registration statements and annual reports. The final rules will require information about a registrant's climate-related risks that have materially impacted or are reasonably likely to have a material impact on, its business strategy, results of operations, or financial condition. In addition, certain disclosures related to severe weather events and other natural conditions will be required in a registrant's audited financial statements. Companies have to include climate-related information disclosed in their official filings[39]:

▶ *Climate-Related Risks.*

Any climate-related risks significantly affecting or likely to affect the company, including its strategy, operations, or finances.

▷ *Impact of Climate-Related Risks.*
How these risks could materially influence the company's strategy, business model, and future outlook, including plans for transitions and scenario analysis.

▷ *Governance and Management.*
How the company's board and management handle climate-related risks.

▷ *Risk Management.*
The methods used to identify, assess, and manage these risks.

▷ *Targets and Goals.*
Any climate-related objectives impacting or likely to impact the company significantly.

▷ *Financial Statement Effects.*
Financial consequences of severe weather and natural events, and costs related to climate initiatives.

▷ *GHG Emissions.*
Direct and indirect greenhouse gas emissions data for certain companies, requiring third-party verification over time.

Compared to the EU CSRD (ESRS E1[40]), the proposed SEC rules mandate companies to divulge details regarding both direct greenhouse gas (GHG) emissions (Scope 1) and indirect emissions arising from purchased electricity or other energy sources (Scope 2). Additionally, companies must disclose GHG emissions from upstream and downstream activities in their value chain (Scope 3) only if these are material or if the company has set a GHG emissions target or goal that includes Scope 3 emissions.

The CSRD, however, goes beyond the SEC's proposed rules: in addition to reporting on climate-related risks, companies are asked to report on (among other things) water and marine resources-related risks, biodiversity and ecosystems-related risks and risks in relation to workers in the value chain, all on a 'double materiality' basis.

15.5   SUSTAINABILITY ASSURANCE PROCESS

Note

In this section we refer to the **Exposure Draft (ED) of the International Standard on Sustainability Assurance 5000 (ISSA 5000)**, published by the IAASB in 2023. The final standard is expected at the end of 2024. At the time of writing this book, more than 140 comments have been submitted on the draft standard. It is therefore very likely that the final standard deviates from the draft used in this book, both in terms of content and numbering of the articles. After the publication of the final standard ISSA 5000, an overview of relevant changes and references to the numbering of the articles of the standard will be provided on the website associated with this textbook (https://principlesofauditing.com/).

15.5.1 INTRODUCTION

A study by IFAC[41] (2023) indicates that 95% of large companies already disclosed some level of sustainability data and that 64% obtained assurance of the information. For 80% of those, it was limited assurance. As accountants possess a unique combination of skills, qualifications, experience, and the professional ethical obligation to act in the public interest they are well positioned to carry out such assignments. It is expected a framework of ethical provisions for use by all sustainability assurance practitioners regardless of their professional backgrounds, as well as professional accountants involved in sustainability reporting will be established by the International Ethics Standards Board (IESBA)[42]. It is this combination of professional requirements that leads to meaningful assurance, which brings trust and confidence to sustainability information (IFAC, AICPA & CIMA, 2021)[43].

The European CSRD includes specific requirements aimed at ensuring the accuracy and reliability of sustainability information provided by companies. Companies in scope are required to obtain limited assurance from a third-party verifier[44] in their first reporting year. Towards 2030 it will become 'reasonable assurance'[45].

Several standards and supportive materials on sustainability assurance are already issued, including[46]:

- ▶ International Standard on Assurance Engagements (ISAE) 3000 (Revised), Assurance Engagements Other Than Audits or Reviews of Historical Financial Information (see chapter 14).
- ▶ ISAE 3410, Assurance Engagements on Greenhouse Gas Statements (see chapter 14).
- ▶ The package of non-authoritative guidance on sustainability and other extended external reporting assurance engagements (EER).
- ▶ The Staff Audit Practice Alert, The Consideration of Climate-Related Risks in an Audit of Financial Statements.

The remainder of this chapter will discuss Sustainability Assurance in more detail[47]. The phases of this assurance process are shown in illustration 15.13[48]:

ILLUSTRATION 15.13

SUSTAINABILITY ASSURANCE PROCESS MODEL

Acceptance and continuance	Understanding and risk analysis	Building and executing assurance plan	Evaluating and completion
• Acceptance and Continuance	• Planning activities • Materiality Assessment • Using the Work of an External Expert • Assessing RMM	• Responding to Identified RMM • Evidence and Sources • Building and Executing further Procedures	• Accumulation and Consideration of Identified Misstatements • Forming the Assurance Conclusion • Preparing the Assurance Report

15.5.2   ACCEPTANCE AND CONTINUANCE

Under ISSA 5000 the practitioner provides reasonable or limited assurance on sustainability information[49]. If an ISSA objective cannot be met, she should adjust the conclusion or consider withdrawal, following applicable laws. Instances of unmet objectives must be documented in the assurance file[50].

Before accepting the engagement, the practitioner will ascertain that the preconditions essential for an assurance engagement are present. Pursuant, there must be a shared understanding between the practitioner and the client regarding the terms of the engagement.

The practitioner bears the responsibility for achieving the desired quality standards as well as ensuring that all engagement team members are informed of the applicable ethical prerequisites[51]. As in a financial statement audit, commitment to upholding professional scepticism is required throughout the engagement. This entails recognition of the significant risks arising from fraudulent activities, even in the presence of positive prior experiences with the integrity and ethical conduct of the entity's management[52].

To effectively execute this role, the practitioner must have acquired considerable expertise in general assurance techniques and methodologies through training and practical application (assurance competence)[53]. Furthermore, specialized knowledge and proficiency in the realm of sustainability is indispensable (subject matter competence). The complexity of the assignment dictates the involvement of a multidisciplinary team, which requires assurance competence and the insights of experts from pertinent fields[54]. This expertise should be cultivated through a combination of training and hands-on experience[55].

The engagement can be complex because of the diverse nature of the sustainability information and various levels of assurance. Also, the information in the report could be more qualitative, emphasizing future projections while the entity's procedures and controls might not be as robust and effective as those governing financial reporting leading to a higher risk of a material misstatement (RMM). Furthermore, the presence of internally developed criteria could introduce bias into the engagement's scope. Therefore, the practitioner determines if this precondition is present[56].

The practitioner starts evaluating if underlying subject matters in scope are appropriate, identifiable and capable of consistent measurement and evaluation, such that sufficient appropriate evidence can be obtained[57]. Even though her scope might be limited to assuring specific disclosures, it's vital to possess a broader awareness of the entire sustainability information landscape. This broader knowledge helps preventing that she is inadvertently linked to information that could be materially inaccurate or deceptive[58].

The practitioner and management establish a shared understanding of sustainability matters in scope and the degree of assurance to be achieved. Selecting only those parts of the information included in scope that are easier to assure or that present the entity in a favourable light is not appropriate[59]. The scope of the engagement could include:

▶ The whole sustainability report.
▶ Specific topics or areas of information within the report, for example environmental or social matters.
▶ Individual items within specific topics or areas of information within the report. For example, waste generated within the 'environmental' topic or area, or gender pay within the 'social' topic; or

▶ Different levels of assurance for different aspects of the sustainability information, for example limited assurance on the 'social' topic and reasonable assurance on the 'environmental' topic.

▶ The reporting boundary might encompass the reporting of a single entity, multiple entities, the complete value chain of an entity, specific geographic areas, activities, operations, or facilities.

Example of Reporting Boundary in the Supply Chain of a Supermarket[60]

In the supply chain, gathering sufficient evidence about how salmon is farmed and reaches consumers through a supermarket can sometimes be unfeasible. In this situation, the AP might not be able to draw a conclusion about the supplier's adherence to salmon farming regulations, as stated in the supermarket's sustainability report[61].

As discussed in section 14.3, assurance engagements require criteria suitable for the circumstances considering, entity-developed criteria or a combination of both and must be available to all stakeholders (as intended users of the report)[62]. As mentioned earlier, sustainability information and criteria can be different and are currently being developed, so assessment of suitability is very important.

Suitable criteria exhibit the following characteristics, while the relative importance of each characteristic is a matter of professional judgement (illustration 15.14)[63].

ILLUSTRATION 15.14

CHARACTERISTICS OF SUITABLE CRITERIA

Relevance: Relevant criteria result in sustainability information that assists decision making by the intended users (double materiality consisting of financial and impact materiality, see section 5.2);

Completeness: Criteria are complete when sustainability information prepared in accordance with them does not omit relevant factors that could reasonably be expected to affect decisions of intended users made on the basis of that sustainability information. Complete criteria include, where relevant, benchmarks for presentation and disclosures;

Reliability: Reliable criteria allow reasonably consistent measurement or evaluation of the sustainability matters, when used in similar circumstances by different practitioners;

Neutrality: Neutral criteria result in sustainability information that is free from bias as appropriate in the engagement circumstances; and

Understandability: Understandable criteria result in sustainability information that can be understood by the intended users.

Example of Considerations for Determining the Suitable of Criteria for Social Matters

When the intended users include trade unions or the entity's employees, the entity may consider that it is appropriate to use criteria that require reporting about matters such as gender diversity, training, and health and safety incidents, and how to measure or evaluate those matters, which, in addition to gender pay gap reporting, are likely to be of interest to trade unions and employees.

Example of Considerations for Determining the Suitability of Criteria for Governance Matters (Processes, Systems and Control)

The practitioner may consider whether the criteria encompass the following:

If the assurance engagement includes the description of the entity's process, systems or controls:

▶ The control objectives and controls designed to achieve those objectives.

▶ The procedures and records, within both information technology and manual systems, by which the sustainability matters, and significant events and conditions, relevant to the sustainability information are recorded, processed, corrected as necessary, and transferred to the sustainability information reported.

If the assurance engagement includes the suitability of the design of the processes, systems or controls:

▶ Identification of the risks that threaten achievement of the control objectives stated in the description of the processes, systems or controls.

▶ Whether the controls identified in that description would, if operated as described, provide reasonable assurance about the achievement of the control objectives.

If the assurance engagement includes the operating effectiveness of the processes, systems or controls:

▶ Whether the controls were consistently applied as designed throughout the specified period.

▶ whether manual controls were applied by individuals who have the appropriate competence and authority.

If all pre-conditions are met, the practitioner will decide whether to accept or continue the sustainability assurance engagement. Irrespective of the level of assurance, the preconditions underpinning an assurance engagement remain constant. The absence of necessary preconditions in a reasonable assurance engagement cannot be rectified merely by transitioning the engagement to a limited assurance engagement[64]. Should the necessary preconditions not be met, an engagement conducted under such circumstances does not align with (ED) ISSA 5000.

As in an audit of financial statements, agreed terms of the assurance engagement have to be specified in sufficient detail in an engagement letter or other suitable form of written agreement[65].

15.5.3 UNDERSTANDING AND RISK ANALYSIS

▶ PLANNING ACTIVITIES

As mentioned in section 14.3, effective planning is essential, involving team composition, task allocation and active team participation. Based on understanding the client, the assessment of risks of material misstatements due to fraud or error leads to a focus on critical areas. The nature, timing, and extent of procedures align with an overarching strategy, refined into a detailed plan. Professional judgment guides procedures, considering how the entity organizes sustainability information. Adaptability is crucial in the continuous and iterative planning phase, allowing for revisions based on unforeseen events or new evidence, maintaining effectiveness and relevance. The practitioner retains overall responsibility for the strategy and plan.

▸ MATERIALITY ASSESSMENT

As explained in chapter 15.3.1, the process applied by the entity to determine the sustainability matters to be reported, often referred to as the 'process to identify reporting topics,' 'materiality assessment,' or 'materiality process,' relates to management's determination of the topics (subject matters) that may be relevant for intended users. Management's 'materiality process' differs from materiality determined by the practitioner who determines materiality as input for performing risk procedures, determining further procedures and evaluating whether the sustainability information is free from material misstatement due to fraud or error.

The concept of 'financial materiality differs from direct material financial implications (as determined by financial statement materiality thresholds) as discussed in chapter 6. A financial material issue (like expected rises in sea water levels as a consequence of climate change) which could lead to significant investments in insulating buildings could be material for the current year financial statements (tangible fixed assets).

The concept of materiality from the practitioner's perspective includes the following principles[66]:

> ▸ Misstatements due to fraud or error are considered to be material if they, individually or in the aggregate, could reasonably be expected to influence decisions of intended users taken on the basis of the sustainability information.
> ▸ Judgements about matters that are material to intended users of the sustainability information are based on a consideration of the common information needs of intended users as a group.

It is assumed that intended users will make reasonable decisions on the basis of sustainability information and have sufficient knowledge and understanding of sustainability matters and concept of materiality. Unless the engagement has been designed to meet the particular information needs of specific users, the possible effect of misstatements on specific users, whose information needs may vary widely, is not ordinarily considered[67].

Materiality is considered in qualitative and, when applicable, quantitative factors[68]. For different sustainability disclosures, the same intended users may have different information needs, and a different tolerance for misstatement. As shown in illustration 15.15 the consideration of factors may help the practitioner to identify the *qualitative* disclosures that may be more significant to the intended users.

Qualitative factors may also be Important in considering the way in which the sustainability information is presented. For example, when the preparer presents the disclosures in the form of graphs, diagrams or images, materiality considerations may include whether using different scales for the x- and y-or images of a graph may result in materially misstated or misleading information.

ILLUSTRATION 15.15

ASSESSING QUALITATIVE MATERIALITY

Examples of Factors for Assessing Qualitative Materiality

The number of persons or entities affected by, and the severity of the effect of, the sustainability matter. For example, a hazardous waste spill may impact a small number of people, but the effect of that spill could lead to serious adverse consequences to the environment.

The nature of a potential misstatement and when it would be considered material. For example, the nature of observed deviations from a control when the sustainability information is a statement that the control is effective.

For narrative disclosures, whether the level of detail of the description or the overall tone of the words used to describe the matter may give a misleading picture to users of the sustainability information.

Whether a potential misstatement would be significant based on the practitioner's understanding of known previous communications to users, for example, in relation to the expected outcome of goals or targets, the degree to which a potential misstatement would impact the entity achieving the goal or target.

Quantitative factors relate to the magnitude of misstatements relative to the disclosures that are expressed numerically or related to numerical values (e.g., the number of observed deviations from a control may be a relevant quantitative factor when the sustainability information is a statement that the control is effective)[69].

If the applicable criteria specify a percentage threshold for materiality, this may provide a frame of reference to the practitioner in determining materiality for the disclosure. Examples of thresholds may include x% of investment in community projects (in hours or monetary terms), y% of energy consumed (in kWh), or z% of land rehabilitated (in hectares).

The applicable criteria may require disclosures of financial information. For example, topics reported may include community investment, training expenditures, or taxes by jurisdiction. These may also be reported in the entity's financial statements. The materiality used for these aspects of the disclosures need not be the same as the materiality used in the audit of the entity's financial statements[70].

For *quantitative* disclosures, aggregation risk, which is the probability that the aggregate of uncorrected and undetected misstatements exceeds materiality, should also be assessed. Aggregation risk arises because the sustainability information may be disaggregated by management for purposes of applying the applicable criteria, or by the practitioner for the purpose of designing assurance procedures. It is therefore appropriate when planning the nature, timing and extent of procedures to:

▷ Consider setting performance materiality for quantitative disclosures to reduce aggregation risk to an appropriately low level; or

▷ Consider what types of errors or omissions would potentially constitute a material misstatement when aggregated with other misstatements.

As in other assurance engagements, factors relevant to the practitioner's consideration of materiality for qualitative disclosures or determination of materiality for quantitative disclosures, have to be documented as well as the basis for determination of performance materiality.

▶ USING THE WORK OF AN EXTERNAL EXPERT

As in the audit of financial statements, when the work of an external expert is planned, the practitioner[71]:

- ▶ evaluates whether the expert has the necessary competence, capabilities and objectivity for the practitioner's purposes;
- ▶ when evaluating objectivity, inquire regarding interests and relationships that may create a threat to that expert's objectivity;
- ▶ obtains a sufficient understanding of the field of expertise of the expert to determine the nature, scope and objectives of that expert's work for the practitioner's purposes;
- ▶ agrees with the expert on the nature, scope and objectives of that expert's work; and
- ▶ evaluates the adequacy of the expert's work for the practitioner's purposes.

▶ ASSESSING THE RISK OF MATERIAL MISSTATEMENTS

DESIGNING AND PERFORMING RISK PROCEDURES

The sustainability assurance team (and external experts) discuss the susceptibility of the disclosures to material misstatements to share insights and enhance understanding by all team members[72]. Designing and performing risk procedures may also involve interactions with management, those charged with governance, personnel within the entity, external parties and relevant publicly available information.

Risk procedures by themselves do not provide sufficient appropriate evidence on which to base the assurance conclusion[73]. Inquiry alone ordinarily does not provide sufficient evidence. Other procedures to get sufficient understanding include among others analytical procedures and observation and inspection[74].

UNDERSTANDING THE SUSTAINABILITY MATTERS, SUSTAINABILITY MATTERS AND INFORMATION, APPLICABLE CRITERIA, THE ENTITY AND ITS ENVIRONMENT AND COMPONENTS

As in auditing financial statements, having a thorough 'understanding' is a prerequisite for assessing the risk of a material misstatement (RMM) due to fraud or error. This understanding involves knowing both the main sustainability topics and the details of the information provided. It's about being aware of events and situations that could lead to wrong or missing information that matters a lot, whether because of fraud or errors. As in an audit of financial statements, the practitioner should assess fraud risk based on evaluating fraud risk factors (see chapter 12). All of this needs to be considered by the practitioner when getting an 'understanding'.

ILLUSTRATION 15.16

EXAMPLES OF FRAUD RISK FACTORS

Giving wrong sustainability info (or leaving out info) to avoid getting in trouble, like being fined.

Setting unrealistically high goals, either inside the company or for the public, to boost share prices or enhance the entity's sustainability reputation, such as falsely labeling a bond as a sustainability bond.

Saying things that aren't true about products or the company to mislead people.

Changing sustainability data on purpose to make the company seem better for future plans or to get money from suppliers or customers.

Giving false info about sustainability to pay less in taxes or get more carbon credits than deserved.

Deliberately reporting biased sustainability information related to performance or compensation incentives to influence the outcomes of reward or compensation programs.

Feeling pressure to meet certain standards or conditions, like getting a special 'green' label or satisfying a contract. Promoting a product as being made from recycled materials while intentionally concealing the use of forced labor in its production.

Manipulating baseline information to make subsequent sustainability data appear more favorable.

As mentioned in section 15.3.2, greenwashing implies a non-neutral and overly positive presentation of information and is a RMM due to greenwashing. Let's consider an example[75].

A company consistently reduces its waste figures by ten percent for three consecutive years. The company has several options to communicate this achievement:

1 Incorporate the data over the years on the page with key figures.
2 Highlight the accomplishment on the same page with an explanation, such as 'a decrease in waste figures for three years in a row.'
3 Feature a statement in the waste section, like 'Proud of our double-digit reduction in waste over several years.'

While all three statements are factually accurate, they may convey different impressions to the reader. Although none of the options can be labelled as providing incorrect information, you might sense that options 2 and 3 present a more positive image.

What would / should you do?

Considerations
Beyond ensuring accuracy and completeness, sustainability reports must offer a balanced view of a company's sustainability performance and future. Balance stands as a fundamental principle in sustainability reporting, preventing users from being misled by the tone and presentation of the report. The subtlety of greenwashing poses a challenge – it's not typically evident in a single statement but rather in the overall 'tone of the report,' including word choices and overall presentation. Sustainability assurance providers need to enhance their skills (professional scepticism) in detecting such practices and develop effective strategies for engaging

in discussions with client's management. Given the limitations of laws and rules in addressing these nuances, they must employ alternative conversation techniques. This involves navigating discussions adeptly and, when necessary, standing firm to uphold integrity in reporting practices by enforcing a more balanced view or, if needed, modifying the assurance report.

Assessing sustainability risks and how they'll affect the entity, and its supply chain can be both complex and uncertain. This uncertainty makes it hard to assess likelihood and impact of risks of material misstatements due to error or fraud[76]. Therefore, an in-depth understanding of sustainability goals, targets, and strategic objectives and information is indispensable as well as understanding of the environment and relevant rules and laws.

Inquiries and discussion with appropriate parties can assist in 'understanding' and identifying disclosures where material misstatements are likely to arise or identifying RMMs[77]. Illustration 15.17 gives some examples of such inquiries[78].

ILLUSTRATION 15.17

EXAMPLES OF INQUIRIES

Inquiries directed towards those charged with governance may help the practitioner understand the extent of oversight by those charged with governance over the preparation of the sustainability information.

Inquiries of management may help the practitioner to evaluate the appropriateness of the selection and application of the applicable criteria Inquiries directed towards in-house legal counsel may provide information about matters such as litigation, compliance with laws and regulations, knowledge of fraud or suspected fraud affecting the sustainability information.

Inquiries directed towards the risk management function (or inquiries of those performing such roles) may provide information about operational and regulatory risks that may affect the sustainability information.

Inquiries directed towards IT personnel may provide information about system changes, system or control failures, or other IT-related risks

---

UNDERSTANDING COMPONENTS OF THE ENTITY'S SYSTEM OF INTERNAL CONTROL[79]

As sustainability reporting includes an increasing amount of non-financial information, the reliability is not (yet) as high as that of financial information. This is caused by[80]:

Qualitative information sometimes more difficult to measure and to evaluate	Inconsistent processes because of several reporting frameworks and standards	Variation in technology platforms
Inconsistent or nonexistent data streams and data governance	Third party data	Increasing regulation

Application of the COSO 2013 Internal Control Framework for Sustainability Reporting can enhance the overall effectiveness, efficiency, and accuracy of the underlying processes and internal controls as well as the accuracy of this reporting[81]. Understanding the internal control system is a prerequisite for assessing control risk.

Illustration 15.18 provides examples of sustainability factors per internal control component.

EXAMPLES OF SUSTAINABILITY FACTORS PER INTERNAL CONTROL COMPONENT[82]

Component	Example of application
Control environment	▸ Company values statement ▸ Board/executive oversight of ESG issues, including charters ▸ ESG governance model and organization chart ▸ Defined sustainability job roles/responsibilities and personnel requirements ▸ Policies and procedures for ESG program ▸ ESG performance targets aligned with incentives and rewards
Risk assessment	▸ ESG risk assessment, including climate risks and opportunities ▸ Company strategic ESG risk profile ▸ Interaction of financial materiality, double materiality and dynamic materiality ▸ Integration of ESG risks into ERM program and action plans ▸ Assessment of new laws and regulations over human rights ▸ Fraud risk assessment related to sustainable business activities and reporting
Control activities	▸ Internal controls framework to address risks in ESG operational and reporting processes ▸ IT controls over systems used for ESG data and reporting ▸ Oversight of third-party service providers gathering or processing ESG and sustainability information
Information and communication	▸ ESG communications plan for internal and external stakeholders ▸ Employee training on relevant ESG topics ▸ ESG data collection and reporting processes and procedures
Monitoring activities	▸ Periodic evaluation of design and operation of internal controls (e.g., internal and external audits) ▸ ESG scorecards to monitor progress toward goals and targets ▸ Protocols for reporting deficiencies to management and the board

DESIGN AND IMPLEMENTATION OF INTERNAL CONTROL

In chapter 7 (Understanding and Assessing Control Risk), we learned how important it is to consider whether internal controls can prevent and detect material misstatements due to error or fraud, when identifying the risk of material misstatements and determining control deficiencies. An improperly designed control may represent a control deficiency. If deficiencies are identified related to the control environment, this may affect the practitioner's overall expectations about the operating effectiveness of control activities[83]. In such cases, she may need to test the operating effectiveness of internal controls to a greater extent.

When the information system and control activities form part of the sustainability matter (e.g., when the sustainability information includes a management's internal control statement), more assurance procedures, evidence and documentation of the information system and control activities are expected.

When comparing the procedures in reasonable versus limited sustainability assurance engagements, the key difference is in their depth and scope. Reasonable assurance engagements require more in-depth testing and evaluation. Reasonable assurance provides a higher level of assurance, aiming to offer an opinion, whereas limited assurance aims to state that nothing has come to the auditor's attention to suggest that the internal control system is not adequately designed or implemented.

Below we illustrate some examples of differences in nature and extend of work between limited and reasonable assurance related to the components of the system of internal control.

Limited Assurance[84]	Reasonable Assurance[85]
▶ **Obtain an understanding of certain components** of IC relevant to the sustainability matters and the preparation of sustainability information (control environment, results of the entity's risk assessment process, and the information system and communication)	▶ **Obtain an understanding of all components of IC** relevant to the sustainability matters and the preparation of sustainability information (control environment, **t**he entity's risk assessment process, the entity's process to monitor the control activities and the information system and communication.
Control Activities	
▶ **Conditional requirement to obtain an understanding** of controls (and related IT general controls) **if the practitioner plans to obtain evidence by testing the operating effectiveness of controls**	▶ **Obtain an understanding of control activities** for which the practitioner plans to obtain evidence by testing their operating effectiveness, related IT general controls, and other controls that the practitioner judges are necessary to identify and assess the risks of material misstatement at the assertion level for disclosures and design further procedures responsive to those assessed risks
Design and Implementation	
▶ Evaluating whether the identified control is **designed effectively to accomplish the control objective, or effectively designed to support the operation of other controls** and evaluate the design and determine the implementation in addition to inquiry of the entity's personnel.	▶ Evaluating whether the identified control is **designed effectively to address the risk of material misstatement at the assertion level, or effectively designed to support the operation of other controls** and evaluate the design and determine the implementation in addition to inquiry of the entity's personnel.
Identifying Control Deficiencies	
▶ Based on the understanding of the components of internal control, **consider** whether one or more control deficiencies have been identified	▶ Based on the understanding of the components of internal control, **determine** whether one or more control deficiencies have been identified

RISK OF MATERIAL MISSTATEMENTS (RMM) AND THE ASSURANCE RISK MODEL

RMMs are assessed on a spectrum ranging from low to high, based on the likelihood of a misstatement occurring and its potential magnitude were it to occur. The higher the combination of likelihood and magnitude, the higher the assessment of risk and the more work the practitioner should perform to prevent exceeding acceptable assurance risk. Examples of risk factors are measuring device limitations such as a lack of water meters or infrequent calibration. Measurement errors can also be caused by poor judgement in measurement leading to incomplete data. Risks of missed aspects such as undetected wastewater leaks or internal control weaknesses like unauthorized interventions, are also examples of sources causing high RMM. Illustration 15.19 shows situations where material misstatements in sustainability information may occur[86].

ILLUSTRATION 15.19

SITUATIONS WHERE MATERIAL MISSTATEMENTS MAY OCCUR[87]

▶ Inaccuracies in gathering or processing information used for sustainability reporting.

▶ Manipulating or obscuring sustainability data in a way that misleads intended users.

▶ Management's judgements involving estimates that are deemed unreasonable by the AP.

▶ Including inappropriate information that doesn't meet applicable criteria or including excessive immaterial information that distorts required sustainability data.

▶ Including information that lacks sufficient appropriate evidence to support it.

▶ Omitting required sustainability information or elements of it, such as disclosures or significant subsequent events.

▶ Presenting sustainability information ambiguously or in a vague manner.

▶ Making unexplained changes to sustainability information from the previous reporting period.

▶ Presenting sustainability information out of context, in an unbalanced manner, or with undue prominence not supported by evidence.

▶ Drawing inappropriate conclusions based on selective information, such as using misleading superlatives or adjectives. For example, claiming 'a large number of companies worldwide' based on data from only a hundred companies without disclosing the small base. Similarly, stating that 'the numbers have doubled since last year' without disclosing the small initial numbers.

As in a financial statement audit, an assurance risk model can be applied as also explained in section 6.3. The model is a flexible tool that helps the practitioner to:

▶ Identify the factors that could affect the likelihood and magnitude of a misstatement in the sustainability information.

▶ Assess the RMM for each assertion.

▶ Determine the appropriate level of evidence to collect[88].

The assurance risk factors mirror the components of the audit risk model (also see illustrations 6.2-6.4):

▶ Assurance risk (AR) is the risk that the practitioner will issue an inappropriate assurance conclusion.

▶ Inherent risk (IR) is the susceptibility of an assertion to a material misstatement due to fraud or error, assuming there are no related controls. IR is assessed based on the nature of the assertion and the characteristics of the entity, its environment and transactions.

▶ Control risk (CR) is the risk that a material misstatement will not be prevented, or detected and corrected, by the entity's internal controls. CR is assessed based on the design and effectiveness of the entity's internal controls.

▶ RMM is the product of inherent risk (IR) and control risk (CR). These risks can be assessed separately, with the impact on the disclosures being the same for both (magnitude), but the likelihood being different. The risk can be determined at the RMM level, but it is recommended to determine both component risks separately (i.e., IR and CR)[89]

▶ Detection risk (DR) is the risk that the practitioner will not detect a material misstatement, even if it exists.

The relationship between acceptable assurance risk and the risk factors can be shown in the following algorithm:

▶ AR is a function of IR * CR * DR
▶ DR is a function of AR / (IR * CR)

RMM AND ASSERTIONS

As in a financial statement audit, assessing RMM, assertions can be used to consider the different types of potential misstatements that may occur. In a sustainability assurance engagement, assertions as described below may be used[90]:

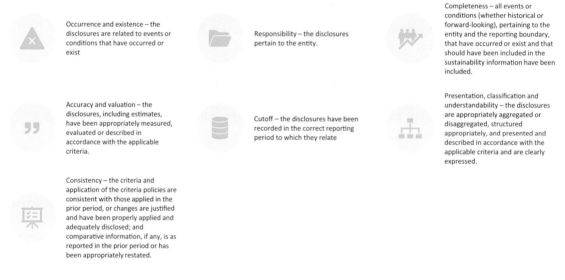

Occurrence and existence – the disclosures are related to events or conditions that have occurred or exist

Responsibility – the disclosures pertain to the entity.

Completeness – all events or conditions (whether historical or forward-looking), pertaining to the entity and the reporting boundary, that have occurred or exist and that should have been included in the sustainability information have been included.

Accuracy and valuation – the disclosures, including estimates, have been appropriately measured, evaluated or described in accordance with the applicable criteria.

Cutoff – the disclosures have been recorded in the correct reporting period to which they relate

Presentation, classification and understandability – the disclosures are appropriately aggregated or disaggregated, structured appropriately, and presented and described in accordance with the applicable criteria and are clearly expressed.

Consistency – the criteria and application of the criteria policies are consistent with those applied in the prior period, or changes are justified and have been properly applied and adequately disclosed; and comparative information, if any, is as reported in the prior period or has been appropriately restated.

Illustration 15.20 depicts examples of different types of possible misstatements that may occur at the assertion level.[91]

ILLUSTRATION 15.20

EXAMPLES OF TYPES OF POSSIBLE MISSTATEMENTS AT ASSERTION LEVEL

▶ False claims in information (occurrence and existence, or responsibility assertion) – for example, an entity's reported community investment or environmental clean-up did not actually occur, or was made by another party, but with responsibility being falsely claimed as the entity's own.

▶ Recording information in the incorrect period (cut-off assertion) – for example, recording an entity's water used in the period preceding or following the period in which the water was actually used.

▶ Inaccuracies in information (accuracy and valuation assertion) – for example, arising from inaccurately calibrated measuring devices, transposition or other errors in the recording of measurements, or use of inappropriate conversion factors, such as use of a carbon dioxide conversion factor for nuclear energy when the entity has coal and oil-fired facilities.

▶ Omission of information (completeness assertion) – for example, a company reports on its land rehabilitation program for three of its mining sites but remains silent about two sites where significant degradation has occurred and where there are no plans to rehabilitate the land.

▶ Incorrectly classified information (presentation, classification and understandability assertion) – for example, the entity classifies seasonal contractors (mainly female) as permanent full-time employees, which results in erroneous reporting about gender representation on its permanent work force.

▶ Misleading or unclear representation of information (presentation, classification and understandability assertion) – for example, the preparer gives undue prominence to favourable information by using large, bold or brightly-coloured text and images, or other ways to emphasize the presentation, but presents unfavourable information less conspicuously), for example, by using small or light-coloured font, and less extensive text.

▶ Bias in information that focuses on positive aspects of performance and omits negative aspects (presentation, classification and understandability assertion).

In limited assurance engagements, it is not required to assess RMM at the assertion level for each disclosure. However, factors for identifying potential material misstatements in disclosures can help to tailor procedures effectively. Such as[92]:

▶ *Nature of sustainability data:* Material misstatements may be more likely in disclosures involving complex calculations (e.g., mass balance) compared to straightforward readings (e.g., water consumption).

▶ *Organizational complexity:* The complexity of an organization, including its ownership, control structures, and geographical reach, can influence the risk of misstatements.

▶ *Systems and processes:* Greater reliance on manual processes or evolving automated systems can increase the likelihood of human errors, processing issues, or unauthorized intervention.

▶ *Incentives to misstate:* External pressures, like the need to meet performance targets for regulatory compliance or stakeholder expectations, can incentivize misstatements.

Finally, the practitioner determines whether the evidence obtained from the risk procedures provides an appropriate basis for the assessment of RMM.

15.5.4   BUILDING AND EXECUTING ASSURANCE PLAN

▶ EVIDENCE AND SOURCES

Responding to identified risks of material misstatement in a sustainability audit involves inquiries, inspection, observation, confirmation, recalculation, reperformance and analytical procedures (just as in a financial statement audit, see section 8.5). For obtaining sufficient appropriate evidence, procedures must be performed in a manner that is neither biased towards obtaining evidence that may be corroborative, nor towards excluding evidence that may be contradictory. Also, the nature, timing and extent of assurance procedures should be appropriate in the circumstances.

As mentioned in section 14.3, the sufficiency and appropriateness of evidence are interrelated and together affect the persuasiveness of evidence[93]. Qualitative disclosures are common in a sustainability report and could be worded in a way that is impossible to gather sufficient appropriate evidence. An assertion like 'we are the most loved employer in our region' may be inherently judgmental, not observable and susceptible to management bias. In these circumstances the practitioner needs to be sceptical and exercise significant professional judgment in evaluating if sufficient appropriate evidence can be gathered.

If it is impossible to obtain sufficient appropriate evidence this is a limitation in scope if it cannot be obtained through alternative procedures. Reasons could be due to restrictions by law or regulation, as a result of impediments imposed by management or due to war or outbreak of disease. Such an inability requires the practitioner to express a qualified conclusion or disclaim a conclusion on the sustainability information.

SOURCES OF INFORMATION

Sustainability information intended to be used as evidence may come from internal or external sources which may affect the availability, accessibility and understandability of that information[94]. For example, information may come from:

- ▶ The entity's records, management or other sources internal to the entity.
- ▶ Other entities within the entity's organizational boundary or value chain.
- ▶ A management's expert.
- ▶ A practitioner's expert.
- ▶ Independent sources external to the entity, other than a management's or practitioner's expert, that provide information, such as the entity's legal counsel, customers, suppliers, governmental agencies, NGOs, bank, or general data providers (e.g., entities providing macro-economic, industry or social data).
- ▶ A service organization.

The source of the information also affects how the practitioner responds to matters such as doubts about the reliability of the information, or inconsistencies in evidence[95]. If the information comes from a reputable external source, such as an authorized jurisdictional environmental agency, the work effort in considering the reliability of the information may not be extensive. But if the information is provided by management, the practitioner needs to consider obtaining additional evidence about the accuracy and completeness of the information.

Example of factors that may be important when considering the relevance and reliability of information obtained from an external information source:

- ▶ The ability of management to influence the sustainability information obtained through relationships between the entity and the external information source, for example an entity may be able to influence, through contractual arrangements, what information is to be reported along its supply chain.
- ▶ Whether the entity has in place controls to address the relevance and reliability of the information obtained.
- ▶ The competence and reputation of the external information source including whether the information is routinely provided by a source with a track record of providing reliable information.
- ▶ Whether there is disclosure of the information used by the external information source as a basis, and the methods used in preparing the information; for example, a pricing agency may compile pricing data and report an external market price but may not control how the information is prepared at its original source.
- ▶ Whether the information is suitable for use in the manner in which it is being used for example, ratings agencies may publish companies' ESG ratings, but may be using information that has not been prepared on a consistent basis between those companies or may have used models in the absence of actual company information.
- ▶ The nature and authority of the external information source; a central bank or government office with a legislative mandate to provide information to the public is likely to be an authority for certain types of information, for example the Intergovernmental Panel on Climate Change is generally regarded as an authoritative source on climate-related scenarios.

▶ BUILDING AND EXECUTING FURTHER PROCEDURES

Following the risk procedures, the practitioner proceeds with the execution of additional steps, tailored to address potential material misstatements in disclosures, whether arising from fraud or error. In a reasonable assurance engagement, procedures are crafted in response to the assessed RMM at the assertion level. The additional procedures are not only responsive to identified risks but also tailored to the unique characteristics of each disclosure.

As in a financial statement audit, evidence gathering procedures in a sustainability assurance process encompass both tests of operating effectiveness of internal controls and substantive procedures (chapter 8). These further steps can encompass a variety of procedures, including but not limited to:[96]

- ▶ Inspection
- ▶ Observation
- ▶ Confirmation
- ▶ Recalculation
- ▶ Reperformance
- ▶ Reconciliations
- ▶ Cut-off procedures
- ▶ Analytical procedures
- ▶ Inquiry

CHAPTER 15 ▶ SUSTAINABILITY ASSURANCE ENGAGEMENTS

Given the diverse nature of sustainability information, the characteristics of these procedures–such as their nature, timing, and extent–are expected to exhibit significant variability from one engagement to another. Selecting the appropriate procedures for a specific engagement is a matter of professional judgement.

Given a lower level of assurance in limited assurance engagements, the nature, timing, and extent of further procedures may differ.

ANALYTICAL REVIEW IN A LIMITED LEVEL OF ASSURANCE ENGAGEMENT

In an L-assurance engagement:

* the practitioner may determine that it is appropriate to place greater emphasis on inquiries of the entity's personnel and analytical procedures, and less emphasis, if any, on testing of controls than may be the case for an R-assurance engagement.
* the practitioner may select fewer items for examination, visit fewer locations or perform fewer procedures (e.g., perform only analytical procedures in circumstances when, in an R-assurance engagement, both analytical procedures and other procedures would be performed).
* when undertaking analytical procedures, if significant fluctuations are identified, appropriate evidence may be obtained by making inquiries and considering responses received in light of known engagement circumstances. Also, the practitioner may use data that is more highly aggregated or use data that has not been subjected to separate procedures to test its reliability to the same extent as it would be for an R-assurance engagement.

In an R-assurance engagement:

* analytical procedures pinpoint material misstatements precisely, while in limited assurance, they support trends and relationships without the same precision. Practitioners may use more aggregated data, e.g., regional instead of facility-level data, or monthly instead of weekly data or employ less rigorously tested data compared to the thorough testing in reasonable assurance engagements.

If the practitioner encounters a situation indicating the likelihood of material misstatements across the entire sustainability information, the overall response should be tailored to manage RMM[97]:

▶ When the control environment evaluation reveals:
  ▶ Lack of an ethical and honest culture fostered by management and governance.
  ▶ An inadequate control environment that doesn't support other internal control components considering the entity's nature and complexity.

> ▶ Control weaknesses in the control environment that affect other internal control components.
> ▶ When fraud or suspected fraud, or non-compliance or suspected non-compliance with laws or regulations, are identified[98].
> ▶ When RMM is pervasive throughout the sustainability information.

Overall responses typically involve heightened professional scepticism and may include[99]:

> ▶ Assigning and supervising personnel, considering their knowledge, skills, and abilities.
> ▶ Performing more procedures at the end of the reporting period instead of interim dates.
> ▶ Gathering more extensive evidence from procedures other than control testing.
> ▶ Expanding sample sizes and the scope of procedures, such as conducting procedures at more facilities.
> ▶ Introducing unpredictability in selecting the nature, timing, and extent of procedures.

As in financial statement audits (chapter 12), responding appropriately to fraud or non-compliance with law or regulation, whether actual or suspected, identified during the engagement, depends on the circumstances and may include taking action, such as sketched in illustration 15.22[100].

ILLUSTRATION 15.22

RESPONDING TO (SUSPECTED) FRAUD AND NON-COMPLIANCE WITH LAW OR REGULATION

Discussing the matter with the entity	Requesting the entity to consult with an appropriately qualified third party, such as the entity's legal counsel or a regulator.	Inspecting correspondence, if any, with the relevant licensing or regulatory authorities.	Considering the implications of the matter in relation to other aspects of the engagement, including the practitioner's risk assessment and the reliability of written representations from the entity.
Obtaining legal advice about the consequences of different courses of action.	Communicating with third parties (for example, a regulator).	Withholding the assurance report.	Withdrawing from the engagement.

TESTING EFFECTIVENESS OF INTERNAL CONTROLS

In case internal controls over sustainability reporting are adequately designed and implemented, the initial assessed control risk (CR) is relatively low. The practitioner may test the operating effectiveness to assess final control risk. Tests includes procedures and inquiries to evaluate how controls were applied throughout the reporting period, their consistency, and the responsible parties. These tests span the entire reporting period and assess potential consequences of deviations.

The practitioner decides whether test of controls provides sufficient evidence. If more convincing evidence is needed, the extent of control testing should be increased. Factors influencing this extent include the frequency of control performance, the reliance duration, expected deviation rates, relevance and reliability of evidence at the assertion level, and evidence obtained from related control tests. Automated application controls, combined with evidence of IT general controls, offer substantial evidence due to inherent IT processing consistency.

Previous engagement evidence may be relevant if its applicability is verified. This comprehensive approach ensures the effective design and consistent application of controls, providing confidence in the accuracy and completeness of sustainability reports.

Testing controls, the practitioner may examine whether the organization has established clear procedures for waste management, including segregation, recycling, and responsible disposal. The test could involve reviewing records and documentation to ensure that employees are trained and consistently follow the waste reduction policies. Additionally, the practitioner may conduct interviews with relevant personnel to verify their understanding of the procedures and confirm their adherence to the sustainability controls in place. This helps ensure that the internal controls designed to promote sustainability are not only established but are also operating effectively in day-to-day operations.

SUBSTANTIVE PROCEDURES

As in the audit of financial statements (chapter 8) the practitioner performs substantive procedures to address detection risk (DR), given the acceptable assurance risk (AR) and assessed RMM.

Substantive procedures comprise tests of details (illustration 15.23) and analytical procedures as well as substantive analytical procedures for reasonable assurance engagements[101].

ILLUSTRATION 15.23

EXAMPLE OF TESTS OF DETAILS[102]

- ▷ Agreeing emissions factors to appropriate sources (for example, government publications) and considering their applicability in the circumstances.
- ▷ Reviewing joint venture agreements and other contracts relevant to determining the entity's organizational boundary.
- ▷ Reconciling recorded data to, for example, odometers on vehicles owned by the entity.
- ▷ Reperforming calculations and reconciling differences noted.
- ▷ Sampling and independently analysing the characteristics of materials such as coal or observing the entity's sampling techniques and reviewing records of laboratory test results.
- ▷ Checking the accuracy of calculations and the suitability of calculation methods used.
- ▷ Agreeing recorded data back to source documents, such as production records, fuel usage records, and invoices for purchased energy.
- ▷ Assertions about child labour were selected and compared with reports produced by an independent NGO about compliance with (draft) European Sustainability Reporting Standard S4 'Other work-related rights'.[103]

In cases involving actual or suspected fraud or non-compliance with laws or regulations, the practitioner must understand the nature of the fraudulent or non-compliant act and evaluate its potential impact on sustainability information and the assurance engagement. Appropriate actions should be taken, aligning with the principles outlined in ISA 240 and 250, akin to procedures followed in financial statement audits (see chapter 12).

When substantive procedures are conducted at an interim date and the intention is to extend the conclusion to a later period, the practitioner should either perform substantive procedures along with tests of controls for the intervening period after the interim date, or if sufficient, conduct further substantive procedures only for the extended period.

As with the financial statement audit, information to be used as evidence that has been prepared by a management's expert must be evaluated[104]. Therefore, she:[105]

> ▶ Evaluates the competence with respect to sustainability matters, capabilities and objectivity of that expert. The objectivity of that expert may inform her consideration of the attribute of bias while expert's work should be subject to technical performance standards or industry requirements.

> ▶ Obtains an understanding of the work performed by that expert; and how the information prepared by that expert has been used by management in the preparation of the sustainability information.

> ▶ Evaluates whether the expert's findings or conclusions have been appropriately reflected in the sustainability information.

Illustration 15.24 sketches steps for evaluating accuracy, reliability, and completeness of greenhouse gas (GHG) data prepared by a management's expert.

ILLUSTRATION 15.24

EVALUATION OF GHG DATA PREPARED BY AN EXPERT

Check Data Sources
Examine the sources of the data. Ensure that reputable and reliable sources were used. Verify if the data is collected from direct measurements, remote sensing, or modelling.

Review Methodology
Understand the methodology used for data collection and analysis. Ensure it follows accepted standards and protocols. Check if the expert used recognized GHG accounting methodologies (e.g., IPCC Guidelines) and if any assumptions made are reasonable.

Data Quality
Assess the quality of the data. Look for any gaps, inconsistencies, or outliers that might indicate potential issues. Evaluate the precision and accuracy of measurements or estimates provided by the expert.

Consider Temporal and Spatial Coverage

Ensure that the data covers the appropriate time period and spatial scale for the intended analysis or decision-making. Verify if the data is representative of the relevant geography and timeframe.

Check for Transparency

A transparent methodology is essential. Ensure that the expert provides clear documentation of their procedures and data sources. Transparency helps others understand and replicate the analysis, which adds credibility to the GHG data.

Peer Review

If possible, seek peer reviews from other experts in the field. Peer-reviewed work is generally more reliable. Look for any feedback or critiques from other professionals who have expertise in GHG emissions.

Consistency and Comparability

Check if the data is consistent with other available information or historical trends. Ensure that the data can be compared to similar datasets to assess its reliability.

Check for Industry Standards

Ensure that the expert adheres to industry standards and guidelines for GHG accounting. For example, the Intergovernmental Panel on Climate Change (IPCC) provides widely accepted guidelines.

Understand Limitations

Recognize the limitations of the data. No dataset is perfect, and understanding the potential shortcomings is crucial for accurate interpretation.

Expert's Credentials

Assess the qualifications and expertise of the individual or team presenting the GHG data. Their background in the field adds credibility to their work.

Data Accessibility

Check if the expert provides access to the raw data or detailed information about the methodology. This allows for independent verification and validation.

As example of another substantive procedure, the practitioner may perform external confirmation procedures to request information regarding disclosures or specific assertions, disclosures to provide relevant evidence about such information as activity data collected by a third party or industry, benchmark data used in calculations or results of laboratory analysis of samples. In an audit of a sustainability report, external confirmations could be used to validate the accuracy of certain environmental data or sustainability performance metrics reported by a company (also see section 8.3).

Below you will find an example of a confirmation request for Volunteer Hours Reported by SolarTech Inc.

Background: SolarTech Inc. reported in its annual sustainability report that its employees contributed 5,000 volunteer hours to community service over the past year, demonstrating its commitment to social responsibility.

Objective: To verify the reliability of SolarTech Inc.'s reported volunteer hours as part of the sustainability assurance engagement.

Step 1: Identify External Parties
Community Organizations: Select NGOs and local community groups supported by SolarTech Inc.
Local Government: Engage with local authorities involved in community volunteering efforts.

Step 2: Draft Confirmation Letter
Include:
- Introduction to the assurance engagement's purpose.
- Request to confirm the volunteer hours (5,000 hours) contributed by SolarTech Inc.'s employees.
- Contact information for responses and inquiries.

Step 3: Send Confirmation Requests
Dispatch letters or emails to the community organizations and local government bodies involved.

Step 4: Collect and Analyse Responses
Record confirmations matching the reported hours and note any discrepancies.
Investigate differences to reconcile the reported figures with external confirmations.

Step 5: Document Evidence and Conclusions

Assemble all confirmations and correspondence.

Evaluate the credibility of SolarTech Inc.'s reported volunteer hours.
Summarize findings in the assurance report, including any suggestions for enhancing future report accuracy and reliability.

Outcome
This approach secures credible evidence about SolarTech Inc.'s reported volunteer activities, enhancing the trustworthiness of its sustainability report and underscoring the value of precise, transparent social information reporting.

As in a financial statement audit (chapter 9), analytical procedures serve as another example of substantive procedures that are typically carried out when there's a reasonably predictable connection between sustainability data and financial or non-financial data[106]. The latter might involve assessing relationships like the link between Scope 2 emissions[107] from electricity and factors such as hours of operation or the general ledger balance for electricity purchases. Additionally, analytical procedures can encompass comparing an organization's sustainability data to external benchmarks like industry averages or scrutinizing trends over time to spot irregularities that warrant further investigation. These trends should also be evaluated for consistency with other factors like facility acquisitions or disposals.

Analytical procedures can also be applied to qualitative information. An example of the latter procedure is a text analysis based on (big) data generated from social media platforms to generate evidence about a disclosure asserting the (good) reputation of the company.

If these procedures reveal irregularities or relationships that don't align with other relevant information or significantly deviate from expected values, the following steps should be taken:

- ▶ Consult with management and gather additional evidence to address these discrepancies.
- ▶ Conduct any necessary supplementary procedures as dictated by the circumstances.

When the practitioner opts for sampling to select items for testing, the purpose of the procedure and the characteristics of the population from which the sample will be drawn must be considered. Of course, the sample size should be adequate to minimize sampling risk to an acceptable level[108]. When conducting a sample[109]:

▶ *Select items fairly*
Choose sample items to ensure each unit in the population has an equal chance of selection.

▶ *Perform Appropriate Procedures*
Carry out the required procedures for each selected item based on the sampling purpose.

▶ *Investigate Deviations*
If discrepancies arise, investigate their nature and causes.

▶ *Evaluate Results*
Assess the overall findings and their significance for the entire population or sampling objectives.

ESTIMATES AND FORWARD-LOOKING INFORMATION[110]

Estimates are approximations used when precise measurement isn't possible, often due to estimation uncertainty. This uncertainty can result from a lack of technology to measure precisely or from relying on forecasts for one or more events or conditions. Forward-looking information, like forecasts or future plans, can also contribute to this uncertainty, especially in sustainability matters where future events are less predictable than historical data.

FORWARD LOOKING INFORMATION, CISCO, PURPOSE REPORT 2022, P. 49[111]

'Increasing our use of renewable electricity is a fundamental part of our strategy. In fiscal 2022, 89 percent of our global electricity came from renewable energy sources, including 100 percent in the United States, Canada, and several European countries. We are ramping up both our onsite and offsite renewable energy efforts, targeting approximately 5 MW of new onsite solar and securing over 500 MW of new long-term renewable energy contracts by the end of fiscal 2025. In India and Europe, we are actively evaluating long-term power purchase agreements (PPAs) that would collectively add over 100 MW of new solar and wind developments to these regions.'

When conducting further procedures in a limited assurance engagement the practitioner:

▷ Determines if management has correctly adhered to the requirements of the applicable criteria relevant to estimates or forward-looking information.

▷ Assesses whether the methods used to develop estimates or forward-looking information are appropriate and have been consistently applied.

▷ Examines whether any changes in reported estimates or forward-looking information, or changes in the method used for developing them compared to the prior period, are suitable in the given circumstances.

One or more of the following actions should be performed if a RMM is identified (in a reasonable assurance engagement)[112]:

▷ Gather evidence from events that have occurred up to the date of the practitioner's report.

▷ Examine how management arrived at the estimate or forward-looking information, including the supporting data and disclosures. This entails assessing whether:

  ▷ The chosen method is appropriate and consistent with prior periods, or if changes have been made, whether these changes are suitable.

  ▷ The assumptions used, including any alterations from prior periods, are appropriate.

  ▷ The data used, including any changes from prior periods, are appropriate.

  ▷ Develop either a single-point estimate or a range to evaluate management's estimate or forward-looking information. In this process, the practitioner must ensure that the range only includes amounts supported by sufficient evidence and deemed reasonable within the criteria's context.

These actions are crucial to ensure the accuracy and reliability of disclosures involving estimates and forward-looking information in sustainability reports.

15.5.5 EVALUATING AND COMPLETION

▷ **ACCUMULATION AND CONSIDERATION OF IDENTIFIED MISSTATEMENTS**

In this section steps will be described that should be performed while accumulating and considering identified misstatements. Most of these steps are similar to those to be taken in a financial statement audit (ISA 450, 700) and are performed during the evaluation and completion phase of the assurance engagement.

IDENTIFIED MISSTATEMENTS

All misstatements, except for those that are clearly trivial[113] must be accumulated. As in other assurance engagements, any accumulated misstatements must be communicated to management, along with a request to correct them[114]. Additional procedures will then be conducted to ascertain whether any material misstatements persist. If management declines to adjust misstatements, the practitioner seeks to determine the reasons behind their decision and takes this understanding into account when forming the final conclusion.

The practitioner also assesses whether these identified misstatements could be attributed to fraud and takes appropriate action if fraud is suspected. Examples of misstatements due to fraud in sustainability information[115]:

- Misstating sustainability information to avoid penalties or fines.
- Intentionally inaccurate or misleading public statements or claims that will favourably impact share price or an assessment of the entity's sustainability credentials, such as an inaccurate statement that a bond is a sustainability bond.
- Intentionally reporting sustainability information relating to performance or compensation incentives in a biased way to influence the outcome of the performance reward or compensation.
- Emphasizing a product was produced using recycled materials but intentionally not reporting that the product was produced using forced labour.
- Intentionally reporting topics for which the entity has positive impacts and omitting topics for which the entity has negative impacts.
- Misstating baseline information to make sustainability information look more favourable in subsequent periods.
- Misstating sustainability information associated with specific project milestones, budget approval, or rights to access certain markets or begin projects in certain markets or geographies.

EVALUATING THE EFFECT OF UNCORRECTED MISSTATEMENTS

After gathering sufficient and appropriate evidence, the practitioner determines if uncorrected misstatements are material, individually or in the aggregate. When sustainability information is measured using a common basis, like monetary amounts or physical units, misstatements of the same nature together can often be aggregated. However, sustainability disclosures can encompass multiple topics, involve various aspects of those topics, and employ different measurement bases. In such cases, she isn't required to convert misstatements in different measurement bases into a common one for aggregation purposes. It's important to note that misstatements in qualitative information hold the same significance as those in quantitative information.

If management does not correct misstatements in qualitative information, the practitioner can accumulate them by listing, marking, or highlighting them in a copy of the sustainability information. When it's not feasible to add misstatements together for aggregate assessment, she considers[116] whether there are commonalities among the misstatements. For instance, they may collectively lead to a more favourable outcome that is materially significant, or they could indicate a bias on the part of management.

If there are signs of possible management bias, it's crucial to assess the impact on the assurance engagement. Intentional management bias constitutes fraudulent behaviour.

When assessing the materiality of uncorrected misstatements in sustainability information, the practitioner considers qualitative factors, including:[117]

Sustainability Matter
▶ Misalignment of reporting topics with the objective.
▶ Misstated information on significant aspects.
▶ Multiple misstatements on the same topic with consistent direction (positive or negative).

External Factors
▶ Non-compliance with severe legal consequences.
▶ Implications for a large number of stakeholders or material implications for a small group.

Nature of Sustainability Information
▶ Doubts about the feasibility of management's plans or sustainability claims.
▶ Misstatements in commonly used peer comparison disclosures.
▶ Errors that impact meeting targets or thresholds.
▶ Reporting significant changes or reversals of trends.

Presentation
▶ Misleading presentation due to unclear wording leading to different interpretations.

Management's Behaviour
▶ Misstatement due to management fraud.
▶ Reluctance to correct misstatements for reasons other than immateriality.
▶ Aggressive targets, estimates, or defensive explanations.

These factors help assess the potential materiality of misstatements in sustainability information and their impact on user decisions. Additional factors that assist the practitioner in assessing the materiality of misstatements include:

▶ *Understanding the underlying cause.*
Investigating why misstatements occurred is crucial. If a qualitative misstatement results from intentional misrepresentation by management, indicating fraud, it is considered material.

▶ *Consideration of indirect effects.*
Assessing whether a misstatement may indirectly impact misstatements identified in other areas of the engagement is essential. The interconnectedness of misstatements across different aspects of the engagement can affect their collective materiality.

EVALUATING THE DESCRIPTION OF APPLICABLE CRITERIA[118]

It's crucial to assess whether the sustainability information adequately references or describes the applicable criteria and their sources. This becomes particularly important when there are notable differences in the criteria applied by similar entities in the same industry, region, or jurisdiction that the practitioner expects to have similar circumstances or equivalence.

SUBSEQUENT EVENTS

As in the audit of financial statements, relevant events occur up to the date of the assurance report (chapter 10). These events may have an effect on the sustainability information and the assurance report. The practitioner must perform procedures and consider if these events must be reflected in the sustainability information.

Examples of subsequent events[119]:

▶ The publication of revised factors, assumptions or benchmarks by a body such as a government agency (e.g., revised emissions factors).
▶ Changes to relevant legislation or regulations.
▶ New relevant scientific knowledge.
▶ Significant structural changes in the entity.
▶ The availability of more accurate quantification methods.
▶ The discovery of a significant error.
▶ Water pollution resulting in loss of license.
▶ Fatality and other significant health and safety events.

If facts that become known after the date of the assurance report that, had they been known at that date, may have caused the practitioner to amend the assurance report, appropriate response is necessary.[120] In these exceptional circumstances, she must thoroughly document the following:

▶ The specific circumstances encountered that necessitated these actions.
▶ A detailed account of the new or additional procedures performed, the evidence obtained through these procedures, and the conclusions reached as a result. This documentation should also include an assessment of how these new findings impact the content of the assurance report.
▶ Information about when these changes to assurance engagement documentation were made and who was responsible for making and reviewing these changes.

▶ WRITTEN REPRESENTATIONS

The practitioner follows a structured process regarding written representations, similar to ISA 580 in a financial statement audit (chapter 10). The so-called Letter of Representation (LoR) serves to remind management and, where applicable, those charged with governance, of their primary responsibility for creating the sustainability report. It confirms in writing that they have fulfilled their duty for preparing the sustainability information, including comparative data where relevant, in line with the criteria agreed in the engagement terms. Furthermore, the LOR includes confirmations that:

▶ All relevant information and access, as agreed upon in the engagement terms, have been provided to the practitioner.
▶ Uncorrected misstatements, individually and collectively, are immaterial to the sustainability information. A summary of such items should be included in or attached to the written representation.
▶ Significant assumptions used in estimates and forward-looking information are considered reasonable.
▶ Any deficiencies in internal control, not trivial in nature, have been communicated to the practitioner.

▷ They have disclosed any knowledge of actual, suspected, or alleged fraud or non-compliance with laws or regulations that could materially affect the sustainability information.

▷ Adjustments and disclosures have been made for events occurring after the sustainability information's date, as required by applicable criteria.

▷ The date of the written representations should be as close as possible to, but not later than, the date of the assurance report.

If any of the requested written representations are not provided, or there are doubts about the competence, integrity, ethics, or diligence of those providing them, the practitioner engages in discussions with management and, if relevant, those charged with governance. This includes assessing the impact on the reliability of representations, evidence, and the overall integrity of the process. Appropriate actions, such as issuing a disclaimer of conclusion on the sustainability information or withdrawing from the engagement, are taken if the integrity of the representations or the individuals providing them is in doubt or if the entity fails to provide the required representations.

OBTAINING, READING AND CONSIDERING THE OTHER INFORMATION

As in the audit of financial statements, it's also crucial to acknowledge that sustainability reports are often published alongside various documents, including financial reports and references to online information (see chapter 10). Here's a breakdown of the steps followed in handling other information within such engagements:

▷ *Obtaining Other Information*
Identify and arrange to obtain documents containing sustainability information while understanding their issuance timing.

▷ *Review and Assessment*
Examine the other information to spot material inconsistencies with either the sustainability information or the practitioner's insights gained during the engagement.

▷ *Responding to Inconsistencies or Misstatements*
If a material inconsistency arises or if other information is materially misstated:
  ▷ Engage in discussions with management.
  ▷ Conduct additional procedures to assess misstatements in other information or sustainability
  ▷ information and determine if an update to understanding is required.

▷ *Handling Material Misstatements in Other Information*
If a material misstatement in other information is confirmed:
  ▷ Request correction from management.
  ▷ Confirm the correction or escalate the matter to those charged with governance if management refuses.

▶ *If Misstatements Persist in Other Information*
   ▶ Evaluate the implications of the material misstatement for the assurance report.
   ▶ Communicate with those charged with governance about how to address the misstatement.
   ▶ If legally feasible, consider withdrawing from the engagement.

▶ *Responding to Material Misstatements in Sustainability Information or Updates to Understanding*
   Take appropriate actions if a material misstatement in the sustainability information is identified or if an update to understanding is required. The specific actions depend on the circumstances and nature of the issue.

▶ SUFFICIENT APPROPRIATE EVIDENCE

In the final stage of the sustainability assurance engagement, the practitioner assesses the sufficiency and appropriateness of the gathered evidence. This includes evidence from external experts, other practitioners, or the internal audit function. If needed, the practitioner seeks additional evidence. When conducting this assessment, all evidence, whether it supports or contradicts other evidence, should be considered.

   In case of evidence that conflicts with other findings, she:
   ▶ Identifies necessary modifications or additional procedures to understand and address the inconsistency.
   ▶ Evaluates any potential effects on other aspects of the assurance engagement.

To arrive at a conclusion, the sufficiency and appropriateness of the evidence obtained should be evaluated. Additionally, the practitioner considers whether uncorrected misstatements are material. It's also crucial to ensure that the sustainability information accurately reflects the core sustainability matters and is presented fairly.

SCOPE LIMITATION

If it is not possible to obtain sufficient appropriate evidence, a scope limitation exists. They may arise from[121]:
   ▶ Uncontrollable circumstances, like accidental destruction of essential documents.
   ▶ Timing-related issues, such as missing a critical event.
   ▶ Restrictions imposed by management or governance, affecting the engagement's procedures and overall risk assessment.

In case of a scope limitation the practitioner will issue a qualified conclusion or a disclaimer of conclusion or withdraw from the engagement, where withdrawal is possible under applicable law or regulation is appropriate.

▶ TAKING OVERALL RESPONSIBILITY[122]

In line with ISA 220, prior to dating the assurance report, the practitioner takes full responsibility for determining:

> ▶ engagement documentation and discussion with the engagement team, that sufficient appropriate evidence has been obtained to support the conclusions reached and for the assurance report to be issued.
> ▶ the sustainability information and the assurance report, to determine that the report to be issued will be appropriate in the circumstances.
> ▶ the sufficiency and appropriateness of the practitioner's involvement in (for example) significant judgments and conclusions reached.
> ▶ compliance with the firm's related policies and with the requirements of (ED) ISSA 5000.

If the engagement is subject to an engagement quality review, the practitioner determines that the engagement quality review has been completed. Illustration 15.26 provides some examples of indicators that the engagement leader may not have been sufficiently and appropriately involved[123].

ILLUSTRATION 15.26

INDICATORS OF INSUFFICIENT INVOLVEMENT OF ENGAGEMENT LEADER

> ▶ Lack of timely review by the engagement leader of the engagement planning, including reviewing the risk procedures performed.
> ▶ Evidence that those to whom tasks, actions or procedures have been assigned were not adequately informed about the nature of their responsibilities and authority, the scope of the work being assigned and the objectives thereof; and were not provided other necessary instructions and relevant information.
> ▶ A lack of evidence of the engagement leader's direction and supervision of the other members of the engagement team and the review of their work.

▶ **DOCUMENTATION AND COMMUNICATION**

The engagement documentation should include the reasons for the practitioner's decision that sufficient appropriate evidence is gathered. Another element in the documentation is the basis for the practitioner's determination that her involvement in the engagement has been sufficient and appropriate.

Consistent with other assurance engagements, significant matters that have been captured during the sustainability assurance process must be communicated[124] with management, those charged with governance or other pertinent stakeholders.

15.5.6 THE ASSURANCE REPORT

The assurance report serves as the means to communicate the results of the sustainability assurance engagement to the intended users. Clear communication is essential for these users to comprehend the assurance conclusion. The practitioner cannot rely solely on oral communication or symbols; they must also issue a written assurance report. This report should be easily accessible whenever an oral report is given, or a symbol is used to prevent any misunderstandings. For instance, a symbol indicating that disclosures underwent an assurance engagement could be linked to a written assurance report on the internet[125].

The conclusion in the assurance report should be distinctly separated from any other information or explanations that do not impact the practitioner's conclusion. This includes, as in auditor's opinions (chapter 11), Emphasis of Matter or Other Matter paragraphs or additional information contained within the assurance report[126].

▶ ASSURANCE REPORT CONTENT[127]

A sustainability assurance report includes the following key elements[128]:
- ▶ A clear title indicating it's an independent practitioner's limited or reasonable assurance report.
- ▶ An addressee.
- ▶ The conclusion, which varies based on the type of assurance engagement:
  - ▶ For unmodified conclusions, a 'Reasonable Assurance Opinion', 'Limited Assurance Conclusion' or an appropriate heading for an assurance report for both levels of assurance.
    For modified conclusions, the heading a prefixed with 'Qualified', 'Adverse,' or 'Disclaimer of' as appropriate, and, for an assurance report for both levels of assurance, clear identification of which opinion(s) or conclusion(s) are modified.
  - ▶ In a reasonable assurance engagement, the opinion shall be expressed in a positive form, that the sustainability information is prepared or fairly presented, in all material respects, in accordance with the applicable criteria.
  - ▶ In a limited assurance engagement, a conclusion conveying whether any matter(s) came to the practitioner's attention during procedures performed and evidence obtained that cause the practitioner to believe that the sustainability information is not prepared or fairly presented, in all material respects, according to the applicable criteria.
- ▶ The basis for the conclusion, following the Conclusion section. For reasonable assurance reports, it's titled 'Basis for Opinion,' for limited assurance, 'Basis for Conclusion,' or an appropriate heading for combined assurance reports.
- ▶ If applicable, a section titled 'Other Information.'
- ▶ A section explaining 'Responsibilities for the Sustainability Information.'
- ▶ If applicable, a section with the heading 'Inherent Limitations in Preparing the Sustainability Information.'
- ▶ A section detailing 'Practitioner's Responsibilities.'
- ▶ In limited assurance engagements, a 'Summary of Work Performed'.
- ▶ The practitioner's name and signature.
- ▶ The location where the engagement leader practices in their jurisdiction.
- ▶ The date of the assurance report.

If the practitioner mentions a practitioner's expert in the report, it should not imply a reduction in her responsibility for the conclusion expressed in that report[129].

OTHER REPORTING RESPONSIBILITIES

If disclosures are different to that of the sustainability information subject to the assurance engagement, the practitioner includes a separate section in the assurance report with a heading such as 'Report on Other Legal and Regulatory Requirements'. If the topics are the same as those in the sustainability information covered by this ISSA, the other reporting responsibilities can be included in the same section as the required report elements. However, it's essential to clearly differentiate them.

UNMODIFIED CONCLUSIONS

The practitioner is required to express an unmodified reasonable assurance conclusion when they determine that:

- For compliance criteria, the sustainability information has been prepared in all material respects in accordance with the applicable framework or criteria.
- For fair presentation criteria, the sustainability information is fairly presented in all material respects in accordance with the applicable criteria.

On the other hand, an unmodified limited assurance conclusion is issued when no issues have come to the attention of the practitioner that cause them to believe that:

- For compliance criteria, the sustainability information is not prepared in all material respects in accordance with the applicable criteria.
- For fair presentation criteria, the sustainability information is not fairly presented in all material respects in accordance with the applicable criteria.

As in the auditor's report on the financial statements, 'Key Assurance Matters' can be included in the sustainability statement. Also, to bring to the intended users' attention a crucial matter presented or disclosed in the sustainability information, an Emphasis of Matter paragraph may be added. If there is a matter outside of what is presented or disclosed in the sustainability information that is relevant to the intended users' understanding of the engagement an Other Matter Paragraph can be included separately in the assurance report. All 'matter paragraphs' are further described in chapter 10.

OTHER INFORMATION

When it comes to 'Other Information', the assurance report explicitly states that no conclusion is provided on it. Additionally, the report includes the following[130]:

- Responsibilities of the practitioner in relation to reading, considering, and reporting on other information, as mandated by the ISSA.
- Any uncorrected material misstatement, if such misstatement exists, is also disclosed in the report.

MODIFIED CONCLUSIONS

In assurance engagements, including financial statement audits and sustainability assurance engagements, circumstances can arise that prevent the practitioner from issuing an unmodified opinion. When a scope limitation exists, and its effect could be material, the practitioner must express either a qualified conclusion or a disclaimer of conclusion.

Similarly, if the sustainability information is materially misstated, the practitioner is required to express either a qualified conclusion or an adverse conclusion.

When the effects of a matter are both material and pervasive, an adverse conclusion or a disclaimer of conclusion is necessary. However, if these matters are material but not pervasive, a qualified conclusion should be expressed with the qualification stating 'except for' the effects of the matter to which the qualification pertains.

In the case of a modified conclusion, it is essential to provide a clear description of the scope limitation and/or the matter(s) that cause the sustainability information to be materially misstated. This description should be included in the assurance report for transparency.

Examples of Modified Conclusions[131]

Examples of a qualified conclusion for a limited assurance engagement (with a material misstatement) are:
▶ Qualified conclusion (compliance framework) – 'Based on the procedures performed and the evidence obtained, except for the effect of the matter described in the Basis for Qualified Conclusion section of our report, nothing has come to our attention that causes us to believe that the [sustainability information] is not prepared, in all material respects, in accordance with XYZ criteria.'
▶ Qualified conclusion (fair presentation framework) – 'Based on the procedures performed and the evidence obtained, except for the effect of the matter described in the Basis for Qualified Conclusion section of our report, nothing has come to our attention that causes us to believe that the [sustainability information] is not fairly presented, in all material respects, in accordance with XYZ criteria.'

Examples of qualified conclusion for a reasonable assurance engagement (with a material misstatement):
▶ Qualified conclusion (compliance framework) – 'Except for the effect of the matter described in the Basis for Qualified Conclusion section of our report, the [sustainability information] is prepared, in all material respects, in accordance with XYZ criteria.'
▶ Qualified conclusion (fair presentation framework) – 'Except for the effect of the matter described in the Basis for Qualified Conclusion section of our report, the [sustainability information] is fairly presented, in all material respects, in accordance with XYZ criteria.'

Examples of adverse conclusions and a disclaimer of conclusion for both limited and reasonable assurance engagements are:
▶ Adverse conclusion (an example for a material and pervasive misstatement for information prepared under a compliance framework) – 'Because of the significance of the matter described in the Basis for Adverse Conclusion section of our report, the [sustainability information] is not prepared in accordance with XYZ criteria.'
▶ Adverse conclusion (an example for a material and pervasive misstatement for information prepared under a fair presentation framework) – 'Because of the significance of the matter described in the Basis for Adverse Conclusion section of our report, the [sustainability information] does not present fairly the entity's compliance with XYZ criteria.'
▶ Disclaimer of conclusion (an example for a material and pervasive limitation of scope) – 'Because of the significance of the matter described in the Basis for Disclaimer of Conclusions section of our report, we have not been able to obtain sufficient evidence to form a conclusion on the [sustainability information]. Accordingly, we do not express a conclusion on that [sustainability information].'

COMPARATIVE INFORMATION[132]

In general, when applicable criteria require comparative information to be included in the current sustainability report, the practitioner assesses whether this comparative information is consistent with the disclosures from the prior period. If inconsistencies are found, they are addressed in accordance with the applicable criteria in the current period. Any changes made to address these inconsistencies are adequately disclosed.

If the comparative information underwent an assurance engagement in the prior period, the assurance report should include details about that previous engagement in an Other Matter Paragraph.

If the practitioner becomes aware of a potential material misstatement in the comparative information, this will be discussed with management, and appropriate procedures will be conducted. If a material misstatement in the comparative information that falls within the scope of the current engagement is not adjusted, the conclusion in the assurance report will be modified accordingly. If the misstatement is not within the scope of the current engagement, it will be described in an Other Matter Paragraph for transparency.

15.6   SUMMARY

As time has passed, there has been a steadily increasing recognition of the critical need to address climate change and its wide-ranging societal consequences. The main drivers of increased recognition are: stakeholder expectations, global sustainability agreements, legal requirements, investor priorities, risk management, reputation and brand value, comparative analysis, comparative analysis, and long-term business resilience.

Theories that help explain sustainability reporting are agency theory, stakeholder theory, and signalling theory. Driven by shareholders, stakeholders, law and regulation, markets, public opinion and press, more and more company boards now see the advantages of transparency.

The concept of double materiality requires companies to report relevant information from both an 'inside-out' and 'outside-in' respectively. When a company determines which topics in its reports have or can affect its financial performance, this is called 'financial materiality' (outside-in). There may also be impacts on the environment, and perhaps on local communities using the river for fishing or a water supply. Such an effect the company has on the economy, environment, or society, is called 'impact materiality' (inside-out)·

In sustainable information, there is a risk that the portrayed image is intentionally more favourable than the reality and that is called 'greenwashing'. In case of greenwashing, stakeholders, such as consumers, often feel misled because companies claim to offer environmentally friendly products that are not as environmentally friendly as advertised. Fraudulent reporting risk increases as rewards become more dependent on sustainability KPIs/goals.

The International Integrated Reporting Council (IIRC) is a global coalition of regulators, investors, companies, standard setters, the accounting profession, and NGOs. It promotes sustainability through integrated reporting, which combines financial and non-financial information to provide a comprehensive view of an organization's performance.

Many large corporations follow the Global Reporting Initiative (GRI) standards for environmental and social reporting. These guidelines are designed to help organizations report on the economic, environmental, and social aspects of their activities, products, and services.

Recognizing the need for standardized sustainability reporting, the International Financial Reporting Standards (IFRS) Foundation established the International Sustainability

Standards Board (ISSB) to develop sustainability standards. The ISSB has issued IFRS S1 General Requirements for Disclosure of Sustainability-related Financial Information and IFRS S2 Climate-related Disclosures.

In 2023, the European Commission adopted the Delegated Act on the first set of European Sustainability Reporting Standards (ESRS). These standards include cross-cutting standards (ESRS 1 and 2) and topical standards (E, S, and G). Cross-cutting standards address disclosures that are essential for understanding the relationship between sustainability matters and the company's strategy, business model, governance, organization, and materiality assessment. Topical standards focus on specific sustainability topics or subtopics related to the environment, social, and governance aspects.

Two important government directives for social and environment include EU Corporate Sustainability Reporting Directive (CSRD) and rules by the US Securities and Exchange Commission (SEC). The CSRD aims to provide comprehensive and standardized reporting on sustainability matters, ensuring that relevant information is disclosed consistently across various entities. The SEC established a rule requiring disclosure on workforce diversity, pay equity, and employee health and safety. An amendment to that rule requires additional disclosures on climate-related risks that could significantly impact an entity's business, financial condition, or results of operations.

International Standard on Sustainability Assurance 5000 (ISSA 5000) is the IAASB's standard on sustainability assurance. The scope of the assurance engagement (limited and reasonable) could include:

▶ The whole sustainability report.
▶ Specific topics or areas of information within the report, for example environmental or social matters.
▶ Individual items within specific topics or areas of information within the report.
▶ Different levels of assurance for different aspects of the sustainability information.
▶ The reporting boundary might encompass the reporting of a single entity, multiple entities, the complete value chain of an entity, specific geographic areas, activities, operations, or facilities.

Responding to identified risks of material misstatement in a sustainability (reasonable) assurance engagement involves inquiries, inspection, observation, confirmation, recalculation, reperformance and analytical procedures (just as in a financial statement audit). For obtaining sufficient appropriate evidence, procedures must be performed in a manner that is neither biased towards obtaining evidence that may be corroborative, nor towards excluding evidence that may be contradictory.

All misstatements, except for those that are clearly trivial must be accumulated. As in other assurance engagements (i.e. ISA 450, ISA 700), any accumulated misstatements must be communicated to management, along with a request to correct them. Additional procedures will then be conducted to ascertain whether any material misstatements persist.

As in the audit of financial statements, relevant events occur up to the date of the assurance report. These events may have an effect on the sustainability information and the assurance report. The practitioner must perform procedures and consider if these events must be reflected in the sustainability information.

15.7 QUESTIONS, EXERCISES AND CASES

QUESTIONS

15.2 Setting the Scene

15-1 What are the main drivers of the increased recognition of need to address climate change and social issues?

15-2 What do you think of the statement by Peter Bakker that 'Accountants will save the world' (see endnote 4)? Motivate.

15-3 What are the key distinctions between using stakeholder theory versus agency theory to explain the phenomenon of Sustainability Reporting?

15-4 Any idea how Shell's 'big sisters' reacted when Shell started sustainability reporting? (The 'sisters' were the seven major oil companies that dominated global oil production, refining, and distribution between the 1940s and the 1970s.)

15.3 Sustainability Reporting

15-5 What is the relevance for stakeholders of ESG factor 'G'?

15-6 Describe the difference between financial materiality and impact materiality.

15-7 How can companies define the most important stakeholders to engage with?

15-8 List the major steps to be taken in a double materiality analysis?

15-9 What is meant by 'greenwashing'?

15-10 What are the main differences between ICFR (internal controls over financial reporting) and ICSR (internal controls over sustainability reporting)?

15.4 Sustainability Reporting Goals, Regulations and Standards

15-11 List the UN Sustainability Goals.

15-12 Describe the role of the IIRC.

15-13 What is the role of the 'Value Creation Process' (illustration 15.9) in sustainability reporting?

15-14 Why is CSRD a big deal for supply chain sustainability?

15-15 Why do you think organizations that choose to report only specific information for certain purposes should include a GRI content index making reported information traceable?

15-16 What is meant by Sustainability Due Diligence?

15.5 Sustainability Assurance Process

15-17 Describe the Sustainability Assurance Process Model.

15-18 When should a sustainability assurance engagement not be accepted?

15-19 What could be the scope of a sustainability assurance engagement?

15-20 What are suitable sustainability criteria?

15-21 List most relevant planning activities in a sustainability assurance engagement.

15-22 Describe some qualitative factors the practitioner may consider in assessing materiality.

15-23 What steps should be taken when the work of an external expert is planned?

15-24 Give some examples of misstatements in sustainability reports due to fraud.

15-25 What is the role of internal controls over sustainability reporting in the assurance process?

15-26 What is the difference between the initial assessment of CR and final assessment?

15-27 Describe the Assurance Risk Model. What is the role of assessing Risk of a Material Misstatement (RMM)?

15-28 List some examples of sustainability factors per internal control component.

15-29 What are the main assurance procedures for obtaining sufficient, appropriate audit evidence?

15.5.4 **15-30** Describe the difference between 'Testing Controls' and a 'Substantive Procedures' approach.

15-31 Sketch some examples of analytical procedures to gather evidence about the reliability of management's assertion: 'At our production site in Rio de Janeiro (Brazil), no child labour has occurred throughout the year.

15-32 What are challenges in gathering evidence about assertions related to 'Estimates' and 'Forward-Looking Information'?

15.5.5 **15-33** When is an identified misstatement clearly trivial? What does that mean?

15-34 Describe how to accumulate and aggregate the effect of misstatements in qualitative information.

15-35 List some potential subsequent events and the effect they can have on sustainability information and the assurance report.

15-36 Why is it required to obtain, read and consider 'other information' that are published together with sustainability reports?

15.6 **15-37** List the key elements that should be included in a sustainability assurance report.

15-38 What are the main differences in the sustainability assurance report in case of limited versus reasonable assurance?

15-39 Describe the different modified sustainability assurance opinions that can be issued.

15-40 What can be consequences of management refusal to adjust material misstatements in comparative information?

PROBLEMS AND EXERCISES

15.2 **Setting the Scene**

15-41 Shell has been voluntarily reporting on ESG (Environmental, Social, and Governance) information since the late 1990s. The reporting was verified by the joint auditors KPMG and Price Waterhouse. After a few years, Shell ceased to provide this assurance engagement.

A. What could have been the reasons for this decision?

B. What is your opinion on this matter?

15- 42 British Airways, Philips, ING, H&M, Nike, Shell, Heineken, Volkswagen, Coca-Cola and Samsung are companies that produce annual sustainability verification statements. Required:

Choose two of the companies listed above.

A. Download a copy of their sustainability verification statements from their websites.

B. Compare the two reports on the basis of GRI guidelines (most recent ones).

Sustainability Reporting

15-43   Internal Control Over Sustainability Reporting: Information and Communication
This case study examines the internal control measures implemented by a multinational corporation (MOON) to ensure the accuracy, reliability, and transparency of its sustainability reporting. MOON operates in various industries, including manufacturing, retail, and technology, and is committed to integrating environmental, social, and governance (ESG) considerations into its business practices. MOON applies the COSO Integrated Framework to ESG. You are as a senior assurance practitioner partner of F&Z Auditors, engaged to deliver assurance on MOON's sustainability report. Based upon understanding internal controls of sustainability reporting (ICSR) your assurance team's evaluation of the design of (COSO) ICSR Component *'Information and Communication'*:

- ▷   While MOON collects vast amounts of data for sustainability reporting, it struggles to discern the most relevant metrics aligned with ESG objectives, goals, targets, and commitments.
- ▷   Internal communication regarding sustainability objectives and responsibilities is inconsistent. While senior management emphasizes the importance of sustainability, there's a lack of structured training programs and communication channels to ensure that all employees understand their roles in supporting the company's sustainability agenda.
- ▷   MOON disseminates sustainability information to external stakeholders, such as investors, regulatory bodies, customers, and the broader community, through various channels, including annual sustainability reports, stakeholder meetings, and dedicated sustainability websites. It strives to provide reliable and comprehensive data to meet the diverse needs of external parties.
- ▷   MOON lacks robust procedures to validate and verify sustainability data. Manual data checks are infrequent, and there's a heavy reliance on outdated or unreliable data sources.
- ▷   Documentation of sustainability reporting processes and controls is complete and up to date.

Question 1:   Summarize deficiencies in ICSR for this component of internal control.

Question 2:   Based upon this evaluation, how do you assess initial control risk (CR)? Motivate per finding.

Question 3:   What are the consequences of your initial assessment of the risk of this internal control component for the further procedures to be included in the assurance plan?

15-44   As mentioned in section 15.3.2, greenwashing indicates that stakeholders feel misled because companies claim to offer environmentally friendly products that are not as environmentally friendly as advertised. Intentional misleading is an indication of fraud.

Question 1:   What steps should the assurance practitioner take in case of this kind of suspected fraud?

Question 2:   In sustainability information in reporting or advertisements, there can be both deception and seduction. Is seductive information fraudulent? What is the difference, and what are the relevant criteria that the assurance practitioner uses to make the distinction?

Case Study: Ambiguous Sustainability Information

A multinational brewery (BEST SpA) has recently launched a sustainability campaign promoting its commitment to environmental and social responsibility. The campaign includes advertisements, social media posts, and sustainability reports highlighting the company's efforts to reduce carbon emissions, promote fair labour practices, and support community initiatives.

As part of the campaign, BEST publishes a sustainability report detailing its achievements and goals in various sustainability areas. The report emphasizes the company's dedication to sustainable sourcing, eco-friendly packaging, and ethical supply chain practices. Additionally, the BEST showcases its partnerships with environmental organizations and its investment in renewable energy projects.

Upon reviewing the sustainability report and campaign materials, stakeholders are unsure whether the information presented is genuinely reflective of the company's sustainability efforts or if it is designed to create a positive image without substantial action behind it. The language used in the advertisements and reports is persuasive and optimistic, leading to questions about the authenticity of the company's sustainability claims.

While some stakeholders view BEST's sustainability initiatives as genuine and impactful, others are sceptical, pointing to instances of greenwashing or superficial gestures. Its sustainability efforts may be perceived as both deceptive, in terms of exaggerating achievements or misrepresenting data, and seductive, in terms of appealing to consumers' desire for eco-friendly products and corporate social responsibility.

The ambiguity surrounding the sustainability information makes it challenging to definitively conclude whether it is deceptive or seductive.

Question 3:   What could you (as the assurance practitioner) do to address this issue?

15-45   **Assessing Double Materiality in Sustainability Reporting – Smurfit Kappa**

Smurfit Kappa, a leading provider of sustainable packaging solutions, has recently released its annual sustainability report. https://www.smurfitkappa.com/sustainability/reporting

As assurance practitioner you are tasked with evaluating the company's sustainability practices; we must assess the concept of double materiality to ensure that the report accurately reflects both the environmental and social impacts of Smurfit Kappa's operations.

Smurfit Kappa's sustainability report outlines its commitment to sustainability across various areas, including environmental stewardship, social responsibility, and governance practices. The report highlights key achievements, initiatives, and challenges faced by the company in its pursuit of sustainable business practices.

As assurance practitioner you are responsible for evaluating the double materiality of Smurfit Kappa's sustainability report. This involves assessing the significance of sustainability issues to both the company's operations and its stakeholders, considering both internal and external perspectives.

Question 1:   What is the objective of presenting the process and outcome of 'double materiality' in Smurfit's Sustainability Report?

Question 2:   Describe the key steps and procedures you will perform to conduct a comprehensive assessment of the double materiality as presented in Kappa's sustainability report.

15.4 Sustainability Reporting Goals, Regulations and Standards

15-46 Search the internet for the latest developments in the field of sustainability reporting standards ESRS and IFRS. Evaluate to what extent further convergence has been initiated. What are the main differences between the two sets of standards? Why do you think regional (EU) standards are 'necessary'?

15.5 Sustainability Assurance Process

15-47 **Spanish Supermarket Chain Selling Salmon from Norway**

GIGA Group S.L., a Spanish supermarket chain, committed to sustainability, sources its salmon from Anjo-Fish AS, a small Norwegian aquaculture company. Anjo-Fish AS places a strong emphasis on adhering to the Aquaculture Stewardship Council (ASC) standards to ensure responsible fish farming practices.

The ASC standards serve as a guiding framework for Anjo-Fish's sustainability journey. These standards cover various aspects of aquaculture, including fish welfare, environmental impacts, labour rights, and community relations. Anjo-Fish's dedication to meeting these standards reflects its commitment to sustainability and responsible business practices.

In its sustainability report, GIGA Group includes the following sustainability information: *'All Norwegian salmon we sell is farmed in accordance with ASC standards (including a link to these standards.'*

To support this assertion about its supply chain, GIGA received the following written information from Anjo-Fish's management:

▷ We have made significant strides in reducing the use of copper-based anti-fouling nets, which can have harmful environmental effects. This demonstrates the company's proactive approach to minimizing its ecological footprint.

▷ We have implemented measures to reduce reliance on medicinal treatments for parasitic salmon lice, prioritizing alternative methods such as biological control. This approach promotes the health of the salmon population while minimizing the use of chemicals in aquaculture.

▷ We place a strong emphasis on transparency and dialogue with local communities. By engaging stakeholders in meaningful conversations, we foster trust and cooperation, ensuring that the company's operations benefit both the environment and the communities in which it operates.

Your role: You are the assurance practitioner engaged to provide limited assurance about this statement in the Sustainability Report of GIGA Group S.L.

Question 1: If you concluded only 10% of the salmon sold was delivered by Anjo-Fish AS what would be your response?

Question 2: In case GIGA Group would decide not to refer to ASC standards in its sustainability report, what would you do?

Question 3: Describe the assurance procedures to gather sufficient and appropriate evidence to be able to issue limited assurance about the reliability of this assertion.

15-48   ING Group 2023 Climate Report, Text Derived from the Limited Assurance Report[133]
Inherent limitations

Non-financial performance information, such as the Information in the report, is subject to more inherent limitations than financial information, given the characteristics of the non-financial information and the methods used for determining such information. It is generally acknowledged by stakeholders globally, including regulators, that there are significant limitations in the availability and quality of data from third parties, resulting in reliance by ING on proxy data. These limitations are reflected in the section 'Data quality and limitations' of Appendix A of the 2023 Climate Report. It is anticipated that the principles and methodologies used to measure and report the Information in the report will develop over time and may be subject to change in line with market practice and regulation, impacting comparability between reporting entities and year-on-year.

Limitations to the scope of our limited assurance engagement.

The Information in the report includes prospective information such as ambitions, strategy, plans, expectations and estimates. Inherently the actual future results are uncertain. We do not provide any assurance on the assumptions and achievability of prospective information in the Information in the report. References to external sources or websites in the Information in the report are not part of the Information in the report itself as reviewed by us. Therefore, we do not provide assurance on this information. The other information comprises all of the information in the 2023 Climate Report other than the Information in the report and our limited assurance report. The Executive Board is responsible for the other information. Our limited assurance conclusion does not extend to the other information and, accordingly, we do not express any form of assurance thereon. Our conclusion is not modified in respect of these matters.

Question 1:   What is difference between 'Inherent limitations' and 'Limitations to the scope'?

Question 2:   Why is non-financial information subject to more inherent limitations than financial information? Give some examples of inherent limitations in the provision of non-financial information.

Question 3:   References to external sources or websites in the Information in the report are not part of the Information in the report itself as reviewed by the assurance practitioner. Therefore, she does not provide assurance on this information. Assume that during the assurance process she detects a material error in an external source that is being referred to in the Climate Report. As this information is not being assured, she decides not to take any further action. What are your thoughts about this? Motivate.

15.8   NOTES

1.   In this chapter, we use the term sustainability reporting instead of ESG reporting in line with reporting- and assurance standard setters like ISSB and IAASB (see section 15.3).

2.   Several early key events raised climate change awareness:
   ▶ In 1972, the United Nations Environment Program (UNEP) was established, focusing on environmental issues and promoting global awareness of climate change.

> ▸ The Club of Rome's 1972 report warned about environmental and climate consequences, advocating for a shift toward a circular society, emphasizing reduced resource use and environmental mitigation. The Club of Rome's model for global development focused on five major trends – accelerating industrialization, rapid population growth, widespread malnutrition, depletion of nonrenewable resources, and a deteriorating environment. However, achieving a self-imposed limitation to economic growth would require considerable effort, a massive change of mindset, and political practice.
>
> ▸ The 1979 First World Climate Conference, organized by the World Meteorological Organization (WMO), convened scientists and policymakers to discuss global warming's potential impacts.
>
> ▸ The Intergovernmental Panel on Climate Change (IPCC) formed in 1988, serving as a crucial scientific body informing policymakers and heightening awareness of the climate crisis.

3. The goals include zero hunger, health and water, and aim for responsible consumption with people having the relevant information and awareness that foster lifestyles in harmony with nature.

4. 'Accountants Will Save the World', Peter Bakker, President of the World Business Council for Sustainable Development, Harvard Business Review, March 5, 2013.

5. CSR Initiatives as Market Signals: A Review and Research Agenda, Fabrizio Zerbini, Journal of Business Ethics volume 146, page 6 (2017).

6. Activism regarding corporate social responsibility generally improves ESG practices and corporate sales and is profitable to the activist. This information serves to provide valuable insights into the investees' governance and strategies to address both short- and long-term material risks and opportunities for value creation. Journal of Business Ethics, Shareholder Engagement on Environmental, Social, and Governance Performance, 20 July 2021, Volume 180, pages 777–812 (2022).

7. For further philosophical aspects see Thompson. J., Environmentalism: Philosophical Aspects in International Encyclopedia of the Social & Behavioral Sciences, 2001.

8. A study of Higgins, 2006, indicates that despite overtures towards stakeholders and promises of organisational transformation, the complex texturing of the Shell reports positions Shell and others within fairly traditional neo-liberal discourses of organisation and society. Business organisations and others have clearly defined and objective functions and social/environmental issues are externally-generated objective threats. As such, the social/environmental reports produced by this company operate to legitimise and normalise the global, western capitalist business system. Social/environmental reporting by Shell: A critical discourse analysis, C. Higgins, July 2006, Deakin University. https://www.academia.edu/1593531/Social_environmental_reporting_by_Shell_A_critical_discourse_analysis

9. https://www.shell.com/sustainability/transparency-and-sustainability-reporting/sustainability-reports/_jcr_content/root/main/section/list/list_item.multi.stream/1657185136417/8c7cf7e17abcd9772af39994b88ed37a5a86e216/shell-sustainability-report-1998-1997.pdf https://www.shell.com/sustainability/transparency-and-sustainability-reporting/sustainability-reports.html

10. Because of the non-financial scope, the label 'Independent Verifiers' was introduced.

11. The G250 refers to the world's 250 largest companies by revenue as defined in the Fortune 500 ranking.

12. Big shifts, small steps. Global Survey of Sustainability Reporting 2022, KPMG. https://assets.kpmg.com/content/dam/kpmg/se/pdf/komm/2022/Global-Survey-of-Sustainability-Reporting-2022.pdf

13. The Greenhouse Gas Protocol (GHG Protocol) serves as a widely used international accounting tool to understand, quantify, and manage greenhouse gas emissions, co-developed by the World Resources Institute (WRI) and the World Business Council for Sustainable Development (WBCSD).

14. International Audit and Assurance Standards Board 2023, Proposed International Standard on Sustainability Assurance 5000 (ED ISSA 5000), International Federation of Accountants, New York, para. A157 and A158.

15. Source is Guidelines on reporting climate-related information European Commission, 2019. https://ec.europa.eu/finance/docs/policy/190618-climate-related-information-reporting-guidelines_en.pdf

16. Management's 'materiality process' differs from materiality determined by the practitioner. The practitioner determines materiality in planning the approach for obtaining evidence and when evaluating identified the context of misstatements of the sustainability information (section 15.6.4).

17. www.barry-callebaut.com/system/files/2023-11/Barry%20Callebaut%20Double%20Materiality%20Report%202023.pdf

18. https://www.barry-callebaut.com/system/files/2023-11/Barry%20Callebaut%20Double%20Materiality%20Report%202023.pdf

19. Ibid. ED ISSA 5000, para. A405.

20. Managing Fraud Risks in an Evolving ESG Environment, ACFE, 2023. https://www.acfe.com/fraud-resources/esg-report-gt-2022

21. https://www.greenhive.io/blog/greenwashing-examples#:~:text=For%20instance%2C%20an%20automobile%20manufacturer,production%20or%20limited%20recycling%20options

22. Maria Tymtsias, Group ESG Expert @ Nortal, Founder and Senior Sustainability Consultant @ Ethicality, GRI Sustainability Professional, https://www.linkedin.com/posts/maria-ochakovska_aiforsustainability-gptforsustainability-activity-7155152171943014401-9jYE/?utm_source=share&utm_medium=member_ios

23. https://unglobalcompact.org/

24. https://www.integratedreporting.org/

25. https://www.integratedreporting.org/what-the-tool-for-better-reporting/get-to-grips-with-the-six-capitals/

26. Over the past 23 years the GRI Standards have become the world's most widely used and internationally accepted tool for corporate transparency. More than 10,000 companies around the world communicate their impacts using the GRI Standards. GRI Global Standards Fund, 2021. https://www.globalreporting.org/media/11jdjwuu/brochure-global-standards-fund-2021.pdf

27. https://www.globalreporting.org/media/wtaf14tw/a-short-introduction-to-the-gri-standards.pdf

28. https://www.globalreporting.org/how-to-use-the-gri-standards/gri-standards-english-language/

29. https://www.globalreporting.org/media/wtaf14tw/a-short-introduction-to-the-gri-standards.pdf

30. Concepts of the Integrated Reporting Framework have been embedded in the heart of IFRS S1.

31. https://www.ifrs.org/content/dam/ifrs/publications/pdf-standards-issb/english/2023/issued/part-a/issb-2023-a-ifrs-s1-general-requirements-for-disclosure-of-sustainability-related-financial-information.pdf

32. https://dart.deloitte.com/USDART/home/publications/deloitte/heads-up/2023/global-esg-disclosure-standard-coverage-issb-finalizes-ifrs-s1-s2

33. https://eur-lex.europa.eu/legal-content/EN/TXT/?uri=CELEX:32022L2464

34. https://www.pwc.nl/en/topics/sustainability/esg/corporate-sustainability-reporting-directive.html

35. Under the CSRD, all large companies that meet two of the following three criteria: turnover exceeding €50 million per year, a balance sheet total of more than €25 million more than 250 employees (averaged over a year). https://www.pwc.nl/en/topics/sustainability/esg/corporate-sustainability-reporting-directive.html

36. https://www.efrag.org/Assets/Download?assetUrl=%2fsites%2fwebpublishing%2fSiteAssets%2fWorking%2520Paper%2520ESRS%25201%2520General%2520Provisions.pdf

37. On March 15, 2024, the EU Council agreed on the Corporate Sustainability Due Diligence Directive (CSDDD), aimed at improving corporate accountability for social, human rights, and environmental impacts within companies and its business partners. This directive, which is still awaiting approval from the European Parliament and European Commission, requires EU companies to undertake rigorous due diligence to address these impacts. Additionally, large companies must develop a plan for transitioning to a sustainable business model in line with the Paris Agreement's 1.5 °C goal. The directive will be implemented in stages based on company size and turnover, with strict enforcement and sanctions for non-compliance. Companies must also engage meaningfully with stakeholders and provide them with requested information.

38. https://vinciworks.com/blog/supply-chain-management-and-the-corporate-sustainability-reporting-directive-csrd/

39. https://www.sec.gov/rules/2022/03/enhancement-and-standardization-climate-related-disclosures-investors#33-11275

40. Like ESRS E1 Climate change Disclosure Requirement E1-6, the company has to disclose its gross Scope 1, 2 and 3 GHG emissions and total GHG emissions.

41. https://www.ifac.org/knowledge-gateway/contributing-global-economy/publications/state-play-sustainability-disclosure-assurance-2019-2021-trends-analysis.

42. IESBA issued an Exposure Drafts regarding International Ethics Standards for Sustainability Assurance (IESSA) and other revisions to the code relating to sustainability assurance and reporting. The proposed standards aim to establish clear ethical frameworks for sustainability assurance practitioners and professional accountants involved in sustainability reporting, with the goal of enhancing the quality of sustainability information and combating greenwashing. https://www.ethicsboard.org/publications/proposed-international-ethics-standards-sustainability-assurance-including-international?utm_source=Main+List+New&utm_campaign=28a2abd83f-EMAIL_CAMPAIGN_2024_02_06_08_37&utm_medium=email&utm_term=0_-28a2abd83f-%5BLIST_EMAIL_ID%5D

43. IFAC, AICPA & CIMA. (2021). The State of Play in Sustainability Assurance. https://www.ifac.org/_flysystem/azure-private/meetings/files/Agenda-Item-5B-June-2021-IFAC-AICPA-CIMA-Report-The-State-of-Play-in-Sustainability-Assurance.pdf

44. Independent verifiers include professional accountants and other (independent) verifiers.

45. As by the deadline of 1 October 2026, the Commission is will adopt standards for limited assurance and for reasonable assurance no later than October 1, 2028.

46. The Netherlands already has a specific assurance standard for sustainability information in place, the NBA Standard 3810N.

47. The further elaboration is mainly based on ED ISSA 5000 as a stand-alone chapter. As much as possible repetition of other ISAs and ISAEs already covered in the previous chapters are avoided.

48. The structure of the sustainability assurance process is similar to the audit process of financial information (see chapters 4 and 6). Both are in line with the iterative empirical cycle of observation, expectation, testing, analysis, conclusion, publication, review, replication, oversight).

49. Ibid. ED ISSA 5000, para. 22-23. In extraordinary cases, deviations from requirements in the standard are allowed, and the practitioner should use alternative procedures aligned with the objectives.

50. Ibid. ED ISSA 5000, 20-23.

51. For details we refer to Ibid. ED ISSA 5000, para. 33.

52. Maintaining professional scepticism requires an ongoing questioning of whether the information and evidence obtained suggests that a material misstatement due to fraud may exist. It includes considering the reliability of the information intended to be used as evidence and the controls over its preparation and maintenance where relevant. Due to the characteristics of fraud, the practitioner's professional scepticism is particularly important when considering material misstatement due to fraud, which may include omission of information and/or deliberate bias. (Ibid. ED ISSA 5000.A.131)

53. Ibid. ED ISSA 5000, para. 31.

54. Ibid. ED ISSA 5000, para. 40.

55. As outlined in paragraph 31 of ISAE 3000.

56. In some circumstances, the practitioner may carry out a separate non-assurance engagement with the purpose of ascertaining the presence of necessary preconditions. This type of engagement is occasionally denoted as a 'readiness assessment'.

57. Ibid. ED ISSA 5000, para. 70.

58. Ibid. ED ISSA 5000, para. A156.

59. Extended External Reporting (EER), IAASB, page 94.

60. Ibid. ED ISSA 5000, para. A159.

61. Salmon farming is subject to strict regulations and controls and most salmon farms are ASC (Aquaculture Stewardship Council) certified. Pressure from environmental organizations also plays a role in this. The maximum number of salmon per cage is set at 2.5 percent salmon in 97.5 percent water.

62. Framework criteria that are embodied in law or regulation or are issued by authorized or recognized bodies of experts that follow a transparent due process are presumed to be suitable. In the absence of indications to the contrary. As are criteria issued by authorized or recognized bodies of experts that follow a transparent due process if they are relevant to the intended users' information needs. Such criteria are referred to as framework criteria in this ISSA.

63. Ibid. ED ISSA 5000 A179-186.

64. Ibid. ED ISSA 5000, para. Application Materials Part 3.A6D.

65. Ibid. ED ISSA 5000, para. 77.

66. Ibid. ED ISSA 5000, para. A266.

67. Ibid. ED ISSA 5000, para. A267.

68. Qualitative factors considered by the entity and the practitioner may overlap but need not be identical. Also, for quantitative disclosures, the practitioner and entity will not necessarily arrive at the same materiality threshold.

69. Ibid. ED ISSA 5000, para. A279.

70. Ibid. ED ISSA 5000, para. A281.

71. Ibid. ED ISSA 5000, para. 48-9.

72. The engagement leader shall determine which matters are to be communicated to members of the engagement team, and to any practitioner's external experts not involved in the discussion. (Ibid. ED ISSA 5000.96).

73. Ibid. ED ISSA 5000, para. A281.
74. Ibid. ED ISSA 5000, A286.
75. Alweer fraude (Again fraud), blog Wim Bartels, 10 October 2023, NBA, Accountant.nl, https://www.accountant.nl/discussie/columns/2023/10/alweer-fraude/
76. Framework criteria may not be considered suitable on their own (e.g., may be incomplete or subject to interpretation in application). Therefore, the entity may supplement the framework criteria so that the applicable criteria are suitable. The process of developing the applicable criteria and applying it to the underlying subject matter may be complex, require judgment, and may be susceptible to bias. Based on the evaluation, AP identifies disclosures where there is an increased susceptibility to misstatement or cause the practitioner to re-evaluate the suitability of the applicable criteria. Ibid. ED ISSA 5000, para. AM.6.A23.
77. ... where material misstatements are likely to arise (in a limited assurance engagement) or identifying RMMs (in a reasonable assurance engagement).
78. Ibid. ED ISSA 5000, para. A306.
79. https://www.ey.com/en_us/cro-risk/how-new-coso-guidance-will-help-with-internal-control-over-esg-reporting
80. COSO ICIF for ESG Reporting: Building confidence in sustainable business information through the COSO Framework, KPMG 2023. https://kpmg.com/kpmg-us/content/dam/kpmg/pdf/2023/coso-icif-for-esg-reporting.pdf
81. COSO, 2023, Achieving effective internal control over sustainability reporting (icsr): building trust and confidence through the COSO internal control—integrated framework, P5.
82. https://www.ey.com/en_us/cro-risk/how-new-coso-guidance-will-help-with-internal-control-over-esg-reporting
83. Ibid. ED ISSA 5000, para. 109.
84. Ibid. ED ISSA 5000, para. 102L, 107L,108L, 109L.
85. Ibid. ED ISSA 5000, para. 102R, 107R,108R, 109R.
86. Ibid. ED ISSA 5000, para. A401.
87. Ibid. ED ISSA 5000, para. A401.
88. A risk-based approach to the sustainability assurance process is based on the idea that the AP should focus on the areas of the sustainability report that are most likely to contain material misstatements.
89. ED ISSA 5000 does not make a statement on this, although assessment of CR is the complement of effectiveness of IC if this is a sustainability matter (a Governance topic disclosure).
90. Ibid. ED ISSA 5000, para. A351R.
91. Ibid. ED ISSA 5000, para. A355.
92. Ibid. ED ISSA 5000, para. A361L.
93. Ibid. ED ISSA 5000, para. A214-8.
94. Ibid. ED ISSA 5000, para. A234.
95. Ibid. ED ISSA 5000, para. A240.
96. Ibid. ED ISSA 5000, para. A356.
97. Ibid. ED ISSA 5000, para. A365.
98. The risk of not detecting a material misstatement due to fraud or non-compliance with law or regulation is higher than the risk of not detecting one resulting from error. Furthermore, these risks are higher in a limited assurance engagement than in a reasonable assurance engagement.
99. Ibid. ED ISSA 5000, para. A366.
100. Ibid. ED ISSA 5000.A370.
101. Substantive analytical procedures are a subset of analytical procedures that focus on specific account balances or classes of transactions. The primary purpose is to obtain substan-

tive evidence regarding the completeness, accuracy, and validity of the financial statement amounts. Ibid. ED ISSA 5000, para. A359.

102. Ibid. ED ISSA 5000, para. A357.

103. https://www.efrag.org/Assets/Download?assetUrl=%2Fsites%2Fwebpublishi ng%2FSiteAssets%2FESRS%2520S4%2520n%2520Own%2520workforce%2520– %2520Other%2520work-related%2520rights.pdf

104. Ibid. ED ISSA 5000, para. 84.

105. Ibid. ED ISSA 5000, para. A246-250.

106. Ibid. ED ISSA 5000, para. 129/130, A378.

107. See section 15.4.4.

108. Sampling risk is the risk that the practitioner's conclusion based on a sample may be different from the conclusion if the entire population were subjected to the same procedure.

109. Ibid. ED ISSA 5000, para. A380.

110. For the assurance engagement Examination of Prospective Financial Information (ISAE 3410) we refer to chapter 14.5 and for auditing Estimates in the context of the audit of financial statements to chapter 13.5.

111. https://www.cisco.com/c/dam/m/en_us/about/csr/esg-hub/_pdf/purpose-report-2022.pdf

112. Ibid. ED ISSA 5000, para. 133.

113. 'Clearly trivial' is not another expression for 'not material.' Misstatements that are clearly trivial are of a wholly different (smaller) order of magnitude, or of a wholly different nature than those that would be determined to be material, and are misstatements that are clearly inconsequential, whether taken individually or in aggregate and whether judged by any criteria of size, nature or circumstances. When there is any uncertainty about whether one or more items are clearly trivial, the misstatement is considered not to be clearly trivial (Ibid. ED ISSA 5000.A391).

114. Ibid. ED ISSA 5000, para. A393.

115. Ibid. ED ISSA 5000, para. A406.

116. Ibid. ED ISSA 5000, para. 142/3.

117. Ibid. ED ISSA 5000, para. A411.

118. Ibid. ED ISSA 5000, para. 144.

119. Ibid. ED ISSA 5000, para. A422.

120. Ibid. ED ISSA 5000, para. A427.

121. Ibid. ED ISSA 5000, para. A451.

122. Ibid. ED ISSA 5000, para. 165.

123. Ibid. ED ISSA 5000, para. A454.

124. Ibid. ED ISSA 5000, para. 61 and 62.

125. For example, as in the Shell's verification report 1998 as illustrated in section 15.2.3.

126. Ibid. ED ISSA 5000, para. 167.

127. The structure of the statement accompanying the annual accounts differs little from the structure of an assurance report. Therefore, see the description of the statement accompanying the annual accounts as set out in chapter 11.

128. Ibid. ED ISSA 5000, para. 169.

129. Ibid. ED ISSA 5000, para. 171.

130. Ibid. ED ISSA 5000, para. 178.

131. Ibid. ED ISSA 5000, para. A509.

132. Ibid. ED ISSA 5000, para. 184-6.

133. https://www.ing.com/Sustainability/Performance-and-reporting/Reporting.htm

INDEX